Social Psychology and Behavioral Medicine

Social Psychology and Behavioral Medicine

Edited by

J. RICHARD EISER

Department of Psychology
University of Exeter

JOHN WILEY & SONS

Chichester · New York · Brisbane · Toronto · Singapore

302
S6786

bc

British Library Cataloguing in Publication Data:

Social psychology and behavioral medicine.
  1. Social psychology
  I. Eiser, J. Richard
  302   HM251   80–42062
ISBN 0 471 27994 3

Text set in 10/12pt Linotron 202 Times, printed and bound
in Great Britain at The Pitman Press, Bath

List of contributors

ANTONY J. CHAPMAN	*University of Wales Institute of Science and Technology, Cardiff, Wales*
JOHN B. DAVIES	*University of Strathclyde, Glasgow, Scotland*
THEODORE M. DEMBROSKI	*Eckerd College, St Petersburg, Florida, USA*
DON DITECCO	*University of Waterloo, Waterloo, Canada*
CHRISTINE EISER	*University of Exeter, Exeter, England*
J. RICHARD EISER	*University of Exeter, Exeter, England*
RICHARD I. EVANS	*University of Houston, Houston, Texas, USA*
MARTIN FISHBEIN	*University of Illinois at Urbana-Champaign, Illinois, USA*
HUGH C. FOOT	*University of Wales Institute of Science and Technology, Cardiff, Wales*
BERNARD H. FOX	*National Institutes of Health, Bethesda, Maryland, USA*
W. DOYLE GENTRY	*University of Texas, Medical Branch, Galveston, Texas, USA*
KENNETH J. GERGEN	*Swarthmore College, Swarthmore, Pennsylvania, USA*
MARY GERGEN	*Swarthmore College, Swarthmore, Pennsylvania, USA*
MICHAEL GOSSOP	*Bethlem Royal and Maudsley Hospitals, Beckenham, England*
ROBERT W. HALEY	*Center for Disease Control, Atlanta, Georgia, USA*
RAY J. HODGSON	*Institute of Psychiatry, University of London, London, England*
PHILIP LEY	*University of Sydney, Sydney, Australia*

v

JAMES M. MacDOUGALL   *Eckerd College, St Petersburg, Florida, USA*

JAMES M. OLSON   *University of Western Ontario, London, Canada*

BERTRAM H. RAVEN   *University of California, Los Angeles, California, USA*

COLETTE RAY   *Brunel University, Uxbridge, England*

MICHAEL ROSS   *University of Waterloo, Waterloo, Canada*

RONALD P. SCHLEGEL   *University of Waterloo, Waterloo, Canada*

RICHARD SCHULZ   *Portland State University, Portland, Oregon, USA*

NOEL P. SHEEHY   *University of Wales Institute of Science and Technology, Cardiff, Wales*

SEIGFRIED STREUFERT   *Pennsylvania State University, Hershey, Pennsylvania, USA*

SUSAN C. STREUFERT   *National Institutes of Health, Bethesda, Maryland, USA*

MARGARET S. STROEBE   *University of Tübingen, Tübingen, Germany*

WOLFGANG STROEBE   *University of Tübingen, Tübingen, Germany*

PETER SUEDFELD   *University of British Columbia, Vancouver, Canada*

STEPHEN R. SUTTON   *Institute of Psychiatry, University of London, London, England*

RICHARD TOTMAN   *University of Sussex, Falmer, England*

FRANCES M. WADE   *University of Wales Institute of Science and Technology, Cardiff, Wales*

Contents

PART IV: COMMUNICATION AND INFLUENCE

PART V: REACTIONS TO ILLNESS, TREATMENT, AGING, AND BEREAVEMENT

Preface

Since before history the control and explanation of health and illness has been a fundamental human concern. The range of rituals, concoctions, devices, and procedures to which people have turned may seem limited only by the boundaries of imagination. Yet throughout many centuries and many cultures people have found it quite natural to assume that the ways they behaved could profoundly influence their health and happiness. The observance of codes of behavior, states of physical health, and feelings of general well-being have been seen as intimately and causally interrelated. It is only quite recently, however, that the nature of any such interrelationships has been the subject of scientific inquiry.

At the same time, our present-day conceptions of health and illness in many respects seem to play down the possibility of such interrelationships. The dramatic recent successes in many fields of curative medicine have much to do with this. If we fall ill, we no longer ask ourselves how we or our kinsmen have sinned, or what deity requires propitiation. We go to the doctor. We expect to get treated, and we expect such treatment to be effective. We place on the medical profession the responsibility of making us 'better', and in return allow that profession the right to intrude into the innermost parts of our bodies. Yet (with the exception of psychiatrists) doctors are not generally given the same right to invade the privacy of people's conducts and feelings. In many respects the personal has come to be differentiated from the physical and the boundary between the two is touchy.

The development of the behavioral sciences similarly has deliberately sought to achieve an 'objective' view of behavior, which involves describing what people do and why they do it, but has generally veered away from asking whether such behavior is good or bad. Questions of morality have acquired their own taboo, yet many of the contexts in which issues of behavior and issues of health have been considered in relation to each other have traditionally involved explicitly moral assumptions.

The deliberate study of the relationship between behavior and health thus poses challenges both to medical and behavioral sciences. Impressive though the advances in techniques of hospital treatment may have been, the major contributions to reduction of morbidity and mortality have been made through preventive measures, such as public sanitation and mass immunization. As a result one is left, at least in developed countries, with a situation where many of the major causes of disease and death directly relate to how people behave and take care of their *own* health. The preventability of behavior-related disease thus depends on the modifiability of health-related behavior. Furthermore, the effectiveness of many of the activities of medical practitioners can depend on a variety of psychological and social factors. The very definition of health and illness also involves assumptions of a psychological nature—if a particular physical condition causes no feelings of distress, by what criteria is it to be classified as an illness, or as a matter for medical concern? Even the criterion of the relationship between a physical condition and life-expectancy begs the question of whether longevity is necessarily a desirable end in itself.

To the behavioral scientist, becoming involved in issues of physical health also leads to the questioning of traditional roles. When certain behavior demonstrably increases the probability of death and disease, can one retain a scientific neutrality, and describe the processes underlying such behavior with as much empathy as when describing the processes which underlie its avoidance, or should one apply one's skills to the task of changing such behavior in a 'healthier' direction? This is a dilemma to which different answers may be offered, and there is no single solution suggested by the various chapters in this book. Involvement with issues of physical health is also leading to a redefinition of the professional roles of behavioral scientists within the health services and medical research. Clinical psychology feels this challenge most acutely, having been closely tied to psychiatry and problems of mental health and mental handicap, rather than with more general issues of physical illness and its prevention. Should clinical psychology acquire a wider territory of competence and responsibility, or should a place be found for a variety of specialties within a broader field of 'health psychology'? Hopefully both developments will occur.

It is against this background that the new field of behavioral medicine has sought to establish its identity. The driving force behind its development has been the age-old assumption of interrelationships between health, feelings, and behavior, now given a firmer foundation of scientific evidence, and a conviction that health is too important a topic to be the prerogative of any one profession or academic discipline. As an interdisciplinary field behavioral medicine requires not only contributions from many different disciplines, but also the integration of these different contributions into a coherent body of knowledge.

It would be wrong to pretend that this integrative ideal has yet been achieved, though it is far less of a fantasy now than, say, a decade ago. We are still at the stage of looking for the contributions which different disciplines and specialties can make, and exploring a few of the more obvious areas of contact and overlap. This book is intended to illustrate *some* of the ways in which empirical and theoretical research in social psychology can play a part in the development of this field. No claim is made that the topics discussed in the various chapters can only be approached from a social psychological perspective—such a claim, indeed, would be contrary to the whole spirit of the behavioral medicine movement. Nor are the topics represented, by any stretch of the imagination, the only ones where a social psychological approach may be fruitful. Rather, our purpose has been to give the reader a feel for what a social psychological approach may have to offer, and for some of the directions in which the field may develop.

To talk of a 'social psychological approach' might convey the impression that there is unanimity among social psychologists concerning the particular methods and theories to be applied in the field of behavioral medicine. There is not, and this volume does not seek to impose a premature consensus. This is not to say that there is no coherence nor any common themes underlying the work that has been done so far. Social psychology is the behavioral science concerned with the study of psychological processes in a social context. That is, it is concerned on the one hand with how 'individual' psychological factors and processes—attitudes, decisions, emotional states, interpretations of information and events, learning, memory, development, and many others—affect people's behavior in the world outside the experimental laboratory, in interaction with others, as members of social groups and as performers of social roles. On the other hand it is concerned with how social factors—interactions with others, social group membership, performance of social roles, attempts to achieve socially valued goals, and so on—may influence so-called 'individual' processes, which can include physiological functioning.

Much health-related behavior occurs or is learned in a social context. A purely individualistic psychological approach is thus likely to offer only a very limited perspective on the relationship between health and behavior. At the same time, most social psychologists have long subscribed to the view that even apparently 'irrational' destructive or self-destructive behavior can be better understood by attempting to understand the *subjective* rationality on which it is based. According to this view, behavioral 'failures' and apparent stupidity reflect the limitations and selectivity of powers of reasoning, rather than their absence or suspension.

A vital part of a social psychological approach is thus a consideration of people's own interpretations of the situations in which they find themselves—of their own personal and occupational goals, of their own physical feelings and symptoms, of the value to themselves of health and longevity, of medical encounters and procedures, and of the outcomes of medical intervention for themselves and others, of public or personal communications about health and illness, and of the social and material constraints upon their behavior.

The chapters have been arranged in five sections. Part I, entitled *The development of behavioral medicine*, gives a foretaste of some of the themes to be considered in more detail in later chapters, but is intended mainly to describe the historical and organizational context within which behavioral scientists in general, and social psychologists in particular, have come to be involved with behavioral medicine. Part II, *Antecedents of illness and injury*, looks at some of the areas where relationships have been postulated between psychosocial and behavioral factors, and vulnerability to illness or injury. Empirical findings, methodological issues, and broader theoretical questions are considered in relation to coronary heart disease, road accidents, cancer, and more general notions of psychological stress. Part III follows directly on, considering some of the most important behavioral antecedents of illness— *Smoking, alcoholism, and addiction*. The major problem here is not so much that of deciding how or whether the behavior involves a risk to health, but that of explaining why people persist in such behavior in spite of apparent acknowledgement of the dangers they incur. Part IV, *Communication and influence*, proceeds to the pragmatics of changing people's behavior. As the work in Part III shows, it is one thing to know that a particular behavior is damaging to health, and quite another thing to know how such behavior may be changed. The distinctive contributions of social psychological research in this area are the examination of notions of attitudes and persuasion, and of the *interpersonal* nature of influence and communication. Health behavior is embedded in a social context, and it may often be the behavior of health professionals (not to say policy-makers), which may need changing, at least as much as that of their 'unhealthy' clients. Finally, Part V, *Reactions to illness, treatment, aging, and bereavement*, looks at how people's own interpretations and resources can influence the effects and effectiveness of medical procedures, and their ability to cope with the stresses of illness in themselves and in those close to them. Illness, treatment, aging, and bereavement have long been known to influence different people in different ways, and social psychological research may suggest some of the reasons for these differences.

Finally, a small disclaimer. This book is not intended to provide a definition or exhaustive taxonomy of the ways in which social psychology can be relevant to problems of health and illness. Nor is the selection of chapters necessarily representative, in any strictly proportionate sense, of the areas of research on which most effort has so far been expanded. Rather, the hope is simply to provide a small stimulus to a field already rapidly expanding and developing, by bringing together empirical reviews, methodological critiques and theoretical analyses on a variety of topics, so demonstrating the wide range of opportunities for research that now exist.

J RICHARD EISER

PART I

The Development of Behavioral Medicine

Social Psychology and Behavioral Medicine
Edited by J. Richard Eiser
© 1982 John Wiley & Sons Ltd

Chapter 1

What is behavioral medicine?

W. DOYLE GENTRY

The question 'What is behavioral medicine?' is itself misleading. It implies that there is consensus among professionals regarding the definition of *behavioral medicine*, as well as the subject-matter and methods which might logically fall under such a rubric. Unfortunately, at this point, there is no such consensus. Rather, there appear to be at least three different ways in which the term is being used, each with its own proponents and statement of explicit aims and objectives. The purpose of this chapter is not to judge which of these ways is best, but rather to distinguish clearly between the three so as:
(a) to eliminate some of the confusion that has already arisen with respect to this newly emerging concept, and
(b) to provide a background against which the present volume can be viewed in terms of its unique contribution to the field of medicine.

The first public use of the term 'behavioral medicine' is credited to Birk (1973), who coined the term to describe the merits of biofeedback in treating medical disorders such as asthma, tension and migraine headaches, epilepsy, and Raynaud's disease. Birk noted (p. 362) that:

> it is perhaps not an exaggeration to point out that a new 'behavioral medicine', biofeedback, now still in its infancy, may in fact represent a major new developing frontier of clinical medicine and psychiatry.

In effect, Birk saw behavioral medicine as synonymous with biofeedback and, in more general terms, as the application of 'behaviorism' to medicine. That is, he stressed the need to identify a 'behavioral control mechanism, in which the patient can, for the first time, take a fully active and direct role in literally learning not to be sick' (p. 362). Accordingly, he focused almost exclusively on the work of individuals such as Neal Miller, Leo DiCara, Gary Schwartz, David Shapiro, Richard Surwit, Bernard Engel, Johann Stoyva, Thomas Budzynski, and Elmer Green, all of whom were linked both by their common background of training in psychology and their specific interest in visceral and autonomic conditioning.

3

Birk's pioneering use of the term behavioral medicine served not only to stimulate research and clinical application in the field of biofeedback (Ray *et al.*, 1979; Schwartz and Beatty, 1977); it legitimized the role of the 'behavior therapist' in medical settings. Whereas very little systematic attention had been devoted to the use of behavioral techniques in treating somatic disorders prior to 1970, a virtual explosion of interest occurred thereafter. Excellent summaries of the wide range of behavioral techniques used, and types of patients treated, are presented by Gentry (1975), Katz and Zlutnick (1975), Pomerleau *et al.* (1975), Williams and Gentry (1977), Gentry (1976), Pomerleau and Brady (1979), and McNamara (1979).

It is clear from these writings that this particular view of behavioral medicine has expanded far beyond the boundaries of biofeedback, yet has maintained a central focus on the 'behavioral' aspects of assessment and treatment. In this regard, Pomerleau and Brady (1979, p. xii) defined behavioral medicine as:

(a) the clinical use of techniques derived from the experimental analysis of behavior—behavior therapy and behavior modification—for the evaluation, prevention, management, or treatment of physical disease or physiological dysfunction; and (b) the conduct of research contributing to the functional analysis and understanding of behavior associated with medical disorders and problems in health care.

They and others in this field have noted the successful use of behavioral techniques such as self-monitoring, relaxation training, contingency contracting, stimulus control, punishment, modeling, and assertive training in treating patients with medical disorders. The latter includes disorders such as: chronic pain, sexual dysfunction, essential hypertension, alcoholism, obesity, enuresis and fecal incontinence, insomnia, neurodermatitis, spasmodic torticollis, and spasms associated with cerebral palsy.

Specific attention has also been given to topics such as behavioral paediatrics (Christopherson and Rapoff, 1979), use of behavioral techniques in treating dental problems such as bruxism and temporomandibular joint (TMJ) syndrome (Masur, 1979), health risk behaviors such as smoking (Boudewyns, 1977) and the Type A behavior pattern (Suinn, 1977) which is linked to increased incidence of coronary heart disease, issues of noncompliance (Gentry, 1977), behavioral assessment and medicine (Keefe, 1979), behavioral epidemiology (Sexton, 1979), application of behaviorism to health care delivery (Epstein and Ossip, 1979) and training of health-care personnel (Mastria and Drabman, 1979), interactions between drugs and behavior therapy (Whitehead and Blackwell, 1979), and finally the use of behavioral techniques in occupational (work) settings (Chesney and Feuerstein, 1979).

The newly organized Society of Behavioral Medicine, a professional group closely affiliated with the American Association for the Advancement of

Behavior Therapy (AABT), currently serves as a forum for proponents of this definition of behavioral medicine, the majority of whom continue to be psychologists (Stewart Agras, personal communication).

A second widely used definition of behavioral medicine came out of a Conference on Behavioral Medicine sponsored by Yale University in early 1977. This conference brought together senior researchers in several behavioral science (psychology, sociology, epidemiology) and biomedical (psychiatry, medicine) disciplines for the purpose of (a) defining, if possible, a concept of behavioral medicine which would be acceptable across disciplines, and (b) defining those areas of investigation which would be included under such a definition. The resulting definition is as follows (Schwartz and Weiss, 1978a):

> Behavioral medicine is the field concerned with the *development* of *behavioral science* knowledge and techniques relevant to the understanding of *physical health* and *illness* and the *application* of this knowledge and these techniques to prevention, diagnosis, treatment and rehabilitation. Psychosis, neurosis, and substance abuse are included only insofar as they contribute to physical disorders as an endpoint.

In arriving at this definition, the Yale Conference members emphasized the facts that:

(1) behavioral medicine should be defined as a field of endeavor (rather than a specific discipline, theoretical approach, and/or set of techniques) in order to highlight its interdisciplinary nature;

(2) a distinction had to be made between 'developments in the behavioral sciences of knowledge and techniques' *vs.* 'development of behavioral science knowledge and techniques' so as not inadvertently to exclude persons lacking formal credentials in the behavioral sciences from working in the field of behavioural medicine;

(3) an emphasis needed to be placed on health-promoting factors as well as those contributing to disease;

(4) it was important to focus on physical health problems *per se*, since most of the attention of behavioral scientists in the past had been devoted to issues of mental health.

In addition, the Yale Conference group devised the matrix shown in Figure 1.1 as a means of organizing the basic content and subareas comprising the field of behavioral medicine. This matrix was designed to illustrate the fundamental similarites in the structure of behavioral medicine research and that of traditional biomedical research. That is, it began with a focus on issues of prevention, etiology/pathogenesis, diagnosis, treatment, and rehabilitation. From there, the matrix became open-ended in that it allowed for an unspecified range of target problems, e.g. hypertension, asthma, myocardial infarction, and so on, and most importantly for contributions from an unspecified range of biobehavioral disciplines, including ones not mentioned on the matrix such as health economics, education, nutrition, and so forth. The latter aspect of the matrix perhaps represents the most unique feature of the behavioral medicine concept espoused by this group.

In essence, this matrix represents the 'big picture' or 'puzzle' one often hears talked about in discussions about the complexities of human disease. It can also be viewed as an attempt at 'holistic' problem-solving in the field of medicine.

Finally, the Yale group suggested a general list of contemporary research problems in the field of behavioral medicine. This list, which is by no means inclusive, illustrates the way in which one can fill in various cells in the matrix. Included were (Schwartz and Weiss, 1978a):

(a) sociocultural influences on physical health and illness, including epidemiological, sociological, and anthropological studies;
(b) psychological factors contributing to physical health/illness, including social psychology, personality, and psychophysiological studies investigating social, behavioral, and emotional stresses and their consequences;
(c) the study of pain and its regulation;
(d) factors contributing to adherence to medical regimens and research on behavioral approaches to substance abuse (addiction);
(e) the need to distinguish between health behavior, illness behavior, and sick-role behavior;
(f) development of behavioral diagnostic techniques, including psychophysiological assessment procedures (e.g. stress testing);
(g) application of behavioral therapies (biofeedback, relaxation training, stress management techniques) to physical disorders and the evaluation of these against traditional psychotherapeutic techniques;
(h) behavioral approaches to prevention of physical disease and promotion of health, including interdisciplinary research derived from education, economics, and social systems theory.

As Schwartz and Weiss (1978a) pointed out, this initial attempt to define the concept of behavioral medicine was viewed more as a 'point of departure' rather than as 'the final word'. Thus, it was not unexpected when a revised definition of behavioral medicine was offered by this same group a short time later (Schwartz and Weiss, 1978b). In an effort to avoid the classic problems of mind/body dualism (which might arise from the earlier attempt to exclude mental disorders *per se*) and to highlight more explicitly the concept of *integration of thought and technology* between biomedical and behavioral science disciplines, the Yale group redefined behavioral medicine (p. 250) as:

the *interdisciplinary* field concerned with the development and *integration* of behavioral *and* biomedical science knowledge and techniques relevant to health and illness and the application of this knowledge and these techniques to prevention, diagnosis, treatment and rehabilitation.

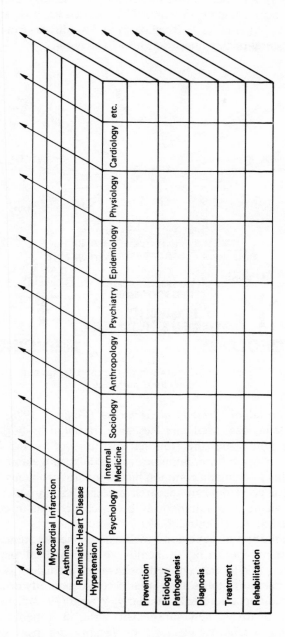

Figure 1.1 Matrix of problems in behavioral medicine

Masur's (1979) graphic representation of the interdisciplinary thrust of behavioral medicine, shown in Figure 1.2, illustrates how specialty areas within different disciplines (e.g. Psychology and Medicine) can interface so as to contribute *jointly* to this important new field.

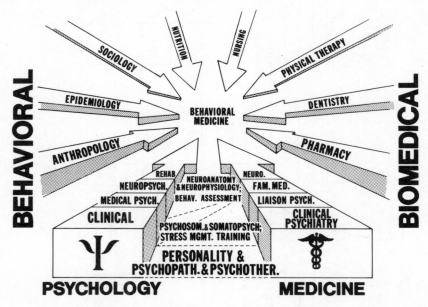

Figure 1.2 Graphic representation of the interdisciplinary thrust of behavioral medicine

The new *Journal of Behavioral Medicine* (Gentry, 1978) and the new Academy of Behavioral Medicine Research, initiated by both the National Academy of Sciences and the National Institutes of Health in the United States, provide a forum for communication and exchange among researchers from many fields working on common biobehavioral problems. It should also be noted that a good deal of research meeting this broader definition of behavioral medicine is simultaneously being carried out in countries other than the United States (Gentry, 1980).

The third definition of behavioral medicine is one that tends to confuse it with developments occurring in health and/or medical psychology. For example, Asken (1979) has defined behavioral medicine as 'the study of *psychological reactions* [italics mine] that occur secondarily or as the result of physical illness and its treatment'. Similarly, Wright (1979) defines behavioral medicine as a 'relatively new subspecialty area identified by a variety of labels, including *pediatric, medical,* or *health care* psychology'. As an example, Wright focuses on the role of the medical psychologist in dealing with issues of organic or illness-related psychopathology (e.g. anorexia nervosa, intellectual sequelae of meningitis, noncompliance in children with encopresis). Thus, behavioral medicine involves:

(a) a multifactorial system of describing and classifying disorders such as hyperactivity and anorexia;
(b) psychological assessment of patients with physical illness to determine the nature and extent of accompanying psychopathology and to address the issue of whether psychological factors precipitate or exacerbate symptoms;
(c) psychological treatment of patients with physical symptoms, which is evaluated via patient protocols;
(d) psychological prediction of patients 'at risk' for medical–psychological problems (e.g. who might be prone toward repeated episodes of poisoning or ingestion of toxins); and
(e) attention to compliance problems from a behavioral, psychological perspective.

For purposes of further discussion we might label these three uses of the term behavioral medicine as the 'behaviorism', Yale and psychological definitions respectively. As such, we can then examine their similarities and differences and the implications each has for further developments both in health care and health research.

Given the above, it seems clear that all three definitions of behavioral medicine have certain common properties and/or goals. For example, all three address biobehavioral problems in a wide, and increasing, variety of physically ill persons. In addition, the 'behaviorism' and Yale definitions include focusing attention on individuals 'at risk' for certain illnesses because of unhealthy patterns of behavior (smoking, alcoholism, obesity), i.e. a concern with preventive intervention and/or health promotion. All three viewpoints also stress the role of psychological factors in influencing the etiology, pathogenesis, treatment, and rehabilitation of disease and the valuable contribution of behavior therapy and behavior modification techniques in altering disease behavior; the latter holds true whether one considers subjective reports of symptom relief or actual objective changes in various organ systems (e.g. decreased premature ventricular contractions or ectopic beats, decreased airway resistance in the lungs, or decreased sweating in patients with chronic hyperhidrosis). Finally, all three definitions address issues of integration with regard to such things as: interactions between drugs and behavior therapy, the need to control for known non-behavioral factors (age, social class, diet) before investigating the influence of behavioral factors, and the modifying effect behavioral factors can have on one another in determining a person's health status. An example of the latter is found in a study by Graham et al (1978) where the authors noted that frequent church attendance was significantly related to lower levels of systolic blood pressure, but *only* for non-obese individuals; in effect, one behavioral factor (being overweight) cancelled out the otherwise positive influence of a second behavioral factor (church attendance) on elevated blood pressure.

There are, on the other hand, a number of important differences between these three definitions of behavioral medicine. The *psychological* definition offered by Asken (1979) and Wright (1979) is limited solely to the psychological causes and consequences of physical illness and as such excludes any emphasis on other influences such as cultural, sociological, economic, nutritional, and so forth. It also focuses exclusively on clinical issues and persons manifesting disease symptoms and/or illness behavior, i.e. healthy persons and those 'at risk' but not yet ill are not discussed. In short, this particular type of activity probably falls more appropriately under the rubric of 'medical psychology' than it does that of behavioral medicine (Stone *et al.*, 1979).

Similarly, the 'behaviorism' definition focuses exclusively on the clinical application of behavioral psychology—behavior therapy and behavior therapy and behavior modification—to traditional medical problems, e.g. reduction of chronic pain, increasing compliance to medical regimen, alleviating tension headaches and other stress disorders, and also in reducing unhealthy behaviors in persons 'at risk' for certain illnesses. Unfortunately, this definition also overlooks the valuable contributions of other behavioral science disciplines and even those of psychologists who are not characterized as 'behaviorists' in the usual sense of the term. Pomerleau and Brady (1979), for example, distinguish between persons working in medical psychology (i.e. those concerned with psychometric assessment, projective testing, and personality theory) versus those working in behavioral medicine, the latter being categorized as having a specific set of behavioral principles and techniques which guide their efforts primarily in the area of therapy. McNamara (1979) also noted the emphasis this definition has on 'medical practice' and the belief that behavioral medicine represents essentially a merging of the 'paths of medicine and behavioral psychology'.

The Yale definition of behavioral medicine is the one that offers an inclusive and broadly integrative approach to health care and health research. As was mentioned earlier in this chapter, the Yale group made a conscious effort initially to include all persons and disciplines which might ultimately shed some light on the complexities of health and disease in humans, regardless of whether one was interested primarily in diagnostic or therapeutic issues. The key to this definition is integration of ideas and technology and also a balanced perspective about health that was heretofore not available. It represents, in Neal Miller's terms, an attempt to develop 'two skills in one skull' (Schwartz and Weiss, 1978a).

The need for this integrated, broad-spectrum approach is pointed out nicely by Hull (1977) in a study reviewing a decade of cross-discipline research on the topic of 'life circumstances and physical illness'. She noted that each of the behavioral science and biomedical disciplines tended to conduct studies in this area along the lines of specific variables with little overlap between the disciplines. That is, epidemiologists tend to study the effect of variables such as age, sex, race, occupation, place of residence, and social class as they relate to critical life events–stress–illness susceptibility, while psychologists tend to investigate the singular effects of emotional traits (personality) on this sequence. Hull also noted that these different disciplines tend to publish their findings in their own 'disciplinary' journals, that they tend to rely on different research methods and different levels of precision in defining both their independent and dependent variables, and that they evidence divergent (and changing) levels of interest in various topics of health research over time. She concluded that, while the different behavioral science disciplines may appear more or less interested in certain topic areas during a given time-period, the desired goal of 'greater interdisciplinary participation' has to date not emerged.

Clearly, the major impact of the Yale definition of behavioral medicine on the health field will come not from its attempt to legitimize further the contributory roles of various single disciplines (e.g. medical psychology, medical sociology, medical anthropology) to medicine, but rather from its attempt to encourage, foster, and *shape* a new integrative, biobehavioral way of conceptualizing health problems and conducting health research. In this sense the Yale definition is the only one of the three which focuses primarily on future activity (i.e. behavioral medicine as an *ideal* rather than a *reality*) as opposed to highlighting events in the present.

It is not surprising that psychology has played a key role in the early development of this field. Psychologists not only constitute the largest single group of non-physician behavioral scientists employed in medical schools in the United States (Buck, 1961)—far outnumbering sociologists and anthropologists—they also possess a unique capacity to intervene in health and illness behavior (Stone, 1977). This no doubt provides the impetus behind both the 'behaviorism' and psychological definitions of behavioral medicine, as well as simultaneous developments in the field of health or medical psychology (Budman and Wertlieb, 1979; Gentry and Matarazzo, 1981; Stone *et al.*, 1979).

While the field of behavioral medicine is in its infancy and there is some lack of consensus about how one should define it, there is no question that it represents 'an idea whose time had come' (Weiss, 1979). Its ultimate success, however, rests on the premise that *all* relevant disciplines will collaborate and contribute equally to a greater understanding of the complexities of human health and illness. The present volume, which provides an excellent summary of the contribution of social psychologists to this field, is a necessary and important step toward this goal.

References

Asken, M. J. (1979). Medical psychology: toward definition, clarification, and organization', *Professional Psychology*, **10**, 66–73.

Birk, L. (ed.) (1973) *Biofeedback: Behavioral Medicine*. Grune & Stratton, New York.

Boudewyns, P. A. (1977). 'Cigarette smoking', in Williams, R. B., and Gentry, W. D. (eds), *Behavioral Approaches to Medical Treatment* pp. 99–111. Ballinger, Cambridge, Mass.

Buck, R. L. (1961). 'Behavioral scientists in schools of medicine', *Journal of Health and Human Behavior*, **2**, 59–64.

Budman, S. H., and Wertlieb, D. (eds) (1979). 'Psychologists in health care settings', *Professional Psychology*, **10**, 397–644.

Chesney, M. A., and Feuerstein, M. (1979). 'Behavioral medicine in the occupational setting', in McNamara, J. R. (ed.), *Behavioral Approaches to Medicine* pp. 267–290. Plenum, New York.

Christopherson, E. R., and Rapoff, M. A. (1979). 'Behavioral pediatrics', in Pomerleau, O. F., and Brady, J. B. (eds), *Behavioral Medicine: Theory and Practice* pp. 99–124. Williams & Wilkins, Baltimore.

Epstein, L. H., and Ossip, D. J. (1979). 'Health care delivery: a behavioral perspective', in McNamara, J. R. (ed.), *Behavioral Approaches to Medicine*, pp. 9–32. Plenum, New York.

Gentry, W. D. (1975). 'Behavior modification of physical disorders', in Gentry, W. D. (ed.), *Applied Behavior Modification*, pp. 130–147. Mosby, St Louis.

Gentry, W. D. (1976). 'Behavioral treatment of somatic disorders, in Spence, J. T., Carson, R. C., and Thibaut, J. W. (eds), *Behavioral Approaches to Therapy*, pp. 169–184. General Learning Press, Morristown, New Jersey.

Gentry, W. D. (1977). 'Noncompliance to medical regimen', in Williams, R. B., and Gentry, W. D. (eds), *Behavioral Approaches to Medical Treatment*, pp. 203–208. Ballinger, Cambridge, Mass.

Gentry, W. D. (1978). 'About the *Journal of Behavioral Medicine*', *Journal of Behavioral Medicine*, **1**, 1–2.

Gentry, W. D. (1980). 'Behavioral medicine abroad', *International Journal of Mental Health*, **9**, 197–203.

Gentry, W. D., and Matarazzo, J. D. (1981). 'Medical psychology: three decades of growth and development', in Bradley, L. A., and Prokop, C. K. (eds), *Medical Psychology: A new Perspective*, pp. 5–15. Academic Press, New York.

Graham, T. W., Kaplan, B. H., Cornoni-Huntley, J. C., James, S. A., Becker, C., Hames, C. G., and Seyden, S. (1978). 'Frequency of church attendance and blood pressure elevation', *Journal of Behavioral Medicine*, **1**, 37–44.

Hull, D. (1977). 'Life circumstances and physical illness: a cross disciplinary survey of research content and method for the decade 1965–1975', *Journal of Psychosomatic Research*, **21**, 115–140.

Katz, R. C., and Zlutnick, S. (eds) (1975). *Behavior Therapy and Health Care: Principles and Applications*. Pergamon, New York.

Keefe, F. J. (1979). 'Assessment strategies in behavioral medicine', in McNamara, J. R. (ed.), *Behavioral Approaches to Medicine*, pp. 101–130. Plenum, New York.

Mastria, M. A., and Drabman, R. S. (1979). 'The development of behavioral competence in medical settings', in McNamara, J. R. (ed.), *Behavioral Approaches to Medicine*, pp. 33–64. Plenum, New York.

Masur, F. T. (1979). 'An update on medical psychology and behavioral medicine', *Professional Psychology*, **10**, 259–264.

McNamara, J. R. (ed.) (1979). *Behavioral Approaches to Medicine*. Plenum, New York.

Pomerleau, O., Bass, F., and Crown, V. (1975). 'Role of behavior modification in preventive medicine', *New England Journal of Medicine*, **292**, 1277–1282.

Pomerleau, O. F., and Brady, J. P. (1979). *Behavioral Medicine: Theory and Practice*. Williams & Wilkins, Baltimore.

Ray, W. J., Raczynski, J. M., Rogers, T., and Kimball, W. H. (1979). *Evaluation of Clinical Biofeedback*. Plenum, New York.

Schwartz, G. E., and Beatty, J. (eds) (1977). *Biofeedback: Theory and Research*. Academic Press, New York.

Schwartz, G. E., and Weiss, S. M. (1978a). 'Yale conference on behavioral medicine: a proposed definition and statement of goals', *Journal of Behavioral Medicine*, **1**, 3–12.

Schwartz, G. E., and Weiss, S. M. (1978b). 'Behavioral medicine revisited: an amended definition', *Journal of Behavioral Medicine*, **1**, 249–252.

Sexton, M. M. (1979). 'Behavioral epidemiology', in Pomerleau, O. F., and Brady, J. P. (eds), *Behavioral Medicine: Theory and Practice*, pp. 3–22. Williams & Wilkins, Baltimore.

Stone, G. C. (1977). 'Health and behavior'. Paper presented at the American Psychological Association, San Francisco.

Stone, G. C., Cohen, F., and Adler, N. E. (eds) (1979). *Health Psychology*. Jossey-Bass, San Francisco.

Suinn, R. M. (1977). 'Type A behavior pattern', in Williams, R. B., and Gentry, W. D. (eds), *Behavioral Approaches to Medical Treatment*, pp. 55–66. Ballinger, Cambridge, Mass.

Weiss, S. M. (1979). 'Behavioral medicine: an idea . . . ', in McNamara, J. R. (ed.), *Behavioral Approaches to Medicine*, pp. ix–xiii. Plenum, New York.

Whitehead, W. E., and Blackwell, B. (1979). 'Interactions between drugs and behavior therapy', in McNamara, J. R. (ed.), *Behavioral Approaches to Medicine*, pp, 157–190. Plenum, New York.

Williams, R. B., and Gentry, W. D. (eds) (1977). *Behavioral Approaches to Medical Treatment*. Ballinger, Cambridge, Mass.

Wright, L. (1979). 'A comprehensive program for mental health and behavioral medicine in a large children's hospital', *Professional Psychology*, **10**, 458–466.

Social Psychology and Behavioral Medicine
Edited by J. Richard Eiser
© 1982 John Wiley & Sons Ltd

Chapter 2

Training social psychologists in behavioral medicine research

RICHARD I. EVANS

The Need for Training Programs

An obvious problem in the more traditional pre- and postdoctoral training of social psychologists is the increasing decline of job placement opportunities for the products of traditional programs. Base on his recent survey dealing with academic job placement possibilities for those receiving Ph.D.s in social psychology, Levy (1979) concludes that academic placements will be increasingly scarce. He sees a reluctance on the part of most social psychology graduate programs to gear themselves for preparation of students for non-academic, applied positions. In fact, he appears to have determined that the need for social psychologists in non-academic applied positions is already exceeding the number of appropriately trained social psychologists. He might have further stated that one reason for the reluctance to shift to more applied programs might be the conventional belief that experimental social psychology encompasses a fairly basic research focus and its integrity may be compromised by moving into applied problem areas. He might also have suggested that, even if they wish to train applied researchers, many social psychology doctoral training faculty members may not be entirely certain what the content and focus of that training should be.

Both of these latter points must be taken quite seriously. Clearly, if social psychologists, in their effort to 'go applied', lose sight of the continuing importance of maintaining the integrity that is intrinsic in strong theoretical and methodological training, then applied programs will quickly warrant the criticisms of them by many of the more traditional social psychologists. As to the matter of content and focus of more applied programs, we had an opportunity to confront this problem as trainers of graduate students in social psychology in the early 1960s. We noticed even then that there was a discernible tendency within the behavioral sciences, and even within social

15

psychology, to consider at least some applied problems. For example, there were opportunities to become involved in applied interdisciplinary research areas emanating from the health service professions (this trend has recently been predominantly localized within the area of Behavioral Medicine). Because of the proximity of our university to the massive Texas Medical Center, we were increasingly being called upon to participate in research activities related to health.

Among the interesting developments during this period were the formation of separate departments of behavioral sciences in medical schools, for example, the University of Kentucky (Straus, 1959) and the University of Oregon (Matarrazo, 1979). In addition, departments such as psychiatry, public health, epidemiology, physiology, and surgery within medical schools had begun to staff individuals who were involved in various psychological specialities to provide capabilities similar to those discussed by Straus (1961, p. 7) when he stated in summary:

> Department[s] of Behavioral Science should be in a strong position to fulfill these major objectives: first, the delineation and synthesis of principles and content from the behavioral sciences which are specially pertinent to the understanding of human behavior in health and disease, and the correlation of these principles with those of the biological and physical sciences in the development of a conceptual frame of reference useful for the practice of comprehensive medicine; second, the application of behavioral science concepts and research findings to a further understanding of the diagnostic, treatment, and management process, to the understanding of interpersonal relationships and social structure within medical institutions themselves; third, the provision of instruction and research consultation in biostatistics; and fourth, the development of curricula and research around concepts of communication and small human interaction.

During the 1960s the training of researchers to meet such goals had not been sufficiently conceptualized by the National Institutes of Health in the United States to the point where academic graduate programs in social psychology in universities could be attracted to engage in such training.

Training in Applications of Social Psychology to Dentistry

My interest in this field began to become crystallized when contacts with the Texas Medical Center led to my being invited to serve as a psychological research consultant to the University of Texas Dental School. In this capacity I had an opportunity to observe and thus to become acutely aware of the many provocative psychological research areas inherent in the patient–dentist situation, as well as within the general field of health behavior. It seemed that social psychologists could find challenging research problems in this field. So when the National Institute of Dental Research became actively interested in the behavioral sciences and financial support for a special research training program in social psychology at both the pre- and postdoctoral levels was now possible, we applied for funding for such a program. The proposal was acted upon favorably and a program was set up within the University of Houston's Department of Psychology and its Social Psychology Doctoral Program (Evans, 1966).

In the process of their training, the students were oriented toward the special problems of dentistry in order to acquaint them with some of the fundamental social psychological research areas which are relevant. This orientation was accomplished in the following manner, aside from the basic training in theory and methodology which was part of our then traditional social psychology doctoral program:

(1) Students were enrolled each semester in a research practicum which was designed to involve the students in the problems of dentistry. It was required that such research areas be intrinsically significant enough to social psychology so that findings will contribute to social psychology aside from their relevance to dentistry. This was intended to encourage more fundamental research and thus to overcome the superficiality of results emanating from some of the narrowly applied interdisciplinary research efforts in which social psychologists had participated in the past. In the final analysis, such research did not make a truly fundamental contribution either to social psychology or to the discipline to which the social psychologist was relating (Evans, 1967).

(2) Extended liaison with the University of Texas Dental School was effected when the Dean appointed a Faculty Liaison Committee, representative of both the clinical and the preclinical (basic science) areas. This committee met regularly with the social psychology trainees, proving helpful to the students in providing resources for both clinical and preclinical research problems, experimental subjects, and access to the facilities and equipment necessary to carry out the research in which the trainees become involved.

(3) Seminars were scheduled throughout the year. Participating in addition to the Program Director, interested Psychology Department faculty members, trainees, and members of the Dental School Faculty Liaison Committee were a group of consultants who were productive social psychological researchers from other institutions. These consultants were not necessarily required to have addressed themselves, prior to being invited to participate in this program, to research problems specific to the field of dentistry. By virtue of their proven research experience in various fields of social psychology it was felt that they would provide a new perspective with respect to dental problems as they viewed them in this context. The seminar discussions of various research possibilities and their implications were taped and transcribed, so on-going records were made accessible at a later time to the trainees in this program, as well as interested individuals in other institutions.

Education Committee. I was asked to consider how our dental study in persuasive communications and fear-arousal could be brought to bear on various risk factors in the prevention of cardiovascular disease, such as smoking. This area became particularly intriguing to us, so as we phased out of the National Institute of Dental Research-supported program, we applied for support for a pre- and postdoctoral social psychology research training program which addressed itself to the prevention of cardiovascular disease (Evans, 1980b). It was funded in 1978 by the National Heart, Lung, and Blood Institute for five years. The rationale for the program suggests that if we accept the assumption that a significant impact on morbidity and mortality would result if individuals could be trained in modifying behaviors involved in *preventing* as well as in rehabilitating heart attack and stroke patients, then the role of the social psychologist in such programs would obviously be an important one.

Examples of research areas in which the trainees could be involved include evaluation of strategies for enhancing communication between post-coronary patient and cardiologist, the evolution of sociopsychological stress in the developing child as related to hypertension, the problem of increasing adherence to various therapeutic regimens prescribed by cardiologists, the evaluation of the effects of training cardiologists in dealing with the post-coronary patient and his or her family, the evaluation of strategies for dealing with lifestyle changes of patients with heart disease and the whole range of developing and evaluating strategies for modifying various types of coronary-prone behaviors (e.g. smoking, diet, Type A, exercise).

In addition to the general training format of our earlier applied social psychology doctoral program, the trainees in this program are required to attend a series of monthly presentations coordinated by cardiovascular investigators which deal with such topics as environmental factors in hypertension, advances in lipid and atherosclerosis research, practice of medicine with consideration of risk factors, problems of individual compliance with physicians' instructions, basic correlates of hypertension, and conscious and conditioned control of cardiovascular function. Attendance is required at the regularly scheduled weekly meetings of the Baylor College of Medicine National Heart and Blood Vessel Research and Demonstration Center of which our long-term 'Social Psychological Deterrents of Smoking in Adolescents' project (to be detailed later) is one component. Also required is participation in the regularly scheduled orientation to cardiovascular disease sessions for cardiovascular Fellows.

To engage in this research focus, the social psychologist should have a reasonable knowledge of the physiological components of the risk factor as it relates to cardiovascular disease. The social psychologist developing intervention programs should learn how to select and collaborate with appropriate researchers and clinicians dealing with cardiovascular disease. In this program such individuals are available to work with the trainees throughout the course of the training program.

In order to obtain the skills necessary to develop intervention and research programs of their own, both the pre- and postdoctoral trainees are active in ongoing research projects in the Baylor National Heart Center. These include our long-range adolescent smoking prevention project, a Type A (coronary-prone) behavior investigation, a diet-modification program, a neighborhood clinics hypertension control study, and various public education and school education projects. Theoretical training which might be related to providing a conceptual base for such research is obtained in social psychology seminars which deal in part with social psychological concepts as they pertain to program development in health behavior.

Perhaps one of the most vital skills a social psychologist should have if he or she is to work effectively in a preventive medicine or health care setting is how to evaluate programs once they are developed. In the opinion of this writer, such evaluation skills must be predicated on both extensive knowledge of classical experimental design and quasi-experimental research methodology (e.g. Campbell and Stanley, 1963), general program evaluation skills, and proficiency with appropriate statistical techniques and computer resources. All trainees in the program are required to enroll in seminars in program evaluation and other aspects of research methodology.

In the last several years social psychologists have been investigating the use of various techniques that might be useful in dealing with problems such as patient compliance or adherence in taking drugs (e.g. hypertension control), self-management following input from health professionals, and improving already existing health maintenance programs. Examples of specific techniques that are proving to be useful are behavior modification, modelling and other derivatives from the social learning paradigm, skills for enhancing group interaction (group dynamics), attribution theory, survey research, focused interviewing and testing, and use of persuasive communication models. The trainees in this program are also required to enroll in various seminars that acquaint them with such techniques.

The training related to prevention and control of cardiovascular disease is a full-time three-year program including summer sessions. From experience with our previous NIDR-supported social psychology research training program and as incorporated in our present program, it has become clear that the best structure for the formal academic training component of such a program continues to be a balance between a standard set of requirements in the first stage of training to insure a reasonable level of basic competence and enough flexibility in the second stage to allow for individual interests and abilities.

Depending on the extent of previous training in psychology of the predoctoral trainees and particularly the postdoctoral trainees, aside from the fairly structured theoretical and methodological training in the program, as suggested earlier, it is shaped to focus particularly on the prevention and control of cardiovascular disease. The trainees are encouraged to engage in independent study and research in this area and are financially supported in any independent research which they begin to develop. To illustrate how outside consultants are involved, some recent program activities might be mentioned. In response to the interest of several of the trainees who were becoming involved in research in the Type A behavior area, cardiologist Ray Rosenman, co-developer of the Type A research area, was invited to spend several days in Houston with our group, sharing various aspects of the state-of-the-art in this field and providing training in the Type A Structured Interview. Theodore Dembroski, a Ph.D. from our earlier program, also visited us and is helping in the development of a research program in which even those students not primarily interested in Type A behavior will become at least peripherally involved.

Research on Prevention of Cigarette Smoking

A more detailed example of one of the current research areas in which our trainees are involved is illustrated by our 'prevention of cigarette smoking' investigation. The difficulties in altering behaviors such as cigarette smoking, which involve drug addiction or dependence, and which have been integrated into our lifestyles in a complex manner, suggested to us that we might focus more of our efforts toward developing strategies that would influence children to resist the pressures to begin a high-risk behavior, that is, focus on prevention rather than cessation. The work of McGuire (1974) investigated verbal inoculations against the influence of persuasive communications which were directed at altering cognitions. Why could inoculation strategies not be developed against the social pressures to begin a behavior such as smoking? So we developed a five-year longitudinal investigation which began with this conceptual base. This would involve training adolescents to resist the social pressures to begin smoking or advance toward frequent addictive smoking. In-depth interviews, conducted prior to both a pilot study (Evans, 1976) and the longitudinal study (Evans et al., 1978), with a large population of seventh-graders, suggest that peer pressure, models of smoking parents, and the mass media (e.g. cigarette advertising), may, individually or collectively, outweigh the belief of children that smoking is dangerous. Recent explorations of this problem at Stanford and Minnesota corroborate our findings (Hurd et al., 1978; McAllister et al., 1978).

Furthermore, we now have some evidence (Evans et al., 1979b) that in addition to depending too heavily on fear as a deterrent to smoking, anti-smoking messages in schools fall into a 'time perspective' trap. That is, they focus too much on the future consequences of smoking. To be more meaningful to teenagers, who tend to be present-oriented, smoking messages should emphasize more immediate effects of smoking on the teenager.

We are using the strategy of 'inoculation against pressures to smoke' predicated on the following theoretical notion concerning the development of addicted smokers: If students can be 'nursed' through the period during which they are particularly vulnerable to social influences to smoke (the junior high years) by teaching them how to resist such influences, they will be sufficiently fortified so that the heavy addictive smoking, which is generally first found as students progress into high school, will be less likely to occur. By then students may be more independent, and may be less likely to respond to social pressures to begin smoking. A social learning approach (e.g. Bandura, 1971) to developing such training interventions is being utilized.

To summarize our methods and results, first the ten-week pilot investigation was completed with 750 male and female students entering the seventh grade in the Houston Independent School District. The message portion of the pilot study consisted of short videotapes approximately ten minutes in length. Rather than relying upon adult authority figures as communicators, as health education programs generally do, the videotapes feature adolescents of approximately the same age as the target population, who present the smoking information and role-play certain social situations where the pressure to smoke is encountered (see Figure 2.1). Furthermore, the roles of the

Figure 2.1 Still from videotape illustrating resistance to social pressure

students in the tapes are presented honestly, since the student spokespersons state that they have been asked to present the messages and to play certain roles. This approach has appeared to be better received by student viewers who may have been adversely affected by the authority figures and the artificiality of many health communication efforts, such as drug control films.

Table 2.1 Social-psychological deterrents of smoking in schools, 1975 pilot study research (evaluation) design

Group	Pretest	Experimental condition	Two-day posttest	Eight-week posttest	Ten-week posttest
Experimental 1	0_1	Message focused discussion* feedback	0_2 F_1	0_3 F_2	0_4 F_3
2	0_1	Nicotine videotape plus testing	0_2	0_3	0_4
3	0_1	Feedback on measurement	0_2 F_1	0_3 F_2	0_4 F_3
Control 4	0_1	Nicotine videotape plus pretest and posttest only			0_4
5		Nicotine video plus posttest only			0_4

0: Observation.
F: Feedback delivery.
* Discussion of coping alternatives.

Table 2.1 summarizes the research design of this investigation. Four different videotapes were presented to subjects on each of four consecutive days. The video presented on the first day included information about the dangers of smoking to health, and, most prominently, a section describing and illustrating peer pressure and its effect on smoking behavior.

The videotape presented on the second day recapped the first tape and presented information about parental influence on smoking behavior, including a depiction of parental pressure to smoke and not to smoke, and children's modeling of parents' smoking behavior.

The third videotape recapped the first two tapes and presented information dealing with pressures to smoke emanating from the mass media. This tape included a pictorial analysis of such advertising techniques as artistically hiding the Surgeon General's warning on cigarette packages, and appeals based on implied sexual attractiveness and popularity.

The fourth and final videotape was a general recap of the first three tapes. The message portion of the pilot study was either present in its entirety (all four videotapes presented) or absent (no videotapes presented) in various experimental and control groups.

Following the videotapes, students were involved in written and oral responses to questions. The experimenter distributed brief questionnaires for subjects' written responses. Four sets of questions were prepared; one presented in conjunction with each videotape. The questions, which incorporated a quasi-roleplaying device of allowing the respondent to make decisions concerning whether or not to respond to social pressures to smoke, were formulated in such a way as to attribute motivation to resist pressures to smoke to persons who have seen the videotape, and attribute ability to decide whether or not to smoke to persons subjected to smoking pressures.

Present in some experimental classes and absent in others was feedback to subjects concerning group smoking behavior in their respective classes. The experimenter presented this feedback with a chart that reflected the degree of smoking or smoking-related behavior. This feedback was delivered during each posttest, with feedback given at the time of the second posttest based on the data gathered in the first posttest, and so on. Feedback on each occasion was delivered after the administration of that day's posttest to avoid contamination by the feedback.

Following each video presentation, and accompanying a discussion designed to reinforce the messages in the videotape, a carefully designed poster representing a scene from the videotape was displayed in the classroom. Figure 2.2 is the poster dealing with peer pressure. It portrays a student

Figure 2.2 Poster illustrating resistance to peer
pressure

visibly turning down an offer of a cigarette from members of a group of students who are all smoking. The wording on the poster is: 'You don't have to smoke just because your friends do. YOU can resist peer pressure'.

Even if your parents smoke, you don't have to imitate them.
YOU can decide for yourself.

Figure 2.3 Poster illustrating resistance to
parent pressure

Figure 2.3 is the poster dealing with parent pressure. It depicts a daughter obviously annoyed at smoke from her mother's cigarette. The message reads: 'Even if your parents smoke, you don't have to imitate them. YOU can decide for yourself'.

Finally, following the media pressure videotape, a poster (Figure 2.4) is displayed. It depicts a large 'Marlboro Man' reaching out from a billboard and offering a cigarette to a passing student, who visibly indicates that he does not want the cigarette. This poster states: 'Cigarette ads are a rip-off. YOU can resist media pressure to smoke'.

The posters served as a continuous reminder of the videotape messages. A preliminary test of student reaction to them indicated that they were

**Cigarette ads are a rip-off!
YOU can resist media
pressure to smoke.**

Figure 2.4 Poster illustrating resistance to media pressure

attention-getting and were preferred to other poster formats which we had designed.

As the studies mentioned earlier indicate (Evans *et al.*, 1970, 1975), repeated testing may be perceived by subjects as a monitoring of their behavior. Therefore testing is treated as an independent variable, and a testing-only group is included to assess the effect of testing by itself on the dependent variables.

The five dependent variables measured include smoking information, smoking attitudes, intention to smoke, and reported smoking behavior, as well as the Horning *et al.* (1973) nicotine-in-saliva analysis which was used as an objective measure of the presence or absence of smoking. The amount of nicotine present in the saliva samples is determined by a mass spectrometric analysis, and inferences can be made about the degree of smoking behavior practiced by the subjects. Cost of operation of the mass spectrometer precludes analysis for each subject on each testing occasion, but saliva samples were collected from each occasion, and a sampling of specimens from each group was analyzed. Investigations by Evans *et al.* (1977, 1980a), found that when subjects learned from a short film that their saliva could be analyzed their self-reports of smoking became more accurate. This technique was used to increase the validity of self-reports of smoking.

As indicated in Figure 2.5, and as reported in Evans *et al.* (1978), rates of onset of smoking in the full treatment, the feedback and the testing-only groups were significantly lower than the onset rates in the pretest–single

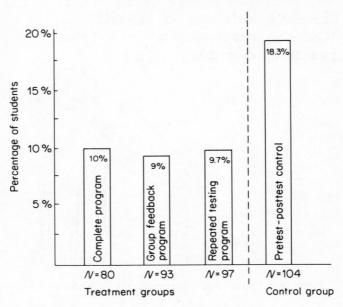

Figure 2.5 Results of 1975 ten-week pilot study. Percentage of students who began smoking (one or more cigarettes a month) during the first quarter of the seventh grade, as reported at the end of the term. *Note*: Treatment *vs.* experimental groups: $\chi^2 = 4.51$; $p < 0.05$

posttest control groups. Over 18 percent in the experimental groups had begun smoking while less than 10 percent in the experimental groups had begun smoking. (The small number of already-smoking subjects in the various experimental groups precluded a statistical comparison of onset rates among the experimental groups and the control group.) These results suggest that such interventions may prove more useful in deterring smoking among junior high students than merely instructing them in the long-term dangers of smoking. Perhaps most importantly, these findings suggest that various kinds of interventions may be effective, particularly if they have a reasonable conceptual base supported by data from the target audience concerning their perceptions of the determinants of smoking.

The five-year longitudinal study initially involving approximately 4500 students is presently under way, using modifications of the pilot study methodology, tracking students through the seventh, eighth, ninth, tenth, and eleventh grades. Through the second year of the study, preliminary data analysis suggests promising impact of the interventions. As indicated in Fig 2.6, 80 percent of the students in a random sample of all students in the experimental groups claim that the films had influenced their decision not to

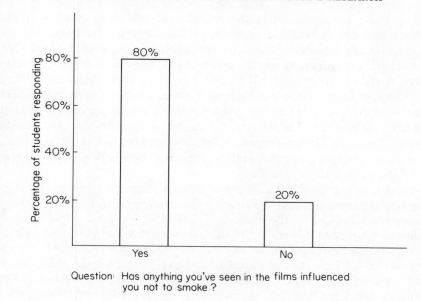

Figure 2.6 Three-year longitudinal study, social-psychological deterrents of smoking in schools project. Open-ended interviews with a sample ($n = 61$) of the students in the full-treatment condition following the second year intervention, 1977–78

smoke. At the end of the ninth grade, analyses of the data support the hypothesized significant relationship between knowledge of the social coping techniques and incidence of smoking (Evans *et al.*, 1980b; 1981).

Further Research Studies on Smoking Prevention

Several individual research studies were carried out by social psychology graduate students in conjunction with this project. They are summarized as follows. The first study is entitled: 'Feedback about immediate consequences: strategy to control children's smoking' (Hansen and Evans, 1978). Within the context of our larger field study of smoking in adolescents, the smoking behavior of an additional sample of 365 sixth-grade children was examined. Subjects in treatment conditions were presented with information about the immediate consequences of smoking and, as is suggested by social learning theory, subjects were also presented with several forms of direct and vicarious feedback about the levels of carbon monoxide found in the breath. After viewing a film about how carbon monoxide immediately enters the smoker's body and can be measured in the breath, subjects were given vicarious feedback via a live demonstration of the detection process using smoking and non-smoking adult models. Subjects in the first feedback group then had their breath tested for carbon monoxide and received immediate feedback on the results. A second group received feedback on the carbon monoxide content of their breath after a one-week delay and subjects in a third group produced breath samples but were never given feedback on the results. A fourth feedback group was not monitored for carbon monoxide but did view the vicarious feedback demonstration. Control conditions included a pretest–posttest-only control group, as well as an information-only group who only viewed the carbon monoxide film.

Although low rates of smoking prohibited a sufficiently rigorous statistical analysis of the results, rates of smoking indicated that the numbers of subjects who reported smoking in the immediate feedback and the information-only conditions were reduced, while the subjects who received delayed feedback had the smallest increase in the number of new smokers. Further analysis revealed that subjects in the delayed and withheld-feedback conditions made significant decreases in their estimates of how soon large amounts of carbon monoxide could be found in their bodies. Overall, this study suggests a social-psychological technique for presenting meaningful information to children which may be used to reduce or deter their experimenting with the use of cigarettes. However, the sixth grade may be too early for the maximum effectiveness of feedback programs, because of the still limited smoking experience of the group.

Another spin-off study completed is entitled 'Role of information and belief in adolescents' smoking behavior' (Bane and Evans, 1978). This study dealt with the possibility that the apparent failure of traditional attempts to deter smoking among schoolchildren may be in the children's failure to attend to or to believe the information presented. To explore this possibility a social-psychological investigation of the relationships between 498 sixth-, seventh-, and eighth-graders' smoking behavior and their awareness of and belief in the negative consequences of smoking was undertaken also within the context of our larger longitudinal study. Junior high school (eighth-grade) subjects in a separate sample responded to questionnaire items measuring their recall of smoking-and-health information and their belief in that information. Smoking behavior was determined by the use of the nicotine-in-saliva technique used in the principal investigation.

Correlations between subjects' reported frequency of cigarette smoking and their beliefs about several negative consequences of smoking suggest that anti-smoking campaigns may have had some impact on the incidence of smoking. However, the variance unaccounted for by the belief items included in this investigation was so great (about 66 percent for the eighth grade) as to suggest that traditional anti-smoking programs were unable to overcome immediate pressures to smoke for a substantial percentage of the children studied. The fact that 85 percent of the self-identified eighth-grade smokers indicated beliefs in the unhealthiness of smoking demonstrates the inadequacy of using merely informational messages as a smoking deterrent, and appears to support the value of the approach utilized by our major study. Students are being trained to cope with immediate social pressures and other social influences to smoke, rather than depending primarily on communicating information concerning the dangers of smoking.

Still another investigation is entitled 'Communicating imminent health consequences: smoking control strategy for children' (Mittelmark and Evans, 1978). A low-fear appeal smoking control intervention stressing immediate effects of smoking (i.e. *carbon monoxide*) was compared to a high-fear appeal Cancer Society-developed, long-term consequences message in a ten-week field study. Also within the context of our larger study, a separate sample of 240 sixth-grade students participated. Subjects in the *carbon monoxide* message group viewed two films, saw in-class demonstrations, and participated in short question-and-answer sessions. The *cancer* message group was exposed to a typical school health anti-smoking program. The pretest–multiple posttest study design also included repeated testing and pretest–final posttest control groups.

It was hypothesized that, as compared to the *cancer* message and control groups, the *carbon monoxide* message group would:

(1) evidence a lower smoking onset rate;
(2) less frequently report intentions to begin smoking;
(3) show evidence of having gained new knowledge;
(4) be more likely to perceive smoking as an immediate detrimental behavior; and
(5) judge immediate effects to be the most important health consideration for children exposed to pressure to begin smoking.

To increase the validity of responses obtained on the dependent measure instrument, the three-step procedure employed in the major investigations in the 'prevention of smoking' project was used during testing occasions. Subjects were first shown how specimens of their saliva could be analyzed, for nicotine content by a mass spectrometer. They were then requested to produce saliva specimens. Finally, subjects responded to a 19-item questionnaire which included items which elicited responses concerning self-reports of smoking.

Due to the very low smoking onset rates which were also observed in this study sample as a whole, the hypothesized reduced smoking onset rate was not observed in the *carbon monoxide* message group. However, results did confirm the remaining hypotheses. It was concluded that low-fear appeal messages which stress short-term consequences of smoking may be more successful deterrents against early experimentation with cigarettes than are high-fear appeal messages which stress long-term serious health consequences. Again some support was gained for the use of another component of the major study, emphasizing *immediate* physiological effects.

Based at least on our research so far (Evans, 1978a; 1978b; Evans, *et al.*, 1980b; 1981), it would appear useful to deal with the problem of influencing preaddictive smokers to curtail the incidence of smoking before they become addicted or nicotine-dependent, or to focus on preventing individuals from beginning to smoke in the first place. This would, of course, necessitate the increased targeting of smoking prevention programs to non-smokers or preaddicted smokers beginning with preteenaged children and progressing to teenagers. Strategies for intervention with this group must move away from depending solely on fear-arousal and the mere dissemination of facts about the long-term health consequences of smoking. Preteens and teenagers must be taught to cope 'on the spot' with the pressures to smoke which they encounter. We should encourage efforts to build into school curricula sophisticated programs which inoculate against the social pressures to smoke, in lieu of the frequently used high-fear-arousal, information-centred programs, which may well even be counterproductive.

Other Training Programs

As our Houston program illustrates, a major trend in social psychology in recent years has been a refocusing of basic and theoretical knowledge and research skills on issues relating to health. This trend is well presented in a recent article by Taylor (1978). A further example of the efforts of this trend on doctoral education in social psychology is presented in the training program in Social and Personality Factors in Health, offered at the University of California, Los Angeles (UCLA), with support of the National Institute of Mental Health (NIMH), a new direction for support from this Institute. Graduate students, in conjunction with their basic predoctoral training, and a few postdoctoral trainees, work in collaboration with the UCLA social psychology faculty in such endeavors as health implications of close interpersonal relationships; health implications of psychosexual interrelationships; and cognitive, perceptual, and attributional factors in health. Elsewhere in this volume the director of this program, Bertram Raven, discusses a research outgrowth of this program dealing with social and interpersonal influence, including studies of effectiveness of various social power strategies in implementing infection-control programs in hospitals.

Another program in this area supported by NIMH is the program of Judith Rodin in the Yale University social psychology doctoral program. Training in this program is similar to the Houston and UCLA programs with an emphasis on research on obesity, aging and substance abuse, as well as cognitive, perceptual, and attributional factors in health.

Examining the various cardiovascular interdisciplinary multi-risk factor intervention programs supported by the National Heart, Lung, and Blood Institute within the Baylor College of Medicine National Research and Demonstration Center as a model, it is evident that there is a developing employment base for graduates of such a training program in medical schools (e.g. Departments of Community and Preventive Medicine, Internal Medicine, Continuing Education Programs, or Epidemiology). For some time now schools of public health, as they look at cardiovascular disease prevention and control, have indicated an interest in individuals with such training. Also, as our own experience has indicated, faculty members of psychology departments can profitably work in this area. Graduates of this program employed by university psychology departments are continuing research in this field by developing an appropriate interface with medical schools or schools of public health. As more programs in behavioral medicine begin to develop during the coming years, as encouraged by the Yale Conference on Behavioral Medicine, support by the National Institutes of Health, and the creation of the Academy of Behavioral Medicine Research (Laman and Evans, 1980), openings for graduates of a social psychology program in various aspects of behavioral medicine should become increasingly available. In fact, both pre- and postdoctoral graduates of our program have been successfully placed in a number of positions (e.g. Brown University, University of Colorado, University of Minnesota, University of California at Los Angeles) that would not be open to them if they had completed a traditional doctoral program in experimental social psychology. The bottom line for such interest in social psychologists trained in behavioral medicine research may be cost-effectiveness. Preventing disease is far less costly than treating it!

References

Arnim, S. S. (1963). 'The use of disclosing agents for measuring tooth cleanliness', *Journal of Periodontology*, **34**, 227–245.

Bandura, A. (1971). *Social Learning Theory*. General Learning Press, New York.

Bane, A. L., and Evans, R. I. (1978). 'Role of information and belief in adolescents' smoking behavior'. Paper presented at the 86th annual meetings of the American Psychological Association, Toronto, Canada, 28 August–1 September.

Cambell, D. T., and Stanley, J. C. (1963). *Experimental and Quasi-experimental Designs for Research*. Rand McNally, Chicago.

Evans, R. I. (1966). 'A new interdisciplinary dimension in graduate psychological research training: dentistry', *American Psychologist*, **21** (2), 167–172.

Evans, R. I. (1967). 'Social and behavioral sciences research: 1962–1966', *Journal of the American Dental Association*, **74**, 1500–1511.

Evans, R. I. (1968). *B. F. Skinner: The Man and his Ideas*, E. P. Dutton, New York.

Evans, R. I. (1975). *Carl Rogers: The Man and his Ideas*. E. P. Dutton, New York.

Evans, R. I. (1976). 'Smoking in children: developing a social psychological strategy of deterrence', *Journal of Preventive Medicine*, **5** (1), 122–127.

Evans, R. I. (1978a). 'Social psychological deterrents of smoking in schools: further results'. Paper presented at the Symposium on Primary Prevention in Childhood of Atherosclerotic and Hypertensive Diseases, Chicago, Illinois, 18–20 October.

Evans, R. I. (1978b). 'Deterring smoking in adolescents: a social psychological perspective'. Paper presented at the Symposium on Primary Prevention in Childhood of Atherosclerotic and Hypertensive Diseases, Chicago, Illinois, 18–20 October.

Evans, R. I. (1980a). *The Making of Social Psychology: Discussions with Creative Contributors*. Gardner Press, New York.

Evans, R. I. (1980b). 'Behavioral medicine: a new applied challenge to social psychologists', in Bickman, L. (ed.), *Applied Social Psychology Annual*, pp. 279–305. Sage, Beverly Hills.

Evans, R. I., Hansen, W. B., and Mittelmark, M. B. (1977). 'Increasing the validity of self-reports of behavior in a smoking in children investigation'. *Journal of Applied Psychology*, **62** (4), 521–523.

Evans, R. I., Henderson, A. H., Hill, P. C., and Raines, B. E. (1979a). 'Current psychological, social, and educational programs in control and prevention of smoking: a critical methodological review', in Gotto, A. M., and Paoletti, R. (eds), *Atherosclerosis Reviews*, vol. 6, pp. 203–243. Raven Press, New York.

Evans, R. I., Henderson, A. H., Hill, P. C., and Raines, B. E. (1979b). 'Smoking in children and adolescents—psychosocial determinants and prevention strategies', chapter 17 in US Public Health Service: *Smoking and Health:* A Report of the Surgeon General. US Department of Health, Education, and Welfare, Washington, DC.

Evans, R. I., Rozelle, R. M., Henderson, A. H., Hill, P. C., Bray, J. H., Dill, C. A., and Gilden, E. R. (1980a). 'Methodological considerations in longitudinal field research: an examination of the Houston adolescent smoking project'. Paper presented at the meetings of the American Educational Research Association, Boston, Massachusetts, April.

Evans, R. I., Rozelle, R. M., Lasater, T. M., Dembroski, T. M., and Allen, B. P. (1968). 'New measure of effects of persuasive communications: a chemical indicator or toothbrushing behavior', *Psychological Reports*, **23** (2), 731–736.

Evans, R. I., Rozelle, R. M., Lasater, T. M., Dembroski, T. M., and Allen, B. P. (1970). 'Fear arousal, persuasion, and actual versus implied behavior change: new perspective utilizing a real-life dental hygiene program', *Journal of Personality and Social Psychology*, **16** (2), 220–227.

Evans, R. I., Rozelle, R. M., Maxwell, S. E., Raines, B. E., Dill, C. A., Guthrie, T. J., Henderson, A. H., and Hill, P. C. (1980b). 'The Houston Project: focus on target-based filmed interventions'. Paper presented as part of the symposium Deterrents of Smoking in Adolescents: Evaluation of Four Social Psychological Strategies, at the 88th annual meetings of the American Psychological Association, Montreal, Canada, 1–5 September.

Evans, R. I., Rozelle, R. M., Maxwell, S. E., Raines, B. E., Dill, C. A., Guthrie, T. J., Henderson, A. H., and Hill, P. C. (1981). 'Social modeling films to deter smoking in adolescents: results of a three year field investigation', *Journal of Applied Psychology*, in press.

Evans, R. I., Rozelle, R. M., Mittelmark, M. B., Hansen, W. B., Bane, A. L., and Havis, J. (1978). 'Deterring the onset of smoking in children: knowledge of immediate physiological effects and coping with peer pressure, media pressure, and parent modeling', *Journal of Applied Social Psychology*, **8** (2), 126–135.

Evans, R. I., Rozelle, R. M., Noblitt, R., and Williams, D. L. (1975). 'Explicit and implicit persuasive communications over time to initiate and maintain behavior change: a new perspective utilizing a real-life dental hygiene program', *Journal of Applied Social Psychology*, **5** (2), 150–156.

Hansen, W. B., and Evans, R. I. (1978). 'Feedback about immediate consequences: strategy to control children's smoking'. Paper presented at the 86th annual meetings of the American Psychological Association, Toronto, Canada, 28 August–1 September.

Higbee, K. L. (1969). 'Fifteen years of fear arousal: research on threat appeals: 1953–1968', *Psychological Bulletin*, **72**, 426–444.

Horning, E. C., Horning, M. G., Carroll, D. I., Stillwell, R. N., and Dzidic, I. (1973). 'Nicotine in smokers, non-smokers, and room air', *Life Sciences*, **13**, 1331–1346.

Hurd, P. D., Johnson, C. A., and Pechacek, T. (1978). 'Peer, physiological monitoring, and commitment effects in antismoking interventions'. Paper presented at the 86th annual meetings of the American Psychological Association, Toronto, Canada, 28 August–1 September.

Janis, I. L., and Feshbach, S. (1953). 'Effects of fear-arousing communications', *Journal of Abnormal and Social Psychology*, **48**, 78–92.

Laman, C., and Evans, R. I. (1980). 'Behavioral medicine: the history and the past', *National Forum*, **60** (1), 13–18.

Leventhal, H., Singer, R., and Jones, S. (1965). 'Effects of fear and specificity of recommendations upon attitudes and behavior', *Journal of Personality and Social Psychology*, **2**, 20–29.

Levy, S. G. (1979). 'Graduate training and prospects in social psychology', *Personality and Social Psychology Bulletin*, **5** (4), 504–506.

Marston, M. V. (1970). 'Compliance with medical regimes: a review of the literature', *Nursing Research*, **19**, 312–323.

Matarazzo, J. (1979). 'Behavioral health and medicine: new frontiers for psychology'. Paper presented at the 87th annual meetings of the American Psychological Association, New York, 1–5 September.

McAllister, A. L., Perry, C., and Maccoby, N. (1978). 'Systematic peer leadership to discourage onset of tobacco dependency'. Paper presented at the 86th annual meetings of the American Psychological Association, Toronto, Canada, 28 August–1 September.

McGuire, W. J. (1974). 'Communication-persuasion models for drug education: experimental findings', in Goodstadt, M. (ed.), *Research on Methods and Programs of Drug Education*, pp. 1–26. Addiction Research Foundation, Toronto, Canada.

Mittlemark, M. B., and Evans R. I. (1978). 'Communicating imminent health consequences: smoking control strategy for children'. Paper presented at the 86th annual meetings of the American Psychological Association, Toronto, Canada, 28 August–1 September.

Straus, R. (1959). 'Philosophy, program objectives, and organization of the department of behavioral science', *Journal of Medical Education*, **34**, 662–666.

Straus, R. (1961). Philosophy, program objectives, and organization of the department of behavioral science, University of Kentucky, Lexington (mimeo).

Taylor, S. E. (1978). 'A developing role for social psychology in medicine and medical practice', *Personality and Social Psychology Bulletin*, **4** (4), 515–523.

PART II

Antecedents of Illness and Injury

Social Psychology and Behavioral Medicine
Edited by J. Richard Eiser
© 1982 John Wiley & Sons Ltd

Chapter 3

Coronary-prone behavior, social psychophysiology, and coronary heart disease*

THEODORE M. DEMBROSKI and JAMES M. MACDOUGALL

Despite the fact that cardiovascular-related diseases remain the principal cause of death in Western industrialized societies, the best combination of the standard risk factors of age, levels of serum cholesterol, systolic blood pressure, and cigarette smoking do not predict a simple majority of the new cases of coronary heart disease (Jenkins, 1976). Moreover, these risk factors are related to coronary heart disease (CHD) in different ways in different cultures (Keys *et al.*, 1970). Finally, neither the dramatic twentieth-century emergence of death due to this disease nor its recent declines can be entirely explained by alterations in diagnostic procedures, age structure of the population, genetic factors, diet, cigarette smoking, or physical exercise (Rosenman and Friedman, 1974). These deficiencies in our knowledge concerning the etiology of CHD have prompted scientists to expand the scope of their research in an effort to identify additional risk factors for CHD. This search has included examination of the potential role which psychosocial factors may play in the prediction, control, and understanding of this disease.

An excellent two-part article by Jenkins (1976) contains reviews of the research linking CHD to such psychosocial factors as anxiety, depression, social mobility, status incongruity, occupational stress, and the like. However, the only psychosocial factor to emerge with enough evidence to strongly suggest risk factor status for CHD is the Type A coronary-prone behavior pattern (Jenkins, 1978). The Type A pattern is characterized by a variety of psychological, emotional, and behavioral attributes, which include *excessive* hard-driving behavior, job involvement, impatience, time urgency, competitiveness, aggressiveness, and hostility (Rosenman and Friedman, 1974). In

* Research for this article was supported in part by research grant HL–22809-01 awarded to the authors by the National Heart, Lung, and Blood Institute, National Institutes of Health, United States Department of Health, Education, and Welfare.

their conceptualization of the Type A pattern, Rosenman and Friedman recognize that the defining attributes are not invariably manifest in an individual, but are most readily observed in the presence of situational provocation or challenge from the environment. Thus, the Type A pattern as defined by Friedman and Rosenman involves both a series of action–emotion responses and an appropriate environmental setting to trigger the responses.

Association between Type A Attributes and Coronary Disease

Speculation concerning an association between behavioral attributes and the cardiovascular system can be traced back nearly 2000 years, when Celsus (AD 30) recognized that '. . . bathing, exercise, fear, and anger and any other state of the mind may often be apt to excite the pulse'. Interestingly, the great physician and pioneer researcher Dr William Harvey commented in 1628 that: 'Every affection of the mind that is attended with either pain or pleasure, hope or fear, is the cause of an agitation whose influence extends to the heart'. In this connection, Heberden underlined in 1772 the importance of emotional states as predisposing factors in coronary disease. Dr John Hunter, who in 1793 died shortly after participating in a boisterous and heated board meeting at St George's Hospital, unfortunately had been correct when he previously proclaimed that '. . . my life is at the mercy of any rascal who chooses to put me in a passion'. A German physician, Van Dusch, observed in 1868 that coronary-prone individuals spoke in a loud voice and worked through the night. The French physician Trousseau suggested in 1882 that anger may aggravate heart disease to such a degree as to precipitate death. Shortly thereafter, Sir William Osler in 1897 attributed coronary disease to 'the high pressure at which men live and the habit of working the machine to its maximum capacity'. Psychiatrists such as the Menningers in the 1930s associated coronary disease with compulsive achievement concerns, intense competitiveness, and aggressiveness. However, it was not until the 1950s that the relationship between behavioral characteristics and clinical manifestation of CHD was studied in a systematic fashion. During that period two pioneering cardiologists, Drs Meyer Friedman and Ray Rosenman (1959) organized such attributes into a coherent behavioral concept, which they designated the Type A coronary-prone behavior pattern. To assess this behavior pattern, Rosenman and Friedman devised a structured diagnostic interview (SI) in which voice stylistics (loudness, rapidity of speech, etc), psychomotor mannerisms, and verbal reports could be reliably used to classify subjects as Type A or Type B (Friedman *et al.*, 1969; Rosenman, 1978). Early prevalence research by these investigators (Friedman and Rosenman, 1959, 1961) revealed a strong association between the occurrence of CHD and the Type A pattern. Subsequent publicity stimulated both additional prevalencer research and substantial criticism of this research, including complaints of small sample sizes, inadequate controls, biases in assessment, patient misattribution of characteristics to themselves, and other criticisms commonly associated with retrospective research. Thus, an essential step forward in establishing the Type A pattern as a risk factor for CHD was the conduct of a prospective study in which it was demonstrated that the Type A pattern predicted the *future* emergence of CHD in the same manner as the traditional risk factors. Under the direction of Ray Rosenman, the Western Collaborative Group Study (WCGS) was launched to accomplish this purpose (Rosenman *et al.*, 1964, 1975, 1976).

Men free of clinical manifestations of CHD ($n = 3154$), aged 39–59 were followed for 8.5 years. Approximately one-half were classified at intake as Type A as judged from the SI. The final results showed that Type A subjects were slightly more than twice as likely as Type B subjects to develop clinical CHD. Moreover, the two-to-one risk ratio remained after statistical adjustment for the four traditional risk factors (levels of age, serum cholesterol, systolic blood pressure, and smoking). In other words, the significant adjusted remainder (1.97, to be precise) was the amount of risk that was *independent* of traditional risk factors. It is also reported that the Type A pattern significantly predicted the incidence of new CHD among subjects in the WCGS who had remained free of CHD for the first 4.5 years of the study, despite the time lag between the event and the initial assessment of the pattern, and significantly predicted recurring clinical events. In sum, subjects in the WCGS with the Type A behavior pattern were approximately twice as likely as Type B subjects to exhibit clinical manifestations of CHD. This amount of risk was approximately equal to that incurred by any of the other traditional risk factors (for a review of the WCGS data, see Brand, 1978).

Although the Type A pattern was graded on a five-point scale (A_1, A_2, X, B_3, B_4), no convincing linear relationship was observed between these levels and incidence of CHD in WCGS. This lack of a linear association between different levels of Type A behavior and CHD may have been due to reductions in group sizes produced by finer discriminations beyond the A/B dichotomy. It is also possible that certain components in the Type A pattern are more predictive of CHD than others, but did not receive appropriate weighting in the initial classification. In other words, it appears useful to draw a distinction between the Type A pattern as a concept and coronary-prone behavior as a concept, which recognizes that not all components in the current definition of Type A may qualify as coronary-prone behavior, and that other yet unidentified behavioral attributes may be discovered by future research (Dembroski *et al.*, 1978a).

Matthews *et al.* (1977), who conducted component reanalyses of taped interviews from the WCGS, offered support for this distinction. They rated separately the numerous characteristics included in the Type A syndrome and showed that only a few of more than 40 attributes assessed in the interview significantly discriminated WCGS cases from controls. The key items primarily reflected potential for hostility, irritability, impatience, competitiveness, and vigorous voice stylistics. These findings raise the question, for example, of whether being hard-working, achievement-oriented, and getting things done quickly without at the same time being excessively and chronically competitive, hostile, impatient, or irritable in the process should qualify as coronary-prone behavior. If the definition of coronary-prone behavior is to be further refined and extended, more component analyses of this sort are essential.

Since coronary atherosclerosis is the disease often implicated in sudden cardiac death, it is very important to know whether this disease is related to the Type A pattern. Autopsy data from the WCGS showed that subjects classified as Type A possessed significantly greater degrees of atherosclerosis than Type B subjects (Friedman *et al.*, 1968). In addition, recently reported findings also showed through coronary angiography that the atherosclerotic process was significantly more advanced in Type A relative to Type B subjects (Blumenthal *et al.*, 1978; Frank *et al.*, 1978).

The findings reported above were derived from subjects designated as Type A or B by the interview assessment method. Another means of assessing the Type A pattern uses a computer-scored questionnaire, called the Jenkins Activity Survey (JAS). Unlike the interview, the JAS relies exclusively on self-reports of subjects to derive Type A and B classification. Seven independent retrospective studies conducted in the US and one in Poland have reported that the JAS A/B scale significantly discriminated coronary patients from controls. It is noted that these case–control studies contained a variety of population groups, and since random phenomena usually do not replicate, the results offer additional support for the association of the Type A pattern and CHD.

The JAS was also used to assess the Type A pattern in the WCGS (Jenkins *et al.*, 1974). The findings showed that it successfully predicted the incidence of CHD independent of standard risk factors. Although significantly related to CHD in the WCGS, the JAS was the weaker predictor of CHD of the two methods of assessment (Brand *et al.*, in press). However, the fact that an independent means of assessing the Type A pattern was used successfully in this study to predict CHD casts doubt on any classification bias interpretation of the findings. It is also noted that the JAS A/B scale was a stronger predictor of recurring myocardial infarction (MI) than of initial events and, in fact, was the strongest predictor of recurrent MI among all predictor variables available, including the standard risk factors. Finally, the JAS has also been retrospectively related to the severity of arteriographically determined atherosclerosis (Zyzanski *et al.*, 1976), although not in all studies (Dimsdale *et al.*, 1978) (for a review of the relation between JAS scores and CHD, see Zyzanski, 1978).

In summary, substantial evidence links the Type A pattern to the prevalence of CHD, incidence of CHD, recurrent MI, and the severity of atherosclerosis. In addition, further epidemiologic research support for the relationship between Type A behavior and CHD is available from numerous retrospective *and* prospective studies which measured Type A attributes by means other than the interview or JAS (Jenkins, 1976). Particularly noteworthy in this regard are very recent findings from a reanalysis of questionnaire data from the Framingham study, in which a subset of questions selected specifically to assess Type A behavior was found to predict both *prevalence* and *incidence* of CHD for *both* men and women (Haynes et al., 1978, 1980).

As Jenkins (1978) has pointed out, this is the first time in medical history that a behavior pattern not directly associated with consummatory behaviors or clinical symptoms has successfully and consistently predicted the emergence of chronic disease.Component anlyses of the Type A pattern suggest that behavioral attributes of hostile competitiveness, impatience, irritation, and vigorous voice stylistics appear to play a more important role in the association with CHD than other attributes of the pattern. Moreover, it may be the case that some of these attributes confer risk independently of others, which makes possible the intriguing notion that different behaviors may be equally coronary-prone and certain behaviors in combination may jointly intensify coronary risk. Much more research is needed, however, before a *definitive* list of coronary-prone behavioral characteristics is firmly established. Important to this effort is a careful examination of the current methods used to assess coronary-prone behavior.

Measurement of the Type A Pattern

The two most frequently used methods of assessing the Type A pattern, and the ones considered most reliable and valid, are the Rosenman et al. (1964) SI and the JAS developed by Jenkins et al. (1967).

The Structured Interview

The SI is a 10–15-minute interview, which consists of a series of questions concerning the subject's ambition, job involvement, work style, competitiveness, aggressiveness, impatience, and sense of time urgency. Most commonly, interviewers are trained by Rosenman and associates in order to insure that the SI is administered in a highly standardized manner. The major purpose of the interview is to determine the relative presence of Type A voice and psychomotor mannerisms, which include: loud, explosive, rapid, and accelerated speech stylistics; short latency answers; tautness of musculature and vigorous gestures; verbal competitiveness; and mannerisms of responding indicative of hostility (for a detailed account, see Rosenman, 1978). Although content of the answers is considered, Type designation is based primarily on the criteria described above.

At the present time, subjects are classified on a four-point scale: extreme A (A_1), predominantly Type A (A_2), indeterminant or mixed (Type X), and Type B, when a relative absence of Type A attributes is observed. Independent raters' interscorer agreement of Type classification most often ranges between 75 and 90 percent and usually hovers around 85 percent for the simple A/B dichotomy (Dembroski, 1978; Rosenman, 1978). Test–retest reliability of dichotomous typing in a study of over 1000 subjects in the WCGS was approximately 80 percent (tetrachloric correlation coefficient = 0.82) for periods that ranged between 12 and 20 months. Both test–retest and interjudge agreement typically are slightly lower for the four-point scale (A_1, A_2, X, B), but the simple A/B dichotomy is used most often in epidemiological research (Jenkins *et al.*, 1968).

To date, most of the data have been collected from white, employed, middle-aged male subjects. It is therefore unknown how interview-defined Type A's and B's are distributed in groups differing in age, sex, socioeconomic class, ethnicity, etc. However, some data suggest that the Type A pattern is more prevalent by a ratio of roughly 2 to 1 than the Type B pattern in managers and high-level executives (Howard *et al.*, 1976). Although the relative percentages change with different convenience samples, we also have found a higher prevalence of Type A's among male college students. Recently, Chesney *et al.* (in press), using *unequivocal* agreement between two independent raters as a criterion, were able to type 56 percent of a sample of 385 male employees of the Lockheed Space and Missile Company as Type A, but only 14 percent as Type B. Since their sample was very similar to subjects used in the WCGS, the results raise the question of whether the prevalence of Type A behavior has increased over the past 15 or 20 years, or whether the scoring procedures have changed over time.

In the future the use of component scoring would be highly desirable in order to provide data on the distribution of different elements of the Type A pattern (e.g. potential for hostility *vs.* explosive speech). In fact, this approach appears to be essential because if researchers continue to find disproportionate numbers of Type A's in their samples, the specificity value of the A/B dichotomy will be sharply diminished. Component analyses of the Type A pattern are needed, then, both to determine which components of the pattern are most predictive of clinical CHD and other relevant end-points *and* to improve the discriminability of the SI. Past research has been consistent in showing that voice stylistics account for the greatest amount of variance and reported content the least amount of variance in final Type designation (Schucker and Jacobs, 1977). However, other components, e.g. potential for hostility, show intermediate and only modest correlations with global Type A

(Dembroski *et al.*, 1978), but, as noted above, show a stronger relationship with clinical CHD than other components, e.g. speed of activity (Matthews *et al.*, 1977). Ours and others' factor-analytic studies have revealed such factors as competitive drive, vigorousness of response, impatience, hostility, voice stylistics, speed of activity, and job involvement (Matthews *et al.*, 1977). In our own work, independent raters routinely score three voice stylistics (loud and explosive, rapid and accelerated, and response latency), two attitudinal–behavioral mannerisms (verbal competitiveness and potential for hostility) and a variety of content dimensions reflecting such attributes as hard-driving competitive, hostility, speed of activity, and impatience (for details on this component scoring system see Dembroski, 1978). Correlations between raters for the above components are usually in the 0.80 range, indicating that components of the pattern can be reliably scored.

Jenkins Activity Survey

The JAS is a self-administered paper-and-pencil questionnaire, which consists of four subscales. The A/B subscale of the JAS was developed by systematically retaining those items that successfully discriminated A's and B's in repeated samples using the SI designation as the criterion (for a review of JAS development, see Jenkins, 1978). The remaining three factor-analytically derived subscales are: (a) hard driving (H); (b) speed and impatience (S/I); and (c) job involvement (J). However, it is important to note that only the empirically derived A/B subscale of the JAS predicted CHD in the WCGS. In this regard it should be remembered that reanalysis of WCGS data done by Matthews *et al.* (1977) suggested that individual items in the interview reflecting drive level, speed, and job involvement were not predictive of CHD.

At both one and four-year intervals the test–retest reliability of the JAS A/B scale in the WCGS was approximately 0.65, suggesting moderate but acceptable reliability (Jenkins *et al.*, 1974). Reliability of the subscales was comparable to that of the A/B scale. Over the years the JAS has been revised several times to enhance improvement of agreement with the SI, and it therefore would be desirable to re-examine the reliability of the currently used forms in a variety of population groups (for what is known about JAS scores in various population groups, see Zyzanski, 1978).

Interview *vs.* JAS Comparisons

Agreement between the SI and JAS in designating subjects as Type A and B has ranged between 56 and 75 percent (Brand *et al.*, in press; Chesney *et al.*, in press; Dembroski and MacDougall, 1978; Jenkins *et al.*, 1967; Kittel *et al.*, 1978; MacDougall *et al.*, 1979; Matthews and Saal, 1978). Based on a variety of studies, it is our belief that agreement between the SI and JAS will most often range between 60 and 65 percent both for college students and working adults (Chesney *et al.*, in press; MacDougall *et al.*, 1979). Corresponding Pearson correlations between JAS A/B scores and the four-point rating of the SI most often can be expected to range between 0.20 and 0.35 (Chesney *et al.*, in press; MacDougall *et al.*, 1978). It is thus abundantly clear that an SI-defined A is by no means synonymous with a JAS-defined A. This fact should be clearly recognized by researchers, and specification of the type of assessment procedures used to identify A's and B's should be common practice in discussions of the Type A concept.

The SI appears to be superior to the JAS in predicting clinical manifestations of CHD in the WCGS (Brand *et al.*, in press). According to the latter authors, the JAS derived nearly all of its predictive strength from its ability to duplicate the SI designation in the WCGS. Likewise, the SI has been shown to be a better predictor of angiographically determined severity of atherosclerosis, especially when large numbers of rural or female subjects are included in the sample (Blumenthal *et al.*, 1978). In addition the SI has also been shown to be a better predictor of challenge-induced cardiovascular reactivity than the JAS (Dembroski *et al.*, 1978b, 1979a).

In reflecting on the comparison between the two methods it should be remembered that the SI is actually a behavioral test in which speech characteristics and behavioral cues rather than verbal content are the primary bases for classifying subjects as Type A and B. Voice stylistics are much less prone to conscious or unconscious dissimulation (Ekman and Friesen, 1974; Jenkins, 1978; Rosenman, 1978). Indeed, such characteristics as vigorousness of response and explosive speech stylistics are sometimes unrelated to content of answers, although our work suggests that content of answers correlates between 0.35 and 0.50 with speech stylistics.

A great strength of the JAS relative to the interview is that it is scored as a continuous variable and, in fact, showed a linear relationship with clinical CHD in WCGS (Jenkins *et al.*, 1974). It also possesses the advantages of relatively easy, cost-efficient standardized group administration, and objective computerized scoring, which does not depend upon clinical or subjective judgments in designating subjects as more or less Type A. If the JAS predicted clinical CHD, the severity of atherosclerosis, and potentially damaging hemodynamic activity as well as the SI, it would clearly be the more desirable of the two measures. Unfortunately, at least with respect to the available data, this does not appear to be the case.

Occasionally researchers elect to use instruments other than the SI and JAS as measures of Type A. An important cautionary note to keep in mind is that *none of these measures* has been related to clinical CHD through programmatic research. The results of some of these studies do suggest, however, that other more effective methods than the JAS may be developed in the future to replace or supplement the SI. In the interim, however, researchers should be discouraged from using measures other than the SI or JAS as the *sole* means of assessing Type A behavior, since there is no guarantee that they will be measuring Type A behavior as it was defined in the major validity studies.

To summarize, assessment of the Type A pattern has included both speech-psychomotor characteristics and self-reports of a variety of behaviors. When possible, *both* the SI and JAS should be used as measures of coronary-prone behavior. Moreover, by this time it should be clear that present research suggests that some of the measured characteristics of the Type A pattern may be more potent predictors of CHD than others. In addition, other attributes not presently included in the Type A concept or the operational procedures of the SI and JAS may prove to be candidates for inclusion in the concept of coronary-prone behavior. Taken together, these results suggest that future research might profit from expansion of multi-dimensional component analyses of (a) self-reports of attitudes and be-haviors, (b) speech characteristics, (c) motor-behavior mannerisms, (d) psychological attributes, and (e) relevant physiological responses (Tasto *et al.*, 1978). In any case, it is emphasized that any new generation of measures of coronary-prone behavior should be validated against a variety of end-points including the SI, JAS, relevant physiological processes, and indices of CHD (MacDougall *et al.*, 1979).

Social Psychological Studies of Type A Individuals

A number of psychological tests have been administered to various samples to determine whether the Type A pattern is related to standard measures of personality. Briefly, the results of these studies showed that the Type A pattern, in general, reflects characteristics which are independent of tradi-tional measures of personality or psychopathology (Caffrey, 1968; Chesney *et al.*, in press; Rosenman *et al.*, 1974). A possible exception to this generaliza-tion is the finding in some studies that JAS-defined Type A but not SI-defined Type A tends to correlate positively with various measures of psychological distress, e.g. anxiety, neuroticism, depression (Chesney *et al.*, in press). The latter findings are worth remembering in view of the fact that historically psychological distress has been related to angina symptoms. It will be of interest to determine whether future research links JAS-defined Type A more with angina symptoms than myocardial infarction. In any event, psychological attributes that do correlate with SI-defined Type A tend to reflect trait characteristics consistent with the conceptual definition of Friedman and Rosenman. For example, attributes that have correlated with SI-defined Type A include self-reports of activity level, aggressiveness, dominance, self-confidence, achievement, impulsiveness, and the like. However, it is noteworthy that a study by Matthews and Saal (1978) found no correlation between McClelland's concept of need for achievement motivation (nAch), power, or affiliation and SI-defined Type A. The same study did disclose a modest positive relationship between resultant achievement motivation high nAch and low test anxiety and JAS Type A scores. All told, however, the use of other standard paper-and-pencil tests may not be the most fruitful approach to uncovering important behavioral characteristics associated with the Type A pattern, or in validating the concept of Type A as an organized and coherent behavioral–psychological attribute.

In regard to the latter issue, note that the definition of the Type A pattern emphasizes that the enhanced aggressive, impatient, and hard-driving behaviors which characterize the pattern occur most readily when appropriate social and/or physical environment challenges are present, and observations of such behavior derived from the interview or questionnaire methods are used to classify subjects as Type A or B. However, it is important to determine whether subjects typed as A or B by these methods do indeed behave in predictable ways when actually confronted with appropriate environmental conditions. Said another way, the validity of the Type A concept and the procedures used to assess it must be established by means other than interview and questionnaire methods.

Preliminary steps in this direction have been undertaken by Dr David Glass and his associates, who have conducted controlled social psychological laboratory and field research specifically designed to investigate the validity of the Type A concept (for a summary of this research, see Glass, 1977). For example, a study with college students was arranged so that the cooperative task performance of JAS-defined Type A subjects was deliberately slowed by another person. JAS-defined subjects, primarily those high on speed and impatience, compared to their Type B counterparts responded to the person with significantly more behavioral signs of impatience and irritation. In a more recent experiment, JAS-defined, Type A's relative to Type B's responded with greater behavioral aggression towards a person who interfered with their performance on an important task (Carver and Glass, 1978).

Another study showed that JAS-defined Type A's performed more poorly than B's on a task requiring slow, paced responding in order to achieve maximum reward (Glass et al., 1974). Presumably, the impatience of the Type A person makes it more difficult to inhibit behavior for prolonged periods of time. Additional differences between JAS-defined A's and B's were found in a study in which Type A's worked at near maximum capacity on a task, whether or not there was a deadline, while Type B's increased their effort only in response to the presence of a deadline. The same program of research also showed that JAS-defined Type A's physically exerted themselves (as measured by oxygen consumption) more than B's on a treadmill, but reported significantly less feeling of exhaustion than Type B's (Carver et al., 1976). In a related study Glass (1977) and his associates found that Type

A subjects endured an apparently incidental tone of ever-increasing loudness for a longer time than Type B's before making some effort to turn it off. This occurred in spite of the fact that both Types reported the sound to be equally obnoxious. Most recently, Weidner and Matthews (1978) reported an interesting study of symptom-reporting by Type A and B subjects. In this experiment independent groups of JAS-defined Type A and B female subjects were allowed to work on arithmetic problems for four minutes while experiencing either no background noise, predictable noise, or unpredictable noise. One-half of each group was led to expect that the experiment would terminate after four minutes while the other half believed that a second four-minute session would be forthcoming. At the end of the four minutes all subjects completed a 14-item symptom checklist and rated their level of fatigue. Type A's who believed that further testing would ensue reported less severe symptoms and fatigue than did either Type A's who believed that the experiment was terminating or Type B's in both conditions. These results suggest that Type A's experience subjectively equal fatigue to Type B's, but will suppress or more likely deny the symptoms if they believe that further effort is required. In all, these experiments offer some support for the construct validity of the Type A pattern by demonstrating that at least *JAS-defined Type A subjects* appear to be more aggressive, more impatient, and more hard-driving than their JAS-defined Type B counterparts under appropriate conditions.

Apart from directly evaluating the validity of the current Type A construct, social psychological laboratory research of this sort offers a convenient model through which additional attributes associated with Type A behavior can be uncovered. For example, Glass (1977) found some evidence that JAS-defined Type A subjects respond more vigorously than Type B's when threat of failure on an important task becomes salient, but give up trying to solve the problem sooner than B's. The behavioral and physiological implications of this apparent initial heightened concern with control of the environment followed by helplessness-prone tendencies deserves more attention in view of the fact that Glass (1977) has also associated the occurrence of severe non-controllable stressors (e.g. loss of job) with prevalence of CHD in Type A subjects. In other words, it is possible that pronounced uncontrollable stressors encountered in life may have more detrimental effects on Type A than Type B individuals However, until additional data are available, caution should be exercised in attributing this characteristic to Type A individuals.

Systematic investigations of actual differences between Type A and B individuals in naturalistic settings have not yet been reported, but findings from *self-report* correlational studies suggest that Type A's and B's may differ in predictable ways in everyday work-related situations. For example, a recent study of 236 managers in 12 different companies found that *SI*-defined Type A's compared to B's reported greater self-confidence, more dissatisfaction with having responsibility for supervising others, and more complaints about conflicting work demands and heavy workloads (Howard *et al.*, 1976, 1977). In another study of working men ($n = 943$), Type A scores were correlated positively and significantly, although very modestly, with a variety of indices of job status and success (Mettlin, 1976). The results of these studies offer some additional support for the validity of the Type A concept and, in addition, suggest that the work environment may be instrumental in inducing and maintaining Type A behavior. Alternatively, the research by Glass (1977) suggests that hard-driving behavior in the work situation may be self-imposed by Type A's in response to needs to control their environment. Findings from an experiment conducted with college students in our laboratory are consistent with this latter interpretation (Dembroski and Mac-Dougall, 1978). The results of this experiment showed that JAS-defined Type A's significantly more than B's actually elected to work alone rather than with others when under stress. Parallel correlational studies showed that a marked preference for working in solitude when under pressure was likewise characteristic of adult patients with coronary disease and the Type A pattern as assessed by the SI. Verbal probing of the reasons for this preference in both Type A students and adults indicated that the desire to work alone when under pressure arose from needs to control the work situation closely and guard against incompetence on the part of coworkers. In a somewhat related approach to the problem, Gastorf *et al.* (1980) subjected JAS-defined A's and B's either to a simple or complex task in the presence of others or while working alone, and found that the presence of others facilitated the performance of A's on the simple task, but impaired performance on the complex task. By contrast, no social facilitation effects were observed for Type B's. Moreover, Van Egeren (1979) has recently demonstrated that JAS-defined A's will more frequently elect to compete rather than cooperate in a mixed motive game. Again, these results can be interpreted as offering modest support for the validity of the Type A concept and also offer leads to other behavioral dimensions that might be associated with the Type A pattern.

In reviewing this literature, however, it is important to note that virtually all of the construct validity research has used the JAS to designate subjects as Type A and B. As we have noted in discussing the assessment of the Type A pattern, research now strongly indicates that the SI and JAS correlate rather poorly, and it is likely that the two instruments are defining only partially overlapping attributes. Thus, greatest weight should be placed on findings replicated using both assessment techniques. Unfortunately, very few studies have used the SI in construct validity research. In addition to the studies by Howard *et al.*, mentioned above, some early and informal observations by Rosenman and Friedman (1961) indicated that interview assessments of Type A/B tended to agree well with informal ratings made by colleagues and friends, suggesting a degree of generalizability to the behavior pattern. These observations were more formally replicated by Caffrey (1968) who found strong correlations between behavior assessments of trained interviewers and independent ratings made by superiors and peers of Trappist and Benedictine monks. However, if SI-defined Type A individuals are indeed generally competitive, impatient, hard-driving, and aggressive in their behavior, it remains to be demonstrated in research paradigms similar to those used by Glass and his associates.

Moreover, it must be emphasized that even if subsequent research shows unequivocally that either SI or JAS-defined Type A relative to Type B subjects are behaviorally more impatient, more aggressive, more competitive, and the like, there is absolutely no guarantee that all or even most of these behaviors are differentially exciting physiological processes that may be instrumental in the etiology of CHD. A more direct means of investigating the latter possibility is to record physiological responses while Type A and B subjects are engaged in similar behaviors.

Social Psychophysiological Studies of Type A Individuals

The rationale for social psychophysiological study of the Type A pattern rests on the major assumption that chronic and excessive sympathetic nervous system (SNS) arousal and related neuroendocrine activity can play a role in atherogenesis and precipitate clinical coronary events. While there is no programmatic research that has linked such physiological arousal directly to the emergence of CHD in humans, there is abundant animal research that makes plausible the latter hypothesis. A number of stress-induced physiological derangements have been observed in animals, including myofibrillary degeneration of the heart, atherosclerosis, arterial hypertension, and exaggerated levels of serum cholesterol. These pathologies are primarily observed under conditions in which the animal is actively coping with environmental stressors. On the other hand, ventricular arrest, bradycardia, hypotension, renal defects, and gastrointestinal ulceration are frequently observed when the animal lacks an effective means of coping with stressors (for a review of these effects, see Herd, 1978; Schneiderman, 1978).

In humans environmental stressors have been shown to increase serum cholesterol, blood pressure, heart rate, circulating catecholamines, and other related activity associated with defensive physiological arousal (e.g. Peterson *et al.*, 1962). Theoretically, a variety of mechanisms exist through which such physiological responses can excite pathophysiological processes, especially if the situation does not permit appropriate musculo-skeletal discharge of the arousal state (see, for example, Buell and Eliot, 1979; Davis, 1974; Eliot, 1979; Herd, 1978; Williams, 1978). In this connection, modern twentieth-century existence presents numerous circumstances that induce such defensive physiological arousal under relatively sedentary conditions. If it can be demonstrated that Type A's relative to Type B's respond to physical and/or social environmental challenges with enhanced SNS and neuroendocrine activation, then a plausible means is suggested through which the behavior pattern might be translated into CHD and clinical events.

In a lengthy program of early research, Friedman and Rosenman discovered a number of differences in physiological functioning between Type A and B individuals. For example, compared to their Type B counterparts, middle-aged male SI-defined Type A_1 subjects (behaviorally extreme Type A's)

(a) showed elevated urinary and serum levels of norepinephrine during their working day and in response to the challenge of a competitive contest;
(b) exhibited hypercholesterolemia;
(c) showed elevated triglycerides before and after ingestion of a test fat meal, and marked postprandial sludging of erythrocytes;
(d) exhibited higher serum levels of ACTH and subnormal secretion of 17-hydroxy-corticosteroids in response to an injection of ACTH;
(e) showed diminished serum levels of growth hormone both before and after arginine challenge;
(f) displayed a hyperinsulinemic response to a glucose challenge, although not showing an abnormal glucose tolerance; and
(g) exhibited more rapid blood clotting (for a review of this research, see Friedman, 1977, 1978).

Following the lead of Rosenman *et al.* (1964) and Friedman *et al.* (1975), more recent research has been directed toward investigating psychophysiological responses of Type A and B subjects subjected to a variety of psychological and performance challenges. Such research is predicated on the dual assumptions that:

(a) non-invasive measures of blood pressure, heart rate, and peripheral vasomotor activity can be used to index the individual's tendency to evidence fundamentally more pathogenic adrenocortical and sympathetic ANS adrenomedullary responses which have been linked to CHD in animal research; and
(b) social psychological manipulations of dimensions of threat, demand, and challenge in the laboratory are accurate simulations of experiences encountered by the individual in day-to-day life, and thus allow one to identify features of the environment and characteristics of the individual which are strongly related to a tendency to evidence potentially pathological physiological responses.

Initial demonstration studies of this sort revealed that although not differing in baseline levels, both SI- and JAS-defined Type A college students showed greater elevations in SBP (and in one study, HR) to a psychomotor performance challenge than did their Type B counterparts (Dembroski *et al.*, 1977; Manuck *et al.*, 1978). Subsequent research has focused on:

(a) identifying the social psychological variables which are important in provoking the differential arousal; and

(b) differentiating which components of the Type A pattern are most predictive of such ANS arousal.

Studies of the first sort have focused on the concept of environmental challenge as an elicitor of A–B differences in physiological arousal. This attention is a logical outgrowth of the basic conceptualization of Type A as a behavioral response to environmental demand. The results of such studies are not entirely consistent. Dembroski *et al.* (1979a) found that under verbal instructions designed to minimize the perceived difficulty of both a cold pressor and reaction time task, SI-defined Type A and B subjects showed rather small differences in blood pressure and heart rate. However, where the instructions emphasized the difficulty and challenge of the task, the differences between the two groups were magnified. By contrast, although obtaining an overall A–B difference in reactivity, Manuck and Garland (1979) found no differential effect on the cardiovascular responsivity of JAS-defined Type A and B subjects from a challenge manipulation involving no incentive *vs.* a monetary incentive for criterion performance on a concept formation task. Most recently, Glass *et al.* (1980), using a within-subject design with SI-defined A's and B's, also found an overall A–B difference in blood pressure, heart rate, and serum epinephrine to the challenge of a television game, but no differential effect of an added monetary incentive. In a separate experiment involving face-to-face competition with a trained confederate, while A–B differences in physiological reactivity were not observed when the confederate simply played the game without comment, in a condition where the confederate derogated the subject's performance, Type A's showed markedly greater cardiovascular and catecholaminic reactivity than Type B's.

A tentative interpretation of all of these findings is that Type A's are primarily responsive to the social or interpersonal aspects of performance challenge, while monetary incentive of themselves are less significant in evoking physiological arousal. This hypothesis is consistent with other findings that both male (Dembroski *et al.*, 1979b) and female (MacDougall *et al.*, in press) Type A's are more physiologically aroused than their Type B counterparts during both the SI and a challenging history quiz. This interpretation is complicated, however, by the failure in the Glass *et al.* study to observe reactivity differences between the Types during simple face-to-face competition. This latter observation argues that the differences between Type A and B subjects in this regard are not absolute, but may reflect threshold differences in the perception of varying levels of interpersonal challenge, with Type A's evidencing greater arousal at lower thresholds.

In contrast to the general pattern of differences in physiological reactivity between Type A and B subjects reported in the above studies, several researchers have failed to observe physiological differences between the Types. Scherwitz *et al.* (1978), using both the SI and JAS, and Lott and Gatchell (1978), using the JAS alone, have reported no significant cardiovascular reactivity differences between Type A and B subjects in response to psychomotor tasks and physiological stressors (cold pressor test). Moreover, Frankenhaeuser *et al.* (1978a) found no heart rate or catecholamine differences between JAS-typed Swedish subjects in response to a choice reaction time task, although a subsequent study did find A–B differences in epinephrine secretion in response to forced inactivity (Frankenhaeuser *et al.*, 1978b). These negative findings emphasize the fact that Type A is not synonymous with a tendency to show consistently higher levels of physiological reactivity. Rather, it seems that the Type A individual is statistically more prone than his Type B counterpart to show such responses under appropriate environmental conditions.

In addition to investigating the environmental determinants responsible for differential arousal in Type A subjects, social psychophysiological research has begun to distinguish which aspects of the pattern are most closely related to the greater reactivity in Type A's. Dembroski *et al.* (1978b) found that of all stylistics observed in the SI, clinical judgments of potential for hostility bore the strongest relationship to challenge-induced arousal in *both* Type A's and B's, with Type A's showing greater average levels of hostility. More recently, Dembroski *et al.* (1979a) found that high-hostile Type A's were prone to show large cardiovascular reactions regardless of the level of challenge while low-hostile Type A's could be provoked only under conditions of marked interpersonal appeals for heightened performance. The results of these two studies present an interesting parallel to the findings of the Matthews *et al.* (1977) reanalysis of the WCGS data, where hostility and irritability were found to be among the factors associated with CHD incidence, and to the Williams *et al.* (1978) study linking measures of hostility from the Minnesota Multiphasic Personality Inventory (MMPI) to severity of atherosclerosis. Other investigators have reported some evidence suggesting the importance of self-involvement (Scherwitz *et al.*, 1978), and cognitive complexity (Streufert *et al.*, 1979) to the greater cardiovascular reactivity seen on the part of Type A subjects. Finally, MacDougall *et al.* (1981) have presented some preliminary findings which suggest that female Type A subjects are differentially responsive to social, but not psychomotor, performance challenges, which is not the case for Type A males.

Thus, while the foregoing social psychophysiological research has yielded some preliminary insight into both the environmental and person variables which modulate the greater physiological reactivity of Type A subjects, it must be said that the work is still in its infancy. Again and again we have observed that in the face of identical challenges, one clear-cut Type A may evidence large and sustained cardiovascular arousal, while another apparently equally clear-cut Type A may show modest or no reactivity. If, indeed, the tendency to evidence exaggerated ANS and related neuroendocrine arousal predisposes one to greater risk of CHD, it remains to identify the entire range of situational and individual difference variables responsible for such differences. To the degree that analyses of this sort allow one to transcend the simple A–B dichotomy in identifying coronary-prone individuals, then future research may begin to identify various maneuvers that may be used to test the hypothesis that challenge-induced physiological reactivity is a better predictor of CHD than purely behavioral assessment procedures.

Efforts directed toward the latter end will need to demonstrate that physiological response to a single or perhaps a series of psychophysiological maneuvers in the laboratory can predict with good reliability the physiological reactions of individuals in their everyday life. In pursuing this aim it will be worthwhile to continue assessment of the Type A pattern and its components to determine whether physiological reactivity in the laboratory predicts arousal in everyday life more accurately in some individuals than others. For example, we have found clear tendencies for some individuals to show a marked increase and then decrease in physiological response during performance, while others maintain a high level of arousal throughout the time-frame of the task.

If it can be determined that some individuals habitually respond to the demands of daily existence with enhanced physiological response, then intervention tactics can be tested to determine the best means of reducing such arousal. At present, only minimal research has been devoted to altering behavioral and physiological manifestations of the Type A pattern, but future work in this area can be expected to suggest techniques that may reduce excessive physiological reactivity.

Intervention

Extensive clinical trials are currently under way both in the United States and in Europe to assess the causal status of the traditional CHD risk factors. However, intervention research in the Type A area is only preliminary despite the fact that such research is badly needed for at least two major reasons. First, the clinical trials are needed to firmly establish the causal association between Type A behavior and CHD. Second, intervention research is a potent procedure for refining the more general concept of Type A and coronary-prone behavior. As noted earlier, it appears that only some components of the Type A pattern are actually associated with CHD, while other attributes may be merely benign correlates. Well-designed intervention studies can be launched to change certain aspects of the behavior pattern in order to determine the effects on such end-points as levels of serum cholesterol, blood pressure, physiological reactivity to laboratory or day-to-day demands, coronary atherogenesis, and incidence of CHD.

To date, however, only a few preliminary studies have emerged. Suinn (1975) has developed the Cardiac Stress Management Program which consists of anxiety management training and image-based rehearsal of non-Type A behavioral responses to daily stressors. Suinn and Bloom (1978) attempted to apply the anxiety management portion of their program to healthy JAS-defined Type A volunteers in an effort to assess the primary prevention potential of the training. Type A's ($n = 7$) received three weeks of therapy, while seven other Type A's served as wait-list controls. The results revealed that treated subjects showed some reduction in scores on the H/D scale of the JAS (but not on the A/B scale) and in state and trait anxiety. However, no significant reduction was observed in cholesterol and triglyceride levels, nor were any changes observed in blood pressure. Similarly, in an unpublished study by Jenni and Wolersheim a mixed group of healthy individuals and heart patients, typed as A's by the SI, were treated either with cognitive insight therapy or an anxiety management program. As in the Suinn study, both groups achieved reductions in state and trait anxiety, which appeared to be somewhat better maintained for the anxiety management group. However, therapy effects on serum cholesterol in the latter study were ambiguous with the cognitive therapy subjects showing a mild reduction in levels, and stress management subjects a substantial increase.

Based on their extensive clinical experience, Rosenman and Friedman (1977) maintain that significant and enduring behavioral changes are difficult to achieve until individuals gain sufficient insight into the pervasive and potentially destructive role which Type A behavior plays in their lives. Thus, a major focus of a pilot study they have conducted is a group therapeutic regimen involving the achievement of insight into the dynamics of the behavior pattern. They also included skill training in the development and practice of alternatives to Type A behavioral responses, the discovery of protective avocational interests, and the reduction in motor activity and level of tension. In short, their techniques aim at significant reorientation in the patient's lifestyle. Although formal data are not available as yet, the anecdotal reports given by the authors are certainly encouraging.

A similar but more focused approach has been attempted by Roskies and her co-workers (Roskies *et al.*, 1978, 1979). Professional and executive volunteers who had been identified as extreme Type A's by the SI ($n = 25$) received either 14 group sessions of traditional insight-oriented therapy or 14 group sessions of behaviorally oriented training with daily home-based exercises. An additional six subjects possessed of unknown clinical symptomatology of CHD were subjected to a second behavior therapy group which received treatement identical to that of the healthy volunteers. All three groups showed significant *reductions* in serum cholesterol, systolic and diastolic blood pressure, several psychological symptoms and level of experienced time pressures, and *increases* in general life-satisfaction. The two behavior groups showed significantly greater reduction in serum cholesterol than did the psychotherapy group. All groups maintained significant decreases in both blood pressure and amount of reported overtime at six-month follow-up, but members of the psychotherapy group showed marked recidivism in serum cholesterol, number of psychological symptoms, and life-satisfaction. Of the members of the two behavior therapy groups, those with ECG abnormalities showed somewhat more improvement in levels of psychological symptoms. One reason for these follow-up differences between the psychotherapy and behavior therapy groups might have been the continued availability of specific relaxation techniques and exercises learned during the behavioral training.

The research reported to date has been extremely restricted in size and has aimed at producing reductions in psychological and biological end-points once or twice removed from clinically manifest CHD. The major outcome that must be demonstrated is to show that alterations in Type A behavior actually reduce the incidence of CHD. The only study employing CHD as an end-point is presently under way under the direction of Dr Meyer Friedman at the Harold Brunn Institute. This five-year prospective study is aimed at the comparison of 600 post-MI Type A and B subjects receiving a broadly based group therapy regimen with 300 post-MI controls who receive only the standard medical treatment and health information. Although early results are encouraging at the present time, sufficient data are not yet available concerning morbidity and mortality among the groups to assess the effectiveness of the treatment in any definitive manner.

In sum, intervention research at the present time has been most tentative in terms of the questions asked and quite mixed in the conclusions obtained. It is not yet established that intervention-induced alterations of Type A behavior are effective in reducing CHD. Moreover, we can draw no firm conclusions concerning the most effective way to intervene in changing important parts of the behavior pattern or in insulating individuals from the effects of their behavior or their physiology. However, there appears to be a sufficient number of positive findings to encourage researchers to undertake conceptually more refined and more tightly controlled studies. In this regard, a recently constituted NIH review panel concerned with the Type A pattern and its association with CHD has concluded that future research must specifically address the problems of:

(a) consistent assessment procedures for defining Type A;

(b) the development of more appropriate control procedures to provide reference points against which treatment effects can be assessed; and

(c) the development of more medically meaningful and artifact-free therapeutic end-points.

Test–retest study of the behavior pattern shows that it is relatively stable over time and it is likely that the physiological concomitants of the pattern are as well. Once the situational variables which evoke those behaviors that are coronary-prone are identified, it may then be possible to alter such elements in the environment. If this is not feasible, it may be possible for individuals to learn to (a) avoid the provocative situations, (b) perceive the events differently, (c) behave in a manner that diminishes the impact of the situation, or (d) control emotional and physiological reactions to the situation. Pharmacological interventions might also be used, either independently of, or in conjunction with, behavioral interventions, to block potentially damaging physiological reactions associated with Type A behaviors. Any one or combination of the above strategies can be applied in controlled studies aimed at reducing risk factors or CHD. It is noteworthy that attempts to alter traditional risk factors and reduce CHD have not so far yielded encouraging results. If CHD is indeed caused by multiple factors, surely intervention on multiple factors, including coronary-prone behaviors, is the strategy that offers the greatest hope of reversing the pandemic of CHD.

References

Blumenthal, J. A., Williams, R., Kong, Y., et al. (1978). 'Type A behavior and angiographically documented coronary disease', Circulation, 58, 634–639.

Brand, R. J. (1978). 'Coronary-prone behavior as an independent risk factor for coronary heart disease', Dembroski, T. M., Weiss, S. M., Shields, J. L. et al. (eds.), Coronary-prone Behavior. Springer-Verlag, New York.

Brand, R. J., Rosenman, R. H., Jenkins, C. D., et al. (in press). 'Comparison of coronary heart disease prediction in the Western Collaborative Group Study using the structured interview and the Jenkins Activity Survey assessments of the coronary-prone Type A behavior pattern', Journal of Chronic Diseases.

Brand, R. J., Rosenman, R. H., Sholtz, R. I., and Friedman, M. (1976). 'Multivariate prediction of coronary heart disease in the Western Collaborative Group Study compared to the findings of the Framingham Study', Circulation, 53, 348–355.

Buell, J. C., and Eliot, R. S. (1979). 'Stress and cardiovascular disease', Modern Concepts of Cardiovascular Disease, 4, 19–24.

Caffrey, B. (1968). Reliability and validity of personality and behavioral measures in a study of coronary heart disease', Journal of Chronic Diseases, 21, 191–204.

Carver, C. S., Coleman, A. E., and Glass, D. C. (1976). 'The coronary-prone behavior pattern and the suppression of fatigue on a treadmill test', Journal of Personality and Social Psychology, 33, 460–466.

Carver, C. S., and Glass, D. C. (1978). Coronary-prone behavior pattern and inter-personal aggression. Journal of Personality and Social Psychology, 36, 361–366.

Chesney, M. A., Black, G. W., Chadwick, J. H., and Rosenman, R. H. (in press). 'Psychological correlates of the coronary prone behavior pattern', *Journal of Behavioral Medicine*.

Davis, R. (1974). 'Stress and hemostatic mechanisms', in Eliot, R. S. (ed.), *Stress and the Heart*, pp. 97–122. Futura, Mount Kisco, NY.

Dembroski, T. M. (1978). 'Reliability and validity of methods used to assess coronary-prone behavior', Dembroski, T. M., Weiss, S. M., Shields, J. L. *et al.* (eds.), *Coronary-prone Behavior*, Springer-Verlag, New York.

Dembroski, T. M., Caffery, B., Jenkins, C. D., *et al.* (1978a). 'Section summary: assessment of coronary-prone behavior', in Dembroski, T. M., Weiss, S. M., Shields, J. L. *et al.* (eds.), *Coronary-prone Behavior*. Springer-Verlag, New York.

Dembroski, T. M., and MacDougall, J. M. (1978). 'Stress effects on affiliation preferences among subjects possessing the Type A coronary-prone behavior pattern', *Journal of Personality and Social Psychology*, **36**, 23–33.

Dembroski, T. M., MacDougall, J. M., Herd, J. A., and Shields, J. L. (1979a). 'Effects of level of challenge on pressor and heart rate responses in Type A and B subjects', *Journal of Applied Social Psychology*, **9**, 209–228.

Dembroski, T. M., MacDougall, J. M., and Lushene, R. (1979b). 'Interpersonal interaction and cardiovascular response in Type A subjects and coronary patients', *Journal of Human Stress*, **5**, 28–36.

Dembroski, T. M., MacDougall, J. M., and Shields, J. L. (1977). 'Physiologic reactions to social challenge in persons evidencing the Type A coronary-prone behavior pattern', *Journal of Human Stress*, **3**, 2–10.

Dembroski, T. M., MacDougall, J. M., Shields, J. L., *et al.* (1978b). 'Components of the Type A coronary-prone behavior pattern and cardiovascular responses to psychomotor performance challenge', *Journal of Behavioral Medicine*, **1**, 159–176.

Dimsdale, J. E., Hackett, T. P., Hitter, A. M., *et al.* (1978). 'Type A personality and extent of coronary atherosclerosis', *American Journal of Cardiology*, **42**, 583–586.

Ekman, P., and Friesen, W. V. (1974). 'Detecting deception from the body or face', *Journal of Personality and Social Psychology*, **29**, 288–298.

Eliot, R. S. (ed.) (1979). *Stress and the Major Cardiovascular Diseases*. Futura, Mount Kisco, NY.

Frank, K. A., Heller, S. S., Kornfeld, D. S., *et al.* (1978). 'Type A behavior pattern and coronary angiographic findings', *Journal of the American Medical Association*, **240**, 761–763.

Frankenhaeuser, M., Lundberg, U., and Forsman, L. (1978a). 'Dissociation between sympathetic–adrenal and pituitary–adrenal responses to an achievement situation characterized by high controllability: comparison between Type A and Type B males and females'. Report from the Department of Psychology, Rep. 540. University of Stockholm.

Frankenhaeuser, M., Lundberg, U., and Forsman, L. (1978b). 'Note on arousing Type A persons by depriving them of work'. Report from the Department of Psychology, Rep. 539. University of Stockholm.

Friedman, M. (1977). 'Type A behavior pattern: some of its pathophysiological components', *Bulletin of the New York Academy of Medicine*, **53**, 593–604.

Friedman, M. (1978). 'Type A behavior: its possible relationship to pathogenetic processes responsible for coronary heart disease', In Dembroski, T. M., Weiss, S. M., Shields, J. L. *et al.* (eds), *Coronary-prone Behavior*. Springer-Verlag, New York.

Friedman, M., Brown, A. E., and Rosenman, R. H. (1969). 'Voice analysis test for detection of behavior pattern: responses of normal men and coronary patients', *Journal of the American Medical Association*, **208**, 828–836.

Friedman, M., Byers, S. O., Diamant, J., and Rosenman, R. H. (1975). 'Plasma catecholamine response of coronary-prone subjects (Type A) to a specific challenge', *Metabolism*, **4**, 205–210.

Friedman, M., and Rosenman, R. H. (1959). 'Association of a specific overt behavior pattern with increases in blood cholesterol, blood clotting time, incidence of arcus senilis and clinical coronary artery disease', *Journal of the American Medical Association*, **169**, 1286–1296.

Friedman, M., Rosenman, R. H., Straus, R., *et al.* (1968). 'The relationship of behavior pattern A to the state of the coronary vasculature: a study of 51 autopsied subjects', *American Journal of Medicine*, **44**, 525–538.

Gastorf, J. W., Suls, J. S., and Sanders, G. S. (1980). 'The Type A coronary-prone behavior pattern and social facilitation'. *Journal of Personality and Social Psychology*, **38**, 773–780.

Glass, D. C. (1977). *Behavior Patterns, Stress and Coronary Disease*. Lawrence Erlbaum, Hillsdale, NJ.

Glass, D. C., Krakoff, L. R., Contrada, R., *et al.* (1980). 'Effect of harassment and competition upon cardiovascular and plasma catecholaminic responses in Type A and B individuals', *Psychophysiology*, **17**, 453–463.

Glass, D. C., Snyder, M. L., and Hollis, J. F. (1974). 'Time urgency and the Type A coronary-prone behavior pattern', *Journal of Applied Social Psychology*, **4**, 125–140.

Haynes, S., Feinleib, M., and Kannel, W. (1980). 'The relationship of psychosocial factors to coronary heart disease in the Framingham Study: eight-year incidence of coronary heart disease', *American Journal of Epidemiology*, **111**, 37–58.

Haynes, S., Feinleib, M., Levine, S., *et al.* (1978). 'The relationship of psychosocial factors to coronary heart disease in the Framingham study: prevalence of coronary heart disease', *American Journal of Epidemiology*, **107**, 384–402.

Herd, J. A. (1978). 'Physiological correlates of coronary prone behavior', in Dembroski, T. M., Weiss, S. M., Shields, J. L. *et al.* (eds.), *Coronary-prone Behavior*. Springer-Verlag, New York.

Howard, J. H., Cunningham, D. A. and Rechnitzer, P. A. (1976). 'Health patterns associated with Type A behavior: a managerial population', *Journal of Human Stress*, **2**, 24–32.

Howard, J. H., Cunningham, D. A., and Rechnitzer, P. A. (1977). 'Work patterns associated with Type A behavior: a managerial population', *Human Relations*, **30**, 825–836.

Jenkins, C. D. (1976). 'Recent evidence supporting psychologic and social risk factors for coronary disease', *New England Journal of Medicine*, **294**, 987–994, 1033–1038.

Jenkins, C. D. (1978). 'Behavioral risk factors in coronary artery disease', *Annual Review of Medicine*, **29**, 543–562

Jenkins, C. D., Rosenman, R. H., and Friedman, M. (1967). 'Development of an objective psychological test for the determination of the coronary-prone behavior pattern in employed men', *Journal of Chronic Diseases*, **20**, 371–379.

Jenkins, C. D., Rosenman, R. H., and Friedman, M. (1968). Replicability of rating the coronary-prone behavior pattern. *British Journal of Preventive and Social Medicine*, **22**, 16–22.

Jenkins, C. D., Rosenman, R. H., and Zyzanski, S. J. (1974). 'Prediction of clinical coronary heart disease by a test for the coronary-prone behavior pattern, *New England Journal of Medicine*, **290**, 1271–1275.

Keys, A. (1970). 'Coronary heart disease in seven countries: XIII multiple variables', *Circulation*, **41**, 138–144.

Kittel, F., Kornitzer, M., Zyzanski, S. J., *et al*. (1978). 'Two methods of assessing the Type A coronary-prone behavior pattern in Belgium', *Journal of Chronic Diseases*, **31**, 147–155.

Lott, G. G., and Gatchel, R. J. (1978). 'A multi-response analysis of learned heart rate control', *Psychophysiology*, **15**, 576–581.

MacDougall, J. M., Dembroski, T. M., and Musante, L. (1979). 'The structured interview and questionnaire methods of assessing coronary-prone behavior in male and female college students', *Journal of Behavioral Medicine*, **2**, 71–83.

MacDougall, J. M., Dembrowski, T. M., and Krantz, D. (1981). Effects of types of challenge on pressor and heart rate responses in Type A and B women. *Psychophysiology*, **18**, 1–9.

Manuck, S. B., Craft, S. A., and Gold, K. J. (1978). Coronary-prone behavior pattern and cardiovascular response. *Psychophysiology*, **15**, 403–411.

Manuck, S. B., and Garland, F. N. (1979). Coronary-prone behavior pattern, task incentive and cardiovascular response. *Psychophysiology*, **16**, 136–147.

Matthews, K. A., Glass, D. C., Rosenman, R. H., and Bortner, R. W. (1977). 'Competitive drive, Pattern A, and coronary heart disease: a further analysis of some data from the Western Collaborative Group Study. *Journal of Chronic Diseases*, **30**, 489–498.

Matthews, K. A., and Saal, F. E. (1978).'The relationship of the Type A coronary-prone behavior pattern to achievement, power, and affiliation motives', *Psychosomatic Medicine*, **40**, 631–636.

Mettlin, C. (1976). 'Occupational careers and the prevention of coronary-prone behavior', *Social Science and Medicine*, **10**, 367–372.

Peterson, J. E., Keith, R. A., and Wilcox, A. A. (1962). 'Hourly changes in serum cholesterol concentration: effects of the anticipation of stress', *Circulation*, **25**, 798–803.

Rosenman, R. H. (1978). 'The interview method of assessment of the coronary-prone behavior pattern', in Dembroski, T. M., Weiss, S. M., Shields, J. L. *et al*. (eds), *Coronary-prone Behavior*. Springer-Verlag, New York.

Rosenman, R. H., Brand, R. J., Jenkins, C. D., *et al*. (1975). 'Coronary heart disease in the Western Collaborative Group Study: final follow-up experience of 8½ years', *Journal of the American Medical Association*, **223**, 872–877.

Rosenman, R. H., Brand, R. J., Sholtz, R. I., and Friedman, M. (1976). 'Multivariate prediction of coronary heart disease during 8.5 year follow-up in the Western collaborative Group Study', *American Journal of Cardiology*, **37**, 903–910.

Rosenman, R. H., and Friedman, M. (1961). 'Association of a specific overt behavior pattern in females with blood and cardiovascular findings', *Circulation*, **24**, 1173–1184.

Rosenman, R. H., and Friedman, M. (1974). 'Neurogenic factors in pathogenesis of coronary heart disease', *Medical Clinics of North America*, **58**, 269–279.

Rosenman, R. H., and Friedman, M. (1977). 'Modifying Type A behavior pattern', *Journal of Psychosomatic Research*, **21**, 323–331.

Rosenman, R. H., Friedman, M., Straus, R., *et al*. (1964). 'A predictive study of coronary heart disease: the Western Collaborative Group Study', *Journal of the American Medical Association*, **189**, 15–22.

Rosenman, R. H., Rahe, R. H., Borhani, N. O., and Feinleib, M. (1974). 'Heritability of personality and behavior'. *Proceedings of the First International Congress of Twin Studies*, Rome, Italy, November.

Roskies, E., Kearney, H., Spevack, M., *et al.* (1979). 'Generalizability and durability of the treatment effects in an intervention program for coronary-prone (Type A) managers', *Journal of Behavioral Medicine*, **2**, 195–207.

Roskies, E., Spevack, M., Surkis, A., *et al.* (1978). 'Changing the coronary-prone (Type A) behavior pattern in a nonclinical population', *Journal of Behavioral Medicine*, **1**, 201–216.

Scherwitz, L., Leventhal, H., Cleary, P., and Laman, C. (1978). 'Type A behavior: consideration for risk modification', *Health Values: Achieving High Level Wellness*, **6**, 291–296.

Schneiderman, N. (1978) 'Animal models relating behavioral stress and cardiovascular pathology,' in Dembroski, T. M., Weiss, S. M., Shields, J. L. *et al.* (eds), *Coronary-prone Behavior*. Springer-Verlag, New York.

Schucker, B., and Jacobs, D. R. (1977). 'Assessment of behavioral risks for coronary disease by voice characteristics', *Psychosomatic Medicine*, **39**, 219–228.

Streufert, S., Streufert, S., Dembroski, T., and MacDougall, J. (1979). 'Complexity, coronary-prone behavior and physiological response,' in Oborne, D., Grunberg, M., and Eiser, J. R. (eds), *Research in Psychology and Medicine*. Vol. 1. Academic Press, London.

Suinn, R. (1975). 'The cardiac stress management program for Type A patients', *Cardiac Rehabilitation*, **5**, 13–15.

Suinn, R. M., and Bloom, L. J. (1978). 'Anxiety management training for pattern A behavior', *Journal of Behavioral Medicine*, **1**, 25–35.

Tasto, D. L., Chesney, M. A., and Chadwick, J. A. (1978). 'Multi-dimensional analysis of coronary-prone behavior', in Dembroski, T. M., Weiss, S. M., Shields, J. L. *et al.* (eds), *Coronary-prone Behavior*. Springer-Verlag, New York.

Van Egeren, L. F. (1979). 'Cardiovascular changes during social competition in mixed motive game', *Journal of Personality and Social Psychology*, **37**, 858–864.

Weidner, G., and Matthews, K. A. (1978). 'Reported physical symptoms elicited by unpredicatable events and the Type A coronary-prone behavior pattern', *Journal of Personality and Social Psychology*, **36**, 213–220.

Williams, R. B. (1978). 'Psychophysiological processes, the coronary-prone behavior pattern, and coronary heart disease', in Dembroski, T. M., Weiss, S. M., Shields, J. L. *et al.* (eds), *Coronary-prone Behavior*. Springer-Verlag, New York.

Williams, R. B., Haney, T., Gentry, W. D., and Kong, Y. (1978). 'Relation between hostility and arteriographically documented coronary atherosclerosis', *Psychosomatic Medicine*, **40**, 88.

Zyzanski, S. J. (1978). 'Coronary prone behavior pattern and coronary heart disease: Epidemiological evidence', in Dembroski, T. M., Weiss, S. M., Shields, J. L. *et al.* (eds), *Coronary-prone Behavior*. Springer-Verlag, New York.

Zyzanski, S. J., Jenkins, C. D., Ryan, T. J., *et al*, (1976). Psychological correlates of coronary angiographic findings', *Archives of Internal Medicine*, **136**, 1234–1237.

Social Psychology and Behavioral Medicine
Edited by J. Richard Eiser
© 1982 John Wiley & Sons Ltd

Chapter 4

Experimentation in behavioral medicine: in search of an applicable method

SIEGFRIED STREUFERT and SUSAN C. STREUFERT

Current Research Methods

Behavioral medicine is not a discipline, but rather a cooperative venture among a number of disciplines. Each of these areas of scientific endeavor not only contributes its knowledge and its theories, but also its typical research methods. Despite the potential richness of methodologies that might have grown out of this cooperation we often find ourselves in difficulties when we intend to demonstrate causal relationships between our independent and dependent variables. For example, research on coronary-prone behavior has clearly established that *some* relationship between such variables as stress experience, behavioral style, and reinforcement on the one hand, and physiological disease on the other hand, does exist. Yet despite valiant efforts we have so far not been able to demonstrate what the causal linkages between behavior and disease are. At present we must still speculate about what this causal link is likely to be. Two difficulties stand in our way: the first is concerned with our lack of knowledge about the physiological mechanisms that (we believe) translate perception, information-processing, personality, or response style into organ damage. Overcoming that problem must be left to a good amount of cooperative research by behavioral and biomedical scientists. The second difficulty concerns the very research methods which behavioral and biochemical scientists have brought to bear on behavioral medicine problems. Much of the past research in behavioral medicine has been observation or has used *post-hoc* analysis of existing data. Other research has utilized quasi-experimental designs (often with clinical populations) to trace the effects of certain personal characteristics on long-range clinical outcomes. Only a few researchers have employed experimental laboratory procedures, typically focusing on relatively restricted questions.

The familiar gap between univariate laboratory research (with its exemplary control over variables but its frequently lacking external validity) on the one side, and the larger-scale quasi-experimental, correlational or observational research (with its obvious applied value yet frequently lacking causal inference potential) on the other side, exists in behavioral medicine as well as in so many other scientific approaches. Most readers would probably agree that tight experimental design in behavioral medicine would represent an ideal form of research. Can this goal be achieved? Some scientists have argued that experimental laboratory research in behavioral medicine would necessarily result in 'trivial' data. This chapter proposes an experimental approach which would eliminate most, if not all, of the objections to laboratory research in behavioral medicine which have been voiced by other writers.

In presenting our arguments we shall continue to focus on coronary-prone behavior as an example of research in need of an experimental approach permitting causal inference. A conference of experts from various fields was convened by the National Institutes of Health (NIH) in December 1978. It concluded that there *is* evidence of a relationship between Type A coronary-prone behavior and heart disease. The members of the conference, however, indicated that little knowledge exists to date about the potential causal linkage from behavior to disease. Certainly there has been at least preliminary research attempting to establish parts of a causal link in this relationship. Most exemplary is probably the experimental work of Dembroski and associates (e.g., Dembroski *et al.*, 1977, 1978, 1979) who have clearly shown that challenges presented to the Type A person under specific, relatively uncomplicated laboratory conditions tend to produce physiological arousal. For example, responding to reaction-time tasks or cold pressor tasks under instructions to excel, compete, etc. results in considerable increases in blood pressure and heart rate when compared to values obtained when the person is at rest or performs without challenge. This research does permit inference of causality (albeit only from stressor and stylistic variables to arousal, but not to disease), yet so far only for arousal responses due to relatively simple (experimental) settings. Since other researchers have shown that Type A persons have about twice the incidence of cardiovascular disease when compared to Type B persons (with other risk factors controlled), it appears as though challenge-induced arousal (as measured by increases in blood pressure, heart rate, etc.) *may*—via catecholamine secretion and subsequent processes—produce cardiovascular damage. However, are Dembroski's 'challenges' under laboratory conditions similar or identical in their effect to all the challenges which a person experiences in his or her daily life? Can immersion in cold water (the cold pressor task) as used by Dembroski and others be compared to an argument with the boss or a last-minute rush to finish an important task? We do not yet know the answer to such questions. In addition, it may not merely be the difference in the specific *characteristics* of the task that might be important (e.g. cold water immersion *vs.* an argument), but likely also the *complexity* of the challenge in the 'real world' in comparison to the greater simplicity of the challenge in the laboratory.

Effects of Multiple Variables

Without question, the vast majority of behavior occurs in complex settings, i.e. people are exposed to a number of stimuli simultaneously. Considerable research has shown that complex settings have a number of effects above and beyond the kind of simple settings that are more easily (and more typically) reproduced or created in the majority of laboratory experiments. For example, findings from stress research show that any single stressor has quite limited effects on human responding until that stressor reaches quite severe levels. Several stressors operating simultaneously, even at relatively mild levels, can combine to produce increased physiological arousal, dissatisfaction and serious detriments in task performance. In other words, it appears to be quite necessary to obtain research data on the additive or interactive effects of *normal day-to-day* challenges and the resultant physiological responses that could lead to disease. Obviously, the ideal research setting where such data should be collected would permit experimental control over several environmental events (stressors) to which persons are exposed, so that causal inferences about the complex linkages from environment to behavior to physiological response to disease can be made. This chapter proposes the use of experimental simulation methods to achieve that end, at least in part.

Behavioral and Stylistic Predictors

So far we have been concerned with the number of environmental variables that might affect a person's responses. Similar complexity exists in the behavioral/stylistic component of our environment–behavior–physiology–disease chain. The majority of behavioral medicine research to date has utilized a single behavioral predictor (possibly in addition to other non-behavioral predictors) for example, Type A as the measured antecedent of a physiological or of a disease target variable.* Certainly such an approach is reasonable, particularly during the beginning stages of a new field. As a result of this approach, we have obtained some knowledge about specific relationships among certain variables; e.g. we have learned that some kind of relationship between the Type A behavioral style and coronary disease does exist. The use of a single predictor, however, does not provide us with

* One of the notable exceptions are those clinical trials where more than one behavioral variable (Type A, smoking, etc.) has been included together with physiological variables (blood pressure, cholesterol, etc.), e.g. the MRFIT Program of the US National Institutes of Health (in progress).

information about potential other behavioral predictor variables which may operate in addition to, or in interaction with, the variable we may have selected for analysis. To stay with our example, we might ask whether Type A represents the only coronary-prone behavior. For that matter, we may wonder whether Type A might be broken up into some components that relate to heart disease and others that are rather harmless. For example can one, as some have suggested, focus on hostility as a separate aspect from Type A time-urgency? Is accelerated speech a marker variable for coronary-proneness, or is it not? Is there yet another, or are there several other, coronary-prone behavior styles? For example, can cognitive complexity which has been shown to predict arousal as well as Type A (Streufert et al., 1979) be related to heart disease? What other stylistic or personality variables might be identified? How do these various potential coronary-prone behaviors *interact*, *sum*, or *coact* to produce arousal and/or physiological damage? Obviously, answers to questions of this kind cannot come from simple experiments which measure the effects a single variable has on one or a few physiological responses. Similarly, the final answer cannot easily be obtained from quasi-experimental field research with clinical or organizational populations and from observational research (even though these methods may provide hypotheses that need to be experimentally explored). What appears to be needed is an experimental approach that contains the necessary complexity at all levels of the environment–behavior–physiological response–disease chain.

Beneficial Effects of Additional Variables

So far we have considered how a number of environmental and/or a number of behavioral variables may interact to produce physiological effects which, in turn, may lead to disease. Yet the interactive relationship among environmental stressors, among behavioral styles and among both groups of variables may not have any deleterious effects at all; in fact, their interaction *could* be beneficial. Specific variables which are by necessity not included in simple experimental research designs, or that might well be overlooked in quasi-experimental or observational studies, may in some cases have ameliorating effects. For example, would someone who is having a fight with the boss respond (in terms of physiological arousal) as severely if he or she knows that there will be someone at home an hour from now comforting her or him? On the other hand, could that response be expected to be different if yet another argument can be expected at home? At present we can only guess. We believe that research which is to be realistically predictive of disease must take into account as many potential detrimental and potential ameliorating variables (i.e. boundary variables; cf. Fromkin and Streufert, 1976) as possible. It is of considerable importance, for example, if a challenge is perceived as even more challenging under some conditions but not challenging under others, or if certain styles of behavior or personality characteristics are displayed in the presence or absence of specific boundary variables. To return to our example of coronary-prone behavior: we know that some Type A persons remain free of heart disease. Why do they? Of course the reason may be found in some physiological protective mechanism, or in the absence of some part of the environment–disease cycle. On the other hand, the absence of disease in these Type A persons may reflect a protective behavioral component or some specific component of the many environmental events experienced by these persons. Again, the answer to questions about ameliorating effects of certain variables is not likely to be found in the data obtained from standard laboratory experimentation.

A Proposal for Simulation Research

To be able to begin to answer some of the questions we have raised, we need a research method which:

(1) approaches the complexities of 'real life', i.e. method should allow us to measure the additive or interactive detrimental or beneficial effects of a combination of stressor variables and behavioral variables;
(2) permits control over experimental variables, i.e. leads to potential causal inference;
(3) permits selection of subjects to reflect specific personality or stylistic variables of interest;
(4) permits the experimental (controlled) induction of a variety of stressors;
(5) operates over considerable time;
(6) involves subjects to such a degree that they 'forget' that their behavior is being measured;
(7) permits interpersonal as well as task-oriented behavior;
(8) permits repeated measurement of a number of physiological and be-havioral responses *without* serious interference with ongoing behavior.

It appears to us that the method which most closely fits the requirements we have just listed is *experimental simulation research* (cf. Fromkin and Streufert, 1976). We shall describe the characteristics, the advantages, and the dis-advantages of that research method in the following section of this chapter. Finally, we will attempt to evaluate the extent to which the experimental simulation method may or may not aid in resolving the problems of behavioral medicine research discussed earlier. We will again draw our examples from research on coronary-prone behavior.

Characteristics of the Experimental Simulation

Simulation techniques were first used by engineers. For example, placing a *precise* miniature model of a planned aircraft into a wind tunnel to measure its flight characteristics constitutes a simulation. There are, however, limits to the necessary precision of the miniature model which is utilized in the simulation. For example, the engineer need not place the pilot's seat into the inside of the miniaturized airplane, as long as the weight distribution of the various parts of the model are equivalent to the weight distribution of the planned aircraft. After all, the shape of the pilot's seat has no effects on the flight characteristics of the plane's fuselage. The weight distribution, on the other hand, does. All external parts of the planned aircraft, however, must be precisely replicated in the exact scale chosen for the miniature. In other words, all components that are *essential* for the aircraft's flight characteristics must be painstakingly reproduced.

The same necessity to reproduce precisely all essential characteristics of behavioral settings holds when we wish to design a simulation in the behavioral and social sciences. Introduced to the sciences concerned with human behavior and human interaction primarily by Guetzkow (1959) and associates, simulation procedures for our research area have typically attempted to capture the essential components of human interaction in task-oriented settings. For example, simulations have been concerned with international decision-making, military activities, executive performance, labor–management negotiations, and more. They have not, however, been utilized in behavioral medicine research.

Early simulations have typically presented participant groups of subjects with a setting and with conditions which were common from one group of participants to the next. The groups would make decisions (within the limitations of their given capacity) which would modify the initial conditions. The potential modifications over any run of the simulation was typically limited by parameters developed by the experimenter. Nonetheless, participants typically had considerable effects on the progress (change) in their simulated environment over time. Because the participants were given the *freedom* (within constraints) to modify their environments, Fromkin and Streufert (1976) defined this kind of simulation technique as *free simulation*.

To Guetzkow and his associates the free simulation represented a *theory* of some behavior under analysis. The goal of a free simulation is most often the prediction of real-world events that might defy understanding by the human mind because of their complexity. For example, if some event is determined by an interaction of fifty or so variables, we cannot learn to understand it. Nonetheless, the proponents of free simulations would argue we might replicate historical complex events and learn to anticipate future events if these events will naturally occur in a simulated setting that contains all essential variables. Because of its capacity to predict future events the free simulation (often later computerized) may be considered to be a theory.

As an attempt at successive approximations at a better and better theory (with repeated improvements of parameters), the free simulation lacks the needed ingredients to be widely useful for experimental research on the relationship among specific variables. Since the participants in free simulations are able to modify their environments, groups of subjects in one simulation would produce and consequently experience quite divergent environmental stressors (after some time) than any other group placed into the same simulation. Experimental comparison among groups of participants in free simulations is consequently limited to the interpretation of outcomes as a function of common (or diverse) starting points.

To make simulation more useful for experimental research purposes, Streufert and associates (e.g. Streufert *et al.*, 1965, 1967) modified simulation techniques from theory-oriented to data-oriented methods. In their 'experimental simulations' (cf. Fromkin and Streufert, 1976), the events experienced by participants reflect the manipulation of an independent (within) variable over time. This method permits the experimenters to measure the (randomized or sequential) outcome of specific levels of single or multiple environmental stressor conditions. For example, the experimental simulation technique has been utilized to determine the effects of information stress levels (e.g. Streufert and Driver, 1965; Streufert and Schroder, 1965), effects of increasing success and failure (Streufert, 1969, 1972), effects of information relevance levels (Streufert, 1973), and more.

An example of a specific experimental simulation might be useful here. Among other simulated environments Streufert and associates developed the Tactical and Negotiations Game, where participant subjects make decisions about the economic, military, intelligence, and negotiation components of a small international conflict. The participants arrive at the laboratory and are presented with a manual which informs them in detail about history, current conditions, and their task in a country called 'Shamba'. They are to resolve the Shamba conflict, a small international conflict situation with some similarity to several real-world problems in recent history. Via the manual and some video presentations, the participants spend about three hours in which they receive the necessary pretraining and the persuasive communications that may lead them to 'believe in' the cause they are representing.

As the simulation begins, they consider themselves faced by an opposing decision-making group that presents the other side. They may interact with that other group in any way they wish (at a distance) as long as they do so within the resources they have according to the manual. It appears to them that the events which occur with time are the direct effects of their own decisions as they interact with the decisions of their opponents. In other words, they learn to believe that they can and do have a direct effect on their own future. However, as stated above, the information reaching the participants has been carefully preprogrammed. Outcomes are determined by the experimental manipulation (the independent variable). Nonetheless, the programming is done carefully enough to make the events *appear* relevant to the decisions participants made previously.

For example, if the experimenter wished to manipulate the amount of information reaching participants per unit of time (information load stress), he or she may predetermine how many items of information would reach the participants at any time interval. In addition, the experimenter would decide in advance what proportion of these messages would communicate success, would communicate failure, or would be neutral in content.

Streufert and Schroder (1965) used such a manipulation and found that an optimal load for quality decision-making can be determined: strategic decision-making in complex settings appears to reach its best level when cooperating participants (irrespective of how many there are) receive one item of information every three minutes. Less frequent or more frequent receipt of information turns out to be stressful and results in decreasing decision-making quality as well as in other effects of experienced stress.

One of the most striking observations in experimental simulations (e.g. the Tactical and Negotiations Game) is the high level of involvement by participants. A well-designed simulation of this type and a well-conceived and pre-tested manipulation of the independent variable is highly believable. In other words, the Tactical and Negotiations Game and other similar experimental simulations permit the experimenter to measure complex real-world behavior under natural conditions. By introducing certain levels of stress at will (within limits that are tolerable and do not damage the participants), the experimenter can nearly duplicate events in the outside world which would not permit experimental manipulation, yet have theoretical or empirical impact potential for health and illness.

Advantages of Experimental Simulations

Advantages of simulation methods, in particular of the experimetal simulation techniques, are primarily found in the combination of real-world-like complexity of setting and events with the ability to manipulate experimental variables at will (without appearing unrealistic). Another advantage is the involvement of subject participants. This involvement easily reaches levels that are observed in the real-world environments which are simulated (and may, if the experimenter is careless, even exceed those levels). In other words, experimental simulation techniques permit us to use controlled manipulations of independent variables and precise measurement of dependent variables (as we know it from the small-scale laboratory experiments favored by those who like to argue for 'experimental realism'). Yet the research is accomplished in a task environment which contains as many components of the complex real world (to achieve mundane realism) as the experimenter wishes to introduce. In other words, we have an experimental environment which allows us to infer causality from our research data relevant to applied complex problems.

Disadvantages

All simulations, including experimental simulations, are to some degree compromises. Some of the control which we know from research in the small-scale laboratory could be lost. Difficulties may occur because variables which would be eliminated from the standard laboratory experiment as potential 'confounds' are without question part of the 'real world' we want to simulate. Such variables may be interactive with the experimental variables of interest and must consequently be included in the simulation as additional manipulated variables or at constant or randomized levels.

Comparisons of stimulations with observational techniques and quasi-experimental research also points out some shortcomings. Some of the complexities of the 'real-world' settings may be lost. Excellent design work can, however, limit potential effects of this shortcoming: if we know (just as it is done in the wind tunnel) what the *essential* components of the real-world setting which we have chosen to simulate are, we can most likely include all or most of these in the simulation design.

The most serious shortcomings of simulations for the research in behavioral medicine is, hopefully, a temporary one. If we are interested in physiological responding, we often wish to obtain continuous physiological measurements of our participants. Such continuous measurement represents a problem (but certainly no more of a problem than it is in the real world). Most real-world settings, and consequently most simulations which are designed to parallel them, allow the people involved to move around freely to feel unencumbered from measurement equipment. However, physiological measurement requires electrodes and other apparatus. In the ideal simulation we should be able to attach devices which measure heart function, blood pressure, etc. to the body of any participant. Ideally, the equipment should be mobile enough so that the subject can forget its presence. The subject should be able to engage in a task without being encumbered. In other words, the information gained should be collected in a mobile person and transmitted by telemetry to some central processor that stores or compares these analog measures together with any digital information that is received from the environment to which the participants are exposed and the information gathered from the behavioral actions of the participants. Blood pressure measurement, particularly, has not yet advanced to that stage. It is hoped that we will soon have equipment available that eliminates these problems. Some significant progress in this direction has recently been made.

Potential Experimental Simulation Research in Behavioral Medicine

Earlier, we listed a number of characteristics which any research method we would wish to employ in behavioral medicine should have. In this final section of our chapter we shall attempt to show where experimental simulation does, and where it does not, fulfill the demands we would have on such an 'ideal' method.

Duplicating the Complexity of 'Real-Life'

To the degree to which events can occur in the limited space of a simulation laboratory, all complexities of the setting and of a series of environmental events we wish to simulate can be duplicated. Experimental control over the introduction of environmental stressors presents no problem. The selection of subjects according to some characteristic of interest may require that subjects who are medically endangered should probably not be exposed to certain severe environmental stressors. Research has shown that the time over which a simulated event takes place in the real-world represents very little problem: participants in simulations can very well adjust to condensed or expanded time. As suggested earlier, the experimenter may not want to include all the complexities of real life, however. Only those that are *essential* for the research must be included. Which are to be considered essential and which are superfluous may, however, require some preliminary investigations.

Interpersonal and Task-oriented Behavior

The choice of the simulated setting rests with the experimenter. If interpersonal behavior is of interest, then of course a setting requiring interaction (or coaction) among persons would be chosen. If we are interested in the effects of task demands on persons, then an appropriate task setting should be simulated. Ideally, a simulation environment might be designed to allow the experimenter to include and exclude conditions of interest at will. Pretesting and designing a simulation requires much time and effort. One single simulation technique that can fulfill a number of purposes is consequently more efficient.

Operation Over Time

By definition, all simulations operate over time. The length of actual time participants spend in the simulation may be chosen by the experimenter. However, participants (in any complex real-world-like simulated task) require at least one or two hours of pretraining. Further, serious data should not be collected during the first 30 to 60 minutes of the simulation to eliminate spurious 'warm-up' effects. In other words, we can expect simulations to produce data continuously after about three hours into the experiment. At that time, a large amount of data can be collected simultaneously,* making simulations, despite their expense per run, a very cost-effective research method. Collecting data over considerable time has additional advantages: 'within' comparisons often permit a clearer identification of the effects which stressor levels have on behavior and physiological response.

Obviously, a simulation cannot go on for ever, since participants (and experimenters) do get tired, setting a limit to the length of any single run. Of course, participants may be brought back to continue their efforts at a later time. A word of caution is necessary here: unless one is simulating a real-world task which is similarly interrupted, the interim periods can have deleterious effects on the data: participants do not remain inactive during the intermissions: they may seek out additional (uncontrolled) information, may communicate with one another, etc.

Involvement

Simulations are known for their levels of involvement. The degree of involvement is easily controlled via kind of task and setting chosen, via the participants' (apparent) effect on their environment. Care must be taken, however, that the involvement generated does not differ from that of the real-world setting which the simulation represents.

Experimental Control, Subject Selection and Casual Inference

As we had described earlier, experimental control, despite the complexity of the setting, is the major advantage of experimental simulations. For behavioral medicine research, where we are interested in human physiological responding to a variety of simultaneous (potentially interacting) stressors, the method is in effect ideally suited. We can manipulate variables to obtain causal inference from changes in environmental stressors as they interact with behavioral (stylistic, personality, etc.) variables (based on participant selection or training) to produce physiological responses. However, this is where the chain ends. Experimental research on stressor variables and behavioral variables as they affect disease in humans is not possible. Obviously, we would not want to induce disease in healthy human subjects, but even if that were our intent, simulations would not permit us to do so. The amount of

* Simultaneously collected data may be subject to 'common error' (if any). The experimenter may wish to include partial replications in later simulation designs to demonstrate that obtained data do not include such error.

time any participant spends in a simulation (even if it should be several days) is simply not long enough to observe the entire environment–behavior– physiological response–disease chain. For the completion of the chain, we need to develop interlocking research with the quasi-experimental methods used, for example, in clinical trials research.

Repeated Measurement

To the degree to which behavior is necessarily repetitive, it can be measured without difficulty. For example, if participants are placed into a simulated decision-making environment we can repeatedly measure the number and quality of decisions they make. The participants would not even be aware of this measurement. On the other hand, if we wish to collect responses to scales repeatedly, we must interrupt the participants from time to time. Experience suggests that such interruptions should be kept to a minimum, and should take as little time as possible. Much more problematic is the repeated measurement of physiological responding, a *sine qua non* in this kind of behavioral medicine research. We have already suggested the (hopefully only current) problems of measuring responding in freely mobile subjects. As long as all data could be collected via electrodes which are placed, say, on the inside of a belt around the body of a subject with telemetry transmission to a central recording system, we would anticipate few problems with repeated measurement: the subject would soon become unaware that we are monitoring his or her physiological responses. The frequently inflating cuff for blood pressure measurement is quite another problem. Here the subject typically is constrained by the tubes connecting the device to a central system and (even if the previous problem is eliminated via some device which the subject would have to carry with him) would become aware of the pressure that from time to time compresses his arm. One can only hope that time and involvement in the simulated task would help to decrease or eliminate the direct effects of repeated collection of physiological data. Of course this limitation is common to all methods where physiological response data are gathered.

Some Final Thoughts

On review, it appears as though the experimental simulation method does as well as, or better than, other methods and has distinct advantages over others in most instances. Its primary shortcomings are in the realm of physiological measurement (a problem it shares with all other methods), and in its lack of applicability to the physiological response–disease part of the environment– behavior–physiological response–disease chain. We would consequently propose that closely interlocking research methods utilizing experimental simulation (to trace the causal connection between the first three components of that chain) and quasi-experimental techniques (and potentially physiological experimentation to indentify clearly the connection between the last two components of the chain) be developed. As in all other areas of behavioral medicine, such an effort would require cooperation among a number of scientists from diverse disciplines, something that fortunately has become a standard in this endeavor.

Finally, we wish to emphasize that we are *not* proposing experimental simulation as the one and only panacea for what may ail behavioral medicine research. Certainly there are areas in behavioral medicine where other methods may be more useful; and there are probably other methods which could be developed that might do as well. Whatever method is chosen, however, where physiological responding and potential subsequent disease is a function of a complex set of environmental stressors and where a number of behavioral characteristics are at play, the research method should allow us to determine realistically the causal chain linking interactions or coactions of environmental and behavioral variables with their biomedical outcome.

References

Dembroski, T. M., MacDougall, J. M., Herd, J. A., and Shields, J. L. (1979). 'Effects of level of challenge on pressor and heart rate responses in Type A and Type B subjects', *Journal of Applied Social Psychology*, **9**, 208–229.

Dembroski, T. M., MacDougall, J. M., and Shields, J. L. (1977). 'Physiologic reactions to social challenge in persons evidencing the Type A coronary prone behavior pattern', *Journal of Human Stress*, **3**, 2–10.

Dembroski, T. M., MacDougall, J. M., and Shields, J. L., Petitto, J., and Lushene, R. L. (1978). 'Components of the Type A coronary prone behavior pattern and cardiovascular responses to psychomotor performance challenge', *Journal of Behavioral Medicine*, **1**, 159–176.

Fromkin, H. L., and Streufert, S. (1976). 'Laboratory experimentation', in Dunette, M. D. (ed.), *Handbook of Industrial and Organizational Psychology*, pp. 415–465. Rand McNally, Chicago.

Guetzkow, H. (1959). 'A use of simulation in the study of international relations'., *Behavioral Science*, **4**, 183–191.

Streufert, S. (1969). 'Increasing failure and response rate in complex decision making', *Journal of Experimental Social Psychology*, **5**, 310–323.

Streufert, S. (1972). 'Success and response rate in complex decision making', *Journal of Experimental Social Psychology*, **8**, 389–403.

Streufert, S., Clardy, M. A., Driver, M. J., Karlins, M., Schroder, H. M., and Suedfeld, P. (1965). 'A tactical game for the analysis of complex decision making in individuals and groups', *Psychological Reports*, **17**, 723–729.

Streufert, S., and Driver, M. J. (1965). 'Conceptual structure, information load and perceptual complexity', *Psychonomic Science*, **3**, 249–250.

Streufert, S., Kliger, S. C., Castore, C. H., and Driver, M. J. (1967). A tactical and negotiations game for the analysis of decision integration across decision areas', *Psychological Reports*, **20**, 155–157.

Streufert, S., and Nogami, G. Y. (1979). '*Der Mensch im beengten Raum*. Steinkopff Verlag, Darmstadt, Germany.

Streufert, S., and Schroder, H. M. (1965). 'Conceptual structure, environmental complexity and task performance', *Journal of Experimental Research in Personality*, **1**, 132–137.

Streufert, S., Streufert, S. C., Dembroski, T. M., and MacDougall, J. M. (1979). 'Complexity, coronary prone behavior and physiological response', in Oborne D. J., Gruneberg, M. M., and Eiser, J. R. (eds), *Research in Psychology and Medicine*, Vol. 1. *Physical Aspects: Pain, Stress, Diagnosis and Organic Damage*. Academic Press, London.

Streufert, S. C. (1973). 'Effects of information relevance on decision making in complex environments', *Memory and Cognition*, **1**, 224–228.

Social Psychology and Behavioral Medicine
Edited by J. Richard Eiser
© 1982 John Wiley & Sons Ltd

Chapter 5

The social psychology of child pedestrian accidents

ANTONY J. CHAPMAN, HUGH C. FOOT, NOEL P. SHEEHY, and
FRANCES M. WADE

According to everyday usage an 'accident' is an unexpected event. Yet when we consider 'accidents', in the plural, it cannot be said that they are unexpected. For instance, in the case of pedestrian accidents—the focus of this chapter—broadly equivalent numbers of people are killed and injured from one year to the next; and much the same distributions of accidents, according to age and sex for example, are seen for each year.

One can choose to regard an accident either as an event which did not have to happen but which, through a coincidental combination of circumstances, did happen; or, alternatively, as something which had to happen because it did happen. Although both positions reflect a common sentiment about the inevitability of accidents, they have quite distinct origins and implications. The first has its origins in a belief that 'chance' plays a significant role in patterning our lives; but it does not exclude the possibility of effective intervention. The second reflects a conviction in a 'hidden purpose' behind major transitions in our lives; and it assumes a more fatalistic stance on the issues of prevention and intervention. Both positions are inadequate to an understanding of the phenomenon of accidents, although the second is more threatening in the degree to which it promotes an attitude of complacency about accident statistics.

The concept of 'intentionality' is central in discussions of accident causation: accidents are typically taken to be unintentional, either in aspects of their performance, or associated consequences, or both. The concept of intentionality is also invoked when discussing injuries that have resulted from deliberate self-mutilations, or from deliberate acts of violence perpetrated on the individual by others, but it is scarcely considered in the context of most other causes of death, disease, and disability. Presumably this is because intervention by man is not seen to be sufficiently close to the cause to be relevant.

The assignation of the term 'accident' to certain classes of injury but not to others is somewhat arbitrary. Injuries sustained through chemical, electrical, and mechanical agents are usually classified as accidents, whereas injury which results from biological agents, such as harmful bacteria or viruses, are classified as diseases. The unexpected and chance qualities associated with accidents are not exclusive to events so classified. The sudden realization of diseases such as poliomyelitis, leukemia, cancer, or coronary thrombosis can be as traumatic and as unexpected as the news of the occurrence of an accident. Other causes of death and disease, say through food poisoning, may be regarded as the result of freak combinations of events concerning interactions between the agent, behavior, and the environment; but these are not generally classified as accidents.

The term 'accident' has not always been used to classify non-biological injury, but nowadays one is encouraged by the community to subscribe to the view that an accident is *by definition* an event which occurs by chance, cannot be foreseen, and cannot be prevented. There is an implication that we must learn to live with accidents; that they are 'facts of life'. In contrast there is an implication that *diseases* can be eradicated, given sufficient resources and research. Yet, even in a society which is relatively 'caring', there is a reluctance to accept that people may not be masters of their own fate. They are taken to be accountable for their actions, and so we regularly seek to identify the causes of accidents through complex social processes of responsibility attribution and apportionment of blame.

Society's attitudes towards accidental injury are shown in various ways. Let us take two examples, the first relating to the role of the Coroner in Britain. Coroners investigate deaths which may have been violent or sudden, or unusual in other respects. Their general function is to provide a quasi-judicial explanation when no immediate medical explanation is available. The range of possible verdicts takes in addiction to drugs, suicide, self-neglect, justifiable homicide, murder, manslaughter, infanticide, misadventure, accidental death, and natural causes. Traumas which are readily incorporated within the present-day medical framework of disease are deemed 'natural' and other types of trauma, by implication, are regarded as 'unnatural'.

Our second example relates to the completion of Death Certificates in Britain. Standard and permitted entries do not allow for the possibility that death may *not* have followed a protracted illness. The Certificate may be issued only by a 'Registered Medical Practitioner WHO HAS BEEN IN ATTENDANCE during the deceased's last illness . . .'. Any emphasis on a fatal illness having been protracted can be inappropriate for those, say, who die relatively young: accidental injury is the most common cause of death in those who are aged 35 or less.

From the above examples it is evident that society regards accidents in a manner which is different from other causes of death and disability. To some extent it can be said that accidents are tolerated because its members place a premium on individual freedoms. For example, reducing speed limits, restricting vehicles within residential estates, and compulsory use of seatbelts are interventions which reduce accidents and/or the severity of accidents, yet they are regarded by many as intolerable infringements on personal liberty. On the other hand, compulsory inoculation before entry to some foreign countries and the establishment of legal standards for food preparation are regarded as perfectly legitimate and acceptable. Such contrasting reactions reflect the fact that while the layman will happily admit to a degree of ignorance in respect of medical matters, he views himself as something of an expert in matters relating to the conduct of his daily affairs and thereby he is, in his everyday practices, less willing to tolerate constraints imposed by society.

In providing within this chapter a methodological and theoretical structure for the study of accidents—a framework which we choose to describe, albeit somewhat broadly, as 'epidemiological'—we are seeking to advance a common frame of reference for evaluating the contributions of conceptually diverse schools of thought within psychology. In so doing we anticipate improvements in the explanatory clarity and readability of otherwise abstruse, or poorly formulated, theories. Thereby we can begin to evaluate the value of these various approaches. A representative review of social psychological perspectives is offered, but it is not our objective to provide an exhaustive account of social aspects of child pedestrian accidents. For example, we have not included detailed discussion of information-processing approaches, nor approaches which lean towards the sociological pale of the theoretical continuum. We would not wish to underplay the significance of these and other perspectives; quite the contrary, we wish to provide a sound basis from which one can make excursions into these and related areas of psychological theorizing.

The Epidemiological Approach

Epidemiology is 'the study of the distribution of disease in human populations and of the factors which determine that distribution' (MacMahon, 1967, p. 81). Its predominant, though not exclusive, purpose is the understanding of disease etiology and the identification of preventive measures. Disease has been defined by Clark (1967, p. 4) as the 'failure of the adaptive mechanisms of an organism to counteract adequately the stimuli and stresses to which it is subject, resulting in a disturbance in function or structure of some parts of the body'. This definition views disease in a multifactorial way, and it implies an ecological conception, rather than confining explanations to any single cause. Hence the focus is upon the individual, and not upon the disease as an entity with a life of its own which attacks man from without. Therefore, within an epidemiological framework, accidents are taken to result from maladaptive behavior on the part of the victim. As Clark asserts, this conceptual framework has broad implications: 'it is possible . . . to conceive of disease manifestations and causes at any level from the molecular to the social. This widens the range of theoretical perspective for characterizing the processes of disease and their methods of control' (Clark, 1967, p. 4). These comments apply to all types of disease, but they are particularly pertinent to accidents (Wade *et al.*, 1979a).

The first step in descriptive epidemiology is to examine the frequency and distribution of a disease in terms of characteristics of persons, time and place: that is, who is affected, when and where. Specific characteristics most frequently examined are:

(1) in relation to persons—age, sex, ethnic group, occupation, education, socioeconomic status and marital status;
(2) in relation to time—changes during the day, the week, the year, and changes according to seasons and decades; and
(3) in relation to place—areas within a community, degree of urbanization, variations across countries, counties, states, and so forth.

Hypothesis formulation is the second step. Ideally hypotheses should contain statements as to the nature of the causal factors or experiences, the disease or manifestation that is the supposed effect, the quantitative relationship between the two, and the time that elapses between exposure to the cause and the appearance of the effect. The third step concerns putting the hypotheses to empirical test by applying either analytic or experimental methods. Some experimental and descriptive work relating to pedestrian accidents is outlined below.

Characteristics of Persons

In the 5–9 age-bracket twice as many boys as girls are involved in UK pedestrian accidents. This sex difference is not so marked in other age-categories, but generally males are affected to a greater degree than are females; a corresponding picture emerges in countries other than the UK. Descriptions of accidents in terms of ethnic group, socioeconomic status, and marital status, etc., are not presently available for the UK.

Characteristics of Time

The UK pedestrian accident rate has fallen consistently over the last 10 years for all age-categories. Trends within the day, within the week, and within the year have remained substantially the same since statistics were first published (cf. Foot *et al.*, 1982). On Mondays to Fridays the peak time for child accidents is between 3 pm and 6 pm, and at weekends most accidents to children occur during the afternoons. For adult pedestrians broadly similar patterns are evident. There is, however, an additional peak in the late evening, especially on Fridays and Saturdays, the high point of which is at 11 pm.

Characteristics of Place

In the UK 96 percent of all child pedestrian accidents occur in built-up areas. For adult pedestrians, the corresponding statistic is 93 percent. For children under 5 years of age most accidents occur on minor roads within 100 yards of their homes. For pedestrians aged 10–15 years most accidents take place on more major roads, at distances of more than a quarter of a mile from home (cf. Wade *et al.*, 1981).

Many hypotheses have been formulated to explain the occurrence of pedestrian accidents. Because children are particularly vulnerable, some theoretical perspectives have been developed specifically to account for children's accidents. Others advance a broad framework, covering accidents as a whole. Before discussing these various hypotheses, let us examine some of the general analytic studies.

General Analytic Studies

Analytic studies focusing on family and social factors associated with pedestrian accidents have been undertaken by three research teams (Backett and Johnston, 1959; Ekström *et al.*, 1966; Read *et al.*, 1963). The consensus from these analytic case-history studies is that of the many antecedent factors investigated, family illness and overcrowding in some manner contribute to child pedestrian accidents (cf. Wade *et al.*, 1979b). In arriving at such conclusions it is assumed that a particular factor may be a cause of a disease if it is found under various circumstances to be associated with that disease: this is referred to in epidemiology as the *method of agreement*. An alternative, the *method of concomitant variation*, seeks to identify factors which vary in strength or frequency as the disease itself varies. The following studies adopt this alternative method.

Routledge *et al.* (1974) surveyed children's exposure to accident risk on homeward school journeys. The study indicated that, despite their greater involvement in accidents, younger children were actually exposed to traffic risk less than older children. Also, despite having more accidents, boys were not exposed to risk more than girls. Thus Routledge *et al.* concluded that differential exposure to risk is not a major contributory factor to child pedestrian accidents (however, see p. 90).

Aspects of pedestrian behavior have been examined in an attempt to investigate the possibility that in routine pedestrian activities the most vulnerable groups of individuals exhibit styles of behavior which distinguish them from other groups. Grayson (1975b) and Routledge et al. (1976) observed pedestrians across the widest age-band possible. Both investigations yielded an adult/child difference in crossing busy streets. Adults appear to assess gaps in traffic before they reach, or turn to, the kerb; they are more likely to start crossing before the road is 'clear'; they tend to cross at an angle; and they move towards the path of oncoming cars and cross immediately behind a passing car, thus maximizing the gap between themselves and any oncoming vehicle. Children, on the other hand, tend to pay little attention to crossing until they arrive at the kerb; they stop at the kerb to wait for a suitable gap; they typically delay longer than adults before deciding to cross; gaps are very seldom anticipated by walking into the road and passing immediately behind a car; and more head movements are made at the kerb and during crossing. These studies found few sex differences in the most vulnerable age group—the 5–9-year-olds—which is the group for which there are approximately twice as many male as female fatalities. The interpretation proffered by Routledge et al. emphasizes the contradiction in the ways children are instructed to cross roads and the ways in which adults are observed to cross. The adult strategy is sophisticated and skilful and as such is not appropriate for teaching to young children. It utilizes infrequent and brief opportunities to cross, rendering necessary the rapid execution of skills involving anticipation and judgment of (a) speed, (b) distance, and (c) future position of vehicles and self. Other analytic studies relate to observations of pedestrian gap acceptance (Cohen et al., 1955; Routledge et al., 1976) and analyses of some of the features of city environments associated with high accident rates (Preston, 1972).

There are several studies which may be grouped under the general rubric of experimental epidemiological investigations. These include experiments concerned to establish the efficacy of prophylactic measures and experiments concerned with particular aspects of behavior. In relation to speeding, for example, the value of speed control humps ('sleeping policemen') has been investigated experimentally in several locations in Britain (Sumner and Baguley, 1979). At one site (Cowley, in Oxfordshire) control humps were introduced on an access road to an estate of local authority housing in which 28 accidents had been recorded in the previous 46 months. Only one accident occurred during the year of the experiment, and this represented a major decrease in accidents compared with a control location. Other experimental studies have been attempts to assess various educational programs and/or the bases of such programs (cf. Singh, 1982). For example, some studies have investigated children's knowledge and understanding of road safety vocabulary and materials (e.g. Cattell and Lewis, 1975; Sheppard, 1975; Sheppard and Colborne, 1968); instructional packages have been evaluated in terms of induced behavioral changes (e.g. Yeaton and Bailey, 1978); knowledge and use of protected crossings have been explored; and personal attributes, relevant to the avoidance of accidents (England, 1976), have been investigated, such as motion prediction skills (e.g. Kenchington *et al.*, 1977; Salvatore, 1974) and perception of hazard (Bongard and Winterfeld, 1976; Martin and Heimstra, 1973).

Accident Proneness

The concept of 'accident proneness' involves the notion that a series of accidents incurred by an individual is explicable in terms of an unfortunate and abnormal personality characteristic. Definitions abound (cf. Shaw and Sichel, 1971), and sometimes an exposure-coping model is invoked in which accidents are viewed as normal, non-pathological aspects of behavior. Generally, however, accident proneness is viewed as a clinical problem and from that perspective accidents are seen as neurotic manifestations of repressed emotions. Accident-prone persons are described as 'acting out' and discharging forbidden and unconscious impulses (cf. Alexander and Flagg, 1965). It is said that they have been subject to particularly strict upbringings and hence they develop unusual amounts of resentment against persons in authority and against various forms of external coercion. A series of accidents befalling an individual is thus taken to emanate from unconscious guilt which the victim tries to expatiate in suffering through self-punishment.

Clinical explanations have been tested by examining accident victims, particularly children, under experimental conditions. For example, Krall (1953) observed 32 5–8-year-olds who had a record of three or more accidents in the preceding four-year period. A control group of 32 accident-free children was selected from the same school. The children were requested to make up a story using a dolls' house and a family of parent and children dolls, and they were observed for two 20-minute periods. The accident-repeating children demonstrated significantly more aggressive behavior in doll play than the accident-free children, and results in general were interpreted as indicating that accident-repeating children came from socially disorganized homes.

Occasionally clinical studies conducted outside the laboratory have focused on the victims of accidents. For example, Burton (1968) studied an accident group of children aged between 5 and 15 years who had been victims of pedestrian or cycling accidents. The empirical hypotheses related children's anxiety, assertiveness, and guilt to their mothers' dominance and repressiveness and rejection of them. Testing was underaken just after accidents had occurred, and the study incorporated a control group of matched subjects. The group of accident children was found to be more hostile, assertive, and dominant; but, contrary to prediction, the mothers of these children were not found to be more dominant, punitive, or aggressive. However, they did manifest a greater need for assertion, and they apparently experienced more stressful pregnancies and greater incidences of feeding and sleeping problems with their children.

Some studies draw upon the statistical concept of 'accident liability'—the probability that an individual will experience a given number of accidents during a particular period of time. For example, Manheimer and Mellinger (1967) in their study of accident children took account of accident liability in terms of:

(1) the extent to which a child exposes him/herself to hazards; and
(2) the extent to which a child possesses psychological or physical traits that impair his/her ability to cope with hazards.

The accident experiences of 8874 4–18-year-olds were analyzed, and it was observed that individual differences in accident liability persisted over time. Children high on accident liability were more likely to be considered by their mothers as daring, active, exploring, and extraverted; and, of course, these are characteristics which are likely to increase exposure to hazards. From the ratings of mothers it was also reported that children who were high on accident liability tended to possess characteristics that impaired ability to cope with hazards; for instance, they were relatively low on self-control and high on distractibility, they were more impulsive, and they were more easily angered when frustrated. There was also found to be a relatively high degree of accident liability among maladjusted children and, to explain this, Mellinger and Manheimer (1967) subsequently invoked an extension to the exposure–coping model. They suggested that maladjusted children are inclined to indulge in risk-taking behavior and this naturally brings them into contact with physical hazards.

In studies testing clinical hypotheses it is rarely possible to deduce that observed differences between accident and control groups are due to antecedent factors rather than to the occurrence and experience of the accident itself. It is quite feasible that the trauma of accidents and/or the resulting injuries cause heightened anxiety and assertiveness on the part of the children, as well as reports of difficult pregnancies, etc., on the part of mothers. In Burton's (1968) work, for example, tests were administered just after accidents had occurred and sometimes the 'accident children' were still in hospital; control children had not usually experienced any comparable period of hospitalization and medical treatment was rarely a feature of their immediate past. Information given to the two groups of mothers may have disposed them differently towards their involvement and towards their children. Each 'accident mother' was told that a survey was being undertaken of children admitted to hospital, including her child; the other mothers were told that they were selected because their children had not experienced hospitalization as a result of any accident. Hence, the accident mothers may have been sensitized to the negative aspects of their offspring and the mothers of children in the control group may have been encouraged to concentrate on the positive features of their children.

Another difficulty with these studies is that some of the findings are not sufficiently definitive to sustain the theoretical frameworks into which they are incorporated. For example, it is a moot point whether soliciting affection reflects limited affectionate contacts; it could reflect an atmosphere in which overt acts of affection are encouraged. To interpret such findings as indicative of social disorganization and stress is to go beyond the data.

Yet another area of difficulty concerns the practical significance of the clinical perspective and whether a clinical framework is consonant with the attainment of goals typically associated with a theoretical perspective. The clinical orientation does point to possible interrelationships between abnormal, maladaptive phenomena, and it does attempt to discern lawful relations between observations and theory. But it does not have the virtue of simplification or parsimony, and it does not allow prediction of behavior. Then again, initiation of prophylactic measures based upon theoretical predictions is rarely possible. If it is the case that the clinical perspective has no practical utility then it is redundant within the epidemiological framework. Returning squarely to accident proneness, clinical studies may not have helped to clarify that issue, but it would be unnecessarily dismissive to conclude that the concept of 'accident proneness' has no place in accident epidemiology.

The exposure–coping approach is more satisfactory than the clinical perspective in that it incorporates both normal and abnormal behavior, and thereby findings can be integrated and simplified. Again, however, the practical value of this approach can be called into question. It is not clear how it promotes knowledge having prophylactic applications. The practical utility of identifying high-risk individuals depends upon the availability of techniques for modifying their high-risk behavior, or upon selectively altering the environment of such individuals to render it potentially less hazardous. For some disease entities it is possible to reduce risk either by behavioral or environmental means: for example, the risk of lung cancer may be reduced by giving up smoking, and immunization protects against rubella. However, according to the exposure–coping model, behavioral changes required to reduce the risk of accidents involve fundamental restructuring of characteristic styles of behavior, and it is not easy to envisage how this can be implemented in any effective way.

Cognitive–Developmental Approaches

It is commonly held, by drivers at least, that many pedestrian traffic accidents are attributable to an inexplicable tendency on the part of pedestrians to wander off the pavement into the carriageway or traffic flow. This is particularly true for child pedestrian accidents in which it is frequently the case that the primary cause of an accident is identified with carelessness and negligence on the part of the child who, in 'dashing out' in the path of oncoming traffic, provides no opportunity on the part of the driver to engage in effective evasive action. Such a view betrays ignorance on the part of adults. It fails to take adequate cognizance of the developmental limitations which bound the behavior of children. Sandels (1970, 1971, 1975) argues that 'young children have completely different prerequisites compared with those of the normal adult, and . . . they act in a manner determined by their age and degree of development' (1975, p. 129). The most serious consequence of failing to take adequate account of this developmental progression is that, as adult motorists, we fail to appreciate fully the circumstances of the child and we do not modify our behavior in appropriate ways.

In literature on accident research, Sandels (1975) has documented the various developmental competencies which differentiate the behavior of the adult and child pedestrians. These differences may be grouped under three broad headings: physical, perceptual–cognitive, and social–attitudinal. With respect to physical differences it is clear that child pedestrians are limited in their rate of movement: this should obviously be taken into account, for example, when calculating the crossing phase of signalized pedestrian crossings. The child's stature affects his/her field of vision; and, by the same token, drivers find child pedestrians difficult to see. Also, their diminutive body size predisposes child pedestrians to certain forms of injury: head, pelvic and abdominal injuries predominate. In adults, injuries are sustained primarily to the head and lower body region (Aldman, 1966; Ryan, 1969).

With respect to perceptual limitations, Sandels (1975) on the basis of her own findings contends, first, that children are relatively poor at judging the direction of sound and, second, that peripheral vision is of less value in children than in adults. However, there is a need for caution in generalizing from Sandels' laboratory context to everyday pedestrian–driver activities. For example, in the laboratory the sound was from a static source, whereas most street sounds are, of course, from moving sources; and a developmental effect in a simple and contrived laboratory arrangement may not be manifested in a complex and noisy street environment. Intuitively one would certainly doubt that the adult's capacity to make fine discriminations in the laboratory confers correspondingly sizeable benefits in the road.

Sandels' studies on peripheral vision used a technique in which subjects, by locating a target at various points, constructed composite maps of their peripheral visual fields. The results suggest that in peripheral vision children are less sensitive than adults. However, Sandels herself has pointed to the possible effects of experimental demands in this task, and indeed Whiteside (1976) has reported that there is only a very slight narrowing of the visual field in 6-year-olds. Again it is conceivable that, in the street environment, any such difference may be of no practical consequence. Neither the Sandels nor the Whiteside research yields information about the processes through which we identify, recognize, and extract cues from peripheral vision. Yet these processes may be vital in differentiating adult and child perceptions of traffic. Liss and Haith (1970) note that, although the static visual acuity of young children does not improve appreciably beyond 1 year, 5-year-olds are inferior to adults in searching for specific peripheral targets. Research by Cohen and Haith (1977) indicates that some distortion of the visual field occurs when a difficult information-processing task is encountered; but apparently the distortions are equivalent in children and adults. While impairments in the visual apparatus may sometimes contribute to pedestrian accidents, these impairments would have to be unusually severe before they could justifiably be invoked as primary or even secondary causal factors.

In discussing children's cognitive abilities, Sandels (1975) maintains that children find it difficult to concentrate on traffic as a dynamic unit. They fixate on items within the whole and hence they tend to perceive discrete, independent events. In similar vein, Deutsch (1964) has argued that children do not always perceive the dangers in relating themselves to their environment: this is because they are limited in their ability to relate antecedent events to consequences and because their experiences are frequently inadequate to cope with new situations. Sandels (1975) also provides data which suggest that many of the most important road signs and markings are not easily understood by children. It is not unusual to find that a child cannot comprehend a basic traffic expression; and many children (as well as some adults) confuse right from left. Cattell and Lewis (1975) report that children as old as 11 years of age misunderstand terms such as 'danger', 'kerb', and 'pedestrian', and of course these are words which have common currency, and which are usually central, in road safety education. Hence some road safety propaganda directed at children—perhaps even a substantial amount—must be ineffective because of the language employed (cf. Singh, 1982).

Investigations of pedestrian behavior have all but ignored another crucial aspect of social and intellectual development, namely the child's ability to adopt the perspectives of others—in the present context, the perspectives of drivers. The ability to assume the perspective of others, especially drivers, is often essential for understanding the meanings and functions of road safety rules and practices. In their analysis of the child's perspective-taking abilities, Piaget and Inhelder (1956) concluded that children up to the age of 4 to 6 could not adopt another's perspective. According to the Piagetian position there is a gradual progression from a typically egocentric outlook to a more social, altrocentric viewpoint, so that by about the seventh or eighth year the child is capable of construing another person's viewpoint with comparative ease. However, it should be noted that Piaget's analysis has undergone considerable criticism (cf. Borke, 1977).

The social–attitudinal differences between children and adults, noted by Sandels (1975), are loosely defined but they refer essentially to children being more playful, impulsive, and spontaneous in their actions. By virtue of such differences children are taken to be relatively less differentiated in their pedestrian styles and habits. They are relatively inconsistent and unpredictable as pedestrians, and many children use pavements and roads for play (cf. Chapman *et al.*, 1981). However, to imply that children are by nature unpredictable is to oversimplify the true state of affairs. Their behavioral styles are in large part determined by child-rearing practices, educational policies, and social norms. This is a point which is elaborated in the section on social learning below.

The relevance of a developmental perspective for understanding *adult* pedestrian accidents is valuable in at least one respect. The developmental explanation proceeds by specifying a competence-performance account of behavior, and it applies across the entire lifespan. According to this account there is an imperfect correlation between the behavioral competence of the person and the performance of specific acts, such that on occasions one can witness instances of what might be termed maladaptive or regressive behavior. These instances of inappropriate behavior may contribute to the occurrence of accidents. The developmental perspective may also provide insights into sex differences in pedestrian accidents: for example, the accident rate for primary school boys is appreciably higher than for girls (cf. Foot *et al.*, 1982). There is a substantial body of research evidence indicating that throughout childhood girls are generally more psychologically advanced than boys (cf. Maccoby and Jacklin, 1975): consequently it might be expected that as pedestrians girls would draw upon a more sophisticated repertoire of skills. The sex difference in accident rates diminishes appreciably in adolescence but is evident again in old age. Both of these trends are explicable in terms of a developmental account. During late adolescence and adulthood male development accelerates and then approximates that of the female. But then, in old age, women tend to remain physically, mentally, and socially more active than men (Coleman, 1981), and they are less inclined to exhibit such impairments as presbyacusis and presbyopia.

The developmental explanation is attractive as much for the weight of evidence in its support as for its conceptual simplicity; but whether it is applicable to all pedestrian accidents is doubtful. It fails to take account of the social environment in which people develop and the manner in which individuals interpret that environment. It makes only tangential reference to the ways in which people may receive differential treatment by virtue of their sex, age, socioeconomic/occupational status, and a host of other characteristics which go towards defining the social identity of the person.

We would argue that the developmental limitations and requirements of pedestrians are important to any complete understanding of pedestrian accidents, particularly accidents involving children. We would also argue that those developmental features which are proposed as differentiating pedestrians' competences (say adult and child competences) should be of a type and degree which can account for pedestrian accidents in an empirically verifiable manner. At the very least the cognitive–developmental perspective has already highlighted a general imperialism on the part of adults in their accounts of accidents involving child pedestrians.

Social Learning Approaches

Social learning theory constitutes an important source of hypotheses concerning the causes of pedestrian accidents. Most human learning is fundamentally social in character, for the acquisition of items of knowledge is dependent upon the social values, attitudes, and social relationships which underlie both the act of learning and its context. However, the term 'social learning' has come to signify a particular area in psychology, referring to the acquisition of those behavior patterns which specifically enable an individual to function as an effective member of a social group.

Social learning theory may, for example, throw some light on the sex difference in children's accident rates, in that it gives reason to believe that different socialization practices for boys and girls may affect their pedestrian activities. Some behaviors, known as 'sex-typed' behaviors, typically elicit different rewards for the two sexes: in other words, the consequences of sex-typed behaviors vary according to the gender of the performer (cf. Weinreich, 1978). According to social learning theory, sex-typed behaviors are acquired by the same learning principles which give rise to any aspect of behavior; but as far as sex-typed behaviors are concerned boys and girls, from a very early age, are expected to behave differently in various respects. Hence by the age of 3 or 4 years there tend to emerge definite sex-appropriate perferences with respect to toys and games; the strength of these preferences tends to increase rapidly with age. To some extent learning the appropriate sex role is a consequence of direct training procedures employed by parents; procedures which may be conceptualized in terms of the application of reinforcement schedules designed to elicit and strengthen particular kinds of behaviors seen as socially desirable, and to inhibit or extinguish others which are less 'desirable'—in this case, less sex-appropriate. The consequence of this kind of differential response selection is that 'by the age of seven, in a whole variety of ways, the daily experience of little boys in terms of where they are allowed to go, how they spend their time and to what extent they are kept under adult supervision is already markedly different from that of little girls' (Newson and Newson, 1976, p. 100).

Evidence relating to pedestrian activities emerges from several sources. Newson and Newson (1976) interviewed 697 mothers of 7-year-old children and found that while as many as 67 percent of boys were described as 'outdoor children' only 52 percent of girls were similarly described. Supervision was also observed to be substantially greater for girls in that mothers tended to place daughters under greater obligation to provide notice of journeys and destinations prior to travelling anywhere. Earlier research by Sadler (1972), in which over 2000 mothers were interviewed, found that at each of seven age-levels, from 2 to 8 years, more mothers of boys than of girls indicated that they worried about the possibility of road accidents. In fact, and as already intimated, accident trends indicate that mothers of boys are justified in feeling more worried and, from the Newsons' data, they are yet more justified if they have relatively little information about the whereabouts of their (male) children. Both the Newsons and Sadler observed that young girls were more often chaperoned in their journeys to and from school and, taken together, their research would seem to point to the existence of an important exposure difference according to the sex of the child. Such a difference could be contributing significantly to the large sex difference in child pedestrian accident rates. However, Routledge et al. (1974) did not encounter exposure differences in the observation studies which they conducted. There are various methodological differences in the studies by these three groups of researchers; and overall it appears that exposure differences can often be quite marked but that sometimes there is little or no difference. Sadler (1972) noted that there are no sex differences in children making shopping errands (i.e. destination-specific journeys), while a new study from Chapman et al. (1981) reports that streets are used for recreational purposes more by boys than by girls. The research by the Newsons, which also hints at an exposure difference, likewise incorporates observations from a wide range of street use. It appears, then, that whereas there are negligible exposure variations for boys and girls engaged in purposive journeys, there may be substantially greater variability for less goal-oriented pedestrian activity. A firm conclusion remains in abeyance until studies are replicated and extended.

Social learning theory is intended to encompass the entire lifespan, and hence it may be useful when considering sex differences in styles of road usage for drivers and/or pedestrians of all ages. Sex-typing does not stop in childhood but carries on through life and has progressively deeper repercussions for the structure and organization of social affairs. Ross (1974) points to the existence of important sex differences in terms of the level of manifest risk associated with particular occupations and leisure activities. The male stereotype, more than the female, incorporates a love of danger, while feminine interests tend to be directed away from hazardous activities. Women more than men may suffer social sanctions as a consequence of failing to succumb to sex-role demands, and they may be perceived as losing certain attributes of femininity in the event of prolonged engagements in masculine-linked activity (Fransella and Frost, 1977). We would contend, through our everyday observations, that driving has tended to foster a chauvinistic image of being predominantly a male preserve, and it is not unlikely that styles of pedestrian activities exhibited by male and female pedestrians reflect this image. If so, one would expect men to display more assertive and potentially more dangerous styles than women; and one would expect too that such differences would be evident in adolescents if not in younger boys and girls.

Some of the procedures characteristically adopted by adult pedestrians are reported in the enquiries of Grayson (1975b) and Routledge et al. (1974). These enquiries have shown that there are systematic differences in strategies used by adults and children in road crossing (see p. 82). A paradox is revealed in that the strategies adopted by adults, which cannot be regarded as anything other than successful and mature, differ in fundamental respects from the ways in which children are instructed to proceed. A social learning perspective may offer a solution to the paradox: children presumably model the more sophisticated road crossing skills of the adult pedestrian and thus become progressively more adult-like in their behavior. However, they may fail to take adequate cognizance of the additional attentional demands required of such strategies, and so they place themselves in considerable danger. Unfortunately the research bearing directly on this issue is exceedingly sparse, but a study of note, by Russell et al. (1976), used confederates as jay-walkers and found that 'high-status' models recruited more adult observers than 'low-status' models. It is reasonable to conjecture that a similar process operates for child pedestrians and, if it does, there is a clear need to educate adults about the potentially detrimental and dangerous consequences of their behavior. At the same time it would be sensible to instruct children that they should not model their own pedestrian behavior on typical adult examples. However, such instructional exercises would be formidable to put into practice: they would require large-scale, integrated campaigns, and these would be enormously expensive. It would be an extremely difficult enterprise to change adult habits, and it would be no less difficult to persuade children that they should not aspire to adult modes of operation.

It may be surmised that if the social learning account is to deal adequately with sex differences in children's accident rates, it will be necessary to demonstrate, first, that there are sex differences in adult crossing strategies, and second, that behavioral differences in boys and girls can be regarded as precursors of the differences in men and women. The latter condition would have to be fulfilled because children would be expected to align themselves more to same-sex models. With regard to the first condition, Mackie and Older (1965) and Jacobs and Wilson (1967) have submitted corroborative data. They observed that considerably more women than men utilized crossing facilities when available. They also observed that children made still more use of these facilities; a sex difference corresponding to that in adults emerged in the Jacobs and Wilson study but not in the Mackie and Older study. Cohen *et al.* (1955) found that men tend to accept smaller inter-vehicle gaps than do women, and they intepreted this as indicative of a greater risk-taking tendency among men. However, there is the possibility that their intepretation is unjustified. The male subjects could not be regarded as more risky if it were the case that, in accepting smaller gaps, they continued to perform within their capabilities. Some marginal support for this possibility is given in the work of Salvatore (1974). He found that girls make more conservative judgments of oncoming vehicle velocity but boys make more correct estimates across the entire range of speeds examined in the study. Girls, he argued, tend to display more caution under all traffic conditions. It is conceivable that some of the sex differences in adult behavior arise because men and women tend to be pedestrians for different reasons. Systematically different styles of road crossing may be adopted when adults are engaged in professional and occupational activities than when they are engaged in family and domestic concerns; and, of course, sex differences in occupational roles (e.g. 'breadwinner' and 'housewife') continue to be salient in our society.

It would not be appropriate to assume that only adults serve as models for children. On the contrary, it has long been established that a vast range of experiences may be promoted by peer groups (cf. Foot *et al.*, 1980). Members of these groups can serve both as models to be imitated and as purveyors of behavioral norms, some of which are group-prescribed and which must be complied with by aspiring group members. Research on pedestrian activities as a function of companionship is long overdue. Thus far there is a study reporting that children in groups are more likely to begin to cross before the road is clear (Grayson, 1975b), and there is some suggestion that immediately preceding road accidents children tend to have been engaged in a peer-group encounter (Sandels, 1971, 1974, 1979).

We are also of the view that an understanding of the structure, determinants, and correlates of relevant *attitudes* may facilitate a wider comprehension of pedestrian accident phenomena. It would be invaluable to know how people construe their pedestrian and traffic environments: knowledge of a person's affective and cognitive outlook could provide a sound basis for predicting behavioral intention and behavior *in situ*. Unfortunately our knowledge of any of these three attitude components and of relations between them is sparse. With regard to children's knowledge about traffic regulations there is some indication that boys possess a more extensive knowledge than do girls (Bongard and Winterfeld, 1976; Sandels, 1975), yet this is not evident in Grayson's (1975a,b) observational studies and it runs counter to what would be predicted on the basis of even the briefest inspection of the accident statistics. The discrepancy may arise in part because most of the non-behavioral measures used to date have involved rather simple recognition tasks, and these fail to take account of the child's depth of comprehension.

We would argue that social learning theories contribute prominently to an understanding of pedestrian accidents. However, we would wish to sound a caveat: approaches which seek to modify pedestrian behavior on the basis of elaborated S–R learning paradigms (cf. Reading, 1973) do so at the expense of potentially serious oversimplification. Road crossing involves considerably more than learning a series of discrete responses in the presence of specifiable stimulus configurations. It demands interpretation of those configurations and the elicitation of simultaneous and juxtaposed responses, coupled with a continuous monitoring of stimulus complexes with a view to making appropriate changes in responses. In the social cognition account to follow the basis for a workable theory is outlined. It treats pedestrian behavior as intentional and purposive, while retaining those features of social learning theory which have made it so potent in the past.

Social Cognition

Social cognition is concerned with the influence which social learning exerts on the structure and processing capacity of the individual's abilities and, reciprocally, with the manner and degree to which the individual's cognitive development patterns and promotes various kinds of learning experiences. Most significant in the social cognition approach is that it adopts as its primary unit of analysis the individual in the context of others: that is, the individual as *communicator*, rather than simply the abstracted notion of the individual *per se*. Applied to pedestrian accidents this conceptual analysis treats pedestrian and vehicular traffic as, at base, a complex communication system, the conduct of which is sanctioned by highly sophisticated social controls. Traditionally road-user activity has been conceptualized as relatively rule-governed, and this accords a degree of face validity to the present analysis. Considerable resources are also directed towards the development and enforcement of rules designed to impart a degree of mandatory compliance about the conduct of co-user activity.

In this account persons have learned a set of rules describing how they and others should behave in pedestrian–driver encounters, and they make strategic choices about which rules to follow in order to achieve a satisfactory mode of sociation. The primary advantage of a rule–role account is that the notion of 'accident' can be accommodated in an enlightening way either by treating such a phenomenon as a failure to abide by the rules regulating role relations, or by treating it as a rational outcome of a failure in the role relations. Its major limitation is that pedestrians and drivers do considerably more than behave in accordance with specified road-user protocol (Foot *et al.*, 1981).

A study of pedestrian–driver encounters by Zuercher (1977) gives grounds to believe that over and above explicit rule-following there are processes involving the negotiation and performance of joint actions. Using confederates he reported that drivers differentiated between pedestrians according to age and sex in deciding whether to stop for them to cross: one in five cars stopped for a middle-aged man; one in six stopped for a young attractive woman; and one in eight stopped for an old lady. He also reported that drivers stopped more frequently for pedestrians of the opposite sex. Unfortunately there are few such studies which have attempted an investigation of the patterning of transactions between drivers and pedestrians. It is unfortunate too that official accident statistics are not compiled in a way which is consonant with this type of social-psychological analysis. However, Sandels (1979), working in Sweden, has conducted her own statistical study of pedestrian and driver characteristics, and she particularly notes that women drivers are overrepresented in the incidents of child pedestrian injuries. Any interpretation of this observation would obviously need to consider sex differences in drivers' exposure to child pedestrians: for example, women may tend to take responsibility for child-connected journeys, particularly school trips.

Given that considerations of 'hazard', 'danger', 'safety', and 'warning' are central to the conduct of pedestrian–driver confrontations, an empirical examination of these concepts could constitute an alternative starting point for exploring road-user communications. A study by Martin and Heimstra (1973) is one of very few to adopt this rationale. A 'perception of hazard' test was developed which required subjects (5–18-year-olds) to assess the degree of hazard depicted in a series of life scenes, one of which was a road traffic scene. However, assessment was by means of a rating scale which was almost certainly too difficult to be used by many of the subjects, and considerable doubt is thereby cast upon the validity and reliability of the data accrued. Additionally, hazard was narrowly defined, being considered exclusively in terms of the perceived severity of likely injury. Other dimensions of outcome, notably social and moral dimensions, were neglected.

A potentially fruitful line of enquiry has been initiated by Bongard and Winterfeld (1976). They showed a series of 18 color films of traffic scenes to a group of 400 children. Each film depicted someone wanting to cross the road and a conflict arising because of an implicit requirement to observe traffic regulations. In films of simple street scenes, the child subjects recognized danger reasonably well, but their performances deteriorated when presented with more complex scenes. The road crossing behavior which children deemed appropriate in unfamiliar circumstances was also more parallel to official recommendations than was the behavior which they deemed appropriate in familiar settings. Initially, perhaps, children are only inclined to practice adult strategies when they are in familiar territory; and perhaps only gradually do they generalize their more sophisticated techniques to other contexts. In fact, most accidents occur when children are in quiet streets and near to home, but then they are far more frequently in these streets than in others.

It should be noted that a social cognition approach promotes the kinds of interactive analyses which are also prompted by the epidemiological framework, outlined above. Both epidemiology and social cognition interpret accidents as the statistically probable and psychologically rational outcome of engaging in certain kinds of activities, in specific circumstances, and at particular times. Social cognition attempts to provide an explicative history of pedestrian–driver confrontation with special reference to the interpersonal domain of activity. Thereby it attempts to elucidate some important features of the structure, determinants, and correlates of pedestrian accidents generally.

Concluding Remarks

In this brief discussion various theoretical perspectives have necessarily been omitted, notably perspectives which are rooted in sociological and information-processing approaches (cf. Foot *et al.*, 1982). Our objective has been to indicate that an epidemiological framework can make a significant contribution to the study of pedestrian accidents. Its power resides in its potential to encompass other approaches, particularly social psychological approaches, which have already proved useful. Critics of this objective might reason that epidemiological methods are entirely parallel with those which are used in any systematic enquiry. They might say that any distinction is solely lexical and that any scientific method might be labelled 'epidemiological'. This form of criticism is rendered less compelling when it is recognized that the epidemiological framework goes beyond many alternative methodologies in one major respect: it specifies *a priori* certain structural features of its subject-matter in a manner which serves to clarify the concepts under study.

A second criticism might be that there are already alternative ways of conceptualizing accidents, properly located within the discipline of social psychology, which seem more appropriate to psychological enquiry and explanation. One of the more serious contenders in this respect is the dramaturgical framework developed by Harré and Secord (1972). This attempts to analyze social interactions and their consequences in terms of rule-prescribed role-ascriptions in the context of the social structuring of environmental 'props' and 'scenery'. While this type of analysis approximates an epidemiological view of the world, it is more restricted in that it seeks to specify the nature of intepersonal transactions: the interactions between people and their environments are seen as rule-circumscribed. The epidemiological framework, by contrast, leaves the sequential processing of these kinds of interactions deliberately vague, and thereby allows for a multiplicity of theoretical advances.

An epidemiological framework facilitates the forging of powerful links with other branches of scientific enquiry, particularly those of medicine and demography, and it thereby provides a structured basis for interaction between diverse disciplines. It also provides important aids to classification and clarification of research enquiry. For instance, it aids understanding and differentiation of those studies which are purely descriptive and those which are derived from specific theoretical perspectives; and it can make apparent the ways in which descriptive studies support or refute specific theoretical positions. However, the most powerful reason for our adopting an epidemiological framework lies in the emphasis that it places on promoting understanding with a view to accident prevention. Hence in reviewing the literature in this chapter we have selected and emphasized work for its practical value to assess the prophylactic application, as well as for its scientific merit.

In our view it is encumbent upon any theory that it should seek to explain its referent phenomena in such a way that the evidence cited excludes other theoretical stances. Yet many social psychological theories proffer a single piece of evidence as confirming each of their respective positions, and this is one reason why there is no one theoretical perspective which can provide a totally adequate account of pedestrian accidents. Of course it is not necessarily the theory which is at fault if it cannot deal with all the facts in its domain. Empirical 'facts' are often constituted by older ideologies, so that a clash between facts and theories may itself constitute proof of progress; for it tends to promote, in time, the replacement of the older theory by the better one. Furthermore, it has never been suggested that a single social psychological theory could comprehensively account for the variable distributional structure of the many different types of pedestrian accident. There is no reason to believe that simple unitary explanations could invariably account for the complex multi-causal nature of pedestrian accidents. Hence we view alternative, or complementary, social psychological theories as desirable and necessary. In conclusion, social psychological theories have indicated in what respects the individual is limited in his or her ability to prevent pedestrian accidents. Such accidents represent a massive psychological, social, political, engineering, medical, and planning problem. The contribution of social psychology must be seen and evaluated in this light.

References

Aldman, B. (1966). 'The road accident risks for children and young people: the morbidity and mortality pattern', *Proceedings of the Second Congress of the International Association for Accident and Traffic Medicine*, vol. 1, pp. 203–206. Stockholm.

Alexander, F., and Flagg, G. W. (1965). 'The psychosomatic approach', in Wolman, B. B. (ed.), *Handbook of Clinical Psychology*. McGraw-Hill, New York.

Backett, E. M., and Johnston, A. M. (1959). 'Social patterns of road accidents to children: some characteristics of vulnerable families', *British Medical Journal*, **1**, 409–413.

Bongard, E. V., and Winterfeld, V. C. (1976). 'Children's traffic knowledge and their comprehension of the dangers involved (children aged 5–9)', in Hakkert, A. S. (ed.), *Proceedings of the International Conference on Pedestrian Safety*, vol. 2, pp. 131–135. Michlol, Haifa.

Borke, H. (1977). 'Piaget's view of social interaction and the theoretical construct of empathy', in Siegel, L. S., and Brainerd, C. J. (eds.), *Alternatives to Piaget: Critical Essays on the Theory*. Academic Press, London.

Burton, L. (1968). *Vulnerable Children*. Routledge & Kegan Paul, London.

Cattell, R., and Lewis, G. D. (1975). 'Children's understanding of words used in road safety literature'. UK Department of the Environment, Transport and Road Research Laboratory. Supplementary Report 155UC.

Chapman, A. J., Sheehy, N. P., Foot, H. C., and Wade, F. M. (1981), 'Child pedestrian behaviour', in Foot, H. C., Chapman, A. J. and Wade, F. M. (eds.), *Road Safety: Research and Practice*. Praeger, Eastbourne.

Clark, D. W. (1967). 'A vocabulary for preventive medicine', in Clark, D. W., and MacMahon, B. (eds.), *Preventive Medicine*. Little Brown & Co., Boston.

Cohen, J., Dearnaley, A. J., and Hansel, C. E. M. (1955). 'The risk taken in crossing a road', *Operational Research Quarterly*, **6**, 120–127.

Cohen, K. M., and Haith, M. M. (1977). 'Peripheral vision: the effects of developmental, perceptual and cognitive factors', *Journal of Experimental Child Psychology*, **24**, 373–394.

Coleman, P. G. (1981). 'Ageing and social problems', in Chapman, A. J., and Gale, A. (eds.), *Psychology and People: A Tutorial Text*. British Psychological Society and MacMillan Press, London.

Deutsch, M. (1964). 'On development and learning', in Haddon, W., Suchman, E. A., and Klein, D. (eds.), *Accident Research*. Harper & Row, New York.

Ekström, G., Gästrin, U., and Quist, O. (1966). 'Traffic injuries and accident proneness in childhood', *Proceedings of the Second Congress of the International Association for Accident and Traffic Medicine*, pp. 95–98. Stockholm.

England, E. S. (1976). 'Children's strategies for road crossing in an urban environment'. M.Sc. Dissertation, University of Salford.

Foot, H. C., Chapman, A. J., and Smith, J. R. (1980). *Friendship and Social Relations in Children*. Wiley, Chichester.

Foot, H. C., Chapman, A. J., and Wade, F. M. (eds.) (1981). *Road Safety: Research and Practice*. Praeger, Eastbourne.

Foot, H. C., Chapman, A. J., and Wade, F. M. (1982). 'Pedestrian accidents: general issues and approaches', in Chapman, A. J., Wade, F. M., and Foot, H. C. (eds.), *Pedestrian Accidents*. Wiley, Chichester.

Fransella, F., and Frost, K. (1977). *On Being a Woman*. Tavistock Publications, London.

Grayson, G. B. (1975a). 'The Hampshire child pedestrian accident study'. UK Department of the Environment, Transport and Road Research Laboratory. Laboratory Report 668.

Grayson, G. B. (1975b). 'Observations of pedestrian behaviour at four sites'. UK Department of the Environment, Transport and Road Research Laboratory. Laboratory Report 670.

Harré, R., and Secord, P. E. (1972). *The Explanation of Social Behaviour*. Blackwell, Oxford.

Jacobs, G. D., and Wilson, D. G. (1967). 'A study of pedestrian risk in crossing busy roads in four towns'. UK Department of the Environment, Transport and Road Research Laboratory. Laboratory Report 106.

Kenchington, M. S., Alderson, G. J. K., and Whiting, H. T. A. (1977). 'An assessment of the role of motion prediction in child pedestrian accidents'. UK Department of the Environment, Transport and Road Research Laboratory. SR320.

Krall, V. (1953). 'Personality characteristics of accident repeating children', *Journal of Abnormal and Social Psychology*, **48**, 99–107.

Liss, P. H., and Haith, M. M. (1970). 'The speed of visual processing in children and adults: effects of backward and forward masking', *Perception and Psychophysics*, **8**, 396–398.

Maccoby, E. E., and Jacklin, C. N. (1975). *The Psychology of Sex Differences*. Oxford University Press, London.

Mackie, A. M., and Older, S. J. (1965). 'Study of pedestrian risk in crossing busy roads in London inner suburbs', *Traffic Engineering and Control*, **7**, 376–380.

MacMahon, B. (1967). 'Epidemiologic methods', in Clark, D. W., and MacMahon, B. (eds.), *Preventive Medicine*. Little Brown & Co., Boston.

Manheimer, D. I., and Mellinger, G. D. (1967). 'Personality characteristics of the child accident repeater', *Child Development*, **38**, 491–513.

Martin, G. L., and Heimstra, N. W. (1973). 'The perception of hazard by children', *Journal of Safety Research*, **5**, 238–246.

Mellinger, G. D., and Manheimer, D. I. (1967). 'An exposure-coping model of accident liability among children', *Journal of Health and Social Behavior*, **8**, 96–106.

Newson, J., and Newson, E. (1976). *Seven Year Olds in the Home Environment*. George Allen & Unwin, London.

Piaget, J., and Inhelder, B. (1956). *The Child's Conception of Space*. Routledge & Kegan Paul, London.

Preston, B. (1972). 'Statistical analysis of child pedestrian accidents in Manchester and Salford', *Accident Analysis and Prevention*, **4**, 323–332.

Read, J. H., Bradley, E. J., Morison, J. D., Lewall, D., and Clarke, D. A. (1963). 'The epidemiology and prevention of traffic accidents involving child pedestrians', *Canadian Medical Association Journal*, **89**, 687–701.

Reading, J. B. (1973). 'Pedestrian protection through behaviour modification', *Traffic Engineering*, **43**, 14–16 and 19–23.

Ross, H. E. (1974). *Behaviour and Perception in Strange Environments*. George Allen & Unwin, London.

Routledge, D. A., Repetto-Wright, R., and Howarth, C. I. (1974). 'The exposure of young children to accident risk as pedestrians', *Ergonomics*, **17**, 457–480.

Routledge, D. A., Repetto-Wright, R., and Howarth, C. I. (1976). 'The development of road crossing skill by child pedestrians. *Proceedings of the International Conference on Pedestrian Safety*, vol. 2, pp. 7C1–7C9. Haifa, Israel.

Russell, J. C., Wilson, D. O., and Jenkins, J. F. (1976). 'Informational properties of jaywalking models as determinants of imitated jaywalking: an extension to models, sex, race and number', *Sociometry*, **39**, 270–273.

Ryan, G. A. (1969). 'Children in traffic accidents', *Pediatrics Supplement*, **44**, 847–854.

Sadler, J. (1972). *Children and Road Safety: A Survey Amongst Mothers*. Report SS450. HMSO, London.

Salvatore, S. (1974). 'The ability of elementary and secondary school children to sense oncoming car velocity', *Journal of Safety Research*, **6**, 118–125.

Sandels, S. (1970). 'Young children in traffic', *British Journal of Educational Psychology*, **40**, 111–116.

Sandels, S. (1971). 'A report on children in traffic'. Skandia Report I. Skandia, Stockholm.

Sandels, S. (1974). 'Why are children injured in traffic? Can we prevent child accidents in traffic? Skandia Report II. Skandia, Stockholm.

Sandels, S. (1975). *Children in Traffic* (Revised edition by J. Hartley (ed.), published in Great Britain, 1975.) Elek Books Ltd., London

Sandels, S. (1979). 'Unprotected road users. A behavioural study'. Skandia Report III. Skandia, Stockholm.

Shaw, L., and Sichel, H. (1971). *Accident Proneness*. Pergamon Press, Oxford.

Sheppard, D. (1975). 'To learn or not to learn the Green Cross Code'. *Safety Education*, Spring, 5–7.

Sheppard, D., and Colborne, H. V. (1968). 'Understanding of road safety propaganda', *Safety Education*, Autumn, 12–13.

Singh, A. (1982). 'Pedestrian education', in Chapman, A. J., Wade, F. M., and Foot, H. C. (eds.), *Pedestrian Accidents*. Wiley, Chichester.

Sumner, R., and Baguley, C. (1979). 'Speed control humps on residential roads'. UK Department of the Environment, Transport and Road Research Laboratory. Laboratory Report 878.

Wade, F. M., Chapman, A. J., and Foot, H. C. (1979a). 'Child pedestrian accidents', in Oborne, D. J., Gruneberg, M. M., and Eiser, J. R. (eds.), *Research in Psychology and Medicine*, Vol. II: *Social Aspects, Attitudes, Communication, Care and Training*. Academic Press, London.

Wade, F. M., Chapman, A. J., and Foot, H. C. (1981). 'The physical environment and child pedestrian accidents in the United Kingdom: a review', *Man–Environment Systems*, in press.

Wade, F. M., Foot, H. C., and Chapman, A. J. (1979b). 'The social environment and child pedestrian accidents', *Learning*, **1**, 39–48.

Weinreich, H. (1978). 'Sex-role socialisation', in Chetwynd, J., and Hartnett, O. (eds.), *The Sex Role System*. Routledge & Kegan Paul, London.

Whiteside, J. A. (1976). 'Peripheral vision in children and adults', *Child Development*, **47**, 290–293.

Yeaton, W. H., and Bailey, J. S. (1978). 'Teaching pedestrian safety skills to young children: an analysis and one-year follow up'. *Journal of Applied Behavior Analysis*, **11**, 315–329.

Zuercher, R. (1977). 'Communication at pedestrian crossings, II'. *Proceedings of the International Conference on Pedestrian Safety*, vol. 2, pp. 115–118. Haifa, Israel.

Social Psychology and Behavioral Medicine
Edited by J. Richard Eiser
© 1982 John Wiley & Sons Ltd

Chapter 6

Endogenous psychosocial factors in cross-national cancer incidence

BERNARD H. FOX

Introduction

The cross-national literature on incidence of and mortality from cancer is fairly extensive, and lately a substantial number of works have appeared on survival data. Most of it, however—perhaps one can say the overwhelming bulk of it—after describing statistics about these measures, addresses possible reasons for similarities and differences strictly in terms of the classical etiologic agents: diet, genetic differences, exposure to non-diet carcinogens, infectious agents, specific behaviors exposing the person to carcinogens such as smoking (really a subgroup of carcinogen exposure, above), occupations, age, habits, and climatic features, among others. Some examples are Burdette (1975), Doll *et al.* (1966), Higginson and Muir (1973), Muir (1975), Muir and Péron (1976), Muir and Nectoux (in press), Segi (1960) and Steiner (1954). Many writers on intranational and cross-national cancer epidemiology have addressed psychological factors, but usually from the point of view that such factors are sources of exposure to ultimate carcinogenic factors, e.g. Greenwald *et al.* (1975).

The contributions of such agents and the more proximate psychosocial factors are hard to separate because of the intimate interaction among them. The principal problem here, however, is to assess the possible role of *endogenous* psychosocial factors (EPF). EPF will be defined and specified in the paragraphs below.

Psychosocial factors in general include both psychological factors and social factors. The former are emotional, attitudinal or ideational phenomena within the organism. Social factors are phenomena associated with or arising from the specific group character of the group to which the organism belongs. Such factors are external to the organism but impinge on it, and affect biological or psychological phenomena or both. Psychological factors can be long-term persistent characteristics of the organism, called traits, or short-term ones, called states. (The meaning of 'long-term' and 'short-term' are not well established in the literature, but the arguments below will not be affected by uncertainties about these meanings.) Psychological factors in animals—excitement, fear, anger, quasi-depression, etc.—cannot be measured subjectively as they can in man; they must be inferred from behavior, although many prefer not to draw inferences at all, but merely to describe the behavior. Social factors can affect behavior, which includes biological response, or psychological factors, or both.

Psychological factors can affect biological states or responses to various degrees and in different ways. When these factors *directly* affect cancer -inducing or cancer-protecting conditions within the body—involving hormones, enzymes, the immune system (IS), cell transformations, oxidative or other metabolic body processes, etc.—and not through an external source of cancer induction or protection, they will be called endogenous psychological factors. An example is depression, which, it has been claimed, is a predictor of increased cancer risk (Bieliaukas *et al.*, 1979), and is hypothesized to affect the IS directly (see Bartrop *et al.*, 1977, for example). As above, social factors can affect psychological ones. When social factors produce or influence endogenous psychological factors, they will be called endogenous social factors. We can now define endogenous psychosocial factors (EPF). EPF are endogenous psychological factors or endogenous social factors, but do not include any other psychological or social factors.

At this point, to make sure of the scope of EPF, it is important to specify those psychological and social factors that are not EPF. Social factors or psychological factors that have no influence on cancer incidence are not EPF. A social factor that does have an influence on cancer incidence—e.g. type of diet—but is not thought to do so through an effect on an endogenous psychological factor is not among the EPF. Other examples of social factors that are not EPF are late marriage among women, or bearing a first child at a relatively late age. These events are associated with, and are thought to lead to, increased risk of breast cancer, but not through their effect on psychic processes. Rather, delay in protective changes of hormone concentration associated with one's first childbirth is felt to increase the risk of breast cancer. Such social factors will be called exogenous social factors. As a last example, if a women has early intercourse with many partners, the theory is that she exposes herself more often to carcinogenic agents, particularly herpesvirus 2, and is thereby at greater risk of cervical cancer than other women. Such social behavior is an exogenous social factor. A psychological factor that may affect cancer susceptibility, but which acts only by increasing or decreasing an external carcinogen or protector is not an EPF. An example is having a personality structure that tends to increase probability of smoking. That personality structure does not change cancer susceptibility by its *direct* effect on the body. It does so only by increasing exposure to an external carcinogen, hence it is not an EPF. A psychological factor such as the one just described will be called an exogenous psychological factor.

With that viewpoint, let us narrow the conceptual framework of our task before addressing data.

What kind of endogenous psychosocial states or stimuli could bring about changes in susceptibility that must be distinguished from more clearly etiologic agents? There are two—genetic and imposed. There are clear differences in both biological response and behavioral response among species, strains and individuals within strains, apparently genetically based (Fox, section on genetic attributes, 1981). As for non-genetic sources of difference in animals, there are classical stressful events affecting the immune system or carcinogen-processing enzymes. The former have generally been identified. Here we think of such things as force-breeding; crowding; arousal stemming from noise, light, fear-pheromones, cage discomfort, etc.; social dominance; and artificial stress resulting from shock, immobility, and cold (Riley, 1979). All of these are EPF because they produce internal biological events that could have an impact on cancer susceptibility, and these events do not stem from an external carcinogen such as smoke, arsenic, aflatoxin, X-rays, or newly exposed viruses, nor an external protector such as retinoid, free radical reducer or selenium.

In the human, genetic differences can clearly appear (Omenn, 1977), and form a major source of variation in cancer susceptibility. But the evidence for such differences being associated with psychological differences is very sketchy, both between strains and between individuals. Moreover, as will be expanded on below, much variation resides within human strains because we are only grossly inbred in a geographic sense and not brother–sister inbred to create a deliberately syngeneic group, as in laboratory animals. Also, in the human, artificial stress is really not under consideration, except in special groups like prisoners of war or concentration camp survivors.

In the human, as well, a whole group of additional stimuli must be considered as psychosocial stimuli that do not exist in the animal, but might be EPF—presence or loss of family or social support, bereavement, psychosis, job security, interpersonal family friction, and cultural shock associated with migration, to name just some.

This search will focus on social groups as the main subjects of inquiry, and if biology enters the picture it will do so of necessity, not because of an intent to emphasize that aspect of carcinogenesis, already addressed elsewhere (Fox, 1978; 1981).

Cancer Incidence Rates Within and Between Countries

Cancer incidence rates will be the main variable discussed, although mortality rates will be used where needed to show important implications of such differences or similarities, or where incidence data do not exist. Incidence is the more accurate and reliable statistic of the two, and is less subject to artifactual variation (Muir, 1973). The main reason for using incidence, however, is that the outcome of interest is incidence, not effect of EPF on progress or outcome of cancer.

Cancer incidence rates are normally published by various countries at regular intervals, but some third-world countries have only a limited history of reporting. While the deficiency of early data for some countries is inconvenient, it does not prevent the making of the first major point, which is that there is a large variation within and between countries in the incidence for a given bodily cancer site; further, over the years, incidence for certain sites within various countries has changed markedly.

Cancer incidence rates vary as much as 30 to 1 even within the same country—184/100,000 *vs.* 6/100,000 for esophageal cancer in females in certain regions of Iran (Higginson and Muir, 1976). Variation in rates such as that for colon cancer among male Chinese in Hawaii (36/100,000), 4/100,000 among male Japanese, among Bombay residents and among Colombians, and 3/100,000 among male South Africans (Bantus) is not very unusual. An extreme case is that for incidence of liver cancer—about 1/100,000 in Norwegian males *vs.* 104/100,000 in Mozambique males (Higginson and Muir, 1976). These authors also cite a really extreme case where, among Mozambique males in the 25–34-year age-group, the liver cancer rate is almost 500 times that for a similar age-group in the USA. For other sites, variation may be less between countries. An extreme example of small variation is found in the female incidence rates for cancer of the bone, where the largest rate among 12 representative countries (the same ones used in the liver example above) is about 1.1/100,000 for Israel and the smallest is about 0.5/100,000, for Japan. There are other extremes, but I have not cited those because the lowest rates are often of the order of 0.1/100,000, which could be off by almost 50 percent because they are rounded (e.g., lip, Japan; pharynx, Newfoundland; testis, Nigeria; kidney, Bulawayo (Zimbabwe); melanoma, Japan; all for men—for women, some examples are lip, Norway; tongue, Romania; nasopharynx, Japan; small intestine, Nigeria). Even if one ignores those cases where objection could be made that accuracy is doubtful, the extremes exist.

It is often possible to ascribe causation with some confidence. For example, epidemiologists are convinced that incidence of lung cancer is raised markedly by smoking; that chewing betel with tobacco and lime is a prime cause of the very high rate of mouth cancer in Travancore, India (Orr, 1963), where fully 46 percent of all cancer is oral; that smoking plus drinking of certain alcholic beverages raises the incidence of esophageal cancer markedly in Normandy (Tuyns *et al.*, 1979); that snuff dipping is the reason for the high rate of oral cancer in elderly women in the Appalachians (Blot *et al.*, 1977); and that asbestos inhalation causes a major increase in the rate of mesothelioma (Selikoff and Hammond, 1979). One could go on with a long list (Hiatt *et al.*, 1977).

Some sample rates are displayed in Figure 6.1 (Segi, 1977) for various countries at two sites. Usually female rates differ less between countries than male. This fact is attributed to the extreme rates incurred by men's greater exposure to local carcinogens. For example, men's rates exceed those of women's in these cancers: oropharyngeal (smoking and drinking), esophageal (same), lung (smoking), and bladder (smoking and occupational exposure), among others. But where exposure is more or less the same, there is little difference: colon (common diet), non-melanoma skin (overall sun exposure, genetic stock), brain and nervous system (?) among others.

There are other possibilities. For example, a recent report cited the lesser susceptibility of women's lung tissues to the effect of smoke constituents for equivalent smoke exposure. Was there indeed equivalent smoke exposure? Did the experimenter control for frequency of inhalation, depth of inhalation, length of butt, filter type, duration of inhalation process, interval after inhalation before exhalation? Is there a difference in cancer susceptibility dependent on hormonal balance? For example, in Japan men with stomach cancer showed less baldness of aging than those without. Accompanying this phenomenon was a differential hormone level in controls with greater and lesser baldness of aging (Wakisaka *et al.*, 1972). Another study hypothesizes greater resistance in women because the control mechanism for the immune system is on the X-chromosome, of which women have two and men one (Purtilo and Sullivan, 1979). If one mutates in women to reduce immunocompetence, their theory states, the other X-chromosome can carry the load of protection; in men there is only one. Nevertheless, if the same is true in animals, why, among long-lived strains, do the males live consistently longer (Smith *et al.*, 1973)?

Within countries the variation in rates is usually much less than that between countries, mostly because of the relative homogeneity of genetic stock and of lifestyle within the country (Lilienfeld *et al.*, 1972). Where there are extremes of climate, diet, industrialization, genetic pools, ethnic pools, or lifestyles, they may lead to relative extremes of cancer rates in that country for a given site. The contrast mentioned above for Iranian incidence of esophageal cancer, observed for both sexes, exemplifies this point. In the USA strong differences are found between states such as New Jersey—whose industrialization is extreme, but whose population has habits of eating, drinking, and smoking more or less representative of the USA as a whole—and Utah, whose large population of Mormons smokes and drinks much less than other groups, eats moderately, and has little exposure to carcinogenic industrial products. The annual age-adjusted mortality rates in white males

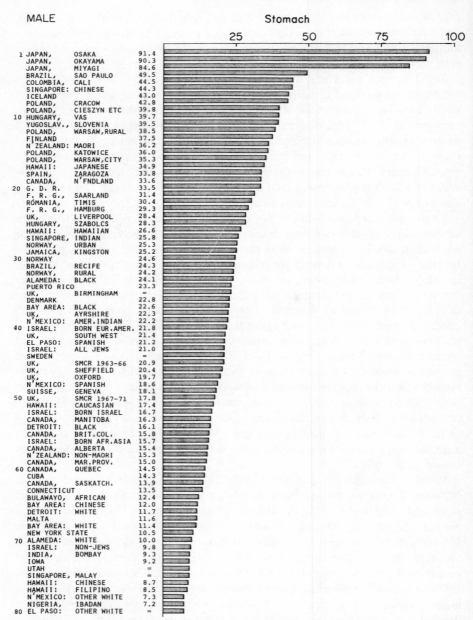

Figure 6.1 Age-adjusted incidence rates (cases/100,000 per year) among 80 world groups, variously late 1960s to early 1970s: stomach cancer in males and breast cancer in females (Segi, 1977. Reproduced with permission). The data source for these charts was Waterhouse, J., Muir, C., Correa, P. and Powell, J., *Cancer on Five Continents,*

FEMALE Breast

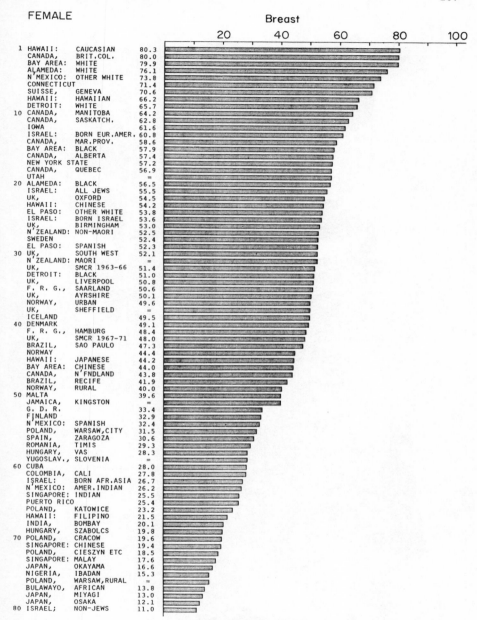

1	HAWAII:	CAUCASIAN	80.3
	CANADA,	BRIT.COL.	80.0
	BAY AREA:	WHITE	79.9
	ALAMEDA:	WHITE	76.1
	N'MEXICO:	OTHER WHITE	73.8
	CONNECTICUT		71.4
	SUISSE,	GENEVA	70.6
	HAWAII:	HAWAIIAN	66.2
	DETROIT:	WHITE	65.7
10	CANADA,	MANITOBA	64.2
	CANADA,	SASKATCH.	62.8
	IOWA		61.6
	ISRAEL:	BORN EUR.AMER.	60.8
	CANADA,	MAR.PROV.	58.6
	BAY AREA:	BLACK	57.9
	CANADA,	ALBERTA	57.4
	NEW YORK STATE		57.2
	CANADA,	QUEBEC	56.9
	UTAH		=
20	ALAMEDA:	BLACK	56.5
	ISRAEL:	ALL JEWS	55.5
	UK,	OXFORD	54.5
	HAWAII:	CHINESE	54.2
	EL PASO:	OTHER WHITE	53.8
	ISRAEL:	BORN ISRAEL	53.6
	UK,	BIRMINGHAM	53.0
	N'ZEALAND:	NON-MAORI	52.5
	SWEDEN		52.4
	EL PASO:	SPANISH	52.3
30	UK,	SOUTH WEST	52.1
	N'ZEALAND:	MAORI	=
	UK,	SMCR 1963-66	51.4
	DETROIT:	BLACK	51.0
	UK,	LIVERPOOL	50.8
	F. R. G.,	SAARLAND	50.6
	UK,	AYRSHIRE	50.1
	NORWAY,	URBAN	49.6
	UK,	SHEFFIELD	=
	ICELAND		49.5
40	DENMARK		49.1
	F. R. G.,	HAMBURG	48.4
	UK,	SMCR 1967-71	48.0
	BRAZIL,	SAO PAULO	47.3
	NORWAY		44.4
	HAWAII:	JAPANESE	44.2
	BAY AREA:	CHINESE	44.0
	CANADA,	N'FNDLAND	43.8
	BRAZIL,	RECIFE	41.9
	NORWAY,	RURAL	40.0
50	MALTA		39.6
	JAMAICA,	KINGSTON	=
	G. D. R.		33.4
	FINLAND		32.9
	N'MEXICO:	SPANISH	32.4
	POLAND,	WARSAW,CITY	31.5
	SPAIN,	ZARAGOZA	30.6
	ROMANIA,	TIMIS	29.3
	HUNGARY,	VAS	28.3
	YUGOSLAV.,	SLOVENIA	=
60	CUBA		28.0
	COLOMBIA,	CALI	27.8
	ISRAEL:	BORN AFR.ASIA	26.7
	N'MEXICO:	AMER.INDIAN	26.2
	SINGAPORE:	INDIAN	25.5
	PUERTO RICO		25.4
	POLAND,	KATOWICE	23.2
	HAWAII:	FILIPINO	21.5
	INDIA,	BOMBAY	20.1
	HUNGARY,	SZABOLCS	19.8
70	POLAND,	CRACOW	19.6
	SINGAPORE:	CHINESE	19.4
	POLAND,	CIESZYN ETC	18.5
	SINGAPORE:	MALAY	17.6
	JAPAN,	OKAYAMA	16.6
	NIGERIA,	IBADAN	15.3
	POLAND,	WARSAW,RURAL	=
	BULAWAYO,	AFRICAN	13.8
	JAPAN,	MIYAGI	13.0
	JAPAN,	OSAKA	12.1
80	ISRAEL;	NON-JEWS	11.0

vol. III. Lyon: International Agency for Research on Cancer, 1976. Please note that Segi chose from these data those incidence rates based on the age distribution of the world standard population he first used in Segi (1960), probably the most representative one

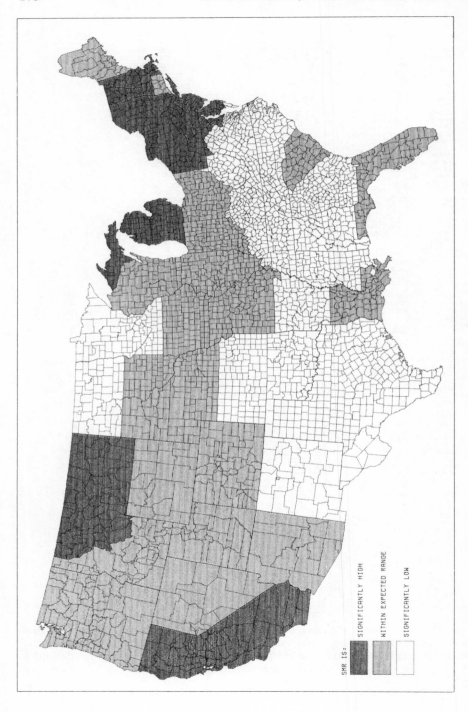

for all sites combined (1950–69) were 174/100,000 for the USA, 205/100,000 for New Jersey, and 133/100,000 for Utah (Mason and McKay, 1974). More extreme contrasts can be found, and less extreme. USA mortality rates by state for two cancer sites are shown in Figures 6.2 and 6.3 (McKay, 1980).

Besides the specific variables associated with cancer incidence to be described below (diet, industrialization, etc.), one non-specific variable is of interest: the change in cancer rates over time. In the USA the incidence rate for stomach cancer has been dropping steadily over the period 1935–71, as has that for cancer of the uterine cervix. During the same period the lung cancer rate has been rising steadily, and the female breast cancer rate has remained almost constant for whites, but has risen somewhat for blacks (Devesa and Silverman, 1978). They show incidence data over 34 years for a number of sites in white females (see Figure 6.4). Recent computerization of data from McKay and Hanson (1980) permits three-dimensional display of trends *by age* for mortality in the USA due to various cancers. Such trend data are shown in Figure 6.5 for cancer of the pancreas in non-whites. More recent trends have been described (Pollack and Horm, 1980), but their stability is yet to be established.

The reasons for these changes are not entirely clear, but reasonable hypotheses have been advanced. For example, colon cancer in Japan is on the rise (Hirayama, 1977), probably because of diet changes. Lung cancer in the USA has been rising, after adjustment for an appropriate lag factor, with cigarette consumption. Stomach cancer started to fall when the US diet moved toward drinking milk and more fresh greens and other vegetables (Higginson and Muir, 1973), at the same time that the preserving techniques used by European immigrants began to decline. We have no clear explanation for the fall in uterine cancer incidence and mortality occurring throughout the western world. It is not fully explainable on the basis of earlier and more efficient detection, but increased survival may account in part for the fall in mortality, and increased rates of hysterectomy must be considered (Devesa and Silverman, 1978).

As an observation preliminary to the more extended discussion below, the hypothesis of increases in stressful living as a potential source of carcinogenesis already encounters difficulties where, over long periods, mortality rates for certain sites stay the same (e.g. breast in white women, prostate,

Figure 6.2 USA age-adjusted mortality by state for bladder cancer in white males, 1968–71 (McKay, 1980). A state's standard mortality ratio (SMR) is 100 × (observed deaths ÷ deaths expected if the overall USA age-specific rates had prevailed in that state). A state's SMR is significant if the SMR ± (1.96 × its standard error (SE)), where the SE is based on the state's own population, does not include the SMR for the total USA (= 100). For calculation of the significance of the SMR, see Bailar and Ederer (1964)

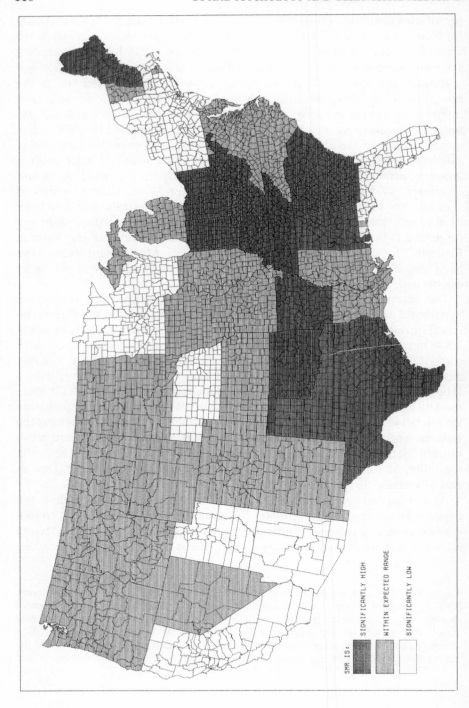

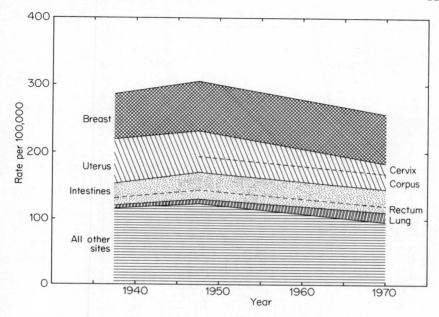

Figure 6.4 Trends in cancer incidence rates (cases/100,000 per year) among white females in the USA, 1935–70, showing high incidence and combined other sites (Devesa and Silverman, 1978)

esophagus, intestines plus rectum, and bladder in white men) or fall (e.g. cervix and stomach) (Devesa and Silverman, 1978). In some cases incidence rates rose while death rates stayed the same. Increased screening efforts that pick diseases up at an earlier stage have been suggested to account for much of this.

Of especial relevance to the present issue are incidence rates among groups who have migrated to other countries, and between different ethnic groups within the same country. In the first category, certain migrant groups have been well studied, e.g. Japanese from Japan who migrated to Hawaii and the US west coast (Haenszel, 1975). Specific organ systems have been examined for effects of migration on cancer incidence in the USA. These sites have been noted to show greater mortality in various white ethnic groups than in native-born whites: oropharynx (Irish and Finnish), large bowel (Irish), esophagus (Irish, Polish, and Russian), stomach (immigrants from many European countries and Japan), larynx (Irish and female Swedish), and thyroid (Norwegian females, Polish, and Russian) (Lilienfeld *et al.*, 1972,

Figure 6.3 USA age-adjusted mortality by state for cervical cancer in whites, 1968–71 (McKay, 1980). For explanation, see Figure 6.2

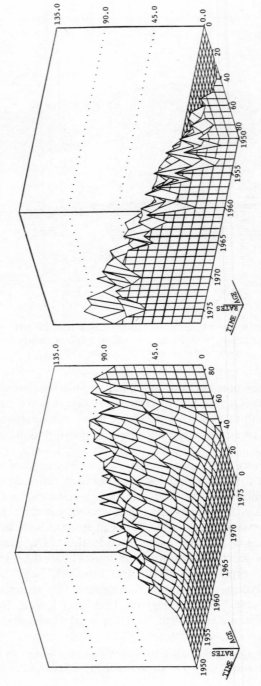

Figure 6.5 USA age-specific mortality rates (deaths/100,000 per year) from cancer of the pancreas among non-white males, 1950–77 (McKay and Hanson, 1980)

cited in Haenszel, 1975). Haenszel makes the following generalizations. For stomach cancer, groups from high-risk countries showed a reduced rate but are still at higher risk than the USA; for lung, groups from both high- and low-risk countries changed to a level intermediate between home and host mortalities; and for large bowel, breast, ovary, corpus uteri, and prostate, rates for migrants in their own lifetime rose to equal the rates of the host country except the Japanese for breast cancer, whose rates remained lower than those of the USA.

A case–control study of Hawaiian Japanese (Haenszel *et al.*, 1972) showed that 'migrants from Japanese prefectures with highest stomach cancer risks continued to experience an excess risk in Hawaii, but this effect did not persist in their Nisei offspring'. Lower risk was found among Nisei who ate western diet, but not among Issei (first generation) who did so. These data support other data suggesting the idea that the critical diet exposure time is during childhood.

Cancer rates among immigrants and ethnic groups have been the subject of considerable study: among sedentes in different countries (Higginson and Muir, 1973; Segi, 1977), between immigrant groups in one country (Haenszel, 1961; Halevi *et al.*, 1971; Steinitz and Costin, 1971), between immigrants and host country natives (Adelstein *et al.*, 1979; Staszewski and Haenszel, 1965), and between different ethnic sedentes in one country (Creagan and Fraumeni, 1972; Donovan, 1970; Young *et al.*, 1978).

The main variables associated with, and probably affecting, incidence rates differ for different sites of cancer. Cigarette smoking, the strongest predictor of cancer risk, has been associated with several sites: lung, bronchus, larynx, esophagus, pancreas, and bladder, among others. Pipe and cigar smoking are associated more with oropharyngeal cancer than lung. Ultraviolet light is associated with skin cancer, ionizing radiation with blood and lymphatic cancer, but most other organs are also affected, though less strongly; benzidine is associated with bladder cancer; benzene with leukemia; vinyl chloride with liver cancer; something in the environment of furniture makers and leather workers causes cancer of the nasal sinuses; arsenic is associated with skin and lung cancer; drinking and smoking with oropharyngeal and esophageal cancer; aflatoxin with liver cancer; schistosomiasis with bladder cancer; late first childbirth, early menarche, late menopause, obesity, and breast cancer-afflicted relatives all increase the chances of breast cancer; etc. (Doll, 1977). Several extensive reviews have dealt with these and other variables (Becker, 1975; Fraumeni, 1975; Hiatt *et al.*, 1977; Holland and Frei, 1973; and Schottenfeld, 1975).

Among the psychosocial variables that may affect cross-national cancer incidences are personality that is associated with smoking patterns; social class, which in turn affects occupation, diet, sexual mores, drinking patterns, attitude toward cancer-prevention activities, age at marriage, age at first childbirth, cleanliness, location of residence, etc.; religion, which can affect many of the just-named variables; economic level, of which the same can be said; and religiosity. One can think of these as affecting physical phenomena that bear on cancer susceptibility.

Those variables that may affect EPF, however, have not been looked at in the context of cancer. Such things come to mind as a national habit of cooperativeness, as in Japan, that might engender reduced worry; suppression of emotional expression, that might increase stress, as in Japan; family support, that might do the same as cooperativeness; and the like. I do not maintain that these consequences have anything to do with cancer incidence. But in the context of the things that affect cancer incidence—hormones, immune responsiveness—they might. Further, EPF include genetic traits as well as environmental traits and states. If they are genetic and are connected to cancer-affecting genetic attributes, such influences might show up in cross-national or cross-ethnic studies.

It is evident that if one looks at the male/female cancer rate ratio for a given site, a large difference, in most cases, can be associated with difference in exposure to a carcinogen. An example is lung cancer, where the excess of smoking in males has led to a male:female ratio in the range of 4:1 to 6:1 over the last 40 years. Males have about twice the female rate in bladder cancer, which increases in populations with heavy smoking and with much exposure to occupational chemicals like certain dyes. Oropharyngeal cancers are three times as frequent in men as women, and esophageal cancer more than three times as frequent. Both are strongly associated with drinking and smoking.

Lastly, large changes such as those experienced by immigrants and their offspring can, with certain exceptions, be traced to changes in known carcinogens. One exception is stomach cancer. Offspring of immigrants from Japan and Europe, which have very high rates, have close to the US native rate, but we have a strong suspicion, not certainty, about the reasons. Most immigrants' daughters increase their rate of breast cancer if they come from a low-rate country. Japanese had been thought to be an exception, and it was suspected that their immunity to the usual immigrant family's rise was genetic, that is, a human strain difference. However, more recent data from preliminary data of the third National Cancer Survey (Cutler and Young, 1975) show that in San Francisco, as Japanese women became westernized, their breast cancer rates moved toward the community norm (Buell, 1973).

In summary, it has been shown that the differences in cancer incidence and mortality between countries can be very large or comparatively small; that within countries, differences between ethnic groups can vary widely, although in general the central tendency of such differences is smaller than that between countries, probably because of the greater homogeneity; that cancer levels can change over time, or remain the same within a country; that by and large for the same site women show lower cancer rates than men; that a large male:female ratio indicates greater exposure to a known carcinogen in the sex with the higher rate; that if a migrant population or their offspring show a major change in incidence of a given cancer site compared to their country of origin, it can be presumed that exposure to an environmental carcinogen has changed; and that there are many cancer-relevant variables of all descriptions.

Claims and Reports in the Literature and their Rationale

Oddly enough, the present subject of inquiry—EPF in cross-national cancer incidence—has received very little attention in the literature. Most of the discussion relating to cross-national or cross-ethnic effects has been addressed to diseases other than cancer. Still, there are a few.

Moss (1980) speculates about the possibility that migration may involve more than the mere physical changes of the new country—diet, drinking, smoking, new occupational hazards, etc. He asks whether there may not also be a social carcinogen in the same sense that high mobility by itself is an independent predictor of increased coronary mortality, and suggests that the effective source of such risk, it present, would reside within the person. (If it exists, this effect may not be so internal as he suggests, since mobility may involve variable sleep habits, activity habits, and diet habits.) He points out that Seventh Day Adventists have a cancer incidence well below that of the US average. This religious group proscribes drinking, smoking, and stimulants of all kinds. They advocate moderation in eating and drinking, and suggest low meat intake. It would be predicted that they would have less cancer associated with smoking and drinking, the etiological effect of meat being uncertain as yet, but they seem to show low rates in almost all cancers (lymphoma and bladder excepted). Moreover, Moss quotes Phillips and Kuzma (1977) as suggesting that due to that group's well-organized, structured, religious lives, many people 'hypothesize that Adventists have decreased stress and anxiety'. Nothing more is said about group incidences. His further discussion revolves around the usual studies of psychological factors as possible percursors to cancer (e.g. Bahnson, 1966; Bahnson and Kissen, 1969; Fox, 1978).

Such factors cannot have value, except in a somewhat distant theoretical way, for the present issue, nor can the Seventh Day Adventist and Mormon data. Except for limited cases (see next paragraph) we do not know what EPF are common to populations as we do when we give tests to experimental and control groups. We cannot control exposure to various carcinogens in populations although we can get rough measures of them. We cannot get direct estimates of EPF relative risk from populations such as these religious groups because we have no measure of their stress levels. Phillips and Kuzma

(1977) are merely speculating. Therefore, except for the record, we cannot make use of the usual studies.

I know of a few major exceptions to the restraint of not having cross-national data on stress. Lynn (1971) examined measures of anxiety in a number of countries and related their ranks to a number of variables—suicide, mental illness, accident-proneness, duodenal ulcers, hypertension, economic growth, sex and celibacy, and calorie intake, among others. He supports the view that anxiety is related to some of these. He used three measures of anxiety. I correlated his preferred measure, a ranking of 11 countries on four variables contributing to anxiety, with the ranking of the same countries on overall cancer mortality (Segi and Kurihara, 1972). The Spearman correlation coefficient for men was 0.02, clearly not significant, and for women it was -0.30 ($0.20 < p < 0.40$) also not significant. When I used Lynn's second measure on anxiety scores based on principal component factor analysis for 18 countries, a similar correlation yielded 0.29 for men ($p \cong 0.21$ not significant) and 0.05 for women, obviously not significant. One is led to a fairly clear position when the anxiety ranks based on the 4-variable scales and the factor analysis ranks are compared with cancer incidences. It can only be concluded that Lynn's measures are not really related to overall cancer mortality. This conclusion avoids the need to bring up objections related to validity, reliability and meaning of his measures.

In a follow-up to Lynn's work, and also using theory and data from Eysenck (1965), Rae and McCall (1973) examined the relationship of lung and cervical cancer mortality to extraversion and anxiety levels as cited by Lynn and Hayes (1969), and yearly adult cigarette consumption in eight advanced countries as cited by Lynn (1971)—USA, UK, Ireland, New Zealand, Canada, West Germany, Australia, and Japan. The data on male lung cancer and female lung and cervical cancer in the same countries came from 1966 reports (World Health Statistics Annual, 1969). Rae and McCall derived rank correlations of mortality rates from these countries with the above-mentioned personality levels. Also, they rank-correlated annual cigarette consumption rates with the cancer mortality rates. These designations will be used—Extraversion, E; Anxiety, A; Male lung cancer, ML; Female lung cancer, FL; Cervical cancer, C; Male and female lung cancer combined, MFL; Cigarette consumption, CC; and '*' for significance at the 5 percent level or better. They found these rank order correlations: $E \times ML$, $+0.66^*$; $E \times FL$, $+0.72^*$; $E \times C$, $+0.64^*$; $A \times ML$, -0.52; $A \times FL$, -0.71^*; $A \times C$, -0.30, $CC \times MFL$, $+0.07$; and $CC \times C$, $+0.45$. They concluded that because $E \times ML$ and $E \times FL$ are positive, and $A \times ML$ and $A \times FL$ are negative, Eysenck's postulate (quoted by Rae and McCall, 1973) is supported: 'persons constitutionally predisposed to take up smoking are also constitutionally predisposed to develop cancer.'

Several questions arise and several problems can be seen in this study, leading to doubts as to the appropriateness of the statistics and the validity of the inferences drawn from the statistics.

1. Every one of the measures used by Rae and McCall appeared as numerical data. It was therefore possible to derive Pearson product-moment correlations, rather than the Spearman rank order correlations that they used, for each of the relationships examined by them. Rank correlation is subject to certain kinds of biases, as is the Pearson correlation. But the former throws away information, and since both statistics are estimates of an underlying population correlation, unless the authors can show a compelling reason to use the rank correlation instead of the Pearson, the latter is preferable. I calculated Pearson correlations from Lynn and Hayes (1969), the source used by Rae and McCall, as follows: (The rank correlation is given first for comparison, then the Pearson; '*' indicates one-sided significance, $p < 0.05$, d.f. = 6): E × ML, 0.66*, 0.61; E × FL, 0.72*, 0.43; E × C, 0.64*, 0.68*; A × ML, −0.52, −0.53; A × FL, −0.71*, −0.46; A × L, −0.30, −0.46; CC × MFL, 0.07, 0.18; and CC × C, 0.45, 0.33. E × FL and A × FL dropped substantially.

2. Rae and McCall made some peculiar choices of data to cite from the source authors' references. Lynn and Hayes (1969) published extraversion and anxiety data in 1969 (manuscript received February, 1969). Lynn published extraversion figures (1971, p. 82) derived from the same source (Cattell's male college student data, available at that time only from Cattell's University of Illinois laboratory—Lynn and Hayes, 1969; Lynn, 1971). When I calculated the respective extraversion correlations using the later and presumably more accurate Lynn data (1971), they differed substantially from those derived from the Lynn and Hayes data, shown above in 1. The Lynn data correlations were, using the same order of Spearman followed by Pearson correlations, E × ML, 0.26, 0.39; E × FL, 0.39, 0.22; and E × C, 0.26, 0.50. With d.f. = 6, none of these except the value 0.50 even approaches significance.

Rae and McCall (1973) say that the correlations of E with cancer that they calculated 'lend tentative support, on a cross-national basis, to Eysenck's postulate' quoted above. These correlations, when calculated on the basis of later data provided by their original source, and that would therefore seem, on the face of it, to be more valid, are no longer in the range $\varrho = 0.5$–0.7 and $r = 0.4$–0.7, with four out of six significant values of ϱ and one of r, but are now in the range $\varrho = 0.2$–0.4, $r = 0.4$–0.5, with no significant values out of six in either (where ϱ indicates the Spearman correlation, following Rae and McCall's notation).

3. To compound the problem, Lynn (1971) cites three measures of A other than those of Lynn and Hayes, *and all different*. The first is a set of values of the eight countries derived from student scores from Cattell (see above), presumably identical to the Lynn and Hayes data, but giving only the ranks.

These differed from the Lynn and Hayes ranks. Lynn also derived ranks on anxiety based on the unweighted averaged of the summed ranks of four variables presumed to be relatively strong reflectors of anxiety: rates of mental illness, suicide, calorie intake and alcoholism. Lastly, he did a principal component factor analysis on 11 variables, emerging with one strong factor and three weak ones. The strong one he identified as anxiety, and provided ranks for this factor on 18 countries. None of the four sources of anxiety ranks were the same: Lynn and Hayes' data from the Cattell students (designated I), Lynn's data from the Cattell students (designated II), Lynns 4-variable data (designated III), and Lynn's 11-variable factor analysis data (designated IV).

I determined rank correlations for II, III, and IV with the cancer mortality data in the eight countries used by Lynn and Hayes, and recalculated those for I. They are $\varrho_{I\times ML} = -0.53$, $\varrho_{II\times ML} = -0.48$, $\varrho_{III\times ML} = -0.31$, $\varrho_{IV\times ML} = -0.48$; $\varrho_{I\times FL} = -0.71^*$, $\varrho_{II\times FL} = -0.48$, $\varrho_{III\times FL} = -0.58$, $\varrho_{IV\times FL} = -0.70^*$; $\varrho_{I\times C} = -0.30$, $\varrho_{II\times C} = -0.74^*$, $\varrho_{III\times C} = -0.12$, $\varrho_{IV\times C} = -0.26$. Lynn sees no reason to depart from his use of II as the basis for the general thesis of anxiety as a common element in the various national characteristics, since, he says, the ranks do not differ much from those of the factor analysis. Yet if one pursues the reasoning of Rae and McCall, it makes a real difference which of those determinations is used. At the very least these variations raise questions about the strength of the true relationship of anxiety to mortality from lung and cervical cancer, using the 1966 mortality data noted.

4. Further, there is a more fundamental and disturbing element of the Rae and McCall analysis, perhaps most important of all. They used 1966 cancer mortality data and University students' extraversion scores from Cattell, the dates of whose data are unknown, but can be presumed to have been derived in the early 1960s. They also used anxiety data cited to have been obtained from Lynn and Hayes, who gave Cattell as their source, also presumably derived in the 1960s. Lynn and Hayes (1973, p. 14) said they calculated anxiety scores using Cattell's second order factor of anxiety in analyzing Cattell's data. It is well known now and it was well known when Rae and McCall wrote (1973), when Lynn wrote (1971), and when Eysenck wrote (1965) that it takes a long time for the carcinogenic effect of smoking to become evident—at the earliest on the order of 20–30 years, and at the median 40–50 years. Eysenck, whom Rae and McCall cite, knew this and specifically pointed it out (1965, p. 41); 'Fig. 6 [that is, Eysenck's Fig. 6] shows the relationship between cigarette consumption and number of deaths for lung cancer in a variety of countries [eleven, including USA, UK, Australia, and Canada]. The consumption figures refer to 1930, the lung cancer figures to 1950; this is done because a period of at least 20 years has to elapse before the results of the earlier smoking can be assumed to issue in deaths from lung cancer. It will be seen that there is quite a reasonable

association between the two variables [$r = 0.73$, $p < 0.01$, d.f. = 9]; as cigarette consumption rises so does the number of deaths from lung cancer.' In a more recent analysis of 1930 smoking and 1950 cancer mortality figures, but corrected by age adjustment and based on industry-reported rather than government-reported consumption figures, the correlation for eight of the same eleven countries is $r = 0.95$ (Clemmesen, 1977). These two figures contrast markedly with the correlation cited by Rae and McCall ($\varrho_{CC \times MFL} = 0.07$). Presumably they cited such a correlation to show that one could not attribute the lung cancer mortality to smoking. In fact, however, that attribution is not at all excluded. To show what they claim Rae and McCall would have to separate the *independent* contribution of smoking to lung cancer from the psychic contribution or, if both are necessary, to specify that value. If they did, they could easily be left with a psychic contribution which could be positive, negative, or zero. In any case a multiple regression including CC as a variable would be far more appropriate than a simple rank correlation.

5. Rae and McCall cite Hagnell (1961), Kissen and Eysenck (1962), and Coppen and Metcalfe (1963) to show a positive relationship of extraversion to cancer, and Kissen and Eysenck (1962) and Kissen (1964) to show a negative one. It is most peculiar that Rae and McCall did not analyze the relationship of other cancers or all cancers combined to personality measures, but only lung and cervix. Moreover, why should cervix be selected from among all the other cancers possible? Both Hagnell and Coppen and Metcalfe related their personality measures to all cancers, and Kissen chose lung because, as a chest physician, that is what he treated. Eysenck followed Kissen's lead with lung cancer, but cited Sheldon *et al.* (1949), who dealt with cancers of the breast and uterine body. It is unfortunate that lung and cervix, together with stomach, were the cancers with the fastest changing rates of mortality of any from the 1940s to 1970 (Devesa and Silverman, 1978)—lung rising and stomach and cervix falling, in the USA and most Western countries. That fact would make lung and cervix even less appropriate as sites to examine in light of the point made in 4, above.

It is appropriate to examine lung cancer because of its specific relation to extraversion through the smoking route. But if, as Rae and McCall claim, they eliminated smoking as a mediating variable, why choose lung specifically? Why choose cervix at all? Why not the hundred odd other cancers, especially the more frequent cancers such as breast, colo-rectum, prostate, stomach? If that were done, a variety of results might be seen. Further, why not take all sites combined, weighting individual sites by adjusting for their mortality frequency, or even not doing so, since the authors' hypothesis, placing no restriction on site, is theoretically unaffected by frequency of site mortalities? Just to show an extreme example, I chose stomach since the rank order of incidence in Japan and USA, the countries with the highest and lowest rates, is almost reversed for this tumor, although the other countries are changed less. Now, the correlations of E and A with male (MStom) and female (FStom) stomach cancer mortality rates are, following the same sequence of ϱ and r, E × MStom, -0.42, -0.63; E × FStom, -0.50, -0.47; A × MStom, 0.33, 0.73^*; A × FStom, 0.34, 0.58. When we compare these results with lung results we find comparable magnitudes, but a *complete reversal of correlation signs,* and the theory has a deep hole in it.

6. Moreover, the values for all ages combined were not age-adjusted, but were crude. They were calculated by dividing the total number of male, female or combined deaths due to the cancer in question by the total number of males, females, or combined sexes in the population and adjusting to a rate per 100,000. The difference between the appropriate age-adjusted values and the inappropriate crude values was likely to vary among different countries, depending on the age distribution. For example, Germany's rates would appear too high and Japan's too low, since a large older population would tend to have more than the average number of such deaths and a small older population fewer than the average number of such deaths. To show the extremity of such a discrepancy, the over-54 male populations of the various countries constituted the following percentages of the total male populations (estimated from the latest census before or during 1966); USA, 16.9; Canada, 14.5; Japan, 13.2; Germany, 21.6; Ireland, 19.8; UK, 21.3; Australia, 15.5; and New Zealand, 15.2. The variation is as great as $(21.6/13.2) - 1 = 0.64$, or 64 percent (Germany *vs.* Japan). The median age for lung cancer incidence is about 56. How much would the ranks have changed if age-adjusted data were used? It is evident that they could have changed substantially, and we really don't have a good idea of the region of values that the age-adjusted data would generally have, nor of the consequent ranks of the countries.

The net result of these several points is the position stated earlier: there is real doubt as to the appropriateness of the statistics used (that is, both the data and the analytic techniques) and the validity of the inferences drawn by Rae and McCall (1973).

Others have looked at consistency of psychological measures across countries and found variable agreement, as did Lynn. It serves no purpose to recount most of these comparisons. One measure, however, is of special interest because it is widely suspected of being related to cancer incidence— frequency and/or importance of stressful life events in the last two years reported by a person. The Holmes–Rahe measures of frequency of stressful events have been shown to have similar rank ordering of such frequencies in different cultures. Holmes and Masuda (1974) describe such relationships in a summary table, where the Spearman rank correlation values of the various life event frequencies in the countries being compared range from 0.75 (American *vs.* Japanese) to 0.88 (Americans *vs.* French and French-speaking Belgians and Swiss). More recently, Junk (1977) created a German version of the Holmes–Rahe measure and found a rank correlation of 0.88 on items when comparing American and German scores. These results say that if one were to use such a measure in other countries in respect to comparing incidence or mortality and Holmes-Rahe scores, such comparisons would have to be taken seriously, and looked at in detail. However, no such comparisons have yet been done, to my knowledge.

A number of authors have dealt with social factors as predictors of cancer, but almost all of their discussions have revolved about exogenous variables (e.g. Graham, 1960; Graham and Schneiderman, 1972; Quisenberry, 1960; Rotkin, 1973). Among such studies, perhaps the most thorough of the ones to date has been the work of Wellington, Macdonald and Wolf (1979). They carried out a regression analysis of cancer mortality associated with 174 variables among whites in the United States: 23 demographic, 6 income, 11 climate, 37 air contamination, 3 radiation, 20 consumption (cigarettes, alcohol, water, milk), and 74 ethnic. They did preliminary modeling of combinations of these 174 variables, in which the intercorrelations, collinearities, and relative contributions to explained variation in submodels were examined. Of the 174 variables, 13 were chosen, four of them composite, from which four basic pools of variables were derived as a basis for producing a number of cancer mortality models. Various combinations of the 13 variables yielded four variable pools, which contained, respectively, 6, 8, 10, and 12 variables. The four composite variables in the respective pools were derived from weights of the subvariables contributing to the first principal component in a principal components analysis. This technique is included in the group of multivariate analyses that some (e.g. Harman, 1967; Morrison, 1976, p. 266) call factor analyses and that others (e.g. Gnanadesikan, 1977, p. 7) call by different terms, e.g., linear reduction techniques. Unlike some techniques with a similar objective, in principal components analysis no subjective judgments enter the process of either specifying the identities of the variables contributing substantially to the principal component—analogous to 'factor' in other techniques—or determining their weights, hence it is preferred by rigorous statisticians. The composite variables were PRELEV, a combination of precipitation and elevation; POLLUT, from 6 air pollutants; ALCO, from malt, wine and distilled spirits consumption; and OTHEUR, other European, from proportion of immigrants in a given state—non-Jews from 10 middle European countries and Jews. For each cancer site, a standardized regression equation was derived to indicate the weight of association of the various predictive variables in the model with that site's mortality. There was no attempt to measure EPF, except that if the data were to show it, we might infer that they are reflected by exogenous variables; for example, ethnic variables could reflect inborn psychological influences. This work has limitations in that the range of the mortality data for some cancer sites was rather restricted, coming only from US data. Some of the predictors were also restricted, e.g. cigarette consumption, alcohol consumption and income; to that extent they tended to parallel the mortality restriction and thereby did not particularly affect the regression coefficients for the restricted sites (Wellington, 1981). But due to the broad range of values of temperature, of PRELEV, and of POLLUT in the USA, these three variables, contributing the major portion of variance explained by the models for the majority of sites, were not restricted, a phenomenon which, in conjunction with the restricted range of some site mortalities, could easily have affected their and other variables' coefficients. The overall movement of US immigrants toward the national norm of consumption forces a less discriminating and encompassing set of factors than might have emerged. Nevertheless, a most important finding should be noted: while urbanization is somewhat related to population density, it is more connected to sociological variables such as income level, alcohol-smoking, and ethnicity, while density, often equated with urbanization but not really the same, reflects environmental variables such as temperature, precipitation, elevation, pollution, and background radiation. Further, outcomes of the ethnic variables (that is, proportion of the US population represented from each of the various countries from which a person or group immigrated and the respective mortality ranks) were strongly related to consumption variables. This finding is consistent with the differences found among ethnic groups in other studies.

Wellington *et al.* (1979) remark briefly (p. 240) on the possibility that stress or tension, cited as a density phenomenon, might have been part of the reason for the higher mortality from cancer in the cities. They reject that idea, pointing to the absence of excess mortality from other diseases such as non-cancer lung, the digestive system, the genito-urinary system, and accidents and violent deaths. If the latter two are combined, the remark about them is true; but there are well-known reasons for the greater number of accidental deaths in rural districts, and similarly, well-known reasons for the greater number of homicides in cities, which almost balance, yielding their observed equality. Further, there is no mention of cardiovascular diseases, which are known to have excess mortality in dense areas for equal smoking levels. Nor is there any mention of mental disorders, hypertension, tuberculosis, and several other diseases, all of which have been shown to increase in families that are socially disorganized (Cassel, 1974)—a more prevalent state in high- than low-density areas.

The results relating mortality, health, and density are confused, showing both positive relationships and negative (Cassel, 1971). It is perhaps better to point to that fact than to select particular diseases with no increase in mortality to make a point, as Wellington *et al.* (1979) seem to have done. Perhaps Cassel's (1974) four theoretical sources of stressful consequences should be examined in this context—social disorganization, domination and subordination, social buffers, and generalized stress.

Within the framework of theory, we are already far enough advanced to refrain from judgments about stress affects based merely on physical phenomena such as crowding or urbanization. We know enough to demand more detail about what seem to be directly relevant phenomena among the presumably stressed population, such as degree of control that a person perceives he has of the environment and of other persons; incongruity between current social status and that during one's upbringing; whether stress as a young person occurred, tending to increase ability to cope with current stress; and Cassel's four sources just mentioned. These are all psychosocial factors that have been linked with excess occurrence of diseases other than cancer.

Unfortunately the analysis by Wellington et al. (1979) fails to satisfy many of the objectives of those who are looking for specific etiological relations to cancer. Within the framework of its objectives the analysis is adequate. But that framework does not seem to yield insights for the present objective. The variables addressed were chosen partly because of their connection with urbanism and other factors, partly because only certain data were available for all states, partly to reduce the number of variables in their models (p. 28), and partly because certain unused variables were so strongly related to some used ones (e.g. pp. 23, 24). The chosen variables, therefore, do not cover many influences that are known to be related to cancer, although a number of variables correlated with these influences are included. Examples of variables not addressed are sex mores, diet, standard classification of industries, education—different from income for certain cancer sites (Devesa and Diamond, 1980)—and age at first childbirth. A second factor of possible importance is that no interactions were included in the final models. Wellington said that they were included in the original models, but they replaced so many of the primary effects even after centering to remove the covariance that they were felt unduly to complicate an already complex study (1981).

The predictor data came largely from 1940 and 1950 data, and the cancer mortality data came mostly from aggregated 1950–1969 data. Because of these facts and the difficulties mentioned above, the weights actually given to the variables from the regression equations were valid only in the context used, and under the assumptions made. In fact, Wellington et al. were well aware of the unique quality of the data since the between-state variation after 1969 is decreasing, as they point out (1979, p. 228 ff.), and use of the coefficient in general for later USA state comparisons would be imprudent.

Speciani (1976, pp. 287–289) suggested EPF as sources of cancer for a number of ethnic groups in his otherwise brilliant exegesis on holism in the history of medicine. He points to reports in Doll, Muir, and Waterhouse (1970) of the relatively high rates in East and West Germany, Sweden, Birmingham and industrial sections of England vs. the low rates in Bombay,

Ibadan (Nigeria), and Bulawayo (Zimbabwe), explaining the differences on grounds of industrial development. But he suggests that where different ethnic groups reside in one country, they are subject to the same cultural and socio-economic environment. In that case variations in cancer incidence cannot be explained, he says, on the grounds of carcinogens due to industrial development. He points out the high rates of cancer incidence among Anglos and the low for Latinos in El Paso, Texas, ignoring completely the major cultural and lifestyle differences between those groups—economic, dietary, occupational, and social. In truth, his basic premise of common culture and lifestyle is wrong in that case. He cites Israel, where, he says, the annual incidence rate of 171.6/100,000 is made up of rates per 100,000 per year contributed by various subgroups: European or American Jewish immigrants, 369.2; Asiatic and African Jewish immigrants, 132.7; Arabs in Israel (actually the data are labelled 'non-Jews') 63.6; and Sabras, that is, native-born Israeli Jews, 30.7.

He expatiates on the reasons for the figures he cites, giving stress differences as the major ones. Euro-Americans, he says, go from a monied, capitalistic system to a socialistic system, having little money, and simultaneously facing risk of violent death; this combination leads to extraordinary stress, he claims. The stress is less among Afro-Asiatics, where pogroms, he suggests, were still fashionable when they left, rendering them less susceptible to stress. Israeli Arabs, he says, with their fatalism, are still less susceptible, and Sabras least of all, with their presence in a land where their 'families have perhaps lived . . . for several generations'. The land is home to them, and they are deemed to be the least stressed of all.

Having a somewhat different suspicion about the reasons for the figures found, I examined the age distributions of the various subpopulations, and found that the median age of the Euro-American immigrants was 46.8; for Asians it was 32.7; for Africans it was 26.0; for non-Jews it was 15.8 (*sic*); *and for Sabras it was 9.4* (*sic*). Among the older age-groups, whose contribution to the incidence of cancer is highest, there were a substantial number of zero entries for the last two groups in a series where the trend is obviously rising. These zeros are almost certainly the result of so few aged people being cohort members in each of those groups, and force the apparent incidence rate down spuriously. No matter how careful one is to adjust for age, if the age distributions contain so few members in certain groups with high incidence that that high incidence cannot emerge, the zero entries will bias the incidence rates downward. In the case of the last two groups the bias was severe. As an aside, in a country where the population has gone from 717,000 in 1948, of whom 253,000 were native-born (Halevi *et al.*, 1971), to 2,115,000 in the early 1960s, as listed in Doll *et al.* (1970), and where 829,000 were Sabras, it is a little misleading to claim that the Sabras' families have perhaps lived there for several generations. The bulk of those families obviously had not.

One cannot discard *in toto* Speciani's speculations, since stresses do exist, and one might suppose that certain subpopulations are subject to such stresses. Moreover, it is possible to conceive that such stresses could yield an increase or decrease of cancer incidence (Fox, 1981). However, the figures cited are not convincing by themselves, as already indicated. The most important reason for not drawing conclusions about stress from these data, however, is that Speciani made no effort, beyond referring to industry and discarding pollution (which has been shown to be at most a minor influence of cancer incidence), to look for differences among known carcinogenic sources to account for differences in the observed data. One cannot even say that the numbers cited are suggestive of stress influence in view of the failure to consider such sources. As a last point, Speciani unfortunately never referred to the cancer rates among the countries of origin of the immigrants, which reflect, among similar age-groups, approximately their experience in the four-fold comparison. No mention of lifestyles of the groups is made, and no suggestion is made as to relative rates for various sites of cancer, that might suggest reasons for the differences: e.g., immigrants from Eastern Europe had high stomach cancer rates; northwest African immigrants had almost double the bladder cancer rate of the average immigrant. All in all, Speciani's proposal is speculative (although that is not a pejorative term in such a case) and his supporting data are themselves applied by him on the basis of an inadequate rationale.

Theory and Inferences

It is possible to arrive at one or two tentative conclusions in our topic, and to indicate certain matters supportive of one conclusion or another without deciding it, but that is all. The data suggest these conclusions and some of these matters.

A large discrepancy between maximum and minimum national rates of cancer, and in fact, a stable gradient of any degree among countries, indicates either an environmental effect, a genetic pool effect, or both. Most researchers who have studied cross-national data tend to think that most, if not all, of these differences are attributable to environmental effects (e.g. Higginson and Muir, 1973), with little coming from genetic effects. The data showing that environmental effects are indeed potent are very clear-cut (e.g. Fraumeni, 1975; Cancer . . ., 1979); but the judgments that genetic effects are small, or that environmental effects operate on a substrate of genetic susceptibility (discussed in more detail below), judgments that fall out as inferences from strong emphasis on the environment, cannot be easily verified, and could in some cases be wrong. We already know about the major differences in animal susceptibilities to cancer when they are closely inbred to produce an almost pure strain (Boraschi and Meltzer, 1979; MacKenzie and

Gardner, 1973; Stutman, 1972). While in many areas cross-breeding among indigenes within a land mass is very likely, it is still evident that there exists much physical difference among peoples. The *statistical* differences are clear in pigmentation (negroid *vs.* caucasoid *vs.* mongoloid); skull conformation, e.g. Alpine brachycephaly *vs.* Nordic dolichocephaly); presence or absence of an epicanthic fold (mongoloid *vs.* other). Anthropologists have outlined clearly the notion of races, and though there is always admixture so that no single individual can be labeled as a pure racial member, they do exist, and in the aggregate display the characteristic features described by the anthropologists. These differences arose through several avenues—mutation, biological selection, genetic drift, environmental effects—but whatever the combination of causes, except for the last, the main source of differences is genetic selection. It is also likely that within a race there are different variations— perhaps one might say lesser, but not necessarily—relating to features other than the ones that identify races. We already know about racial and regional differences in blood groups. What about hormone levels in the blood? What about enzymes that transform carcinogens into harmless substances? What about the reverse, enzymes that make carcinogens out of certain substances? What about enzymes that carry out the DNA repair processes that go along with the regular, unavoidable DNA transformations (in a wider framework these might be called mutations) occurring all the time to all of us? What about efficiency in calling up antibodies? What about normal levels of natural killer cells? All of these things affect cancer susceptibility, as well as many others not mentioned, and all are more or less under genetic control. This fact suggests that we might find basic differences in susceptibility to cancer among various ethnic groups to form their own distribution of prevalence, and perhaps—perhaps—explain in part some of the differences found among ethnic and geographic groups. These contributions to the whole explanation stand beside those suggested by Muir—the environmental, physical ones— but almost certainly contribute far less to the moderate and high cancer rates than the physical ones.

Now we come to EPF. They are made up of inborn and imposed factors. The inborn ones, to the degree that they are related to the genetic factors controlling cancer susceptibility, could also predict cancer. The problem is that there is no evidence to show such a connection, however much evidence there is for genetic transmissibility of psychological characteristics (Cattell, 1965; Gottesman, 1963; Manesovitz *et al.*, 1969; Scarr, 1966). Obviously we cannot reject the possibility of there being cancer predictors, however, merely on those grounds. On the other hand, because there is no such evidence, it is just as inadmissible to make bold claims of such predictability, and even, in some cases, causation itself.

Among the imposed EPF there are learned ones that have assumed the status of traits; and there are states, relatively short-term EPF, the most important of which in the present context are stressor-provoked. If traits persist over generations through social stability, resisting environmental stimuli such as those induced by migration, their contribution is irrelevant to data on trends; if they do change, it is relevant. As for stressor-induced EPF, their contribution is relevant, and will be addressed as a basic issue below.

It has been proposed that the lowest levels of cancer found among diverse ethnic or national groups form a baseline from which one can estimate the relative contribution of various known and unknown environmental carcinogens. This position forms the basis of Higginson's view that two-thirds (Cancer . . ., 1979) or even 80 percent (Higginson, 1969) of cancer can be attributed to environmental conditions. For this proposal to be accepted it is necessary to claim that all other groups, in the absence of such conditions, have a basic susceptibility equal to that of the group with the lowest incidence. Except for extreme genetic susceptibilities to cancer like those for Wiscott–Aldrich syndrome, Fanconi's anemia, retinoblastoma, xeroderma pigmentosum, etc. (Mulvihill et al., 1977), we are unable to find more than some suggestions that genetic factors are indeed active in differentiating national and ethnic groups. In fact, without a rather extreme relative risk for a genetic risk trait, *combined with* a rather extreme prevalence of the trait in a population, it would be quite difficult even to *detect* the risk trait by observing group cancer incidences (Doll, 1978). Doll quotes Peto to the effect that if 10 percent of a population had a recessive trait for greater cancer risk, and if a person having the trait was ten times as likely to get cancer as one without it, then if one twin had the trait, the probability of the other, identical, twin getting cancer is only 1.67 times that of a person in the general population. The probability of a sibling of the twin proband getting cancer is only 1.2 times the population expectation. Thus, single recessive traits are quite unlikely to be detected in the population. The probability that among all the genetic traits that increase (or decrease) susceptibility, those with unidirectional effect should pile up sufficiently in one group to yield a substantial—or even detectable—excess or deficiency of cancers is quite small. It is less difficult to conceive of this happening if the susceptibility resides in one or two genes; but most susceptibilities observed in animal experimentation are polygenic. There is no reason to think that the human forms an exception. This belief is consistent with a second point cited by Doll (1978), which is of considerable importance in supporting the view of distributed susceptibilities (Cook et al., 1969). This is that if a small proportion of the population are highly susceptible to cancer while the rest are immune, the age-specific incidence of cancer would have to stop rising once a substantial number of susceptibles had succumbed. In most of the common cancers this does not happen; the curves rise to age 80 or 85.

On the other hand, most people believe that in any single individual the distribution of genes endangering or protecting the person can vary widely.

Thus one person is more likely to get cancer than another. But since we do not know who is who, we cannot aggregate the people at greater risk before their cancer. For any group of traits to be characteristic of a people, there must have been complete or almost complete isolation for many generations. Up to modern times this may have been possible, and even then social and commercial intercourse among contiguous peoples was usually substantial. If we add to that the admixtures associated with wars, we find only the broad-gauge differences characteristic of races.

To support the notion of approximately equal cancer susceptibilities among nations, when migration takes place high incidences fall—in the second and third generations—to the levels of the host country, and low incidences rise. We have not measured data following immigration to one of the unusually low-incidence countries—perhaps with the exception of Israel—but the low-incidence cancers (cervix, penis) were already low in those immigrants. There is one cultural group isolate which illustrates the point clearly. The incidence of cervical cancer in nuns is exceedingly low (Kessler and Aurelian, 1975), yet the populations from which they come have an average incidence.

It is possible to reconcile low incidences in a population with high genetic susceptibilities if two things are true:

(1) susceptibility differences are peculiar to individual cancer sites; and
(2) the carcinogenic stimulus is absent from the population.

The theory behind this set of requirements is that the genetic factor provides a conditional risk. By itself it will not produce cancer. Thus both conditions must prevail for a country to show a low incidence. However, for moderate and high incidence cancers we can, in almost all cases, find several with very low incidence that are widely separated geographically and include both developed and developing nations or groups. For example, the annual incidence in males of gall bladder and bile duct cancer for Jews in Israel is 7.5, for American Indians in New Mexico, 6.5, for Japanese in Miyagi prefecture, 5.4; but we find among the low incidences these countries: Iceland, 0.0; Ibadan, Nigeria, 0.2; Bulawayo, Zimbabwe, 0.4; blacks in Alameda County, California, and Malays in Singapore, 0.6; Bombay, 0.7; rural Norway, 0.8; and Newfoundland, 0.9. A similar picture obtains in females, whose high incidences are about twice those for males. It is very unlikely that a common carcinogen that affects the groups in higher incidence areas is lacking in every one of the low incidence areas simultaneously with the presence of high genetic susceptibility in every one of the low incidence groups. However, minor differences in genetic susceptibilities between peoples are not only possible but likely, at least for individual cancer sites.

Modern (within the last 2000 years) travel has diluted the purity of many peoples' genetic attributes, and certainly, in a country without massive barriers, has homogenized, to a large degree, the genetic stock in countries as a whole, whether or not they are isolated from other lands.

On the face of it, therefore, genetic differences may exist; but also, on the face of it, the most that such differences can yield are small *absolute* variations in baseline cancer rates for individual sites. 'Absolute' is emphasized because a difference between 0.2/100,000 and 0.8/100,000 is a fourfold difference, but only a 0.6/100,000 difference in absolute annual rate. Higher rates are presumably the result of local carcinogens or *ad hoc* susceptibilities, e.g. high fat and meat intake or local trace-metal deficiencies in the soil.

Stressor-provoked EPF are states, by and large, although some, e.g. Speciani (1976) and Cassel (1970), might disagree. To satisfy possible qualms based on their views, one should specify that the EPF must be short- or long-term, and that the long-term kind of EPF that I am calling stresses could be labeled traits under some definitions.

Such EPF by themselves are not likely to provoke cancer unless they increase the activity of specific enzymes that produce carcinogens in the body from certain substances that themselves are not carcinogens (an example of the latter is benz[*a*]pyrene from cigarettes). What they are theorized to do instead is to change the body's susceptibility to carcinogenic attack. Most researchers in the field have been satisfied to assign the mechanism by which stress in the organism increases cancer incidence to the immune system (IS) without elaborating much on how this happens (e.g. Achterberg *et al.*, 1976; Bahnson, 1966; Bahnson and Kissen, 1969). Others have addressed themselves to the mechanisms in more detail (e.g. Solomon and Amkraut, 1979; Wayner *et al.*, 1979), but confine themselves to the IS, citing the various influences that can effect immune capability—hormones, antibody response, lymphocyte effects, etc., mostly acting through the central nervous system. Morrison (1980, Chapter 2) discusses the IS in regard to EPF, but with a more questioning view of orthodox IS theory as propounded by Burnet (1970) than earlier writers. Fox (1981) also discusses the roles of EPF and the IS in human carcinogenesis, specifically addressing, besides that system, other mechanisms of cancer initiation and protection because they were ignored in almost all previous publications on the subject of EPF and mechanisms—enzymatic transformations between carcinogenic and non-carcinogenic state (forward as well as backward ones) and the processes of DNA repair, both of which precede the fixation of a transformed state that duplicates itself. In addition, in relation to these two processes as well as the IS, he dealt with the notion of precancerous transformations—the concept that cancer yields successive cell dysplasias by stages from an initial non-malignant insult to the final malignant transformation of cells.

If EPF bring about IS changes, these changes are operating on cell transformations that are for the most part already there. That is, these cell changes were produced earlier by carcinogens, changes that yielded cell-

We know that when first asked in 1951, 83 percent of the doctors said they smoked (Doll and Peto, 1976). Now

$$PAR = 0.83 \times 14/(0.83 \times 14 + 1) = 0.92.$$

In this true example, then, 92 percent of all lung cancer deaths among the 34,000 in the original sample can be associated with smoking. If the number who smoked was, say, 10 percent, then PAR might be $0.1 \times 13/(0.1 \times 13 + 1) = 0.57$. For the same outcome, if R of stressor-induced EPF were 2, which is closer to the relative risk envisaged by workers in the field, and 25 percent of the population were stressed we might find PAR for EPF to be $0.25 \times 2/(0.25 \times 2 + 1) = 0.33$.

Now let us look at smoking and lung cancer together with stress. About 42 percent of the US population (men and women combined) smoked 16 years ago and the relative risk of smoking for lung cancer later on was about 4 (this figure is only a gross approximation, since relative risk in the USA is very difficult to ascertain for an overall population, various studies having used different samples and having gotten different figures) (*Smoking and Health*, 1979). Now PAR $= 0.42 \times 4/(0.42 \times 4 + 1) = 0.63$. For a hypothetical PAR of 0.33 associated with EPF, the two factors would account for practically all of the risk factor attribution if the variables were uncorrelated; but they are not. That is, a certain number of people are both stressed and smokers. If all the stressed were smokers, the common PAR would be the same for both, that is, 0.33, and it would be contained in the larger PAR, 0.63, adding to the attributable risk. Statistically more than one attack could be used to determine the independent effects of the two risk factors; e.g. multiple regression if the function were linear, or perhaps, as would be likely to be more appropriate here, a logistic risk function. Both would give weights to the independent components of each contributor, so that the net contributions would be additive in the respective functions. Back transformation could give the raw data ultimately needed if the logistic function were used.

Note that I used a subjunctive equivalent form throughout. This was done because the assumption of independence is untenable. The EPF arising from stressors, like most genetic conditions rendering a person more susceptible to cancer, are conditional on the presence of appropriate carcinogens. They do not cause cancer independently. In such a case a linear or a log-linear model containing the stressor by itself would yield a weight of zero for it, but a non-zero weight for the interaction term between the stressor and a relevant carcinogen. Thus one cannot assign relative or attributable risk to EPF alone. One must use the combination of some carcinogen together with EPF. Such values are not known now, and it is fruitless to try to extrapolate from known studies on EPF for one tumor site or set of carcinogens to others. One can illustrate certain problems related to the interaction issue. It is known that in the case of lung cancer incidence, R for smoking is a function of age. For average smoking experience, incidence of lung cancer rises as the seventh (*sic*) power of age, and the incidence among non-smokers rises as the fourth power of age (Doll, 1978). The function permits a statement about R for any given combination of age and smoking. But if length of time smoked is used, instead of age, incidence rises as the fourth power of smoking duration.

Let us add to that picture. Stressors affect people differently, a fact which led Holmes and Rahe to create their revision in which effect of life changes was estimated by the subject in addition to merely counting the number of events or adding up arbitrarily assigned weights (Holmes and Masuda, 1974; Rahe, 1974). Secondly, stressors can produce different EPF. When an animal, formerly dominant, is placed in another cage with an existing dominant, most often it goes into a state of behavior resembling quasi-depression, at the same time proliferating elevated levels of adrenocortical hormones associated with the pituitary–adrenal axis. When an animal in a new cage is in process of establishing dominance there is an adrenomedullary response, with mineralocorticoids, blood pressure rise and aggressive behavior. It is probably so with humans. Thirdly, the demonstration that stressors can both help and harm in animals, depending on a number of variables, makes the matter even more difficult, if we assume the same holds true for man. If we assume additivity of effects, the net result of good and bad effects in the human would be the algebraic sum of the two, a net outcome less than the larger of the two. Thus, because we are not dealing with individuals, but with geographic or cultural groups, the aggregate result is the only one visible, and it will be more difficult to detect than either one alone.

One could conceive, however, that the converse of the conditional state mentioned above is also true. That is, if an independent carcinogen produces the usual curve of exponentially increasing cancer incidence with age, one cannot assume that the carcinogen was the sole agent. Aside from initiation and promotion, or two- or multi-stage processes, one could well hypothesize that stressors imposed an additional influence. Either they could have lowered the threshold to the independent carcinogen or they could have raised its potency, or both. In either case one would observe a curve higher than would be seen if the carcinogen acted alone. One would want to hypothesize, in addition, some function of the stressors as one grew older and as the aggregate of overall influences raised the cancer incidence level with age. At a gross level, would the stressors act most strongly on the young, the middle-aged, the old? Would one hypothesize an interactive function? What would be the rationale?

Further, because of the biology of cancer one is faced with a most important question. Cancers develop, for the most part, through a serial process of cell transformations. Some examples are skin keratoses, cervical dysplasia, precancerous changes in the prostate, and rectal polyps. These can, in some cases, develop into cancer, although the bulk of them do not. However, when they are present they signal an increased risk of cancer. Do EPF affect the number, progress, type and growth rate of dysplasic tissues on skin, cervix, prostate, rectum before malignant tissue appears? At what stage can one say that EPF are influential? Worse, if EPF increase the chance of a first transformation to dysplasia, how can one carry out experiments testing such an effect if the stressors are short-term or intermittent? This question is important because of the long period between the first application of the carcinogen and the first emergence of a malignant cell, and another long period between the first malignant cell (all cancers arise from single cells, it is believed) and its growth to detectable, diagnosable size. For lymphoma and leukemia, for example, the median interval from X-ray or atomic bomb exposure to diagnosis ran about six years (median because the time distribution is log normal). For lung cancer due to asbestos it ran from 15 to 40 years (Selikoff, 1977); for cervix, endometrium and breast, 10 or more years are necessary (Koss, 1975). For prostate it ranges from 10 to 30 years. How are we to measure the effect of individual stressors if they are spread over that much time? If they relate to a single stressful occasion, how can we tell whether the cancer had already become malignant, was still in the precancerous stage, or was not even in process of developing? For populations, if we can identify the stressors, a study might, with a large enough population, detect a common stressor. For example, one might look at the cancer incidence for short-latency tumors in a group all of whom retired at age 65 or 60.

Last, in respect to carcinogens and EPF, a large, although unknown, number of cancer cases arise strictly by chance, whether or not a stressor is present (Miller, 1980). The usual mechanisms by which cancer occurs would explain the presence of these, and one must assume that the putative effect of stressors rides on top of existing cancer susceptibility, yielding either earlier occurrence or more likely occurrence. If that is so, however, one has the task of separating out the effects. We have already gone through the issue of separating out genetic effects, and the same techniques might apply here. However, instead of anticipating no change in rates for groups with genetically based susceptibility when they migrate, in this case we would expect changes, not stasis, if all other conditions were the same except for a stressful environment. Thus, among Poles who migrated to England (Adelstein *et al.*, 1979), did their rates change? Yes, for some sites; no, for others. This is a point against the stress hypothesis unless the effect of stressors is specific for the changed sites or unless there was no change in stress. Did their culture change? We do not know. But we do know that such changes vary among migrants. Among recent Irish immigrants to England their cultural situation changed and their social adjustment became worse; but for Indian and Pakistani immigrants their culture, by and large, was preserved intact and their social adjustment was good (Cochrane, 1979). Did the Poles' exposure to carcinogens change? Probably to some extent, in view of the fairly substantial differences in dietary habits, availability of certain foods, differences in jobs, trace mineral content of water, use of certain chemical products, etc. As time went on, these changes would become more stable and would form an important environmental impact on the carcinogen exposure of these immigrants. Did stress change? We do not know. But if we did know, there would be no way of disentangling it from the simultaneous impact of a number of environmental carcinogens, particularly what Higginson called 'lifestyle', encompassing food, marriage customs, and other cultural phenomena. The same line of argument holds for any immigrant group. One can say, however, that if migration is supposed to entail an increase of stress and therefore an increase of cancer risk, one has to account for the role of stressors quantitatively with even greater care in the case of *falling* cancer rates, as with cervix in Latinos and with stomach among Japanese and East Europeans.

The only 'experimental' stressor exposures I know of are prisoners of war and concentration-camp survivors. Data on the latter are not easy to come by in respect to cancer, although general statements about changed disease susceptibility showed a rise in most disease classes (World Veterans Federation, 1963). Unfortunately, cancer was not one of the classes (they were given as respiratory, digestive, etc.). It might have been given, but I suspect that the incidence was too small for any useful rates to have emerged. Prisoners of war in World War II (both theaters) and the Korean conflict showed no significant change in their cancer mortality over any period up to 30 years for World War II and for 22 years for the Korean war. If anything, there might have been the suggestion of a deficiency of cancer mortality, but as mentioned it was not significant (Keene, 1980).

Finally, one might try to determine if stressor changes in a people who have not migrated could have an effect. Two questions will be explored. First we look at a people in whom there is a presumption of increased stress over time because of a major increase in commercialization and industrialization. From 1955 to 1970 the mortality rates of the Japanese associated with various cancer sites were observed (Hirayama, 1977). A rise in some occurred, very similar to the rise observed in the USA over the period when similar changes were occurring. Lung cancer deaths went up with smoking. As mentioned (p. 119), the correlation of tobacco consumption levels obtained from tobacco companies in eight countries with lung cancer death rates in those countries was 0.95. Stomach cancer death rate went down, and was strongly associated with specific dietary changes according to locale; essentially there was a dose–response relationship. The rate fell according to the increase in milk, eggs, and green vegetables. Earlier detection contributed somewhat to the picture. Colon cancer death rates went up, and were related to fat and total caloric intake. The age-related statistics showed clear cohort effects for lung and cervix, the earlier-born groups being less subject to the changes for equal ages, since their exposure to environmental changes was less, overall, during their lifetimes. Again, because of the fact that both increases and decreases were observed, we cannot tell whether stressor-induced EPF contributed at all to the general picture. Again, their effect would probably have to be low, in view of the strong correlations observed between changes in known etiological agents and associated cancer mortality rates.

The second issue is related to the first, to a degree. If stressor-induced EPF have even a moderate effect in increasing cancer rates, as the conventional view has it, or even in decreasing them, we would expect most cancers to show corresponding rate rises and falls over time, unless EPF were selective. (But if they were too selective there would be little effect overall.) We assume that with increase in local migration, alienation from one's cultural values, transformation to nuclear rather than extended family structure, mobility, status change, and the other stressors described by sociologists and psychologists in our recently changing society, life stressors would have been increasing over time. If there had been a substantial trend, say upwards, three things would have been true (unless EPF were little or not at all changed by an increase in stressor level—see below—but let us ignore that possibility for the moment). Those cancer sites whose incidence among USA whites has been rising, e.g. pancreas and lung, would have suffered a smaller than apparent rise caused by environmental variables. Those whose mortality has been falling, e.g. cervix and stomach, would have suffered a larger than apparent drop in the environmentally caused rate. But those whose levels has been steady, e.g. breast, colorectal, uterine corpus, breast (see Figure 6.4), would have had to drop due to other causes precisely enough to compensate for the rise due to EPF in order to stay stable. The named ones are not the only ones to stay stable. For all stable ones, an exactly similar compensatory drop would have to take place, if EPF were not selective. If they are selective, the only thing we can do is to exclude most of the stable ones, including some with high rates. (The changes described above appear in Devesa and Silverman, 1978.) Thus, either EPF had no effect to speak of or there was little change in the stressful environment, so that the assumption by the sociologists of social upheaval and stressor rise would not be acceptable.

The possibility spoken of above, that EPF was little or not at all changed by an increase in stressor level, hence the flat cancer rate over time, is not convincing. Assuming that EPF has an effect on cancer rate, the failure of EPF to change could be due to one of three things: (a) There is no effect of stressors on EPF, with consequent cancer rate stability; (b) People adapt to increased stress—that is, they can handle it up to a point, with consequent stability of the cancer rate; or (c) As stressor level rises, EPF are affected up to a ceiling, after which they are stable, and in our picture of events, we have gone beyond the stressor level corresponding to that ceiling. Option (a) is contradicted by the animal data. In fact, the very definition of a stressor is the production of physiological heterostasis. Consciousness of EPF is not necessary, but is usually present. Option (b) may well be true, but then, what of all the psychosomatic data showing effect of various stressors on other diseases? One can argue that the mechanisms for cancer induction have relatively little dependence on the psychosomatic consequences of the usual stressors, contrary to other diseases. That is not a trivial possibility. Option (c) seems very unlikely, and is contradicted by animal data.

The position that EPF have little unidirectional effect could just as well be taken (either because there is little absolute effect or because the positive and negative effects cancel each other out). I am inclined to the view of little unidirectional effect rather than to the view that stressor effects in our society have not increased, and accept, in some degree, the notion that people do adapt to societal stress in respect to cancer-affecting stressor outcomes.

In sum, we have little evidence that stressor-induced EPF affect cancer incidence or mortality rates, either from cross-national or cross-ethnic comparisons, or from changes over time within a people or ethnic group. Further, we have little evidence that genetically based EPF have such effects. This position must be coupled, however, with the simultaneous view that, first, we are at the mercy of circumstances preventing final, definitive judgements on large groups, but allowing probability statements. Second, we must observe that if EPF operate with nearly equal force and frequency to increase and decrease cancer risk in the individual, whatever their source, we would observe just the outcomes that we have seen. I believe (1) that EPF do exert small and theoretically measurable effects, but in both directions (Fox, 1981); (2) that many people, but by no means everyone, adapt to stressors, with a corresponding reduction in the number of people whose EPF has risen with increase in stressor frequency and level; and (3) that the low level of EPF contributions to cancer in general and the algebraic summing of approximately equal good and bad effects to a value close to zero explains the observed outcomes in ethnic and national groups.

References

Achterberg, J., Simonton, O. C., and Matthews-Simonton. S. (eds.) (1976). *Stress, Psychological Factors, and Cancer.* New Medicine Press, Fort Worth, Texas.

Adelstein, A. M., Staszewski, J., and Muir, C. S. (1979). 'Cancer mortality in 1970–1972 among Polish-born migrants to England and Wales', *British Journal of Cancer*, **40**, 464–475.

Bahnson, C. B. (ed.) (1966). 'Psychophysiological aspects of cancer', *Annals of the New York Academy of Sciences*, **125**, 773–1055.

Bahnson, C. B., and Kissen, D. M. (eds.) (1969). 'Second conference on psychophysiological aspects of cancer. *Annals of the New York Academy of Sciences*, **164**, 307–634.

Bailar, J. C. III, and Ederer, F. (1964). 'Significance factors for the ratio of a Poisson surface antigens, which in turn would, under the theory, activate recognizers of these antigens. This activation, through the complex mechanism of the IS, is supposed to destroy the transformed cell. In theory, if EPF decrease (or increase) the activity of the IS, such activation could decrease the efficiency of the IS (or improve it). Few researchers have paid attention to their own data showing lesser risk among stressed humans than unstressed, and none that I know of has even attempted to explain how stress could do such a thing. In the animal sphere, on the other hand, a number of studies have shown both increased and decreased risk under stressors (e.g. Newberry, 1978) and under the stimulation of adrenocortical hormones (e.g., Kripke and Boros, 1974), substances normally proliferated under stress. One can talk, for example, about inhibition of suppressor lymphocytes as a means of decreasing risk.

With this background we can address the question of whether cross-national evidence shows stressor-induced EPF as probable variables in raising or lowering cancer rates.

To deal with the point properly, a preliminary look at relative and attributable risks is necessary. If we use only available data on increased risk, it is obvious that for many high-incidence places a particular carcinogen is at fault. The most prominent of such cases is smoking. Depending on what country we look at, the level of smoking will contribute a particular fraction to the attributable risk of lung cancer, which is a direct function of relative risk (let us call the latter R). We define R as the proportion of those with a risk factor like being a leather worker who get or die from the disease $\div$ the proportion of those without the factor who get or die from the disease ('get' if we are discussing incidence and 'die from' if we are discussing mortality). Another way of defining R is how many times more likely a person with the factor is to get the disease than one without it. Attributable risk (AR) among those who get or die from the disease is $(R - 1)/R$ (Levin, 1953). Attributable risk is the proportional contribution of that factor to all factors associated with the disease.

Let us look at an example of AR, using lung cancer. Because most lung cancer patients die within a year of diagnosis, mortality and incidence for that disease are almost the same. If R of mortality by 1972 among male British doctors who smoked in 1951 was 14 (Doll and Peto, 1976), then AR among those who died of cancer is $13/14 = 0.93$; that is, among those who died of cancer of the lung, 93 percent of their deaths can be associated with smoking. We can also estimate the attributable risk of lung cancer mortality for that whole population of doctors, not merely those who died of cancer. That risk will be called PAR, or population attributable risk. Let us designate the proportion of the population exposed to the factor (proportion of smokers) as b. Now

$$PAR = b(R - 1)/[b(R - 1) + 1] \quad \text{(Levin, 1953)}.$$

variable to its expectation', *Biometrics*, **20**, 639–643.

Bartrop, R. W., Lazarus, L., Luckhurst, E., Kiloh, L. G., and Penny, R. (1977). Depressed lymphocyte function after bereavement. *Lancet*, **1**, 834–836.

Becker, F. F. (ed.) (1975). *Cancer, a Comprehensive Treatise* (4 vols.). Plenum Press, New York.

Bieliauskas, L., Shekelle, R., Garron, D., Maliza, D., Ostfeld, A., Paul, O., and Raynor, W. (1979). Psychological depression and cancer mortality. *Psychosom. Med.*, **41**, 77–78.

Blot, W. J., Mason T. J., Hoover, R., and Fraumeni, J. F., Jr. (1977). 'Cancer by county: etiologic implications', in Hiatt, H. H., Watson, J. D., Winsten, J. A. (eds.), *Origins of Human Cancer*. (Book A). Cold Spring Harbor Laboratory, Cold Spring Harbor, NY.

Boraschi, D., and Meltzer, M. S. (1979). 'Macrophage activity for tumor cytotoxicity: genetic variation in macrophage tumoricidal capacity among mouse strains', *Cellular Immunology*, **45**, 188–194.

Buell, P. (1973). 'Changing incidence of breast cancer in Japanese-American women', *Journal of the National Cancer Institute*, **51**, 1479–1483.

Burdette, W. J. (1979). 'Geoprevalence and etiology of cancer', *Bullétin de la Société Internationale de Chirurgie*, **34**, 345–354.

Burnet, F. M. (1970). *Immunological Surveillance*. Pergamon Press, Oxford.

'Cancer and environment: Higginson speaks out'. *Science* (1979), **205**, 1363–1366.

Cassel, J. (1970). 'Physical illness in response to stress', in Levine, S., and Scotch, N.A. (eds.), *Social Stress*. Aldine Publishing Co., Chicago.

Cassel, J. (1971). 'Health consequences of population density and crowding', in National Academy of Sciences, *Rapid Population Growth. Consequences and Policy Applications*. Johns Hopkins University Press, Baltimore.

Cassel, J. (1974). 'An epidemiological perspective of psychosocial factors in disease etiology', *American Journal of Public Health*, **64**, 1040–1043.

Cattell, R. B. (1965). *The Scientific Analysis of Personality*. Aldine Publishing Company, Chicago.

Clemmesen, J. (1977). 'Correlation of sites', in Hiatt, H. H., Watson, J. D., and Winsten, J. A. (eds.), *Origins of Human Cancer*. Cold Spring Harbor Laboratory. Cold Spring Harbor, NY.

Cochrane, R. (1979). *A Comparative Study of the Adjustment of Irish, Indian and Pakistani Immigrants to England*. The Mahesh Dasai Memorial Lecture of The British Psychological Society.

Cook, P., Doll, R., and Fellingham, S. A. (1969). 'A mathematical model for the age distribution of cancer in man', *International Journal of Cancer*, **4**, 93–112.

Coppen, A., and Metcalfe, M. (1963). 'Cancer and extraversion'. *British Medical Journal*, **2**, 18–19.

Creagan, E. T., and Fraumeni, J. F., Jr. (1972). 'Cancer mortality among American Indians, 1950–1967', *Journal of the National Cancer Institute*, **49**, 959–967.

Cutler, S. J., and Young, J. L., Jr. (1975). Third National Cancer Survey: Incidence Data. *National Cancer Institute Monograph 41*. DHEW Publication No. (NIH) 75–787, National Cancer Institute, Bethesda, MD.

Devesa, S. S., and Diamond, E. L. (1980). 'Association of breast cancer and cervical cancer incidences within income and education among whites and blacks'. *Journal of the National Cancer Institute*, **65**, 515–528.

Devesa, S. S., and Silverman, D. T. (1978). 'Cancer incidence and mortality trends in the United States: 1935–1974', *Journal of the National Cancer Institute*, **60**, 545–571.

Doll, R. (1977). 'Introduction', in Hiatt, H. H., Watson, J. D., and Winsten, J. A. (eds.), *Origins of Human Cancer*, vol. A. Cold Spring Harbor Laboratory, Cold Spring Harbor, NY.

Doll, R. (1978). 'An epidemiological perspective of the biology of cancer', *Cancer Research*, **38**, 3573–3583.

Doll, R., Muir, C., and Waterhouse, J. (eds.) (1970). *Cancer Incidence in Five Continents*, vol. II. International Union Against Cancer. Distributed by Springer-Verlag, Berlin.

Doll, R., Payne, P., and Waterhouse, J. (eds.) (1966). *Cancer Incidence in Five Continents*. International Union Against Cancer. Distributed by Springer-Verlag, Berlin.

Doll, R., and Peto, R. (1976). 'Mortality in relation to smoking: 20 years' observations on male British doctors', *British Medical Journal*, **2**, 1525–1536.

Donovan, J. W. (1970). 'Cancer mortality in New Zealand. 3: Breast and genital organs', *New Zealand Medical Journal*, **72**, 318–322.

Eysenck, H. J. (1965). *Smoking, Health and Personality*. Weidenfeld & Nicolson, London.

Fox, B. H. (1978). 'Premorbid psychological factors as related to cancer incidence', *Journal of Behavioral Medicine*, **1**, 45–133.

Fox, B. H. (1981). 'Psychosocial factors and the immune system in human cancer', in Ader, R. (ed.), *Psychoneuroimmunology*, pp. 103–157. Academic Press, New York.

Fraumeni, J. F., Jr. (ed.) (1975). *Persons at High Risk of Cancer*. Academic Press, New York.

Gnanadesikan, R. (1977). *Methods for Statistical Data Analysis of Multivariate Observations*. Wiley, New York.

Gottesman, I. I. (1963). 'Heritability of personality: a demonstration', *Psychological Monographs*, 77 (Whole No. 572).

Graham, S. (1960). 'Social factors in the epidemiology of cancer at various sites', *Annals of the New York Academy of Sciences*, **84**, 807–815.

Graham, S., and Schneiderman, M. A. (1972). 'Social epidemiology and the prevention of cancer', *Preventive Medicine*, **1**, 371–380.

Greenwald, P., Korns, R. F., Nasca, P. C., and Wolfgang, P. E. (1975). 'Cancer in United States Jews', *Cancer Research*, **35**, 3507–3512.

Haenszel, W. (1961). 'Cancer mortality among the foreign-born in the United States', *Journal of the National Cancer Institute*, **26**, 37–132.

Haenszel, W. (1975). 'Migrant studies', in Fraumeni, J. F., Jr. (ed.). *Persons at High Risk of Cancer*. Academic Press, New York.

Haenszel, W., Kurihara, M., Segi, M., and Lee, R. K. C. (1972). 'Stomach cancer among Japanese in Hawaii', *Journal of the National Cancer Institute*, **49**, 969–988.

Hagnell, O. (1961). 'Epidemiology and the aged'. *Laekartidnirgen*, **58**, 492–499.

Halevi, H. S., Dreyfuss, F., Peritz, E., and Schmelz, U. O. (1971). 'Cancer mortality and immigration to Israel, 1950–1967', *Israel Journal of Medical Science*, **7**, 1386–1404.

Harman, H. H. (1967). *Modern Factor Analysis* (2nd edn.). University of Chicago Press.

Hiatt, H. H., Watson, J. D., and Winsten, J. A. (eds.) (1977). *Origins of Human Cancer*. (3 vols.). Cold Spring Harbor Laboratory, Cold Spring Harbor, NY.

Higginson, J. (1969). 'Present trends in cancer epidemiology', *Proceedings of the Eighth Canadian Cancer Conference*. Pergamon of Canada, Ltd, Honey Harbor, Ontario.

Higginson, J., and Muir, C. S. (1973). 'Epidemiology', in Holland, J. F., and Frei, E., III (eds.), *Cancer Medicine*. Lea & Febiger, Philadelphia.

Higginson, J., and Muir, C. S. (1976). 'Geographical variation in cancer distribution', in Homburger, F. (ed.), *The Physiopathology of Cancer*, vol. 2: *Diagnosis, Treatment, Prevention*. Karger, Basel.

Hirayama, T. (1977). 'Changing patterns of cancer in Japan with special reference to the decrease in stomach cancer mortality', in Hiatt, H. H., Watson, J. D., and Winsten, J. A. (eds.), *Origins of Human Cancer*, vol. A. Cold Spring Harbor Laboratory, Cold Spring Harbor, NY.

Holland, J. F., and Frei, E. III (eds.) (1973) *Cancer Medicine*. Lea & Febiger, Philadelphia.

Holmes, T. H., and Masuda, M. (1974). 'Life changes and illness susceptibility', in Dohrenwend, B. S., and Dohrenwend, B. P. (eds.), *Stressful Life Events*. Wiley, New York.

Junk, J. (1977). *Testung der Social Readjustment Rating Scale (SRRS) im Deutschen Sprachraum*. [Testing of the Social Readjustment Rating Scale (SRRS) in the German language region.] Unpublished inaugural dissertation for the MD degree, Ruprecht-Karl University at Heidelberg.

Keene, R. J. (1980). 'Follow-up studies of World War II and Korean conflict prisoners', *American Journal of Epidemiology*, **111**, 194–211.

Kessler, I., and Aurelian, L. (1975). 'Uterine cervix', in Schottenfeld, D. (ed.), *Cancer Epidemiology and Prevention*. Charles C. Thomas, Springfield, IL.

Kissen, D. M. (1964). Relationship between lung cancer, cigarette smoking, inhalation, and personality. *British Journal of Medical Psychology*, **37**, 203–216.

Kissen, D. M., and Eysenck, H. J. (1962). Personality in male lung cancer patients. *Journal of Psychosomatic Research*, **6**, 123–127.

Koss, L. G. (1975). 'Precancerous lesions', in Fraumeni, J. F., Jr. (ed.), *Persons at High Risk of Cancer*. Academic Press, New York.

Kripke, M. L., and Boros, T. (1974). 'Immunosuppression and carcinogenesis', *Israel Journal of Medical Science*, **10**, 888-903.

Levin, M. (1953). 'The occurrence of lung cancer in man', *Acta; Unio Internationalis contra Cancrum*, **9**, 531–541.

Lilienfeld, A. M., Levin, M. L., and Kessler, I. I. (1972). *Cancer in the United States*. Harvard University Press, Cambridge, MA.

Lynn, R. (1971). *Personality and National Character*. Pergamon Press, Oxford.

Lynn, R., and Hayes, B. (1969). Some international comparisons of tobacco consumption and personality. *The Journal of Social Psychology*, **79**, 13–17.

MacKenzie, W. F., and Garner, F. M. (1973). 'Comparison of neoplasms in six sources of rats', *Journal of the National Cancer Institute*, **50**, 1243–1257.

Manesovitz, M., Lindzey, G., and Thiessen, D. D. (eds.) (1969). *Behavioral Genetics: Method and Research*. Appleton-Century-Crofts, New York.

Mason, T. J., and McKay, F. W. (1974). *U.S. Cancer Mortality by County*. DHEW Publication No. (NIH) 74-615. National Cancer Institute, Bethesda, MD.

McKay, F. W. (1980). Unpublished figures and data. National Cancer Institute, Bethesda, MD.

McKay, F. W., and Hanson, M. R. (1980). Unpublished figures and data. National Cancer Institute, Bethesda, MD.

Miller, D. G. (1980). 'On the nature of susceptibility to cancer', *Cancer*, **46**, 1307–1318.

Morrison, D. F. (1976). *Multivariate Statistical Methods*. (2nd edn) McGraw-Hill, New York.

Morrison, F. R. (1980). 'Psychological Factors in the Etiology of Cancer', unpublished PhD Dissertation, University of California at Berkeley, Berkeley, CA.

Moss, A. (1980). 'Mortality and General Susceptibility: a Study of Heart Disease and

Cancer Mortality in Alameda County, California', unpublished PhD Dissertation, University of California at Berkeley, Berkeley, CA.

Muir, C. S. (1973). 'Geographical differences in cancer patterns', in Doll, R., and Vodopia, I. (eds.), *Host Environment Interactions in the Etiology of Cancer in Man*. World Health Organization, IARC Science Publication No. 7.

Muir, C. S. (1975). 'International variation in high-risk populations', in Fraumeni, J. F., Jr. (ed.), *Persons at High Risk of Cancer*. Academic Press, New York.

Muir, C. S., and Nectoux, J. (In press). 'International patterns of cancer and their epidemiological value', in Schottenfeld, D., and Fraumeni, J. F., Jr. (eds.), *Cancer Epidemiology and Prevention*. W. B. Saunders, Philadelphia.

Muir, C. S., and Péron, Y. (1976). 'Special demographic situations', *Seminars in Oncology*, **3**, 35–47.

Mulvihill, J. J., Miller, R. W., and Fraumeni, J. F., Jr. (eds.) (1977). *Genetics of Human Cancer*. Raven Press, New York.

Newberry, B. H. (1978). 'Restraint-induced inhibition of 7, 12-dimethylbenzanthracene-induced tumors: relation to stages of tumor development', *Journal of the National Cancer Institute*, **61**, 725–729.

Omenn, G. S. (1977). 'Behavior genetics', in Birren, J. E., and Schaie, K. W. (eds.), *Handbook of the Psychology of Aging*. Van Nostrand Reinhold, New York.

Orr, I. (1963). 'Oral cancer and betel nut chewers in Travancore: its etiology, pathology and treatment', *Lancet*, **2**, 575–580.

Phillips, R. L., and Kuzma, J. W. (1977). 'Rationale and methods for an epidemiologic study of Seventh Day Adventists', *Epidemiology and Cancer Registries in the Pacific Basin*. National Cancer Institute Monograph 47, DHEW Publication No. (NIH) 77-1223, National Cancer Institute, Bethesda, MD.

Pollack, E. S., and Horm, J. W. (1980). 'Trends in cancer incidence and mortality in the United States, 1969–1976'. *Journal of the National Cancer Institute*, **64**, 1091–1103.

Purtilo, D. T., and Sullivan, J. L. (1979). 'Immunological bases for superior survival of females', *American Journal of Diseases of Children*, **133**, 1251–1253.

Quisenberry, W. B. (1960). 'Sociocultural factors in cancer in Hawaii', *Annals of the New York Academy of Sciences*, **84**, 795–806.

Rae, G., and McCall, J. (1973). 'Some international comparisons of cancer mortality rates and personality.' *Journal of Psychology*, **85**, 87–88.

Rahe, R. H. (1974). 'The pathway between subjects' recent life changes and their near-future illness reports: representative results and methodological issues', in Dohrenwend, B. S., and Dohrenwend, B. P. (eds.), *Stressful Life Events: Their Nature and Effects*. Wiley, New York.

Riley, V. (1979). 'Cancer and stress: overview and critique', *Cancer Detection and Prevention*, **2**, 163–195.

Rotkin, I. D. (1973). 'A comparative view of key epidemiological studies in cervical cancer related to current searches for transmissible agents', *Cancer Research*, **33**, 1353–1367.

Scarr, S. (1966). 'Genetic factors in activity motivation', *Child Development*, **37**, 663–674.

Schottenfeld, D. (ed.) (1975). *Cancer Epidemiology and Prevention*. Charles C. Thomas, Springfield, IL.

Segi, M. (1960). *Cancer Mortality for Selected Sites in 24 Countries (1950–1957)*. Department of Public Health, Tohoku University School of Medicine, Sendai, Japan.

Segi, M. (1977). *Graphic Presentation of Cancer Incidence by Site and by Area and*

Population. Nagoya, Segi Institute of Cancer Epidemiology, Japan.

Segi, M., and Kurihara, M. (1972). *Cancer Mortality for Selected Sites in 24 Countries, No. 6 (1966–1967)*. Japan Cancer Society, Nagoya, Japan.

Selikoff, I. J. (1977). 'Cancer risk of asbestos exposure', in Hiatt, H. H., Watson, J. D., and Winsten, J. A. (eds.), *Origins of Human Cancer*. Cold Spring Harbor Laboratory, Cold Spring Harbor, NY.

Selikoff, I. J., and Hammond, E. C. (eds.) (1979). 'Health hazards of asbestos exposure', *Annals of the New York Academy of Sciences*, **330**, 1–814.

Sheldon, W. H., Hartl, E. M., and McDermott, E. (1949). *The Varieties of Delinquent Youth*. Harper, New York.

Smith, G. C., Walford, R. L., and Mickey, M. R. (1973). 'Lifespan and incidence of cancer and other diseases in selected long-lived inbred mice and their F_1 hybrids', *Journal of the National Cancer Institute*, **50**, 1195–1213.

Smoking and Health. A Report of the Surgeon General (1979). DHEW Publication No. (PHS) 79-50066. DHEW, Office of Smoking and Health, Washington, DC.

Solomon, G., and Amkraut, A. A. (1979). 'Neoendocrine aspects of the immune response and their implications for stress effect on tumor immunity', *Cancer Detection and Prevention*, **2**, 179–224.

Speciani, L. O. (1976). *L'Uomo senza Futuro* [Man without a Future] (2nd edn). U. Mursia, Milan.

Staszewski, J., and Haenszel, W. (1965). 'Cancer mortality among the Polish-born in the United States', *Journal of the National Cancer Institute*, **35**, 291–297.

Steiner, P. E. (1954). *Cancer: Race and Geography*. Williams & Wilkins, Baltimore.

Steinitz, R., and Costin, C. (1971). 'Cancer in Jewish immigrants', *Israel Journal of Medical Science*, **7**, 1413–1436.

Stutman, O. (1972). 'Immunologic studies on resistance to oncogenic agents in mice', in Gilbert, J. R. (ed.), *Conference on Immunology of Carcinogenesis, National Cancer Institute Monograph 35*. DHEW Publication No. (NIH) 72-334. National Cancer Institute, Bethesda, MD.

Tuyns, A. J., Péquignot, G., and Abbatucci, J. S. (1979). 'Oesophageal cancer and alcohol consumption: importance of type of beverage', *International Journal of Cancer*, **23**, 443–447.

Wakisaka, J., Inokuchi, T., and Kakizoe, K. (1972). 'Correlation between cancer of the stomach and alopecia', *Kurume Medical Journal*, **19**, 245–251.

Wayner, L., Cox, T., and Mackay, C. (1979). 'Stress, immunity and cancer', in Oborne, D. J., Gruneberg, M. M., and Eiser, J. R. (eds.), *Research in Psychology and Medicine*, vol. 1. Academic Press, New York.

Wellington, D. G. (1981). Personnal communication. J.R.B. Associates, McLean, Virginia.

Wellington, D. G., Macdonald, E. J., and Wolf, P. F. (1979). *Cancer Mortality. Environmental and Ethnic Factors*. Academic Press, New York.

World Health Statistics Annual 1966, (1969) vol. 1. Vital statistics and causes of death. WHO, Geneva.

World Veterans Federation International Conference on the Late Effects of Imprisonment and Deportation, Hague, 1961. The Hague: World Veterans Federation and Government of the Netherlands, 1963.

Young, J. L., Jr., Asire, A. J., and Pollack, E. S. (1978). *SEER Program: Cancer Incidence and Mortality in the United States*. DHEW Publication No. (NIH) 78-1837, National Cancer Institute, Bethesda, MD.

Social Psychology and Behavioral Medicine
Edited by J. Richard Eiser
© 1982 John Wiley & Sons Ltd

Chapter 7

Psychosomatic theories

RICHARD TOTMAN

In physical medicine treatments vary considerably in the extent to which they are based on a knowledge of the causes of a complaint. Some drugs are known to be beneficial, although the mechanisms by which they work are virtually unknown. Certain treatments, like the surgical removal of a metastatic tumour, are based on a deliberately planned policy of intervention, although knowledge of the causal chain leading up to the condition being treated is sketchy or non-existent. Other treatments, like antibiotics and vaccination, are the result of a much more thorough understanding of causation and a derived 'theory' of prevention or intervention. In general (although there are exceptions) it is treatments in the latter category which have had the most far-reaching consequences. It is fair to say, for example, that removal of a metastatic tumor serves more to slow down the pathological process than to arrest it.

The roots of behavioral medicine can be traced back many centuries, but as a scientific discipline it is still comparatively young. In the behavioral scientist's repertoire are to be found a wide range of different methods of treatment; biofeedback, meditation, relaxation training, autohypnosis, counseling, assertion training, and the various forms of behavior therapy. But as with early pills and potions, very few if any of these are the product of a systematic knowledge of etiology. In the case of behavior-modification programs based on Skinnerism, there are paradigmatic reasons for not admitting causal theory. Controlled studies of the social and psychological conditions predisposing to illness have proceeded more or less independently of investigations of forms of therapy.

However, recent years have witnessed a revival of interest in the question of why and in what circumstances, when physical risk factors appear to be constant, some individuals are more likely than others to develop symptoms of physical illnesses. My concern in this chapter is to consider this issue, and in particular to consider the main theoretical standpoints from which explanations of consistencies in research findings have been advanced.

Every major research program has an ultimate goal, and that of behavioral medicine and psychosomatic research is the alleviation of misery, sickness and discomfort in favor of good adjustment and effective, contented functioning of the individual in a complementary social environment. The starting point of this discussion is that the narrower the gap between research and theory into causation and considerations of treatment, the better this goal is likely, in the long run, to be served. As in physical medicine, the most powerful and most enduring cures are those grounded in a systematic knowledge of causes.

Recent Psychosomatic Research

If there is a single major theme which has emerged from recent research on stressful life events, personality, and illness this is the highlighting of social factors as significant in the onset and course of a wide range of physical and psychiatric disturbances. It must now be considered well established that life events which threaten health do so primarily on account of their social meaning to the individual (Dohrenwend and Dohrenwend, 1974; Brown, 1976; Cassel, 1976; Brown and Harris, 1978; Totman, 1979a).

At least a dozen studies have purported to show that high rates of illness follow bereavement and other forms of loss (Rowland, 1977; Totman, 1979a; Stroebe et al., see Chapter 22). Other circumstances which have been linked to enhanced susceptibility or poor prognosis are: poor adjustment to a new job or role (e.g. Parens et al., 1966; Jacobs et al., 1970; Hinkle, 1974); social mobility (e.g. Marks, 1967; Jenkins, 1971, 1976); exposure to different status social environments (e.g. Syme et al., 1965; Cobb et al., 1969; Cohen, 1974), frequent residential moves (e.g. Christenson and Hinkle, 1961; Syme, 1967; Rowland, 1977), poor integration within a new and unfamiliar culture (e.g. Marks, 1967; Syme, 1967; Medalie et al., 1973), and rapid cultural change imposed upon a previously 'primitive' social order (Tyrola and Cassel, 1964; Cassel, 1976).

Individual studies and particular methodologies have not gone unchallenged (e.g. Rabkin and Struening, 1976; Minter and Kimball, 1978). Indeed it is probably true that no one study using human subjects, of all those which have been carried out, can be called absolutely definitive. This has to be accepted as in the nature of psychosomatic research. The overall conclusion, however, from what is now a very large body of findings, is that social traumas of various kinds can have an adverse effect upon health independently of effects attributable to diet, exercise, smoking, and other conventionally attested physical risk factors. That this conclusion is gaining acceptance is reflected in the growing use of 'life change' scaling techniques as predictors of disease onset (Rahe, 1972; Johnson and Sarason, 1979). The greatest danger seems to come from changes which somehow disrupt or threaten the social continuity in a person's life, in particular from social deprivations such as the loss of a relationship or a social role which had previously served to sustain action by giving direction and purpose to a person's efforts (Becker, 1962; Brown, 1976; Brown and Harris, 1978; Totman, 1979a).

The likelihood that an individual will adjust to the kinds of social upheaval which constitute a risk to health is known to be moderated by the presence of social support (Cobb, 1976), by the availability of compensating sources of social involvement (Totman, 1979b), and by enduring characteristics of the person himself which, presumably as a result of early learning and experience, determine his resilience in critical situations (Lazarus, 1966; Garrity et al., 1977; Kobasa, 1979).

Attempts to measure individual traits in order to define a disease-prone or a resilient personality have had a much more checkered history than studies of precipitating life events. The reason for this is bound up with the lack of agreement among psychologists as to how personality should be measured and the underlying differences in metatheoretical commitment regarding the nature of personality itself. Little support reamins for old 'specificity' theories, based on the belief that identifiable personality constellations are discretely associated with particular symptom-complexes (Alexander et al., 1968). This is not to say that there have been too few studies of personality in relation to susceptibility. In fact there have been several hundred. The problem lies in cross-relating their findings on account of the diversity of approaches to measuring personality. The result is that patterns and consistencies, if there are any, emerge far less readily than is the case with studies of life events.

There is, however, one notable exception to this; the linking of the Type A behavior pattern with susceptibility to coronary artery disease. Type A individuals are to be distinguished from Type Bs in that they possess at least one of the following traits: competitive achievement striving, hostility–aggressiveness, irritation when impeded, and an ever-present sense of time urgency. The association between the Type A pattern and proneness to coronary disease must now be considered well established in view of the large number of replications of the finding by different workers (Jenkins, 1971, 1976; Dembroski and MacDougall, see Chapter 3). I have argued elsewhere (Totman, 1979a) that a cautionary note must be attached to research on Type A regarding the specificity of the finding. A number of traits which bear more than a passing resemblance to the Type A profile have been described by other authors as distinguishing characteristics of patients with non-coronary diseases, for example, rheumatoid arthritis (Moos, 1964), ulcerative colitis (Engel, 1955) and disseminated lupus erythematosus (McClary et al., 1955). From his extensive longitudinal studies of illness records in several different populations, Hinkle (1974) has concluded that those most prone to ill health are those least flexibly oriented to their goals, duties, and responsibilities.

The idea that Type A behavior may best be regarded as a special instance of a more general trait of rigidity will be returned to later on in this chapter.

I. The Main Theoretical Positions

If, as I have said, the ultimate objective of psychosomatic research and behavioral medicine is to produce a schema for preventive and remedial measures, then a principal objective must be a causal theory of the psychosocial determinants of illness. Moreover, the more general, more encompassing the causal model, the greater will be the range of derivative programs for intervention and prevention. We now have available the findings from a very large number of studies of life events, personality, and illness, which taken together point to some definite themes and patterns. Several contemporary authors have remarked that the onus is now very much on theory to make sense of these. The aim of this chapter is to consider the main paradigmatic attempts at theory construction.

Early Theories

The very first formal theories of psychosomatic influence were based on the Freudian idea that symptoms can be the symbolic expression of unconscious conflicts and repressed wishes and needs, whose origins are to be found in the developmental history of the individual. The problems with these psychodynamic approaches are well known and well documented (MacIntyre, 1958; Weiss, 1977) and so will not be reiterated at length here. Briefly, they hinge on two difficulties:

(a) the definition of processes as unconscious makes them *a priori* difficult to identify and demonstrate convincingly in research; and
(b) the key propositions in many theories were dualistic in nature—explicitly or implicitly it was held that feelings caused physiological states.

Most of the criticisms levied at psychodynamic approaches can be reduced to one or other of these two basic points. The research which was carried out (mainly case-studies) ultimately failed to meet up to the criteria for scientific objectivity which were being applied at this time, with the result that during the late 1950s and early 1960s interest in psychodynamic formulations gradually fell away.

Recently, something similar to early psychodynamic ideas have appeared, in revised and reformulated version in 'systems' and 'information-processing' models, having at their heart the notion of homeostatic equilibrium (Grinker, 1973; Horowitz, 1979), but by and large they have remained out of vogue among researchers. The main reason for the decline of interest in the psychoanalytic tradition was the growing popularity of Skinnerian behaviorism. The general feeling that accompanied this movement—that the only way to avoid ambiguities in research was to concentrate exclusively on exhibited behavior—provided the momentum for the interest in psychophysiology experiments which then ensued.

Based on a philosophy of psychophysical parallelism, the general aim with which psychophysiologists set out, on the face of it a modest one, was to relate aspects of the organism's behavior to temporally associated physiological conditions. The notion of parallelism enabled the body–mind problem to be sidestepped, and the premium was on the accumulation of properly 'objective' data. The reaction against the theory-laden approaches of the psychoanalysts went full swing and theory was generally avoided. The stimulus–response language of behaviorism which became the standard language of psychophysiology had the special appeal that it appeared to provide a means of integrating animal and human research. Hypotheses about human predicaments could be tested in 'laboratory analog' studies or even in studies of animals themselves. Experiences such as anxiety, grief, sickness, even death, came to be regarded as 'responses' to 'stimulus conditions' in people's lives.

The pivotal point of this research for psychosomatic researchers was the concept of *stress*. Many different definitions of stress were put forward by different authors, and common to all of them was the idea of life events and situations associated with specific hormonal and neurohormonal reactions which, when abnormally intense or prolonged, could cause tissue damage directly or could critically upset defence systems such as the immune response. The experiments of Selye and others (Selye, 1956) did much to elucidate physiological interactions towards the end of the causal chain, i.e. from the limbic system down; but very little insight was gained as a result of psychophysiological investigations into predisposing *psychological* conditions. The reason for this is to be found in the stress concept itself.

To refer to as 'stressors' the circumstances in people's lives which predispose them to sickness is quite acceptable in a research program whose aims are confined to teasing out physiological interactions. To incorporate this term into psychological investigations is to be at risk of assuming what it is intended to prove. A researcher wishing to study the physiological consequences of stress who chooses as his research paradigm, say, laboratory studies of people trying to solve unsolvable anagrams, may indeed be able to discover hitherto undocumented physiological patterns. The results of the study will, however, have little bearing on psychological knowledge. The only interesting aspect of this research from a psychological angle is the performance of the researcher himself in planning the study: the tacit use made by him of his own knowledge of the world which enabled him to select one situation rather than another as 'stressful' and therefore as potentially worthy of study.

In fact, behind the veil of objectivity which the stress concept presented was an almost total arbitrariness in the life situations investigated by psychophysiologists. Parachute-jumping, working for exams, performing difficult vigilance tasks, getting electric shocks, crowding, isolation, having a child who is dying of a terminal illness, and watching films of incision rites are just a few examples. The upshot of this research was the uncontroversial conclusion that situations intuitively defined by researchers as stressful do indeed have their physiological counterparts and some pointers as to which aspects of physiological functioning are most affected. Predictably, the qualification was almost invariably appended to discussions that psychophysiological reactions vary enormously from person to person, situation to situation, and in relation to person and situation in interaction. Implicit in such qualifications is an admission that virtually nothing is learned from these studies about the *psychology* of stress. Ultimately responsible for this is the ambiguity and circularity of the stress concept itself, and the exclusive preoccupation with exhibited behavior that was characteristic of the research of these decades.

Much of this research depended on a denial of the common-sense truth that circumstances in a person's life are associated with extreme physiological reactions on account of their meaning to that person. One does not have to be trained as a psychologist to know that if, on being told his wife has been involved in a car accident, a person feels sick, this reaction is not a consequence of the 'stimulus' qualities of the sounds which are heard but of the interpreted meaning of the message. A primary requirement of investigations of stress in people's lives is therefore that account be taken of the meaning of life situations to individuals. The more formal version of this argument runs roughly as follows.

Axiomatic to the Skinnerian paradigm, and underpinning the explanatory force of the stimulus–response (S–R) construct, is the system's rejection of any data other than that which is given in immediate experience. A 'stimulus' is definitionally equivalent to (or different from) others on account of its physical identity (or disparity). A 'response' consists in a more or less perfected sequence of limb movements; but the significance of acts, actions, social encounters, and social messages lies not in their physical constitution and properties but in their value as signs, signifying or marking a meaning which individuals, by virtue of their common membership of a culture, are able to decode and appreciate. To refer to such signs as 'stimuli' and 'responses' is therefore not only inappropriate but is seriously misleading since these terms make it appear that social behavior and social contingencies are explained, whereas in fact they are not explained at all. Continued attempts to use the S–R construct to explain the relation between life experiences and health (or physiology) are thus based on a fallacy; a fallacy which, to the extent that these terms are retained in contemporary accounts, is responsible for holding back progress even today.

One of the most thorough statements of the irrelevance of the behavioristic scheme to the analysis of meaning was made by Harré and Secord in 1972, in their now well-known work, *The Explanation of Social Behaviour*. The basic argument is quite simple and may be summarized thus:

(1) It is possible to envisage behaviorally distinct, even incompatible, performances which have the same social meaning. For example, helping an old person across the road and preventing him from crossing both may be represented as 'considerate' acts and therefore as signifying the same intention.
(2) The same overt behavior may convey quite different meanings. For example, holding a forefinger vertically in the air may denote the quantity 'one' or may represent the provoking insult 'up yours!'.

Conclusion: acts, actions, social contingencies and social messages are understood on the basis of the inferred intention of the actor, not on the basis of their constituent movements. Intentions are inferred from a reading of social context related to an underlying knowledge of social structure and relations.

Not only is it true that the value of social behaviors derives from their role as mediators of meaning, or signs, rather than from any extensional property of the behavior itself, it can also be shown that the relation of the sign to the meaning it signifies is frequently arbitrary. For instance, there is no reason in principle why waving goodbye could not be replaced by tossing back the head or flapping the elbows. The S–R terminology therefore cannot form the basis of a comprehensive social psychological (or psychosomatic) theory because it applies primarily to behaviors, and in social life there are good reasons for taking meanings and intentions as the primary data rather than performance itself. This is not to deny the usefulness of the S–R approach as a program for altering overt behavior, or even as the starting point of more sophisticated intervention such as 'cognitive restructuring' through the modification of behavior. It undoubtedly represents a potentially useful set of therapeutic tools; but its usefulness is strictly as a set of tools and not as a general framework for understanding the nature of the psychological disturbances involved and developing a causal model.

Psychophysiological theories arose out of a dissatisfaction with what appeared to be intractable problems in the psychodynamic scheme. Through an adherence to the behaviorist system of classification which quickly became virtually universal amongst researchers, psychophysiology turned out to be at least as limited *a priori* in its power to produce a causal theory relating onset of symptoms to psychological state as are the theories it set out to replace.

Cognitive, 'Systems', and Information-processing Approaches

A mounting dissatisfaction with the passive model of man on which the S–R construct was built led a number of writers in the 1960s and 1970s to focus their attention on the 'processing' or thinking which takes place before a reaction occurs. Lazarus (1966) was one of the first to discuss these issues; his original account the concepts of 'feedback' and 'cognitive appraisal' are invoked in a system where the central task confronting the organism in a challenging situation is conceived of as coping with threat. The appraisal of threat and the selection from a repertoire of coping strategies are represented as 'intervening variables' between input and output stages.

This style of model, which draws heavily on machine metaphors and depicts man as a processor of information, has enjoyed considerable popularity among researchers interested in stress as a short-term transitory state, governed by variations in the conditions under which a task is performed and differences in the nature of the task itself (see Hamilton and Warburton, 1979, for a review). The performances studied in this research are mostly variations on the classic skill and memory tasks which are easily contrived and studied in the laboratory. Kuhn (1974) has attempted to abstract the elements common to these approaches. Man, Kuhn writes, is regarded as a *system* in an *environment* to which the system reacts with *adaptive behavior*. The essential components of the system are the *detector* which receives information about the environment, the *selector* which enables the system to respond in one way rather than another, and the *effector* which executes the response. The concept of feedback is invoked to account for learning.

Again, different authors define stress in different ways, but unlike in psychophysiology, definitions are in terms of hypothetical intervening cognitive states such as response conflict or information overload. Mandler (1979) offers the following general definition: 'A situation is defined as stressful if and when the interpretative cognitive activities of the organism transform input in such a way that a perceptible internal change results' (p. 184).

Theories in this vein take the important step of addressing levels of activity that are not directly accessible but which have to be inferred from systematic regularities and biases in performance. However, it is important not to lose sight of the strong lead from research on life events and illness referred to at the beginning of this chapter; that the predisposing (and protecting) conditions appear to be essentially social in nature. It is clear that machines, whatever else they are, are not social entities. There is a wide gulf between concepts relating to the handling of 'information' which are germane to traditional information-processing approaches, and the kinds of concept that seem to be required to express the social nature of the contingencies which are important in relation to serious illness. Folkman *et al.* (1979) sum up the state of the field by saying: 'With few exceptions today's information processing, stress and coping researchers seem not to be talking to each other' (p. 267).

Why should this be? Largely to blame is the lingering S–R rhetoric and the commitment of researchers to the idea that cognitive intepretative activity 'intervenes' between input and output stages. The general reluctance finally to abandon the S–R terminology means that the preceding criticisms can often be applied with the same force to cognitive and information-processing theories as to psychophysiology. The analysis still hinges on the extensional properties of action. There are no criteria for the consideration of meaning as symbolically conveyed distinct from the criteria for the consideration of the contents of performance. It is still ultimately behavior that is being explained, not what is signified by that behavior.

Traditional information-processing approaches, then, have little to say about social contingencies. Although some pay lip service to the importance of social factors by acknowledging the significance of 'attitudes', 'values', etc., they lack a conceptual scheme and methodology for investigating these matters.

Sociological Theories

A number of attempts have been made by sociologists and social psychologists to characterize the quality of the disease-prone individual's relation to his immediate social environment. The high-risk individual has been described as alienated from society (Bennette, 1969), the subject of 'information incongruity' (Moss, 1973), status incongruity (Shekelle et al., 1969), role ambiguity (French, 1973), and cultural mobility (Syme et al., 1965). His environment has been epitomized as unpredictable, as lacking social cohesion, as not providing social support (Kiritz and Moos, 1974), as overloading, as not providing the optimal level of stimulation (Lipowski, 1975) and as undergoing rapid and irresistible cultural change or 'development' (Henry and Cassel, 1969).

Social meaning is accorded central importance in these formulations. However, while the hypothetical precipitating conditions are often elaborately described at a collective level, their consequences for the individual are rarely touched upon. There is no proviso for dealing with how and why the person himself comes to be affected. Any theory of illness, in order to be relevant to the study of individual pathology, must incorporate a model of psychological causes at an individual level; illness is something which happens to individuals, not societies or groups. Some account of the individual's cognitive resources for handling social information and for producing social behavior himself is therefore a necessary component of such a theory. Analyses which cut short at the level of the group lack this component. Social theories point to some very important conditions in relation to the interplay between social dynamics and the health of the individual, and are invaluable in sharpening our understanding of when a person is most at risk. Because there is no place in them for consideration of the effects of social forces on the individual they are simply not equipped to make causal assertions regarding the genesis of symptoms.

The Learned Helplessness Model

Originally conceived by Seligman (1975) as an explanation of the etiology of depressive episodes, helplessness is identified as a syndrome said to arise when responses previously instrumental in securing rewards are no longer efficacious. The application by Glass of the Helplessness model to the onset of coronary disease (Glass, 1977) is an interesting attempt to integrate findings from several different areas. Glass's starting point is that the Type A pattern and stressful environmental conditions are each significant in the genesis of coronary disease. Type A behavior is construed as a learned style of coping with a perceived non-contingency between instrumental responding and rewards, a kind of stepping-up of efforts in order to reassert control. Glass admits a 'cognitive' component in the scheme serving to influence expectancy but leaves this aspect of the model largely undeveloped.

However, Abramson *et al.* (1978) have recently proposed a reformulation of Seligman's original model in terms of Attribution Theory. In the reformulated model greater emphasis is placed on the role of cognitive activity in the sequence leading up to the onset of depression. Perceived non-contingency between responding and outcome is said to lead to attributions about the cause of helplessness. Three dimensions are distinguished along which such attributions can be ordered: stable or unstable (non-contingency is attributed to persevering *vs.* temporal factors); global or specific (helplessness deficits occur in a broad *vs.* a narrow range of situations); and external *vs.* internal (relevant others are equivalently helpless *vs.* less helpless in the same situation). The attributions an individual makes influence his expectancies regarding future helplessness, which, in turn, determine the quality and extent of the resultant depression. Further subdivisions of classes of attribution are suggested by Wortman and Dintzer (1978) and by others in a special issue of *Journal of Abnormal Psychology* devoted to the reformulated model. I shall consider the discussions in this volume in some detail as they close in on some centrally important issues.

One of the main controversies concerns whether or not a substantial body of the research carried out on the reformulated model does in fact constitute a test of its predictions. It is noticeable that in the 17 papers which make up the special issue no general consensus emerges as to whether the results of the experiments in question are consistent with the model, several authors expressly questioning the relevance of particular findings (Buchwald *et al.*, 1978; Huesmann, 1978; Wortman and Dintzer, 1978).

Almost all tests of the Helplessness model with people as subjects have been carried out using experimental manipulations presumed to be analogous to Seligman's original experiments with dogs. In those experiments, exposure to inescapable shock was found to result in interference in subsequent learning to escape or avoid shock. In response to the onset of shock, instead of exhibiting the normal pattern of attempting to escape, dogs pretreated with the helpnessness schedule would sit passive and withdrawn. In the human studies, helplessness has been operationalized predominantly in terms of performance deficits in solving anagrams or other laboratory tasks, and expectancy of non-contingency (the independent variable) has been manipulated by pretrained failure to escape aversive stimulation, such as high levels of noise. In the more recent studies, generalized changes in a person's stated expectancy of success at a laboratory task have been incorporated as the dependent measure.

A review of the findings of research into the Learned Helplessness model will not be embarked on here. However, I want to suggest that the general lack of consistency in the findings of laboratory studies of people and the prevailing dissension between authors regarding the relevance of much of the experimental work which has been carried out allegedly as a test of the model's predictions are not a natural function of the comparative youth of the model, as Seligman (1978) gives out, but portents of a much more fundamental problem. The issue at stake has to do with the feasibility of laboratory syntheses of naturally arising social situations.

The particular strength and attraction of the original Learned Helplessness model as this grew out of Seligman's research with dogs was the ease with which the axiomatic concepts of the theory could be operationally realized. There is no problem defining 'uncontrollability', 'outcome', and 'response', etc. in terms of the arbitrarily selected apparatuses available to animal experimenters. The extension of the theory from the animal laboratory to the study of people, and in particular the recent reformulation in terms of Attribution Theory, has taken away from the model precisely the quality that gave it its original intuitive viability as a causal construct.

The issue again turns on the difference between perceived non-contingency as a socially contextual meaning and 'laboratory'-perceived non-contingency as something like manipulated failure on a contextually dissociated task whose meaning is at best highly ambiguous, such as avoiding bursts of white noise or solving anagrams. To admit 'demand characteristics' as extraneous and unwanted noise in the experimental system whose consequence is merely to dilute the effects of the variables under study (Orne, 1962) is not sufficient to answer this criticism, for the problem goes much deeper. Harré (1979) succinctly sums up the real dilemma:

> At the heart of the idea of an experiment is the assumption that the conditions for the production of an effect can be separated into factors which can be varied

independently of one another. If this were so it would be possible to hold all but one of the conditions steady and vary one as an independent variable, looking amongst the products of the activity initiated by that factor for another isolatable feature which seems to vary in a lawful way with the variation of the independent variable. This is the classical methodology of much of physics. . . . If the conditions of social action are a structure of internally related elements, then this condition for the application of the experimental method can never be met. The extraction of an element from the structure and its separation from the relations in which it stood to other elements would, if it were internally related to them, change the nature of the element. It would no longer be what it was in the natural condition (pp. 102–3).

Nowhere can this criticism be more crucially relevant than in the study of depression where the issue of social meaning is inextricably bound up with the nature of the subject-matter itself. Indeed, some comments by authors writing about the Learned Helplessness model foreshadow this very conclusion. Buchwald *et al.* (1978), in their discussion of experiments which have been presented as analogs to therapy procedures, state:

In a sense, it seems misleading to describe much of the work reviewed in this section as 'therapy analogs' or 'prevention analogs', because the interventions are directed at laboratory-produced interference effects. . . . It is by now well established that the results of analog therapy studies show very limited generalization to actual clinical treatment when the analog studies (a) use techniques not directly analogous to actual treatment on (b) mildly distressed persons who have not sought therapy to affect (c) target behaviors that the subjects do not identify as problems.

This last point raises the issue of the generality of the model's predictions, not only from the laboratory to natural settings, but from one natural situation to another. Wortman and Dintzer (1978) cite the hypothetical case of a student who has failed his exams and who attributes his poor performance to inveterate laziness. On the reformulated Helplessness model laziness is an internal, stable and global factor, and therefore this attribution should result in serious deficits. Wortman and Dintzer correctly point out that such deficits will not necessarily follow in these circumstances—the person's estimated degree of control over laziness being a relevant factor in predicting the outcome. The indeterminacy of the model's predictions does not end there, however. What if the subject happens to be part of an anti-establishment clique where laziness and poor academic performance are actually fashionable and therefore in that particular social microcosm condoned? In such unlikely but nevertheless conceivable circumstances it would seem reasonable to conclude that the issue of helplessness and contingent depression does not arise at all. Again one is brought round to the conclusion that it is necessary to have some idea of an individual's personal goals and esoteric social affiliations before being able to decide whether or not a given event constitutes a non-contingency and hence whether or not the attributional analysis becomes relevant. To answer this criticism on the basis that eccentric microsocial patterns 'iron out' using a statistical analysis of a large enough sample is inadmissible in a program of research aimed at laying down the guidelines for therapeutic intervention, because this answer involves the unwarranted assumption that the probability of an individual's exhibiting a particular behavior can be inferred from the statistical incidence of that behavior in a sample of individuals (the fallacy of the assimilation of distributively unreliable statistics to distributively reliable, as this is described by Mackie, 1973).

For these reasons it seems unlikely that the Learned Helplessness model reformulated in terms of Attribution Theory (I shall call this LHAT) can be proved or disproved on the basis of empirical testing in the laboratory using human subjects. Whether it can produce sufficiently sensitive analyses of naturally occurring situations to be of clinical value is at the present time unanswerable on the basis of the few studies in clinical settings which have been carried out.

So where does the reformulated model leave us in respect of our quest for a causal psychosomatic theory which is free of dualism and which treats social observables not as isolated units of primary data, as 'stimuli' and 'responses', but as syntactically related mediators of meaning?

Attributions are interpretative and so the basic assumption of Attribution Theory that people make attributions in social situations is consistent with the general thesis that people impose a meaning structure on social events. To say that poor performance at a skill task is alternatively attributable to: the banality and lack of interest of the task itself, a poor night's sleep or general incompetence, and so to distinguish: global *vs.* specific, persevering *vs.* temporal, and internal *vs.* external dimensions along which attributions are made is to propose an embryo theory of social meaning in terms of accountability of the actors concerned. But accountability according to what criteria? This is the question that must be answered if every attributional analysis of a helplessness situation is not to be subject to the criticism that reasonable mitigating circumstances can easily be thought up—possible exceptions to the Attribution Theory predictions such as the laziness-as-fashionable interpretation of the failing student. One must be especially careful not to make the mistake of arguing that because instances such as these are improbable they can, for the purpose of analysis, be treated as so much error variance. This argument fails because it relies on a picture of contemporary society as a harmonious aggregate of individuals all of whom share the same repertoire of regulative social criteria rather than the more plausible view of society as a mosaic of microsocial units each constitutionally subscribing to esoteric regulative social principles. If the second of these points of view is the more correct (and there are good reasons to suppose it is, for example misunderstanding between people could not occur on the first hypothesis), then any given sample studied is best thought of as containing individuals with a mixture of different social commitments rather than as an overwhelming majority of Mr Normals plus a handful of 'funnies'. Although there might be nobody in the sample who, say, specifically favors the laziness-as-fashionable principle, there is likely to be a fairly high proportion of differently styled social miscreants.

The counterargument might hold that although society is appropriately represented as a conglomerate of different institutions and microsocial units each with its own esoteric customs, definitions, goals, and styles, common to them all are identifiable universal regulative principles making it possible, up to a point, to characterize the attributions a person makes in a rather global way as, say, face-saving, ego-enhancing, defensive, self-esteem-protecting, egotistic, etc. Much of the work on attributions about the cause of one's own behavior has been concerned to demonstrate the egotistic or face-saving nature of such attributions (Snyder *et al.*, 1977).

Taken no further, this position is probably supportable and indeed has its roots back in the history of psychology long before LHAT appeared on the scene in Freudian, Adlerian, and other ego psychologies and in Maslow's idea of self-actualization as well as the copious accounts by different authors of mechanisms of psychological defence and self-esteem. What then does LHAT have which these earlier theories do not? How can we account for its current popularity? I believe that the empirical gains of LHAT over the older theories may in fact be something of a myth and that its current popularity is primarily explicable in terms of an ethical trick which it allows the researcher and therapist to perform, thereby opening up new practical and therapeutic possibilities.

Consider the example of a woman whose husband leaves her. She becomes depressed, and several possible explanations of her husband's departure occur to her: he left her for another woman, he left her because she nagged him, he left her to make her remorseful, he left her because he lost his mind. Now self-esteem theorists and LHAT theorists would have no difficulty agreeing which of these interpretations are most likely to deepen her depression and which are most likely to relieve it. Both concur that the worst consequences would follow from those interpretations which most closely implicate her as the causal agent—e.g. it was her nagging, unattractiveness, or whatever. The essential difference between the two approaches is purely a conceptual one. The Attribution analysis, because it is pitched at the reasons people themselves contrive for events etc., permits each of the reasons in any given series to be treated as equally legitimate. Ontological equivalence of attributions is primary to the study of lay epistemology which Attribution Theory represents. The issue of the authenticity of a particular attribution does not arise, indeed it cannot, as an encumbent consideration for the LHAT researcher in the same way that it does in self-esteem theories which take a much more absolutist position regarding the truth of falsity of people's causal ascriptions. To a self-esteem theorist, one or other of the above list of possible reasons is the true one, or at least is more true than the others. To an attributionist the truth or falsity of attributions is incidental to the main analysis. Because criteria for establishing the authenticity of attributions are axiomatically excluded from the basic theoretical system, it becomes not just theoretically possible to talk about 'cognitive restructuring' by 'changing' the attributions a person makes, but theoretically and ethically expedient to do so.

If this argument is correct then we must expect the predictions of LHAT to be empirically indistinguishable from those of self-esteem theories. As it stands at the present it is difficult to see how there can conceivably be much about it which sets it off from the older theories other than its inherent neutrality over the relative authenticity of attributions, the new ethical guidelines which this sets, and the implications for therapy which follow from these.

Physical and Psychiatric Illness

My concern in this chapter is to establish at least some of the criteria for a theory of how social forces come to affect the risk of physical illness, especially serious degenerative conditions. The Learned Helplessness model, while it has been applied by Glass to the study of Type A behavior and coronary disease, is most commonly discussed as a model of depression. This introduces the question of how far the conclusions from research into the onset conditions for physical illness mesh with what is known about causes of psychiatric episodes. To what extent are the same social conditions implicated? Obviously this is a big question as both 'psychiatric episodes' and 'physical illness' are almost absurdly wide categories; and we know, at least in relation to physical illness, that other factors such as genetic predisposition, diet, and smoking are important. Nevertheless (and surprisingly in view of the roughness of the distinctions involved) recent research in each area shows a more than superficial correspondence.

For example, Kuo (1976), in a study of Chinese immigrants to America, found evidence that social isolation and poor adjustment to the American way of life were associated with poor mental health. In a study of alcoholics, Orford et al. (1976) found that 'marital cohesion' played a large part in contributing to favorable outcome from treatment. Studies by Vaughn and Leff (1976), Ingham and Miller (1976) and Brown and his associates (Brown and Harris, 1978) also provide support for the idea that the onset and relapse of schizophrenia and depression are affected by kinds of life event similar to those which affect the onset of physical illness. There are distinctions which must be made and qualifications which must be drawn regarding the comparability of the social circumstances described by each of these authors and their equivalence with the situations described by authors of studies of physical illness, but consideration of these would be beyond the scope of this chapter. It is sufficient to note that these findings raise the interesting possibility that physical and psychiatric symptoms are alternative products of the same underlying psychological 'malfunction' which it is the job of psychosomatic theory to explicate.

II. The Elements of a Causal Model

It has been said many times by many different authors that we cannot expect to understand mental illness without understanding normal healthy adaptive behavior. The same is true of psychosomatics and behavioral medicine. The overwhelming conclusion we are brought to from the preceding discussion of the main paradigmatic drifts in psychosomatic theory is that we are unlikely to achieve a large-scale psychosomatic model in the absence of a general theory of normal social behavior. The argument is a logical one. If, as recent research indicates, some kind of maladaptive reaction to the social environment is at the root of the psychological risk factor for a large class of physical and psychiatric disturbances, then any model of this maladaptive reaction must be linked in an essential way with a model of normal adaptive social behavior. This is why many of the problems with classical and contemporary psychosomatic theory which were touched on in the previous section really turn out to be problems with the development of an adequate general theory of social behaviour.

To say that until the basic issues in social psychology are resolved we are not in a position to surmise about psychosomatic effects is to look at the situation very one-sidely. Neither form of knowledge is primary to the other. This is especially evident at the present time when social psychological theory is very much in the melting pot (Strickland *et al.*, 1976; Ginsburg, 1979). Our attempts to understand the psychological conditions leading to illness are themselves likely to have important consequences for a general theory of social behavior. The evolution of models of normal social behavior is not dissociable from the evolution of models of maladaptive social behavior, and so it is right that discussions of each should proceed together.

Recent research into the social causation of illness is perhaps most appropriately regarded as providing mainstream social psychology with a metatheoretical heuristic: the possibility of epitomizing 'maladaptive' interaction between the individual and society as the condition which is associated with a high risk of deterioration in health. It enables the tentative setting of a criterion for when the relation between individual and society goes bad. This then is my defense for allowing a discussion of general theoretical issues in social psychology to intrude in the discussion of psychosomatic theory. The second half of this chapter is given over to the more positive task of establishing what must go into a general psychosomatic theory in order for it to be able to account for recent findings while avoiding the classic pitfalls.

Comprehension and Evaluation of Behavior: Constitutive Structure and Regulative Social Rules

The main point to emerge from the preceding discussions is that for a psychosomatic theory to be viable it must invoke the idea of an underlying 'social grammar' in terms of which the individual relates to the social world and against which the meaning of social contingencies is assessed. What more can be said about this as a cognitive resource of the individual?

Firstly, in order to be able to interpret the acts and actions of others, the individual must possess a systematically articulated knowledge, or cognitive map, of the make-up of society and its subdivisions; he must know about the social conventions, rituals, styles, quirks, etc. of those around him. Different writers have used different terms to refer to this knowledge. It has been said to consist in 'cognitive schemata', 'cognitive categories', 'cognitive constructs', 'templates', etc. The common denominator to all these descriptions is the idea of a structurally related constitutive, or normative, body of information. A distinction must be drawn between the structures responsible for the comprehension of the social world and the regulative criteria, or rules, which govern the evaluation of behavior. The constitutive structure defines the parameters of socially intelligible behavior. If an act is not readily assimilable to the constitutive structure it will not be comprehensible. Regulative rules, on the other hand, define the parameters of socially warrantable behavior. If an act is not readily assimilable to regulative criteria it is not acceptable. Both constitutive and regulative information are therefore to an extent local to the particular cultures and microcultures within which an individual moves, and with which he is familiar.

Regulative rules inhere in any socially organized collection of individuals and are the cornerstone of social cohesion and social exclusion within that group. The fact that people are capable of choosing between alternative courses of action and in doing so exhibiting priorities implies that regulative rules, as well as underlying the evaluation of other people's deeds, are also involved in the production of social behavior; in the genesis of acts and actions (Totman, 1980). They guide behavior by prescribing and permitting certain courses of action and by censoring and restricting others. The principle that the same cognitive repertoire of regulative rules is expressed in action and in speech corresponds to the 'accounting as part of the action' assumption of ethogenics (Harré and Secord, 1972; Harré, 1979).

The concepts constitutive structure and regulative social rule are, I believe, preferable on two counts to other expressions coined by cognitivists and to the more conventional terms 'attitude', 'belief', 'value', etc., which, as will be apparent, they underpin. First, they have sounder philosophical and logical foundations (Collett, 1977), and second, they represent a fundamental distinction which is often obscured by the everyday connotations that attach to these other terms.

With this basic distinction it is not difficult to construct a very rough, very general mechanistic model of human social behavior drawing on some major themes in social psychological research and observations it is possible to make regarding the form and logic of people's ordinary language. A necessary condition of a regulative rule is that it can be breached, and it is clear that the prescriptions and constraints which derive from society are not the only determinants of a person's behavior. They describe an ideal state of affairs, the 'competence' component in a competence–performance distinction. The acts and actions a person in reality commits (the performance component) can be construed as the conjoint product of limitations imposed by the physical environment (which I take to include biological aspects of the person himself) and regulative rules. It is hardly necessary to resort to findings from research to know that people tend to justify the acts and actions they have committed, both to others and to themselves. This can be taken to imply that a feedback system exists whereby committed actions are automatically tested and compared against the individual's cognitive repertoire of regulative rules. Research and theory on cognitive consistency (Abelson *et al.*, 1968) suggest that this testing process continues until concordance between action and rule is achieved. The essentials of such a process can be represented in a block diagram (Figure 7.1).

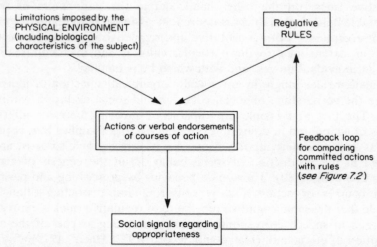

Figure 7.1 The determinants of planned actions and the comparison of committed actions with regulative social rules

What further observations can be made regarding the nature of this consistency-seeking process? The logic of the system in Figure 7.1 and psychological research and theory provide us with several leads. The efficacy of rules to produce actions depends upon a certain resistance to change in the underlying generative rule structure, although this is not to say that rules cannot be changed. Prejudice, and psychological defence acting in favor of consistency—that is, acting generally so as to procure a match between committed actions and regulative rules—are therefore to be anticipated in this scheme *a priori*. These are evident in the distorting, denying, and rationalizing strategies, including face-saving and self-esteem-protecting attributions, which research and observation reveals are employed in the course of justification.

Research into attitude change has made it clear that, as a last resort of the consistency-seeking process, regulative rules may themselves be modified so as to be brought into line with a committed action. So attitudes, beliefs, preferences, styles, appetites—even the experience of pain—may be changed by the forced compliance manipulation of subtly structuring an experimental demand so that a subject is coerced into being something but remains ignorant of the source of the coercion, or at least of its extent (Zimbardo, 1969; Kiesler *et al.*, 1969; Totman, 1976).

The Self-Perception theory proposal that actions can take their cue from behavior (Bem, 1972) suggests that registrations of consistency between committed actions and regulative rules serve to clarify and sometimes to change them in rather the same way that test cases clarify (and occasionally change) new laws. Figure 7.2 illustrates in greater detail this hypothetical consistency-seeking process whereby actions are tested against regulative rules and the rule-structure is clarified or modified as a consequence.

The Attribution Theory postulate that a useful distinction can be made between statements uttered by an individual to the effect that he considers himself responsible for an act or action (internal attributions) and statements indicating that he considers his behavior to have been constrained by circumstances (external attributions) is represented in Figure 7.2 as an early stage of the consistency-seeking process. If an individual is easily able to point to determining influences, that is, if he makes an external attribution, the need to justify his behavior is mitigated and the consistency-seeking process is cut short. If an internal attribution is made, comparison of the committed action to the system of regulative rules becomes necessary. If a rule describing that action is readily identified (i.e. if the justification is obvious and strong) a match is quickly established and consistency-seeking is terminated. If justification is not straightforwardly achieved, then a 'theory' is constructed to account for the action by attempting to define or contrive a new rule, *r*, to which it may be assimilated. Successful contrivance of such a rule leads to its incorporation into the general structure as clarification, or perhaps modifica-

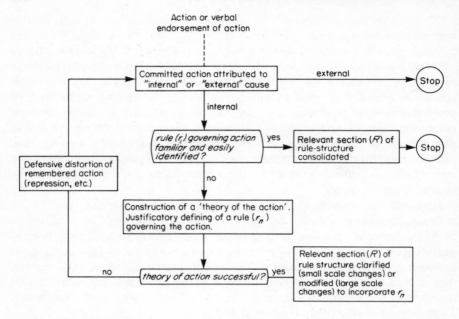

Figure 7.2 The consistency-seeking process, and the consolidation or modification of regulative social rules

tion, of an existing higher-order rule or rule system, R. Such alterations in the general rule structure correspond to processes such as attitude change.

Exactly what counts as the 'successful' definition of a rule, r, clearly needs some amplification. Cultural differences are bound to play a part in this. In Western societies, for example, the contrivance of a rational linguistic structure may be sufficient in itself—'success', in this respect may consist largely in cleverness with the language. Other defensive strategies have been described (e.g. Lazarus, 1966) which might be represented at this stage of the consistency-seeking process. For example, an action may be misattributed or repressed, or the memory of it sufficiently 'processed' so that it is more easily representable as in line with a higher-order regulative rule (. . . 'So you see, it really was in fact an honest thing to do . . .', etc.).

The Verbal Testing of Regulative Rules

Festinger (1954) and others after him (Morse and Gergen, 1970; Suls and Miller, 1977) have used the term 'social comparison' to refer to the evaluative verbal interchanges that take place so copiously during the course of ordinary friendly conversation. Clearly gossip is full of endorsements and criticisms of the acts and actions of others and of specific regulative rules (e.g. attitudes) themselves. The idea that an aspect of conversational language can be treated as an extension of action has also been taken up by several authors (Austin, 1962; Searle, 1970; Bruner, 1977). So it would seem reasonable to propose on the present model that actions can be symbolically conceived and 'committed' in a weak sense by an individual letting others know what he would or would not do in a given (real or imagined) set of circumstances. The performance of, or the commitment to, acts and actions can therefore be regarded as not the only instigator of the consistency-seeking process. Regulative rules may be tested and substantiated or modified through voluntary declarations made in the presence of others, and these publicly avowed opinions can, for the purpose of this analysis, be treated as equivalent to committed actions in their consequences for the consistency-seeking process.

Finally, it must be said that consistency should be conceived as a linear quantity and not a dichotomy. If structures responsible for understanding the social world are deeply hierarchical, as I have suggested (Totman, 1973), then registration of inconsistency and the contingent modification of regulative rules can be associated with changes in the higher levels of the structure while the more normal everyday adaptive process which I have called 'clarification' can be regarded as involving more minor adjustments at lower-order levels.

III. Psychosomatic Hypotheses from the General Model

So far, I have drawn on some of the better-established themes from research in social psychology and linked these in a very basic, very general model of the mechanisms involved in the individual's handling of social meaning. Some inferences were made regarding certain necessary properties of this system, and some further qualifications derived from forms inherent in people's ordinary language. The model illustrated in Figures 7.1 and 7.2 is not the only such model it is possible to conceive, and there can be no doubt that the brief outline of it given here is far from complete. It leaves undiscussed a number of issues; in particular, the establishment of an adequate methodology for the discovery and representation of social rules themselves (see Harré, 1979). But my aim in this chapter is primarily to demonstrate how models of this nature can fill a critical gap in current psychosomatic theory, and so it would be inappropriate to extend the discussion of the basic model any further here (for a more detailed presentation, and a discussion of the use of the concept of social rule in social psychology see Totman, 1980). The rest of this chapter is concerned with illustrating the potential of formulations like the present one as theoretical constructs in psychosomatics. This will be done by demonstrating how a single axiom applied to the present system yields several empirically potent psychosomatic hypotheses.

Axiom

From recent research the assumption can be set up that sustained registration of consistency, or near-consistency, is a necessary condition for maintenance of health through the psychosomatic factor.

Three Theoretical Statements and Derivative Hypotheses Based on this Axiom

STATEMENT 1   For consistency to be sustained, the directives provided by regulative rules must not be incompatible with the physical environment, which is taken to include the biological attributes of the subject himself. In other words, regulative rules must be sufficiently pragmatic and compromising to permit acts and actions which satisfy organismic needs and not to prescribe acts and actions which overstep organismic limitations.

HYPOTHESIS 1   Enhanced susceptibility is associated with the tenure of rigid and extreme criteria for social performance.

There are a number of lines which could be pursued in connection with this hypothesis. One of the more interesting and currently relevant is research linking Type A behavior with proneness to coronary disease. Conceivably, the set of traits which characterize the Type A individual may be attributable to the tenure of extreme and uncompromising criteria relating to achievement and competence. If this is so, one would expect the Type A consistently to construe his achievement as falling short of his desired standards. Is there any evidence for this idea?

Reports from many sources confirm that coronary-prone individuals tend to feel dissatisfied with their achievements (Caffrey, 1967; Theorell and Rahe, 1972; Romo *et al.*, 1974). Bruhn *et al.* (1974) have referred to the 'Sysiphus reaction' as characteristic of coronary patients. Arlow (1945) commented that the coronary patient is 'inwardly convinced that he is a sham and cannot accept success. This inner insecurity and sense of weakness remains unaffected by realistic achievements.' Cathey *et al.* (1962) state that all the coronary patients in their study felt that the work they had undertaken was too difficult and that they had failed in achieving their life's goals. Miller (1965) found that coronary patients scored higher than average on a measure of 'overcontrol' which was said to indicate that they are excessively concerned with the need to feel competent and responsible. Wardwell *et al.* (1963) refer to evidence that coronary patients reveal an 'unstable self concept', and Siltanen *et al.* (1975) have presented evidence showing a greater discrepancy between real and ideal self in coronary patients than in healthy control subjects.

More recent evidence collected by Glass (1977) and his associates offers more direct support for this hypothesis. A series of experiments concerned with subjects' reactions to an uncontrollable stressor has confirmed that Type A individuals respond to high salience uncontrollability cues with an initial period of hyperresponsiveness. Type Bs, in contrast, react more appropriately by relinquishing attempts to control the uncontrollable. Summarizing the results of a series of experiments, Glass (1977) states: 'Pattern B subjects gave up efforts at mastery, whereas pattern As tried harder to do well, presumably in the interests of reasserting environmental control' (pp. 79–80). The correspondence of this conclusion with Hypothesis 1 is readily apparent. However, it is important to keep in mind that the main explanatory construct in Glass's formulation—threatened sense of environmental control—is, as it stands, incompletely defined. As is the case with the reformulated Learned Helplessness model of depression, what constitutes 'control' is easily established according to the arbitrary and rather curious contrivances of the psychologist's laboratory, but becomes much more ambiguous when applied to acts and actions in natural situations.

In addition to the considerable bulk of evidence that coronary patients tend to set themselves rigorous, sometimes even impossible, standards of achievement in their work, other authors have reported similar perfectionist attitudes in different areas of their lives. Minc (1965) found them to be overly concerned to do the socially correct thing. They have also been described as highly self-controlled (Bonami and Rimé, 1972; Thomas and Greenstreet, 1973), as having a very strong sense of duty (Mertens and Segers, 1971), as possessing obsessive traits and tending to overcontrol emotions (Rimé and Bonami, 1973; Dongier, 1974). Liesse et al. (1974) also identified a higher level of rigidity and scrupulousness among coronary patients than in a healthy sample. So the possibility arises that the Type A style is a much-researched special case of a more general disposition relating to the strictness of individual criteria for consistency, and that this more general disposition is associated with a high risk for illnesses of all kinds. Also in line with this intepretation are the numerous reports in the psychosomatic literature of rigid and extreme standards linked with susceptibility to other forms of illness, some of which were mentioned earlier on in this chapter. It is tempting to speculate that the Type A pattern is frequently found in association with coronary disease because of the very heavy physical demands it places on the organism, introducing a 'mechanical' risk factor along with the others.

Findings concerned with many different illnesses have produced agreement that individuals in the sick samples which have been the object of study show more pronounced inhibition of aggressive tendencies than do those in the corresponding healthy control groups (Scotch and Geiger, 1963; Laborsky et al., 1973; Abse et al., 1974; Straker and Tamerin, 1974; Greer and Morris, 1975). On the face of it these findings seem to clash with descriptions of the

Type A person as one who is characteristically irritable and whose temper is easily aroused. But if the expression of hostile feelings can be considered a normal biologically based function, and the several lines of evidence which have led to the discovery of fight–flight centres in the brain (e.g. Gray, 1972) suggest that it can, then moral attitudes which censor or restrict such expression can be regarded as another case of antagonism between directives from social rules and biological proclivities.

STATEMENT 2   Psychological defences act so as to force a match between committed actions and regulative rules. In that such defences act generally in favor of consistency, they act in favor of low susceptibility.

HYPOTHESIS 2   An individual's general defensive competence will be positively associated with low susceptibility.

A large number of different studies have linked unsuccessful psychological defences to rapid progression of cancer and autoimmune conditions (Solomon, 1969). Strong psychological defences have been associated with good prognosis for survival on renal dialysis (Hagburg and Malmquist, 1974), and low levels of body chemicals known to constitute risk factors for various diseases. Lazarus (1966, 1977) mentions and reviews several findings supporting this latter conclusion (see also the study by Knight et al., 1979 and the review by Field, 1979).

Psychiatric states which involve a profound distortion of reality, such as schizophrenia, are considered by many to be an exaggerated form of defence against unresolvable problems and conflicts. Is there any evidence to suggest that abnormal resistance to physical illnesss is to be found among schizophrenics? Huxley et al. (1964), discussing the possibility that schizophrenia is a genetic morphism, summarize the findings of a number of studies by saying:

> Overt schizophrenics are extremely resistant to surgical and wound shock (and recover more rapidly), to visceral perforation, to high doses of histamine (correlated with fewer mast cells in the skin), insulin, thryroxine and other physiologically active substances, to pain, to arthritis, to many allergies and probably to many infections (with the exception of tuberculosis which they are prone to). One of us has seen a schizophrenic recover successfully from the most appalling burns which would have killed any normal person in hours or minutes.

On the other hand, the findings of epidemiological research show reasonable agreement that the risk of death and physical illness in psychiatric populations is *higher* than normal (Sims, 1978). The psychiatric populations studied in epidemiological research, however, typically make up a very heterogeneous group of diagnoses, including neurotics, depressives, schizophrenics, organic psychoses, alcoholics, attempted suicides, and drug addicts. The high incidence of physical degeneracy is often principally attributable to organically based psychoses, suicides, and alcoholism (Babigian and Odoroff, 1969; Innes and Millar, 1970; Sims, 1978).

There is, however, a more obscure problem in interpreting the findings of epidemiological research in relation to the second hypothesis. If it is true, as was suggested earlier, that similar psychosomatic factors are involved in the etiology of physical and psychiatric illnesses, assessment of this hypothesis on the basis of statistical surveys of large samples is virtually impossible. Putting it very crudely: if physical and psychiatric symptoms each represent alternative products of a common cause (an underlying *psychological* problem such as absence of consistency on the present model), then physical symptoms might be expected to be common among individuals classified as psychotic during periods when the psychosis 'fails' as an attempt to cope with this problem; perhaps when treatment of the psychotic state is successful. Epidemiological data are therefore unsuitable for assessing Prediction 2 because it is concerned exclusively with distributively unreliable trends which are not generalizable to the individual case.

The only definitive data can come from small-scale biographical studies. Particularly intriguing in this context are some descriptions by authors of a pattern of 'alternation' between physical and psychiatric symptoms in their patients so that the onset of physical symptoms coincides with remission in psychiatric symptoms and vice-versa (Clow and Prout, 1946; Appel and Rosen, 1950; Doust, 1952; Weblin, 1963; Dubin, 1977). Sachar *et al.* (1963), in a study of endocrine activity during acute schizophrenic reactions, actually identified a period of 'psychotic equilibrium' associated with a significant drop in corticosteroid and epinephrine excretion, preceded and followed by substantially higher levels of these hormones. These accounts lend some support not only to Hypothesis 2 but also to the speculation that physical and psychiatric conditions are alternative reactions to a similar underlying psychological state.

STATEMENT 3   The sustained output of acts and actions (either in performance or by endorsement) is a necessary condition for the achievement of consistency.

HYPOTHESIS 3   'Life events' will be associated with enhanced susceptibility in so far as they reduce the extent of the subject's involvement in goal-directed activities and/or social interaction of a 'social comparison' nature.

A different way of arriving at essentially the same prediction is to argue that the social world is far from stagnant, and the constant output of rule-based behavior, whether in performance or by endorsement, is necessary for the maintenance of adaptive social powers, that is, for continued good adjustment to the social environment. On the model outlined in Figures 7.1 and 7.2 this is the only way in which regulative social rules can be tested and the underlying social grammar consolidated or modified accordingly. Some incidental remarks of authors of studies of life events are broadly in line with this idea. Often it is implied that the critical factor in relation to health is not the occurrence of the event itself so much as the destruction of a well-established social microsystem within which social criteria and desiderata were habitually defined and negotiated. In discussing the consequences of bereavement, for example, the precipitating event has been described as the 'loss of security' (Chambers and Reiser, 1953), 'difficulty in adjusting to the event' (Mei-Tal et al., 1970), 'the erosion of self-esteem' (Jacobs et al., 1970), and the 'loss of a significant relationship that had enabled them [the patients] to sustain conformity of behaviour and self esteem' (Flarscheim, 1958). Again, some of the most valuable information is to be found not in statistical studies of large samples but in the more specific biographical detail.

It is not difficult to derive from this hypothesis a method of estimating the 'risk value' attached to life events. Such a method might be based on a structured interview whose focus is the consequence of recent life events (a) for a person's general involvement in goal-directed activities, and (b) in respect of opportunities to indulge in conversation as a 'social comparison' nature; that is, the two broad classes of social rule-following, as these are defined here. An alternative more sensitive, but more exacting, approach would be to employ the techniques advocated and put into practice by Harré and his associates, involving the discovery of rules and rule structures by analysing speech patterns and by 'negotiating' with subjects accounts of their own actions (e.g. Harré and Secord, 1972; Marsh et al., 1978; Harré, 1979).

I have recently explored the first of these two possibilities in a study of men who had just suffered a first myocardial infarction. Post-infarction patients and age-matched healthy controls were compared using a version of Brown's structured interview method (see Brown and Harris, 1978) specially adapted in some pilot studies to the aim of discovering the consequences of each life event reported according to these two criteria. Patients were questioned about the period in their lives one year prior to the initial onset of symptoms, and controls were questioned about an equivalent period in their lives. The average incidence of life events reported over this period was roughly the same in each group; but the special interview and question routine was successful in discriminating patients from controls. Patients reported a significantly greater reduction in conversational contact following life events than did controls. The differentiation could be improved by also taking into account net changes in average time spent involved in goal-directed activities—doing or planning things with a definable goal. For the coronary patients it appeared that life events had often meant a constriction of opportunities to engage in previously involving projects and/or severance from previously important sources of conversational contact (Totman, 1979b).

Conclusion

The model outlined in this chapter is not intended as unique or prototypic. It is put forward as an example of the kind of psychosomatic model which is required in order to answer the questions posed by recent research findings if the pitfalls into which psychosomatic theories customarily fall are to be avoided. This model does not rely on notions of unconscious wishes and needs, it does not involve dualistic assertions, and it is not limited to the analysis *per se* of observables in the way that S–R and traditional cognitive theories are. Proviso for taking into account the social meaning of situations to people is built into the concepts of constitutive structure and regulative social rule. By taking as its point of departure an individual's cognitive map of society and its subdivisions, and his resources for choosing and acting which are themselves part a function of the microcultures in which he moves, part a function of broader social units, and part a function of society at large, it becomes possible to represent the influence of the collective on the individual without deflecting from what must be the pivotal point of the analysis—the individual himself.

Moreover, there is room in the present scheme for incorporating not only the rough idiographic information which is given in Attribution Theory distinctions, but also the finer-grain biographical detail which is the result of ethogenic and similarly styled approaches as these are advocated by workers such as Brown and Harré. According to Figure 7.2, each of these analyses and its associated methodology is appropriate to a different level of the justificatory or consistency-seeking process.

Finally, a note must be added to the relation of models such as the present one to physiological hypotheses. While this style of model is not reducible to physiology, it is not void of physiological implications. The task of discovering physiological structures underlying human social behavior can be thought of as like the task of constructing a circuit diagram of the constituent electronic logic in a computer without having access to the circuitry itself. The first stage must be to model the machine's languages, operating systems, and programs at a software level. Only with a good set of software models would it be worthwhile starting to set up hypotheses about the constituent electronics. If there is literally no access to the hardware, then the task is an impossible one since there are likely to be many alternative ways of realizing given software functions electronically. Similarly, it is not possible to proceed directly to physiological hypotheses about the mechanisms responsible for human social behavior. The first stage must be the definition of processes, functions, and operations through the construction and vindication of psychological models of the kind outlined in this chapter. These are roughly analogous to models of computer software. An acceptable psychological model will then serve to delimit a field of physiological hypotheses and the ease with which these can thereafter be tested will, as in the computer analogy, be dependent on the extent of access to the relevant cortical structures.

References

Abelson, R. P., Aronson, E., McGuire, W. J., Newcombe, T. M., Rosenberg, M. J., and Tannenbaum, P. H. (eds.) (1968). *Theories of Cognitive Consistency: a Sourcebook.* Rand McNally, Chicago.

Abramson, L. Y., Seligman, M. E. P., and Teasdale, J. D. (1978). 'Learned helplessness in humans: critique and reformulation', *Journal of Abnormal Psychology*, **87**, 49–74.

Abse, D. W., Wilkins, M. M., van der Castle, R. L., Buxton, W. D., Demars, J-P., Brown, R. S., and Kirschner, L G. (1974). 'Personality and behavioural characteristics of lung cancer patients', *Journal of Psychosomatic Research*, **18**, 101–113.

Alexander, F., French, T. M., and Pollock, G. H. (1968). *Psychosomatic Specificity.* University of Chicago Press, Chicago.

Appel, J., and Rosen, S. R. (1950). 'Psychotic factors in psychosomatic illness', *Psychosomatic Medicine*, **12**, 236–243.

Arlow, J. A. (1945). 'Identification mechanisms in coronary occlusion', *Psychosomatic Medicine*, **7**, 195–202.

Austin, J. A. (1962). *How to Do Things with Words.* Oxford University Press, Oxford.

Babigian, H. M., and Odoroff, C. L. (1969). 'The mortality experience of a population with psychiatric illness', *American Journal of Psychiatry*, **126**, 470–480.

Becker, E. (1962). 'Towards a comprehensive theory of depression', *Journal of Nervous and Mental Diseases*, **135**, 26–35.

Bem, D. J. (1972). 'Self-perception theory', in Berkowitz, L. (ed.), *Advances in Experimental Social Psychology*, vol. 6, pp. 1–62. Academic Press, New York.

Bennette, G. (1969). 'Psychic and cellular aspects of isolation and identity impairment in cancer: a dialectic of alienation', *Annals of the New York Academy of Sciences*, **164**, 352–364.

Bonami, M., and Rimé, B. (1972). 'Approche exploratoire de la personalité precoronarienne par analyse standardisée de donées projectives thematiques', *Journal of Psychosamatic Research*, **16**, 103–113.

Brown, G. W. (1976). 'Social causes of disease', in Tucker, D. (ed.), *An Introduction to Medical Sociology*, pp. 291–333. Tavistock, London.

Brown, G. W., and Harris, T. (1978). *Social Origins of Depression.* Tavistock, London.

Bruhn, J. G., Paredes, A., Adsett, C. A., and Wolf, S. (1974). 'Psychological predictors of sudden death in myocardial infarction', *Journal of Psychosomatic Research*, **18**, 187–191.

Bruner, J. (1977). 'The ontogenesis of speech acts', in Collett, P. (ed.), *Social Rules and Social Behaviour*, pp. 88–101. Blackwell, Oxford.

Buchwald, A. M., Coyne, J. C., and Cole, C. S. (1978), 'A critical evaluation of the learned helplessness model of depression', *Journal of Abnormal Psychology*, **87**, 180–193.

Caffrey, B. (1967). 'A review of empirical findings', in Syme, S. L., and Reeder, L. G. (eds.), *Social Stress and Cardiovascular Disease. Milbank Memorial Fund Quarterly*, **45**, pp. 119–139.

Cassel, J. (1976). 'The contribution of the social environment to host resistance', *American Journal of Epidemiology*, **104**, 107–123.

Cathey, C., Jones, H. B., Naughton, J., Hammerstein, J. F., and Wolf, S. (1962). 'The relation of life stress to the concentration of serum lipids in patients with coronary artery disease', *American Journal of Medical Science*, **244**, 421–441.

Chambers, W. N., and Reiser, M. F. (1953). 'Congestive heart failure', *Psychosomatic Medicine*, **15**, 39–60.

Christenson, W. N., and Hinkle, L. E. (1961). 'Differences in illness and prognostic signs in two groups of young men', *Journal of American Medical Association*, **177**, 247–253.

Clow, H. E., and Prout, C. T. (1946). 'Study of modification of mental illness by intercurrent physical disorders in 100 patients', *American Journal of Psychiatry*, **103**, 179–184.

Cobb, S. (1976). 'Social support as a moderator of stress', *Psychosomatic Medicine*, **38**, 300–314.

Cobb, S., Schull, W. J., Harburg, E. M., and Kasl, S. V. (1969). 'The intrafamilial transmission of rheumatoid arthritis: an unusual study', *Journal of Chronic Diseases*, **22**, 193–194.

Cohen, J. B. (1974). 'Sociocultural change and behavior patterns in disease etiology: an epidemiological study of coronary disease among Japanese Americans'. Ph.D. dissertation in Epidemiology, School of Public Health, University of California at Berkeley.

Collett, P. (1977). 'The rules of conduct', in Collett, P. (ed.), *Social Rules and Social Behaviour*. Blackwell, Oxford.

Dohrenwend, B. S., and Dohrenwend, B. P. (eds.) (1974). *Stressful Life Events: their Nature and Effects*. Wiley, New York.

Dongier, M. (1974). 'Psychosomatic aspects in myocardial infarction in comparison with angina pectoris', *Psychotherapy and Psychosomatics*, **23**, 123–131.

Doust, J. W. L. (1952). 'Psychiatric aspects of somatic immunity', *British Journal of Social Medicine*, **6**, 49–67.

Dubin, W. R. (1977). 'A study of the relationship between psychological defences and endocrine function in a patient with cardiovascular disease', *Transactions and Studies of the College of Physicians of Philadelphia*, **45**, 65–73.

Engel, G. L. (1955). 'Studies of ulcerative colitis III. The nature of the psychological process', *American Journal of Medicine*, **19**, 231–256.

Festinger, L. (1954). 'A theory of social comparison processes', *Human Relations*, **7**, 117–140.

Field, H. L. (1979). 'Defence mechanisms in psychosomatic medicine', *Psychosomatics*, **20**, 690–700.

Flarscheim, A. (1958). 'Ego mechanisms in three pulmonary tuberculosis patients', *Psychosomatic Medicine*, **32**, 67–86.

Folkman, S., Schaefer, C., and Lazarus, R. S. (1979). 'Cognitive processes as mediators of stress and coping', in Hamilton, V., and Warburton, D. M. (eds.), *Human Stress and Cognition*, pp. 265–298. Wiley, Chichester.

French, J. R. P. (1973). 'Person role fit', *Occupational Mental Health*, **3**, 15–20.

Garrity, T. F., Soames, G. W., and Marx, M. B. (1977). 'Personality factors in resistance to illness after recent life changes', *Journal of Psychosomatic Research*, **21**, 23–32.

Ginsburg, G. P. (ed.) (1969). *Emerging Strategies in Social Psychological Research*. Wiley, Chichester.

Glass, D. C. (1977). *Behavior Patterns, Stress, and Coronary Disease*. Lawrence Erlbaum, Hillsdale, New Jersey.

Gray, J. A. (1972). 'The structure of the emotions and the limbic system', in *CIBA Foundation Symposium 8: Physiology, Emotion and Psychosomatic Illness*, pp. 87–130. Associated Scientific Publishers, Elsevier.

Greer, S., and Morris, T. (1975). 'Psychological attributes of women who develop breast cancer: a controlled study', *Journal of Psychosomatic Research*, **19**, 147–153.

Grinker, R. R. (1973). *Psychosomatic Concepts*. Jason Aronson, New York.

Hagburg, B., and Malmquist, A. (1974). 'A prospective study of patients in chronic hemodialysis—IV. Pretreatment psychiatric and psychological variables predicting outcome', *Journal of Psychosomatic Research*, **18**, 315–319.

Hamilton, V., and Warburton, D. M. (eds.) (1979). *Human Stress and Cognition*. Wiley, Chichester.

Harré, R. (1979). *Social Being: A Theory for Social Psychology*. Blackwell, Oxford.

Harré, R., and Secord, P. F. (1972). *The Explanation of Social Behaviour*. Blackwell, Oxford.

Henry, J. P., and Cassel, J. C. (1969). 'Psychosocial factors in essential hypertension. Recent epidemiological and animal experimental evidence', *Journal of Epidemiology*, **90**, 171–200.

Hinkle, L. E. (1974). 'The effect of exposure to cultural change, social change and changes in interpersonal relationships on health', in Dohrenwend, B. S., and Dohrenwend, B. P. (eds.), pp. 9–44. Wiley, New York.

Horowitz, M. J. (1979). 'Psychological response to serious life events', in Hamilton, V., and Warburton, D. M. (eds.), pp. 237–263. Wiley, Chichester.

Huesmann, L. R. (1978). 'Cognitive processes and models of depression', *Journal of Abnormal Psychology*, **87**, 194–198.

Huxley, J., Mayr, E., Osmond, H., and Hoffer, A. (1964). 'Schizophrenia as a genetic morphism', *Nature*, **204**, 220–221.

Ingham, J. G., and Miller, P. McC. (1976). 'The determinants of illness declaration', *Journal of Psychosomatic Research*, **20**, 309–316.

Innes, G., and Millar, W. M. (1970). 'Mortality among psychiatric patients', *Scottish Medical Journal*, **15**, 143–148.

Jacobs, M. A., Spilken, A. Z., Norman, M. M., and Anderson, L. S. (1970). 'Life stress and respiratory illness', *Psychosomatic Medicine*, **35**, 433–441.

Jenkins, C. D. (1971). 'Psychologic and social precursors of coronary disease', *New England Journal of Medicine*, **284**, 244–255.

Jenkins, C. D. (1976). 'Recent evidence supporting psychologic and social risk factors for coronary disease', *New England Journal of Medicine*, **294**, 987–995 and 1033–1039.

Johnson, J. H., and Sarason, I. G. (1979). 'Recent developments in research on life stress', in Hamilton, V., and Warburton, D. M. (eds.), *Human Stress and Cognition*, pp. 205–233.

Kiesler, C. A., Collins, B. E., and Miller, N. (1969). *Attitude Change: a Critical Analysis of Theoretical Approaches*. Wiley, New York.

Kiritz, S., and Moos, R. H. (1974). 'Physiological effects of social environments', *Psychosomatic Medicine*, **36**, 96–114.

Knight, R. B., Atkins, A., Eagle, C. J., Evans, N., Finklestein, J. W., Fukushima, D., Katz, J., and Weiner, H. (1979). 'Psychological stress, ego defences and cortisol production in children hospitalized for elective surgery', *Psychosomatic Medicine*, **41**, 40–49.

Kobasa, S. C. (1979). 'Stressful life events, personality and health: an inquiry into hardiness', *Journal of Personality and Social Psychology*, **37**, 1–11.

Kuhn, A. (1974). *The Logic of Social Systems*. Josey-Bass, San Francisco.

Kuo, W. (1976). 'Theories of migration and mental health: an empirical testing on Chinese Americans', *Social Science and Medicine*, **10**, 297–306.

Lazarus, R. S. (1966). *Psychological Stress and the Coping Process*. McGraw-Hill, New York.

Lazarus, R. S. (1977). 'Psychological stress and coping in adaptation and illness', in Lipowski, Z. J., Lipsitt, D. R., and Whybrow, P. C. (eds.), *Psychosomatic Medicine: Current Trends and Clinical Applications*, pp. 14–26. Oxford University Press, New York.

Liesse, M., van Imschoot, K., Mertens, C., and Lauwers, P. (1974). 'Charactéristiques psychologiques et réactions physiologiques au stress de sujets normaux et coronariens', *Journal of Psychosomatic Research*, **18**, 49–54.

Lipowski, Z. J. (1975). 'Physical illness, the patient and his environment: psychosocial foundations of medicine', in Arieti, S., and Reiser, M. F. (eds.), *American Handbook of Psychiatry*, 2nd edition, vol. 4, pp. 3–41. Basic Books, New York.

Luborsky, L., Docherty, J. P., and Penick, S. (1973). 'Onset conditions for psychosomatic symptoms: a comparative review of immediate observation with retrospective research', *Psychosomatic Medicine*, **35**, 187–204.

MacIntyre, A. C. (1958). *The Unconscious: a Conceptual Study*. Routledge & Kegan Paul, London.

Mackie, J. L. (1973). *Truth, Probability and Paradox: Studies in Philosophical Logic*. Clarendon Press, Oxford.

Mandler, G. (1979). 'Thought processes, consciousness, and stress', in Hamilton, V., and Warburton, D. M. (eds.), *Human Stress and Cognition*, pp. 179–201. Wiley, Chichester.

Marks, R. (1967). 'A review of empirical findings', in Syme, S. L., and Reeder, L. G. (eds.), *Social Stress and Cardiovascular Disease. Milbank Memorial Fund Quarterly*, **45**, pp. 51–108.

Marsh, P., Rosser, E., and Harré, R. (1978). *The Rules of Disorder*, Routledge & Kegan Paul, London.

McClary, A. R., Meyer, E., and Weitzman, E. L. (1955). 'Observations on the role of the mechanism of depression in some patients with disseminated lupus erythematosus', *Psychosomatic Medicine*, **17**, 311–321.

Medalie, J. H., Kahn, H. A., Neufeld, H. N., Riss, E., Goldbourt, U., Perlstein, T., and Oron, D. (1973). 'Myocardial infarction over a five year period. I Prevalence, incidence and mortality experience', *Journal of Chronic Diseases*, **26**, 63–84.

Mei-Tal, V., Meyerowitz, S., and Engel, G. L. (1970). 'The role of psychological process in a somatic disorder: multiple sclerosis', *Psychosomatic Medicine*, **32**, 67–86.

Mertens, C., and Segers, M. J. (1971). 'L'influence des facteurs psychologiques dans la gènese des affections coronariennes', *Bulletin de l'Académie Royale de Médicine de Belgique*, **11**, 155–199.

Miller, C. K. (1965). 'Psychological correlates of coronary artery disease', *Psychosomatic Medicine*, **27**, 257–265.

Minc, S. (1965). 'Psychological factors in coronary heart disease', *Geriatrics*, **20**, 747–755.

Minter, R. E., and Kinball, C. P. (1978). 'Life events and illness onset: a review', *Psychosomatics*, **19**, 334–339.

Moos, R. H. (1964). 'Personality factors associated with rheumatoid arthritis: a review', *Journal of Chronic Diseases*, **17**, 41–55.

Morse, S., and Gergen, K. J. (1970). 'Social comparison, self-consistency, and the concept of self', *Journal of Personality and Social Psychology*, **16**, 148–156.

Moss, G. E. (1973). *Illness, Immunity and Social Interaction*. Wiley, New York.

Orford, J., Oppenheimer, E., Egert, S., Hensman, C., and Guthrie, S. (1976). 'The cohesiveness of alcoholism-complicated marriages and its influence on treatment outcome', *British Journal of Psychiatry*, **128**, 318–339.

Orne, M. (1962). 'On the social psychology of the psychology experiment', *American Psychologist*, **17**, 776–783.

Parens, M. D., McConville, B. J., and Kaplan, S. M. (1966). 'The prediction of frequency of illness from the response to separation', *Psychosomatic Medicine*, **28**, 162–171.

Rabkin, J. G., and Struening, E. L. (1976). 'Life events, stress, and illness', *Science*, **149**, 1013–1020.

Rahe, R. H. (1972). 'Subjects' recent life changes and their near-future illness reports', *Annals of Clinical Research*, **4**, 250–265.

Rimé, B. and Bonami, B. (1973). 'Specificité psychosomatiques et affections cardiaques coronariennes: essai de verification de la theorie de Dunbar au moyen de MMPI', *Journal of Psychosomatic Research*, **17**, 345–352.

Romo, M., Siltanen, P., Theorell, T., and Rahe, R. H. (1974). 'Work behavior, time urgency and life dissatisfactions in subjects with myocardial infarction: a cross cultural study', *Journal of Psychosomatic Research*, **18**, 1–8.

Rowland, K. F. (1977). 'Environmental events predicting death for the elderly', *Psychological Bulletin*, **82**, 349–384.

Sachar, E. J., Mason, J. W., Kolmer, H. S., and Artiss, K. L. (1963). 'Psychoendocrine aspects of acute schizophrenic reactions', *Psychosomatic Medicine*, **25**, 510–537.

Scotch, N. A., and Geiger, H. J. (1963). 'The epidemiology of essential hypertension: a review with special attention to psychological and sociocultural factors', *Journal of Chronic Diseases*, **17**, 167–177.

Searle, J. (1970). *Speech Acts*. Cambridge University Press, Cambridge.

Seligman, M. E. P. (1975). *Helplessness*. W. H. Freeman, San Fransico.

Seligman, M. E. P. (1978). 'Comment and integration', *Journal of Abnormal Psychology*, **87**, 165–179.

Selye, H. (1956). *The Stress of Life*. McGraw-Hill, New York.

Shekelle, R. B., Ostfeld, A. M., and Paul, O. (1969). 'Social status and incidence of coronary heart disease', *Journal of Chronic Diseases*, **22**, 381–394.

Siltanen, P., Lauroma, M., Nirrko, O., Punsar, S., Pyrola, K., Tuominen, H., and Vanhala, K. (1975). 'Psychological characteristics related to coronary heart disease', *Journal of Psychosomatic Research*, **19**, 183–195.

Sims, A. (1978). 'Hypotheses linking neuroses with premature mortality', *Psychological Medicine*, **8**, 255–263.

Snyder, M. L., Stephan, W. G., and Rosenfield, D. (1977). 'Attributional egotism', in Harvey, J. H., Ickes, W., and Kidd, R. F. (eds.), vol. 2, pp. 91–117. Lawrence Erlbaum, Hillsdale, New Jersey.

Solomon, G. F. (1969). 'Emotions, stress, the central nervous system and immunity', *Annals of the New York Academy of Sciences*, **164**(2), 335–343.

Straker, N., and Tamerin, J. (1974). 'Aggression and childhood asthma: a study in a natural setting', *Journal of Psychosomatic Research*, **18**, 131–135.

Strickland, L H., Aboud, F. E., and Gergen, K. J. (eds.) (1976). *Social Psychology in Transition*. Plenum Press, New York.

Suls, J. M., and Miller, R. L. (eds.) (1977). *Social Comparison Processes: Theoretical and Empirical Perspectives*. Wiley (Hemisphere), New York.

Syme, S. L. (1967). 'Implications and future prospects' (Editorial), in *Social Stress and Cardiovascular Disease. Milbank Memorial Fund Quarterly*, **45**, 175–180.

Syme, S. L., Hyman, M. M., and Enterline, P. E. (1965). 'Cultural mobility and the occurrence of coronary heart disease', *Journal of Chronic Diseases*, **26**, 13–30.

Theorell, T., and Rahe, R. H. (1972). 'Behavior and life satisfaction of Swedish subjects with myocardial infarction', *Journal of Chronic Diseases*, **25**, 139–147.

Thomas, C. B., and Greenstreet, R. L. (1973). 'Psychobiological characteristics in youth as predictors of five disease states: suicide, mental illness, hypertension, coronary heart disease and tumor', *Johns Hopkins Medical Journal*, **132**, 16–43.

Totman, R. G. (1973). 'An approach to cognitive dissonance theory in terms of ordinary language', *Journal for the Theory of Social Behaviour*, **3**, 215–238.

Totman, R. G. (1976). 'Cognitive dissonance and the placebo response: the effect of differential justification for undergoing dummy injections', *European Journal of Social Psychology*, **5**, 119–125.

Totman, R. G. (1979a). *Social Causes of Illness*. Souvenir Press, London.

Totman, R. G. (1979b). 'What makes "life events" stressful? A retrospective study of men who have suffered a first myocardial infarction', *Journal of Psychosomatic Research*, **23**, 193–201.

Totman, R. G. (1980). 'The incompleteness of ethogenics', *European Journal of Social Psychology*, **10**, 17–41.

Tyrola, H. A., and Cassel, J. C. (1964). 'Health consequences of cultural change: the effect of urbanization on coronary heart mortality in rural residents. *Journal of Chronic Diseases*, **17**, 167–177.

Vaughn, C. E., and Leff, J. P. (1976). 'The influence of family and social factors in the course of psychiatric illness: a comparison of schizophrenic and depressed neurotic patients', *British Journal of Psychiatry*, **129**, 125–137.

Wardwell, W. I., Bahnson, C. B., and Caron, H. S. (1963). 'Social and psychological factors in coronary heart disease', *Journal of Health and Human Behaviour*, **4**, 154–165.

Weblin, J. E. (1963). 'Psychogenesis in asthma: an appraisal with a view to family research', *British Journal of Medical Psychology*, **36**, 211–225.

Weiss, J. H. (1977). 'The current state of the concept of a psychosomatic disorder', in Lipowski, Z. J., Lipsitt, D. R., and Whybrow, P. C. (eds.), *Psychosomatic Medicine: Current Trends and Clinical Applications*, pp. 162–171. Oxford University Press, New York.

Wortman, C. B., and Dintzer, L. (1978). 'Is an attributional analysis of the learned helplessness model viable? A critique of the Abramson–Seligman–Teasdale reformulation', *Journal of Abnormal Psychology*, **87**, 75–90.

Zimbardo, P. G. (1969). *The Cognitive Control of Motivation*. Scott Foresman, Illinois.

PART III

Smoking, Alcoholism, and Addiction

Social Psychology and Behavioral Medicine
Edited by J. Richard Eiser
© 1982 John Wiley & Sons Ltd

Chapter 8

Social psychological analysis of smoking behavior

MARTIN FISHBEIN

Introduction

To date there have been well over 10,000 studies attempting to identify the psychological and sociological factors that underlie a person's smoking decision. A review of this literature (Fishbein, 1977) made it abundantly clear that at the present time there is relatively little that is actually known about the basis for (or the determinants of) a given smoking decision. Despite the enormous amount of research on smoking that has been conducted, all we now know is that there are a virtual plethora of factors that have been found to be related to various smoking behaviors at one time or another. Unfortunately theorists and researchers in the smoking area have been unable to develop an empirically supported, systematic theory of smoking that can account for a person's decision to start, continue, or stop smoking. There is, however, a general consensus that:

(a) different factors underlie different smoking decisions, i.e. the factors underlying the initiation of smoking are different from those underlying the maintenance or continuance of smoking, which in turn are different from those underlying the cessation of smoking;
(b) there are a large number of factors underlying any given smoking decision;
(c) with respect to any given behavior (e.g. continuing to smoke), the factors influencing one person's decision to continue may be very different from the factors that influence this same decision in another person.

As the Advisory Committee to the Surgeon put it:

there is no single cause or explanation of smoking, . . . smokers may start, continue, and discontinue smoking in response to different inner needs and external influences, social and other. (*US Dept. of Health,* 1964, p. 376).

Perhaps as a result of this conclusion, it has often been argued that because of the diversity of needs which impel different persons to smoke . . . no general rule concerning efforts to persuade people not to smoke, or to give up smoking, will be valid or effective . . ., no single approach will be satisfactory for more than a minority of individuals . . . (Larson and Silvette, 1968, p. 304).

Despite this pessimistic outlook, I will argue that there is a social psychological theory of behavior that is directly applicable to an analysis of the factors underlying any smoking or non-smoking decision. For the past several years, my colleagues and I have been attempting to develop a general theory of human behavior. Since the theory is based on the assumption that humans are reasonable animals that systematically utilize or process the information available to them, we have decided to call our theory a theory of reasoned action. Although the theory does not assume that a person's information is either complete or accurate, it does assume that the information is used in a reasonable way to arrive at a behavioral decision. According to this theory, different factors (or beliefs) *should* underlie different smoking decisions, and two people making the same smoking decision could have arrived at this decision on the basis of very different sets of beliefs.

Since the theory has been described in detail elsewhere (e.g., Fishbein and Ajzen, 1975; Ajzen and Fishbein, 1980), I will provide just a brief overview of the theory as it is presently formulated. I will then apply the theory to an analysis of smoking behavior and present the results of some recent research on the smoking decision.

A Theory of Reasoned Action

The ultimate goal of the theory is to predict and understand an individual's behavior. We make the assumption that most behaviors of social relevance are under volitional control and, consistent with this assumption, the theory views a person's intention to perform (or not to perform) a behavior as the immediate determinant of that action. Thus, barring unforeseen events, a person's intention should permit highly accurate prediction of his behavior. It should be obvious, however, that intentions can change over time; the longer the time-interval, the greater the likelihood that events will occur which will produce changes in intentions. It follows that accuracy of prediction will usually increase as the time interval between measurement of intention and behavioral observation decreases.

This does *not* mean that knowledge of a person's intention to perform some behavior will always predict whether or not the person will, in fact, perform that behavior. The performance of a behavior reflects a *decision* on the part of the individual. Unfortunately, the term 'decision' has sometimes been used to refer to what a person 'intends to do' and, at other times it has been used to refer to what a person actually does. In this chapter, the term 'decision' will refer only to a person's behavior.

The term *decision* implies a choice between two or more alternatives. Consistent with the notion of a direct relation between intentions and behavior, the decision can be predicted from a knowledge of the person's intentions to perform each of the alternatives (see, for example, Ajzen and Fishbein, 1969; Fishbein *et al.*, 1976, pp. 58–59). Generally speaking, a person will perform that alternative toward which he or she has the strongest intention. Again, it must be pointed out that this does *not* mean that knowledge of a person's intention to perform some behavior will always predict whether the person performs that behavior.

When a person is confronted with two mutually exclusive and exhaustive alternatives (e.g. to try or not to try a cigarette), knowledge of one of the two intentions will usually be sufficient for predicting the person's decision. This, however, is not the case when more than two alternatives are available or when the individual does not view the alternatives presented as being mutually exclusive and exhaustive. For example, even though a current smoker may have a relatively weak intention to continue smoking at her present level, she may (decide to) do this if her intentions with respect to other alternatives (e.g. decreasing the amount of cigarettes smoked and quitting) are even weaker. Further, although a person might have a strong intention to continue not smoking, he may still try a cigarette since he may not view these two behaviors as mutually exclusive and his intention to try a cigarette might also be quite strong. In order to accurately predict a person's decision, then, it will often be necessary to assess his intentions to perform each of the alternative behaviors available to him.

Since our goal is to *understand* human behavior, nor merely to predict it, the second step in our analysis requires that we identify the determinants of intentions. According to the theory, a person's intention is a function of two basic determinants, one personal in nature and the other reflecting social influence. The personal factor is the individual's positive or negative evaluation of performing the behavior; this factor is termed *attitude toward the behavior*. Note that the theory of reasoned action is concerned with attitudes toward behaviors and not with the more traditional attitudes toward objects, people, or institutions. The second determinant of intention is the person's perception of the social pressures put on him to perform or not perform the behavior in question. Since it deals with perceived prescriptions, this factor is termed *subjective norm*. Generally speaking, people will intend to perform a behavior when they evaluate it positively and when they believe that important others think they should perform it.

Our theory assumes that the relative importance of these factors depends in part on the intention under investigation. For some intentions, attitudinal considerations may be more important than normative considerations while for other intentions normative considerations may predominate. Frequently, both factors are important determinants of the intention. In addition, the relative weights of the attitudinal and normative factors may vary from one person to another. The discussion of out theory up to this point can be summarized symbolically as follows:

$$B \sim I = f[w_1 A_B + w_2 SN]$$ (1)

In equation (1), B is the behavior of interest, I is the person's intention to perform behavior B, A_B is the person's attitude toward performing behavior B, SN is the person's subjective norm concerning performance of behavior B, and w_1 and w_2 are empirically determined weighting parameters that reflect the relative importance of A_B and SN.

For many practical purposes, this level of explanation may be sufficient. However, for a more complete understanding of intentions it is necessary to explain why people hold certain attitudes and subjective norms.

According to our theory, an individual's attitude toward a behavior is a function of his *salient* beliefs about performing the behavior. A belief about any object may be defined as the person's subjective probability that the object has a given attribute. The terms 'object' and 'attribute' are used in the generic sense and they can refer to physical objects, people, actions, events, or any other discriminable aspect of the individual's world. In dealing with attitudes toward a behavior, the object of interest is, of course, performance of the behavior. The attributes associated with this object are usually the consequences or outcomes of performing the behavior in question. To illustrate, a person might indicate a 60 percent chance that her smoking leads to lung cancer. The belief object 'my smoking' is linked to the attribute 'leads to lung cancer' with a belief strength or subjective probability of 0.60.

Generally speaking, a person who believes that performing a given behavior will lead to mostly positive outcomes will hold a favorable attitude toward the behavior, while a person who believes that performing the behavior will lead to mostly negative outcomes will hold an unfavorable attitude toward it. Specifically, the belief that performing a given behavior will produce a certain outcome is assumed to contribute toward the behavior in direct proportion to the subjective probability or strength of the belief (b) and to the degree to which the outcome is positively or negatively evaluated (e). The beliefs that underlie a person's attitude toward a behavior are termed *behavioral beliefs*. The relation between a set of n behavioral beliefs and attitude toward that behavior is summarized in equation (2).

$$A_B = f\left[\sum_{i=1}^{n} b_i e_i \right]$$ (2)

It can be seen that A_B is determined by the sum of the products of belief strength and attribute evaluation over the set of behavioral beliefs that are salient for the individual.

Subjective norms are also assumed to be a function of beliefs, but beliefs of a different kind; namely, the person's beliefs that specific individuals or groups think he should or should not perform the behavior. These beliefs underlying the subjective norm are termed *normative beliefs*. Generally speaking, a person who believes that most referents with whom he is motivated to comply think he should perform the behavior will perceive social pressure to do so. Conversely, a person who believes that most referents with whom he is motivated to comply think he should not perform the behavior will have a subjective norm that puts pressure on him to avoid performing the behavior. The relation between normative beliefs and subjective norm is expressed symbolically in equation (3). Here again, SN is

$$ SN = f \left[\sum_{j=1}^{n} b_j m_j \right] \tag{3} $$

the subjective norm, b_j is the normative belief concerning referent j, m_j is the person's motivation to comply with referent j, and n is the number of salient normative beliefs.

Our discussion of the theory of reasoned action shows how behavior can be explained in terms of a limited number of concepts. Through a series of intervening constructs it traces the causes of behavior back to the person's beliefs. Each successive step in this sequence from behavior to beliefs provides a more comprehensive account of the factors underlying the behavior. That is, each step represents a different level of explanation for a person's behavior. At the most global level, behavior is assumed to be determined by intention. At the next level, these intentions are themselves explained in terms of attitudes toward the behavior and subjective norms. The third level explains these attitudes and subjective norms in terms of beliefs about the consequences of performing the behavior and about the normative expectations of relevant referents. In the final analysis, then, a person's behavior is explained by reference to his or her beliefs. Since people's beliefs represent the information (be it correct or incorrect) they have about their worlds, it follows that their behavior is ultimately determined by this information.

Personal versus General Beliefs and Attitudes

At this point, an often overlooked distinction between general and personal beliefs and attitudes must be made. According to the theory of reasoned action, it is the person's beliefs about, and attitudes toward, his or her *own performance* of the behavior that are directly relevant to the formation of intentions.

Consider, for example, the following two statements: (1) 'Smoking is harmful to health', and (2) 'My smoking is (would be) harmful to my health'. Clearly, a current smoker might agree with (i.e. believe) the first statement but disagree with (i.e. disbelieve) the second. Similarly, although a non-smoker might believe that 'Smoking is relaxing', he or she might not believe that '*My* smoking would be relaxing'.

Unfortunately, in my review of the smoking literature (see Fishbein, 1977), I found that most smoking research utilized questionnaires written in a general, rather than a personalized, format. I have subsequently found that this is true of most behavioral science research. Indeed, to the best of my knowledge, almost all surveys and public opinion polls assess general rather than personal beliefs. This is also true of attitudes. For example, attitudes have not been measured toward 'My smoking', but toward 'Smoking' in general.

There is now considerable evidence to support the argument that it is personalized beliefs and attitudes that influence the formation of behavioral intentions (see, for example, Fishbein, 1980; Chung, 1980; Fishbein *et al.*, 1978). Although a person may believe that 'Smoking increases the chances of lung cancer', this will have little influence on his or her smoking decision if he or she also believes that '*My* smoking is *not* increasing *my* chance of getting lung cancer'. The failure to recognize this distinction, and to assess personal beliefs and attitudes, is probably one of the main reasons for the failure of many behavioral science analyses to obtain consistent results in their attempts to understand social psychological factors underlying a person's smoking or non-smoking decision.

Application of the Theory of Reasoned Action to an Analysis of Smoking Decisions

In the remainder of this chapter we will try to show how the theory of reasoned action can be applied to the study of smoking and non-smoking behaviors. First and foremost, the utility of the theory in this area rests largely on the assumption that a person's smoking (or non-smoking) decision is under volitional control, i.e. that a person's smoking or non-smoking behavior is predictable from his or her intentions. Since we all know people who have intended to quit but have been unable to do so, it might initially appear that this approach is 'doomed' from the start. In point of fact, however, it turns out that intentions are highly accurate predictors of smoking behavior. In retrospect, this finding is not as surprising as it may first appear. Suppose you randomly selected 100 people and asked them if they intended to smoke. Approximately 70 percent of these people will be non-smokers and almost all of them will have non-smoking intentions. Similarly, a substantial majority of the smokers will say they intend to smoke. As you can imagine, if you observe these respondents' behavior one week, one month, two months, or even six or more months later, you will find that very few (if any) of the non-smokers have become smokers and that most smokers have continued to smoke. Overall, then, you would find a very strong relationship between smoking intentions and smoking behaviors.

Predicting Smoking Decisions from Intentions

In order to provide some empirical evidence for this argument 41 young women were asked to indicate their smoking intention on the following scale:

I intend to smoke cigarettes during the next month
likely ____ : ____ : ____ : ____ : ____ : ____ : ____ : unlikely.

One month later these women were recontacted and were asked whether they had or had not smoked during the past month: 31.7 percent indicated they had smoked, while 68.3 percent said they had not. Consistent with expectations, 38 of the 41 (92.7 percent) behaved in accordance with their intentions.* The correlation between intentions and behavior was 0.84.

Although the above findings do provide strong support for the argument that smoking intentions can accurately predict smoking behavior, they do not really address the question of the relationship between quitting intentions and quitting behavior. Before attempting to answer this question, a methodological point must be made. Note that in testing the intention–behavior relationship above, the women were not simply asked if they intended to smoke cigarettes, but instead they were asked to indicate their smoking intentions within a given time-period. This specification of a time-period is a crucial, but often overlooked, factor in many attempts to predict behavior from intention. For example, if you ask cigarette smokers if they intend to quit, over 60 percent will answer in the affirmative. However, if you ask these same smokers whether they intend to quit *in the next week*, less than 5 percent will answer 'yes'. Clearly, then, in order to predict behavior from intentions, the intention must contain a time dimension that corresponds to the time-interval between the assessment of intentions and the observation of the behavior in question.

In order to investigate the relationship between intentions to quit and actual quitting, a new sample of 25 young women smokers were asked to indicate their intentions to quit smoking *in the next two months* on the following scale:

I intend to quit smoking cigarettes in the next two months
likely ____ : ____ : ____ : ____ : ____ : ____ : ____ unlikely.

* One woman who intended to smoke did not do so, while two women who did not intend to smoke reported that they had smoked.

Sixteen women reported that they intended to quit, six said they did not intend to quit, and the remaining three were uncertain. Two months later, the women were recontacted and asked to report their current smoking status. Table 8.1 shows the obtained relation between the women's intentions and

Table 8.1 Prediction of quitting ($n = 25$)

Intention to quit in next 2 months	Behavior	
	Continue smoking	Quit
Yes	10	6
?	2	1
No	4	2
	16	9

their self-reports of behavior. It can be seen that there was no relationship between quitting intentions and behavior; in fact, predictive accuracy was slightly less than the 50 percent expected by chance alone. While such a result may appear discouraging, it was not unexpected. Recall that the performance of any behavior reflects a *decision* (i.e. a choice among alternatives) on the part of the individual. As was indicated above, quitting is not the only behavioral alternative available to smokers. In fact, current smokers have at least four alternatives available to them: (1) they can continue smoking at the same rate; (2) they can increase their smoking; (3) they can decrease their smoking; or (4) they can quit smoking. According to almost all decision theories, all of a person's alternatives must be considered if one wishes to predict that person's ultimate choice. Thus, we would expect the person to choose that alternative toward which he or she has the strongest intention.

In order to test this notion, the 25 young women smokers were also asked to indicate, on 7-place *likely–unlikely* scales, their intentions to: (a) continue smoking at the same rate during the next two months; (b) increase their smoking during the next two months; and (c) decrease their smoking during the next two months. Not surprisingly, none of the women intended to increase their smoking, but many expressed intentions to continue smoking at the same rate or to decrease.

Let us now reconsider the 16 smokers who said they intended to quit (i.e. who checked the 'likely' side of the quitting intention scale). As can be seen in Table 8.2, only two of these women had stronger intentions to quit than to either continue smoking at the same rate or to decrease their smoking, and both of these women did in fact quit. In contrast, five of the women had stronger intentions to decrease or to continue at the same rate than to quit, and all five of these women continued smoking. The remaining nine women

Table 8.2 Analysis of those intending to quit ($n = 16$)

	Behavior	
	Continue smoking	Quit
$I_Q > I_C$ or I_D	0	2
$I_Q = I_C$ or I_D	5	4
$I_Q < I_C$ or I_D	5	0
	10	6

reported equally strong intentions to quit *and* to continue at the same rate or to decrease; five of these women continued smoking and four quit.

Thus, as was pointed out earlier, although a person's intention to perform a given behavior is the best *single* predictor of whether or not the person will perform the behavior in question, it will often be necessary to consider a person's intentions with respect to all of his or her available alternatives in order to predict accurately the person's actual behavioral choice.

Generally speaking, when a person is confronted with two mutually exclusive and exhaustive alternatives, knowledge of one of the two intentions will usually be sufficient for predicting the person's choice. Thus, for example, if smokers are asked their intentions to *both* smoke and not smoke, either of these intentions provide quite accurate predictions of their smoking behavior. In keeping with the notion of *choice*, however, the difference between the two intentions results in a slightly more accurate prediction of the person's actual smoking or non-smoking behavior.

Moreover, when more than two alternatives are available or when the individual does not view the alternatives presented as being mutually exclusive and exhaustive, knowledge of any one intention will not provide highly accurate behavioral prediction. The latter is clearly the case with smokers who do not view quitting and decreasing as mutually exclusive alternatives. Even more important, non-smokers apparently do not view continuing not to smoke and trying a cigarette as mutually exclusive. Although this has important implications for smoking prevention programs, a discussion of these implications is beyond the scope of the present paper (see, however, Fishbein, 1977).

Predicting Intentions from Attitudes and Subjective Norms

Given that a person's smoking decision can be accurately predicted from a knowledge of the person's smoking and not smoking intentions, we can now turn to the question of whether we can predict and understand the determinants of these intentions. According to the theory of reasoned action, the intention to perform any behavior (or behavioral altenative) is a function of the person's attitude toward performing that behavior and/or his or her subjective norm concerning the performance of that behavior.

We have now obtained considerable evidence to support the applicability of the theory of reasoned action in the area of smoking. For example, in one of our first studies Chung and Fishbein (1979) asked 63 young college women to indicate their intentions to smoke, their attitudes toward 'my smoking', and their subjective norms concerning smoking. Consistent with expectations, the young women's intentions were predicted with considerable accuracy from a knowledge of their attitudes and subjective norms ($R = 0.83$).

In other studies (e.g. Fishbein, 1980; Roberts, 1979; Chung, 1980) we have, among other things, examined non-smokers' intentions to start smoking and to try a cigarette, as well as smokers' intentions to quit, to decrease their smoking, and to change brands. As might be expected, measuring intentions within homogeneous groups (e.g. measuring non-smokers' intentions to start smoking) produced highly skewed data (e.g. most non-smokers do not intend to start) with a restricted range. Despite this methodological problem (which serves to attenuate correlations), we have, in every case, obtained highly significant multiple correlations (R ranges from 0.40 to 0.73; $\bar{R} = 0.57$) between the respondents' intentions to perform the behavior in question and their attitudes and subjective norms concerning that behavior.

Recall, however, that the relative importance of attitudes and subjective norms are expected to vary across behaviors and individuals. One of the important implications of this is that very different intervention strategies may be required to change different intentions effectively in the same population or to change the same intention in different populations.

Consistent with expectations, the relative importance of attitudinal and normative considerations does vary across behaviors and populations. As can be seen in Table 8.3, grade-school children's intentions to try a cigarette and to start smoking are influenced almost as much by normative as by attitudinal considerations, while these two intentions are almost entirely under attitudinal control for young college women. In marked contrast, while the grade schooler's intentions to quit are almost entirely under attitudinal control, young women's intentions to perform this same behavior are almost entirely under normative control. The strategic implications of these findings cannot be underestimated. For example, these results suggest that an anti-smoking campaign based on normative pressure may be an effective way to prevent the initiation of smoking in grade-school students, but it will be quite ineffective in reducing young women's intentions to try a cigarette or to start smoking. At the same time, however, the use of normative pressure should be quite effective in increasing young women's intentions to quit smoking, but it will be ineffective if one is trying to convince grade-school students to quit.

Table 8.3 Relative importance of attitudinal (W_1) and normative (W_2) considerations as determinants of different intentions in different populations

	Intention	Population	W_1	W_2	R
A.	*Nonsmokers*				
	Try a cigarette	College women	0.52*	0.05	0.55*
		Grade-school students	0.37*	0.25*	0.54*
	Start smoking	College women	0.52*	0.04	0.54*
		Grade-school students	0.37*	0.35*	0.57*
B.	*Smokers*				
	Quit smoking	College women	−0.02	0.40*	0.40*
		Grade-school students	0.46*	−0.04	0.45*
	Decrease smoking	College women	0.42*	0.01	0.41*
	Change brands	College women	0.50*	0.11	0.56*

* $p < 0.01$.

The Determinants of Attitudes and Subjective Norms

Having found that intentions to engage in various smoking and non-smoking behaviors can be predicted from a knowledge of the attitude toward performing the behavior and/or the subjective norm with respect to that behavior, we can now investigate the determinants of these attitudes and norms.

Predicting Attitudes

Consistent with the theory of reasoned action, we have found that a person's attitude toward engaging in a given smoking or non-smoking behavior is a function of the person's salient beliefs that his or her *own* performance of the behavior will lead to various consequences or outcomes and his or her evaluation of those outcomes. For example, in the study by Chung and Fishbein (1979), 63 young college women were asked to indicate:

(1) their attitudes toward 'My smoking cigarettes' (by rating this concept on a semantic differential composed of three bipolar evaluative scales);
(2) their beliefs that 'My smoking cigarettes' would lead to each of 16 outcomes (by rating statements such as 'My smoking cigarettes will (would) increase my chances of getting lung cancer' on a 7-place bipolar *likely–unlikely* scale); and
(3) their evaluations of each of the 16 outcomes (by rating each outcome, e.g. 'increasing my chances of getting lung cancer' on a 7-place bipolar *good–bad* scale.

The correlation between the direct (semantic differential) measure of attitude and the estimate based on behavioral beliefs and outcome evaluations (i.e. Σbe) was 0.58 ($p < 0.01$). Moreover, despite the restricted ranges and skewed distributions associated with data obtained from homogeneous groups (i.e. smokers and non-smokers), significant correlations have also been obtained with respect to several other attitudes including the attitude toward 'My trying a cigarette' ($r = 0.47$, $p < 0.01$); 'My starting to smoke cigarettes' ($r = 0.53$, $p < 0.01$); and 'My quitting cigarette smoking', ($r = 0.45$, $p < 0.01$). Overall, then, there seems to be strong support for the hypothesis that attitudes toward various smoking and non-smoking behaviors can be predicted from a knowledge of behavioral beliefs and outcome evaluations. Before considering these beliefs and outcome evaluations in more detail, however, let us briefly consider the determinants of subjective norms.

Predicting Subjective Norms

According to the theory of reasoned action, a person's subjective norm concerning a particular behavior should be a function of the person's normative beliefs about the prescriptions of various reference groups and individuals with respect to that behavior and the person's general motivations to comply with these referents. Support for this hypothesis in the smoking area has been obtained with respect to a variety of behaviors. For example, Chung and Fishbein (1979) also asked the 63 young women in their sample to indicate:

(1) their subjective norms (by rating the extent to which they believed that 'Most people who are important to me' thought they should or should not smoke cigarettes on a 7-place *should-should not* scale);
(2) their normative beliefs (by indicating the extent to which six different referents each thought they should or should not smoke cigarettes); and
(3) their motivations to comply with each referent (by indicating the extent to which, on a 7-place scale, they 'wanted to' or 'did not want to' comply with the referent in general).

Consistent with expectations, the correlation between the direct (SN) and indirect measures (Σbm) of the subjective norm was 0.53 ($p < 0.01$). In other studies, the estimate based on normative beliefs and motivations to comply have predicted, among other things, subjective norms with respect to trying a cigarette ($r = 0.68$, $p < 0.01$), starting to smoking cigarettes ($r = 0.45$, $p < 0.01$), decreasing the amount of cigarette smoking ($r = 0.59$, $p < 0.01$), and quitting ($r = 0.64$, $p < 0.01$).

Taken together then, the above findings provide strong support for the applicability and utility of the theory of reasoned action as a basis for understanding various smoking and non-smoking decisions. We saw above that knowledge of a person's smoking and non-smoking intentions allows us accurately to predict his or her ultimate smoking or non-smoking decision. Moreover, we also showed that a given smoking or non-smoking intention can be predicted from a knowledge of the person's corresponding attitudes and subjective norms, which are themselves predictable from a consideration of underlying behavioral beliefs, outcome evaluations, normative beliefs, and motivations to comply. A complete understanding of a given smoking decision thus rests on an analysis of the beliefs, evaluations, and motivations to comply that underlie the decision in question. Although complete analyses of different smoking decisions are beyond the scope of the present paper, a recent study by Fishbein, Loken, Chung, and Roberts (in preparation) will serve to illustrate our approach.

Factors Underlying Young Women's Smoking Decisions

As we saw earlier, whether or not women will smoke can be very accurately predicted from the differences in the women's intentions to smoke and not to smoke cigarettes (i.e. from $I_S–I_{NS}$). In this study, we tried to predict the differential smoking intentions of 193 young college women. Consistent with expectations, we found that the differential intentions (i.e. $I_S–I_{NS}$) could be accurately predicted from the differences in their attitudes toward 'My smoking' and 'My not smoking' (i.e. from $A_S–A_{NS}$) and from their differential subjective norms (i.e. $SN_{S–NS}$). Further, these differential attitudes and subjective norms were in turn predicted from differences in behavioral beliefs and outcome evaluations (i.e. from $\Sigma be_S–\Sigma be_{NS}$) and from differential normative beliefs and motivations to comply (i.e. from $\Sigma bm_{S–NS}$). Thus, we also found that the differential intentions could be predicted quite accurately from a consideration of the women's differential behavioral beliefs, outcome evaluations, normative beliefs, and motivations to comply. More specifically, regressing the differential intentions ($I_S–I_{NS}$) on to the estimates of differential attitudes (i.e. $\Sigma be_S–\Sigma be_{NS}$) and subjective norms (i.e. $\Sigma bm_{S–NS}$) resulted in a multiple correlation of 0.62 ($p < 0.01$). Moreover, at least for this sample of women, this differential smoking intention was more strongly influenced by attitudinal ($W_1 = 0.50$, $p < 0.01$) than by normative ($W_2 = 0.20$, $p < 0.05$) considerations.

An Analysis of Behavioral Beliefs and Outcome Evaluations

Thus, in attempting to explain why some women intend to smoke ($I_S > I_{NS}$) while others do not ($I_{NS} > I_S$) we should first consider their personal beliefs about smoking and not smoking as well as their evaluations of the outcomes they associate with engaging in these two behaviors. Table 8.4 shows the mean differential beliefs ($b_S–b_{NS}$), outcome evaluations (e) and the differential

Table 8.4 Average differential behavioral beliefs, outcome evaluations, and products for women with differential intentions to smoke (DI_S) and not to smoke (DI_{NS})

Outcomes	b_S-b_{NS}		e_i		be_S-be_{NS}	
	DI_S ($n = 36$)	DI_{NS} ($n = 150$)	DI	DI_{NS}	DI_S	DI_{NS}
Harmful to health	4.53	5.37*	−2.17	−2.71*	−9.44	−14.62*
Increase cancer	4.33	5.34*	−1.94	−2.75*	−10.38	−14.97*
Breathing problems	3.89	4.90*	−2.33	2.75*	−9.06	−13.52*
Offensive to others	2.81	4.65*	−2.14	−2.65*	−6.11	−12.52*
Bad breath	3.44	5.09*	−2.50	−2.51	−8.44	−12.82*
Bad odor on clothes	3.67	5.26*	−1.83	−2.52*	−6.72	−13.39*
Increase dependency	4.78	4.93	−2.08	−2.88*	−10.00	−14.31*
Expensive	4.17	5.05*	−0.86	−0.79	−3.53	−4.09
Relieves tension	2.75	−0.48*	2.31	2.47	6.39	−1.17*
Relaxing	2.94	−1.40*	2.56	2.51	7.92	−3.55*
Helps concentrate	0.44	−2.29*	2.31	2.21	1.42	−5.41*
Helps interact	1.28	−1.65*	2.08	2.12	3.47	−3.51*
Acceptance by peers	−0.39	−2.03*	1.67	1.57	−0.56	−3.22*
Something to do with hands	3.75	1.35*	0.58	0.65	2.86	1.63
Keep weight down	1.00	−3.37*	2.72	2.50	2.75	−8.45*
Pleasant taste experience	0.14	−4.76*	2.13	2.03	0.44	−9.41*

* Difference between DI_S and DI_{NS} significant at 0.01 level.

belief-evaluation products (be_S-be_{NS}) for women with intentions to smoke $(I_S > I_{NS})$ and not to smoke $(I_{NS} > I_S)$ cigarettes. Perhaps the first thing to note in the table are the beliefs themselves. According to the theory of reasoned action, attitudes are a function of salient beliefs, and thus one cannot simply sit down and construct a list of beliefs. Instead, it is necessary first to identify those beliefs that are most salient for (i.e. occur with the greatest frequency in) the population under consideration. Thus, prior to conducting the study, an independent sample of young women were asked to tell us what they believed were (or would be) the advantages and disadvantages of their own smoking and not smoking. Table 8.4 shows only those beliefs that were emitted most frequently in response to these questions.*

What is perhaps most striking is the small number of beliefs that refer to the health consequences of smoking or not smoking. Although many health outcomes may be incorporated within the belief that 'My smoking is harmful to my health', it was still surprising to find little or no mention of such things

* The beliefs are not ordered in terms of frequency in Table 8.4. Rather, they have been grouped to illustrate various positive and negative outcomes.

as coronary heart disease, life expectancy, or premature or stillborn births. Equally surprising were the relatively large number of beliefs referring directly or indirectly to interpersonal relations (e.g. offensive to others, bad breath, helps me interact, gives me something to do with my hands). Indeed, even without further analysis, these findings make it clear that young women's smoking decisions are not based primarily on health considerations. Let us consider these beliefs and outcome evaluations in somewhat more detail.

Turning first to the evaluations, it can be seen that both intenders and non-intenders were in general agreement about which outcomes were good (+) and which were bad (−). With respect to six of the eight negative outcomes, however, intenders were significantly *less* negative than non-intenders. Thus, for example, although intenders felt that 'being harmful to health' and 'being offensive to others', were 'bad', they did not view these outcomes as negatively as did the non-intenders. In marked contrast, there were no significant differences between intenders and non-intenders with respect to any of the positive outcomes (e.g. tension relief, acceptance by peers, and having a pleasant taste experience).

The major differences between intenders and non-intenders, however, occur with respect to differential beliefs. All beliefs were scored from +3 (likely) to −3 (unlikely); the difference scores can thus range from +6 to −6, with positive scores indicating that the women believed that the outcome was more likely to be a result of their smoking than of their not smoking and negative scores indicating the opposite. Ignoring, for a moment, the magnitude of the difference scores, it can be seen that although all the young women believed that smoking was more likely to lead to each of the eight negative consequences than was not smoking, they differed markedly in their differential beliefs about the positive consequences. More specifically, while intenders believed that their smoking would be more likely to lead to seven of the eight positive outcomes than their not smoking, non-intenders believed they would be more likely to attain seven of the eight positive outcomes by not smoking.

When the magnitude of the differential beliefs is taken into account, intenders and non-intenders are found to differ significantly in their beliefs concerning almost every outcome, be it positive or negative. For example, although all the women believed that their smoking was more likely to lead to negative health consequences than their not smoking, intenders believe this significantly *less* than do non-intenders. Given this finding, and the previous finding that intenders evaluate health consequences less negatively than do non-intenders, it follows that these health beliefs make a significantly more negative contribution to the differential attitudes of non-intenders than of intenders (see the last two columns of Table 8.4). Thus, despite the fact that almost all the women recognize some of the negative health consequences of smoking, the findings in the first three rows of Table 8.4 make it clear that health considerations do play an important role in influencing the women's smoking or not smoking behaviors. Taken in context, however, it can also be seen that health beliefs are only a small subset of the beliefs that underlie the young women's decisions. In fact, with the exception of beliefs about the relative cost of smoking, and beliefs that smoking (in contrast to non-smoking) gives the women something to do with their hands, all the beliefs considered were found to make significantly different contributions to the different attitudes of intenders and non-intenders (see column 3 of Table 8.4).

An Analysis of Normative Beliefs and Motivations to Comply

In addition to these attitudinal considerations, the women's smoking or not smoking decisions were also influenced by normative factors. Table 8.5 shows

Table 8.5 Average normative beliefs, motivations to comply and products for women with differential intentions to smoke (DI_S) and not to smoke (DI_{NS})

Referents	b_j		m_j		$b_j m_j$	
	DI_S $(n = 36)$	DI_{NS} $(n = 150)$	DI_S	DI_{NS}	DI_S	DI_{NS}
Mother	−2.44	−2.63	5.17	5.69*	−12.53	−15.12*
Father	−2.25	−2.61*	5.17	5.61	−11.69	−14.82*
Other family	−1.44	−2.43†	4.92	5.35	−6.92	−13.45†
Boy friend	−1.69	−2.35†	5.25	5.40	−9.25	−13.15†
Friends	−1.06	−2.09†	4.42	4.75	−4.72	−10.40†
Doctor	−2.61	−2.85	4.86	6.12†	−12.75	−17.62†

* Difference between DI_S and DI_{NS} significant at 0.05 level.
† Difference significant at 0.01 level.

the mean differential normative beliefs (b_{S-NS}), motivations to comply (m), and the differential belief-motivation products (bm_{S-NS}) for women with intentions to smoke $(I_S > I_{NS})$ and not to smoke $(I_{NS} > I_S)$ cigarettes. Note first that all the women believe that the six referents think they should *not* smoke cigarettes (i.e. all normative beliefs are negative), although non-intenders believe their boy friends, fathers, other family members, and friends are more opposed to their smoking than do intenders. Moreover, although the women are motivated to comply with all of these referents, non-intenders are significantly more motivated to comply with their doctors and their mothers than are intenders. In fact, it is interesting to note that non-intenders have stronger motivations to comply with their doctors than with any other referent. Thus, although intenders and non-intenders do not differ in their beliefs and their doctors think they should not smoke, intenders perceive significantly less normative pressure not to smoke from their doctors than do non-intenders (see column 3). Generally speaking, then, although all women report that their referents exert normative pressure not to smoke, this pressure is greater for non-intenders than for intenders with respect to each referent. The finding that many young women intend to smoke despite normative pressure not to, supports our earlier finding that attitudinal considerations are more important determinants of these women's smoking decisions than are normative ones.

Summary and Conclusions

To summarize, young women appear to consider many different factors in arriving at their decisions to smoke or not smoke cigarettes. Women recognize normative pressure not to smoke, and the greater this perceived pressure the less likely they are to smoke (or to become smokers). However, these normative considerations appear to play only a minor role in influencing the women's ultimate smoking decisions. Much more important are their considerations of the relative advantages and disadvantages of smoking.

In addition to considering the effects of smoking and not smoking on a limited number of health outcomes, the women take into account the effects of smoking and not smoking on others (e.g. will it offend them, will I be more or less likely to be accepted?), as well as upon themselves (e.g. will these behaviors lead to bad breath, to weight-gain or tension relief? Will I be more relaxed or better able to interact in social situations?). Finally, they also consider questions of cost and habituation.

Although all the young women believe that their smoking is more likely to lead to the negative consequences than is their non-smoking, some women hold these differential beliefs more strongly than others. Generally speaking, the more strongly a woman holds these beliefs, the less likely she is to be (or to become) a smoker.

More important, some women believe that most of the positive outcomes in Table 8.4 are more likely to be attained by smoking than by not smoking, while others believe these same positive outcomes are more likely to be achieved by not smoking than by smoking. Not surprisingly, the first group of women are likely to be (or become) smokers, while women in the second group are very unlikely to make this decision.

To put this most simply, some women apparently believe that the benefits of smoking (relative to not smoking) outweigh the risks while others see little or no benefits and many risks. These differential beliefs lead to positive differential smoking attitudes in the former group and negative differential smoking attitudes in the latter group. Given that differential smoking intentions (and hence, actual smoking behavior) are more under attitudinal than normative control, the women in the first group are very likely to be (or to become) smokers.

Viewed in this light it can be seen that a woman's smoking decision follows quite *reasonably* from her salient beliefs and outcome evaluations. While one may question the values that some women place on certain outcomes or the accuracy of some of their beliefs, a decision to smoke is actually quite *reasonable* if the decision-maker believes that the net effects of smoking are more positive than the net effects of not smoking.

Thus, if one wished to influence young women's smoking decisions, a reasonable strategy would be to decrease the women's beliefs that smoking leads to positive consequences *and* to increase their beliefs that these outcomes will be attained by not smoking. Clearly, one is unlikely to have a great deal of influence if one simply points out the negative health consequences of smoking. Indeed, to be successful, an intervention attempt will have to consider a wide range of beliefs, most of which are not health-related, about both smoking and non-smoking.

Recall, however, that different interventions could be required if one wished to influence different decisions in this same population (e.g. the decision to try or not try a cigarette or the decision to quit or not quit cigarette smoking) or the same decision (i.e. to smoke or not smoke cigarettes) in a different population. What we have tried to demonstrate is that it is possible to identify the factors underlying a given smoking or not-smoking decision by considering a small set of variables that comprise a theory of reasoned action. It is our contention that to be successful, interventions must be based on a full understanding of the decision in question. Not only must one know whether a particular decision is under attitudinal or normative control, but one must also identify the beliefs, outcome evaluations, and motivations to comply that lead to the different attitudes and/or subjective norms that underlie different decisions.

References

Ajzen, I., and Fishbein, M. (1969). 'The prediction of behavioral intentions in a choice situation', *Journal of Experimental Social Psychology*, **5**, 400–416.

Ajzen, I., and Fishbein, M. (1980). *Understanding Attitudes and Predicting Social Behavior*. Prentice-Hall, Englewood Cliffs, NJ.

Chung, J. (1980). 'Factors influencing young women's smoking intentions and behavior'. Unpublished Master's dissertation, University of Illinois, Urbana-Champaign.

Chung, J., and Fishbein, M. (1979). 'Predicting young women's intention to smoke: Some implications for attitude measurement'. Paper presented at Midwestern Psychological Association, Chicago, May.

Fishbein, M. (1977). 'Consumer beliefs and behavior with respect to cigarette smoking: a critical analysis of the public literature'. A report prepared for the staff of the Federal Trade Commission, submitted to Congress, October.

Fishbein, M. (1980). 'A theory of reasoned action: some applications and implications', in Howe, H., and Page, M. (eds.), *Nebraska Symposium on Motivation, 1978*. University of Nebraska Press, Lincoln. (In press).

Fishbein, M., and Ajzen, I. (1975). *Belief, Attitude, Intention and Behavior: An Introduction to Theory and Research*. Addison-Wesley, Boston.

Fishbein, M. Loken, B., Roberts, S., and Chung, J. (1978). 'Are young women 'informed' about cigarette smoking?' Report prepared for the staff of the Federal Trade Commission, August.

Fishbein, M., Thomas, K., and Jaccard, J. J. (1976). *Voting Behaviour in Britain: An Attitudinal Analysis (Occasional Papers in Survey Research, No. 7)*. SSRC Survey Unit, London.

Larson, P. S., and Silvette, H. (1968). *Tobacco, Experimental and Clinical Studies, Supplement I*. Williams & Wilkins, Baltimore.

Roberts, S. (1979). Beliefs associated with smoking intentions of college women. Ph.D. dissertation, University of Illinois, Urbana-Champaign.

US, Department of Health, Education and Welfare (1964). *Smoking and Health: Report of the Advisory Committee to the Surgeon General of the Public Health Service*. Public Health Service Document No. 1103. US Government Printing Office, Washington, DC.

Social Psychology and Behavioral Medicine
Edited by J. Richard Eiser
© 1982 John Wiley & Sons Ltd

Chapter 9

Alcohol use among young adult males: an application of problem-behavior theory*

DON DITECCO and RONALD P. SCHLEGEL

Introduction

The purpose of this chapter is to investigate the nature of the differences found among various drinker 'types', specifically: problem drinkers, non-problem drinkers, and non-drinkers. This aim immediately gives rise to two questions:

(a) how does one define problem and non-problem drinkers?
(b) what variables are relevant in examining differences between these groups once they are defined?

The first part of the chapter is addressed to these two concerns. A brief review of problem drinking research is presented and Jessor's problem-behavior theory (Jessor and Jessor, 1977), a general social-psychological theoretical framework, is described. The issue of the 'qualitativeness' or 'quantitative-ness' of the differences between drinkers is raised and a specific operationalization of problem and non-problem drinking is suggested. Empirical evidence is then presented which relates certain drinker types to relevant discriminating variables and the theoretical and practical significance of these findings is discussed.

The Status of Problem Drinking

Problems associated with the human consumption of alcoholic beverages appear to be as old as beverage alcohol itself. A great variety of individual and social ills have been attributed to the use of alcohol throughout history.

* This research was supported by Grant No. 1212–105 from the Non-Medical Use of Drugs Directorate, Health and Welfare Canada. The authors wish to thank Ed Ware for his advice on statistical matters, and Gisele DiTecco for preparing the manuscript.

Recently, Room (1977) has distinguished current problems recognized as possible consequences of alcohol abuse as follows:

(1) chronic illness (e.g. cirrhosis);
(2) acute health problems (e.g. delirium tremens);
(3) casualties (e.g. drinking–driving casualties);
(4) problems of demeanor (e.g. public drunkenness);
(5) default of major social roles (e.g. marital problems);
(6) mental problems (e.g. alcohol-dependence).

Although the phenomenon of 'alcohol problems' has been conceived of in varying ways depending upon the point of view of the analyst, the most prevalent orientation in the modern era has been that of the disease conceptualization of alcoholism (Room, 1977). Jellinek (1952), the early leader in the scientific investigation of problem drinking, conceived of alcoholism as a disease (a pathological addiction of unknown psychological or physical etiology) which progressed in stages, the most crucial of these being the incidence of loss of control, that is the inability of the drinker to abstain from drinking or to cease drinking voluntarily once drinking had begun. In his later work, Jellinek (1960) expanded on his notion that not all excessive drinking could be legitimately labeled a disease, and used alcoholism as a generic term covering various manifestations of harmful drinking (only some of which were considered true diseases). More recent investigations (e.g. Cahalan, 1970; Cahalan and Room, 1974) based on general population studies have challenged the notion that alcohol problems are best conceived of as resulting from some common underlying entity or syndrome such as psychological dependence (Room, 1977). These general population studies suggested that problems associated with alcohol use were relatively independent of each other and that the orderly progression of alcoholic stages suggested by Jellinek did not occur (e.g. Roizen et al., 1978; see also Horn and Wanberg, 1969, 1970; and Rohan, 1976, for similar conclusions based on investigations of clinical samples).

Although the argument is partially semantic as to whether or not some form of excessive drinking is a disease (Keller, 1976), it has grown polemical (Schneider, 1978), and interpretation of this question has led to extensive controversy over appropriate intervention and investigatory strategies (e.g. Beauchamp, 1975, 1976; Brandsma, 1977; De Lint, 1971; De Lint and Schmidt, 1971; Hershon, 1973; Keller, 1976; Larkin, 1979; McKechnie, 1976; Robinson, 1972; Rohan, 1975; Siegler et al., 1968). An apparent reaction against the disease conceptualization of alcoholism is the view that problem drinkers should not be conceived of as pathological in any real sense, but simply as individuals on the extreme end of the drinking continuum. Thus, individuals who experience drinking problems are no different than non-problem drinkers except that they drink more, and hence suffer more drinking-related problems. According to this view 'the essential difference between drinkers is quantitative rather than qualitative' (Rohan, 1975, p. 915). The fact that no discrete cutting points have been found in problem *vs.* non-problem drinking levels (e.g. Cahalan, 1970; De Lint and Schmidt, 1971) or in variables relating to intake or problems (e.g. Donovan and Jessor, 1978) has reinforced this viewpoint. This line of reasoning has led to the suggestion, by some, that the focus of alcohol intervention strategies should be on alcohol control policies rather than on the individual problem drinker (e.g. Beauchamp, 1975; De Lint, 1974, 1978; De Lint and Schmidt, 1971; cf. Addiction Research Foundation, 1978; Vladeck and Weiss, 1975).

The argument over whether alcoholism or problem drinking is best conceived of as a disease (or internal disposition) rather than a response to life circumstances (Rohan, 1975) or the social–cultural environment (De Lint, 1974) is reminiscent of the person–situation controversy so well known in the area of personality and social psychology (e.g. Bowers, 1973; Ekehammar, 1974; Mischel, 1977). Recognizing this, Sadava (1978) and Larkin (1979), among others, have recently argued for a multivariate interactionist position in the study of alcohol use.

The present investigation attempts to examine the nature of the differences among problem drinkers, non-problem drinkers and non-drinkers using a multivariate framework which incorporates person and situation factors. It is argued here that the appropriateness of the qualitative *vs.* quantitative conceptualization of drinkers, although partially a semantic issue, can be examined empirically with appropriate methodology. The relevance of the theoretical framework to be presented will be considered in light of research findings from the area of problem drinking.

Distinguishing Problem Drinkers from Non-problem Drinkers

Investigators attempting to understand problem drinking have extensively compared those classified as alcoholics *vs.* normals, or examined correlations among various measures of alcohol intake (or problem drinking definitions) with a host of attributes in normal populations.

The inconclusiveness of assessment techniques based on clinical groups of alcoholics has been reported by Miller (1976). In his review, Miller concludes that no satisfactory procedure for identifying alcoholics has yet emerged. Results have been particularly divergent in the area concerning the 'alcoholic personality'. Consistent with earlier reviews (e.g. Rosen, 1960; Syme, 1957), Miller found that beyond the fact that identified alcoholics typically score higher on the psychopathic deviance (PD) scale of the MMPI, 'there are virtually no established commonalities, either of alcoholics in general or of alcoholic subtypes' (p. 659). The extent of Miller's pessimism concerning the establishment of an alcoholic personality type by means of traditional psychometric instruments is made clear in his conclusions:

> Rosen suggested in 1960 that the personality differences found in some studies are probably due to sample sources rather than to actual differences between alcoholics and others. Fifteen years of additional research with concurrent personality measures have failed to disconfirm this basic contention. With a present growing uncertainty about the defining criteria of alcoholism . . . it seems doubtful that the next fifteen years will be more fruitful in this regard (pp. 659–660).

In a more recent and exhaustive review of the alcoholic personality literature, Barnes (1979) concluded that in addition to high PD scores (weak ego), other characteristics such as neuroticism and field dependence have been found among alcoholics 'with some degree of consistency'.

Aside from the problems of classification, the paucity of longitudinal investigations makes the etiology of problem drinking even more obscure. As Miller (1976) notes, the common finding of high PD scores among individuals classified as alcoholics may be an artifact (i.e. socially deviant alcoholics may be more readily labeled). Barnes (1979) also notes that those *classified* as alcoholics tend to show the traits mentioned above, while the consistency of traits at the 'pre-alcoholic' stage is much less certain.

Studies concerned with relating various attributes to drinking levels or problem drinking in general populations have been in some ways more successful. In their major study of drinking behavior among university students in England, Orford et al., (1974) reported that most investigations which attempted to examine the causes of drinking behavior were based on cross-sectional surveys of young adults. They noted that three basic categories of individual difference variables were related to drinking: (1) social and cultural factors (race, religion, sex); (2) personality; and (3) social influence. Among social influence variables, Orford et al. report repeated demonstrations of the influence of parental example and friendship group consensus. Among the personality variables investigated they list: alienation, self-esteem, expectations for need satisfaction, anxiety and depression, dependency and sex-role conflict, antisocial symptoms (and behaviors) and personality disorders. Orford et al. concluded:

> This is by no means a comprehensive list of personality concepts which have been used in this area of research but it serves to demonstrate the variety, and arbitrariness, of the concepts chosen . . . with rare exceptions . . . the influence of variables from more than one of these broad areas of investigation has not been examined in the same study (p. 1334).

Consistent with the Sadava and Forsyth (1977) criticisms of research in the area of non-medical drug use in general, alcohol-specific research appears to

suffer from similar defects including: problems of definition, lack of longitudinal investigation, unintegrated univariate approaches, and dependency on
small non-representative samples. The lack of an integrated framework
makes the assessment of the relative importance of various factors particularly problematic. However, a noted exception (cf. Cahalan, 1970; Orford
et al., 1974; Mayer and Filstead, 1979) to the more or less *ad hoc* approach
in this area is the work of Richard Jessor (e.g. Jessor and Jessor, 1977). Jessor
has detailed an integrated social-psychological framework aimed at explaining and predicting problem behavior in general.

Problem-behavior Theory

Jessor first elaborated his theory of problem behavior in a major empirical
study of deviance in a tri-ethnic community (Jessor *et al.*, 1968). Jessor's
definition of deviance was a socially relative one, involving behaviors which
were non-conforming in relation to the 'dominant and pervasive norms' of the
society at large. His theoretical orientation was imbedded in Rotter's (1954)
social learning theory and thus deviant behavior was conceived of as
functional and goal-directed occurring 'when the expectation of its maximizing valued goal attainment or preferred outcomes is higher than that for
conforming behavior' (Jessor *et al.*, 1968, p. 42). According to this view, the
focus of explaining problem behavior should not be on the discovery of new
behavioral principles, but rather on identifying those processes in both the
individual and situation which increase the likelihood of a deviant response.
Jessor *et al.* (1968) proposed these processes would be those that affected:

(a) the learning of deviant or conforming behavior respectively:
(b) the expectations held concerning the outcomes produced by deviant or
    conforming behaviors;
(c) the value placed on these outcomes;
(d) the availability of, or access to, various outcomes.

Essentially, then, deviant behavior can be conceptualized as an attempt to
achieve valued goals which are perceived as unattainable through non-deviant
behavior, or as a method of coping with the failure to achieve such goals.

Jessor *et al.* (1968) presented three (interrelated) major predictor systems
which were relevant to the occurrence of deviance:

(a) the sociocultural system (social norms, accessibility to opportunity struc-
    tures, etc.);
(b) the personality system (beliefs and expectations concerning goal attain-
    ment, etc.);
(c) the socialization system (parental influences).

In a series of studies, combinations of variables within the three major systems were successfully used as concomitant predictors of ethnic and individual differences in deviance rates (e.g. heavy alcohol use, arrests, etc.) among adolescents and adults in the tri-ethnic community.

The variables which enter into this framework are not intended to be rigidly fixed but rather to be flexible, depending upon the aims of a specific study. A revised and extended conceptualization of problem-behavior theory has been detailed for application to adolescent and young adult populations (Jessor and Jessor, 1977). This most recent elaboration of the theory de-emphasizes the role of the socialization system (which is relegated to a category of 'background' factors). Demographic variables from the sociocultural system (e.g. socioeconomic status) have similarly been classified as background variables. More generally the orientation toward relatively objective measures of the opportunity, normative, and control structures of the sociocultural system has shifted to a conceptualization emphasizing the phenomenological or *perceived* environment. The personality system now stresses the values placed on goals, as well as the expectations of obtaining the goals, as direct motivators of deviant or conforming behaviors. These two systems (personality and perceived environment) are seen as relating to a behavior system involving participation in conventional or unconventional (deviant) behaviors. Specifically the reformulation involves three systems.

(1) The Personality System

This reflects those values and beliefs of a person which act as instigations towards or controls against problem behavior. Three subsystems are identified:

(a) the motivational–instigation structure which relates to values and expectations concerning various goals (e.g., value on independence);
(b) the personal belief structure which concerns cognitive controls capable of exerting pressure against deviance (e.g. locus of control);
(c) the personal control structure which deals with personal beliefs which relate more directly to deviant behavior than the above (e.g. attitudinal tolerance of deviance).

(2) The Perceived Environment System

This system is concerned with the perception of social support for, or controls against, deviance. A distinction is made between two structures within the perceived environment:

(a) the distal structure which relates to the general valence and consensus of peer and parental supports and controls (e.g., parental standards for behavior);

(b) the proximal structure which relates directly to the prevalence of, and support for, deviance in the perceived environment (e.g. friends' models for problem behavior).

(3) The Behavior System

This is seen as the explanatory focus of the other two systems. However, it also has predictive capacities, since participation in one structure of the behavior system tends to preclude participation in the other. The two structures are:

(a) the problem-behavior structure which is constituted by those actions 'that are considered by the larger society to be inappropriate or undesirable, to depart from widely shared and institutionalized legal or social norms, and to warrant the exercise of social controls' (Jessor and Jessor, 1977, p. 34; e.g. illegal drug use);
(b) the conventional–behavior structure which relates to socially approved and normatively expected activities (e.g. church attendance).

These systems of explanatory variables have been used with reasonable success in the prediction of various problem behaviors among adolescents and young adults including the onset of drinking (Jessor and Jessor, 1975), marijuana use (Jessor et al., 1973), sexual behavior (Jessor and Jessor, 1975) and problem drinking behavior (Donovan and Jessor, 1978; Jessor and Jessor, 1977). One such study will be discussed in detail below.

Problem–behavior Theory and Problem Drinking

Other evidence exists which suggests the potential utility of a problem-behavior orientation to alcohol abuse. Miller (1976) reported on longitudinal studies which identified adolescent behavior predictive of future problem drinking or alcoholic status (Jones, 1968; McCord, 1972; Robins et al., 1962). Although reserving judgment, Miller suggested that the consistent emergence of socially deviant attitudes and behaviors of preproblem individuals in these studies might point to a legitimate component in the etiology of problem drinking (cf. Gomberg, 1968). This is consistent with the findings of an unpublished longitudinal study by Berry (1967, reported by Smart, 1976) in which it was found that pre-alcoholic boys engaged in aggressive delinquency and tended to have parents who stimulated social deviancy. Also consistent with these findings are those of several cross-sectional studies which continue to report that deviant-type behaviors are associated with alcohol misuse (e.g. Bell and Champion, 1979) and the earlier noted finding that alcoholics tend to score higher on PD.

According to Jessor's formulation, problem drinking should be just one possible manifestation of deviance resulting from predisposing social psychological factors. In fact Donovan and Jessor (1978) have gone so far as to state

> Our findings indicate that problem drinking is part of a syndrome, which suggests that attempts at an alcohol-specific understanding of problem drinking may be parochial and, more serious perhaps, that alcohol-specific prevention efforts may be futile (p. 1521).*

This statement is partially supported by the fact that the same pattern of psychosocial variables account for other problem behaviors such as marijuana use. Earlier work (Jessor and Jessor, 1977, pp. 82–89) showed significant interrelationships among problem behaviors such as marijuana use, problem drinking, and general deviance (e.g. petty theft) for high-school students, although results for a college sample were weak and less consistent.

The most recent application of problem-behavior theory to drinking behavior (Donovan and Jessor, 1978) involved a large-scale national probability sample of adolescents in grades 7 through 12. In that study three different criteria were used for problem drinking, involving different combinations of frequency of drunkenness and negative consequences of drinking. Donovan and Jessor found significant mean differences between nonproblem and problem drinkers across the three criteria on virtually all measures from the three major systems. Various combinations of predictor variables produced multiple regression equations which accounted for about 20–44 percent of the variance on different problem drinking criteria. The perceived environment set showed consistently higher relationships to problem drinking than the personality set. This finding was interpreted in terms of the more direct relationship to behavior of the perceived environment variables as compared to the fairly generalized personality measures. Multiple regressions within ethnic group status demonstrated consistent significant results, although only limited information was presented concerning the pattern of predictor variables in the stepwise multiple regressions.

Most relevant to the concerns of the present study are the conclusions reached regarding the nature of the differences between problem and non-problem drinkers:

> We found no discontinuity, no sharp hiatus, between the psychosocial patterns of problem and non-problem drinkers. No special qualitatively unique explanatory concepts have to be invoked to account for problem drinking. Instead of recourse to pathology or maladjustment or even physiology, the stance that is supported by the data is that a common set of psychosocial dimensions accounts for both problem and non-problem drinking, and that variation on those dimensions characterizes adolescents who engage in one or the other kind of drinking. It is

---

* To avoid confusion it should be noted that the 'syndrome' referred to here is a general behavior syndrome of deviant activities.

worth noting that the same dimensions also discriminate the abstainers from the drinkers. In addition, the abstainers, minimal drinkers, non-problem drinkers and problem drinkers are fully ordered in their degree of proneness to problem behavior, abstainers being least prone and problem drinkers most (p. 1521).

While agreeing that, at a certain level, these variables can account for problem *and* non-problem drinking, it is suggested here that all variables may not have an equal status in relation to the two criteria. It is therefore reasonable to examine whether elements of the variable set are differentially important in 'accounting for' problem *vs.* non-problem drinking. It is the purpose of this investigation to attempt such a determination.

An Empirical Investigation of Problem Drinking

Rationale for Study

Jessor's multivariate predictive system has the advantages of theoretical integration and an empirically demonstrated relationship to problem drinking behavior. Jessor concludes that drinkers can be ordered 'quantitatively' on the basis of a common set of psychosocial dimensions. The notion that drinkers are differentiated quantitatively assumes that those factors which distinguish abstainers from infrequent drinkers also distinguish infrequent drinkers from regular drinkers, and regular drinkers from excessive drinkers, etc. That is, there exists some set of drinking-relevant factors which show an equivalent monotonic relationship to consumption *and* degree of problem status.

Before continuing, it is necessary to comment on the use of the terms 'quantitative' and 'qualitative'. There is little doubt that alcohol consumption rates (and possibly associated problems, Cahalan, 1970) show a relatively smooth distribution in the general population (perhaps log normal, De Lint and Schmidt, 1971). Similarly, predictor variables usually employed (e.g. attitudes towards drinking, attitudes towards deviance, etc.) are probably normally distributed. These variables cannot be conceived of as qualitative in any strict technical sense (i.e. they have ordinal properties and unimodal distributions). Thus, from a purely statistically descriptive viewpoint, drinking behavior may be viewed as quantitative *but* different explanations may relate to drinking at different points on the quantitative continuum so as to suggest discretely different 'populations'. Sadava and Forsyth (1977) in a creative application of canonical analysis present preliminary evidence that drug *use* measures and drug *abuse* measures (separate 'criterion' canonical variates) may relate to somewhat different sets of psychosocial variables ('predictor' canonical variates). Put in the multivariate context of Jessor's framework and its relationship to the ordering of drinker types, one could ask: do the variables from problem-behavior theory combine in *one* linear combination to predict differences across *all* levels of drinking status or might a second (unique) dimension exist which might better differentiate problem drinkers from non-problem drinkers specifically? This hypothetical second dimension could be thought of as a qualitative attribute of problem drinkers in the sense that it would not be consistently associated with levels of alcohol consumption in general. More fundamentally, to the extent that a factor (say some combination of phychosocial variables) measures 'whatever-it-is' that is specific to problem drinkers, it should by definition separate them from both non-problem drinkers and non-drinkers, while not distinguishing the other two groups. In the event that relevant variables which produce such a pattern cannot be found, then no justification exists for claiming that problem drinkers are uniquely different (i.e. qualitatively different) from non-problem drinkers.

In order to investigate the above proposition, it is necessary to define problem drinkers and at least two other groups along the supposed drinking continuum (e.g. moderate drinkers and non-drinkers). One reason that groups are created in the first place is that no one variable (e.g. frequency, quantity, number of reported problems, drinking pattern) seems to capture all possible relevant aspects of 'problem drinking', and so an attempt is made to use multiple criteria to triangulate on the concept. At the same time it should be remembered that the nature of the differences one finds between problem drinkers and others will depend on how one classifies the problem and what comparison groups are used. It is argued here that although exception can be taken to any comparison of drinker groups based on necessarily arbitrary definitions, the *major* aspect of 'problem' drinking as opposed to non-problem drinking is consistent heavy consumption. As has often been said, drinking is the *'sine qua non'* of alcoholism. Thus the behavior pattern most relevant to alcohol problems (in terms of most definitions) is regular 'heavy' drinking. Heavy drinking will be defined here as drinking to the point of intoxication. This definition has the advantage of being relatively straightforward, simple, and demonstrably related to other relevant criteria (e.g. social complications, symptomatic drinking, and risk to physical health).

Intuitively, it would seem (and empirically it can be demonstrated) that those drinkers who are most problem-prone are those who frequently drink to intoxication, as opposed to those who limit their intake to levels below that point. Although it may be that a continuum of drinking styles ranging from abstainers to habitual drunkards exists, one can envisage three *archetypical* groups in terms of alcohol consumption:

(1) non-drinkers—individuals who never, or only very rarely and in small quantities, consume alcohol;

(2) moderate drinkers—individuals who drink regularly but usually limit their consumption to small or moderate amounts (i.e. levels which do not result in intoxication);

(3) excessive drinkers—individuals who drink regularly, and consistently consume enough alcohol to result in intoxication.

This grouping suggests that the interesting question is not what distinguishes those people who drink a little from those who drink a lot, but what distinguishes regular drinkers who consistently appear to exercise 'control' over their intake, from regular drinkers who consistently drink to the point of intoxication (and finally what distinguishes these two groups from those who refrain from alcohol consumption almost completely).

Many definitions, theories, and findings concerning problem drinking promote the idea of control, or loss of control, over drinking, as the most important aspect of the behavior. As indicated previously 'loss of control' was the defining characteristic of alcoholism for Jellinek (1952), and Cahalan and Room (1974) have found that self-report measures of loss of control over drinking (e.g. 'once I start drinking I find it hard to stop') were the best predictors of social complications and other problems due to drinking. By selecting as a comparison group individuals who drink regularly but in moderate amounts, it was hoped that differences relevant to this 'control' aspect might be highlighted.

It is proposed here to examine the differences between non-drinkers (ND), moderate drinkers (MD), and excessive drinkers (ED), in terms of Jessor's problem-behavior theory in order to clarify the nature of the relationship among these groups. Multiple discriminant function analysis (MDFA) is a technique which allows such a multivariate comparison of group differences (Klecka, 1975; Tatsuoka, 1970). As is well known, the examination of multiple univariate differences can result in both statistical and conceptual ambiguity. In order to create a more accurate and integrated picture than that obtained by univariate analysis, MDFA creates a linear combination of predictor variables which maximizes the differences between the groups under study. In the present investigation, however, since only two groups are to be compared or 'discriminated' at one time, multiple regression analyses (Cohen and Cohen, 1975; Kim and Kohout, 1975) will be used in lieu of MDFA. Multiple regression analysis is essentially identical to MDFA in the special case where predictor variables are being related to a dichotomous measure (Tatsuoka, 1971). Thus the beta weight which a predictor variable receives in a regression equation relating to a dichotomous dependent measure indicates the relative ability of that variable to discriminate cases on the basis of the dichotomous classification. Multiple regression techniques are generally more familiar to researches and also routinely provide such useful statistics as adjusted R^2s.

The appropriateness of the qualitative *vs.* quantitative distinction of drinkers will be examined by comparing the multiple regression equations which are obtained when different drinker types are discriminated. For example, if the relationship among ND, MD, and ED is consistently 'quantitative' or monotonic across the variables from problem-behavior theory, it would be expected that essentially the same linear function which maximizes the correlation with a ND–MD dichotomy should be obtained when a MD–ED dichotomy is regressed on the same variable set. Put into more relativistic terms, the dimension which distinguishes ED from MD should highlight those variables which are relevant to problem drinking, whereas the dimension which distinguishes MD from ND should reveal those differences which are related to drinking *per se*. To the extent that these two dimensions are similar, problem drinkers are simply 'quantitatively' different from non-problem drinkers, rather than 'qualitatively' different.

Methodology

Design

This study is part of a prospective longitudinal investigation of non-medical drug use among secondary school students which has been ongoing since 1974. The original purpose of the project was to examine the relationship of attitudinal, social expectancy, perceived social environment, and selected demographic variables to a range of non-medical drug use. In 1974 a stratified (across grades 9, 10, 11, 12) random sample of 1751 male and female students was obtained from 14 secondary schools comprising two Ontario school boards (one urban in orientation, the other more rural and small-town). Self-report measures of social psychological and behavioral variables relevant to non-medical drug use, including Jessor's measures of personality and perceived environment factors (e.g. Jessor *et al.*, 1973), were obtained at various time-intervals over a four-year period. Unpaid student volunteers (with parental consent) participated in the study by filling out questionnaires during school hours. However, at the most recent data point (initiated in February of 1978), all subjects were contacted by mail and paid $5.00 for filling out and returning their questionnaires. In all testing sessions subjects responded anonymously—records were based on a code number which was unique to each subject and included on his/her questionnaire. The present investigation is confined to cross-sectional analyses of the responses of male subjects from the last data point ($n = 494$; age range 18–22).

Criterion Groups

Subjects were divided into three groups on the basis of their answers to questions concerning their usual frequency and quantity of use of any type of beverage alcohol. 'Non-drinkers' (ND) consisted of those who were abstainers or who drank alcoholic beverages *less* than once a month and consumed no more than two drinks per drinking occasion. 'Moderate drinkers' (MD) were those who drank regularly—at least once a week, but usually consumed only from one to three drinks per session. 'Excessive drinkers' (ED) were defined as those who drank regularly—at least once a week, and who usually consumed *a minimum* of eight or nine drinks per occasion. A drink was defined as: a 12-ounce bottle of beer (or equivalent), a 4-ounce glass of wine, or a 'shot' ($1\frac{1}{2}$ ounces) of liquor (whiskey, gin, vodka, etc.).

The cut-off chosen for 'excessive drinkers' was selected since:

(a) it is consistent with an estimated blood alcohol level well above that considered 'legally impaired' in most jurisdictions;
(b) it represents an intake approaching that considered to be indicative of a significant risk to health (Fisher, 1975).

The cut-off for 'moderate drinkers' results in an intake usually below that producing 'legal impairment' in most individuals and obviously a relatively lower risk to health. For the three groups in the rural (urban) samples, numbers are: ND—17 (14), MD—37 (44), ED—50 (55).

Although these groups are selected to reflect 'pure' and thus extreme types, one should be concerned with the ecological validity of such groupings. One problem with the study of young adult males (the most highly represented group for problem drinking behavior) is that abstainers are rare. In Jessor's (Jessor and Jessor, 1977) analysis of college data the number of abstainers was so small they had to be combined with non-problem drinkers for analysis. In the two samples available for the present investigation only 10 (rural sample) and 11 (urban sample) subjects indicated that they did not drink. These numbers were augmented to 17 and 14 by including individuals who reported drinking no more than two drinks at infrequent intervals (i.e. less than once a month). Although these samples represent rather small percentages (approximately 6.2 percent of male respondents), the relevance of this category for comparison purposes justifies its inclusion. Moderate drinkers comprise 14.9 and 18 percent of the samples respectively, while excessive drinkers represent 20.5 and 23.3 percent of respondents respectively. Thus substantial minorities are included under the rubric of moderate and excessive drinkers. The total sample included individuals still studying (mostly at university) and those working full time. Non-drinkers were much less likely to be working full time (6.5 percent) than were moderate drinkers (37 percent) or excessive drinkers (39 percent). The mean ages of the groups were 20.5, 20.6 and 20.3 years for ND, MD and ED respectively.

Predictor Variables

The following problem behavior variables were accessed for analysis:

Personality system variables

(1) value on achievement (rating of importance of achieving success at school or in the work place)
(2) value on independence (rating of importance of independent thought or action)
(3) expectations for achievement (subjective probability of achieving success)
(4) expectations for independence (subjective probability of achieving independence)
(5) fatalism scale (internal–external locus of control; Schlegel and Crawford, 1978)
(6) attitudinal tolerence of deviance (rating of 'how wrong' various transgressions such as lying and stealing are)
(7) self-rated religiosity
(8) functions of drinking (reasons for, minus reasons for not, drinking).

Perceived environment system variables
(a) Distal variables

(1) parental support (emotional support offered by parents)
(2) parental controls (strictness of parents)
(3) parental expectations (importance of subject's success to parents)
(4) peer support
(5) peer controls
(6) peer expectations
(7) parent–peer agreement (*re* expectations for subject)
(8) peer influence (relative importance of peer *vs.* parental opinions)
(9) accord with mother (subject's rating of how well he gets along with his mother)
(10) accord with father

(b) Proximal variables

(11) friends' attitudes towards drinking
(12) friends' approval of (subject's) weekly drinking
(13) friends' approval of (subject's) daily drinking
(14) friends' approval of (subject's) getting drunk
(15) friends' pressures (encouragement) to drink
(16) friends' attitude toward marijuana use
(17) friends' pressures for marijuana use

(18) adults' attitudes towards drinking
(19) adults' approval of (subject's) weekly drinking
(20) adults' approval of (subject's) daily drinking
(21) adults' approval of (subject's) getting drunk
(22) adults' pressures for drinking
(23) mother's drinking behavior (7-point scale; does not drink, to drinks much more than average)
(24) father's drinking bahavior
(25) parental drunkenness (frequency of observing parents under the influence of alcohol).

Behavior system variables

(1) frequency of marijuana use
(2) frequency of hallucinogen use
(3) frequency of church attendance
(4) academic achievement in high school.

All data are based on subjects' self-reports. 'Friends' were defined as the subject's two best friends. 'Adults' were defined as individuals over 30 years old whose evaluations of the subject were considered important to the subject. Note that the perceived environment system contains both distal variables (e.g. parental controls) and a range of proximal variables which relate to normative beliefs and models across a range of drinking levels (e.g. weekly drinking, getting drunk, etc.).

Multivariate Strategy*

To validate multivariate results requires an independent replication, with multiple regressions performed on the rural and urban samples separately. Given that the data set consists of variables which are moderately intercorre-

---

* A major concern of multivariate investigations is the danger of multicollinearity which can produce severe problems of interpretation (e.g., Darlington, 1968; Wainer, 1976). In the present situation multicollinearity is high, particularly among the variables of the perceived environment set. Further, the necessity of validation analyses results in small sample sizes and therefore less stability. Although combining variables into factors will improve the stability of the predictors and reduce multicollinearity (increasing the chances for successful replication or cross-validation), this results in a loss of detail, especially in the present analysis where variables which discriminate differentially between two different sets of groups are sought to be identified. For example, although generally friends' attitudes about a range of drinking behaviors (e.g. approval of weekly drinking, approval of getting drunk) cluster together, combining these would eliminate any differential predictiveness which might be expected from normative beliefs concerning moderate *vs.* abusive use of alcohol as they relate to differences among the three groups. Secondly, although some variables are related empirically, they may be conceptually distinct and of interest in their own right. For these reasons it was decided to examine a subset of the initial variables rather than attempting to combine them into factors.

lated and sample sizes are relatively small, instability and suppression effects are probably to be expected. A conservative approach to model testing is thus required. Since suppression effects are often uninterpretable anyway, only variables which significantly differentiated groups at the univariate level were included in the analyses. Further, to ensure findings of some generalizability and replicability, only variables which showed such significance in each sample were included. Specifically, variables were selected within each system if they significantly related to group status (either ND *vs.* MD or MD *vs.* ED) at the $p<0.1$ level for *both* urban and rural samples. Variables thus selected were used in a stepwise multiple regression on each sample, within each system, to determine the similarity (replicability) of the models obtained for distinguishing between ND and MD *vs.* MD and ED.

The suggested strategy, then, was to select variables for analyses which demonstrated reliably significant differences at the univariate level across both samples— rural and urban. This approach ignores sample uniqueness or instability resulting in a more conservative but general model.

Results

Univariate Analyses

Before proceeding with the multivariate analysis described above, it is instructive to examine the relationship of the predictor variables to the two criteria (i.e. ND–MD dichotomy, and MD–ED dichotomy) at the univariate level. The most general and straightforward way of doing this is to examine the simple correlations obtained for both the rural and urban samples combined. These results are presented in Table 9.1. All variables were scored in a positive direction and drinker groups were dummy-coded 1, 2, and 3 for ND, MD, and ED respectively. Thus, positive correlations with the ND–MD dichotomy indicate that the particular attribute is more strongly represented among MD. Positive correlations with the MD–ED dichotomy are indicative of a higher mean value on the variable for ED. As was explained above, these correlations may be thought of in the following manner—the greater the absolute value of the correlation, the better the ability of that predictor variable to distinguish the two groups comprising the dichotomy.

Examination of the univariate findings reveals the following general patterns. The personality variables appear slightly better able to distinguish between MD and ED than ND and MD, although in the case of none of these variables is the correlation with the MD–ED dichotomy significantly greater than that with the ND–MD dichotomy. Perceived environment variables show the opposite tendency, being more likely to reliably differentiate ND from MD than MD from ED. Several variables from this set, including every proximal variable, distinguish ND from MD at highly significant levels while

Table 9.1 Correlations of predictor variables with drinker status dichotomies (combined sample)

	ND *vs*. MD ($n = 112$)	MD *vs*. ED ($n = 186$)
Personality system		
Value on achievement	−0.18*	0.06
Value on independence	0.12	0.10
Expectations for achievement	−0.12	0.09
Expectations for independence	0.07	0.18†
Fatalism	0.21†	0.32§
Tolerance of deviance	0.15	0.25‡
Religiosity	−0.20†	−0.22‡
Drinking functions	0.40§	0.46§
Perceived environment system		
Parental expectations	−0.01	0.04
Peer expectations	−0.03	−0.09
Parental support	−0.07	−0.12*
Peer support	−0.03	−0.09
Parental control	−0.18*	0.03
Peer control	−0.26‡	−0.10
Parental–peer agreement	−0.17*	−0.06
Peer influence	0.10	0.02
Mother's drinking behavior	0.18*	0.04
Father's drinking behavior	0.24†	0.08
Parental drunkenness	0.30‡	0.10
Accord with mother	−0.13	0.05
Accord with father	−0.06	−0.07
Friends' attitudes toward marijuana use	0.50§	0.25‡
Friends' pressures for marijuana use	0.35§	0.21‡
Friends' attitudes toward drinking	0.50§	0.18†
Friends' approval of weekly drinking	0.54§	0.16†
Friends' approval of daily drinking	0.36§	0.10
Friends' approval of getting drunk	0.30§	0.25‡
Friends' pressures for drinking	0.43§	0.11
Adults' attitudes toward drinking	0.33‡	0.14*
Adults' approval of weekly drinking	0.52§	0.02
Adults' approval of daily drinking	0.30‡	−0.05
Adults' approval of getting drunk	0.25‡	0.22‡
Adults' pressures for drinking	0.39§	−0.07
Behavior system		
Marijuana use	0.31‡	0.38§
Hallucinogen use	0.11	0.19‡
Church attendance	−0.50§	−0.15†
Academic achievement	−0.23†	−0.32§

* $p < 0.1$; † $p < 0.05$; ‡ $p < 0.01$; § $p < 0.001$.

Table 9.2 Correlations of selected predictor variables with drinker status dichotomies (rural and urban samples)

	ND vs. MD		MD vs. ED	
	Rural ($n = 54$)	Urban ($n = 58$)	Rural ($n = 87$)	Urban ($n = 99$)
Personality system				
Fatalism	0.20	0.23*	0.29‡	0.34‡
Tolerance of deviance	0.20	0.11	0.28‡	0.22†
Drinking functions	0.48§	0.32†	0.51§	0.42§
Perceived environment system				
Parental drunkenness	0.36‡	0.23*	0.11	0.08
Friends' attitudes toward marijuana use	0.44‡	0.55§	0.23†	0.28‡
Friends' attitudes toward drinking	0.48§	0.52§	0.25†	0.13
Friends' approval of weekly drinking	0.60§	0.48§	0.18*	0.15
Friends' approval of daily drinking	0.50§	0.25*	0.10	0.09
Friends' approval of getting drunk	0.33†	0.27†	0.30‡	0.22†
Friends' pressures for drinking	0.42‡	0.44‡	0.16	0.07
Adults' approval of weekly drinking	0.70§	0.36‡	-0.19*	0.17*
Adults' approval of getting drunk	0.33†	0.16	0.19*	0.25†
Adults' pressures for drinking	0.34†	0.41‡	0.05	-0.18*
Behavior system				
Marijuana use	0.28†	0.32†	0.35‡	0.42§
Hallucinogen use	0.10	0.13	0.22†	0.18*
Church attendance	-0.44‡	-0.57§	-0.14	-0.18*
Academic achievement	-0.35‡	0.09	-0.27†	-0.36§

* $p < 0.1$; † $p < 0.05$; ‡ $p < 0.01$; § $p < 0.001$.

only four variables reach correlations above 0.20 for the MD–ED comparison. It is also interesting to note that among the highest correlations (although still relatively small) with the MD–ED dichotomy are friends' and adults' approval of getting drunk (abusive drinking), whereas the two highest correlations with the ND–MD dichotomy involve friends' and adults' approval of weekly drinking (a relatively moderate drinking level). Parental drinking behavior and drunkenness differentiate ND from MD but not MD from ED. The distal variables (e.g. parental expectations) generally provide little discrimination for either comparison.

Table 9.2 compares the univariate findings in both samples for those variables which showed significant differences with either group dichotomy in each sample. These results are consistent with those presented in Table 9.1, except that several variables significant in the overall sample did not reach the $p < 0.1$ level in each individual sample and so are not represented here. The result is a smaller, and hopefully more reliable, set of predictor variables. Multivariate analyses were based on these variables.

Multivariate Analyses

Because of space considerations multiple regression analyses of the three predictor systems within both urban and rural samples are presented in Appendix A, and analyses of the overall sample (rural and urban combined) are presented in the text. The extent of replicability will be described, although detailed examination of the specific sample findings is left to the reader. The tables to be presented, illustrating the results of stepwise regressions, list variables according to the order in which they were selected and indicate the cumulative multiple correlation at that step. The next column contains the cumulative adjusted R^2. Adjusted R^2 is a more conservative and realistic estimate of the proportion of variance explained in the population since it takes into consideration sample specific error (see Cohen and Cohen, 1975, p. 106). The beta weights given in the tables are based on the equation generated with all variables listed included in the calculation. The F ratios and p values in the last column pertain to these beta weights.

Table 9.3 presents the results of the stepwise multiple regression of the personality system variables selected on the basis of the procedure described previously. (The personality variables appear to replicate well across samples). In the case of the MD–ED correlations all variables, fatalism, tolerance of deviance, and drinking functions receive a significant weight, whereas in the case of the ND–MD dichotomy only drinking functions receive a significant weight. The increment in explained variance provided by the addition of fatalism and tolerance of deviance (calculated on the basis of change in adjusted R^2) is a negligible 0.3 percent in the case of the ND–MD

Table 9.3 Summary tables of stepwise multiple regressions (MR) of drinker status on personality variables

Variables	Cumulative MR	Cumulative adjusted R^2	Simple R	Beta	F
ND vs. MD ($n = 104$)					
Drinking functions	0.41	0.16	0.41	0.38	16.3‡
Fatalism	0.43	0.17	0.20	0.14	2.2
Tolerance of deviance	0.44	0.17	0.13	0.04	<1
MD vs. ED ($n = 174$)					
Drinking functions	0.46	0.21	0.46	0.35	24.9‡
Fatalism	0.51	0.25	0.34	0.23	10.9†
Tolerance of deviance	0.53	0.27	0.25	0.15	5.0*

* $p < 0.05$; † $p < 0.01$; ‡ $p < 0.001$.

Table 9.4 Summary tables of stepwise multiple regressions (MR) of drinker status on reasons for drinking factors

Variables	Cumulative MR	Cumulative adjusted R^2	Simple R	Beta	F
ND vs. MD ($n = 112$)					
Celebration	0.44	0.18	0.44	0.49	21.5‡
Coping	0.45	0.19	0.13	−0.14	1.9
Conformity	0.45	0.18	0.21	0.04	<1
MD vs. ED ($n = 186$)					
Celebration	0.44	0.19	0.44	0.29	15.3‡
Coping	0.51	0.25	0.43	0.28	14.2‡
Conformity	0.51	0.25	0.27	0.05	<1

‡ $p < 0.001$.

discrimination while it is a significant 5.7 percent in these case of the MD–ED dichotomy.

The drinking functions variable, which is obviously the most important predictor for both criteria, is composed of a rating of the importance of reasons for drinking, minus the rated importance of reasons for not drinking. Reasons for drinking have been investigated in some detail in terms of their relationship to problem drinking. Mulford and Miller (1960) attempted to scale the 'social meanings' or 'definitions' individuals give to drinking on a cumulative (Guttman-like) basis. The 'scale' they developed successfully distinguished drinkers from non-drinkers. When the scale was dichotomized as personal-effects definitions (e.g. liquor helps me feel more satisfied with myself) vs. social-effects (e.g. liquor goes well with entertainment) it was found that those who defined alcohol for its personal effects tended to be heavier drinkers than those who defined alcohol on the basis of social effects. Cahalan and Cisin (1968) concluded that 'escape' drinking (drinking to avoid problems, e.g. drinking helps me forget my worries) could help explain some of the variations in heavy drinking. The 'reasons for drinking' rated in the present data set cover a range of personal and social 'effects'. Non-drinkers were asked to rate the importance of these reasons for 'beginning to drink'.

The above literature, plus factor analyses of the present data, suggested three factors which might be examined:

(1) coping reasons (e.g. drinking helps me forget I'm not the person I would like to be; drinking helps me to get over the changes in my life);
(2) celebration reasons (e.g. drinking is just a good feeling at a party; drinking is a good way to celebrate);
(3) conformity reasons (e.g. drinking because I'm expected to drink; drinking to be part of the group).

Multiple regression analyses using these three factors are reported in Table 9.4. The results indicate that, for distinguishing MD from ED, celebration reasons and coping reasons are both significant and equally important. However, coping reasons play no significant role in distinguishing ND from MD. Correlations of drinker status with the conformity factor, although always higher for the MD–ED dichotomy, are similarly and negligibly weighted in the multiple regression equation for both criteria. (Again the findings here demonstrated good cross-sample replication.)

Several variables from the perceived environment set were eligible for analyses and in an effort to reduce multicollinearity stepwise multiple regressions were carried out with a cut-off point set at $p=0.1$. Thus variables were included in the regression only if they added significantly to the variance already explained by the equation at that step. Even under these conditions, however, inconsistencies and suppression effects still emerged in the separate analyses on the urban and rural samples (see Table 9A3). The results appeared rather idiosyncratic to each sample, although one consistency was evident. As was indicated in the univariate findings, the ability of the proximal environment variables to distinguish MD from ED is relatively modest with adjusted R^2s of 0.18 and 0.17. This compares with adjusted R^2s for the ND–MD dichotomy of 0.56 and 0.42. In order to compare models generated for each criterion more directly a multiple regression was run on the combined sample based on those variables from the perceived environment system which entered significantly in any one of the subsample analyses. Table 9.5 presents the results of this comparison. The most salient feature is the reversal in positions of friends' and adults' approval of getting drunk and friends' and adults' approval of weekly drinking. For the ND–MD discrimination, normative beliefs concerning getting drunk are the least important predictors and receive negligible weights in the overall equation. The two most important variables (in terms of order of selection) for this distinction are friends' approval of weekly drinking and friends' attitudes toward marijuana use. Except for friends' attitudes towards marijuana use, the situation is reversed for the MD–ED dichotomy. Adults' and friends' approval of weekly drinking enter the equation last and receive negligible weights, while friends' and adults' approval of getting drunk are among the most highly weighted variables.

Regression analyses of the behavior system variables are presented in Table 9.6. which illustrates the pronounced difference in the discriminating power of the variable church attendance depending upon the criterion. Church attendance is a strong predictor of ND–MD status but a trivial predictor of MD–ED status. Marijuana use, although receiving a significant weight in both equations, appears slightly more relevant to the MD–ED dichotomy than the ND–MD distinction. Academic achievement relates to the criteria in a sample-specific fashion as is indicated by the univariate correlations in Table 9.2. Hallucinogen use, while relating to the MD–ED dichotomy significantly at the univariate level, receives little weight when entered into the multiple regression along with the other variables. (Except for the relationship of academic achievement to ND–MD status, the variables from the behavior system replicate well across samples.)

Discussion

The results demonstrate the utility of problem-behavior theory for prediction of both problem and non-problem drinking status. Variables from all three systems significantly correlate with both criteria, with multiple correlations within systems ranging from 0.40 to 0.68. Most notably, however, the findings support the notion that the predictor variables from Jessor's problem-behavior theory differentially discriminate problem and non-problem drinkers. Personality system variables more readily distinguish problem drinkers

Table 9.5 Summary tables of stepwise multiple regressions (MR) of drinker status on perceived environment variables

Variables	Cumulative MR	Cumulative adjusted R^2	Simple R	Beta	F
ND *vs.* MD ($n = 108$)					
Friends' approval of weekly drinking	0.53	0.28	0.53	0.17	1.7
Friends' attitudes toward marijuana use	0.62	0.38	0.49	0.30	13.6‡
Adults' pressures for drinking	0.66	0.42	0.39	0.15	3.0*
Adults' approval of weekly drinking	0.67	0.43	0.52	0.16	2.4
Friends' attitudes toward drinking	0.68	0.44	0.49	0.16	2.0
Adults' approval of getting drunk	0.68	0.43	0.25	0.02	<1
Friends' approval of getting drunk	0.68	0.43	0.31	0.00	<1
MD *vs.* ED ($n = 179$)					
Friends' attitudes toward marijuana use	0.25	0.06	0.25	0.19	7.2†
Friends' approval of getting drunk	0.33	0.10	0.25	0.14	3.6*
Friends' attitudes toward drinking	0.35	0.11	0.19	0.12	2.1
Adults' approval of getting drunk	0.37	0.12	0.21	0.15	3.8*
Adults' pressures for drinking	0.39	0.13	−0.08	−0.13	2.8*
Friends' approval of weekly drinking	0.40	0.13	0.17	0.07	<1
Adults' approval of weekly drinking	0.40	0.12	0.03	−0.04	<1

* $p < 0.1$; † $p < 0.05$; ‡ $p < 0.001$.

Table 9.6 Summary tables of stepwise multiple regressions of drinking status on behavior variables

Variables	Cumulative MR	Cumulative adjusted R^2	Simple R	Beta	F
ND vs. MD ($n = 109$)					
Church attendance	0.50	0.24	−0.50	−0.44	27.0‡
Marijuana use	0.53	0.27	0.31	0.23	4.6*
Academic achievement	0.55	0.28	−0.23	−0.11	1.5
Hallucinogen use	0.55	0.28	0.12	−0.09	<1
MD vs. ED ($n = 181$)					
Marijuana use	0.39	0.15	0.39	0.35	17.7‡
Academic achievement	0.46	0.20	−0.32	−0.23	11.0†
Hallucinogen use	0.46	0.20	0.19	−0.05	<1
Church attendance	0.46	0.19	−0.15	−0.03	<1

* $p < 0.05$; † $p < 0.01$; ‡ $p < 0.001$.

Table 9.7 Adjusted R^2 for personality system models *vs.* perceived environment system models with drinking status dichotomies

	Rural sample		Urban sample	
	ND–MD ($n = 54$)	MD–ED ($n = 87$)	ND–MD ($n = 58$)	MD–ED ($n = 99$)*
Personality system model	0.21	0.28	0.13	0.24
Perceived environment system model	0.56	0.18	0.42	0.17

* Total ns before exclusion due to missing data.

from non-problem drinkers, while the perceived environment variables are more relevant to a drinker–non-drinker distinction. These findings are replicated across both samples, as is illustrated in Table 9.7, which presents the proportions of variance explained for both systems on each criterion. Most striking is the relatively weak correlations of the perceived environment variables with the MD–ED dichotomy. The perceived attitudes of friends and significant adults, concerning various drinking practices, are only slightly more positive for excessive drinkers than moderate drinkers. Further, although parental and peer controls and parental models for drinking significantly distinguish ND from MD, none of these factors differentiate MD from ED. This suggests that the social environment relevant to drinking practices for ND is quite different from that of both MD and ED, each of which share a similar set of perceived normative beliefs.

What then are the factors which are most likely to discriminate MD from ED? Although fatalism and tolerance of deviance are more strongly correlated with the MD–ED dichotomy, these correlations are not very much larger than those with the ND–MD criterion at the univariate level. The most outstanding difference within the personality system concerns the endorsement of coping reasons for drinking by ED. Moderate drinkers are no more likely to rate coping functions for alcohol as important to drinking than are ND. It would appear that among this age-group, where there are relatively permissive norms concerning drinking (MD report getting drunk 6.7 times per year on average; ED 56.4 times), the perceived role of alcohol for the individual is an important determinant of problem status. However, both celebration and conformity reasons significantly discriminate MD from ED. Thus ED are more likely to rate any reason for drinking as more important than are MD. This holds true for differences between ND and MD, except in the case of coping reasons. Therefore, drinking functions generally differentiate drinker types in a quantitative way, but the endorsement of coping functions appears to be a unique aspect of ED.

It may be that educational attempts which are aimed at teaching individuals to distinguish between positive, social functions of drinking, and potentially problem-linked coping uses of drinking, are desirable. Those who favor the single distribution model of alcohol consumption suggest that teaching 'responsible drinking' may result in a greater frequency of drinking and thus more problems (Smart, 1979). However, Smart (1979) has cautioned that since frequency of drinking explains a small amount of the variance on problem drinking, and since correlations among various kinds of drinking problems are not great, 'it is probably too early to give up on approaches to prevention that involve sensible drinking and do not contribute to increasing the level of consumption' (p. 240). The fact that problem drinkers are more likely to rate any reasons for drinking as more important than MD suggests that one must be wary of increasing consumption when attempting to promote a 'positive' approach to alcohol use. It must also be remembered that positive, socially integrated drinking, although less likely to lead to certain social or psychological problems, can still produce medical complications if pursued too vigorously. It is often said that the Italian culture shows a positive attitude toward moderate drinking and disapproval of drunkenness, but at the same time constant 'moderate' drinking has led to a national cirrhosis rate indicative of a significant alcohol problem (De Lint and Schmidt, 1971; see also Chapter 10).

The perceived environment variables did not replicate well across samples—probably because of their number and degree of intercorrelation. Nevertheless, consistent with the univariate pattern (and common sense) variables relevant to drunkenness were relatively more important in the MD–ED comparisons, whereas variables concerning weekly drinking most strongly differentiated ND from MD. It is important to remember, however, that all proximal perceived environment variables showed a stronger correlation with the ND–MD dichotomy, and even variables which seem directly related to the MD–ED discrimination (e.g. friends' approval of getting drunk) are relatively weak predictors of MD vs. ED status. Even so, to the extent that these perceived norms do discriminate problem drinkers from MD, it makes sense to focus on changing attitudes regarding heavy drinking and drunkenness rather than drinking per se. This is particularly true given the prevalence of drinking among this age-group and the relative improbability of abstinence.

Concerning the behavior variables, church attendance clearly has a differential relationship to each criterion, showing strong correlations with the ND–MD categorization in both samples, and trivial levels of correlation with the MD–ED category. In this aspect ND are uniquely different. The other variables in this system seem more able to discriminate MD from ED, although the degree of difference is not great and in the case of academic achievement the findings are inconsistent across samples.

Overall the data indicate both 'qualitative' and 'quantitative'differences between drinker types. There is some indication of general problem-proneness among ED, in terms of higher levels of tolerance for deviance, fatalism, marijuana and hallucinogen use. However, ED do not differ from MD in terms of their values or expectations for achievement and independence, and report getting along with their parents as well as MD do. There is little suggestion of a general rejection of societal values or an overriding non-conformist stance. It seems more likely that excessive alcohol use for this age-group represents a generalized learned response to a variety of situational and psychological demands. It would seem reasonable, particularly in a treatment situation, that attempts be made to assess personal efficacy in order to ensure that useful substitute behaviors are available to an individual who has learned to use alcohol for coping purposes. This could broaden and perhaps strengthen a more 'alcohol-specific' approach.

Finally, the limitatuions of the data must be recognized. The sample, being composed of individuals still participating in the fifth year of a longitudinal study, cannot be considered representative of any well-defined population. Indications are that the sample is overrepresented by those who are less extreme in their use of drugs and perhaps generally more conventional. Only cross-sectional data have been presented, and so strong statements regarding causal relationships are precluded. Longitudinal analyses, and analyses of female data, currently under way, will hopefully refine and extend the findings of the present investigation.

Appendix 9A: Summary Tables of Stepwise Multiple Regressions for Individual Samples

Table 9A.1 Summary tables of stepwise multiple regressions (MR) of drinker status on personality variables

Variables	MR	Adjusted R^2	Simple R	Beta	F
ND *vs.* MD (rural sample; $n = 50$)					
Drinking functions	0.48	0.21	0.48	0.45	10.6‡
Fatalism	0.48	0.20	0.16	0.07	<1
Tolerance of deviance	0.48	0.18	0.17	0.05	<1
ND *vs.* MD (urban sample; $n = 54$)					
Drinking functions	0.35	0.11	0.35	0.32	5.6†
Fatalism	0.40	0.13	0.24	0.20	2.3
Tolerance of deviance	0.40	0.11	0.11	0.02	<1
MD *vs.* ED (rural sample; $n = 80$)					
Drinking functions	0.52	0.26	0.52	0.42	15.1§
Fatalism	0.54	0.28	0.33	0.18	3.1*
Tolerance of deviance	0.55	0.28	0.28	0.12	1.4
MD *vs.* ED (urban sample; $n = 94$)					
Drinking functions	0.42	0.16	0.42	0.31	10.3‡
Fatalism	0.48	0.22	0.36	0.26	7.8‡
Tolerance of deviance	0.51	0.24	0.23	0.18	3.7*

* $p < 0.1$; † $p < 0.05$; ‡ $p < 0.01$; § $p < 0.001$.

Table 9A.2 Summary tables of stepwise multiple regressions (MR) of drinker status on reasons for drinking factors

Variables	MR	Adjusted R^2	Simple R	Beta	F
ND vs. MD (rural sample; $n = 54$)					
Celebration	0.49	0.22	0.49	0.51	12.7§
Coping	0.49	0.21	0.22	−0.04	<1
Conformity	0.49	0.21	0.22	0.00	<1
ND vs. MD (urban sample; $n = 58$)					
Celebration	0.37	0.12	0.37	0.46	8.8‡
Coping	0.42	0.14	0.03	−0.22	2.3
Conformity	0.42	0.13	0.20	0.05	<1
MD vs. ED (rural sample; $n = 87$)					
Celebration	0.49	0.23	0.49	0.34	9.8‡
Coping	0.54	0.28	0.46	0.27	5.3†
Conformity	0.54	0.27	0.30	0.01	<1
MD vs. ED (urban sample; $n = 99$)					
Celebration	0.41	0.16	0.41	0.29	8.7‡
Coping	0.48	0.22	0.40	0.24	5.3†
Conformity	0.49	0.22	0.25	0.09	<1

† $p < 0.05$; ‡ $p < 0.01$; § $p < 0.001$.

Table 9A.3 Summary tables of stepwise multiple regressions (MR) of drinker status on perceived environment variables

Variables	MR	Adjusted R^2	Simple R	Beta	F
ND vs. MD (rural sample; $n = 52$)					
Adults' approval of weekly drinking	0.69	0.47	0.69	0.47	16.9§
Friends' attitudes toward marijuana use	0.73	0.52	0.43	0.23	5.5†
Friends' approval of weekly drinking	0.76	0.56	0.59	0.26	5.5†
ND vs. MD (urban sample; $n = 55$)					
Friends' attitudes toward marijuana use	0.54	0.28	0.54	0.35	8.9‡
Friends' attitudes toward drinking	0.64	0.39	0.54	0.32	7.1†
Adults' pressures for drinking	0.67	0.42	0.43	0.21	3.5*
MD vs. ED (rural sample; $n = 83$)					
Friends' approval of getting drunk	0.30	0.08	0.30	0.24	5.0†
Friends' attitudes toward drinking	0.37	0.11	0.24	0.25	5.9†
Adults' approval of weekly drinking	0.42	0.15	-0.17	-0.29	7.3‡
Adults' approval of getting drunk	0.47	0.18	0.19	0.22	4.1†
MD vs. ED (urban sample; $n = 94$)					
Friends' attitudes toward marijuana use	0.27	0.06	0.27	0.23	5.9†
Adults' approval of getting drunk	0.34	0.09	0.23	0.21	4.5†
Adults' pressures for drinking	0.41	0.14	-0.19	-0.32	9.3‡
Adults' approval of weekly drinking	0.46	0.17	0.17	0.23	5.0†

* $p < 0.1$; † $p < 0.05$; ‡ $p < 0.01$; § $p < 0.001$.

Table 9A.4 Summary tables of stepwise multiple regressions of drinking status on behavior variables

Variables	MR	Adjusted R^2	Simple R	Beta	F
ND *vs.* MD (rural sample; $n = 52$)					
Church attendance	0.43	0.17	−0.43	−0.35	6.8†
Academic achievement	0.49	0.21	−0.36	−0.17	1.3
Marijuana use	0.50	0.20	0.28	0.16	<1
Hallucinogen use	0.50	0.19	0.10	−0.06	<1
ND *vs.* MD (urban sample; $n = 57$)					
Church attendance	0.57	0.31	−0.57	−0.53	21.7§
Marijuana use	0.60	0.33	0.32	0.26	3.2*
Academic achievement	0.60	0.33	−0.09	−0.10	<1
Hallucinogen use	0.61	0.33	0.13	−0.12	<1
MD *vs.* ED (rural sample; $n = 85$)					
Marijuana use	0.38	0.14	0.38	0.31	6.1†
Academic achievement	0.42	0.16	−0.29	−0.17	2.3
Church attendance	0.42	0.15	−0.15	−0.05	<1
Hallucinogen use	0.42	0.14	0.22	0.02	<1
MD *vs.* ED (urban sample; $n = 96$)					
Marijuana use	0.42	0.16	0.42	0.41	12.3§
Academic achievement	0.49	0.23	−0.36	−0.27	8.4‡
Hallucinogen use	0.50	0.23	0.18	−0.11	<1
Church attendance	0.50	0.22	−0.17	−0.04	<1

* $p < 0.1$; † $p < 0.05$; ‡ $p < 0.01$; § $p < 0.001$.

References

Addiction Research Foundation of Ontario (1978). 'A strategy for the prevention of alcohol problems'. *The Journal*, **7** (7): Special supplement.

Barnes, G. E. (1979). 'The alcoholic personality; a reanalysis of the literature, *Journal of Studies on Alcohol*, **40,** 571–634.

Beauchamp, D. (1975). 'Public health: alien ethic in a strange land?' *American Journal of Public Health*, **65,** 138–139.

Beauchamp, D. (1976). 'Alcoholism as blaming the alcoholic', *International Journal of the Addictions*, **11,** (1), 41–52.

Bell, D. S., and Champion, R. A. (1979). 'Deviancy, delinquency and drug use', *British Journal of Psychiatry*, **134,** 269–276.

Berry, J. C. (1976). 'Antecedents of schizophrenia, impulsive character and alcoholism in males'. Ph.D. thesis Columbia University, 1967. Cited by R. G. Smart, *The new drinkers*. Addiction Research Foundation of Ontario, Toronto, Canada.

Bowers, K. S. (1973). 'Situationism in psychology: an analysis and a critique', *Psychological Review*, **80,** (5), 307–336.

Brandsma, J. M. (1977). 'Alcoholismic dysbehaviourism revisited: a reply to Keller', *Journal of Studies on Alcohol*, **38,** 1838–1842.

Cahalan, D. (1970). *Problem Drinkers: a National Survey*. Jossey-Bass, San Francisco.

Cahalan, D., and Cisin, I. H. (1978). 'American drinking practices: summary of findings from a national probability sample; 1. Extent of drinking by population subgroups', *Quarterly Journal of Studies on Alcohol*, **29,** 130–151.

Cahalan, D., and Room, R. (1974), *Problem Drinking Among American Men*. College and University Press. New Haven, Conn.

Cohen, J., and Cohen, P. (1975), *Applied Multiple Regression/Correlation Analysis for the Behavioral Sciences*. Lawrence Erlbaum Associates, Hillsdale, New Jersey.

Darlington, R. B. (1968). 'Multiple regression in psychology research and practice', *Psychological Bulletin*, **69,** 161–182.

De Lint, J. (1971). 'The status of alcoholism as a disease: a brief comment', *British Journal of Addiction*, **66,** 108–109.

De Lint, J. (1974). 'The prevention of alcoholism', *Preventive Medicine*, **3,** 24–35.

De Lint, J. (1978). 'Total consumption and rates of excessive use: a reply to Duffy and Cohen', *British Journal of Addiction*, **73,** 265–269.

De Lint, J., and Schmidt, W. (1971). 'Consumption averages and alcoholism prevalence: a brief review of epidemiological investigations', *British Journal of Addiction*, **66,** 97–107.

Donovan, J. E., and Jessor, R. (1978). 'Adolescent problem drinking; psychosocial correlates in a national sample study', *Journal of Studies on Alcohol*, **39,** 1506–1524.

Ekehammar, B. (1974). 'Interactionism in personality from a historical perspective', *Psychological Bulletin*, **81,** 1026–1048.

Fisher, A. (1975). 'Sober—yet drinking too much', *The New York Times Magazine*, 18 May.

Gomberg, E. S. L. (1978). 'Etiology of alcoholism', *Journal of Consulting and Clinical Psychology*, **32**, 18–20.

Hershon, H. I. (1973). 'Alcoholism, physical dependence and disease: comment on the alcohologist's addiction', *Quarterly Journal of Studies on Alcohol*, **34**, 506–508.

Horn, J. L., and Wanberg, K. W. (1969). 'Symptom patterns related to excessive use of alcohol', *Quarterly Journal of Studies on Alcohol*, **30**, 35–58.

Horn, J. L., and Wanberg, K. W. (1970). 'Dimensions of perception of background and current situation of alcoholic patients', *Quarterly Journal of Studies on Alcohol*, **31**, 633–658.

Jellinek, E. M. (1952). 'Phases of alcohol addiction', *Quarterly Journal of Studies on Alcohol*, **13**, 673–684.

Jellinek, E. M. (1960), *The Disease Concept of Alcoholism*. Hillhouse Press, New Brunswick, NJ.

Jessor, R., Graves, T. D., Hanson, R. C., and Jessor, S. L. (1968), *Society, Personality and Deviant Behavior: A Study of a Tri-ethnic Community*. Holt, Rinehart & Winston, New York.

Jessor, R., and Jessor, S. L. (1975). 'Adolescent development and the onset of drinking: a longitudinal study', *Journal of Studies on Alcohol*, **36**, 27–51.

Jessor, R., and Jessor, S. L. (1977). *Problem Behavior and Psychosocial Development: A Longitudinal Study of Youth*. Academic Press, New York.

Jessor, R., Jessor, S. L., and Finney, J. W. Jr. (1973). 'A social psychology of marijuana use: longitudinal studies of high school and college youth', *Journal of Personality and Social Psychology*, **26**, 1–15.

Jessor, S. L., and Jessor, R. (1975). 'Transition from virginity to nonvirginity among youth: a social-psychological study over time', *Developmental Psychology*, **11**, 473–484.

Jones, M. C. (1968). 'Personality correlates and antecedents of drinking patterns in adult males', *Journal of Consulting and Clinical Psychology*, **32**, 2–12.

Keller, M. (1976). 'The disease concept of alcoholism revisited', *Journal of Studies on Alcohol*, **37**, 1694–1717.

Kim, J., and Kohout, J. (1975). 'Multiple regression analysis', in Nie, N. H., Hall, C. H., Jenkins, J. G., Steinbrenner, K., and Bent, D. H. (eds.), *Statistical Package for the Social Sciences*, 2nd edn., McGraw-Hill, Inc., New York.

Klecka, W. R. (1975). 'Discriminant analysis', in Nie, N. H., Hall, C. H., Jenkins, J. G., Steinbrenner, K., and Bent, D. H. (eds.), *Statistical Package for the Social Sciences*, 2nd edn., McGraw-Hill, Inc., New York.

Larkin, E. J. (1979). 'Controlled drinking disease, concept controversy: suggestions for synthesis', *Psychological Reports*, **44**, 511–515.

Mayer, J., and Filstead, W. J. (1979). 'The adolescent alcohol involvement scale', *Journal of Studies on Alcohol*, **40**, 291.

McCord, J. (1972). 'Etiological factors in alcoholism: family and personal characteristics', *Quarterly Journal of Studies on Alcohol*, **33**, 1020–1024.

McKechnie, R. J. (1976). 'How important is alcohol in "alcoholism"?', in Madden, J., Walker, R., and Kenyon, W. (eds.), *Alcoholism and Drug Dependence*. Plenum Press, New York.

Miller, W. R. (1976). 'Alcoholism scales and objective assessment methods: a review', *Psychological Bulletin*, **83**, 649–674.

Mischel, W. (1977). 'The interaction of person and situation'. In Magnusson, D., and Endler, N. S. (eds.), *Personality at the Crossroads: Current Issues in Interactional Psychology*. Lawrence Erlbaum, Hillsdale, NJ.

Mulford, H. A., and Miller, D. E. (1960), 'Drinking in Iowa; III. A scale of definitions of alcohol related to drinking behavior', *Quarterly Journal of Studies on Alcohol*, **21**, 267–278.

Orford, J., Waller, S., and Peto, J. (1974). 'Drinking behavior and attitudes and their correlates among university students in England', *Quartely Journal of Studies on Alcohol*. **35**, 1316–1374.

Robins, L. W., Bates, W. M., and O'Neal, P. (1962), 'Adult drinking patterns of former problem children', In Pittman, D. J., and Snyder, C. R. (eds.), *Society, Culture and Drinking Patterns*.Wiley, New York.

Robinson, D. (1972). 'The alcohologist's addiction: some implications of having lost control over the disease concept of alcoholism', *Quarterly Journal of Studies on Alcohol*, **33**, 1028–1042.

Rohan, W. P. (1975). 'Drinking behavior and alcoholism', *Journal of Studies on Alcohol*, **36**, 908–916.

Rohan, W. P. (1976). 'Quantitative dimensions of alcohol use for hospitalized problem drinkers', *Diseases of the Nervous System*, **37**, 154–159.

Roizen, R., Cahalan, D., and Shanks, P. (1978). 'Spontaneous remissions among untreated problem drinkers', in Kandel, D. B. (ed.), *Longitudinal Research on Drug Use*. John Wiley & Sons, Chichester.

Room, R. (1977). *The Scope and Definition of Alcohol-Related Problems*. Social Research Group, School of Public Health, University of California, Berkeley. Working Paper F-58. May 1977.

Rosen, A. C. (1960), 'A comparative study of alcoholics and psychiatric patients with the MMPI', *Quarterly Journal of Studies on Alcohol*, **21**, 253–266.

Rotter, J. B. (1954). *Social Learning and Clinical Psychology*. Prentice-Hall, Englewood Cliffs, NJ.

Sadava, S. W. (1978). 'Etiology, personality and alcoholism', *Canadian Psychological Review*, **19**, 198–214.

Sadava, S. W., and Forsyth, R. (1977). 'Person–environment interaction and college student drug use: a multivariate longitudinal study', *Genetic Psychology Monographs*, **96**, 211–245.

Schlegel, R. P., and Crawford, C. A. (1978). 'Multidimensional locus of control and drug use among high school students. *Canadian Journal of Behavioral Science*, **10**, 141–151.

Schneider, J. W. (1978). 'Deviant drinking as a disease: alcoholism as a social accomplishment', *Social Problems*, **25**, 361–372.

Siegler, M., Osmond, H., and Newell, S. (1968). 'Models of alcoholism', *Quarterly Journal of Studies on Alcohol*, **29**, 571–591.

Smart, R. G. (1979). 'Priorities in minimizing alcohol problems among young people', in Blane, H. T., and Chafetz, M. E. (eds.), *Youth, Alcohol, and Social Policy*. Plenum Publishing, New York.

Syme, L. (1957). 'Personality characteristics and the alcoholic: a critique of current studies', *Quarterly Journal of Studies on Alcohol*, **18**, 288–302.

Tatsuoka, M. M. (1970). 'Discriminant analysis: the study of group differences, *Selected Topics in Advanced Statistics*. Institute for Personality and Ability Testing. Champaign, Illinois.

Tatsuoka, M. M. (1971). *Multivariate Analysis: Techniques for Educational and Psychological Research.* John Wiley & Sons, Toronto.
Vladeck, B. C., and Weiss, R. J. (1975). 'Policy alternatives for alcohol control', *American Journal of Public Health*, **65**, 1340–1342.
Wainer, H. (1976). 'Estimating coefficients in linear models: it don't make no nevermind', *Psychological Bulletin*, **2**, 213–217.

Social Psychology and Behavioral Medicine
Edited by J. Richard Eiser
© 1982 John Wiley & Sons Ltd

Chapter 10

Alcoholism, social policy, and intervention

JOHN B. DAVIES

Four Views of Alcoholism

The type of policy which one prefers to bring to bear on any problem involving people probably depends on whether the people in question are judged to be ill or judged to be healthy. The popular wisdom is that people who do 'bad' things because they are ill are not responsible for their actions, whereas those who do 'bad' things when they are fit and well are doing them 'on purpose'. The above conjunctions between being ill and being not responsible, and not being ill and being responsible, are the two most obvious, but they do not exhaust the possibilities. There are four possible combinations and these are set out in Table 10.1. Each 'cell' is identified by a title which characterizes the nature of the issues raised in that cell.

Table 10.1

'It's a disease'	'It's not a disease'	
Medical/genetic	Social/environmental	'He/she can't help it'
Medical/ personal responsibility	Moral/religious	'He/she does it on purpose'

The *moral/religious* and *medical/genetic* cells have been referred to above and are self-explanatory. The *medical/personal responsibility* cell creates problems by involving the disease concept and the notion of personal responsibility which are not normally related. People do not generally develop disease *symptoms* on purpose. However, a person's voluntary actions and behavior certainly have a bearing on the diseases he or she is likely to catch. D. L. Davies (1979) suggests that the disease model of alcoholism is very attractive to alcoholics because it implies that they have no responsibility for their condition, but goes on to say: 'The illness concept carries no such

235

universal implications, of course. A venereologist who acquires gonorrhea from intercourse with a known prostitute would look very foolish if he were to disclaim responsibility for his illness.' In actual fact, however, it seems as though people's judgements about who *deserves* medical treatment are influenced by the visibility of, or appearance of, personal responsibility. Thus it is not too difficult to find people who feel that mountaineers or racing-car drivers who receive injuries are less deserving of medical treatment than are victims of lung cancer or heart disease. Whilst the mountaineer's or racing driver's decision to climb or race seems to have a perceived direct bearing on his medical need, the fact that the cancer victim or heart patient may have contributed to his own medical need is less directly seen. Studies of the conditions under which people help or do not help each other reveal, amongst other things, that we are more likely to go to the assistance of a person who suddenly collapses if we think he has had a heart attack than if we think he is drunk (Latané and Darley, 1970; Piliavin *et al.*, 1969). Presumably, we think the drunk is less deserving of our attention. In fact, as suggested above, the notions of disease and personal responsibility are by no means necessarily contradictory.

The *social/environmental* cell sees alcoholism as mainly a social, rather than a medical, problem. Whilst this cell is represented as having nothing in common with the medical/personal responsibility cell, the view taken here (as will become apparent later) is that social/environmental factors determine the framework within which alcohol is consumed in a given society, and the nature and magnitude of its overall alcoholism problem; whilst medical factors and perceived personal responsibility characterize the individual's alcohol problem and prognosis.

The Nature of the Evidence

Medical/Genetic Cell

There is much evidence to demonstrate physical, physiological, pharmaco-logical, psychological, and other differences between alcoholics and non-alcoholics. Due to the difficulty of distinguishing whether a particular state or combination of states is a cause of alcoholism, or merely a consequence, the major interest from the present point of view is in conditions which predate the onset of the 'disease'. This leads naturally to the consideration of the possible role of genetic endowment (predisposition) in the development of alcoholism.

Amongst the possible harmful effects in which alcohol consumption is implicated, a recent text (Edwards and Grant, 1977) lists liver diseases, neurological disorders, damage to the pancreas, hypoglycemia, endocrino-pathy and blood disorders as well as broader manifestations like head injuries, road accidents, crime, and suicide. Few workers would dispute the reality of these consequences. With respect to the predisposition argument, however, what appears to be lacking is strong evidence for the existence of some state or cluster of states which is at least fairly specific to alcohol abuse and which predates the onset of 'disease' symptoms. The basic model appears to be that individuals predisposed to alcoholism have some metabolic dysfunction which is *normalized* by the ingestion of alcohol (Clare, 1979) in much the same way that diabetes is 'normalized' by insulin; but such a theory remains somewhat speculative in the absence of evidence which powerfully disentangles the causal sequence. What direct evidence exists comes mainly from animals, and the problem here is that it is possible to argue strongly that alcoholism induced in laboratory animals is very different from alcoholism, induced probably by very different factors, in humans. For example, Segovia-Riquelme *et al.* (1971) and Eriksson (1968) have demonstrated, through inbreeding experiments with rats, that strains having differing degrees of preference for alcohol can be obtained. This does not, unfortunately, demonstrate that alcoholism has a genetic basis in a human population, since the *necessity* for a particular gene combination for the development of the 'disease' is not demonstrated. Humans, and even animals for that matter, can have other reasons for developing the drinking habit. [For example, animals deprived of food will show a 'preference' for alcohol in order to make up their calory intake (Lester and Freed, 1972), and this too casts little light on drinking in humans.] Eriksson concluded that the role of inheritance in alcoholism was probably slight. Despite the failure to demonstrate a specific or fairly specific set of physical, biochemical, physiological (or whatever) states which characterize the pre-alcoholic condition in humans, and which might indicate a genetic predisposition, a genetic component in alcoholism may still be present to some degree. Supportive evidence for this possibility comes from heritability studies, although some of these might underestimate broad cultural effects on drinking, due to lack of variance in base rates (see J. B. Davies, 1981).

Prominent amongst recent workers in this field are Shields and Goodwin. In addition to empirical research, both these workers have produced articles reviewing the area of genetic research and alcoholism (Shields, 1977, 1979; Goodwin and Guze, 1974; Goodwin, 1975). Any reader interested in a more comprehensive and detailed account of this area is advised to examine these reviews as a starting point. Basically, the bulk of the evidence comes from family studies, twin studies, and adoption studies, and involves the usual virtues and vices inherent in these kinds of methods. Amongst the numerous findings are such things as a higher incidence of drinking problems (and divorce) amongst a group of adoptees raised apart from alcoholic biological parents than in a matched control group of adoptees. The groups did not differ in terms of any other variables studied, including depression and 'character disorder' (Goodwin *et al.*, 1973). There was no significant difference in incidence of alcohol problems between the adopted and non-adopted sons of alcoholic parents (Goodwin *et al.*, 1974). There is also the suggestion that a gene for alcoholism is likely to be dominant rather than recessive, from a study of grandsons of alcoholics who were either the sons of the sons of alcoholics, or the sons of the daughters of alcoholics, in that no substantial difference between the groups of grandsons was found (Kaij, 1975).

Mention should perhaps be made of a study by Wolff (1972) which at one level seems to have some bearing on the genetic argument. Wolff compared adult Japanese, Taiwanese, and Koreans in terms of certain responses to alcohol and found that these groups demonstrated marked facial flushing and signs of intoxication to amounts of alcohol that did not affect Caucasians. Similar results were obtained from young infants. The author attributed the results to racial differences in autonomic functioning. The findings are sometimes used as direct evidence of a genetic component in alcoholism, though the author himself confesses that whether they have any bearing on the etiology of alcoholism is an open question. The demonstration of between-group differences does not have any *prima facie* bearing upon the incidence (and causes) of alcoholism *within* a group.

Twin studies using the comparison of monozygotic and dizygotic twins have also been carried out. Overall, the data are not beyond reproach, but are suggestive. Two large-scale studies were carried out in Sweden and Finland. In the Swedish study, Kaij (1974) located 174 pairs of twins where at least one partner was registered at a temperance board because of alcohol problems. The concordance rate for alcohol abuse was significantly higher for the monozygotic twins than the dizygotic. A study by Partanen *et al.* (1966) of 902 male twins produced interesting if slightly different results, in so far as there was greater concordance for (reported) frequency and amount of drinking amongst monozygotes, and also for abstinence; but no evidence was found for heritability of the more severe consequences of alcohol abuse (arrests for drunkenness, or evidence of other social complications) which might normally be thought of as indices of addiction. There does seem to be some ambiguity as to which aspects of drinking have the (most important) genetic component, and also as to the interdependence or independence of the possible genetic factors. Shields (1977) cites evidence from 700 twins who attended the Maudsley hospital over a period of 28 years, and cautiously suggests support for the Partanen view that 'out of control' drinking is *not* under genetic control. In this case, the *failure* of alcoholism to show high concordance rates amongst twins reared together is also interpreted as showing that family environment 'is not the critical factor in addiction'. The review articles mentioned above give more detail of twin studies.

Whatever the truth of the matter, it has to be said that there is a body of accumulating evidence for a hereditary component in alcohol abuse, and that whilst individual pieces of research may not be beyond criticism (as acknowledged by the authors in most cases), there is sufficient evidence to make some kind of genetic hypothesis seem not unreasonable.

There has also been much interest in the notion of psychological, as opposed to physiological, predisposition, and a good deal of energy has been spent in search of the 'alcoholic personality'. Apart from some more or less specific findings, for example, that alcoholics have low self-esteem, or are more field-dependent or whatever, notwithstanding the problems of deciding whether these things are causes or effects, nothing approaching a stable group of traits which might meaningfully be called personality has emerged. Maybe the search for *the* alcoholic personality is misguided; but it may still be the case that some personalities, having little in common, nonetheless predispose to alcoholism. The 'natural' alcoholic personality may come in a variety of forms. As things stand, much of the available evidence is ambiguous or contradictory. A summary of the major studies in this area is given in Williams (1976).

The failure to find strong evidence for a unique and specific predisposing factor creates difficulties for the genetic view. For example, if alcoholism predisposition is related to some other trait, such as a tendency towards depression or neurosis; or if the predisposition requires a multifactorial model taking into account sex, social milieu, psychiatric history and stress (as suggested by Cloninger *et al.*, 1979) the model loses much of its vigor. Perhaps for this reason, some workers (Goodwin *et al.*, 1974) are keen to argue that alcoholism in its severe forms does *not* result from the interaction of multiple causes, though this is not a popular position. A fitting summary comes from Shields (1977) who concludes his review of the genetic theory of alcoholism in the following way:

> Despite many uncertainties and inconsistencies, there is growing evidence—admittedly not satisfactory to everyone—that genetic factors, some general, others perhaps relatively specific, are probably involved (along with others) in the development of alcoholism in man.

Evidence of the type reviewed above is used to support the 'bimodal' theory. According to this, the distribution of alcohol consumption in a population does not form a (log) normal distribution, but is bimodal. 'Normal' drinkers are said to make up the main peak of the distribution, whilst excessive consumers form a small peak at higher consumption levels. The smaller peak comprises individuals genetically predisposed to alcoholism, whereas those in the main mode have no such predisposition. Consequently, 'normal' drinking, and increases or decreases in the normal mode, have no influence on the numbers of heavy drinkers whose drinking has a genetic basis. Alcoholics become alcoholics because in a sense they were alcoholics already. Because of this predisposition, any legal or fiscal attempts to control alcoholism by reducing *consumption generally* are seen as illogical and misguided, within the context of this theory.

The bimodal theory is clearly related to the 'disease' notion, and tends to be the position favored by the alcohol-production industry. The 'disease' notion encounters problems in so far as abstinence is the course of action usually recommended to 'sufferers', for reasons which are not always clear (for example, a diabetic whose metabolism is 'normalized' by insulin becomes ill, not better, if he is recommended to abstain from insulin). An increasing number of workers are demonstrating instances in which alcoholics have returned to 'normal' controlled drinking (D. L. Davies, 1962; Kendell, 1965) showing that movement is possible between the modes postulated by the bimodal theory. The riposte that they could not have been 'real' alcoholics produces a futile semantic cycle.

According to the bimodal theory, 'normal' drinkers form one mode, and those with the 'disease' of alcoholism form the other. This would only be the case, of course, if the predisposition to drink were a predisposition to drink heavily (i.e. more than 'normal') so the ambiguous evidence for the genetic basis of 'loss of control' drinking creates problems for the bimodal model. The distribution will not be bimodal if the predisposition merely predisposes a person to drink 'normal' amounts.

Social/Environmental

Any coverage of possibilities for broad social policy measures must start from the fundamental issues raised by the 'unimodal' model, which contrast sharply with the bimodal model described previously. The controversy about the unimodal model stems from work by Ledermann (1956) in which he proposed that the frequency distribution of drinkers in a population is continuous, unimodal, positively skewed, and approximates a log normal curve. In the light of the nature of this proposition, Ledermann and others have argued that:

(1) it is possible to estimate the proportion of excessive drinkers in a population from knowledge of the mean per capita consumption; and
(2) it is possible to influence the number of heavy drinkers in a population by means of legal and/or fiscal measures aimed at altering the mean per capita consumption.

These two consequences would follow if the Ledermann theory were true, since in the distribution proposed there would be an (almost) invariant relationship between the consumption level in the mode, and the numbers occurring at higher consumption levels.

It appears that Ledermann's distribution theory is far from beyond statistical criticism, as shown by Duffy (1977). In the absence of any data about dispersion, Duffy points out that an infinite number of different estimates of the number of excessive drinkers can be obtained for any particular mean per capita consumption; consequently, some statement about dispersion has to be made if the distribution is to have the properties ascribed to it by Ledermann. In order to make the distribution usable in the way he suggested, Ledermann proposed that one should proceed on the basis that 1 percent of the population consumed in excess of 1 litre of alcohol per day (a dosage, he argued, that would rapidly kill them), hence restricting the range of the distribution, and enabling solution(s) to be derived. Duffy points out that, by this method, unique solutions are not derived for mean and standard deviation of the log-normal distribution, but alternative pairs of solutions (Ledermann proposes that the pair with the smaller dispersion be used); and that for mean per capita consumption levels below a certain value, no sensible solution can be derived since the distribution starts to contain 'negative drinkers' (i.e. those whose alcohol consumption would be less than zero!). To overcome these problems, workers including Ledermann have suggested that the figure of 1 percent be altered to provide real solutions, and that smaller values be used where necessary. It has been suggested that the smaller figure of 0.03 percent be used (De Lint and Schmidt, 1968). It is in this area that problems arise. It appears that the choice of these cut-off points is to a greater or lesser extent arbitrary; that some of them have no very firm roots in empirical evidence; and that others might have been derived *post facto* and adopted as a matter of statistical expediency. Duffy describes Ledermann's original 1 percent suggestion as having 'the status of a mere assumption', and suggests that De Lint's proposal of 0.03 percent 'was suggested by the data considered'. Ledermann's notion is thus a theoretical one, and Duffy demonstrates that if Ledermann's proposals are rigidly adhered to, the model fails to predict accurately certain empirically derived data sets, unless arbitrary manipulations of the above type are employed. Thus, according to Duffy, the model does not *predict* in the way it is claimed to.

According to Bruun *et al.* (1975) the problems of using Ledermann's theory are much simplified by the findng that the dispersion parameter appears to be fairly insensitive to differences in per capita consumption in different populations. They produce data from a range of 'populations and sub-populations' in which mean per capita consumption varies from approximately 1 litre, up to about 18 litres per year, and show that the standard deviation of the log distribution varies only between about 1 and 1.4. A similar argument is also put forward by Skog (1977). However, Duffy is able to use the identical data to illustrate precisely the opposite point of view. By actually solving the equations, Duffy shows that the differences in dispersion which Bruun *et al.* and Skog interpret as evidence for *similarity* of dispersion, produce differences of between 45 and 82 percent in the estimated number of excessive drinkers. In other words, only small variations in the dispersion produce substantial variations in the estimated size of the excessive drinking group.

Ledermann's suggestion is, in itself, theoretical rather than empirically derived. Empirical data, it appears, do not always fit the theory very closely unless certain modifications are made, such as De Lint's modification with respect to the dispersion. Consequently, any claim that *the* Ledermann distribution adequately describes alcohol consumption in a range of different societies, and that accurate predictions can be made from knowledge of the mean per capita consumption alone, must be viewed with strong suspicion. It seems likely, after all, that the heterogeneous or homogeneous nature of a society and its subcultural norms will affect the dispersion. Because of the fact that the unimodal model and Ledermann's hypothesis are often treated as virtually synonymous, it is sometimes assumed that a refutation of Ledermann is a refutation of the unimodal theory; this is not necessarily the case. In addition, because Ledermann's hypothesis fails to have the broad applicability which is claimed, with the consequence that it does not show the invariant relationship between total consumption and number of excessive drinkers, it is sometimes assumed that this is evidence that broad social policies for the control of consumption cannot be effective in reducing the amount of excessive drinking. This is also not necessarily the case.

The fact that the dispersion parameter varies between populations certainly invalidates Ledermann's first claim, that one can automatically predict the number of excessive consumers in a society from knowledge solely of the per capita consumption. The second proposition, however, that the number of excessive drinkers may be influenced by broad policy measures aimed at influencing per capita consumption, remains more or less intact. The reason *why* Ledermann fails to predict is that in different populations the norms and customs surrounding drinking behavior vary, giving rise to different distribution patterns. These patterns, however, are fairly stable so that *within* populations the dispersion parameter remains fairly constant over periods of time. An excellent study by Cartwright (1977) concludes that once these patterns (and hence the dispersion) are known, there is a functional relationship between mean and excessive consumption of the broad type suggested by Ledermann, within a given population.

The fact that *the* Ledermann distribution does not adequately describe certain empirically derived data sets from different populations does not mean that a Ledermann *type* of relationship does not exist *within* any, or indeed each, of those populations. A more parsimonious view, such as that described by Sulkunen (1977), places less emphasis on the precise mathematical form of the Ledermann distribution as originally proposed, and permits the introduction of dispersion parameters that might be more or less unique in particular populations. Thus the theory that a functional relationship exists between average consumption and the number of excessive drinkers within a population remains entirely plausible. Since there is evidence that, between populations, the variance may differ sufficiently to cause problems of prediction, the strongest data for this 'diluted' form of the theory must come from studies carried out within a given population, *over time*, which show sufficient consistency in distribution statistics to allow a stable relationship to be inferred. Unfortunately, for a number of reasons, including unreliability or uncomparability of data from different times, satisfactory data of this type are largely lacking. (Though Schmidt (1977) provides data for the years 1954–73 in the UK, and reports a correlation of 0.98 between cirrhosis mortality and per capita consumption.) It appears then that the promise and power of the original Ledermann theory are somewhat reduced by statistical analyses of between-population differences, and by lack of time-based data within societies.

Fortunately, other kinds of evidence exist. A recent important study described by P. Davies (1979) contains statistical data from the nine EEC countries and from seven non-EEC countries. The report describes a study of alcohol control policies and related data, and a selection from these data helps to resolve the present difficulties. In Table 10.2 are listed the nine

Table 10.2 Rank order of 15 countries according to three criteria*

	(a) Per capita consumption	(b) Percentage heavy drinkers	(c) Deaths from liver cirrhosis
France	1	1	1
Spain	2	3	6
Italy	3	2	3
Luxembourg	3	3	4
West Germany	5	5	5
Austria	6	7	2
Switzerland	7	6	7
Belgium	8	8	8
Denmark	9	9	9
Netherlands	10	11	12
Poland	11	14	10
Ireland	12	13	15
UK	12	10	14
Sweden	14	11	11
Norway	15	15	13

* (a) Per capita consumption, 1976 (source: 'official statistics' of countries concerned); (b) percentage of people consuming more than 15 centilitres of pure alcohol per day, 1976; (source: Vingtième rapport du Comité OMS d'experts de la Pharmacodépendance): and (c) deaths per 100,000 due to cirrhosis of the liver, 1974 (source: World Health Statistics Annual).

common market countries and six non-member countries from which data were obtained (Israel is excluded). The first column of figures gives the *rank order* in terms of per capita consumption. The second column gives the ranks in terms of percentage of persons consuming more than 15 centilitres of pure alcohol per day; and the final column gives rate of deaths per 100,000 of population due to cirrhosis of the liver, again in rank order. The similarity between the rankings is so striking as to make statistical description unnecessary; but for the record, per capita consumption correlates (Spearman) 0.95 with percentage consuming in excess of 15 centilitres, and 0.89 with cirrhosis statistics (both significant beyond 0.01). In the report cited, the author is at considerable pains to point out deficiencies in the collated statistics, and urges utmost caution in their interpretation. This is especially true for the second column of figures, where the exact derivation of the statistics is not known. With respect to the first and third columns, statistics from different countries are not always collected on the same basis, or according to the same criterion. Whatever the error involved, however, the author is still of the opinion that sufficient reliability exists in these data to warrant cautious conclusions. From the point of view of the present discussion, it appears that there is a relationship between per capita consumption and cirrhosis statistics, and possibly also with the percentage of heavy drinkers according to an arbitrary criterion.

Given that these figures represent some broad measure of reality there are two conclusions which are possible. If we apply the statistical criticisms of the Ledermann notion, we conclude that the association between, for example, consumption and cirrhosis, does not represent a statistically valid relationship. Instead, we must argue that the vagaries of distribution parameters between different countries render any such conclusion untenable, and it just happens *by chance* that high levels of one coincide with high rates of the other at this particular time. Such a conclusion seems unreasonable. On the other hand, if we accept the alternative view-point, we conclude that the higher rates of cirrhosis which appear in countries with higher mean consumption are causally connected. The suggestion that mean consumption and the incidence of alcoholism (of which cirrhosis is a useful indicant) are not *necessarily* related thus becomes somewhat esoteric in circumstances where evidence exists to suggest strongly that *in fact*, in broad terms, they are. In so far as this latter is true, a general unimodal theory, of which Ledermann is a specific example, is supported.

Medical/Personal Responsibility

Whether or not a person *really* has control over his/her alcoholism (or the extent of such control) is, at one level, a discussion which concerns the perceived merits and flaws in the genetic evidence; and at another level, depends on certain philosophical conclusions about the nature of man. Independent of these issues, however, exists the possibility of telling a person he/she has such control, or does not have such control, purely as a tactic in the treatment of alcoholism. The issue is clearly related to the notion of 'locus of control' discussed by Phares (1976), as a possible explanation for certain failures of counseling and treatment techniques. A factor in these failures is, according to Phares, the patient's lack of belief that he/she can exert any influence over life events. To use the same terminology, the medical/genetic cell (including the 'disease' notion) suggests an external locus of control (in the sense that the person can do little or nothing about it), whereas the present cell allows for an internal locus. If telling a person that he/she is not the helpless victim of an alcoholism 'disease' but that he/she can exercise some control over what is happening, is shown to have beneficial therapeutic effects, this is a useful tactic regardless of the perceived merits of the 'disease' notion. (By contrast, if telling a person that he/she has a disease worsens his/her chances of recovery, this is unhelpful even if one believes the statement to be true.) There is an ethical issue here; but it is by no means clear where 'the truth' lies, and in the above circumstances the positive consequences would outweigh the possible negative ones.

What evidence is there to suggest that a person with alcoholism stands a better or worse chance of recovery, according to his/her beliefs about the causality of the condition? A paper by Robinson (1972) raises just this issue, though it is not always clear whether certain statements are empirically based or derived inferentially. He writes (p. 1032): 'Widely held ideas do tend . . . to set limits to the range of expectations and beliefs which any person is likely to have about his own condition and about what counts as appropriate behavior in specific situations'. Few would dispute the validity of such an assertion, which involves a number of straightforward concepts from cognitive social psychology, linking as it does consensus views of large groups, the individual's response to such views, and finally beliefs about what counts as appropriate behavior. It is sufficient to say that a vast body of evidence exists linking these broad areas. Robinson's more specific assertions include one to the effect that a person's illness, and helplessness, is legitimated by the authority of the medical profession; and also, discussing an imaginary exchange between a 'non-addictive' (in view of what comes later, it is not clear why Robinson uses this qualification) drinker and a doctor, both of whom adopt a general 'disease' orientation to the condition, he writes, 'Any attempt by the doctor to persuade the alcoholic to change his drinking habits is likely to fail since he will, by definition, believe himself incapable of doing so.' Finally, Robinson also raises the notion of 'addiction' in conjunction with the disease model, and writes: '. . . implied in the notion of the "addictive drinker," is the idea that once the disease has been contracted it can be arrested or cured only by outside intervention.'

The work relating locus of control to drinking (and smoking) behavior has relied frequently on the Rotter Internal–External Control Scale (1966), and has produced ambiguous results. Some workers have found 'problem drinkers' to be more 'external' (e.g. Naditch, 1975) whilst others have found them to be more 'internal' (e.g. Gozali, 1971). There are apparently problems of dimensionality with the Rotter scale, and the studies have concentrated on differences between 'problem drinkers' and 'normals', rather than on differences between those who can and cannot reduce their consumption. These notions are also very relevant to the problem of cigarette smoking, as shown by the work of Eiser and his associates (see Chapter 12).

Are there any studies carried out in a treatment setting, in which prognosis and personal responsibility are experimentally examined? A study by Edwards *et al.* (1977) goes some way towards this. This study involved 100 male alcoholics attending an outpatient Alcoholism Family Clinic (with their spouses). After a number of initial assessment procedures the patients were assigned randomly, but matched for social class and severity of symptoms, to either an 'advice' group or a 'treatment' group. In the *advice* group, the couples were told that responsibility for attainment of the treatment goals *lay in their own hands* rather than being something which could be taken over by others. This message was given in sympathetic and constructive terms. The patient was offered no further appointment at the clinic and no medication was offered. A social worker would call once a month to see how things were.

In contrast to the above, the *treatment* group were offered a far more comprehensive regime, including introduction to Alcoholics Anonymous, prescription of calcium cyanamide, drugs to cover withdrawal, further appointments with the psychiatrist, extensive social work involvement and, if necessary, a 6-week session in an inpatient alcoholism unit, with detoxification, inpatient group therapy, occupational therapy, and other services offered. (The ethical considerations of studies of this type are carefully considered in this paper.) Initial statistical examination showed that randomization to the two groups was satisfactory, no significant differences being observed between the 'advice' and 'treatment' groups in terms of 14 demographic and drinking-history variables.

The results obtained from the study are in the form of 'follow-up' data obtained over a 12-month period following the date of intake. The data reported are extensive. In general terms, the study showed that 12 months after the study was started, a group of alcoholics who were simply told that the responsibility for their condition lay in their own hands made as good a recovery as a matched group offered a comprehensive treatment regime. More correctly, Edwards *et al.* describe this as follows:

> Within the defined alcoholic population, if after assessment and one session of counselling, treatment of the type described is then offered to half the patients,

then on average the 12-month outcome (on the variables delineated) in this half is not much improved as compared with the outcome in the half to whom no such offer is made.

The authors conclude that the research literature is already 'rich in reports which demonstrate that a given treatment is no better than another'; and 'poor in reports which suggest that any particular treatment is advantageous.' They describe their own paper as 'further support for what was already an apparent truth.'

Amongst the implications which the authors draw from their study, one in particular is of special interest with respect to the present topic; namely, 'Until further information is available as to the efficacy of costly and intensive interventions, services should primarily be developed in terms of economic and rather low-key programmes.'

In summary, it appears that the stressing of a 'disease' notion of alcoholism which removes all responsibility from the sufferer has a number of disadvantages, and is potentially damaging in so far as it negates any helpful contribution which the patient can make in his own recovery. Evidence shows that the related notion of 'addiction' predicts greater perceived difficulty in giving up the habit of smoking; and a sample of alcoholics given permission to take some responsibility for their illness show similar prognosis to a group given extensive treatment under a medical model, but no responsibility. The notion of disease and personal responsibility are not regarded as incompatible in this cell.

Moral/Religious

There is very little evidence appropriate to this cell. A number of studies (e.g. Davies and Stacey, 1972; J. B. Davies, 1980; Aitken, 1978) have shown a tendency for heavier drinkers, both young people and adults, to be less likely to report religious involvement and a tendency for abstainers to more freqently show a high degree of religious affiliation, *perhaps* suggesting that the approach might help to protect some individuals for whom religious messages are credible. Some workers (e.g. Benedict, 1967) have stressed the importance of raising alcoholic patients to a 'higher plateau of values', perhaps involving the 'helping hand of a Deity', if the psychotherapeutic treatment of alcoholism is to succeed.

Discussion: Implications and Opinions

Medical/Genetic

There is a sense in which *all* behaviors must have *some* genetic basis. Thus, if the genetic basis for alcoholism is to be seen as important a significantly greater component has to be demonstrated for alcoholism than for other 'average' behaviors. Consequently, a statement to the effect that 'a genetic basis for alcoholism has been demonstrated', whilst literally true, is misleading if it gives the impression that genetic factors have been shown to be the greatest determining influence.

The point at which an individual's drinking becomes labeled 'alcoholic' is arbitrary, and revolves around definitions of alcoholism which are ambiguous. Whether drinking behavior in a population is distributed unimodally or bimodally cannot be taken as evidence that the genes underlying the behavior are either common to all, or specific to one group. It cannot be naively assumed that the distribution of a behavior is isomorphic with the distribution of genes.

Investigations of the notion that particular groups of people who have some identifying characteristic are genetically different from other groups frequently cause controversy. Possibly the best example of this is Jensen's (1969) work on a proposed genetic basis for differences in measured intelligence (IQ) between racial groups. At first sight, the suggestion that research on the genetic basis for alcoholism is similar to IQ research seems somewhat remote, perhaps even hysterical, firstly because the distinction between populations usually takes place within, rather than between, racial groups, so the discrimination does not have offensive racist connotations; and secondly, whereas alcoholism is clearly a form of behavior, IQ is less obviously so. Whatever the merits or demerits of the IQ researches in question, the findings have met with strong reaction because of the fear that they might be used as a justification for particular kinds of social policies. The over-stressing of the genetic evidence for alcoholism in one sense operates in the same way, in so far as it provides the basis for the bimodal theory. Attention is thereby concentrated on the 'problem' group, whilst commercial attempts to increase the consumption of the 'normal' section of the drinking population can proceed unchecked; but more important, attention is directed away from social and environmental factors which are demonstrably involved, the problem being located conveniently *inside* certain people.

The policy issues raised by this cell involve the medical role in alcoholism, the possibility of prediction, eugenic measures and genetic counseling.

Whether or not the *act* of consuming alcohol is properly, or misleadingly, regarded as a manifestation of 'disease' is a matter of opinion, but there is no doubt that consuming too much causes people to become ill. Any overall policy must involve medical services to treat the health consequences of excessive consumption. Detoxification is a necessary adjunct of this. A strictly medical model seems wholly appropriate to the treatment of those aspects which are strictly medical, i.e. illness caused by excessive consumption. The labeling of the actual act of consumption as a disease manifestation seems to be on less firm ground, as is its treatment within an entirely medical framework. A greater stress on personal responsibility for the behavioral aspects of alcoholism seems indicated, especially in the light of findings which relate prognosis to motivation.

Most of the genetic evidence comes from studies of special samples, and casts only a dim light on the predictive value of the genetic hypothesis in less specialized, and larger, groups. The evidence is insufficiently strong at present to make the trade-off between 'correct' identification (disregarding the problem of criterion) and the consequences of (mis-) labeling justifiable. For similar reasons, the notion of a eugenically based alcoholism policy cannot be treated as a serious suggestion, especially when social and cultural factors are known to have effects on drinking patterns.

Genetic counseling generally seems justified where there is powerful evidence for some genetic deficit or damage, as in Downs syndrome, neural tube deficits (spina bifida, hydrocephaly), or phenylketonuria. The genetic evidence for alcoholism is not nearly so precise, which suggests that genetic counseling in this area has no more to recommend it than the 'prediction' or 'eugenic' possibilities discussed earlier. Of some relevance here is the issue of the fetal alcohol syndrome (Streissguth, 1976)—in fact a problem of morphogenesis. There is speculation that the syndrome manifests itself not merely in an extreme form, but also in less striking forms where it might produce more widespread attentional and learning difficulties. If so, there is room for greater dissemination of information about the syndrome, and possibly counseling as well.

The genetic model thus produces no *specific* implications for a policy on alcoholism. There is clearly a central role for medical services in any overall policy, but this is not a unique implication of this cell. Counseling with respect to the fetal alcoholism syndrome is a possibility worth consideration.

Social/Environmental

Whilst the cells involving the 'disease' idea cast useful light on what to do with those alcoholics who exist (prevalence) the 'social' cell perhaps has more to offer by way of trying to reduce the numbers who are likely to emerge in the future (incidence).

Despite the sensational coverage of alcohol research by the popular press, and repeated outcries about the terrible cost of alcoholism to the economy (the *contribution* of alcohol to the economy is seldom mentioned in these arguments; see J. B. Davies, 1980), the best statistical evidence available puts the UK at the bottom of the league table of European Common Market countries in terms of per capita consumption (data for 1950, 1970, 1976) and next but one from the bottom in terms of deaths from liver cirrhosis (1974). France, which heads the league table on both counts consumes, according to the latest figures, over twice as much per capita as the UK (22.3 litres of pure alcohol as opposed to 9.1), and has a rate of deaths due to cirrhosis 8.6 times as great (32.8 per 100,000 population as opposed to 3.8). Perhaps more surprisingly, Scotland's comparable cirrhosis figure is 6.3 per 100,000 which still places it well down the 'league table'. (All data from P. Davies, 1979.)

One disturbing feature of the evidence, however, is that the *percentage increase* both in per capita consumption and cirrhosis in the UK places this nation much higher up the list of EEC nations. This may be artifactual to some degree, since if all countries increase by the same amount, the country with the lowest per capita rate will automatically have the highest percentage increase. Whatever the truth of the matter in relation to other countries, there is no doubt, however, that within the UK *consumption and alcohol-related problems have increased substantially since the mid-1950s.*

The liquor trade takes an interest in the issues surrounding the bimodal and unimodal theories, and tends to favor the former. If one believes this model, one can apparently stimulate per capita consumption with consequent economic advantage, without being 'responsible' for any increases in the alcoholism rate which might subsequently follow. However, even if this model is true (which it isn't), one can't go on selling more alcohol for ever because even so-called 'normal' drinkers encounter alcohol problems if they drink too much. There must come a time when increasing numbers of those currently regarded as 'normals' start to encounter alcohol problems, unless the increase in sales is brought about by selling more alcohol to those already 'predisposed' to alcoholism, which is clearly indefensible. Consequently, even according to this model, one cannot indefinitely go on selling more drink without increasing alcohol problems. The decision about when to introduce measures to prevent any further increase in, or perhaps reduce, per capita consumption thus depends solely on how one perceives the total cost/benefit payoff between the economic gains and the human costs involved; and a reluctance to consider any measure which might reduce consumption is an indication of the extent to which the economic advantage is preferred. A recent report from the Royal College of Psychiatrists (1979) asks the question 'What level of casualty is then to be taken as *acceptable*?'

Legal and fiscal measures are specific ways in which governments have attempted to influence people's drinking behavior, and the Erroll (1972) and Clayson (1973) reports illustrate some of the issues involved. Some of the measures they recommended were intended to reduce the symbolic attraction and 'forbidden fruit' aspect of alcohol consumption, especially for young people, and to encourage its use in normal or more relaxed settings, for instance as an accompaniment to a meal, perhaps involving the whole family; strategies suggested by the 'integration' theory. The integration theory is the third of the three major theories of prevention (the unimodal and bimodal theories being the other two). It has recently come in for much criticism, for example by Schmidt (1977). The central notion in this theory is that the nature of alcohol use in a given population depends on the way in which drinking is integrated into the pattern of norms and social controls which prevail in that society. Where it is properly integrated into a strong set of social controls, consumption, it is predicted, will be low. Consequently, an attempt to change drinking habits can usefully be attempted by trying to influence the informal social controls and pressures which currently operate. The major criticisms of this theory are, firstly, that it relies heavily on cross-cultural information which has been subsequently proved wrong. For example, one widely circulated myth was to the effect that Italians drank mainly at mealtimes and had a low alcoholism rate. This, it turns out, is wrong on both counts. Secondly, like the bimodal model, it apparently permits ever-increasing per capita consumption, since any rise in alcohol problems is a consequence of 'poor integration' and not a necessary effect of the rise in general consumption.

The basic flaw in Schmidt's criticism is to be seen in the original paper in which these three 'prevention theories' were outlined (Popham *et al.*, 1976). Whilst the bimodal and unimodal theories concern the distribution of alcohol consumption in a population, and are exclusive alternatives, the integration theory is not the same category of suggestion. It has nothing to do with any particular form of distribution of consumption, and may be more or less true or false without having any implications for the unimodal theory or the bimodal theory. The integration theory basically says little more than that normative patterns of alcohol consumption in a society are related to social aspects of the situations in which it is consumed. The demonstration that specific pieces of evidence have been misinterpreted, or that liberal attitudes do not always co-exist with lower consumption (Makela, 1972), serves to define the way in which integration operates, rather than invalidating it. Differences in the way in which different sections of communities integrate alcohol into their lifestyle can actually *account for* the failure of a strictly applied Ledermann equation accurately to describe drinking in different populations. By seeing the three models as being mutually exclusive, Schmidt is forced to favor only one of them (in fact, the unimodal theory) and restricts his attention to obvious changes in the law, thus neglecting factors which may have a profound effect on people's drinking behavior within a given society. Schmidt thereby throws out the baby with the bathwater. Despite this, formal governmental controls over the availability of alcohol and the times and places where it may be consumed are well deserving of serious consideration. It appears that out of a number of measures which have been tried in different countries, including state monopoly, control of outlet frequency, restriction of hours of sale, age limits, licensing of *consumers*, and price, the evidence that price changes seem to have the biggest observable effect on per capita consumption seems to be the most convincing. An excellent coverage of these kinds of measures is given in Popham *et al.* (1976).

An essential accompaniment to such measures, whose aim is to influence total (i.e. mean per capita) consumption in the *short term*, is the attempt to change the social controls which surround drinking (i.e. the distribution of consumption in the population) through alcohol education and related propaganda, so that the society becomes more *resistant* to alcohol problems. As pointed out, changing social norms and attitudes is essentially a 'long-term' goal, and immediate short-term effects are unlikely to be achieved; though the long-term goal is likely to be worthwhile.

Education is potentially the most powerful tool for tackling the long-term problem. Studies of the attitudes and myths associated with alcohol and its consumption have suggested ways in which alcohol education in schools might approach the problem with the aim of lessening the symbolic value of drinking and peer group pressures to drink amongst youngsters (Davies and Stacey, 1972; Aitken, 1978). It appears, however, that many adults attach similar symbolic values to drinking (J. B. Davies, 1980, 1981), and also that the range of attitudes associated with heavy drinking is very wide, amounting almost to a 'view of the world'. There is thus a powerful argument not only for health education to cover a wider area (indeed, to be an implicit message which runs through the whole school curriculum) but also for its more widespread dissemination to the whole population, including adults. Furthermore, the attitudes which have been found amongst teenagers to be associated with heavier alcohol consumption seem to resemble those associated with heavier smoking. It may be that particular groups of attitudes or 'views of the world' underlie at least in part a number of other behaviors labeled as 'problems'. This implies that a comprehensive health education program has a very broad base, requiring a thorough integration into all aspects of teaching, rather than a somewhat grudging acceptance as an annoying extra to other 'more important' subjects. The actual title 'health education' is unfortunate in so far as it has implications which delimit the area of its operation. It implies 'education' (i.e. 'facts' and 'school') about topics specifically related to 'health', and can be used to define wider aspects of behavior and society related to smoking, drinking or whatever, as 'out of bounds' or 'inappropriate' to health education.

Changing attitudes is an important aspect of health propaganda; changing people's attitudes, it is assumed, will lead to changes in their behavior. This is a naive view of attitudes as just causal agents (people can in fact change their attitudes without changing their behavior) rather than as themselves having causes. People are not born with attitudes. They form them to help them make sense of the world in which they live, as a result of observations of what happens around them, and the noting of situations and events which prove to have either positive or negative value. Consequently, if particular attitudes are consequences of, and adaptive to, a given set of environmental experiences, then changing these attitudes must involve the attempt to alter those conditions giving rise to the experiences which make the attitudes adaptive (or in behavioristic terms, those conditions which reinforce the behaviors from which the attitudes derive). Changing attitudes involves more than merely changing verbal behavior.

Should it ever become a policy to give alcohol-directed health propaganda a chance to be maximally effective, it would seem logical to try and balance the odds a little by controlling the nature of opposing propaganda. As things stand, the battle is somewhat unequal. In 1975, the UK alcohol industry spent £27 million on advertising, whereas the *total* budget of the Health Education Council was £1½ million. (data from report of Royal College of Psychiatrists, 1979). Advertising performs a useful function in so far as it informs people about what is available and where. It seems desirable, however, to restrict alcohol (and other) advertising more closely to this function, and to outlaw that part of advertising which portrays and educates people to accept as 'normal' particular stereotyped views of the world; or better still, to persuade advertisers to change the nature of their messages so that they help rather than compete. Alcohol manufacturers, however, would need to accept that increasing consumption leads, in one way or another, to an increasing alcohol problem; that the limiting of sales is in all important ways a desirable and honorable aim; and that the argument that 'this makes no economic sense' and 'fails to fully exploit market potential' is shallow by comparison, especially where a powerful drug is involved.

The overall conclusions from this cell are as follows. Specific legal and fiscal measures are possible ways of controlling availability. There is evidence that availability is related to consumption; and also that, of the measures tried, substantially increasing the real price of alcohol seems to be the most effective. Any government instituting such a measure will probably lose some popularity.

Health education is a vital facet of attaining the long-term goal of altering the social climate and norms surrounding alcohol consumption. Its chances of being more effective are increased if the realm of topics to which health education is seen as pertinent is greatly extended. There is a need for integration betweeen the goals of health education, the media, advertisers and the alcohol production industry. If the alcohol-production industry agrees to such an integration policy it will probably lose some money. There has to be some agreement that societal goals are not always synonymous with the maximizing of economic profits. The absence of a common societal goal towards alcohol is striking, and not least within our own profession. The basic difficulty is therefore in deciding how much we *want* to reduce the incidence of alcoholism. Do we really want to improve the quality of our society in human terms, at some material expense, or not?

Medical/Personal Responsibility

Two major issues occur in this cell. The first concerns a belief in personal responsibility, and this is shared with the moral/religious cell. The second concerns medical treatment; in a sense, this cell frees medical interventions from the shackles of the 'genetic' cell. In this latter cell, the argument is such as to lead to a conclusion that medical intervention is essential and must be appropriate, because people are suffering from a 'disease' over which they have 'no control'. In the present cell these constraints are partially removed so that the efficacy of medical strategies can be evaluated alongside other possible courses of action, employed more fruitfully in circumstances where they are shown to be most effective, and not used where they are shown to be ineffective or no more effective than more economical forms of 'treatment'. There is evidence to suggest that the stressing of the notion that undifferentiated alcoholism is a 'disease' may prove unhelpful, especially to those in the earlier stages of the habit. If more evidence on this topic confirms existing trends, one would hope to see medical and alcoholic agencies of all kinds ceasing to spread the undifferentiated disease notion. In so far as belief in personal responsibility is an important factor in enabling a person to cope with alcoholism, Edwards' hopeful suggestions about alternative, cheaper, but equally successful strategies need to be further explored.

The role of medical practitioners may be more important in non-medical interventions than seems at first apparent. Eiser's research shows how people have complicated networks of belief about disease and personal capacity to influence outcomes. Parsons (1951) has earlier described expectations about the sick role. In social psychology a large body of evidence exists to show that the effectiveness of a given message to a given audience is very much influenced by the perceived credibility of the source of the message. Now, in Edwards' research, the message that the outcome of treatment depended on the patients' ability to take responsibility for the condition came from a *medical* source, surrounded by medical trappings, in a hospital. There is no specific evidence on this topic, but it may well be that any message to the effect that the alcoholic does not have a disease of the type he conceptualized and that his recovery is in his own rather than the medical profession's hands, must, ironically, come from a doctor. If a person thinks he has a disease, it seems likely that he will accept the contrary word of a doctor, who 'knows' about these things, more readily than the word of a social worker, counselor, or ex-alcoholic. Only the doctor has perceived competence.

The disease notion appears to be fairly widespread, so a medical component in all treatment regimes, including non-medical ones, may be of considerable advantage. If this is so, one would like to see a lessening of the split between medical treatments and non-medical treatments (counseling, for example); and a closer liaison between the two approaches, with the 'credible' medical practitioners recommending 'patients' to the non-medical aspects of an integrated treatment system when appropriate, until such time as the undifferentiated 'disease' label has died out. Furthermore, Edwards' research does not show that non-medical approaches work as well as medical ones, but rather that an *integrated* system might be as effective, and cheaper. (The economic advantage, it is assumed, would enable services to be more widely distributed, rather than simply reducing spending in this sector.) At the present time, whilst there is contact of some kind between hospital-based medical agencies, and non-medical practitioners such as Councils on Alcoholism, social workers or Industrial Alcoholism Units, there is little close integration of both essential aspects under a single conceptual treatment philosophy. For such a system to evolve, a number of idols (self-images?) would have to be knocked down on *both* sides of the fence.

As a footnote to this section, there seems to be no reason why a closely integrated system might not also make use of the services of religious practitioners (priest, chaplain, rabbi, guru, or whatever) within the framework of 'personal responsibility' which is shared by the present and the moral/religious cell. If a particular 'patient' wishes to use, or seems likely to benefit from, a source with religious credibility, there seems no reason why a comprehensive service should not offer this within a restricted framework, without prejudice to the secular aspects of the program. It appears that particular individuals have had their 'consciousness' (i.e. behavior) changed in ways which are pleasing to themselves and to others by social messages expressed from a religious viewpoint.

Moral/Religious

By and large, these issues are avoided by modern research workers, who prefer approaches which are less value-laden; though as Andreski (1974) points out, in some cases this means preferring a hidden ideology to an obvious one. There are usually felt to be, with some justification, a number of serious problems inherent in the moral/religious approach.

Given the current climate of the times, it is the opinion here that the moral/religious approach to alcoholism does not form a workable basis for broad social measures, though no doubt it proves a very helpful measure in (possibly) a large number of individual cases. Overall, there are a number of serious drawbacks to the approach; but it must be said that objections can be raised to almost any intervention philosophy, so it is not unique in this respect. It appears that at least part of the problem lies in the fact that social scientists feel uneasy about involving God in the treatment of alcoholism.

On the other hand, in a more restricted framework, others have shown less reluctance to involve value systems, including religion, in treatment; and argue strongly that this can be beneficial or even necessary in certain therapeutic situations. A book by Mowrer (1967, part II) gives the views of a number of workers who involve values and/or religious belief in various psychotherapeutic settings, including the treatment of alcoholism.

Psychologists and Social Policy: an Opinion

Decisions as to what should be done, if anything, effectively to limit alcohol-abuse problems are to a large extent political. Indeed, a recent paper by Cahalan (1979) discusses the influence of vested interests both in alcohol production *and in alcohol research*, and raises some extremely disturbing issues. It is essential reading. Another recent paper by Kendell (1979) discusses the politics of alcoholism, and concludes that it is no longer appropriately regarded as a medical problem. The failure to institute strong policies, he implies, indicates that the trade-off between profits and human costs is regarded, at least for the moment, as quite satisfactory. Kendell writes in strong terms:

> We have learnt how long it takes to make any appreciable progress, how spineless ministers can be, and how strongly commercial empires defend their profits. But we have also learnt that if we are sufficiently determined and sufficiently patient we are eventually able to change public attitudes and people's behavior.

It would be comforting to think that Kendell includes psychologists generally in the group he refers to as 'we', but unhappily such a general application is not appropriate. Psychologists are actively involved on both sides of the fence, some trying to persuade people to drink less, while others try to persuade them to drink more. It appears that psychologists, in trying to rid their experiments of subjective bias and values, have sometimes mistakenly expunged these things from their own selves. Endeavoring to increase a population's consumption of a powerful drug is, after all, something about which one ought to have some biased and unscientific opinions.

It is ironic that so much attention is devoted by academic psychologists to the ethics of certain experimental procedures, especially those involving deception. Unfortunately, this debate confines itself largely to condemnations of particular *experiments*, the majority of which have no direct influence on, and are unknown to, ordinary people. (Interestingly, some of the most criticized ones are those which raise disturbing questions.) By contrast, the ethical considerations raised by the nature of the work done by some psychologists in spheres such as marketing and commerce are hardly, if ever, mentioned in this particular debate. This is a pity, since the consequences of this work are often more far-reaching and potentially or actually more damaging.

A more theoretical issue concerns the prominence given to the psychological study of individual differences. The study of these differences is a highly worthwhile and rewarding exercise. However, there has often been a tendency to prize the individual for his/her own sake alone, and to see the study of the subtle ways in which people differ as being more desirable, and more ennobling to mankind (and to the psychologist) than the study of the blatantly obvious ways in which people are the same. The study of individuality cannot, by definition, have very much to say about society; since a social system is a series of agreed contingencies based mainly on those behaviors which are, for better or for worse, similarly elicited from large numbers of people. Anyone can become an alcoholic if he/she drinks enough. The notion that the number of alcoholics in a society is related to the general level of alcohol consumption in that society has already been discussed. It might also be the case that the incidence of other 'problem' behaviors in a society (e.g. delinquency, violence, the extreme alienation we call psychopathic) is related to the general level of that behavior which prevails (at all levels). Too great an emphasis in psychology on the individual may direct attention away from the social/environmental conditions which provide the setting for societal problems regardless of the differences between the individuals involved. These social/environmental conditions are in many respects being actively shaped by people working in commerce, advertising, politics, and the mass media. Within such a context, the reluctance of many psychologists to engage in work which might be construed as influencing the behavior of 'normal' people, may border on self-indulgence.

References

Aitken, P. P. (1978). *Ten-to-fourteen-year-olds and Alcohol*. HMSO, Edinburgh.

Andreski, S. (1974). *Social Sciences as Sorcery*. Penguin, Harmondsworth.

Benedict, P. K. (1967). 'Psychotherapy of alcoholism', in O. H. Mowrer (ed.), *Morality and Mental health*, pp. 87–92, Rand McNally, Chicago.

Bruun, K., Edwards, G., Lumio, M., Makela, K., Pan, L., Popham, R. E., Room, R., Schmidt, W., Skog, O. J., Sulkunen, P, and Osterberg, E. (1975). *Alcohol control policies in public health perspective*, vol. 25. Finnish Foundation for Alcohol Studies, Helsinki (cited in Duffy, J. C., 1977).

Cahalan, D. (1979). 'What I would most like to know: why does the alcoholism field act like a ship of fools?', *British Journal of Addiction*, **74**, 235–238.

Cartwright, A. (1977). 'Population surveys and the curve', in *The Ledermann curve*. Alcohol Education Centre, London.

Clare, A. W. (1979). 'The causes of alcoholism', in Grant, M., and Gwinner, P. (eds.), *Alcoholism in perspective*. Croom Helm, London.

Clayson, C. (1973). *Report of the Departmental Committee on Scottish Licensing Law*. HMSO, Edinburgh.

Cloninger, C. R., Reich, T., and Wetzel, R. (1979). 'Alcoholism and affective disorders: familial associations and genetic models', in Goodwin, D., and Carbon, E. (eds.), *Alcoholism and affective disorders*. Spectrum, New York.

Davies, D. L. (1962). 'Normal drinking in recovered alcohol addicts', *Quarterly Journal of Studies on Alcohol*, **23**, 94–104.

Davies, D. L. (1979). 'Defining alcoholism', in Grant, M., and Gwinner, P. (eds), *Alcoholism in perspective.* Croom Helm, London.

Davies, J. B. (1980).'Drinking and alcohol-related problems in five industries', in Hore, B., and Plant, M. (eds), *Alcohol problems in employment.* Croom Helm/ Alcohol Education Centre, London.

Davies, J. B. (1981). 'The transmission of alcohol problems in the family', in Harwin, J., and Orford, J. (eds), *Alcohol and the Family.* Croom Helm/Alcohol Education Centre, London.

Davies, J. B. and Stacey, B. (1972). *Teenagers and Alcohol.* HMSO, London.

Davies, P. (1979). 'Some comparative observations on alcohol consumption, alcohol-related problems and alcohol control policies in the United Kingdom and other countries of Europe', *British Journal on Alcohol and Alcoholism,* **14,** 208–232.

De Lint, J., and Schmidt, W. (1968). 'The distribution of alcohol consumption in Ontario', *Quarterly Journal of Studies on Alcohol,* **29,** 968–973.

Duffy, J. C. (1977). 'Estimating the proportion of heavy drinkers', in *The Ledermann curve.* Alcohol Education Centre, London.

Edwards, G., and Grant, M. (1977). *Alcoholism: New Knowledge and New Responses.* Croom Helm, London.

Edwards, G., Orford, J., Egert, S., Guthrie, S., Hawker, A., Hensman, C., Mitcheson, M., Oppenheimer, E., and Taylor, C. (1977). 'Alcoholism: a controlled trial of "treatment" and "advice" '. *Journal of Studies on Alcohol,* **38,** 1004–1031.

Eiser, J. R., Sutton, S. R., and Wober, M. (1977). 'Smokers, non-smokers and the attribution of addiction', *British Journal of Social and Clinical Psychology,* **16,** 329–336.

Eriksson, K. (1968). 'Genetic selection for voluntary alcohol consumption in albino rats', *Science,* **159,** 739.

Erroll, Lord, of Hale (1972). *Report of the Departmental Committee on Liquor Licensing.* HMSO, London.

Goodwin, D. W. (1975). 'Genetic determinants of alcohol addiction', *Advances in Experimental Medicine and Biology,* **56,** 339–355.

Goodwin, D. W., and Guze, S. B. (1974). 'Heredity and alcoholism', in Kissin, B., and Begleiter, H. (eds.), *The Biology of Alcoholism,* vol. 3, Plenum Press, New York.

Goodwin, D. W., Schulsinger, F., Hermansen, L., Guze, S. B., and Winokur, G. (1973). 'Alcohol problems in adoptees raised apart from biological parents', *Archives of General Psychiatry,* **28,** 238–243.

Goodwin, D. W., Schulsinger, F., Møller, N., Hermansen, L., Winokur, G., and Guze, S. B. (1974). 'Drinking problems in adopted and non-adopted sons of alcoholics', *Archives of General Psychiatry,* **31,** 164–169.

Gozali, J. (1971). 'Control orientation as a personality dimension among alcoholics', *Quarterly Journal of Studies on Alcohol,* **32,** (1A), 159–161.

Jensen, A. R. (1969). 'How much can we boost IQ and scholastic achievement?', *Harvard Educational Review,* **39,** 1–123.

Kaij, L. (1974). *Studies on the Etiology and Sequels of Abuse of Alcohol.* Department of Psychiatry, University of Lund, Lund (cited in Goodwin and Guze, 1974).

Kaij, L. (1975). 'Grandsons of alcoholics: a test of sex-linked transmission of alcohol abuse', *Archives of General Psychiatry,* **32,** 1379–1381.

Kendell, R. E. (1965). 'Normal drinking by former alcohol addicts', *Quarterly Journal of Studies on Alcohol,* **26,** 247–257.

Kendell, R. E. (1979). 'Alcoholism: a medical or a political problem?', *British Medical Journal*, **1**, 367–371.

Latane, B., and Darley, J. M. (1970). *The unresponsive bystander: why doesn't he help?* Appleton-Century-Crofts, New York.

Ledermann, S. (1956). *Alcool–Alcoolisme–Alcoolisation: Données Scientifiques de Caractère Physiologique, Economique et Social.* Travaux et Documents, Cahier No. 29. Institut National d'Etudes Demographiques. Presses Universitaires de France.

Lester, D., and Freed, E. X. (1972). 'A rat model of alcoholism?', *in* Seixas, F. A., Omenn, G. S., Burk, E. D., and Eggleston, S. (eds), *Nature and Nurture in Alcoholism.* Academy of Sciences, New York.

Makela, K. (1972). 'Consumption level and cultural drinking patterns as determinants of alcohol problems'. Paper presented at 30th International Congress on Alcoholism and Drug Dependence, Amsterdam (cited in Schmidt, 1977).

Mowrer, O. H. (ed.) (1967). *Morality and mental health.* Rand-McNally, Chicago.

Naditch, M. P. (1975). 'Locus of control and drinking pattern in army trainees', *Journal of Consulting and Clinical Psychology*, **43**, (1), 96.

Parsons, T. (1951). *The Social System*, Free Press, Chicago.

Partanen, J., Bruun, K., and Markkanen, T. (1966). *Inheritance of Drinking Behaviour* Rutgers University Center of Alcohol Studies, New Brunswick, New Jersey (cited in Goodwin and Guze, 1974.)

Phares, E. J. (1976). *Locus of Control in Personality.* General Learning Press, Morristown, New Jersey.

Piliavin, I. M., Rodin, R., and Paliavin, J. A. (1969). 'Good Samaritanism: an underground phenomenon?', *Journal of Personality and Social Psychology*, **13**, 289–299.

Popham, R. E., Schmidt, W., and De Lint, J. (1976). The effects of legal restraint on drinking, in Kissin, B., and Begleiter, H. (eds), *The Biology of Alcoholism*, vol. 4: *Social Aspects of Alcoholism*. Plenum, New York.

Robinson, D. (1972). 'The alcohologist's addiction: some implications of having lost control over the disease concept of alcoholism', *Quarterly Journal of Studies on Alcohol*, **33**, (4), 1028–1042.

Rotter, J. B. (1966). 'General expectancies for external versus internal control of reinforcement', *Psychological Monographs*, **80** (1; whole no. 609).

Royal College of Psychiatrists (Report of a special committee (1979). *Alcohol and Alcoholism.* Tavistock, London.

Schmidt, W. (1977). 'Cirrhosis and alcohol consumption: an epidemiological perspective', in Edwards, G., and Grant, M. (eds), *Alcoholism: New Knowledge and New Responses.* Croom Helm, London.

Segovia-Riquelme, N., Varela, A., and Mardones, J. (1971). 'Appetite for Alcohol', in Israel, Y., and Mardones, J. (eds), *Biological Basis of Alcoholism.* Wiley & Sons, Toronto.

Shields, J. (1977). 'Genetics and alcoholism', in Edwards, G., and Grant, M. (eds.), *Alcoholism: New Knowledge and New Responses.* Croom Helm, London.

Shields, J. (1979). 'Alcoholism and adoption', *Eugenics Society Bulletin*, **11**, (1), 9–13.

Skog, O. J. (1977). 'On the distribution of alcohol consumption', in *The Ledermann curve.* Alcohol Education Centre, London.

Streissguth, A. P. (1976). 'Maternal alcoholism and the outcome of pregnancy: a review of the fetal alcohol syndrome', in Greenblatt, M., and Schuckit, M. A. (eds), *Alcoholism Problems in Women and Children*, pp. 251–274. Grune & Stratton, New York.

Sulkunen, P. (1977). 'Behind the curves: on the dynamics of rising consumption level', in *The Ledermann curve*. Alcohol Education Centre, London.

Williams, A. F. (1976). 'The alcoholic personality', in *Social Aspects of Alcoholism*. Kissin, B., and Begleiter, H. (eds), Plenum, New York.

Wolff, P. H. (1972). 'Ethnic differences in alcohol sensitivity', *Science*, **175**, 449–450.

Social Psychology and Behavioral Medicine
Edited by J. Richard Eiser
© 1982. John Wiley & Sons Ltd

Chapter 11

Drug-dependence: the mechanics of treatment evaluation and the failure of theory

MICHAEL GOSSOP

> I wish I could be
> What I was
> When I wanted to be
> What I am now.
>
> *Graffiti written on the wall of the drug-dependence clinic at the Maudsley Hospital by an anonymous addict.*

Few areas of psychological medicine are surrounded by quite so much confusion as drug dependence, and nowhere is this confusion more obvious than in the area of treatment evaluation. More than 50 years ago America saw the closure of 44 clinics that had been set up to treat drug addicts. Their effectiveness had never been evaluated. Since then, hundreds of different treatment programs have been established throughout the world, and there is little convincing evidence about their relative effectiveness.

Treatment evaluation studies are generally agreed to be a good thing. For obvious reasons it is valuable for the clinician to know whether a particular treatment intervention is likely to be beneficial, harmful, or whether it will have no effect upon the patient. As a result there has been an increasing number of evaluation studies in recent years, and administrative and fund-giving authorities are coming to rely upon such research. Indeed, numerous drug treatment programs are having their funds withheld until evaluative research has been completed (Platt, *et al.*, 1977).

The present chapter examines some of the methodological difficulties inherent in attempts to evaluate the effectiveness of treatments for drug addiction. It also looks more broadly at the nature of drug dependence and at the way in which current theories of addiction have influenced the sorts of intervention that are used in treatment programs.

261

Methodology

Broadly speaking, treatment (outcome) evaluation studies are concerned with finding out the effectiveness of particular treatment interventions or treatment programs: they attempt to answer questions of the sort—is this patient or this group of patients more likely to improve given treatment X or treatment Y? Evaluative research is limited by the same sorts of constraint that apply to experimental research; but whereas experimentation usually involves a high degree of control of the relevant variables, this control is less likely in treatment evaluation. Experimental research is frequently based upon a much clearer theoretical model than evaluative research: as a result it is easier to distinguish between those factors that are likely to have an influence upon the dependent variable and those that may safely be disregarded. The effective determinants can then be controlled, measured, or systematically varied according to the experimenter's intentions or the other restraints that exist. As one moves from experimental or theoretical research toward evaluative research, the number of variables which can be controlled usually decreases, while the number of unknown and uncontrolled variables that may affect the results increases. Because of this, one cannot place so much confidence on the results being due to the treatment conditions.

The simplest sort of investigation is the follow-up study, though in practical terms this is so complicated to carry out that only a few such studies have been conducted. In this design, subjects are exposed to a treatment program and then, after a period of time they are retraced, and their drug use, social adaptation, occupational record, etc., is noted. This is the weakest of all experimental designs. It lacks pretreatment measures that can be compared with the follow-up measures, and there is no control or comparison group whose progress can also be monitored. As such the follow-up study can lay little claim to experimental rigor; but in an area which is so poorly understood as drug dependence, longitudinal studies can fulfil a useful function in pointing to the 'natural history' of drug dependence.

In 1969, Stimson contacted a sample ($n = 128$) of the addicts to whom heroin was being prescribed at 13 out of the 15 London drug-dependence clinics (Stimson, 1973). This same group was followed up after 7 years (Stimson et al., 1978). At least 40 people (31 percent) were abstinent from opiates and living in the community. Some of these individuals were using other psychoactive drugs on a regular basis. One person was a heavy drinker (more than 100 ml of alcohol per day), five were using tranquilizers, antidepressants or hypnotics as prescribed by their general practitioner and not used for intoxication, and three were regular cannabis smokers. Stimson suggests that among the 40 people who were no longer using opiates, this amount of drug use corresponds to the incidence of alcohol and drug use in the general population (e.g. Edwards et al., 1972). Of the other subjects in

Stimson's follow-up study, 15 (12 percent) had died and 62 (48 percent) were still using opiates daily. Continued opiate use was found to be rare in patients who stopped attending the clinics to live in the community.

Stimson wisely avoids being tempted beyond the descriptive into the more hazardous area of making conclusions about treatment effectiveness. The 20-year follow-up study by Vaillant (1973), however, does fall into temptation. Like Stimson, Vaillant found that at least 35 percent of his sample of heroin addicts had achieved stable abstinence. It appeared that the addict could move from the daily use of heroin to stable abstinence at any point in his career, though there was a suggestion in Vaillant's data that more addicts gave up drugs when in their late 20s. Unlike Stimson, Vaillant uses the flimsy framework of the follow-up design to comment on treatment effectiveness, and suggests that either imprisonment or voluntary hospitalization on their own were useless in producing abstinence. Prison followed by parole, on the other hand, was described as surprisingly effective. Unfortunately, the methodological deficiencies of this sort of design (no control group, inadequate information both about the social and psychological differences between subjects prior to the investigation and about their different experiences during the study), make conclusions of this sort extremely suspect.

It is an unfortunate feature of drug research that many evaluation studies are riddled with methodological weaknesses, and it is distressing that these are seldom taken into consideration when conclusions are drawn about the effectiveness of treatment. Nowhere is this more apparent than in the evaluation of methadone maintenance programs. These are now widely accepted as of 'completely documentated efficacy' (Cushman, 1974), with a success rate of 70–90 percent (Anderson and Solomon, 1971); and Newman (1976) has asserted that the effectiveness of methadone maintenance is beyond question. When one looks at the report of the Methadone Maintenance Evaluation Committee (1968), the studies cited in support of these conclusions used a number of selection procedures which eliminated the most disturbed patients from the study. Among the patients excluded were multiple drug abusers and addicts with alcohol problems. Since multiple drug abuse is now the most common pattern (certainly in the UK) this would automatically limit methadone maintenance to a very small minority of cases. The strictness of patient selection procedures is also related to the subsequent success rates of treatment, which casts further doubt on the results.

Another flaw in this research is that success rates have usually been quoted for those subjects who remain in the methadone program, and not for the original sample. Since the most disturbed members of a program are likely to constitute many of the drop-outs, this procedure leads to a systematic bias which inflates the apparent effectiveness of treatment. Examples of this sort of data manipulation can be seen in the reports of Dole and Nyswander (1966) and Gearing (1970).

These and several other methodological deficiencies of methadone maintenance evaluation research have been discussed at greater length elsewhere (Gossop, 1978a), and the methodological problems inherent in treatment evaluation research have received considerable attention in recent years (Jeffrey, 1975; Siegel and Platt, 1977). Such methodological limitations make it impossible to know precisely which factors led to the changes that may have occurred after the treatment. It is frequently assumed, however, that these problems can be completely overcome simply through taking more care in the design of evaluation studies, and by introducing greater experimental rigor in conducting such studies. This emphasis upon the 'mechanics' of evaluation obscures the important interaction betweeen the empirical study itself and the theoretical framework (whether explicit or implicit) that underlies the whole investigation.

Some of these methodological deficiencies can be directly related to the lack of any agreed or satisfactory theory of addiction. For instance, it is generally acknowledged that evaluation studies should include a control group in their experimental design. Unfortunately, there is no clear indication of the variables on which the experimental and control groups should be matched. It is not difficult to obtain a control sample matched for patterns of drug-taking, age, sex and educational attainment, but there is little evidence that these variables are especially relevant for the purposes of comparison. In a study of addicts in two different treatment modalities, it is possible that the reasons why each sought their own form of treatment might account for the outcome *irrespective of the treatment intervention* itself. It is clearly not permissible to assume that addicts are assigned at random to diferent treatment programs. A complex set of filtering mechanisms operates upon the drug-using population in such a way that the individuals who eventually attend a drug clinic represent a highly selected minority of drug users (in much the same way that alcoholics receiving treatment represent a highly selected minority among drinkers). There are, in addition, a variety of factors which influence the sort of treatment that drug users will receive when they approach a clinic. Blumberg *et al.* (1974) found that high rates of unemployment, illegal activities, and physical complications from the use of drugs were more frequent among addicts who were *not* given prescribed drugs by the clinic. But although there are suggestions that certain factors do exert a powerful selection effect upon attendance and treatment at drug clinics, these factors remain obscure. They are, nonetheless, the very factors which need to be controlled before any valid conclusions can be drawn from evaluation research findings.

Even the choice of evaluation criteria depends upon theoretical assumptions about the nature of drug dependence. Many methadone maintenance studies which have taken retention rates (i.e. the number of addicts who remain in the treatment program) as a criterion measure, make the implicit assumption that continuing to use daily doses of methadone with medical approval can be regarded as a successful outcome. The use of retention rates as a measure of successful treatment is partly responsible for the inflated claims that have been made for methadone maintenance. On the other hand, the preoccupation with total abstinence as the ultimate criterion of success poses other problems. The use of abstinence as a criterion measure probably reflects moral assumptions as much as medical or scientific ones. Like alcoholics, addicts can sometimes regulate their drug use without total abstinence, though reduction or stabilization of drug use is seldom included as a measure of treatment success.

One of the most important problems involved in treatment evaluation research concerns the way in which addiction and the treatment process are conceptualized. It is often taken for granted that addiction can be regarded as an affliction which is to be treated by specific techniques or procedures. These may include the administration of drugs, the use of behavior therapy techniques such as aversion therapy, or talking psychotherapies intended to modify the patient's personality problems or to resolve intra-family difficulties. In each case, the notion that one is treating the addict by 'doing something' either to him or to his environment obscures the important role played by that person's attitudes, beliefs, and expectations. The idea that addiction is an overwhelming compulsion which the addict is powerless to resist is a myth, albeit one in which the addict himself may believe. The same view is widespread among psychologists and psychiatrists: it is implicit in, or at least encouraged by, the sorts of theory which have been used to explain the phenomena of drug dependence.

Explanations of drug dependence tend to fall into four categories (Gossop, 1979). The addiction is seen as the result of some underlying personality predisposition, of social–cultural factors, of conditioning processes, or of a pharmacologically induced need of drugs.

Personality Theories

The personality approach regards drug dependence as an attempt to cope with some underlying personality difficulty or difficulties. The American Psychiatric Association, for instance, described addiction as the symptomatic expression of an antisocial personality disorder (DSM II, 1968). This is not a satisfactory formulation for several reasons, not the least of which concerns the difficulty of defining what is to count as this sort of personality disorder.

In addition, although several studies have reported unusual personality features among addicts, there is no single distinctive personality pattern. The attempt to identify a set of personality characteristics that differentiate between addicts and non-addicts is increasingly recognized to be non-productive. It has been suggested that the investigation of any trait in alcoholics will show that they have either more or less of it (Keller, 1972), and this observation applies equally well to drug addiction.

There are, however, considerable personality differences between different subgroups of addicts, and one line of research has investigated the relationship between specific styles of addiction and personality. In a study of hostility among addicts, Gossop and Roy (1976) found that intravenous addicts receiving in-patient treatment showed higher levels of measured hostility than oral users: barbiturate users seemed to be the most hostile group. The disinhibiting effects of the barbiturates may reduce the anxiety that the addict experiences in coping with his hostile feelings and increase the chances he will act out his hostility. Addicts who score highly on measures of hostility are more likely to have been convicted of some criminal offence and to have a greater number of convictions for offences involving violence as well as for non-drug offences (Gossop and Roy, 1977).

Opiate addicts were also found to score comparatively highly on the measures of hostility, but in this case it seems likely that the opiates reduced the addicts' experienced (or reported) hostility. Out-patient addicts who were using heroin or methadone at the time of testing scored much lower on measures of hostility than detoxified narcotics users (Gossop and Roy, 1976). Unfortunately, the levels of association between personality factors and particular styles of addiction are rather low, and their value for predicting the addict's response to different treatment options remains unclear.

Social Theories

Unlike the personality approach which locates the causes of addiction within the individual, the social and epidemiological accounts look to external factors that might cause or predispose individuals towards dependence upon drugs. In America, for instance, addiction is particularly prevalent among certain ethnic minorities in deprived inner-city areas. Chein et al. (1964) suggested that low educational attainment, low economic status, disrupted family life, and crowded housing conditions were among the important social determinants. Duncan (1977) also found that addicts scored higher than a normal group of adolescents on measures of life stress, and argued that this supports the notion of drug dependence as a response to a stressful environment. These factors should not be seen as inevitable determinants, however. In the UK there is little evidence that social disadvantage leads to addiction, and the incidence of drug dependence among West Indians and Asians in Britain seems to be very low.

One social factor that has often been neglected—perhaps because it is so obvious—is the availability of drugs. Where drugs are easily obtained more people tend to use them. The rate of addiction among medical personnel, for instance, has been estimated to be ten times greater than that for the general population (Maddux, 1965). Lee Robins investigated the illicit use of drugs by US servicemen in Vietnam where heroin and other drugs were freely available. Almost half of all enlisted men used narcotics at some time during their Vietnam tour, and 20 percent became addicted (Robins *et al.*, 1974). Nonetheless, even where drugs are easily obtained many people do not try them, and of those who do only a minority become addicted. Availability is best seen as a necessary rather than a sufficient condition for drug dependence. The less accessible drugs are to the individual, the more powerful the other factors must be.

Physiological Theories

The medical background of many workers in addiction has encouraged them to look for biochemical or physiological explanations of drug dependence. One of the most influential models was proposed by Dole and Nyswander (1965), and this is closely related to the widespread use of methadone maintenance as a treatment for heroin addiction. The heroin addict is seen as suffering from a metabolic disorder caused by his use of drugs: he is suffering from a physiological disorder which is to be treated by drugs in the same way that diabetes is to be treated by insulin (Dole and Nyswander, 1965). The clearest statement of this position is that 'Drug addiction is a distinct medical entity which ravages the patient, destroys the entire fabric of his life. . . As in every major disease, the patient is *helpless* before its destructive inroads' (Nyswander, 1956; my italics). This metabolic disease may be permanent and irreversible, and abstinence from heroin is to be achieved by the substitution of another daily medication. Methadone maintenance is therefore presented as the same sort of intervention as the medical treatment of other illnesses (Newman, 1977).

In recent years there has been a revival of interest in neurochemical models of addiction after the discovery of naturally occurring polypeptides in the CNS. These brain endorphins and enkaphalins are highly complex agents whose functions are, as yet, far from clear. It seems that they act as neurotransmitters and that the opiates may have similar sites and actions. There has been some speculation that addiction may be caused by exogenous opiates taking over the control of inhibitory mechanisms normally controlled by the enkaphalins: when the opiates are withdrawn, the inhibitory mechanisms may have lost their power to stimulate the tolerant opiate receptors (Kosterlitz and Hughes, 1977). Although the interaction between exogenously administered opiates and endogenous opiate peptides may play a considerable part in the development of tolerance and dependence, Kosterlitz and Hughes (1978) conclude that metabolic changes appear to play only a minor (if any) role in addiction.

Conditioning Theories

A quite different approach is that of the conditioning theorists. Rather than look for common underlying 'defects' in the histories, environments, personalities, and physiologies of addicts, Kumar and Stolerman (1977) argued that a more profitable research policy might set up experimental models to generate reproducible patterns of drug self-administration. Such studies have generally involved animals (largely for ethical reasons).

Experimental studies of the primary reinforcing properties of drugs have shown that animals will increase their rate of operant responding when this is followed by intravenous morphine, CNS stimulants such as the amphetamines and cocaine, or sedative–hypnotic drugs such as the barbiturates (Schuster and Thompson, 1969; Deneau et al., 1969). There has also been considerable interest in ways that conditioning processes can modify the pharmacological effects of drugs. Wikler (1948) first proposed that conditioning factors may play an important role in leading to the addict's craving for drugs after detoxification and his all-too-frequent relapse. After repeated pairings of the narcotic withdrawal syndrome with previously neutral environmental stimuli, those stimuli may themselves precipitate the signs and symptoms of withdrawal. This account corresponds to the observation by several addicts that when they visited certain parts of the West End of London (e.g. Piccadilly Circus or Gerrard Street) they experienced a craving for drugs. It is also interesting that several ex-addicts who managed successfully to stay off drugs have said that they deliberately avoided going near these places.

Theory and Therapy

These accounts have been among the most influential in the field of drug dependence, and treatment programs have reflected their influence. Physiological theories, for instance, have tended to restrict their definition of drug dependence to the twin phenomena of tolerance (decreased responsiveness to the actions of a drug after repeated experience of that drug) and withdrawal (the occurrence of a physical withdrawal syndrome when the drug is not taken). As a result, this model of addiction encourages a medical and physical approach to treatment which over-values the importance of detoxification or, failing that, of some form of drug maintenance. Methadone maintenance is one example of this latter approach; the use of narcotic antagonists such as naloxone. naltrexone, and cyclazocine is another. Schecter (1978) suggests that 'Antagonists offer an ideal post-methadone short-term program leading to a drug-free state.' Whereas on theoretical grounds these antagonist drugs might appear to be a valuable method of treating a physiological disorder, in fact most drug addicts generally reject such forms of treatment.

In the context of the various attempts to discover an effective medical treatment, it is quite instructive to look at the history of opiate addiction in the United States. By the end of the nineteenth century America already had a large drug addict population. This may well have been largely a result of the ready availability to troops both of narcotics and of hypodermic syringes during the Civil War. At this time, terms such as 'army disease' and 'soldier's illness' were used to refer to opiate addiction. But whatever the reasons, by 1914 it was estimated that there were at least 200,000 addicts in America (Jones *et al.*, 1969).

In 1898 a new drug, supposedly free from addictive properties, was synthesized and this was soon being recommended as a safe and effective treatment for morphine addiction (cf. Szasz, 1975). This new preparation was heroin; and although most addicts who received the new treatment gave up their use of morphine, there was an unfortunate tendency to transfer their addiction to heroin. The resultant heroin addiction was then treated by the Towns–Lambert method. This involved the daily administration of another medication containing a cathartic followed by fluid extract of prickly ash bark and also hyposcyamus combined with tincture of belladonna (Kleber, 1978). Again, the new medical treatment was enthusiastically received both by physicians and by the policy-makers. As a treatment it seems to have few supporters today. As so often in the history of medicine, treatments that were once widely accepted as beneficial have turned out to be either useless or dangerous.

The synthesis of methadone during the 1940s led to another outburst of optimism about the possibility of a medical treatment for opiate dependence. Since that time, methadone has been extensively used in the treatment of heroin addiction despite the fact that as early as 1948 there had been warnings that users found the effects of this new drug to be highly pleasurable (Isbell *et al.*, 1948). The appeal of methadone as an addictive drug in its own right has since been amply confirmed. The medical model of treatment is epitomized by the use of methadone maintenance. This has received approval from many addicts largely because it provides them with a free supply of narcotics (which could be useful if it encouraged the addict to avoid criminal activities, obtain a job, and regulate his style of life). On the other hand, the American street addict is using extremely poor-grade narcotics. In their analysis of samples of New York street heroin, Primm and Bath (1973) found the modal content of heroin to be less than 1 percent. When the addict is given a daily dose of as much as 180 milligrams of methadone, the fact that he stops craving heroin is more likely to reflect the fact that he is stoned on methadone than any euphoria-blocking effect. On the evidence of studies from both Britain and America, it is now quite clear that some addicts prefer methadone as a drug of abuse even to heroin (Gossop and Connell, 1975; Agar and Stephens, 1976). In Levy's (1972) follow-up study of 50 narcotic addicts, he found that after 5 years, nine had stopped using opiates and 11 had reverted to occasional use only. Whether or not they had received methadone treatment had no relationship to their subsequent use of, or abstinence from, drugs. Rather than accept the weaknesses of their approach to addiction, however, proponents of the medical model continue to believe that another medication will be discovered that will provide an effective treatment for drug dependence (e.g. Kolb, 1962).

Unlike the physiological model, personality disorder formulations of addiction encourage an individual-oriented approach to treatment. A variety of individual and group-psychotherapy interventions have been tried, and although clinical case studies have reported successful outcomes (e. g. Kraft, 1970), the long-term effects of psychotherapy as a treatment for drug dependence seem to be poor (Harding, 1975). Again, this formulation is predicated upon the assumption that some sort of pre-existing personality disorder impels the addict towards drug dependence, and subsequently towards relapse, unless the underlying disorder itself can be changed. This position is really an intrapsychic re-statement of the medical model. One might expect the social theories of addiction to counterbalance these 'hidden factor' explanations. Unfortunately, most social accounts also fall into the trap of setting up pre-existing 'causes', though in this case the causes are of a social rather than a medical sort.

The influence of social theories of addiction upon treatment approaches can be illustrated by Kaufman and Kaufman's (1978) attempt to treat the families of drug addicts. The addict's drug abuse is seen as symptomatic of the social pathology of the interactions within the family, and the aim of therapy is to create structural changes in the family. The social approach should be valuable in its attempt to place addiction in a wider social context than the intra-individual formulations of personality and physiological theories. When stated in this form, however, it retains the assumptions that addiction can be seen as an end-product of forces acting upon the individual; i.e. it is seen as symptomatic of some sort of 'family pathology'. Others have taken the more profitable line of looking for the social factors that support or interfere with the individual in his efforts to do without drugs. In more detailed analyses of Stimson's group of heroin addicts it was found that those individuals who achieved abstinence were more likely to have a regular job, a legitimate source of income, permanent accommodation, and to be least involved with other drug addicts (Oppenheimer et al., 1979).

Conditioning models of the sort proposed by Wikler (1965) encourage forms of therapy which are designed to break down the reinforcing consequences of drug-taking. This has been attempted by associating the drug-taking with aversive consequences. Teasdale (1973) used an aversion therapy procedure in which drug-related stimuli were paired with electric shock. This seemed to lessen the craving that the addict experienced when he was presented with the experimental stimuli, but the effect failed to generalize to other stimuli, and several subjects relapsed soon after treatment. Teasdale suggests that conditioned abstinence syndromes are likely to be only one of a number of factors leading to relapse. Even if the aversion therapy had successfully eliminated the conditioned abstinence symptoms, the other factors could have remained operative. There has also been some recent interest in the use of covert (or imaginal) sensitization, but although this has been said to yield encouraging results, most investigations have been in the form of clinical case studies with small numbers of subjects, and few experimental controls (e.g. Copemann, 1977).

The actual series of events that make up the treatment intervention are themselves extremely complex. They occur within a confused system of social, psychological, legal and quasi-medical pressures; and despite the concise accounts given in the research journals the treatment is seldom a precise and delineated procedure, but an uncontrolled and poorly understood series of events. Indeed, when we use the word 'treatment' in this context, we are using the term metaphorically and not literally (the exception to this are those physicians who still cling to the belief that addiction is a specific physical disorder).

'Treatments' are essentially instrumental by nature; they consist of *what is done*; but rather than being an event that *happens to* the addict, treatment in the field of drug addiction is a process in which the addict takes an active role. Copemann and Shaw (1976) looked at a group of addicts who had been admitted to a treatment program as an alternative to imprisonment. The treatment approach was described in broadly operant terms. The authors suggest that their results point to a positive relationship between length of stay in treatment and improved outcome (measured by qualitative estimates of clinical improvement rather than by measures of behavioral adjustment). Copemann and Shaw argue that this relationship is not surprising because the longer an addict remains in treatment, the greater his exposure to the treatment regime. Kolb (1962) has also assumed that there exist specific techniques for the treatment of addiction and that 'many voluntary patients would be permanently cured if they could be compelled to remain in the hospital for at least four or five months'. Whereas there may be some empirical relationship between the length of time that an addict chooses to remain in a treatment program and his chances of staying off drugs afterwards, the effects underlying this relationship are not known, and the level of correlation is likely to be low. It certainly should not be assumed (as by Kolb, and by Copemann and Shaw) that some simple positive linear relationship exists between the two.

Both of these reports illustrate the insidious way in which the treatment of addiction can come to be seen as a sort of mechanical process whereby the greater the exposure, the greater are the chances of improvement. Neither gives proper consideration to the ways in which the attitudes and intentions of the addict himself may play a significant part in the process. For instance, Copemann and Shaw found that addicts who are under threat of a court sentence do as well as others who are not under this sort of pressure. This finding could easily be seen as reflecting the worries of the person about the social complications entailed by any continued drug use. This interpretation is supported by the results of Gossop (1978b) who found that addicts who have the longest criminal histories, and who are most worried about getting into further trouble with the law, are likely to remain in treatment for longer periods than addicts who do not face such pressures. The most important single factor associated with the period of time that the addict decided to remain in treatment, however, was his own desire for treatment. By searching for a 'hidden factor' type of explanation of why an addict remains in treatment or why he does well, it is possible to underrate the importance of the addict's own expectations and intentions.

Using an operant conditioning model, Meyer and Mirin (1979) have attempted to reformulate the 'heroin stimulus' in cognitive terms. They suggest that the primary reinforcement of opiates may be associated with specific effects within the central nervous system, but that drug users ascribe different meanings to the effects of heroin and to the environmental stimuli that are associated with the use of drugs. It is the symbolic significance of drug-taking that has such a powerful influence upon addiction. Similarly, in treatment, the addict's decision to cooperate with, or to resist, the aims of a treatment program will depend upon the way in which he perceives his own drug use, upon his beliefs about how and why the use of drugs has become so important in his life, and upon his expectations about his ability to cope without drugs in the future. In short, the external treatment procedures are of less importance than the *meaning* that they have for the addict.

In an investigation of 40 former opiate addicts who had achieved abstinence, Wille (1980) found that a unilateral decision on the part of the doctor to reduce the addict's maintenance prescription usually failed to produce any improvement in the addict's behavior. In certain cases it led to serious adverse effects, as when the addict transferred his use of drugs to black market supplies. Those addicts who did manage to give up their use of drugs reported that they had intended to do so, and that they felt that they could control the process of reduction themselves. Indeed, a small number of Wille's sample (4 out of 40) withdrew themselves from opiates voluntarily and spontaneously over a period of a few days. More than half of the addicts who achieved abstinence did so as out-patients in the community and without any in-patient treatment. These results are based upon retrospective interviews, and are therefore liable to certain biases (e.g. once an individual has successfully given up his dependence upon drugs, he may subsequently overrate his own part in this, and underestimate the contribution of other factors). Nonetheless, it is difficult to ignore the increasing weight of evidence that points to the important role played by the addict's beliefs, intentions, attitudes, and expectations.

An important consequence of this is that one can no longer apply specific treatment procedures to a group of addicts and expect them to have predictable outcomes. By concentrating upon the treatment itself, and upon the question of the effectiveness of specific interventions, evaluative research has frequently served to obscure the crucial role of individual differences within the addict population. Einstein and Garitano (1972) have pointed out that many drug-dependence treatment programs fail to take account of these individual differences. By continuing to act as if drug dependence were a homogeneous disorder which could be treated by some specific technique, the general air of confusion and misunderstanding that surrounds this issue is perpetuated. There is the further sophistry that whenever there is a favorable outcome and the addict gives up using drugs, this success is usually attributed to the treatment process itself. The addict is relegated to the role of a passive recipient of the treatment. When the addict returns to his use of drugs after treatment, however, instead of regarding this as a treatment failure, the addict is suddenly credited with the capacity to control his own actions, and the relapse is seen in terms of the addict's lack of motivation or his resistance to treatment. It is a most curious paradox that the addict's cognitions are omitted from any consideration of the reasons for achieving a successful outcome, and are invoked only to legitimize the failure of treatment, and implicitly to denigrate the individual.

Cognition and Drug Dependence

The well-known experiments of Schachter and Singer (1962) demonstrated how drugs depend for their effect upon the cognitive interpretation of the person who takes them; and among marihuana smokers, Becker (1966) described how the effects of the drug are themselves dependent upon the users' social experiences with the drug. At first the drug effects may be perceived as physically unpleasant, or at least ambiguous. The user learns from others how he should enjoy their effects. He also acquires a conception of the meaning of drug-taking, which makes the use of cannabis both possible and desirable. The same process of learning, and of cognitive integration, occurs with such other drugs as heroin, barbiturates, amphetamines, and the other drugs of dependence.

The impact of the individual's cognitions can also be seen in Schasre's (1966) study of a group of narcotic addicts who had subsequently given up their use of heroin. The most interesting finding concerned those individuals who stopped using heroin after making a deliberate decision. The most common reason for giving up was that the users realized they were *physically dependent.* This is quite contrary to the usual assumptions (e.g. Lindesmith, 1968) that once the user is physically dependent or becomes aware of his physical dependence, he is inevitably committed to the further use of drugs. Among the other reasons that led people to give up heroin were the shock of being arrested, of seeing a friend convicted for possession, or having a friend die of an overdose.

Schasre's report touches upon an exchange between a number of heroin addicts and those ex-users who cited physical addiction as their reason for giving up heroin. The addicts refused to accept that this was possible and argued that once a person was physically addicted they were 'hooked' and unable to control their habit. This interesting conversation receives only a brief mention by Schasre, but it is suggestive of the crucial role of the addict's attitudes and beliefs about his own drug-taking.

Eiser and Gossop (1979) conducted a study of individuals attending an out-patient drug-dependence clinic at the Maudsley Hospital in London. This study looked at the ways in which addicts interpreted their own dependence upon drugs. One way was to regard it as a form of sickness, or as symptomatic of some underlying disorder most appropriately treated by doctors. Another group (mainly heroin addicts) emphasized their physical dependence upon drugs, and their unwillingness and inability to give them up. These two factors bear an interesting resemblance to Parsons' (1951) concept of the sick role. The addict has little confidence in his ability to get better through his own efforts, and he may also see his addiction as a form of illness and expect to be cured as a result of medical intervention. But whereas Parsons' notion of the sick role tends to combine the 'hooked' and 'sick' aspects, it seems likely that these two ways of interpreting one's addiction may be largely independent. Similar results have also been reported in a study of the ways in which cigarette smokers perceived their smoking (Eiser, Chapter 12); a principal-components analysis revealed the same sort of hooked and sick factors that emerged in the drug clinic investigation.

It is not altogether encouraging that some addicts tended to define themselves as 'sick'—an explanation which seems to account for their addiction and simultaneously absolve them from altering it, whereas those other addicts who regarded themselves as 'hooked', emphasized their compulsion to go on using drugs, their physical addiction, and their resistance to change. A further investigation of the addict's perceptions of his own drug-taking (Gossop, Eiser, and Ward, in preparation) suggests that there are a number of such factors which relate to the addict's decision to seek in-patient treatment for his drug dependence. Whereas out-patients were terrified of withdrawal, the in-patient group did not share this same fear: interestingly, the in-patients regarded the out-patient clinic as merely providing a maintenance prescription. The out-patients felt that it offered more than just a script. Among the in-patient group, the patients who stayed longest (as voluntary patients), were the least afraid of withdrawal, whereas the patients who only stayed on the unit for a short period of time were, like the out-patient group, inclined to fear the experience of withdrawing from drugs. The short-stay patients were also more inclined to believe that they were really addicted, as well as that drugs helped them to cope, and that they had other problems beyond their drug difficulties.

The addict's beliefs and attitudes, and the meaning that drug-taking has for him, therefore appear to have clear implications for those who are involved in the business of helping addicts to do without their drugs. Ignoring these attitudes is likely to lead the addicts and helpers into mutual misunderstandings and hostility. Non-cognitive models of addiction which encourage the helper to ignore the addict's interpretation of his own behavior, not only lead to interventions which are likely to be irrelevant and ineffective, but they are also likely to lead to unnecessary confrontations between the addict and those who are trying to help him. It is ironic that almost the only time that the addict is credited with the power to control his own behavior is when he deliberately acts against the wishes or instructions of the professional helper. Until then he was a passive victim of his addiction: suddenly he becomes an active, but malign, influence, sabotaging an otherwise effective treatment program.

The addict is not passively compelled to use drugs; he can and does control his own drug-taking. In recognizing this, the helper should try to work with the addict's beliefs about his drug use. Both parties must explore, and try to understand, th social and psychological meaning that drug-taking has for the addict before they can attempt to effect any changes. Too often those involved in the 'treatment' of drug addicts attempt to deny or ignore the addict's own perceptions of his drug-taking, and this is usually reinforced by the non-cognitive theories that have traditionally been used to explain drug addiction. Such failures to acknowledge the personal significance of drug-taking to the individual are liable to provoke hostility or resistance on the part of the addict, and may well play an active part in interfering with the addict's attempt to do without drugs.

Of course, the approach to drug dependence suggested in this chapter requires a considerable revision of much of the received wisdom in this area. It also requires a fundamental change in the ways in which we conceive of the relationship between patient and therapist, and indeed, a revision of the traditional idea of 'treatment' in this context. Drug addiction is a far more complex human problem than has generally been assumed. It will not respond to the simple mechanical interventions of the sort that too many therapists have attempted to impose upon the problem. Those evaluation studies which have made extravagant claims for high success rates in this area are deluding themselves and misleading others. There are few clearer statements on this subject than that of Einstein (1966):

> There is no relationship between time spent in treatment and the outcome of treatment. There is no relationship between the type of treatment and the outcome of treatment. Whoever the agent of therapy is, whether he be the aggressive social worker, the Rogerian counselor, the pastoral counselor, the psychoanalytically oriented psychotherapist, the clinician who uses methadone maintenance, or the ex-addict giving mutual aid, the end result is not significantly different. The great majority of addicts simply resume drug use.

Similar conclusions have been reached about the effectiveness of treatments for other forms of addictive behavior. In a review of the treatments available for alcoholism, Clare (1977) concluded that a minority of alcoholics will achieve abstinence regardless of the nature, intensity, and duration of treatment, and that there is no difference between the remission rate for different treatments. In smoking, too, most studies suggest that regardless of the sort of treatment (whether behavior modification, formal psychotherapy, re-education programs, or drug treatments), only a small proportion of the cigarette smokers who give up, manage to remain non-smokers (Bernstein, 1969; Hunt and Matarazzo, 1973).

Many individuals return to drug-taking after treatment. This could be seen simply as a failure of the treatment itself. In view of the fact that many interventions have been tried and none have had any marked success in the treatment of drug dependence, it could be seen as an indication that the model of 'treatment' is itself inappropriate in this instance. It should also alert us to the fact that drug dependence is a far more complex problem than has usually been assumed: the apparently high 'relapse rate' is a measure of the difficulties inherent in any attempt to change a person's beliefs about some centrally important aspect of their lives.

References

Agar, M. H., and Stephens, R. C. (1976). 'The methadone street scene—the addict's view', *Current Therapy*, **17**, 100.
Anderson, D., and Solomon, P. (1971). 'Drug dependence', Solomon, P., and Patch, V. D. (eds), *Handbook of Psychiatry* Large Medical Publications, Los Altos, Calif.
Becker, M. S. (1966). 'Becoming a marijuana user', in O'Donnell, J., and Ball, J. (eds), *Narcotic Addiction*. Harper & Row, New York.
Bernstein, D. A. (1969). 'Modification of smoking behaviour: an evaluative review', *Psychological Bulletin.*, **71**, 418–440.
Blumberg, H., Cohen, S., Dronfield, E., Mordecai, E., Roberts, J., and Hawks, D. (1974). 'British opiate users': II. 'Differences between those given an opiate script and those not given one', *International Journal of the Addictions*, **9**, 205–220.
Chein, I., Gerard, D. L., Lees, R. S., and Rosenfeld, E. (1964). *Narcotics Delinquency and Social Policy. The Road to H.* Tavistock, London.

Clare, A. W. (1977). 'How good is treatment?' in Edwards, P., and Grant, M. (eds), *Alcoholism: New Knowledge and New Responses*. Croom Helm, London.

Copemann, C. D. (1977). 'Treatment of polydrug abuse and addiction by covert sensitisation: some contraindications', *International Journal of the Addictions*, **12**, 17–23.

Copemann, C. D., and Shaw, P. L. (1976). 'Readiness for rehabilitation', *International Journal of the Addictions*, **11**, 439–445.

Cushman, P., Jr. (1974). 'Methadone maintenance treatment: and appraisal', *Journal of Drug Issues*, **4**, 376–380.

Deneau, G., Yanagita, T., and Seevers, M. H. (1969). 'Self-administration of psychoactive substances by the monkey', *Psychopharmacologia (Berl.)*, **16**, 30–48.

Dole, V. P., and Nyswander, M. E. (1965). 'A medical treatment for diacetylmorphine (heroin) addiction', *Journal of the American Medical Association*, **193**, 646–650.

Dole, V. P., and Nyswander, M. E. (1966). Rehabilitation of heroin addicts after blockade with methadone. *New York State Journal of Medicine*, **66**, 2011–2017.

DSM II (1968). *Diagnostic and Statistical Manual of Mental Disorders*, 2nd edn. American Psychiatric Association, Washington.

Duncan, D. F. (1977). 'Life stress as a precursor to adolescent drug dependence', *International Journal of the Addictions*, **12**, 1047–1056.

Edwards, G., Chandler, J., and Hensman, C. (1972). 'Drinking in a London suburb: I. Correlates of normal drinking', *Quarterly Journal of Studies on Alcohol*, suppl. 6, 69–93.

Einstein, S. (1966). 'The narcotic's dilemma: who is listening to what?', *International Journal of the Addictions*, **1**, 1–6.

Einstein, S., and Garitano, W. (1972). 'Treating the drug abuser: problems, factors and alterations', *International Journal of the Addictions*, **7**, 321–331.

Eiser, J. R., and Gossop, M. R. (1979). ' "Hooked" or "Sick": addicts' perceptions of their addiction', *Addictive Behaviors*, **4**, 185–191.

Gearing, F. (1970). 'Evaluation of methadone maintenance treatment program', *International Journal of the Addictions*, **5**, 517–543.

Gossop, M. R. (1978a). 'A review of the evidence for methadone maintenance as a treatment for narcotic addiction', *Lancet*, **1**, 812–815.

Gossop, M. R. (1978b). 'Drug dependence: a study of the relationship between motivational, cognitive, social and historical factors, and treatment variables', *Journal of Nervous and Mental Diseases*, **166**, 44–50.

Gossop, M. R. (1979). 'Drug dependence: a re-appraisal', in Oborne, D. J., Gruneberg, M. M., and Eiser, J. R. (eds), *Research in Psychology and Medicine*, vol. 2. Academic Press, London.

Gossop, M. R., and Connell, P. H. (1975). 'Attitudes of oral and intravenous multiple drug users toward drugs of abuse', *International Journal of the Addictions*, **10**, 459–472.

Gossop, M. R., Eiser, J. R., and Ward, E. (in preparation). Implications of the addict's perceptions of his own drug taking, for the treatment of drug dependence.

Gossop, M. R., and Roy, A. (1976). 'Hostility in drug dependent individuals: its relation to specific drugs, and oral or intravenous use', *British Journal of Psychiatry*, **128**, 188–193.

Gossop, M. R., and Roy, A. (1977). 'Hostility, crime and drug dependence', *British Journal of Psychiatry*, **130**, 272–278.

Harding, G. T. (1975). 'Psychotherapy in the treatment of drug dependence', in Bostram, H., Larsson, T., and Ljungstedt, N. (eds), *Drug Dependence in Treatment and Treatment Evaluation*. Almgvist & Wiksell, Stockholm.

Hunt, W. A., and Matarazzo, J. D. (1973). 'Three years later: recent developments in the experimental modification of smoking behaviour', *Journal of Abnormal Psychology*, **81**, 107–114.

Isbell, H., Wikler, A., Eisenman, A. J. *et al.* (1948). 'Liability of addiction to 6-dimethylamino-4-4-diphenyl-3-heptanone (methadone, "amidone", or "10820") in man', *Archives of Internal Medicine*, **82**, 362–392.

Jeffrey, D. B. (1975). 'Treatment evaluation issues in research on addictive behaviours', *Addictive Behaviors*, **1**, 23–26.

Jones, K., Shainberg, L. W., and Byer, C. O. (1969). *Drugs and Alcohol*. Harper & Row, New York.

Kaufman, E., and Kaufman, P. (1978). 'Multiple family therapy: a new direction in the treatment of drug abusers', *Drug and Alcohol Abuse*, **4**, 467–478.

Keller, M. (1972). 'The oddities of alcoholics', *Quarterly Journal of Studies on Alcohol*, **33**, 1147–1148.

Kleber, H. D. (1978). 'Treatment—past and future', in Schecter, A. (ed.), *Treatment Aspects of Drug Dependence*. CRC Press.

Kolb, L. (1962). *Drug Addiction: A Medical Problem*. Thomas, Springfield, Ill.

Kosterlitz, H. W., and Hughes, J. (1977). 'Opiate receptors and endogenous opioid peptides in tolerance and dependence', in Gross, M. M. (ed.), *Alcohol Intoxication and Withdrawal*. Plenum, New York.

Kosterlitz, H. W., and Hughes, J. (1978). 'Biological, significance of the endogenous opioid peptides and the opiate receptors', in Israel, Y. *et al.* (eds), *Research Advances in Alcohol and Drug Problems*, vol. 4. Plenum, New York.

Kraft, M. B. (1970). 'Successful treatment of "Drinamyl" addicts and associated personality changes', *Canadian Psychiatric Association Journal*, **15**, 223–227.

Kumar, R., and Stolerman, I. P. (1977). 'Experimental and clinical aspects of drug dependence', in Iverson, L. I., and Iverson, S. D. (eds), *Handbook of Psychopharmacology*. Plenum Press, New York.

Levy, B. S. (1972). 'Five years after: a follow-up of 50 narcotic addicts', *American Journal of Psychiatry*, **128**, 868–872.

Lindesmith, A. R. (1968). *Addiction and Opiates*. Aldine, Chicago.

Maddux, J. F. (1965). 'Hospital management of the narcotic addict', in Wilmer, D. M., and Kassebaum, G. C. (eds), *Narcotics*. McGraw-Hill, New York.

Methadone Maintenance Evaluation Committee (1968). 'Progress report of evaluation of methadone maintenance treatment programme as of March 31, 1968', *Journal of the American Medical Association*, **206**, 2712–2714.

Meyer, R. E., and Mirin, S. M. (1979). *The Heroin Stimulus*. Plenum, New York.

Newman, R. G. (1976). 'Methadone maintenance treatment: will it survive?', *New York State Journal of Medicine*, **76**, 1536–1537.

Newman, R. G. (1977). *Methadone Treatment in Narcotic Addiction*. Academic Press, New York.

Nyswander, M. E. (1956). *The Drug Addict as a Patient*. Grune & Stratton, New York.

Oppenheimer, E., Stimson, G. V., and Thorley, A (1979). 'Seven-year follow-up of heroin addicts: abstinence and continued use compared', *British Medical Journal*, **2**, 627–630.

Parsons, T. (1951). *The Social System*. Free Press, Chicago.

Platt, J. J., Labate, C., and Wicks, R. J. (1977). *Evaluative Research in Correctional Drug Abuse Treatment*. Heath, Lexington.

Primm, B. J., and Bath, P. E. (1973). 'Pseudoheroinism', *International Journal of Addictions*, **8**, 231–242.

Robins, L. N., Davis, D. H., and Goodwin, D. W. (1974). 'Drug use by U. S. Army enlisted men in Vietnam: a follow-up on their return home', *American Journal of Epidemiology*, **99**, 235–249.

Schachter, S., and Singer, J. E., (1962). 'Cognitive, social and physiological determinants of emotional state', *Psychological Review*, **69**, 379–399.

Schasre, R. (1966). 'Cessation patterns among neophyte heroin users', *International Journal of Addictions*, **1**, 23–32.

Schecter, A. (1978). 'An overview of the use of Lowinson, J. H. *et al.* (eds), *Critical Concerns in the Field of Drug Abuse*. Marcel Dekker, New York.

Schuster, C. R., and Thompson, T. (1969). 'Self-administration of and behavioral dependence on drugs', *Annual Review of Pharmacology*, **9**, 483–502.

Siegel, J. M., and Platt, J. J. (1977). 'Basic principles of evaluation methodology in correctional drug abuse treatment', in Platt, J., Labate, C., and Wicks, R. (eds), *Evaluative Research in Correctional Drug Abuse Treatment*. Heath, Lexington.

Stimson, G. V. (1973). *Heroin and Behaviour*. Irish University Press, Shannon.

Stimson, G. V., Oppenheimer, E., and Thorley, A. (1978). 'Seven year folow-up of heroin addicts: drug use and outcome', *British Medical Journal*, **1**, 1190–1192.

Szasz, T. S. (1975). *Ceremonial Chemistry*. Routledge & Kegan Paul, London.

Teasdale, J. (1973). 'Conditional abstinence in narcotic addicts', *International Journal of Addiction*, **8**, 273–292.

Vaillant, G. E. (1973). '20-year follow-up of New York narcotic addicts', *Archives of General Psychiatry*, **29**, 237–241.

Wikler, A. (1948). 'Recent progress in research on the neurophysiologic basis of morphine addiction', *American Journal of Psychiatry*, **105**, 329–338.

Wikler, A. (1965). 'Conditioning factors in opiate addiction and relapse', in Wilmer, D., and Kassebaum, G. (eds), *Narcotics*. McGraw-Hill. New York.

Wille, R. (1980). 'Case Studies I. Natural processes of recovery', in Edwards, G., and Aris, A. (eds), *Drug Dependence in Socio-Cultural Context*. WHO, Geneva.

Social Psychology and Behavioral Medicine
Edited by J. Richard Eiser
© 1982 John Wiley & Sons Ltd

Chapter 12

Addiction as attribution: cognitive processes in giving up smoking

J. Richard Eiser

One of the difficulties of doing social psychological research in applied contexts is the way in which issues become defined as 'problems' for psychologists and others to solve. Often the applicability of familiar methods and theories becomes less easily recognized, simply because of the form in which the questions are put. An instance of this is in the field of addiction research, and is particularly true with respect to cigarette smoking.

How, then, has cigarette smoking come to be defined as a problem? Whilst tobacco has enjoyed many periods of favor and disfavor over the centuries since it was introduced into Europe, it is only recently that the associated health risks have been recognized. This recognition is a result not only of improved techniques of medical and epidemiological investigation, but also of changes in the pattern of tobacco use. More traditional tobacco products (cigars, pipes, chewing tobacco, snuff) seem to allow the absorption of nicotine from the tobacco (into the bloodstream and thence to the brain) through the buccal and nasal membranes. Nowadays, however, most tobacco is consumed in the form of manufactured cigarettes, which operate on a rather different principle. With a manufactured cigarette relatively little nicotine appears to be absorbed into the bloodstream through the nose and mouth. Instead, most of the nicotine is absorbed when the smoke is inhaled into the lungs. The inhaled smoke, however, contains not just nicotine, but also carbon monoxide and carcinogenic tar which is deposited in the lungs.

There can be no doubt that the diseases caused or exacerbated by cigarette smoking are among the major problems in medicine today. It has been calculated that there are about 50,000 premature deaths per annum in the United Kingdom attributable to smoking (Royal College of Physicians, 1977). In spite of massive public and private endowments for research, there remains little sign of a 'magic cure' for the majority of lung cancer patients. Attention has therefore appropriately shifted toward the question of prevention. With

281

this shift in attention, however, has come a subtle, but important, shift in definition. Smoking has come to be seen not only as a behavior which *causes* disease, but as a behavior which is *itself* an appropriate target for medical study and intervention. Smoking has become labeled as a disorder *in itself*—more specifically, as a form of addiction or dependence disorder (Russell, 1971), and even as a 'mental disorder' (Jaffe, 1977).

Smoking as an Addiction

In terms of conventional behavioral and pharmacological criteria, the label of 'addiction' can be applied to cigarette smoking as appropriately as it can to the use of a number of other legal and illegal drugs, such as alcohol and opiates. Established smokers certainly experience great difficulty in doing without cigarettes for extended periods of time, and among those who come to clinics for help with giving up, the percentage remaining abstinent up to (say) one year after treatment is consistently low (roughly 25 percent), whatever the method of treatment employed (Raw, 1978). It has been argued that the process of relapse is essentially the same whether one is dealing with cigarettes, alcohol or heroin (Hunt and Matarazzo, 1973), although this conclusion, based on group rather than individual data, is open to important methodological objections (Litman *et al.*, 1979; Sutton, 1979).

The pharmacological evidence points to nicotine as the main psychoactive substance in tobacco smoke. Smokers will respond to changes in the nicotine content of cigarettes (Russell, 1977) or to changes in their salivary and urinary pH which affects absorption and excretion of nicotine (Schachter *et al.*, 1977) by adjusting the number of cigarettes they smoke, the number of puffs they take, the amount they inhale, etc., so as to maintain a relatively constant level of nicotine in their bloodstream. There is also evidence of the development of tolerance to nicotine (as in the case of other drugs) and of withdrawal symptoms (albeit relatively mild, such as perceived inability to concentrate) when the drug is withdrawn. Nicotine appears to have both stimulant and relaxant properties, depending on the dose and on other factors. It should also be noted that the cigarette is an extremely effective means of self-administering nicotine. It has been calculated that the nicotine from an inhaled puff hits the brain in about 7 seconds—faster than the heroin from an intravenous injection (Russell, 1977).

Addiction: the Popular Stereotype

To say that smoking has these characteristics, however, does not amount to saying that smoking is an addiction in the popular stereotypical sense of the term. Indeed it is questionable how addictive any drugs are in this sense. According to the popular stereotype, once an addictive drug has been used, there is little hope of the user being able to escape from its clutches ever again. The drug-user's addiction is a 'sickness' which can only be cured by medical intervention, if indeed it is curable at all. Striking counter-evidence on this point comes from a study by Robins *et al.* (1974), which found an extremely high rate of 'spontaneous recovery' from opiate dependence among American servicemen returning from Vietnam (see Chapter 11).

Other problems associated with thinking of addiction as a 'sickness' can be learned from considering the 'disease' concept of alcoholism (Jellinek, 1960). Whilst acceptance of this concept may shift the emphasis away from mere moral censure, it may have a number of problematic implications for how the alcoholic's drinking is viewed by himself and by therapists and helping agencies, as discussed in Chapter 10.

Apart from this issue of personal responsibility and control, another important aspect of sick-role theory (Parsons, 1951) is the notion that the role of a sick person can in some way be marginal or deviant. Seeing drug users and smokers as 'addicted', and hence 'sick', makes it easier to regard them as 'different'. The question of why people smoke thus becomes translated into one of how smokers are different from 'normal' healthy people. A fair number of studies have been unsuccessful in their attempts to explain sizeable portions of variance in terms of personality, as opposed to demographic, factors (e.g. Jacobs *et al.*, 1966; Matarazzo and Saslow, 1960). Also if the drug user defines himself as 'sick', he has an explanation which seems both to account for his behavior, and absolve him from personal responsibility for altering it.

The concept of addiction is thus very much bound up with how people *explain* each other's use of drugs. When one starts talking about interpersonal explanations of behavior, however, one moves into the territory of social psychology generally and of attribution processes in particular. In what follows, I shall describe some findings which show that concepts developed from an attributional perspective may be relevant to a consideration of smoking attitudes and behavior.

Attribution Theory

For readers less familiar with the social psychological literature, a brief account of attribution theory may be useful here. Attribution research is the field of social psychology concerned with people's everyday explanations for events and experiences. Stemming from the early work of Heider (1958), the field has expanded to include a wide range of topics from the perception of cause–effect relationships to broader questions under the headings of what used to be more frequently termed person perception and moral judgment.

An example of a specific area within this field is attribution of responsibility (e.g. Fincham and Jaspars, 1980). This combines the traditional interests in questions of perceived causality, impressions of personality and moral judgment by employing research paradigms in which subjects typically are presented with descriptions of episodes in which the actions of one person have certain, often undesirable, consequences for another, and are asked to rate the perpetrator of the act in terms of various criteria. Sometimes such judgments are presented as analogous to those made by jurors when appraising a defendant. Another area is that of attribution for success and failure at achievement tasks (e.g. Weiner and Kukla, 1970). This can involve both teachers' explanations for why pupils succeed or fail (which can lead on to the question of the possibility of self-fulfilling prophecies instituted within educational systems), and the attributions made by individuals themselves for their *own* success and failure. Indeed, the continuity between people's explanations for others' behavior, and their explanations for their *own* behavior and experiences (*self-attributions*) is a recurrent theme in attribution research, bearing on such issues as self-attribution of emotional states (Schachter and Singer, 1962) and of attitudes (Bem, 1967; Cooper *et al.*, 1978). In spite of this continuity, however, there are certain differences between self-attributions and attributions for others' behavior, which will be discussed below. Research on personality variables such as internal–external locus of control (Rotter, 1966) may also be incorporated within an attributional approach, in that it can be taken to refer to individual differences in attributional style.

Attribution *theory* (e.g. Kelley and Michela, 1980) is the name given to a set of propositions concerned primarily with the conditions under which one type of explanation for an event or experience is likely to be *perceived* as more appropriate than another. Although the theory presents an apparently rationalistic 'model of man', it is not a theory about how people *ought* to explain events in accordance with the canons of logic or scientific method, but rather a theory about how 'commonsense notions' or 'lay conceptions of personality'—what Heider (1958) called 'naive psychology'—get translated into people's explanations for behavior.

Smokers *vs.* Non-smokers: Actors *vs.* Observers?

A central distinction in attribution theory is that between explanations of a person's behavior in terms of the kind of person he is (internal or personal attributions) and explanations in terms of the stimulus environment in which he finds himself (external or situational attributions). Jones and Nisbett (1971) have argued that people called upon to account for their *own* behavior ('actors') tend to offer situational explanations, but that, when they take the role of independent 'observers' of another's behavior, they tend to make more internal attributions in terms of the characteristics of the other person.

This seems very much what happens with respect to how the explanations offered by smokers for their own smoking differ from those given by non-smokers asked to account for the behavior of smokers.

We have investigated this in two studies in which we sent short questionnaires concerning smoking to representative samples of the adult population who were participating in the Independent Broadcasting Authority's weekly survey of audience reactions to television programs. In the first study (Eiser *et al.*, 1977) the final sample included 105 smokers, 155 who had never smoked regularly, and 108 ex-smokers. Smokers were asked how difficult they thought it would be to give up cigarettes, how much they would like to give up cigarettes, whether they thought they were addicted, and whether they got real pleasure from a cigarette. Non-smokers responded to similar items, reworded so that they were asked whether they thought cigarette smokers, on average, would find it difficult to give up, would like to, were addicted and got real pleasure from a cigarette. The responses of smokers and non-smokers were then compared, controlling for sex, age, and social class. The first two items showed no significant differences. Non-smokers were much more likely to label the average smoker as addicted than the smokers, on average, were prepared to label themselves. Also non-smokers significantly underestimated the amount of pleasure obtained by smokers (see Table 12.1).

The second study (Eiser *et al.*, 1978b) followed similar lines, with a sample of 115 smokers, 117 never-smokers, and 82 ex-smokers. Comparisons were made between smokers and non-smokers on items concerning the difficulty of giving up cigarettes, whether smokers would like to give up, whether they got real pleasure from a cigarette, and whether they were frightened that cigarette smoking might seriously damage their own health. Again, there were no significant differences between smokers and non-smokers on the first two items. However, non-smokers again underestimated the amount of pleasure obtained by smokers, as well as the extent to which smokers were frightened about the risks to their health. Thus, in view of the non-smoker, the average smoker is clearly addicted, does not always obtain pleasure from smoking, and is relatively unconcerned about the risks to his health. For the non-smoker, it would seem that the apparent irrationality of smokers is explained by means of the personal attribution that smokers are 'addicted', and negligent of the health risks.

A recent report by Wright (1980) focused more specifically on the attributions made by ex-smokers, as distinct from both smokers and never-smokers. When asked to rate how much their own, or the average smoker's, failure to give up smoking was due to the factors of lack of effort, lack of ability, task difficulty, or bad luck, both smokers and ex-smokers emphasized task difficulty and effort relative to ability, whereas the reverse was true for never-smokers.

Table 12.1 Comparisons between smokers, never-smokers, and ex-smokers (means)

(a) First study (Eiser et al., 1977)

	Smokers ($n = 105$)	Never-smokers ($n = 155$)	Ex-smokers ($n = 108$)
1. 'How easy or difficult would it be for you to give up cigarettes if you wanted to?' 1 = Very easy; 5 = Very difficult.	3.64	3.85	3.53
2. 'How much would you like to give up cigarettes?' 1 = Not at all; 2 = Somewhat; 3 = Very much	2.15	2.06	2.19
3. 'Do you think you are addicted to cigarettes?' 1 = No; 2 = Don't know; 3 = Yes.	2.19 $\xleftrightarrow{*}$ 2.70		2.71
4. 'Do you get real pleasure from a cigarette?' 1 = Hardly ever; 2 = Sometimes; 3 = Almost always	2.50 $\xleftrightarrow{\dagger}$ 2.18		2.22

(b) Second study (Eiser et al., 1978b)

	Smokers ($n = 115$)	Never-smokers ($n = 117$)	Ex-smokers ($n = 72$)
1. 'How difficult would it be for you to give up cigarettes if you wanted to?' 1 = Not at all difficult; 2 = Fairly difficult; 3 = Very difficult.	2.24	2.32	2.22
2. 'Would you like to stop smoking altogether if you could do so easily?' 1 = No; 2 = Yes.	1.70	1.73	1.77
3. 'Do you get real pleasure from a cigarette?' 1 = Hardly ever; 2 = Sometimes; 3 = Almost always	2.37 $\xleftrightarrow{\ddagger}$ 2.20		2.28
4. 'Are you frightened that your cigarette smoking might seriously damage your own health?' 1 = No; 2 = Don't know; 3 = Yes	2.15 $\xleftrightarrow{\S}$ 1.70		1.79

* $F(1, 314) = 30.99$; $p < 0.001$.
† $F(1, 314) = 17.95$; $p < 0.001$.
‡ $F(1, 261) = 8.13$; $p < 0.01$.
§ $F(1, 261) = 13.56$; $p < 0.001$.

'Dissonance' and the Self-attribution of Addiction

One of the most influential concepts in the smoking literature is the distinction between 'consonant' and 'dissonant' smokers introduced by McKennell and Thomas (1967). Smokers who say they would like to give up smoking if they could do so easily are assumed to be in a state of cognitive dissonance regarding their smoking. It is suggested that there is little point in exhorting such smokers to give up, since they already hold negative beliefs about smoking and their problem is not whether they want to stop, but how. The idea that these smokers are the most addicted is used by McKennell and Thomas to explain this apparent discrepancy between attitudes and behavior. 'Consonant' smokers, who say they do not want to give up, are presumed to be a better target for health education, since there is still room for their attitudes to change.

There is a difference, though, between asking someone 'Do you want to stop smoking *now?*' and the hypothetical question 'Would you like to stop smoking altogether if you could do so easily?' The qualification 'if you could do so easily' offers a huge loophole to any smokers who might wish to escape from the implications for their own behavior of admitting that smoking is dangerous. In formal terms, this is because dissonance does *not* arise merely from holding negative attitudes concerning the consequences of one's behavior. It arises from the cognition that one has *chosen freely,* but that one's choice was wrong. Reducing perceived freedom of choice thus reduces or eliminates cognitive dissonance (Linder *et al.*, 1967). If the smoker feels he could *not* stop smoking easily, no dissonance is implied by his saying that he would like to stop if he could, and the label of 'dissonant smoker' is, in this context, a misnomer (Eiser, 1978).

In the second of the two studies already mentioned, we included a question which allowed us to classify smokers as 'consonant' and 'dissonant' by the McKennell and Thomas (1967) criterion, and we also asked them if they thought they were addicted. We found (Eiser *et al.*, 1978a) that over half our smokers were prepared to label themselves as addicted. There was also a clear association between smokers seeing themselves as addicted and being 'dissonant' (see Table 12.2). We next conducted a step-wise discriminant analysis to see which items in the questionnaire best predicted which smokers were 'consonant' and 'dissonant'. The clearest discriminator was the item 'Are you seriously frightened that cigarette smoking might seriously damage your *own* health?' Those who said 'yes' to this item were much more likely to be 'dissonant'. The inference drawn from these results is that fear of the health consequences remains a powerful motivator for smokers to want to give up, but that the self-attribution of addiction may furnish the smoker not only with an explanation for his previous failures at doing without cigarettes, but also with a means of dissonance reduction, and hence (in some cases at least) with an excuse for continuing to smoke.

Is There Still Room for Informational Influence?

It is generally taken for granted that smokers know they are putting their health at risk. Smokers' subjective expected utilities (SEUs) for giving up smoking indeed tend to be more positive than their SEUs for continuing to

Table 12.2 Differences between 'consonant' and 'dissonant' smokers

(a) Discriminant analysis: Means of variables leading to significant improvements in discrimination

Variables (as entered in step-wise discriminant analysis)	Means		F
	Consonant ($n = 35$)	Dissonant ($n = 80$)	$(1, 113)$
1. Frightened	1.54	2.41	25.99†
2. Tried to give up ever	1.43	1.80	17.76†
3. Addicted	1.74	2.38	12.57†
4. Pleasure	2.54	2.30	5.50*
5. No. of cigarettes per day	15.60	20.70	6.17*

    * $p < 0.05$; † $p < 0.001$.
    Note: response categories for:
      Variables 1 and 3: 1 = No; 2 = Don't know; 3 = Yes
      Variable 2:   1 = No; 3 = Yes
      Variable 4:   1 = Hardly ever; 2 = Sometimes; 3 = Almost always

(b) Frequencies of 'Consonant' and 'Dissonant' smokers who did or did not regard themselves as addicted ('Don't knows' included in 'Not addicted' category)

	Addicted	Not addicted
'Consonant'	11	24
'Dissonant'	50	30

    $\chi^2 = 8.23$; $p < 0.01$.

(c) The McKennell and Thomas (1967) criterion

'Would you like to stop smoking cigarettes altogether if you could do so easily?'

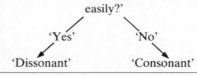

smoke (Eiser and Sutton, 1977; Mausner and Platt, 1971), although the problem remains whether the beliefs measured are those most salient to the subjects (see Chapter 8). It is by no means clear, though, whether smokers have an *accurate* idea of the degree of risk they are running. As part of a more recent study using the same postal survey procedure (Eiser *et al.*, 1979) we compared 109 smokers with 168 never-smokers and 101 ex-smokers in terms of their responses to a number of statements concerning the consequences of smoking. Smokers clearly held less negative beliefs about these consequences than did non-smokers. Just less than 50 percent of smokers, as against about

85 percent of non-smokers, believed smoking to be 'really as dangerous as people say'. Just under one in four of all our subjects realized that smoking caused more deaths in the United Kingdom than road accidents. For smokers the frequency was under 14 percent. Conversely, over 18 percent of smokers, as against less than 7 percent of ex-smokers, accepted the argument that 'if you've been smoking for more than about ten years, there's no point in stopping, as any damage has probably been done already'. These are both examples of where factual information could be presented so as to lead smokers to increase their estimates of the importance and benefits of stopping smoking.

Wanting to Stop

Even if one objects to the McKennell and Thomas picture of hordes of fully informed smokers in states of unresolved dissonance, it is still quite clear that very many smokers would like to give up if the process of giving up could be made easier, and they could be assured a greater chance of success. One might expect smokers' clinics offering psychological support to would-be ex-smokers to fulfil this demand, but it seems that such clinics tend to attract the heavier smokers and, presumably as a part consequence of this, traditionally have unimpressive success rates (where proper records are available) and seem relatively ineffective in terms of the therapists's time (Raw, 1978). Nonetheless, there is a continued interest in anti-smoking 'aids', of which nicotine chewing-gum seems, among the more recently available, to be both publicly credible and demonstrably helpful (Raw et al., 1980).

It was in the context of this public interest in anti-smoking aids (but before the availability of this more recent gum), that the British independent broadcasting company Granada Television rashly offered, during a program in October 1977, free anti-smoking kits to any smokers who wrote in or telephoned for them. They had some 10,000 'kits' available, mostly consisting of samples of products already commercially available, the claimed effectiveness of which relied upon widely varying amounts of scientific evidence. As it turned out, they were flooded by over half-a-million requests, and finding themselves completely unable to meet the demand, turned to the government for help. For a variety of reasons, the government decided it could not finance the provision of more kits, and so what the great majority of the half-million received was a broadsheet 'newspaper' containing a more or less predictable mixture of exhortation and advice—not at all the 'magic cure' no doubt hoped for. Another function of the government's involvement was support for a number of evaluation studies, and as part of this, we gained access to a sample originally of 20,000 selected at random from those who asked for the kits.

These 20,000 were all sent a questionnaire, asking a variety of questions about their smoking habits, attitudes and intentions, and of these 2000 were at the same time sent a supplementary questionnaire, to be described below. The response rate was, low—under 12 percent—but perhaps not surprisingly so granted the disappointment, or indeed anger, of many who had hoped for a kit and received pieces of paper instead. A follow-up on a subsample of non-responders does not suggest any obviously damaging bias, however, among those who responded. Nonetheless, no claim is made that the findings are necessarily representative of the general smoking population. The respondents also were sent a follow-up questionnaire after 1 year, primarily to check on their success or failure, according to their own reports.

Within the main questionnaire, the main dependent variable was a measure of behavioral intention:

'Do you intend to try to stop smoking in the near future?', with responses in terms of the categories 'No, definitely not', 'No, probably not', 'Yes, probably' and 'Yes, definitely'.

This measure of intention was related in later analyses to self-reported attempts at stopping smoking at the 1-year follow-up. Among the predictor variables, two items were intended to tap attributional processes. The first of these asked simply:

'How addicted do you think you are to smoking? (responses: 'Extremely', 'Fairly', 'Slightly', 'Not at all')'

The second was a more complex item modeled mainly on the Weiner and Kukla (1970) attributional analysis of achievement motivation. This asked subjects to rank (from 1 to 5 in decreasing order of importance) the following five possible reasons why 'so many smokers fail when they try to stop smoking':

(a) 'Because it's just too difficult for them';
(b) 'Because they don't try hard enough';
(c) 'Because they don't know the best way to set about it';
(d) 'Because of the kind of people they are';
(e) 'Because of bad luck'.

Since very few subjects attached much importance to 'bad luck', this last category was analyzed separately for the other four, which were combined to form two separate indices. The first index ('Stable') was presumed to reflect the extent to which subjects attributed failure to factors such as task difficulty (a) and personality (d) which could be seen as likely to remain stable over time, as opposed to effort (b) and knowledge (c) which could be seen as changeable. This index was calculated as the sum of the rank scores for (b) and (c) minus the sum of the rank scores for (a) and (d). The second index ('Internal') was calculated on the rank scores as (a) + (c) − (b) − (d), and was presumed to reflect attributions of greater personal responsibility for failure. Note that we assumed, at least within the context of this study, that the 'knowledge' factor (c), could be treated as 'external', in that it could be taken to reflect a feeling that 'other people need to tell smokers the best way to set about it'. The broadcast, indeed, seemed to promise just such new help and knowledge.

Among the other items, there were three particularly relevant to a subjective expected utility analysis of the decision to stop smoking. These were:

'If you stopped smoking altogether do you think *your* chances of getting lung cancer would be lower than if you continued to smoke?' (responses: 'About the same', 'A bit lower', 'Much lower').

'How important is it to you to reduce your chances of getting lung cancer?' (responses: 'Not important', 'Fairly important', 'Extremely important').

'If you tried to stop smoking altogether, how likely do you think you would be to succeed' (responses: 'Very unlikely', 'Fairly unlikely', Fairly likely', 'Very likely').

The data were analyzed by means of a series of path analyses. By far the most important predictor of intention was the expectancy measure, i.e. subjects' perceptions of their chances of success at stopping. The measure of the self-attribution of addiction correlated significantly with intention, as did the 'Stable' index, but in both cases the path analyses indicated that their effect on intention was indirect. These variables influenced intention by influencing expectancy. The direction of these effects was as predicted: those who saw themselves as more addicted, and made more stable attributions for failure, had lower expectancies of success and less firm intentions to stop. The 'Internal' index, on the other hand, showed no direct or indirect link to intention.

The items concerning the perceived chances of, and importance of, avoiding lung cancer, both had direct effects on intention. As predicted, those who thought their chances of avoiding cancer would be improved by stopping, and who attached more importance to this, had stronger intentions to stop. These data, however, did not suggest that subjects made decisions on the basis of the multiplicative rule specified by subjective expected utility theory (see Chapter 13).

The 1-year follow-up produced finally just over 1,800 returns. The main concern of this was to determine if subjects had in fact tried to stop, and if so, if they had succeeded.

These data indicated a highly significant link from intention to behavior—those who intended most strongly to try to stop were the most likely in fact to attempt to do so. The other variables considered related to behavior (trying to stop) only indirectly, through their effects on intention.

A discriminant analysis was next performed to distinguish *among those who actually made the attempt*, those who had stopped and were still not smoking after 1 year (in fact approximately 14 percent) from those who were smoking again. The most powerful predictor of success was an item in the main questionnaire not so far mentioned—the longest period they had managed to stop for in the past. Thereafter, the most important predictors were the two 'motivational' variables—the importance of avoiding cancer and the perceived chances of doing so if one stopped. Successes were less likely also than failures to have seen themselves as addicted, and had higher expectations of success.

Smoking and the 'Sick Role'

As mentioned, a subsample of those who received the main questionnaire simultaneously received a supplementary questionnaire. This was entitled 'How do you feel about stopping smoking?' and subjects had to respond to each of 20 statements in terms of four categories from 'Not at all' to 'Very much how I feel'.

These statements were partly modeled on those used by Eiser and Gossop (1979) in a study of drug-dependence clinic patients (see Chapter 11). This study had distinguished two factors in a similar set of statements concerning drug addicts' views of their addiction—a 'Hooked' factor, represented by items concerned with a perceived inability to give up drugs, and a 'Sick' factor, reflecting a concern with the health dangers of drug use, and the perception of their addiction as a sickness which doctors could cure. Note that the traditional notion of the 'sick role' (Parsons, 1951) implies both that the sick person, once sick, cannot be blamed for remaining so, and that it is the responsibility of the medical profession to provide treatment. The Eiser and Gossop data suggest that, for the drug clinic patients in question, this notion confounds empirically distinguishable dimensions.

The data from the questionnaire sent to the smokers revealed a very similar two-factor structure. This time it was the first factor which we labeled 'Sick', and was represented by strongest loadings on such statements as 'I think of my smoking as a sickness which needs to be cured' and 'I'm frightened about what smoking may be doing to me'. The second factor ('Hooked') was represented by such items as 'If I wanted to I could give up smoking' (negative loading), 'I'm not going to be able to give up smoking unless someone helps me', as well as items concerned with a resentment of anti-smoking influence attempts, e.g. 'I feel I'm constantly being "got at" nowadays because I'm a smoker' (see Table 12.3).

Subjects' scores on these two factors were then considered in relation to measures derived from the main and follow-up questionnaires. The 'Sick' factor correlated significantly *negatively* with the 'Internal' index, supporting the intuition of an association between sick role perceptions and external locus of control (Rotter, 1966) but contributed *positively* to expectancy of

Table 12.3 Principal component factor matrix (two factors, oblique rotation) and means for 'Very dissonant' and 'Not very dissonant' smokers: Granada TV sample

	Factor 1 'Sick'	Factor 2 'Hooked'	Mean for 'Very dissonant smokers'	Mean for 'Not very dissonant smokers'	F (1, 231)
1. I'm frightened about what smoking may be doing to me	0.72	0.06	2.62	3.13	7.13‡
2. Even if I stopped smoking for a while, I'm sure that other people would persuade me to start again	0.07	0.28	1.97	1.99	0.01
3. I resent other people telling me that I shouldn't smoke	−0.25	0.49	2.52	2.61	0.14
4. I don't think I'm really prepared to give up smoking if it proves too difficult or distressing	−0.05	0.57	1.83	2.63	14.12§
5. I've never made a serious effort to give up smoking completely	−0.06	0.26	2.45	2.37	0.09
6. If life was easier, I'd have less need to smoke	0.28	0.48	1.83	2.40	5.70†
7. I feel I'm constantly being 'got at' nowadays because I'm a smoker	0.03	0.51	2.31	2.06	1.14
8. I know that some people die because they smoke, but I think most smokers stay just as healthy as non-smokers	−0.47	0.45	1.86	2.01	0.52
9. I'd like to give up smoking if I could do so easily	0.12	0.21	—	—	—
10. If I really wanted to, I could give up smoking	−0.04	−0.47	2.38	2.26	0.28
11. I'm not going to be able to give up smoking unless someone helps me	−0.38	0.59	2.55	2.84	1.49
12. I think you have to smoke a lot more than I do to put your health at serious risk	−0.28	0.15	1.69	1.65	0.03
13. I'd feel very ashamed of myself if I tried to give up smoking and failed	0.29	0.31	1.86	2.20	2.05
14. If I gave up smoking, I'd expect to feel a lot healthier than I do now	0.51	0.12	3.31	3.53	1.59
15. I find smoking helps me cope when I've got problems	0.05	0.41	3.28	3.39	0.40
16. I think of my smoking as a sickness which needs to be cured	0.73	0.21	2.38	2.83	3.18*
17. I think that the government should do more to persuade people not to smoke	0.61	0.00	2.86	2.91	0.03
18. What I feel I really need is a pill or some sort of medicine that'll stop me wanting to smoke	0.50	0.42	2.90	3.42	6.67†
19. I feel that other people are partly to blame for the fact that I became a smoker	0.14	−0.01	2.34	2.02	1.57
20. I really want to stop smoking, but I need somebody to tell me how to do it	0.58	0.40	3.00	3.14	0.39

* $p < 0.1$; † $p < 0.05$; ‡ $p < 0.01$; § $p < 0.001$.
Note: Items were scored from 1: 'Not at all how I feel' to 4: 'Very much how I feel'.

success. The 'Hooked' factor (as well as correlating positively with the self-attribution of addiction item) correlated significantly *positively* with the 'Stable' index, and contributed *negatively* to expectancy of success. Even on this much-reduced sample size, expectancy of success was still a very reliable predictor of intention, and intention of behavior. As regards predictions of success at stopping, higher scores on the 'Hooked' factor were predictive of failure, among those who tried, but scores on the 'Sick' factor did not discriminate successes from failures.

More Evidence on the 'Dissonant' Smoker

One of the 20 items was derived from the McKennell and Thomas (1967) 'consonant–dissonant' distinction. This was 'I'd like to give up smoking if I could do so easily'. This produced a highly skewed distribution with 204 of the 233 subjects responding 'Very much the way I feel'. This was perhaps only to be expected from such a peculiar sample. A stepwise discriminant analysis was therefore conducted to discriminate these 204 'very dissonant' smokers from the remaining 29 ('not very dissonant'), on the basis of their responses to the remaining 19 items. This means of each item for the two groups are shown in Table 12.3, together with the results of univariate *F* tests on the mean differences.

The two most important discriminators were the statements 'I don't think I'm really prepared to give up smoking if it proves too difficult or distressing' (loading heavily on 'Hooked') and 'I'm frightened about what smoking may be doing to me' (loading heavily on 'Sick'). The means for the 'very dissonant' group were significantly higher than those of the 'not very dissonant' group on both these statements. After inclusion of these two statements the improvement in discrimination at each further step was non-significant.

As in the Eiser *et al.* (1978a) study, therefore, greater so-called 'dissonance' was associated with greater fear of the effects of smoking and also with items expressing a lack of confidence in one's ability to give up. For such 'very dissonant' smokers, no real commitment seems to be involved in the declaration that they would like to give up *if they could do so easily*, since they have an armory of reasons ready for why they could *not* do so easily.

Conclusions

Practical Implications

It has been assumed, throughout this research, that people will seek explanations for why others may behave differently from themselves, and will also try to see, and present, their own behavior as reasonable under the circumstances. Whether such attributions are 'true' is as much a judgment of value as one of scientific fact. Either way, it is not a question which social psychology need be in the business of answering.

Where social psychology can make a contribution is by showing how such attributions may shape, and be shaped by, the behavior of those who hold them—of the teenager experimenting with cigarettes, alcohol, or other drugs; of the established smoker deciding whether to try to give up smoking; of the non-smoker frustrated in his attempts to persuade smokers to stop; and of the ex-smoker in his new-found virtue. For non-smokers, such attributions serve to 'explain' why others smoke, primarily in terms of distinctive attributes of smokers, rather than in terms of the positive and negative reinforcing properties of tobacco itself. For smokers, such attributions provide a defence against the behavioral imperatives implied by the weight of evidence on the dangers of cigarette smoking.

Such attributions, however, do not come out of thin air. They are, in a very real sense, public property, established and reinforced by mass and interpersonal communication. An especially important feature of such attributions at the present time is the definition of smoking, drinking, and the use of other drugs as a *medical* problem, not just in the sense that these behaviors may produce disease, but in the sense that they are to be regarded as diseases *in themselves*. The 'sick role' has thus been offered to smokers and, to a large extent, has been accepted.

There is, however, room for hope even within a preconception of smoking (and other types of drug-use) as a disease. As suggested by analyses designed to distinguish between different aspects of the sick role, perceiving smoking or drug-use as a 'sickness' (which can be dangerous to one's health, and which is appropriate for medical intervention) does not necessarily involve perceiving oneself as addicted or 'hooked' in the sense of being unable to give up the drug. In the data reported, feeling 'hooked' led to lower expectancy of success at giving up, less strong intention to try, less likelihood of making an attempt, and less success if an attempt was made. This was not true of those who saw their smoking as a sickness, these people being generally less skeptical about the health risks involved. Ideally, what seems needed is to separate the concept of addiction as a major source of self-inflicted disease, as well as of numerous 'abnormal' physiological changes, from the concept of addiction in the folk-psychology sense, with its implications of helplessness and diminished (or non-existent) responsibility.

I am not claiming that giving up smoking is easy for the typical smoker. Appreciation of the pharmacological basis of tobacco may well lead to changes in ideas of what might count as 'safer smoking' (Russell, 1974), with major commercial and therapeutic implications. At the same time, the idea that giving up smoking, or any other drug, is *absolutely* impossible without external intervention is a myth which is likely to militate against the success of even the most pharmacologically sophisticated therapeutic techniques.

Theoretical Implications

Finally, the studies I have briefly described were an attempt to apply notions from a major theoretical approach in experimental social psychology to new fields. How well can it be said that attribution theory has survived this encounter? To a great extent, conceptual distinctions derived from an attributional perspective have been shown to have empirical implications, and this is perhaps enough to earn a favorable verdict for any theory. Attribution theory, however, contains not only conceptual distinctions but also a number of propositions about what goes on in the heads of individuals in social situations. It implies a pre-eminent concern with the business of explaining, and drawing causal inferences from, past and present experience. It deals far less directly with how individuals make predictions concerning the future. Indeed, Kelley and Michela (1980) distinguish between, on the one hand, 'attribution theories', which are concerned principally with the antecedents of interpersonal perceptions, and, on the other hand, 'attributional theories', which are primarily concerned with the consequences of such attributions— for example, changes in expectancy and behavior.

In so far as the studies reported in this chapter are concerned simply with questions such as 'when do smokers think they are addicted?', the data fit within an attribution theory framework. Once we move on to consider questions such as 'what happens when smokers think they are addicted?', we have crossed into the territory of 'attributional theory'. Within this territory, some of the most influential work has been that derived from the Weiner and Kukla (1970) model of achievement motivation. Yet this work does not always provide a compelling case for the idea that behavioral decisions depend critically on the sophisticated processes of causal explanations posited by attribution theory. Weiner (1979), for instance, now argues that the attribution of previous success or failure experiences to stable or unstable factors makes a considerable difference to expectancy for future success, but that attribution to internal or external factors makes no difference to expectancy, although it may influence emotional reactions. This is borne out by the findings of Weiner *et al.* (1976), and is entirely consistent with our own findings of the predictability of expectancy from our 'Stable' but not our 'Internal' index.

In that attribution theory *per se* has been less concerned with behavioral consequences, its practical applicability in its present form is open to question. Expectancy seems to be the critical link between attributions and behavior, but the concept itself is treated as relatively unproblematic in much attributional research. On the other hand, research on the psychology of prediction (e.g. Fischoff, 1976; Nisbett and Ross, 1980) suggests that people's calculations of the likelihood of future events are open to numerous biases. As for factors other than expectancy that may affect behavior, we are at the moment almost in a theoretical and empirical vacuum. As I have argued elsewhere (Eiser, 1981), what seems to be needed in this area is a more integrative approach to social cognition that deals both with processes of explanation and with processes of prediction, and also indicates when and how each type of process is engaged.

If such an approach can be developed it may then be possible to turn our attention more fruitfully to the issue of the relationship between cognitions and behavior. This issue is the one, more than any other, on which the practical applicability of current social psychological theory depends. Behavioral medicine cannot afford to dodge this issue, since it *is* concerned with behavior and its consequences for health and not simply with perceptions and inferences as an end in themselves. The point may therefore have been reached where it is from applied research that new developments in theory should be sought.

References

Bem, D, J. (1967). 'Self-perception: an alternative in interpretation of cognitive dissonance phenomena', *Psychological Review*, **74**, 183–200.

Cooper, J., Zanna, M. P., and Taves, P. A. (1978). 'Arousal as a necessary condition for attitude change following compliance', *Journal of Personality and Social Psychology*, **36**, 1101–1106.

Eiser, J. R. (1978). 'Discrepancy, dissonance, and the "dissonant" smoker', *International Journal of the Addictions*, **13**, 1295–1305.

Eiser, J. R. (1981). 'Attribution theory and social cognition', in Jaspars, J., Fincham, F. D., and Hewstone, M. (eds), *Attribution Theory: Essays and Experiments*. Academic Press, London.

Eiser, J. R., and Gossop, M. R. (1979). ' "Hooked" or "sick": addicts' perceptions of their addiction', *Addictive Behaviors*, **4**, 185–191.

Eiser, J. R., and Sutton, S. R. (1977). 'Smoking as a subjectively rational choice', *Addictive Behaviors*, **2**, 129–134.

Eiser, J. R., Sutton, S. R., and Wober, M. (1977). 'Smokers, non-smokers, and the attribution of addiction', *British Journal of Social and Clinical Psychology*, **16**, 329–336.

Eiser, J. R., Sutton, S. R., and Wober, M. (1978a). ' "Consonant" and "dissonant" smokers and the self-attribution of addiction', *Addictive Behaviors*, **3**, 99–106.

Eiser, J. R., Sutton, S. R., and Wober, M. (1978b). 'Smokers' and non-smokers' attributions about addiction: a case of actor–observer differences?', *British Journal of Social and Clinical Psychology*, **17**, 189–190.

Eiser, J. R., Sutton, S. R., and Wober, M. (1979). 'Smoking, seat-belts and beliefs about health', *Addictive Behaviors*, **4**, 331–338.

Fincham, F. D., and Jaspars, J. M. (1980). 'Attribution of responsibility: from man-the-scientist to man-as-lawyer', in Berkowitz, L. (ed.), *Advances in Experimental Social Psychology*, Vol. 13. Academic Press, New York.

Fischhoff, B. (1976). 'Attribution theory and judgment under uncertainty', in Harvey, J. H., Ickes, W. J., and Kidd, R. F. (eds). *New Directions in Attribution Research*, Vol. 1. Lawrence Erlbaum, Hillsdale, NJ.

Heider, F. (1958). *The Psychology of Interpersonal Relations*. Wiley, New York.

Hunt, W. A., and Matarazzo, J. D. (1973). 'Three years later: recent developments in the experimental modification of smoking behavior', *Journal of Abnormal Psychology*, **81**, 107–114.

Jacobs, M. A., Anderson, L. S., Champagne, E. Karush, N., Richman, S. J., and Knapp, P. H. (1966). 'Orality, impulsivity and cigarette smoking in men: further findings in support of a theory', *Journal of Nervous and Mental Diseases*, **143**, 207–219.

Jaffe, J. H. (1977). 'Tobacco use as a mental disorder: the re-discovery of a medical problem', in Jarvik, M. E. *et al.* (eds), *Research on Smoking Behavior*. NIDA Research Monograph 17. Rockville, Md; DHEW 1977.

Jellinek, E. M. (1960). *The Disease Concept of Alcoholism*. Hillhouse Press, Highland Park, NJ.

Jones, E. E., and Nisbett, R. E. (1971). 'The actor and observer: divergent perception of the causes of behavior', in Jones, E. E. *et al.* (eds), *Attribution: Perceiving the Causes of Behavior*. General Learning Press, Morristown, NJ.

Kelley, H. H., and Michela, J. L. (1980). 'Attribution theory and research', *Annual Review of Psychology*, **31**, 457–501.

Linder, D. E., Cooper, J., and Jones, E. E. (1967). 'Decision freedom as a determinant of the role of incentive magnitude in attitude change', *Journal of Personality and Social Psychology*, **6**, 245–254.

Litman, G. K., Eiser, J. R., and Taylor, C. (1979). 'Dependence, relapse and extinction: a theoretical critique and a behavioral examination', *Journal of Clinical Psychology*, **35**, 192–199.

Matarazzo, J. R., and Saslow, G. (1960). 'Psychological and related characteristics of smokers and non-smokers', *Psychological Bulletin*, **57**, 493–513.

Mausner, B. and Platt, E. S. (1971). *Smoking: A Behavioral Analysis*. Pergamon, New York.

McKennell, A. C., and Thomas, R. K. (1967). *Adults' and Adolescents' Smoking Habits and Attitudes*. Government Social Survey. SS 353/B. HMSO, London.

Nisbett, R. E., and Ross, L. (1980). *Human Inference: Strategies and Shortcomings of Social Judgment*. Prentice-Hall, Englewood Cliffs, NJ.

Parsons, T. (1951). *The Social System*. Free Press, Chicago.

Raw, M. (1978). 'The treatment of cigarette dependence', in Israel, Y. *et al.* (eds), *Research Advances in Alcohol and Drug Problems,* vol. 4. Plenum, New York.

Raw, M., Jarvis, M. J., Feyerabend, C., and Russell, M. A. H. (1980). 'Comparison of nicotine chewing-gum and psychological treatment for dependent smokers'. *British Medical Journal*, **281**, 481.

Robins, L. N., Davis, D. H., and Goodwin, D. W. (1974). 'Drug use by US Army enlisted men in Vietnam: a follow-up on their return home', *Americal Journal of Epidemiology*, **99**, 235–249.

Rotter, J. B. (1966). 'Generalised expectancies for internal versus external control of reinforcement', *Psychological Monographs*, **80** (whole No. 609).

Royal College of Physicians (1977). *Smoking or Health*. Pitman Medical, London.

Russell, M. A. H. (1971). 'Cigarette smoking: natural history of a dependence disorder', *British Journal of Medical Psychology*, **44**, 1–16.

Russell, M. A. H. (1974). 'Realistic goals for smoking and health: a case for safer smoking', *Lancet*, **1**, 254–257.

Russell, M. A. H. (1977). 'Smoking problems: an overview', in Jarvik, M. E. *et al.* (eds), *Research on Smoking Behavior*. NIDA Research Monograph 17. Rockville, Md: DHEW 1977.

Schachter, S., Silverstein, B., Koslowski, L. T., Perlick, D., Herman, C. P., and Liebling, B. (1977). 'Studies of the interaction of psychological and pharmacological determinants of smoking', *Journal of Experimental Psychology: General*, **106**, 3–40.

Schachter, S., and Singer, J. E. (1962). 'Cognitive, social and physiological determinants of emotional state', *Psychological Review*, **69**, 379–399.

Sutton, S. R. (1979). 'Interpreting relapse curves', *Journal of Consulting and Clinical Psychology*, **47**, 96–98.

Weiner, B. (1979). 'A theory of motivation for some classroom experiences', *Journal of Educational Psychology*, **71**, 3–25.

Weiner, B., and Kukla, A. (1970). 'An attributional analysis of achievement motivation', *Journal of Personality and Social Psychology*, **15**, 1–20.

Weiner, B., Nierenberg, R., and Goldstein, M. (1976). 'Social learning (locus of control) versus attributional (causal stability) interpretations of expectancy of success', *Journal of Personality*, **44**, 52–68.

Wright, S. J. (1980). 'Actor–observer differences in attributions for smoking: introducing ex-actors and attributions for failure to give up', *British Journal of Social and Clinical Psychology*, **19**, 49–50.

PART IV

Communication and Influence

Social Psychology and Behavioral Medicine
Edited by J Richard Eiser
© 1982 by John Wiley & Sons Ltd

Chapter 13

Fear-arousing communications: a critical examination of theory and research

STEPHEN R. SUTTON

The main causes of premature death and disablement are preventable—or at least postponable—at the level of individual behavior. If we didn't smoke, drank less, drove more carefully, wore our seat-belts, ate more prudently and did more exercise, we would be healthier and live longer. In the course of everyday life we are frequently exposed to information about such risks and other non-lethal ones such as tooth decay. Much of this information comes to us via the mass media in the form of articles, posters, and television programs—some of which are designed to persuade us to change our behavior in appropriate ways, and some of which simply report 'the facts'. Such communications typically contain information about the health consequences that may ensue from performing, or failing to perform, a particular behavior. Are such communications effective in influencing people to change their attitudes and behavior? How can we explain the success or failure of such communications? The area of research that has attempted to answer these questions is known by the rubric 'fear-arousing communications', the name reflecting the emphasis that has been placed on the role of fear in the mediation of communication effects. This chapter presents a comprehensive review of theories and findings on the effects of fear-arousing communications.

Plan of the Chapter

The first section of the chapter discusses the *fear-drive model* which has guided the bulk of the studies in this area, and the non-monotonic models proposed by Janis and McGuire. The difficulties of conducting an adequate test of these models are emphasized. Then we review the findings from experimental studies of fear-arousing communications that have been pub-

303

lished between 1953, when the first paper was published, and 1980. The main conclusions drawn are:

(1) that increases in fear produce increases in acceptance of the recommended action; and
(2) that the interactions predicted by the fear-drive model are not supported by the findings.

Leventhal's (1970) alternative to the fear-drive model—the *parallel response model*—is then considered. This is followed by the exposition of a decision-making approach based upon subjective expected utility (SEU) theory (Edwards, 1961), which emphasizes cognitive factors (subjective probabilities, utilities) rather than fear in the mediation of communication effects. The model represents an application to the area of fear-arousing communications of an approach that is being increasingly employed in many different areas of psychology. Finally, the SEU model is compared with the *protection motivation theory* of Rogers (1975) which has a similar expectancy-value orientation.

The Fear-drive Model

Most of the research on fear-arousing communications has been guided by the fear-drive model. This was adapted from the drive-reduction models employed by animal learning theorists such as Miller (1951). The fullest exposition of the model can be found in Hovland *et al.* (1953). The basic assumption is that fear serves as a drive to motivate trial-and-error behavior. A reduction in the strength of fear reinforces the learning of any new response that accompanies it. When a communication arouses fear the recipient will become highly motivated to try out various responses to alleviate the unpleasant state. If the communication presents a reassuring recommendation to the effect that if the recipient adopts the recommended response he will avoid the threat, and if mental rehearsal of this recommendation is followed or accompanied by a marked reduction in fear, then this verbal response will be reinforced and will tend to occur on subsequent occasions when similar external and internal stimuli are present. If cognitive rehearsal of the recommendation fails to reduce the fear level (i.e. if there is *residual fear*), spontaneous responses will be tried out until one is hit upon that reduces the tension. This is likely to be some form of defensive reaction such as denying the threat or subsequent avoidance of the fear-arousing cues (*defensive avoidance*).

As an illustration, consider a highly effective communication on the subject of dental hygiene. By spelling out the unpleasant consequences of poor dental hygiene practices (decayed teeth, diseased gums), the communication is likely to arouse fear in the audience. If the audience are then told that cleaning their teeth in the recommended way with the proper kind of toothbrush will be successful in preventing these consequences, they will imagine themselves taking this preventive action, and this cognitive response will be accompanied by a reduction in emotional tension and will thereby be reinforced. Subsequently, they will tend to think about the recommended action whenever the appropriate cues are present, and they will therefore be more likely to clean their teeth properly.

There are a number of logical and theoretical problems with the formulation of the fear-drive model. The first concerns the nature of fear. Close adherence to the animal origins of the model would imply that the essence of fear is autonomic and skeletal activity which comes to be associated through classical conditioning with formerly neutral cues. Hovland *et al.*, however, though they talk of habit chains and Pavlovian conditioning, seem to regard fear in largely cognitive terms, i.e. anticipation of unpleasant consequences, and in later writings Janis (e.g. 1967) develops these ideas in his concept of *reflective fear*. On this view, however, fear-arousal would seem to involve not classical conditioning (without there necessarily being any awareness of the link between stimulus and response) but *belief formation* in which the recipient consciously forms a cognitive link between the object (e.g. my smoking) and the attribute (e.g. lung cancer). To the extent that fear is conceived of as a cognitive response, the fear-drive model can be viewed as an odd mixture of fear-arousal, which involves higher mental processes, and fear-reduction and resultant behavior change, which involve low-level animal-like processes.

Secondly, it is not clear whether the important factor determining the probability of repetition of the response is the *amount* of fear-reduction or the *completeness* of the reduction. Consider a situation in which a recommendation of given efficacy completely reduced a 'moderate' but not a 'high' level of fear, the size of the reduction being greater in the latter case. In which condition would the probability of acceptance be higher?

Finally, if mental rehearsal of the recommendation is successful in reducing fear, it is not clear why this cognitive response should lead to a behavioral one. *Thinking* about averting the threat, if it alleviates fear, should be sufficient.

Since reduction of fear is held to be the crucial mediating variable, an adequate test of the fear-drive model would require that fear-reduction is measured and related to acceptance of the recommendations. In the typical study, however, fear is measured only once, immediately after the communication, i.e. immediately after the recommendation. Depending on how soon and how quickly the supposed fear-reduction occurs, this measure of fear could reflect the initial level of fear aroused, the final level of residual fear, or some intermediate level of partially reduced fear. The only solution to this methodological problem would seem to be to employ continuous or near-continuous measurement of fear. This can obviously be done more easily with physiological indices of fear than with subjective reports, repeated measures of which would probably distract the subject from the communication and be subject to carry-over effects, i.e. one measurement affecting a later one. However, physiological indices may not be measuring the same thing as subjective reports. Mewborn and Rogers (1979) found only moderate (though significant) correlations between autonomic indices and mood ratings during a fear-arousing film (0.36 for mean heart-rate; 0.39 for skin conductance). The correlations were lower and non-significant during the reassurance communication which ensued.

Non-monotonic Models

Implicit in the fear-drive model is the notion that the relationship between fear and acceptance is non-monotonic. Other things being equal (e.g. if the perceived efficacy of the recommended action remains constant), an increase in fear will produce first an increase in probability of acceptance (when the level of fear is such that rehearsal of the recommendation successfully reduces it) and then a decrease in acceptance (when the level of fear is such that the recommendation fails to reduce it to zero level). The optimal level of fear will be the maximum level that can be successfully reduced by thinking about the recommendations.

The non-monotonic relationship was elaborated by Janis (1967) in his *family-of-curves model*. The model assumes that increases in fear have multiple effects, some of which facilitate persuasion and others of which have an interfering effect. For example, an increase in fear may increase motivation to find a means of averting the danger (facilitation) and at the same time lead to a more critical evaluation of the recommended action (interference). It is assumed that facilitation increases more rapidly than interference as fear level increases from zero level, but that at some point interference starts to increase at a faster rate. The resultant relationship between fear and acceptance takes the form of an inverted U-shaped curve with the optimal point occurring at that level of fear at which the interfering effects start to increase at a faster rate than the facilitating effects. The optimal level of fear-arousal will depend upon the value of any variable that affects the relative strength of facilitating and interfering effects. One such variable would be the perceived efficacy of the recommended action. For each different level of efficacy there will be a corresponding inverted U-shaped curve representing the relationship between acceptance and fear-arousal.

Janis reviews the literature on fear-arousing communications and shows how the inconsistent findings can be reconciled by the postulated curvilinear model. Unfortunately, as clearly shown by Leventhal (1970), the model is so flexible that it can accommodate virtually any pattern of findings. In his view, it is little more than a *post hoc* descriptive schema. It should be emphasized, however, that the model does generate some testable predictions. In particular it predicts, over the normal range of fear aroused by persuasive communications, an interaction effect between fear and any other factor that affects the balance of facilitating and interfering effects, e.g. an increase in, say, communicator credibility will produce a greater increase in acceptance at levels of fear that approach the new optimal level than at lower levels of fear. Unfortunately, an adequate test of such a prediction would involve quite a complex factorial design with multiple levels of fear, which would allow at least three points on each curve to be plotted. The problem is compounded if the interacting factor is itself expected to have a curvilinear effect on acceptance (see Janis, 1970, p. 601). Thus, apart from the criticisms expounded in the previous section, all of which apply here too, the main problem with the curvilinear model is the practical difficulty of testing out its predictions.

Another non-monotonic model was proposed by McGuire (1968). According to McGuire, the amount of attitude change produced by a communication depends upon *reception* of the message (the degree to which it is attended to and understood) and, given adequate reception, the amount of *yielding* to the arguments. The amount of aroused fear, like many other independent variables, is assumed to be related in a compensatory fashion to these two mediators of attitude change. In particular, consideration of the drive properties of fear leads to the expectation that it will be *positively* related to yielding. As a cue, on the other hand, fear evokes habitual responses which will tend to interfere with reception of the message; thus fear is expected to be *negatively* related to reception. Given appropriate assumptions concerning different rates of change, the resultant relationship between fear and acceptance will be an inverted U-shaped curve as in Janis' model, the optimal level occurring at the point at which the negative curve starts to decrease at a faster rate than that at which the positive curve is increasing. If post-exposure anxiety level is assumed to be a simple additive function of the individual's chronic anxiety level and the anxiety aroused by the communication, then the model predicts an interaction between these two variables on acceptance. In particular, a given increase in message fear should increase acceptance among individuals of low chronic anxiety and reduce acceptance among individuals of high chronic anxiety. (Note that precisely the same prediction can be derived from the other models.)

Furthermore, the model predicts that fear level (chronic or message or both) will interact with situational factors that affect the relative importance of reception and yielding in mediating the effect of fear on attitude change. For example, a message that is extremely easy to understand would virtually remove individual variation in reception and thus magnify the importance of yielding in mediating the effect of fear on acceptance. One would predict therefore that, relative to a difficult message, an easy message would shift the optimal level of fear in the direction of higher fear, i.e. that a given increase in fear would lead to a greater increase in acceptance for an easy than for a difficult message.

Janis (1967) criticized McGuire's model for being oversimple in assuming that the only responses cued off by fear are interfering responses and that the only responses energized by fear are facilitating responses. For instance, contrary to the latter assumption, Janis' model postulates that high fear is likely to produce motivated defensive reactions which interfere with acceptance.

Apart from these criticisms, which simply reflect a different viewpoint, McGuire's model is open to the same objections as Janis' model with regard to its ability to accommodate opposite findings *ex post facto* and the requirement for elaborate factorial designs to test its predictions. There has been only one empirical test of McGuire's model as applied to fear-arousing communications (Millman, 1968), and it yielded only partial support for the model.

Review of Findings from Studies of Fear-arousing Communications, 1953–80

This review is limited to published studies that (a) attempted to manipulate fear by presenting communications with different fear-provoking potential; (b) included a check on the effectiveness of the manipulation (i.e. a post-exposure measure of fear); and (c) included a measure of acceptance that had a clear behavioral referent. To elaborate on the last part, studies were excluded if they did not include a measure of either attitude toward the behavior (e.g. desire to have an X-ray), behavioral intention (e.g. intention to have a tetanus inoculation), reported behavior (e.g. whether or not the subjects say that they have changed their toothbrushing practices), actual behavior (e.g. whether or not the person has an X-ray), or behavioral outcome (e.g. weight loss). The rationale for this strict selection criterion can be found in the work of Fishbein and Ajzen (e.g. Ajzen and Fishbein, 1977) which shows the importance of distinguishing between different kinds of 'attitude' when the object is to predict and explain behavior (see also Chapter 8).

Some 35 studies were found that satisfied these criteria. They are listed chronologically in Table 13.1, together with three other studies (Goldstein, 1959; Hass *et al.*, 1975; Skilbeck *et al.*, 1977, Expt 2) which are also discussed in this chapter. In the remainder of the chapter, whenever a particular study in Table 13.1 is discussed, the reference will include the study number (in italics) so that the reader can quickly locate the study in the table.

As is clear from a glance at Table 13.1, the studies cover a wide range of topics, subject groups and communication media. Fear has been operationalized in a variety of ways, the two most common being the subject's summed

Table 13.1 Selected experimental studies of fear-arousing communications published in the period 1953–80

Study	Topic	Subjects	Medium[a]	Comparison[b]	Fear Sig.?[c]	Intention Z[e]	Intention df	Behavior Z	Behavior df
1. Janis and Feshbach (1953, 1954)	Dental health	High-school freshman	T+S	HF–LF	No			-1.96	100
				HF–DT	Yes			+0.59	100
2. Moltz and Thistlethwaite (1955)	Dental health	Airforce recruits	T+S						
3. Goldstein (1959)	Dental health	High-school freshman	T+S						
4. Leventhal and Niles (1964)	Smoking	Non-students	F	HF–RO	Yes	-1.88	73 (smoking)		
				HF–LF	Yes	+0.69	118 (smoking)		
5. Haefner (1965)	Dental health	High-school freshman	T+S	HF–LF	Yes			+2.40[g]	252
6. Insko et al. (1965)	Smoking	7th graders	T+S	HF–LF	Yes	+3.40	264 (immediate)[h]		
						+1.61	264 (at 1 week)		
7. Leventhal and Niles (1965)	Safe driving	Students	F	HF–LF	No	+3.20[i]	196		
8. Leventhal et al. (1965)	Tetanus	Students	P	HF–LF: eligibles	Yes	+1.28	136	-0.42	59
				HF–RO eligibles	Yes	+3.80	136	+2.06	60
				HF–LF: ineligibles	Yes	+1.36	136		
9. Radelfinger (1965)[j]	Tetanus	Stanford students	T	HF–LF	Yes	+1.72	36	-1.32	68
				HF–DT	Yes	+2.26	33	+0.85	72
10. Radelfinger (1965)	Tetanus	San José students	T	HF–LF	Yes	+0.17	26		
				HF–DT	Yes	+2.02	28		
11. Beach (1966)	Seatbelts		F	HF–LF	Yes[g]	-0.88	26 (immediate)	+0.95	40 (at 6 months)
				HF–LF	No[k]	-0.69	26 (immediate)		
12. Chu (1966)	Roundworms	5th- and 6th-graders (Taiwan)	P	HF–LF:H Efficacy-imminent	No	+2.06	123		
				HF–LF:H Efficacy-remote	Yes	+3.69	108		
				HF–LF:M Efficacy-imminent	Yes	+1.68	129		
				HF–LF:M Efficacy-remote	Yes	+1.97	113		
				HF–LF:L Efficacy-imminent	Yes	+0.93	122		
				HF–LF:L Efficacy-remote	Yes	+1.65	118		
13. Dabbs and Leventhal (1966)	Tetanus	Students	P	HF–QO[l]	No	+1.76	393	+1.40	134
				HF–LF	Yes	+1.37	179	+2.34	120
				HF–RO	Yes	+2.90	179		
14. Leventhal et al. (1966)	Tetanus	Students	P	HF–(QO+RO)[m]	Yes	+2.70	399	+1.88	236
				HF–LF (overall)	Yes	+2.11	399	+1.78	417
				HF–LF: Eligibles-male-specific	Yes	0.00	399		
				HF–LF: Eligibles-male-non-specific	Yes	+1.09	399		
				HF–LF: Eligibles-female-specific	Yes	+1.40	399		
				HF–LF: Eligibles-female-non-specific	Yes	+1.50	399		

Table 13.1 Selected experimental studies of fear-arousing communications published in the period 1953–79

Study	Topic	Subjects	Medium[a]	Comparison[b]	Fear Sig.[c]	Results — Intention[d] z[e]	Intention[d] df	Results — Behavior[d] z	Behavior[d] df
15. Leventhal and Singer (1966)	Dental health	Non-students	T+S	HF–LF: Ineligibles–male-specific	No	−0.33	399		
				HF–LF: Ineligibles–male-non-specific	No	+0.78	399		
				HF–LF: Ineligibles–female-specific	Yes	+0.39	399		
				HF–LF: Ineligibles–female-non-specific	Yes	+2.01	399		
16. Leventhal and Watts (1966)	Smoking	Non-students	F	HF–LF	Yes	+3.80	297		
17. Leventhal et al. (1967)	Smoking	Student smokers	F	HF–LF	Yes	+2.70	101		
			F	HF–RO	Yes	+1.30	101		
18. Leventhal and Trembly (1968)	Safe driving	Male high-school students	F						
19. Evans et al. (1970)	Dental health	Junior high-school students	L+S	HF–LF[n]	Yes	0.00			
20. Rogers and Thistlethwaite (1970)[f]	Smoking	Students	F	HF–LF	Yes	+1.45	36		
21. Kirscht and Haefner (1973)	Heart disease	Non-academic University employees	F						
22. Krisher et al. (1973)	Mumps	Male students	T+S						
23. Ley et al. (1974)	Obesity	Overweight women	L						
24. Evans et al. (1975)	Dental health	Female junior high-school students	F						
25. Hass et al. (1975)	Energy consumption	Students	P						
26. Rogers and Deckner (1975)[o]	Smoking	Smokers	F	HF–DT	Yes	+1.57	115		
27. Rogers and Deckner (1975)	Smoking	Smokers	F+P	HF–LF	Yes	+2.60	152		
28. Griffeth and Rogers (1976)	Safe driving	High-school students	F+P	HF–LF	Yes	+2.10[p]	136	+5.50[q]	135
29. Ramirez and Lasater (1976)	Dental health	6th, 7th- and 8th-graders	T+S						
30. Rogers and Mewborn (1976)	Smoking, Safe driving, Venereal disease	Students	F+P						
31. Dziokonski and Weber (1977)	Dental health	Female students	T+S						

	Topic	Subjects	Communication	Comparison	Significant	Z	n
32. Ramirez and Lasater (1977)	Dental health	5th, 6th, 7th- and 8th-graders	T+S	HF-LF	Yes	+2.05 +1.68	196 (recency) 196 (Patient Hygiene Performance)
33. Skilbeck et al. (1977)	Obesity	Overweight ♀	L				
34. Skilbeck et al. (1977)	Obesity	Overweight ♀	L				
35. Dembroski et al. (1978)	Dental health	Black 9th graders	T+S				
36. Dembroski et al. (1978)	Dental health	6th, 7th- and 8th-graders	T+S				
37. Kirscht et al. (1978)	Obesity	Mothers of obese children	L+P	HF-LF	Yes	+3.14	109 (at 2 weeks)
38. Mewborn and Rogers (1979)	Venereal disease	Students	F+T				

[a] T = tape recording; S = slides; F = film; P = printed; L = lecture

[b] HF = highest experimental fear group; LF = lowest experimental fear group; DT = control group given a communication on a different topic; RO = control group given recommendations and/or specific instructions only; QO = questionnaire only control group.

[c] Is the difference in fear significant at the 0.05 level on a one-tailed test?

[d] *Intention* subsumes measures of attitude toward the behavior and intentions; *behavior* subsumes measures of reported behavior, actual behavior, and behavioral outcome.

[e] Z is the standard normal deviate for the comparison; *df* is the degrees of freedom (or, in the case of a comparison between proportions, the number of observations) involved in the comparison.

[f] Only the results for smokers are reported. For rationale, see section on Relevance.

[g] Conformity to recommended dental hygiene practices.

[h] The 'immediate' measure of intention was used in the Z analysis.

[i] The intention measure averaged over four different delay times.

[j] In both Radelfinger studies measures of intention were obtained on only 50 percent of the total sample.

[k] This study employed physiological measures of fear-arousal (skin conductance and heart-rate).

[l] Chu included a second control group but did not report its mean fear level.

[m] The two control groups were combined for this comparison.

[n] HF and LF here refer to Evans et al. 'high-fear' and 'low-fear' groups.

[o] See Rogers et al. (1978) for the results of the 1-year follow-up for the two Rogers and Deckner samples combined.

[p] Only one intention item out of six showed a significant difference between the two noxiousness (fear) conditions.

[q] There was a significant three-factor interaction on behavior.

[r] This study differed from the others in that it was the mothers who received the fear-arousing communication but the children whose weight was measured.

response to a number of mood adjectives (e.g. frightened, anxious, worried, nauseous), and a rating of worry or concern about the threat depicted in the message. Frequently, the effects of factors other than fear have also been examined (e.g. the perceived efficacy of the recommended action, chronic anxiety).

This section of the chapter will attempt to draw together and summarize the finding from these studies, and to assess their bearing on the validity of the fear-drive model. Discussion of findings that bear more directly on the proposed decision model will be postponed to a later section.

Main Effect of Fear

Are increases in fear associated with increases in acceptance? Although the critical predictions of the fear-drive model are in terms of interactions rather than main effects, this is the obvious question to consider first. When the number of studies on a given topic is large, rather than simply presenting a catalog of findings study by study, it is both more economical and more informative to summarize the findings by means of *overall* statistics i.e. to employ what has come to be known as *meta-analysis* (Cooper, 1979; Glass, 1978; Rosenthal, 1978). Where the traditional review combines the results from a number of studies intuitively, the meta-analytic review does so systematically and quantitatively.

To integrate the findings on the main effect of fear, the technique of adding Zs (standard normal deviates) was employed (see Rosenthal, 1978). This yields a combined Z value whose associated probability can be found from tables. A more elaborate analysis involving effect sizes will be reported elsewhere.

The procedure used was as follows. The data from each study were reanalyzed in the form of single degree of freedom comparisons between the highest experimental fear group and the lowest experimental fear group (E–E comparisons) and/or between the highest experimental fear group and one or more control groups (E–C comparisons). (For these purposes an experimental fear group was defined as one that received a communication designed to arouse some degree of fear, and a control group as one that either received no communication at all or received a non-fear-arousing communication on a different topic.) These comparisons were computed for the measure of fear-arousal and for the one or more measures of acceptance. When significant interactions were reported in the original paper, wherever possible comparisons were computed *at each level* of the interacting factor (e.g. Chu, 1966; *12*). Where multiple fear measures were reported, the comparison was designated significant if at least one of the measures showed a significant difference on the relevant comparison. When, as was sometimes the case for behavioral measures, the acceptance measure was based on a sample consisting of less than 80 percent of the original sample on which fear was measured, the comparison for that measure was not computed.

The results of the comparisons for level of fear aroused are reported in Table 13.1 simply in terms of whether or not that comparison was significant in the expected direction on a one-tailed test at the 0.05 level. The results of the comparisons for the acceptance measures are given in terms of the Z value associated with the one-tailed probability for the relevant comparison and the degrees of freedom or sample size (df) on which the comparison was based.

The column labeled *intention* subsumes the results of comparisons on measures of attitude toward the behavior and intention; the column headed *behavior* subsumes the results of comparisons on measures of reported behavior, actual behavior and behavioral outcome. (For comparisons involving proportions, the Z value was obtained directly from the difference-of-proportions test; similarly, the *critical ratio* value yielded by the Hovland *et al.* (1949) test for the difference between the net proportion who change was treated as a Z value.)

It was possible to carry out this procedure for 21 of the 35 studies. Selecting only those comparisons that produced a significant difference in fear-arousal, a combined Z was computed by adding all the individual Z values for the acceptance measure and dividing by the square root of the number of Z values. The one-tailed probability associated with this combined Z value is directly analogous to a probability from a single study; i.e. it tells us how likely a set of results as extreme as, or more extreme than, the observed set would occur by chance alone, if there were really no relationship between fear and acceptance. Separate combined Zs were computed for E–E and E–C comparisons, first for intention and then for behavior measures of acceptance. The results are shown in Table 13.2. It should be noted that E–E

Table 13.2. Results of the meta-analysis of the main effect of fear on acceptance

Comparison	N	Combined Z	One-tailed probability	Number of unretrieved studies
Intention				
E–E comparisons	24	7.95	$< 10^{-8}$	537
E–C comparisons	8	5.19	$< 10^{-7}$	72
Behavior				
E–E comparisons	8	5.14	$< 10^{-7}$	70
E–C comparisons	5	3.45	$< .0005$	17

N is the number of comparisons. E–E comparisons are comparisons between the highest and lowest experimental fear groups. E–C comparisons are comparisons between the highest experimental fear group and a no-fear control group. The method of adding weighted Zs (weighted by the degrees of freedom or number of observations) yielded similar results.

comparisons and E–C comparisons will not be completely independent since for some studies the highest experimental fear group is common to both comparisons; similarly, neither will the comparisons for intention and behavior be completely independent. The last column of Table 13.2 gives an estimate of the number of unretrieved studies showing on average a null result that would have to exist to bring the overall probability to chance level ($p = 0.05$). This is a way of taking into account the *file drawer problem*, i.e. the strong likelihood that published studies are a biased sample of the studies that are actually conducted, the bias being in the direction of showing a significant difference (Rosenthal, 1979). Generally, the findings summarized in Table 13.2 suggest that we can be confident that increases in fear are associated with increases in acceptance, though the results are less definitive for behavior than for intention. In interpreting the results yielded by this meta-analysis it should be borne in mind that whereas the intention measures are relatively homogeneous, consisting of questionnaire measures of intention or attitude toward the behavior obtained immediately after exposure to the communication, the behavior measures are a mixed bag of different kinds of measures assessed at different intervals after exposure (e.g. mean cumulative weight loss at 8 weeks; whether or not the subject obtained a chest X-ray on the day of exposure to the communication; number of errors on a driving simulator at one or two days).

Non-monotonic Effect of Fear

A total of 20 studies included three or more fear conditions and thus enabled an assessment of the inverted-U hypothesis. However, significant increases in fear were accompanied only rarely by an inverted-U-shaped pattern in the response variable. The two clear cases in point are Janis and Feshbach (1953; *1*) and Krisher *et al.* (1973; *22*). In the latter study the high-fear message had a greater effect on shot-taking than either the low-fear message or the high-fear message accompanied by false physiological feedback; however, there was no significant difference in intention. This represents meager support for the curvilinear hypothesis.

Efficacy of the Recommended Action

As well as manipulating fear level, many of the fear-arousal studies also involved a manipulation of one or more additional factors. Often these were factors that from the standpoint of the fear-drive model should influence fear reduction and thereby modify the fear-acceptance relationship. The factor that has received the most attention is the *efficacy* of the recommended action. The effect of a fear-arousing communication should depend upon the amount of reassurance the recipient is given as to the effectiveness of the recommended action in averting the threat. If the recommended action is perceived by the recipient to be highly effective, then increasing fear should lead to more acceptance (assuming that there is no residual fear in the high-fear condition). If, on the other hand, the action is perceived to be ineffective, then increasing fear should lead to defensive reactions and hence less acceptance. Thus, a crossover interaction is predicted. Although the fear-drive model specifies interaction effects, main effects of efficacy are of interest too, particularly when alternative theoretical formulations are considered.

Eight studies have examined the effect of varying the efficacy of the recommended response (2, 12, 13, 20, 27, 28, 30, 38). In the first of these, Moltz and Thistlethwaite (1955; 2) found that reassurance of efficacy significantly reduced anxiety (one-tailed test), but had no significant effect on self-reports of toothbrushing (direction not given). There was no mention of an interaction with fear which was anyway not successfully manipulated.

Rogers and Thistlethwaite (1970; 20) found a significant fear by reassurance interaction on smokers' beliefs that smoking causes lung cancer, with the high-fear–low-reassurance group showing the least acceptance, a pattern suggestive of a defensive reaction; a similar interaction was not found for intention, however. The main effect of reassurance on intentions was significant among the smokers, with higher reassurance producing stronger intentions.

Rogers and Deckner (1975; 27), whose sample consisted only of smokers, did not mention any effect of reassurance on beliefs, but found a significant effect on reported cigarette consumption: the high-reassurance group was smoking less at 1 week and 1 month after exposure than the low-reassurance group. An effect in the same direction was found for intentions to stop smoking, but this was not significant.

Rogers and Mewborn (1976; 30) found a significant main effect for efficacy (higher efficacy producing stronger intentions) for all three topics that they studied. There was also a significant interaction between fear and efficacy for one of the topics (venereal disease). The pattern, however, was not consistent with the fear-drive model which would predict that the least acceptance would occur in the high-fear–low-efficacy condition, as in the Rogers and Thistlethwaite study. They also found, among the smokers, a significant interaction between efficacy and probability of the threat on intention to stop smoking, with the least acceptance occurring in the low-efficacy–high-probability condition (owing to the unexpected effects of the manipulations, this group would also have a relatively high perceived severity). This suggests that resistances are aroused when individuals expect a severe threat that they feel unable to avoid (see Rogers and Mewborn, 1976, p. 60).

In the remaining four studies it was possible to examine the effect of reassurance on fear. Chu (1966; 12) found that higher efficacy led to significantly higher(!) anxiety, but also to significantly greater willingness to adopt the recommended action. There was a marginally significant inter-action between efficacy and fear but this was not consistent with the fear-drive model. Dabbs and Leventhal (1966; *13*) found that describing the recommended tetanus inoculation as perfect versus imperfect protection had no significant effects on fear, intentions to take shots, or actual shot-taking. There was no mention of any interactions. Griffeth and Rogers (1976; *28*) successfully manipulated the efficacy of safe-driving practices in avoiding accidents but found no significant effect on intentions to drive safely or number of errors made on a driving simulation task, apart from a three-factor (probability × efficacy × noxiousness) interaction on the latter measure. Finally, Mewborn and Rogers (1979; *38*) found that reassurance significantly reduced self-reports of fear but did not affect physiological indices (heart-rate, galvanic skin response). Higher reassurance significantly strengthened intentions to use 'wonder' drugs for venereal disease, but there was no interaction with fear. It should be noted, however, that their reassurance manipulation confounded efficacy and the probability of occurrence of the undesirable consequence.

One clear finding emerges from the catalog of results presented above. Excluding the Mewborn and Rogers (1979) study, in six studies in which intentions were measured, greater efficacy produced stronger intentions to act in four cases; significantly so in three. In the other two studies information on the direction of the difference was not supplied. Under the null hypothesis of no relationship between efficacy and intentions, the probability of obtain-ing at least three significant results in one direction out of six is less than 0.0025 (calculated by means of the binomial distribution). We can therefore state with some confidence that greater efficacy produces stronger intentions to adopt the recommended response. Furthermore, there would have to be at least 54 unretrieved studies showing no significant effect to increase the probability to 0.05. On the other hand, there is no consistent evidence for the predicted interaction between efficacy and fear.

Specific Instructions

Another factor that might be expected to be important is the giving of specific instructions on how to carry out the recommended action. From the point of view of the fear-drive model specific instructions should have a similar effect to reassurance of the effectiveness of the recommendation, i.e. there should be a crossover interaction on acceptance. Furthermore, and more generally, providing specific instructions would be expected to facilitate implementation of the decision to adopt the recommended action. Put simply, if one knows *how* to do something one will be more likely to achieve it.

Leventhal and his colleagues have examined the effect of specific instructions in three studies (*8, 14, 17*). In two studies on tetanus the instructions consisted of information about the location of the clinic and the opening times. Instructions had no effects on fear apart from significantly reducing nausea in the Leventhal *et al.* (1965; *8*) study. Furthermore, no significant effects on intentions were found except in the Leventhal *et al.* (1966; *14*) study, in which specific plans strengthened intentions to take a shot among ineligible subjects but not among eligible subjects. By contrast, instructions affected behavior in all three studies. In the two tetanus studies, the provision of instructions led to more shot-taking. However, the fact that none of the subjects in the recommendations-only control groups obtained an inoculation suggests that specific information *alone* is not sufficient to influence behavior. In the smoking study (Leventhal *et al.*, 1967; *17*), instructions on how to stop smoking helped smokers to maintain their reduced consumption.

Position of Recommendations

From the standpoint of the fear-drive model the position of the recommendations should be crucial in influencing the effectiveness of a communication. Given that the recommendation is perceived to be effective, the optimum position should be immediately after the fear-arousing part of the message when the level of aroused fear is presumably at its peak and hence the amount of potential fear reduction is greatest. The effect of varying the position of the recommendations has been examined in two studies.

In the first study, Leventhal and Singer (1966; *15*) compared the effect of placing the recommendations before, intermixed with, or after the fear-arousing material, and found that this had the expected effect on fear. In the high-fear condition there was a progressive reduction in reported fear, while in the low-fear condition there was no significant difference. Despite the success of the manipulation, however, position had no significant effect on intention to follow the recommended dental hygiene practices. From the fear-drive model one would have expected to see a difference in intention in the high-fear condition.

Skilbeck *et al.* (1977; *34*) compared the following three conditions: fear material immediately followed by recommendations (FR), fear followed by recommendations but with other neutral material in between (FDR), and recommendations preceding fear material (RF). They found as predicted that the FR condition was significantly superior to the other two conditions which were mutually similar in their effect on weight change. It was the RF group, however, that reported the most fear.

In attempting to interpret these findings the reader should remember the problems discussed in an earlier section of the chapter, in particular the need for a continuous measure of fear to track fear-arousal and reduction. Furthermore, it should be noted that it is difficult to exclude the alternative hypothesis that differences produced by varying the position of the recommendations are due to cognitive structuring, e.g. the superiority of the FR condition in the Skilbeck *et al.* study might be due to the logical ordering of material which would enable the recipient to process the information relatively easily.

Other Communication Factors

Occasionally, studies have examined the effect of manipulating other aspects of the communication. The only two factors to have received more than isolated attention are the *number of exposures* and the *sidedness* of the communication.

Kirscht and Haefner (1973; *21*) exposed subjects once, twice, or three times to the same communication on heart disease with 1-day intervals. Although the amount of fear was not affected by repetition, some intentions were strengthened by repeated exposures for women, but were weakened for men. The percentage of subjects who reported taking a 'specific and immediate health-related action' increased with more exposures. Skilbeck *et al.* (1977; *33*) compared a single exposure to a fear-arousing lecture with multiple exposures achieved by attaching a reminder of the main message to each daily record sheet. They found that a single exposure was significantly more effective in reducing weight and that its advantage over multiple exposures improved with time. It is probable that the number and the timing of exposures will prove to be crucial factors.

Communicator Factors

Communicator factors have been relatively little studied in the research on fear-arousing communications.

The *race of the communicator* was varied in three studies of dental hygiene using schoolchildren as subjects (*32, 35, 36*). In the first of these, Ramirez and Lasater (1977; *32*) found that the Anglo-American communicator aroused significantly more fear than the Chicano-American communicator, though this depended on the self-esteem of the subjects, who, it should be noted, were predominantly Anglo-American. On the index of tooth cleanliness (PHP score), the group who had heard the Anglo-American communicator had significantly cleaner teeth 1 day and 6 days after exposure, though there were no significant differences in reported frequency and recency of toothbrushing or intentions to brush one's teeth more frequently. The other two studies (Dembroski *et al.*, 1978; *35, 36*) used black or white communicators in all black schools and found that the black communicator did not arouse significantly more fear but did generate significantly more immediate behavior change in terms of PHP scores. In both cases, however, the pretest

PHP scores of the experimental groups were not equivalent. The results of these three studies suggest that greater communicator–recipient similarity (in terms of race) produces more immediate behavior change without necessarily affecting fear level.

Recipient Factors

A number of studies of fear-arousing communications have investigated the effect of personality factors, again with the expectation of interactions between the personality factor and fear level. One obvious problem is that differences on a given personality factor may be confounded with other subject factors.

Chronic anxiety was the first personality factor to be investigated. Assuming that an increase in the fear level of a communication will be especially effective in increasing anxiety in chronically anxious people, then one would expect more defensive responses (i.e. less acceptance) amongst such people as fear level increases. On the other hand, less chronically anxious people should show more acceptance under high-fear than under low-fear. Janis and Feshbach (1954; *1*) reanalyzed data from part of their original 1953 sample and found evidence for the predicted interaction on self-reports of dental hygiene practices but not on resistance to counterpropaganda. Dabbs and Leventhal (1966; *13*) also measured chronic anxiety but found no significant effects on intention to take a tetanus shot.

A similar personality factor that has been investigated is the person's characteristic *way of coping with threat*. Some people apparently tend to recall fear-arousing stimuli better than neutral stimuli, while for others the reverse is true. If so, Goldstein (1959; *3*) argued, one would predict an interaction between fear level and this personality characteristic similar to the one predicted for chronic anxiety. Goldstein compared 'copers' and 'avoiders', categorized on the basis of an emotional version of the Sentence Completion Test, and found a marginally significant ($p < 0.05$ on a one-tailed test) interaction on net change in self-reported dental hygiene practices. However, contrary to expectation, copers did not respond particularly well to either the high-fear or the low-fear message. (It should be noted that Goldstein did not say whether or not fear was successfully manipulated.) Furthermore, analysis of learning scores provided no evidence of differential recall.

In another study on dental health, Dziokonski and Weber (1977; *31*) divided subjects into three groups according to their scores on a scale of *repression–sensitization* derived from the MMPI (Byrne *et al.*, 1963). This was found to be related to three items measuring 'vulnerability' to gum disease ('repressors' felt less vulnerable), but not to attitudes, intentions, or learning; there were no interactions.

Leventhal and Trembly (1968; *18*) found that *self-esteem* was significantly related to several mood measures (activation, concentration, and impotence) but not to desire to take protective actions (safe driving practices). They reported an interesting interaction between intensity of the communication (size of picture and loudness) and self-esteem on protective intentions. Low-self-esteem subjects showed decreases as the stimulus became more intense, whereas medium- and high-self-esteem subjects showed increases. There was no evidence for emotional mediation, and Leventhal and Trembly prefer a cognitive interpretation: they suggest that among the low-self-esteem subjects the large picture created feelings of helplessness which led to breakdown of the coping mechanism.

Dabbs and Leventhal (1966; *13*) also found an interaction between self-esteem and fear level on intentions to take a tetanus shot. Low-self-esteem subjects increased their intentions to take shots from the control to the low-fear condition; but they showed no further increase under high fear. High-self-esteem subjects, on the other hand, showed increased intentions only from low-fear to high-fear conditions.

Ramirez and Lasater (1977; *32*) found that high-self-esteem subjects were significantly less anxious about their dental health than low-self-esteem subjects (especially when the message had been delivered by the Chicano-American rather than the Anglo-American communicator). High-self-esteem subjects also expressed significantly stronger intentions to perform the recommended dental hygiene practices and when questioned at 1 week had cleaned their teeth significantly more recently than low-self-esteem subjects. There was no main effect on PHP score, but there was a significant interaction, with high fear and low fear equally effective in the case of high-self-esteem subjects but low fear less effective than high fear in the case of low-self-esteem subjects, a different pattern from that reported by Dabbs and Leventhal. A similar interaction was obtained on self-reports of tooth-brushing frequency. By contrast, Krisher *et al.* (1973; *22*) found no significant effects for self-esteem or for their facilitation–inhibition and hypochondriasis scales.

Leventhal and Watts (1966; *16*) examined the effect of *perceived suscepti-bility* (to illness, lung cancer and car accidents) and found that high-susceptible subjects, despite being significantly more frightened by the communications, did not differ from low-susceptibles on intentions to take an X-ray or decrease smoking, or in actual behavior. Susceptibility has sometimes been seen as related to the concept of *relevance*, but it will not necessarily be true that high-relevant subjects will perceive themselves to be more susceptible to accidents and illness than low-relevant subjects; in fact, one can argue plausibly for just the opposite relationship (see the section on Relevance).

Kirscht *et al.* (1978; *37*) found significant positive correlations between *illness threat* (a combination of perceived susceptibility and severity) and several other health beliefs measured before exposure, on the one hand, and their outcome measure (cumulative weight change) on the other; there were apparently no significant interactions. Dabbs and Leventhal (1966; *13*) measured susceptibility and coping but found no effects for either factor on intentions to take a tetanus shot.

Ley *et al.* (1974; *23*) measured Extraversion, Neuroticism and Internal–External control. Of these, only the last correlated significantly with the behavior measure (weight loss); high scorers actually lost weight significantly faster. Finally, Rozelle *et al.* (1973) reported results from the Evans *et al.* (1970; *19*) sample showing a significant effect of need-for-social-approval on toothbrushing intentions; there was no significant interaction with the fear manipulation.

In conclusion, the results of fear-arousal studies that have investigated personality characteristics are inconsistent and complex. It is impossible to draw any firm conclusions from these studies except to say that clearly more work is needed. It would be helpful to have more information about the relationships among the various personality measures. It is interesting to note, for example, that Goldstein's copers and avoiders did not differ significantly on Janis and Fesbach's (1954; *1*) chronic anxiety scale.

Relevance

Many studies of fear-arousing communications have divided subjects on the basis of some behavioral criterion into those for whom the communications are *relevant* and those for whom they are *irrelevant*. To the extent that these two groups react with different degrees of fear, one can derive from the fear-drive model the simple prediction of an interaction between relevance and fear level on acceptance similar to that predicted for chronic anxiety and repression–sensitization.

In four studies of tetanus, subjects who had had a recent shot (*ineligibles*) have been compared with those who had not (*eligibles*). Radelfinger (1965; *9, 10*) found that, except in the no-fear control conditions, eligible subjects were more frightened than ineligibles. He omitted to say, however, whether or not there were any significant differences in shot-taking intentions or behavior. Leventhal *et al.* (1965; *8*) found that eligibles were more frightened and expressed significantly stronger intentions to obtain a shot, but there was apparently no interaction between eligibility and fear. Leventhal *et al.* (1966; *14*) found as in the previous studies that eligibles were significantly more frightened. However, there was an interaction with fear level: the fear manipulation was effective only for the eligible subjects. The results for intentions were complex. Fear level had no significant effect for eligibles or ineligibles. Among ineligibles, men expressed stronger intentions than women and specific instructions strengthened intentions. Neither effect occurred among eligibles; in fact the means were reversed. Surprisingly, eligibility was unrelated to shot-taking.

Other studies have compared the response of smokers and non-smokers to communications about smoking and lung cancer. This distinction is rather different from, say, the distinction between people who travel by car several times a week versus those who travel once a week or less. In particular, a communication about smoking and lung cancer that recommends that people should stop smoking is irrelevant to non-smokers in the sense that, for them, it has no implications for behavior change; they already perform the recommended action. As such it would not be surprising to find differences between smokers and non-smokers in their response to a fear-arousing communication on that subject, and such differences would be only of secondary importance, both practically and theoretically. Distinctions among smokers based on cigarette consumption, on the other hand, are of more interest, since such a communication would have behavioral implications for light and for heavy smokers. Only two studies have compared light and heavy smokers.

Leventhal and Watts (1966; _16_) found that light smokers (< 15/day) were more frightened by the communications than non-smokers, who were in turn more frightened than heavy smokers. However, there were no significant differences between light and heavy smokers in intentions to stop/decrease smoking or to take a chest X-ray. For the analysis of X-ray-taking, light and heavy smokers were combined and only eligible subjects (no X-ray in the previous 6 months) were considered. A significantly _lower_ proportion of those in the high-fear condition than in the moderate-fear or low-fear conditions took an X-ray. It is interesting to note that in a similar study Leventhal and Niles (1964; _4_) found a different result: more subjects in the high-fear condition took X-rays, but the difference was not significant. Leventhal and Watts also reported a non-significant tendency for greater fear to produce a greater decrease in smoking, though subject loss was a problem here.

In the second study, Leventhal et al. (1967; _17_) found no significant differences between light and heavy smokers (defined as in the previous study) on fear or desire to stop/reduce smoking. With regard to changes in cigarette consumption, light smokers showed little change after the 1-week stage while heavy smokers, though they continued to smoke more than light smokers, showed a further decrease.

The findings regarding relevance provide no support for the fear-drive model. In only one study (Leventhal et al., 1966; _14_) was the predicted Eligibility × Fear interaction on reported fear observed; and in no case was a similar interaction obtained on measures of intention or behavior. In the tetanus studies eligibles were consistently more frightened by the communications than ineligibles, but in only one case did this fear difference clearly produce a difference in intentions. On the other hand, in the Leventhal and Watts (1966; *16*) study, heavy smokers, the 'more relevant' subjects, were *less* frightened than light smokers. As these findings indicate, notions about relevance in the literature on fear-arousing communications have been too simplistic. The assumption that there is a necessary connection between engaging to a greater extent, or more frequently, in the target behavior and being more frightened by the communication is clearly not tenable. A person who engages to a greater extent in the target behavior may do so precisely *because* he is less concerned or more skeptical about the possible health consequences than his 'low-relevant' fellow. He may therefore be less frightened by a fear-arousing communication. Clearly, in order to predict the response of high-relevant and low-relevant subjects to persuasive communications, one needs to know how the two groups differ with regard to their attitudes and beliefs toward the target behavior and the recommended alternative. It should be added that the same reasoning applies to *any* subject factor.

Summary and Conclusions

The main findings of the studies of fear-arousing communications can be summarized in the following six statements:

(1) increases in fear are consistently associated with increases in acceptance (intentions and behavior);
(2) there is no evidence that fear and acceptance are related in a non-monotonic fashion;
(3) increasing the efficacy of the recommended action strengthens intentions to adopt that action;
(4) providing specific instructions about how to perform the recommended action leads to a higher rate of acting in accordance with the recommendation;
(5) greater similarity between communicator and recipient in terms of race produces more immediate behavior change without necessarily affecting fear;
(6) there is little support for the interactions predicted by the fear-drive model.

It should be noted that conclusions (4) and (5) are based upon comparatively few studies. One cannot therefore make these statements with much confidence, and they should be regarded as suggestions or trends to be investigated further.

Leventhal's Parallel Response Model

The *parallel response model* was proposed by Leventhal (1970) as an alternative to the fear-drive model. The model assumes that the response to a fear communication involves two separate parallel processes, *danger control* and *fear control*. The danger control process involves the selection and guidance of responses aimed at averting the danger. The information used in this process consists largely of information about the environment. Fear control, on the other hand, involves the initiation of responses in an attempt to reduce the unpleasant feeling of fear, and is guided largely by internal cues. Examples of fear control responses would be avoidance of fear-arousing stimuli, denying the threat, and drinking alcohol to alleviate anxiety. In some instances actions that are instrumental in coping with the danger may have the additional effect of reducing fear; in others, fear control and danger control may involve quite different responses. The two processes may sometimes interfere with one another as when, for example, strong fear motivates avoidance behaviors which disrupt danger control.

The importance of the parallel response model lies largely in its movement away from the notion of fear as the central explanatory concept in persuasion towards a recognition that an individual's response to a fear-arousing communication involves adaptive behaviors motivated by a desire to avert the anticipated danger. The model is not sufficiently precise, however, to enable specific predictions to be made about the factors mediating acceptance of the communicator's recommendations. It is more a general paradigm that raises new questions for research than a tightly articulated theory capable of generating testable predictions. For instance, the model suggests the following questions:

(1) What aspects of the communication arouse fear and what aspects create an awareness of danger? To what extent do these two aspects overlap?;
(2) What factors determine whether it is fear control or danger control that takes precedence?;
(3) What factors determine the actions adopted to cope with the danger/fear?

Such questions invite the development of more specific theoretical formulations which do generate testable predictions. The decision-making model discussed in the following section is one approach that will hopefully serve this purpose. It emphasizes the cognitive processes involved in the arousal of fear and in the selection of a response to avert the anticipated danger.

A Cognitive Decision-making Model Based on SEU Theory

The model presented in this section is a cognitive mediation model based on *subjective expected utility* (SEU) theory (Edwards, 1961). Incipient SEU notions have been employed from time to time in the literature on fear-arousing communications. Indeed, in Hovland *et al.*' (1953) seminal chapter the subjective probability of the threatened event was discussed, albeit briefly. In the related area of health decisions, the *Health Belief Model* (Becker, 1974), which can be regarded as a loose version of the SEU model, has been extensively researched, and the subjective-probability-like concepts of perceived *susceptibility* and *vulnerability* found their way into the fear-arousal literature. With the emphasis given to fear, however, these SEU notions remained undeveloped until 1975 when Rogers published his *protection motivation theory* (Rogers, 1975). The model presented here is an attempt to apply SEU ideas more comprehensively and systematically to explaining the effects of fear-arousing communications. The relationship between fear and the SEU concepts of subjective probability and utility—a special instance of the more general problem of the relationship between feeling and thinking (Zajonc, 1980)—is also considered at some length. A detailed comparison of the SEU model and protection motivation theory will be presented in a later section.

Exposition of the Model

According to SEU theory, a person faced with two or more alternative courses of action will choose the one with the greatest SEU. The SEU for an alternative is a function of the subjective values or *utilities* attached to the possible outcomes of the alternative and the *subjective probabilities* that the alternative will lead to those outcomes. It is computed by multiplying the utility of each outcome by its subjective probability and summing over outcomes.

SEU theory offers a way of explaining the effects of communications that are designed to influence the recipient to discontinue his present course of action in favor of a recommended alternative. It suggests that a communication will be successful if, by inducing changes in utilities and subjective probabilities, it increases the individual's SEU for the recommended action so that it is greater than his SEU for each available alternative, including continuing the current course of action.

In order to convey the basic ideas of the SEU approach to fear-arousing communications, we will consider the example of a communication on the subject of heart disease which includes an implicit or explicit recommendation to do more exercise. For the purpose of this example we will assume that only one outcome (heart disease) is taken into account by the individual in making his decision. The model is shown in Figure 13.1. The choice facing the individual is seen as one of continuing his current course of action (doing no exercise) or adopting the recommended response (doing more exercise).

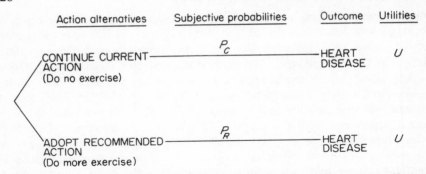

Figure 13.1 The decision facing the recipient of a fear-arousing communication on the subject of heart disease and exercise

According to the model, the individual's decision will depend upon the following variables:

(1) the person's utility for heart disease, which we will symbolize by U (being an undesirable outcome, the utility will be negative);
(2) the person's subjective probability of that outcome occurring, given that he continues his current course of action (P_C); and
(3) his subjective probability of the outcome occurring given that he adopts the recommended action (P_R).

Given multiplicative combination of subjective probabilities and utilities, the person's SEU for continuing (SEU_C) and his SEU for adopting the recommended response (SEU_R) will be equal to $P_C . U$ and $P_R . U$ respectively (both SEU values will be negative). According to the model, the individual will choose the alternative that has the higher SEU value and hence, in this situation, the one that is associated with the *lower* subjective probability of occurrence of the unpleasant consequence. Thus, if the communication affects the relative size of the subjective probabilities such that, after exposure, $P_R < P_C$ (or, equivalently, $P_C - P_R > 0$), then the individual will decide to adopt the recommended action. (Note that this can occur in three distinct ways: by increasing P_C, by reducing P_R, or by doing both.) In terms of our heart disease example, to be effective the communication must convince the recipient that his probability of getting heart disease would be lower if he did more exercise.

The probability difference ($P_C - P_R$) is a convenient way of defining the concept of the *perceived efficacy* of the recommended action. The recommended action will be perceived to be effective to the extent that it is perceived to reduce the risk of occurrence of the undesirable consequence. This definition is consistent with the way in which the concept of perceived efficacy, or reassurance as it is sometimes called, has been employed in the literature, with the exception of the Mewborn and Rogers (1979; *38*) study.

It is possible to state the model in an alternative form in which the variables are related in a continuous rather than in a threshold fashion. In this form, the probability of deciding to adopt the recommended action is held to be monotonically related to the difference in SEUs ($\text{SEU}_R - \text{SEU}_C$); the greater this difference, the more likely the person will be to adopt the recommended action. In this alternative formulation, changes in U as well as in $(P_C - P_R)$ will affect the decision. In particular, given that $P_R < P_C$, then decreasing U (i.e. making it more negative) will lead to a higher probability of adopting the recommended action. For example, given that the person believes that he is less likely to get heart disease if he does more exercise, then changing his evaluation of heart disease by making him realize that it is worse than he thought will make him more likely to decide to do more exercise. Furthermore, the multiplicative combination implies that probability difference $(P_C - P_R)$ and utility will interact so that a given decrease in utility will be more effective the greater the probability difference. In the special case in which the two subjective probabilities are equal ($P_R = P_C$), altering the utility will have no effect on the probability of adopting the recommended action. Thus, it doesn't matter how serious the person believes heart disease to be, if his subjective probability of getting it is the same under the two alternatives, he will not have any preference. Similarly, when utility is zero, changing the probability difference will have no effect on the probability of adopting the recommended action. Thus, if he doesn't care whether or not he gets heart disease, he will have no preference for either action, irrespective of the associated probabilities.

To summarize, a communication on heart disease will be effective in persuading the person to (decide to) do more exercise if it convinces him (a) that heart disease is a bad thing to get, and (b) that he will be less likely to get heart disease if he does more exercise.

While the single-outcome model serves a useful didactic purpose in presenting the basic ideas of the approach, it is unlikely in a real decision situation that an individual will take account of only one outcome in making his decision. Other consequences of the alternatives may be important. For example, the individual may anticipate financial outlay and risk of injury, two possible undesirable consequences of adopting the recommendation to do more exercise. The probabilities and utilities associated with these other consequences may also be influenced by the communication, that is, *impact effects* may occur, and they may of course be influenced in ways which make it *less* likely that the individual will adopt the recommended action. It is not necessary here to present the algebraic formula for the multiple-outcome SEU model. The interested reader can find this elsewhere (e.g. Edwards, 1961). It is sufficient for present purposes to point out that the approach adopted here can be easily extended to incorporate multiple outcomes as well as multiple-action alternatives.

It should be noted that, according to the model, the person's decision is held to depend *only* upon the SEUs of the action alternatives. Other variables, whether individual (e.g. self-esteem, perceived vulnerability to injury and illness) or situational (e.g. communicator credibility, modality of communication), can influence the decision only *indirectly*, by influencing the subjective probabilities or utilities associated with outcomes of the action alternatives. A corollary of this is that the model says nothing about the determinants of subjective probabilities and utilities and hence how one might influence these key components of the model.

What factors affect, for instance, subjective probabilities? One obvious factor would be information about *objective* risks. However, in practice this information is nearly always oversimplified. It is given in a form that applies to some general group of people (e.g. the national population); rarely is it broken down into the many categories into which the person may classify himself (e.g. male, late-20s, living in London, etc.). Seldom are we given information about our *own* probability of, say, dying in a road accident which takes into account our special circumstances and lifestyle.

Probably more important are the several *heuristics* or cognitive simplification strategies identified by Tversky and Kahneman (1974). The most relevant to the present discussion is the *availability* heuristic according to which people assess the probability of an event by the ease with which instances can be imagined or recalled. Thus, one's subjective probability of getting heart disease may be high if a close friend of the same age has recently had a heart attack. Reporting of events in the mass media probably plays an important role here. Sensational, dramatic causes of death like tornadoes, plane crashes, food poisoning, and homicide receive heavy media coverage and probably as a result people tend to overestimate their frequency (and hence their probability) relative to unspectacular causes like diabetes, asthma, and emphysema (Lichtenstein *et al.*, 1978).

Related to the above discussion is the question of the relationship between subjective probabilities and utilities. Classical SEU theory assumes that the two components are independent, i.e. that they do not affect each other (Behling and Starke, 1973). It would seem more realistic, however, to expect them to be mutually dependent to some extent. For example, one may overestimate the probability of desirable events ('wishful thinking').

These questions concern the input side of the model. What about the output side? The SEU model deals with a cognitive event—the decision to adopt some action. Generally, it is assumed that the decision will be implemented; i.e. that the appropriate behavior will ensue. This will not always be so, however, as Fishbein and Ajzen (1975) point out. For example, the individual may change his mind as a result of exposure to counter-propaganda, or he may for some reason be unable to perform the appropriate behavior.

A possible limitation of the model as it stands is that it does not take into account the subjective probability of successfully carrying out the recommended action, given that an attempt is made. This variable, which can be called *confidence*, should be distinguished from the subjective probability that the action, if successfully performed, will avert the unpleasant consequence; the latter subjective probability enters into our definition of the perceived efficacy of the recommended action. Confidence is likely to be a crucial factor whenever the recommended response is difficult and requires sustained effort over a period of time (e.g. giving up smoking). When, on the other hand, the protective response involves a very simple action (e.g. obtaining a tetanus shot), confidence should be far less important. Incorporating this factor into the SEU model requires a reconceptualization of the decision to one involving a choice between continuing the current course of action and *attempting* to adopt the recommended response. The latter choice may lead either to success (with a given subjective probability—confidence) or to failure. For an example of such an extended SEU model applied to smoking behavior, see Sutton (1979).

The Role of Fear

The SEU model presented above makes no mention of fear. Fear is not one of the components of the model (unless of course it is defined in terms of subjective probability or utility). However, feeling frightened, anxious or worried is an almost ubiquitous aspect of a person's response to a threatening future event. So it is reasonable to ask how fear relates to the components of the SEU model. In discussing this question we will focus on the affective experience of fear which we will take to be primary in relation to other indices of fear such as physiological changes (e.g. increased heart-rate).

From the standpoint of the model presented here, fear is assumed to have no causal role in mediating the effects of fear-arousing communications. It is regarded merely as an epiphenomenon that may reflect in part the person's cognitions concerning the unpleasant consequences in question. In particular, in the single-outcome model we would expect fear to depend upon P_C and U. The higher P_C is, and the lower (more negative) U is, the greater the level of fear. For example, the more likely the person believes he is to get heart disease, and the more unpleasant he perceives getting heart disease to be, the more frightened he should feel. (Indeed, one might predict a multiplicative interaction between P_C and U on fear level.) However, fear will also depend on P_R. If P_R is also high (i.e. if the individual feels that the threatening event is highly likely to occur whatever he does) then we would expect him to feel much more frightened than if P_R is very low (i.e. if he is virtually certain that he can avert the danger by adopting the recommended action). One implication of this is that we would not necessarily expect to find a simple one-to-one correspondence between the level of reported fear and the probability of adopting the recommended response.

A Note on 'Rationality'

The SEU model and similar approaches are sometimes dismissed on the grounds that they make the unrealistic assumption that people are 'rational'. However, the model assumes only that individuals behave in a way that is *subjectively* rational. Thus the model permits many kinds of 'irrational' behavior. For instance, people's subjective probabilities may be imperfectly related to the objective probabilities. They may make mistakes in making decisions; they may fail to take into account all the relevant consequences and possible alternative courses of action available to them. Having made a decision, they may change their minds as a result of reconsidering the outcomes or receiving further information. Moreover, in many cases what seems from the observer's point of view to be irrational, stupid behavior may from the actor's viewpoint be entirely rational. For example, many non-smokers probably regard smoking as irrational, self-destructive behavior, but from the smoker's point of view the short-term benefits of satisfying a craving, or feeling more relaxed, may outweigh the long-term risks of lung cancer.

Comparison with Protection Motivation Theory

Another recent application of expectancy-value concepts to fear-arousing communications is Rogers' (1975) *protection motivation theory*. The theory distinguishes three crucial determinants of the individual's response to a fear-arousing communication: (a) the severity of the depicted event; (b) the probability of the event's occurrence; and (c) the efficacy of the recommended response. Each of these communication variables is assumed to initiate corresponding cognitive processes which mediate attitude change by arousing 'protection motivation'. The amount of protection motivation (and hence attitude change) is postulated to be a monotonically increasing function of the product of these three cognitive variables.

The theory is similar to the single-outcome version of the SEU model presented here. Both have the subjective probability of the event's occurrence (under the current course of action) as a key component; and the perceived severity of a negative outcome can be considered equivalent to its utility. Furthermore, perceived efficacy is defined operationally by Rogers (e.g. Rogers and Mewborn, 1976; *30*) as the reduction in the probability of the event's occurrence that is associated with taking the recommended protective action, i.e. efficacy can be considered equivalent to our probability difference concept $(P_C - P_R)$.

Though the models are similar in many ways, protection motivation theory suffers from a number of logical–theoretical problems. First, in protection motivation theory, unlike the model presented here, the variables are combined arbitrarily. In particular, though there is a rationale for multiplying together severity and probability of occurrence—namely, that the model is a special instance of the general class of expectancy-value models in which values and probabilities are combined multiplicatively—there is no basis for multiplying this product by perceived efficacy.

Second, since efficacy (E) is defined in terms of probability (P_C) the variables are not, as Rogers states, independent of one another. This dependence creates a practical difficulty. Since it will usually be the case that $P_R \leqslant P_C$, it follows that $0 \leqslant E \leqslant P_C$, that is, the range of E is restricted by P_C. This makes it difficult to test the model experimentally in the way that Rogers attempts to do, that is, by independently manipulating P_C and E, because subjects in the low-P-high-E condition are given inconsistent information. For example, they are told both (a) that if they continue to smoke, the probability of getting lung cancer is low, and (b) that giving up smoking would greatly reduce their chances of getting lung cancer. This probably accounts for the failure in Rogers and Mewborn's (1976; 30) study to obtain an independent manipulation of P_C and E; they reported a significant interaction between these two variables on a measure of perceived efficacy of the recommended response included as a manipulation check.

Third, on the input side, protection motivation theory assumes a simple correspondence between information about objective probabilities and subjective assessments, i.e. Rogers seems to assume that all information presented to the subject will be accepted. He thus glosses over the crucial question of how subjective probabilities and utilities (or health beliefs in general) are formed and changed.

One can also question the need to postulate a special type of motivation, *viz.* the motivation to protect oneself against threatening events. The SEU approach, by contrast, assumes that all decisions are guided by one motivation, *viz.* to maximize one's outcomes. Thus, from the SEU standpoint, health behaviors are not seen as fundamentally different from other kinds of behaviors and hence they are not seen as requiring a different kind of explanation.

Finally, the SEU model recognizes that a person's intention to adopt the recommended response (and hence his subsequent behavior) after exposure to a fear-arousing communication depends not only upon the utility and subjective probabilities associated with the event depicted in the communication but also upon the utilities and subjective probabilities associated with *other* consequences of the available courses of action. Although Rogers briefly mentions other factors (Rogers, 1975, p. 221), these are not explicitly incorporated into the model.

Evidence for the Proposed Model

As yet, there is little experimental evidence that bears directly upon the validity of either the proposed SEU model or protection motivation theory. With a few exceptions, the research on fear-arousing communications has not systematically examined the effect on decisions and behavior of manipulating probabilities and utilities.

One important exception concerns the effect of the perceived efficacy of the recommended action, which has been investigated in a number of studies. As noted above, perceived efficacy has been operationally defined as $(P_C - P_R)$, i.e. the reduction in the subjective probability of the danger that is associated with (successfully) carrying out the recommended action. The SEU model predicts that, given that the consequence has a negative utility, an increase in $(P_C - P_R)$ will produce an increase in probability of acceptance, i.e. it predicts a main effect for perceived efficacy on acceptance; protection motivation theory generates the same prediction. As we saw previously, the experimental results support this prediction.

Three recent studies by Rogers and his associates are relevant in so far as they involved manipulations of the probability and noxiousness of the threatening event. Hass et al. (1975; 25) gave their subjects a written communication which argued that an energy crisis was likely (or unlikely) and that if it occurred the consequences for one's lifestyle would be drastic (or minor). Noxiousness but not probability was found to have a significant effect on an immediate measure of intentions to use less energy; the predicted interaction was not confirmed.

Rogers and Mewborn (1976; 30) attempted to manipulate noxiousness, probability, and efficacy independently in three separate experiments on smoking, safe driving, and venereal disease. Unfortunately, their manipulation checks yielded strange results, making their other findings difficult to interpret. Fear-arousal but not perceived severity were affected by the noxiousness manipulation. Furthermore, although the probability manipulation was effective, rather surprisingly it also influenced perceived severity. Also, as discussed above, there was an efficacy by probability interaction effect on perceived efficacy. There was no suggestion of the predicted three-factor interaction effect on intention to adopt the recommended response. Separate analysis of the results of the smoking experiment revealed a significant interaction effect between efficacy and probability on intentions to stop/reduce smoking. Compared with the low-probability (low-severity) condition, the high-probability (high-severity) condition was associated with an increase in intention when giving up smoking was perceived as highly effective, and with a decrease in intention when the response was seen as ineffective. While the former arm of the interaction is consistent with both models, the latter arm would seem to be inconsistent with a rational model;

why should the combination of high probability, high severity and low efficacy lead to *lower* intentions to act than low probability combined with low severity and low efficacy (if, indeed, this difference was significant)?

Griffeth and Rogers (1976; *28*), in a study on safe driving, again attempted to manipulate orthogonally the three components of protection motivation theory. The noxiousness manipulation influenced fear as well as perceived severity; the probability manipulation was unsuccessful. None of the independent variables significantly affected intentions to drive safely (based on six items combined). However, one item when analyzed separately (intention 'to never ride with a reckless driver') was found to be significantly affected by noxiousness, with high noxiousness more effective than low. Furthermore, subjects in the high noxiousness condition made significantly fewer errors on the driving simulator. There was also a significant three-factor interaction effect, but this did not follow the expected pattern.

Finally, Dziokonski and Weber (1977; *31*) examined the effect of manipulating perceived vulnerability, which was equivalent in their operationalization to subjective probability. The high-vulnerability communication said that females were three times more likely to contract gum disease than males; the low-vulnerability version indicated that females were three times more resistant than males. The sample consisted of female undergraduates. Vulnerability apparently had no significant effects on dental health intentions, though it should be noted that only one of the three vulnerability measures confirmed the success of the manipulation.

These findings represent rather mixed support for the proposed SEU model and protection motivation theory. Part of the problem stems from the difficulty of producing clean manipulations of the relevant probabilities and utilities. An adequate test of the models would seem to require a different approach to data analysis. If path-analytic techniques were employed, one could examine the extent to which a particular treatment effect (produced, say, by an attempted manipulation of utility) on intentions or behavior was mediated by measures of the key components of the models. One could also test the predicted interactions directly, i.e. in relation to the measures of the components rather than to the experimental manipulations designed to influence those measures.

Conclusions

This chapter began with a consideration of the fear-drive model and related approaches. These were shown to be extraordinarily difficult to test. Furthermore, a review of the findings on fear-arousing communications yielded little support for these approaches. The main positive result to emerge was that increases in fear are consistently associated with increases in intentional and behavioral measures of acceptance. Leventhal's parallel response model was then considered and criticized on the ground that it is not refutable. A decision-making model derived from SEU theory was proposed as an alternative to these approaches. The model has two advantages over its rival formulations. First, it is able to generate testable predictions and is therefore refutable, at least in principle. Second, it is not limited to explaining the effects of communications that arouse fear. It can be seen as a *general* model of the cognitive processes that mediate the effects of any kind of persuasive communication (or indeed any information the individual receives). As yet, there is little evidence bearing on the validity of the SEU model in this context. It is hoped that this chapter will stimulate research specifically designed to test the proposed model, as well as to address the more general questions of how people form their subjective probabilities and utilities, and how they combine them in making the numerous decisions, health-related and otherwise, with which they are faced in the course of everyday life.

References

Ajzen, I., and Fishbein, M. (1977). 'Attitude-behavior relations; a theoretical analysis and review of empirical research', *Psychological Bulletin*, **84**, 888–918.

Beach, R. I. (1966). 'The effect of a "fear-arousing" safety film on physiological, attitudinal and behavioral measures: a pilot study', *Traffic Safety Research Review*, **10**, 53–57.

Becker, M. H. (ed.) (1974). *The Health Belief Model and Personal Health Behavior*. Slack, New Jersey.

Behling, O., and Starke, F. A. (1973). 'The postulates of expectancy theory', *Academy of Management Journal*, **16**, 373–388.

Byrne, D., Barry, J., and Nelson, D. (1963). 'Relation of the revised Repression–Sensitization Scale to measures of self-description', *Psychological Reports*, **13**, 323–334.

Chu, G. C. (1966). 'Fear arousal, efficacy and imminency', *Journal of Personality and Social Psychology*, **4**, 517–524.

Cooper, H. M. (1979). 'Statistically combining independent studies: a meta-analysis of sex differences in conformity research', *Journal of Personality and Social Psychology*, **37**, 131–146.

Dabbs, J. M., and Leventhal, H. (1966). 'Effects of varying the recommendations in a fear-arousing communication', *Journal of Personality and Social Psychology*, **4**, 525–531.

Dembroski, T. M., Lasater, T. M., and Ramirez, A. (1978). 'Communicator similarity, fear arousing communications, and compliance with health care recommendations', *Journal of Applied Social Psychology*, **8**, 254–269.

Dziokonski, W., and Weber, S. J. (1977). 'Repression–sensitization, perceived vulnerability, and the fear appeal communication', *The Journal of Social Psychology*, **102**, 105–112.

Edwards, W. (1961). 'Behavioral decision theory', *Annual Review of Psychology*, **12**, 473–498.

Evans, R. I., Rozelle, R. M., Lasater, T. M., Dembroski, T. M., and Allen, B. P. (1970). 'Fear arousal, persuasion, and actual versus implied behavioral change:

new perspective utilizing a real-life dental hygiene program', *Journal of Personality and Social Psychology*, **16**, 220–227.

Evans, R. I., Rozelle, R. M., Noblitt, R., and Williams, D. L. (1975). 'Explicit and implicit persuasive communications over time to initiate and maintain behavior change: new perspective utilizing a real-life dental hygiene situation', *Journal of Applied Social Psychology*, **5**, 150–156.

Fishbein, M., and Ajzen, I. (1975). *Belief, Attitude, Intention and Behavior: An Introduction to Theory and Research*. Addison-Wesley, Reading, Mass.

Glass, G. V. (1978). 'Integrating findings: meta-analysis of research'. *Review of Research in Education*, **6**, 351–379.

Goldstein, M. J. (1959). 'The relationship between coping and avoiding behavior and response to fear-arousing propaganda', *Journal of Abnormal and Social Psychology*, **58**, 247–252.

Griffeth, R. W., and Rogers, R. W. (1976). 'Effects of fear-arousing components of driver education on students' safety attitudes and simulator performance', *Journal of Education Psychology*, **68**, 501–506.

Haefner, D. P. (1965). 'Arousing fear in dental health education', *Journal of Public Health Dentistry*, **25**, 140–146.

Hass, J. W., Bagley, G. S., and Rogers, R. W. (1975). 'Coping with the energy crisis: effects of fear appeals upon attitudes toward energy consumption', *Journal of Applied Psychology*, **60**, 754–756.

Hovland, C. I., Janis, I. L., and Kelley, H. H. (1953). *Communication and Persuasion*. Yale University Press, New Haven, Conn.

Hovland, C. I., Lumsdaine, A. A., and Sheffield, F. D. (1949). *Experiments on Mass Communication*. Princeton University Press, Princeton.

Insko, C. A., Arkoff, A., and Insko, V. M. (1965). 'Effects of high and low fear-arousing communications upon opinions toward smoking', *Journal of Experimental Social Psychology*, **1**, 256–266.

Janis, I. L. (1967). 'Effects of fear arousal on attitude change: recent developments in theory and experimental research', in Berkowitz, L. (ed.), *Advances in Experimental Social Psychology*, vol. 3. Academic Press, New York.

Janis, I. L., and Feshbach, S. (1953). 'Effects of fear-arousing communications', *Journal of Abnormal and Social Psychology*, **48**, 78–92.

Janis, I. L., and Feshbach, S. (1954). 'Personality differences associated with responsiveness to fear-arousing communications', *Journal of Personality*, **23**, 154–166.

Kirscht, J. P., Becker, M. H., Haefner, D. P., and Maiman, L. A. (1978). 'Effects of threatening communications and mothers' health beliefs on weight change in obese children', *Journal of Behavioral Medicine*, **1**, 147–157.

Kirscht, J. P., and Haefner, D. P. (1973). 'Effects of repeated threatening health communications', *International Journal of Health Education*, **16**, 268–277.

Krisher, H. P. III., Darley, S. A., and Darley, J. M. (1973). 'Fear-provoking recommendations, intentions to take preventive actions, and actual preventive actions', *Journal of Personality and Social Psychology*, **26**, 301–308.

Leventhal, H. (1970). 'Findings and theory in the study of fear communications', in Berkowitz, L. (ed.), *Advances in Experimental Social Psychology*, vol. 5. Academic Press, New York.

Leventhal, H., Jones, S., and Trembly, G. (1966). 'Sex differences in attitude and behavior change under conditions of fear and specific instructions', *Journal of Experimental Social Psychology*, **2**, 387–399.

Leventhal, H., and Niles, P. (1964). 'A field experiment on fear arousal with data on the validity of questionnaire measures', *Journal of Personality*, **32**, 459–479.

Leventhal, H., and Niles, P. (1965). 'Persistence of influence for varying duration of exposure to threat stimuli', *Psychological Reports*, **16**, 223–233.

Leventhal, H., and Singer, R. P. (1966). 'Affect arousal and positioning of recommendations in persuasive communications', *Journal of Personality and Social Psychology*, **4**, 137–146.

Leventhal, H., Singer, R. P., and Jones, S. (1965). 'Effects of fear and specificity of recommendation upon attitudes and behavior', *Journal of Personality and Social Psychology*, **2**, 20–29.

Leventhal, H., and Trembly, G. (1968). 'Negative emotions and persuasion', *Journal of Personality*, **36**, 154–168.

Leventhal, H., and Watts, J. (1966). 'Sources of resistance to fear-arousing communications on smoking and lung cancer', *Journal of Personality*, **34**, 155–175.

Leventhal, H., Watts, J., and Pagano, F. (1967). 'Effects of fear and instructions on how to cope with danger', *Journal of Personality and Social Psychology*, **6**, 313–321.

Ley, P., Bradshaw, P. W., Kincey, J., Couper -Smartt, J., and Wilson, M. (1974). 'Psychological variables in the control of obesity', in Burland, W. D., Samuel, P. D., and Yudkin, J. (eds), *Obesity Symposium*. Churchill Livingstone, London.

Lichtenstein, S., Slovic, P., Fischhoff, B., Layman, M., and Combs, B. (1978). 'Judged frequency of lethal events', *Journal of Experimental Psychology: Human Learning and Memory*, **4**, 551–578.

McGuire, W. J. (1968). 'Personality and attitude change: an information-processing theory', in Greenwald, A. G., Brock, T. C., and Ostrom, T. M. (eds), *Psychological Foundations of Attitudes*. Academic Press, New York.

Mewborn, C. R., and Rogers, R. W. (1979). 'Effects of threatening and reassuring components of fear appeals on physiological and verbal measures of emotion and attitudes', *Journal of Experimental Social Psychology*, **15**, 242–253.

Miller, N. E. (1951). 'Learnable drives and rewards', in Stevens, S. S. (ed.), *Handbook of Experimental Psychology*. Wiley, New York.

Millman, S. (1968). 'Anxiety, comprehension, and susceptibility to social influence', *Journal of Personality and Social Psychology*, **9**, 251–256.

Moltz, H., and Thistlethwaite, D. L. (1955). 'Attitude modification and anxiety reduction', *Journal of Abnormal and Social Psychology*, **50**, 231–237.

Radelfinger, S. (1965). 'Some effects of fear-arousing communications on preventive health behavior', *Health Education Monographs*, **19**, 2–15.

Ramirez, A., and Lasater, T. L. (1976). 'Attitudinal and behavioral reactions to fear-arousing communications', *Psychological Reports*, **38**, 811–818.

Ramirez, A., and Lasater, T. M. (1977). 'Ethnicity of communicator, self-esteem, and reactions to fear-arousing communications', *The Journal of Social Psychology*, **102**, 79–91.

Rogers, R. W. (1975). 'A protection motivation theory of fear appeals and attitude change', *The Journal of Psychology*, **91**, 93–114.

Rogers, R. W, and Deckner, C. W. (1975). 'Effects of fear appeals and physiological arousal upon emotion, attitudes and cigarette smoking', *Journal of Personality and Social Psychology*, **32**, 222–230.

Rogers, R. W., Deckner, C. W., and Mewborn, C. R. (1978). 'An expectancy-value theory approach to the long-term modification of smoking behavior', *Journal of Clinical Psychology*, **34**, 562–566.

Rogers, R. W., and Mewborn, C. R. (1976). 'Fear appeals and attitude change: effects of a threat's noxiousness, probability of occurrence, and the efficacy of coping responses', *Journal of Personality and Social Psychology*, **34**, 54–61.

Rogers, R. W., and Thistlethwaite, D. L. (1970). 'Effects of fear arousal and reassurance upon attitude change', *Journal of Personality and Social Psychology*, **15**, 227–233.

Rosenthal, R. (1978). 'Combining results of independent studies', *Psychological Bulletin*, **85**, 185–193.

Rosenthal, R. (1979). 'The "file drawer problem" and tolerance for null results', *Psychological Bulletin*, **86**, 638–641.

Rozelle, R. M., Evans, R. I., Lasater, T. M., Dembroski, T. M., and Allen, B. P. (1973). 'Need for approval as related to the effects of persuasive communications on actual, reported and intended behavior change—a viable predictor?', *Psychological Reports*, **33**, 719–725.

Skilbeck, C., Tulips, J., and Ley, P. (1977). 'The effects of fear arousal, fear position, fear exposure, and sidedness on compliance with dietary instructions', *European Journal of Social Psychology*, **7**, 221–239.

Sutton, S. R. (1979). 'Can subjective expected utility (SEU) theory explain smokers' decisions to try to stop smoking?', in Oborne, D. J., Gruneberg, M. M., and Eiser, J. R. (eds), *Research in Psychology and Medicine*, vol. 2. Academic Press, London.

Tversky, A., and Kahneman, D. (1974). 'Judgment under uncertainty: heuristics and biases', *Science*, **185**, 1124–1131.

Zajonc, R. B. (1980). 'Feeling and thinking: preferences need no inferences', *American Psychologist*, 151–175

Social Psychology and Behavioral Science
Edited by J. Richard Eiser
© 1982 John Wiley & Sons Ltd

Chapter 14

Giving information to patients

PHILIP LEY

Introduction

This chapter will review a number of topics in the general area of giving information to patients. Certain fields of research have had to be excluded, especially that of the effectiveness of the mass media in health education. Rather the concern has been with face-to-face interaction between physicians, other health care workers, and patients and, within such interactions, almost exclusively with the problems and effects of providing information. While at first glance this might seem to be an arbitrary limitation, it is hoped that what follows will show that the limitation is justified in terms of practical and theoretical interest. In addition it will soon become apparent that even this small area of the field has generated enough research to fill a large number of pages. The questions to be addressed are:

(1) Do patients receive enough information?
(2) Do patients understand the information given to them?
(3) Do patients want more information?
(4) What criteria might be used to decide what information should be given to patients?
(5) What are the effects of giving threatening information?
(6) What methods can be used to improve communications?
(7) What are the effects of improved communications?

In answering these questions a wide variety of problems will be touched on, ranging from the measurement of comprehensibility to professional non-compliance.

The Adequacy of Information Currently Provided to Patients

A variety of criteria could possibly be used to assess the adequacy of information given to patients. In fact three have been used with some frequency in surveys. These are:

(1) the extent to which patients feel satisfactorily informed;
(2) the extent to which patients have knowledge that clinicians wish them to have; and
(3) whether patients are actually given the information that it would reasonably be expected that they be given.

Each of these criteria has some problems associated with it. Patients' satisfaction with communications can, in theory, be influenced by a variety of factors other than whether or not the clinician has provided information. Further, high satisfaction is no guarantee that information has been transmitted successfully. The second criterion gives no indication of whether *adequate* information has been provided. The final criterion begs the question of what expectations are reasonable. Nevertheless, these criteria have been the ones most frequently used, and the results of research based on them will now be reviewed.

Patients' Satisfaction With the Information Given Them

Ley (1972a) has reviewed a number of British studies of patients' satisfaction with communications. All of the patients involved were, or had been, hospital in-patients. Surgical, medical, and maternity cases were included in the samples reviewed. The range of percentages of patients dissatisfied with communications was from 11 to 65 percent with a median of approximately 35 percent. It has also been shown that dissatisfaction rates are just as high in samples with whom clinicians had made special efforts to communicate (Ley, 1976). Some more recent surveys, which follow the same pattern, are summarized in Table 14.1. It can be seen from this summary that the problem of patients' dissatisfaction with communications is not limited to a given type of patient, nor is it limited to only one country. Nor is there any evidence in these survey results to suggest that the problem is decreasing as time passes.

Patients' Possession of Knowledge that Clinicians Wish Them to Have

A simple way of assessing the extent to which patients have knowledge that clinicians wish them to have is to see how much patients recall of what they are told. It can be safely assumed that clinicians wish their patients to have the information that they have given them. Investigations of patients forgetting are summarized in Table 14.2. Although at first glance these data would seem to suggest that patients will often not have the knowledge that clinicians wish them to have, there is a major problem in generalizing from these studies to clinical situations as a whole. This arises from the fact that because the

Table 14.1 Surveys of patients' satisfaction with communication

Investigation	Patients		Percentage dissatisfied
(1) *UK studies*			
Raphael and Peers (1972)	Psychiatric in-patients	Median =	39
	(nine hospitals)	Range	31–54
Ley *et al.* (1974)	Surgical in-patients		23
Ley *et al.* (1976a)	Medical in-patients		53
Mayou *et al.* (1976)	Coronary in-patients		65
Parkin (1976)	Medical in-patients		57
Kincey *et al.* (1975)	General practice patients	Median =	26
	(various topics)	Range	21–39
Ley *et al.* (1975)	General practice patients	Median =	37
	(various topics)	Range	30–51
Ley *et al.* (1976b)	General practice patients	Median =	35
	(various topics)	Range	21–46
(2) *USA studies*			
Fischer (1971)	Medical out-patients		20
Jolly *et al.* (1971)	Pregnant women		40
De Castro (1972)	Child out-patients		8
Hospital Affiliates Inc. (1978)	National sample (various	Median =	48
	topics)	Range	32–51
(3) *Summary*		Median	Range
Ley (1972)		35	11–65
UK studies (above)		38	21–65
USA studies (above)		36	8–51

investigations summarized above were interested in memory, the patients involved were usually studied on their first visit with their particular illness. How much these patients would be able to recall after a number of visits cannot be ascertained from these results.

Fortunately Hulka and her associates have provided information on patient's knowledge after repeated contacts with their doctors. Hulka *et al.* (1975a) reported that a sample of diabetics had acquired 67 percent of the information that their physicians wanted them to have. This compared with 68 percent for pregnant women, and 88 percent for mothers of infants studied by Hulka *et al.* (1975b). Hulka *et al.* (1975a) also reported that there was a significant correlation between amount of knowledge and duration of illness. In general these results for knowledge are a little better than those for memory after the first visit, but not much better. Diabetic patients and pregnant mothers still lacked about a third of the knowledge that their doctor wished them to have.

The investigations summarized above have all calculated success rates by directly comparing what the patient knew with what the patient had been

Table 14.2 Patients' recall of information presented by doctors

Investigation	Type of patient	Mean number of statements made by doctor	Time between consultation and recall	Percentage recalled
1. Ley and Spelman (1965)	47 medical out-patients	5.6	10–80 minutes	63
2. Ley and Spelman (1967)	(a) 22 medical out-patients	7.0	10–80 minutes	61
	(b) 22 medical out-patients	7.9	10–80 minutes	59
3. Joyce et al. (1969)	(a) 30 out-patients	9.5	Immediately after consultation	48
	(b) 24 out-patients	11.9	1–4 weeks	46
4. Ley et al. (1973)	20 general practice patients	7.2	Less than 5 minutes	50
5. Ley et al. (1976b)	157 general practice patients	5.1	1–2 weeks	56
6. Anderson (1979)	151 out-patients	12.2	?	39

told. Other investigations have been conducted in which only the patients' knowledge has been assessed. These studies implicitly assume that patients should have certain types of information, e.g. names of drugs they are taking, their diagnosis and so on. A review of early studies in this field is provided by Ley and Spelman (1967). More recent examples of these investigations include that of De Castro (1972) who found that 32 percent of mothers did not know their child's diagnosis, 45 percent did not have adequate knowledge of the treatment, and 30 percent did not know that they were supposed to bring the child for follow-up visits to an out-patient clinic. Boyd et al. (1974) found that 60 percent of patients did not know the names of drugs they were taking, and that 20 percent did not know the purpose of the medication. Even lower levels of knowledge were found in a sample of discharged general medical in-patients studied by Ellis et al. (1979), who found that the percentages lacking adequate knowledge were as follows: diagnosis, 69 percent; advice, 88 percent; drug treatment, 56 percent; prognosis, 54 percent; and follow-up arrangements, 31 percent. Finally Grennan et al. (1978) found that 36 percent of their patients with arthritis did not know the names of their drugs, nearly three-quarters did not know of the side-effects, and 14 percent did not know their diagnosis. Results of investigations such as these confirm that patients often lack knowledge that they would be expected to possess.

Are Patients in Fact Given Information?

In the past, and in some places in the present, doctors have been reluctant to inform patients that they are fatally ill, or have cancer. In some hospital settings (McIntosh, 1977), and in general practice in the UK (Cartwright, 1967) it would seem that patients are often not given this information. However, there are probably great differences in policy between institutions and between countries, and indeed the situation might be changing quite rapidly. For example, in surveys conducted in the USA, the percentages of doctors who would not usually or would never tell their patients if they had cancer have changed as follows: Fitts and Ravdin (1953), 69 percent; Oken (1961), 90 percent; Friedman (1970), 9 percent; Novack et al. (1979), 2 percent. Interestingly, clinicians justify their beliefs by appeal to clinical experience whether or not they approve of telling (Novack et al., 1979). Unfortunately these surveys have not been conducted with national samples of physicians and surgeons, but have been usually of those at a single hospital or small group of hospitals. Added to this, response rates have also been low, so it is not possible to regard these data as more than suggestive. However, it is clear that despite the large numbers of doctors who do tell their patient there are many who do not (Ley and Spelman, 1967; Koenig, 1969; McIntosh, 1974, 1977). So, many of these patients will often not in fact be given information.

In less dramatic areas it also seems that patients are not given adequate information. Direct observation, or examination of transcripts of consultations, has revealed that patients can receive surprisingly little information in key areas. For example Webb (1976) found that in none of 50 consultations did her general practice patients receive adequate information about treatment, while Svarstad (1974) reported that in 63 percent of her sample of 221 consultations information about treatment was inadequate.

Other investigators have looked at the extent to which pharmacists provide proper advice to their customers. Rowles et al. (1974) reported that of a sample of 100 pharmacists only 20 percent saw that the patient was properly informed about the medication. Even more alarming is an investigation by Knapp et al. (1969) who found that 11 of a sample of 12 pharmacists were prepared to fill a prescription which would lead to the patient taking a dangerous combination of drugs without warning of the dangers. Finally Campbell and Grisafe (1975), in an investigation using surrogate patients, found that 53 percent of a large sample of randomly selected pharmacists were not giving patients adequate information about their medication.

These observational studies of the behavior of health-care personnel confirm that patients are often not given adequate information. Thus the conclusions of these observational studies are in agreement with those based on patient self-report and patients' levels of knowledge.

Patients' Understanding of Information Given to Them

Criteria for judging how well patients understand what they have been told
have included:

(1) patient's own reports of not understanding;
(2) indirect assessment of comprehensibility by readability formulae;
(3) direct tests of patients' comprehension of information given to them.

Patients' own reports might, of course, be in error in that patients will not
necessarily know whether they have really understood something said to
them. It is also true that indirect measurement by use of readability formulae
presents some difficulties, which will be discussed later. Of the three criteria
the best is probably the use of direct tests of comprehension.

Another possible criterion is also an indirect one. This is the use of tests of
general medical knowledge or vocabulary. This type of measure is probably
the least satisfactory of all, as levels of knowledge might well be expected to
change rapidly, with increasing exposure to press articles and televison
features on medical matters. For reviews and examples of these sorts of
investigations see Ley and Spelman (1967); Boyle (1970); Tring and Hayes-
Allen (1973); and Ley (1977).

Patients' Self-reported Failures to Understand Information Presented to Them

Several studies have shown that patients frequently claim not to have
understood what they have been told. For example Korsch et al. (1971) found
this to be true of mothers of children attending a pediatric clinic. Evidence

Table 14.3 Patients' reported failures to understand what their general
practitioner had told them

Investigation	Percentage not understanding			
	Diagnosis	Aetiology	Treatment	Prognosis
Kincey et al. (1975)	7	17	14	13
Ley et al. (1975)	47	47	43	53
Ley et al. (1976b)	30	43	—	35

that this also occurs in general practice settings is provided in a number of
investigations by Ley and his co-workers, which are summarized in Table
14.3. It will be seen below that this reported inability to understand gains
some support from less subjective measures of frequency of not understanding.

The Understandability of Information Presented to Patients

It has also been demonstrated that patients are not likely to understand what they are told by applying readability formulae to materials issued to them. Several formulae exist (see Klare, 1974, for a review), but the one most commonly used to assess clinically relevant information is the Reading Ease Formula devised by Flesch (1948). Ley (1977) briefly reviewed investigations into the validity of this formula and concluded that scores derived by use of it are correlated with:

(1) standardized reading tests (Flesch, 1948; Peterson, 1956; Powers *et al.*, 1958; Klare, 1963);
(2) the speed with which a passage can be read (Brown, 1952; Klare *et al.*, 1957);
(3) the probability that an article in a newspaper will be read (Swanson, 1948; Ludwig, 1949);
(4) the rated difficulty of a passage (Gilinsky, 1948; Russell and Fea, 1951; Carter, 1955; Klare *et al.*, 1955);
(5) knowledge of contents after reading the passage (Allen, 1952; Klare *et al.*, 1957; Keeran and Bell, 1968; Ley *et al.*, 1972; Bradshaw *et al.*, 1975; Ley *et al.*, 1979).

While there were some negative findings (e.g. Wodeman, 1956; Marshall, 1957), it was apparent that the Reading Ease Formula had some predictive validity. The Flesch Formula is as follows:

Reading Ease $= 206.84 - 0.85\,W - 1.02\,S$
where: $W =$ number of syllables per 100 words;
             $S =$ average sentence length in words.

The scores are interpreted by reference to a normative table which indicates, in terms of grade level, the reading ability required to understand the material. From knowledge of the percentage of the US population with a given level of reading ability it is then possible to translate the score into an estimate of the percentage of the US population who would understand it (Miller, 1963; Ley, 1973).

Inspection of the formula shows that in effect it is saying that difficulty level is determined largely by the length of the words and sentences used. Another obvious potential determiner of difficulty is the commonness of the words used in the passage. The use of rare esoteric words should make things harder. Not surprisingly, therefore, some formulae include a measure of this variable. For example the Dale–Chall Formula reads:

Reading Grade Score $= 0.1579\,X + 0.0496\,Y + 3.6365$
where: $X =$ Dale Score, i.e. percentage of words not in the Dale list of 3000 common words;
                       $Y =$ average sentence length in words.

The Dale–Chall Formula correlates fairly highly (approximately +0.8) with the Flesch Formula, and also with a variety of external validity criteria. However, like other formulae using a vocabulary rarity measure, it is likely to be less useful in assessing clinical material than the Flesch Formula. This is simply because it is likely that clinical information will contain illness and drug names, anatomical terms, and other uncommon words. The effect of this might be to overestimate the difficulty of the material to be assessed.

A number of investigations which have used readability measures are summarized in Table 14.4. The range of material assessed has been wide. Ley

Table 14.4 The understandability of leaflets issued by health-care agencies as assessed by readability formulae

Material	Number of leaflets likely to be understood by stated percentage of readers			
	25% or less	26–40%	41–74%	75% or more
X-ray leaflets (F) (Ley et al., 1972)	—	2	—	3
Dental leaflets (F) (Ley, 1974)	1	1	—	3
Prescription drug leaflets (F) (Liguori, 1978)	—	2	—	2
Opticians' leaflets (F) (French et al., 1978)	7	20	9	2
OTC drug leaflets (DC) (Pyrczak and Roth, 1976)	6	3	—	1
Social security leaflets (DC) (Bendick and Cantu, 1978)	26	24	22	9

F = Flesch Formula; DC = Dale–Chall Formula.

et al. (1972) assessed the difficulty of X-ray leaflets issued by a hospital with a largely working-class clientele. Ley (1974) assessed a variety of leaflets issued by an English dental hospital. Pyrczak and Roth (1976) investigated the difficulty of leaflets accompanying over-the-counter drugs in the USA; while Liguori (1978) conducted an assessment of leaflets accompanying prescription drugs. In England the difficulty level of 38 booklets and pamphlets issued by opticians was investigated by French et al. (1978). Finally a survey by Bendick and Cantu (1978) is also worthy of inclusion. This study was concerned with information about social security benefits and the like in the USA. As judged by these results it is clear that probably the majority of leaflets issued to patients will be at too hard a level for substantial proportions of them.

Before leaving this topic it is worth mentioning some disquieting findings reported by Morris *et al.* (1979). This investigation assessed four leaflets about diazepam using 13 different formulae. It was found that the difficulty grades assigned to the leaflets showed an alarming range (in the case of one leaflet from Grade 5 to Grade 16). However, the two formulae for which most validation data are available, the Flesch Formula and the Dale–Chall, agreed very closely; it was also true that within formulae the rank order of difficulty of leaflets was very consistent. Thus there was disagreement on absolute level of difficulty, but not on relative difficulty. The implication of this is that the formula chosen will affect the conclusions drawn. Investigators will probably do well to use either the Flesch or the Dale–Chall formulae. These will agree with one another, and both appear to be valid as assessed by external criteria.

Kintsch and Vipond (1979) have pointed out the lack of theoretical rationale of current readability measures, and have argued for more concern with theory of text comprehension, and the use of more sophisticated measures of text comprehensibility (Kintsch and van Dijk, 1978; Kintsch, 1979). It is impossible to deny that to date approaches to readability have been technological rather than scientific, and it will be interesting to see if analyses of the Kintsch type lead to better predictability and control of comprehension.

Finally it is plausible to suppose that the effectiveness of increasing readability will depend on the level of ability of the reader. It would be expected that material could be made too easy, and thus offputting. The hypothesis that the relationship between readability and the effectiveness of the communication might be curvilinear, is worth bearing in mind.

Direct Assessment of Patients' Understanding of What They Are Told

Several researchers have studied the problem of how well patients understand instructions given to them. Riley (1966) investigated lay persons' understanding of seven pieces of advice commonly given by doctors, and was able to show that many mistakes would be made in following the advice because it was not properly understood. For example, many people told to avoid substances containing aspirin would not know about the presence of aspirin in several of the compound medications in which it occurs. Similarly, patients told to take a medicine four times a day would take it at very different times.

This last problem, the interpretation of instructions about taking medicine, has received attention in studies by Hermann (1973), Mazzullo *et al.* (1974), Boyd *et al.* (1974), and Parkin *et al.* (1976). Hermann investigated 381 prescriptions issued by Ohio State University's Hospital Out-Patients Department. Patients were asked when they would take their medicines. Fifteen percent of the prescriptions could not be interpreted at all by patients, and very wide variation was found in interpretation of instructions to take medicines two, three, four, or five times a day. Many of the errors in interpretation were major ones. For example some patients would think it correct to take four doses of antibiotic at hourly intervals. Mazzullo et al. reported similar findings for New York patients. Thus the instruction to take nitrofurantoin with meals would be interpreted by 54 percent as meaning before meals; by 33 percent as during meals; and by 13 percent as after meals. The prescriber's intention had been that it should be taken immediately after meals. Instructions accompanying furusemide 'for fluid retention' were interpreted by 52 percent as meaning that the drug was given to create fluid retention. Boyd et al. (1974) reported that patients frequently make errors. These occurred in 143 out of 256 prescriptions, and were judged by the authors to be clinically significant in one case in eight. Further evidence of failures to understand treatment advice is provided by Parkin et al. (1976) who found that 35 percent of 134 discharged medical in-patients did not understand how and when to take their medicines.

Beyond a point there is no need to list further investigations. It is clear that patients are often issued with instructions that they do not understand. However, it should be mentioned that in the case of chronic illnesses involving frequent contact with the physician some of these difficulties of interpretation are sorted out. For example, Hulka (1979) reported that error rates due to scheduling misconceptions were very low (about 3 percent) in her samples of diabetic and congestive cardiac failure patients. This does not, of course, lessen the problem in the case of shorter-term illnesses, nor is there any reason why the information should not be put in a completely unambiguous form initially.

Patients' Desire for Information

It would appear from survey evidence that the majority of patients wish to know as much as possible about their illness, its causes its treatment, and its outcome (Cartwright, 1964; Ley and Spelman, 1967), and of course the implication of patients' dissatisfaction with communications is that they feel that they should be told more than they are.

The finding that patients desire fairly full information is confirmed in surveys which focus on just one specific aspect of health care, such as medication. In fact patients probably want to know more about their medication than the professionals would wish to tell them. Evidence of this was provided by the investigations conducted by Joubert and Lasagna (1975) and Fleckenstein (1977), which are summarized in Table 14.5. There is also some evidence from studies of reactions to information about contraception to support the belief that patients want as full information as possible. Benson et al. (1977) found that there was a more favorable reaction to a 12-page than to a 4-page booklet giving information about an intrauterine contraceptive

Table 14.5 Patients' and professionals' views as to the information patients should be given about medication

Type of information	Percentage thinking patients should be informed		
	Patients	Physicians	Pharmacists
Name of drug	97	92	93
Common risks of normal use	89	85	71
Overdose information	86	76	84
Risks of using too little	80	52	74
Risks of not using at all	79	46	76
All possible risks of normal use	77	25	39
Other important uses	75	20	12

device. Similarly Morris *et al.* (1977) found that women preferred a longer rather than a shorter booklet about their oral contraceptives.

Most surveys have also shown that lay persons are in favor of patients being told they have cancer or are dying (Kelly and Friesen, 1950; Cappon, 1962; Ley and Spelman, 1967; McIntosh, 1974), although there are patients who do not want to be told (McIntosh, 1977). Medical opinion has always been more mixed (Ley and Spelman, 1967; Koeing, 1969; Cartwright *et al.*, 1973; McIntosh, 1977). However, as mentioned above, survey evidence suggests that it is possible that, in the USA at least, medical opinion is switching to the position that patients should be told if they have cancer (Novack *et al.*, 1979).

In view of this desire for information, and the fact that patients clearly do not receive as much information as they wish, it will be worthwhile considering the criteria which could possibly be used to decide what information should be given to patients.

Criteria for Deciding What Information Should be Given to Patients

A number of criteria suggest themselves as being important when making this decision. These include:

(1) legal requirements;
(2) patients' desires;
(3) professionals' views;
(4) behavioral objectives;
(5) rationality;
(6) empirical criteria.

It is obviously possible for governments and their agencies to pass laws requiring that patients be given certain information about their illness or its treatment. Thus, for example, in 1970 the US Food and Drug Administration required that printed material be issued with oral contraceptive pills. This material had to contain basic warnings of the main risks and contraindications (Food and Drug Administration, 1976).

Patients' desire for information has already been discussed and from a consumer viewpoint this should presumably be the main criterion. It is likely, however, that this will provoke clashes with the views of professionals, who are frequently less willing to share information with patients. Sometimes no reason is given for this unwillingness to communicate, but often the reason given is that the provision of information will lead to excessive anxiety, non-compliance, or other undesirable outcomes.

In the field of medication it is possible to use behavioral objectives to provide a criterion of what information patients should be given. Hermann *et al.* (1978) provide an example of something approaching this. For example in relation to knowledge about how the drug is expected to help they suggest that the patient must be able to:

(1) recall the basic facts about the complaint;
(2) recognize the desired effect of the drug and act if it is absent.

The first of these objectives requires that the patient be given information about:

(1) the disease or symptoms to be affected;
(2) potential consequences of compliance;
(3) potential consequences of non-compliance.

In turn the second objective requires that the patient should be informed about:

(1) events showing the effect;
(2) time at which to expect the effect;
(3) what to do if no effect occurs.

Obviously it is possible that it might be difficult to obtain agreement on the major categories of knowledge that the patient should have. However, once this is obtained the lower-order objectives seem to flow logically enough from the higher-level categories.

The next criterion—rationality—can also be used in relation to informational needs concerning treatment. Rationality as a criterion demands that the patient should be given enough information to make rational decisions about treatment. If we construct the outline of an oversimplified payoff matrix it might look something like Figure 14.1. To fill in the cells of the payoff matrix the patient needs to know at least:

(1) the probabilities of improvement, no improvement, and of deterioration—both with and without treatment;

Patient's choices

Outcomes   Accept treatment *X*   Refuse treatment *X*

Improvement

No improvement plus side-effects

No improvement

Improvement plus side-effects

Deterioration of condition

Figure 14.1 Simplified payoff matrix

(2) the nature and probabilities of occurrence of side-effects and adverse reactions.

Once more clinicians are likely to object that the provision of this information will lead to greatly increased non-compliance, and other undesirable outcomes.

The final possible criterion—the empirical one, depends on having established correlations between the provision of certain information and particular outcomes. If the outcome is then desired, the appropriate information can be given. Evidence on the effects of giving information will be reviewed below, after consideration of these investigations relating to the possibility that giving information might have harmful effects, and of methods by which communications could be improved.

The Effects of Giving Potentially Threatening Information to Patients

Those health professionals who do not believe that patients should be informed about such matters as a diagnosis of cancer, the risks of treatment, or the risks of investigations, predict that the provision of such information will lead to the following consequences:

(1) undesirable emotional reactions;
(2) reduced compliance;
(3) anxious over-concern;
(4) more frequent reporting of side-effects of drugs.

A small number of investigators have attempted empirical tests of these propositions, and in general found no support for them. Gerle *et al.* (1960) found that informed incurable cancer patients had better adjustment during their remaining life, and Gilbertsen and Wangensteen (1962) found that their informed patients saw many advantages in having been told. In a group of patients who had been successfully treated, 93 percent indicated that it had been of distinct advantage to them to know, and of a group of patients who were going to die from cancer, 87 percent said that it had been advantageous to know. Both groups listed number of concrete advantages in knowing, ranging from the opportunity to settle financial affairs to an increase in peace of mind. The majority of cancer patients studied by Kelly and Friesen (1950) also approved of being told, as did those of Aitken-Swan and Easson (1959).

Greenwood (1973) studied the effects of telling parents whenever innocent heart murmurs were discovered in their children. Parents were told that these should occasion no concern: 14 percent of the parents showed some anxiety on being told, and 5 percent did not believe that the murmur was really normal.

More adventurously Golodetz et al. (1976) gave 124 consecutive patients open access to their case records, and found that only 4 percent of patients did not respond favorably to this move. A similar lack of predicted disasters from giving hospital in-patients access to their case notes has been reported by Stevens et al. (1977). These investigators compared anxiety, depression, and satisfaction in patients who were given such access and a control group who were not. No differences were found between the groups. Access to the information had not caused problems.

A number of investigations have explored the question of whether or not the provision of information about side-effects increases the frequency with which patients experience them. These include those of Newcomer and Anderson (1974) who found that such information did lead to increased reports of side-effects, and those of Eklund and Wessling (1976). Paulson et al. (1976), Suveges (1977), and Weibert (1977) who found that it did not. In addition Myers and Calvert (1973, 1976, 1978) reported that in none of their three studies did the provision of such information produce either more frequent side-effects nor reduce compliance.

Alfidi (1971) was convinced that telling patients about the risks of angiographic procedures would have adverse results. Accordingly he studied two samples of patients to whom he gave explicit information about the possible risks and complications (including death) involved in the procedures. Five of the first sample of 132 patients refused to go through with the procedure, as did two out of the 100 patients in the second sample. Patients in both samples were overwhelmingly in favor of the information being given (90 percent of the first sample and 97 percent of the second sample). These findings changed Alfidi's views on the desirability of informing patients. A summary of these investigations is given in Table 14.6.

Methods for Improving Communications

Attempts to improve communications have involved:

(1) altering the way in which clinicians orally present information to patients (Ley, 1979a, 1979b; Kupst et al., 1975);

Table 14.6 Effects of giving patients 'bad news'

Investigators	Topic	Effect
Kelly and Friesen (1950)	Diagnosis of cancer	89 percent approved of being told
Aitken-Swan and Easson (1959	Diagnosis of cancer	66 percent approved of being told
Gilbertsen and Wangensteen (1962)	Diagnosis of cancer	93 per cent of successfully treated, and 87 percent of those who were told, claimed that knowing was a distinct advantage
Gerle *et al.* (1960)	Diagnosis of inoperable cancer	Better adjustment in those told than in a control group who were not told
Greenwood (1973)	Informing parents of innocent heart murmurs in their children	14 percent showed anxiety, 5 percent thought that conditions was dangerous (despite reassurance)
Golodetz *et al.* (1976)	Giving patients access to their case records	4 percent would have preferred no access
Stevens *al.* (1977)	Giving patients access to their case records	No more anxiety or depression than in controls not given access
Alfidi (1971)	Informing fully of risks of angiographic examination	3 percent refused examinations; 93 percent approved of being told
Myers and Calvert (1973, 1976, 1978)	Informing of side-effects of drugs orally or in writing	No more side-effects and no less compliance in medicine-taking, in any of the three separate studies
Newcomer and Anderson (1974)	Written information about side-effects	More side-effects reported
Eklund and Wessling (1976)	Written information about side-effects	No more side-effects reported
Paulson *et al.* (1976)	Written information about side-effects	No more side-effects reported
Suveges (1977)	Written information about side-effects	No more side-effects reported
Weibert (1977)	Written information about side-effects	No more side-effects reported

(2) making written materials easier to understand and remember (Ley *et al.*, 1972; Ley *et al.*, 1979);
(3) using illustrations to reinforce written information (Lovius *et al.*, 1973);
(4) attempts to make information more readable by introduction of humor in the form of cartoons (Moll and Wright 1972; Moll *et al.*, 1977);

(5) providing the patient with a tape-recording of the consultation (Butt, 1977; Reynolds *et al.*, 1979);

(6) providing access to taped information about the illness and its treatment (Midgley and Macrae, 1971).

Methods advocated for improving oral communication with patients include the use of primacy and importance effects to control the content of what is forgotten (Ley, 1972b). To control the amount forgotten the following techniques are available: explicit categorization (Ley *et al.*, 1973); simplification (Ley *et al.*, 1972; Bradshaw *et al.*, 1975); repetition by the clinician (Kupst *et al.*, 1975; Ley, 1979b); repetition by the patient (Kupst *et al.*, 1975); and use of specific rather than general advice statements (Bradshaw *et al.*, 1975). Finally one investigation used a mixture of these techniques (Ley *et al.*, 1976b). The effectiveness of these techniques is summarized in Table 14.7.

Table 14.7 The effects of memory-enhancing techniques on recall of orally presented clinical information

Investigation	Technique	Percentage improvement in recall	p
Ley (1972)*	Primacy	+74	<0.01
	Stressing of importance (medical out-patients)	+38	=0.06
Ley *et al.* (1973)	Explicit categorization (general practice patients)	+24	<0.01
Ley (1979b)	Explicit categorization (7 analog studies)	+31	<0.01
Reynolds *et al.* (1979)†	Explicit categorization (cancer patients)	−18	ns
Bradshaw *et al.* (1975)	Simplification	+48	<0.01
	Use of specific advice statements (obese females)	+219	<0.001
Kupst *et al.* (1975)	Repetition by clinician	+20	<0.01
	Repetition by patient (child out-patients)	+20	<0.01
Ley (1979b)	Repetition (six analog studies)	+31	<0.01
Ley *et al.* (1976b)	Mixture of techniques (general practice patients)	+27	<0.001

* This study attempted to increase memory for advice statements only.

† Control patients received only 65 percent of the information given to the experimental group.

ns = not significant.

The percentage improvement is calculated by the formula:

$$\% \text{ improvement} = \frac{E - C\%}{C\%}$$

where: $E\%$ = percentage recall in experimental condition;
              $C\%$ = percentage recall in the control condition.

Recall has been assessed either by asking patients to recall all that they can of the material presented, or by asking patients to answer a set of questions concerning the material. It can be seen that a number of techniques are effective in increasing recall of orally presented information.

One obvious technique for enhancing the effectiveness of communication is to provide written information in addition to orally presented information. This is commonly done in the case of medication; usually with some success. Morris and Halperin (1979) reported that groups receiving written information showed better knowledge than controls, in at least some areas, in eleven of the investigations that they reviewed, and failed to show superior knowledge in only three. Ellis et al. (1979) compared medical in-patients who received written as well as oral information on discharge from hospital and found significantly greater knowledge of diagnosis, advice, and treatment. In an interesting investigation of cancer patients Reynolds et al. (1979) found that the provision of written information increased patients' knowledge in an unusual way, in that having to provide it led to clinicians giving information on more topics.

Recall of written information can also be increased by the use of the techniques used in the case of orally presented information. Table 14.8 summarizes relevant findings. It can be seen that the results obtained are very mixed. Simplification sometimes makes a large difference to the total amount recalled, and sometimes leads to slightly less being recalled. This reinforces Kintsch's (1979) pleas for more refined methods of analyzing text comprehension and memory. The failure of the use of illustrative material to increase recall is also of interest. These findings echo the mixed findings reported from non-clinical fields, e.g. Dwyer (1972), Snowman and Cunningham (1975), Willows (1978), and the general difficulties in using diagrams for instruction (Marcell and Barnard, 1979).

Presumably there should be an interaction between the benefits of using illustrations and the nature of the task illustrated. Thus it might be expected on common-sense grounds that illustrations would help understanding of how to put eye-drops in. On the other hand a picture of the heart might not help a patient recall details of his heart medication regimen. Indeed it is likely that pictures will often serve as distractors and, further, that where they are incompatible with the patient's own spontaneous imagery (evoked by the material), they could cause interference and lead to less recall. This might

Table 14.8 The effects of memory-enhancing techniques on the recall of written clinical information

Investigation	Technique	Percentage improvement in recall	p
Ley et al. (1972)	Simplification (X-ray information)	(1) −6 (2) +34	ns <0.01
Bradshaw et al. (1975)	Simplification	(1) +29 (2) +72	ns <0.05
	Use of specific advice statements (dieting advice)	(1) +350 (2) +158	<0.001 <0.001
Ley et al. (1979)	Simplification (menopause leaflet)	+22	<0.05
	Mixture of techniques (contraceptive booklets)	−6	ns
Lovius et al. (1973)	Illustrations (dental leaflets)	No significant improvement	
Moll et al. (1977)	Cartoons (booklet about gout)	(1) −2 (2) +4	ns ns

ns = not significant.

have happened on the investigation by Moll and Wright (1972) who reported less recall of illustrated than unillustrated items in the handbook on gout that they studied (illustrations were in cartoon form). However, pictures were not randomly assigned to items, so this evidence is correlational rather than experimental.

As an alternative to a written record Butt (1977) reported that he had provided patients with a taped record of their final interview: 91 percent of patients claimed to have found this helpful and it was especially appreciated by the spouses of elderly patients. Patients claimed to have listened to the recording an average of 3.5 times. Reynolds et al. (1979) also provided patients with a tape and found that this form of communication was appreciated. It led to the same level of knowledge as the provision of written information.

An alternative method of enhancing the presentation of information has been urged by Midgley. This is the provision of audiovisual materials in a studio at the surgery. The patient can then, at leisure, listen to and see material designed to increase understanding of the illness, and easily ask the doctor for clarification of any problems. Midgley and Macrae (1971) reported that patients with angina exposed to this procedure knew significantly more about their condition than those not so exposed.

Mention should also be made of the effectiveness of training clinicians to be better interviewers. Although this will not necessarily ensure that patients receive more information, it will lead to the clinician acquiring a more accurate picture of the patient's condition. One promising program currently undergoing evaluation is that of Maguire and Rutter (1976a, b). Research to date has shown that clinicians trained by this method elicited far more relevant symptoms from patients than those not so trained (Rutter and Maguire, 1976; Maguire et al., 1977), and were rated more favorably by the interviewees (Maguire et al., 1977).

Radical Approaches to the Improvement of Communication

Several methods for improving the traditional system of doctors giving information to patients have been outlined above. However, some writers have argued that much more drastic changes are required. One suggestion has already been mentioned. This is the idea that patients should be allowed full access to their case records, and it has been shown that this does not seem to lead to undue difficulties (Golodetz et al., 1976; Stevens et al., 1977). A more radical proposal has been put forward by Shenkin and Warner (1973). This is that patients should be given a complete unexpurgated copy of their case records updated at each new encounter with physicians and other health-care personnel. These authors list a number of advantages including: patient satisfaction; patient education; patient autonomy; increased pressure on clinicians to provide better care; avoidance of unnecessary duplication of investigations; better continuity in patient care—the patient being able to provide the physician with a record of all previous consultations. This proposal should therefore improve the lot of patients, and by its effects on clinicians improve the standard of care that they offer.

A further ingenious proposal for improving communication has been put forward by Fischbach et al. (1979, 1980). This is that patients should be made co-authors of their medical records. This proposal would also be expected to improve patients' knowledge, the doctors' communicative skills, and the standard of clinical care. Maguire and Rutter (1976b) have pointed out that doctors frequently fail to elicit important symptoms from patients. The proposals of Fischbach et al. would reduce this possibility in that the patient could point out the omissions when helping to compose the case record. The proposed method would also ensure that the clinician obtained plenty of feedback about the comprehensibility of the information he had provided. Fischbach and her colleagues reported that in pilot studies of this method there appeared to be no great disadvantages; the main problem being that there was greater physician time per patient needed.

Another method for improving communication is patient activation, which is a term covering a number of techniques for making the patient more demanding in the physician–patient interaction. A good example of this is the investigation by Roter (1977). Roter arranged for patients to be interviewed by health educators before seeing the physician. During these interviews the health educator discovered what the patient wished to find out, and made sure, by teaching and rehearsal if necessary, that the patient knew how to ask for the desired information, should the physician not provide it. Roter found that this technique produced more direct questioning by patients, led to more negative affect being expressed by both doctors and patients, but also led to more patients attending for follow-up. Once again the proposed technique is likely to affect both patient knowledge and physician behavior, the clinician being provided with feedback about patients' informational needs. Finally, as much of this evidence implies, it must be stressed that it is not only patients whose behavior could be improved. Although beyond the scope of this chapter, the issue of health professionals' non-compliance with recommended good health-care practices deserves a great deal of further research (see Ley, 1981; also Chapter 17).

Effects of Improved Communication

Compliance With Advice

The attempt to increase patients' compliance presents both ethical and practical problems. For present purposes a detailed examination of the ethical problems concerned would be inappropriate. However, they should be mentioned even if only in passing. Many of them would disappear if compliance-inducing attempts were always preceded by providing the patient or client with full information, in understandable form, so that an informed decision could then be made. The information provided would have to include benefits and risks of the proposed, of alternative, and of no, treatments. If a decision to try the treatment was made, then presumably attempts to see that the treatment regimen was adhered to would not be ethically repugnant, as long as a regular informed review of progress was given to the patient, along with the opportunity to withdraw. While many situations would be simply dealt with by this procedure it would be idle to pretend that some would not present much more complex dilemmas. For a recent general discussion of this area see Jonsen (1979).

The magnitude of the non-compliance problem is shown in Table 14.9, which summarizes data from surveys reported by Ley (1972c), Food and Drug Administration (1979) and Barofsky (1980), Ley's data were derived from investigations conducted before the end of 1970; the Food and Drug Administration survey was of studies conducted since the beginning of 1969; and Barofsky's survey consisted of all of the investigations discovered by that reviewer. Not included here are the data collected as part of the Food and Drug Administration survey of controlled trials of amphetamine-like com-

Table 14.9 Frequency with which patients fail to follow
advice about medication (% not complying)

Type of medication	Ley (1972c)	Food and Drug Administration (1979)	Barofsky (1980)
Antibiotics	49	48	52
Psychiatric	39	42	42
Antihypertensives	—	43	61
Antituberculosis	39	42	43
Other medication	48	54	46
Range of percentages not complying	8–92	11–95	6–83

pounds in the treatment of obesity (Scoville, 1975). In summarizing data from 8000+ patients on the active drug, or placebo, it was found that non-compliance rates were 48 percent and 49 percent respectively. Ley (1972c) also summarized data about diet where it was found that 49 percent were non-compliant; and about other forms of advice, where it was found that 55 percent were non-compliant. Ley (1978) reported a median non-compliance rate in returning for follow-up of 48 percent in 14 experiments on the treatment of obese women. These figures show that non-compliance is common. The role of improved communication in reducing it will now be discussed.

Ley (1977, 1979b) argued that not only are understanding and memory necessary conditions for compliance, but that it is empirically true that much of the variance in compliance can be attributed to failures of comprehension and memory. It should follow from this that attempts to increase understanding and memory should lead to increased compliance, and Ley et al. (1975) and Ley (1977) have presented some evidence that this is so. Further there is correlational and experimental evidence to suggest that increased understanding leads to greater patient satisfaction (Ley et al., 1976a; Ley, 1977). As one of the correlates of patient satisfaction is patient compliance, it would be expected that increases in understanding and memory would have not only direct effects on compliance, but indirect effects mediated through increased satisfaction. This model is illustrared in Figure 14.2.

In addition to the studies of Ley and his co-workers, relevant evidence is available from a study by Parkin et al. (1976) who studied 130 patients after discharge from hospital. Sixty-six patients did not comply with the drug regimen prescribed on discharge; of these 46 (nearly two-thirds) did not understand the regimen. Thus it could be argued that twice as many patients were non-compliant through non-comprehension as for other reasons.

The main criticism of this hypothesis is simply that attempts to increase understanding do not always lead to increased compliance. Relevant literature

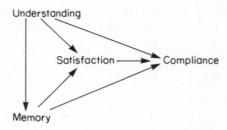

Figure   14.2 Relationships   between
understanding, memory, satisfaction,
and compliance

on the effects of written information on patients' compliance has been
reviewed by Morris and Halperin (1979). These authors reported that, while
in six out of seven studies involving short-term (mainly anti-microbial)
medication, written information improved compliance, this was true in only
six out of eleven studies involving long-term medication. A particularly
striking failure to improve compliance by patient education was the investigation of Sackett *et al.* (1975). These investigators found that compliance was
unaffected by learning about hypertension and its treatment, even when
patients had completely mastered the information presented to them.

However the conclusions of Morris and Halperin cannot be taken as ruling
out the role of increased comprehension in inducing compliance. To do this
the investigations would have had to involve presenting information to
patients that they did not have previously, in such a way as to ensure an
increase in patients' understanding. A re-examination of the studies reviewed
by Morris and Halperin reveals that in only five of them where compliance
was assessed did a comparison of knowledge levels show a significant
difference in favor of the experimental group. In four out of these five studies
the informed group was significantly more compliant than the group not
receiving written information.

An investigation which did present patients with information that they
lacked, and investigated the role of understandability of that presentation, is
that of Ley *et al.* (1975). They first found out what information patients
lacked, and then assigned two series of 80 patients randomly to receiving the
usual information orally presented, or to receiving in addition a written leaflet
giving the information that they lacked. There were three versions of the
leaflet. All contained the same information, but the three leaflets were at
different levels of difficulty. It was found that the most difficult leaflet failed
to increase compliance, but that the two easier ones did.

However, it is not possible to conclude that the only reasons for the failure
of the investigations summarized by Morris and Halperin to show the
expected association between increased information and compliance are

those just suggested. The study by Sackett *et al.* (1975) has already been mentioned, and Ley (1978) reported two experiments involving obese females in which the presentation of easy-to-understand-and-remember material failed to affect weight loss. It is clear that even properly prepared and understandable information does not always increase compliance.

Part of the reason for this is that non-compliance is probably not a unitary phenomenon. Ley (1979c) has argued that types of non-compliance can be graded according to whether it is intentional or unintentional, and as to whether the patient is adequately or inadequately informed. This classification is shown in Table 14.10. Adequately informed patients who are

Table 14.10 Different types of non-complier and the types of techniques likely to affect them

Type of non-compliance	Knowledge and comprehension	
	Adequate	Inadequate
Intentional	persuasive techniques needed	correct information needed
Unintentional	mechanical aids	correct information needed

intentionally non-compliant will not be affected by messages conveying mere information. If they are to become compliant they will require persuasive communications. Information will, however, have an effect on the inadequately informed intentional non-complier. The effect of the provision of information to this group will be to move them to one of the other three groups. The adequately informed unintentional non-complier is the person who is forgetful about medicine-taking. Provision of mechanical devices such as the noise-emitting pill-box of Azrin and Powell (1969), calendar packs, or other mechanical aids should affect compliance by this group. Finally the inadequately informed unintentional non-compliers require correct information about medicine-taking and its rationale. This group thinks that it is complying with advice but because of inadequate understanding is not in fact doing so.

Another reason for the failure of increased information to improve compliance is, of course, that this is only one of many factors in the compliance equation. Figure 14.3 attempts a brief partial listing of the other variables involved, and their likely relationships with each other. The treatment variables listed are the complexity of the treatment in terms of the numbers of drugs prescribed, and the duration of the treatment. Evidence that these two variables exert an effect has been reviewed by Blackwell (1979) and Haynes (1979).

Doctor variables include those behaviors which lead to the patient being satisfied with the consultation (Haynes, 1979), satisfied with communications (Ley, 1979c), and the provision of supportive follow-up (Barofsky, 1980). Haynes summarizing eight investigations, reported that in all of them higher satisfaction was associated with compliance, and Ley summarized four studies reporting correlations between satisfaction with communications and reported compliance, in all of which there was a positive association between these two variables. Barofsky's review provided evidence of significantly higher compliance rates amongst patients receiving antihypertensive, antibiotic, antituberculosis, or psychiatric medication when there was regular, supportive, medication-related follow-up by the physician. This also seems to be true in the case of obesity (Ley, 1980a).

Patient variables are mainly those associated with the Health Belief Model (Becker, 1974) and include perceived seriousness of the illness and perceived effectiveness of treatment. Ley (1979c) has analyzed relevant studies summarized by Haynes and Sackett (1977) and reported that, of eight investigations into the relationship between perceived seriousness/vulnerability, six showed that medication compliance was greater the more the patient felt at risk from the illness; while of six investigations into the relationship between perceived effectiveness of treatment and medication compliance, four gave the predicted result.

It can be seen from Figure 14.3 that improving communication by

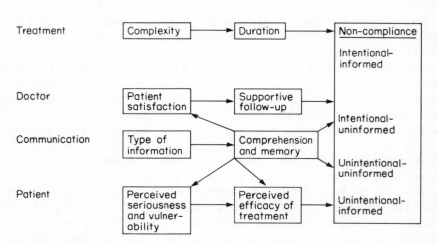

Figure 14.3 Relationships between communication, other variables, and non-compliance

increasing comprehensibility and memorability is expected to have both (a) direct effects on non-compliance of the uninformed varieties, and (b) indirect effects via influence on patients' satisfaction, the perceived seriousness of the illness, and the perceived efficacy of treatment. However whether improved communication has the desired effects will depend (a) on the relative strengths of the other variables, and (b) on the frequency of the various types of non-compliance in the sample under investigation.

Response and Reaction to Treatment and Investigations

There are a number of possible mechanisms by which the provision of information might affect emotional responses to treatment and investigatory procedures. These include:

(1) opportunities for covert rehearsal, and thus of habituation prior to the experience;
(2) provision of labels for experiences and sensations which would otherwise be unlabeled, and thus possibly interpreted as negative affect;
(3) increasing the patients' feeling of control;
(4) stimulation of moderate fear and realistic expectations.

In addition discussions with the patient, of reactions to the impending procedures, might reduce fear by catharsis.

However each of these possibilities receives only partial support in the literature. Thus Janis's theory that there will be a curvilinear relationship between preoperative fear and postoperative recovery is certainly not generally true (Levy and McGree, 1975; Sime, 1976; Ley, 1977; Leventhal et al., 1979; see also Chapter 13). Nor does perceived control always reduce distress from noxious stimulation (Leventhal, 1979). Much of this research has been carried out with laboratory stressors, but Leventhal's group has conducted studies both in laboratory and clinical settings. The outcome of these investigations is to lay great stress on the provision of information about sensations to be experienced in the affected part. It is likely that this type of communication will be successful in directing attention to informational components and distracting attention from the emotional components of the distressing experience. Laboratory studies using ischaemic pain (Johnson, 1975); cold pressor stress (Leventhal et al., 1979); and investigations in clinical settings on gastroendoscopy (Johnson et al., 1973); and plaster cast removal in children (Johnson et al., 1975) have provided results consistent with this interpretation. This reseatch has, however, been mainly concentrated on relatively short-lived procedures, which the subjects had not previously experienced. To assess the general practical value of providing information about sensations, research is needed to see whether the distraction effect can overcome distress in previously experienced painful situations, e.g. dentistry, and whether it has the same effects on longer distress experiences, e.g. major surgery. It might be expected that the pain distress-coding and memory systems would be much more easily triggered off in situations where pain had been previously experienced. Further, in longer-term distress situations it might be expected that (a) there would be more stimuli likely to arouse the pain-distress systems, and (b) that attending to sensation components would be subject to fatigue effects and thus impossible to sustain. However Leventhal and Everhart (1979) report on two unpublished investigations which make it seem likely that sensation information might well be effective in the case of major surgery. One of these studies found that recovery in cholecystectomy patients was fastest in a group given sensation information (Johnson *et al.*, 1977). A second investigation reported similar findings for cholecystectomy and hysterectomy patients (Wilson, 1977).

Ley (1977) has also reviewed evidence on the effectiveness of preoperative communications in reducing postoperative distress as measured by analgesic requirements, and in speeding up recovery. Preoperative communications were classified as: *technical instruction*, i.e. how to cough, how to breathe, how to use a trapeze; *informational*, i.e. what would happen, and when; and *quasi-psychotherapeutic*, i.e. giving the patient the opportunity to air fears and discuss reactions. The effectiveness of these communications in reducing distress and speeding recovery is summarized in Table 14.11. What is

Table 14.11 Effects of preoperative communication on postoperative progress

Type of communication	Number of comparisons showing			
	Analgesic requirement		Days in hospital	
	Fewer	Same	Fewer	Same
Instruction	1	1	2	0
Information	3	1	3	1
Quasi-psychotherapeutic	1	0	2	0
Mixtures of the above	2	0	3	0
Summary	7	2	10	1

particularly interesting, in view of spiralling health costs, is that preoperative communication can shorten hospital stay. This was true in ten of the eleven comparisons, and the mean reduction in stay was approximately 2 days. Johnson *et al.* (1977) and Wilson (1977) also report reduced stay in their informed groups.

Conclusions

The evidence reviewed above has shown that:

(1) patients do not seem to receive as much information as they desire, or as professionals judge adequate;
(2) the information provided to patients is often not understood by them, and patients frequently forget what they are told;
(3) provision of further information does not lead to the adverse consequences often feared by clinicians;
(4) it is possible to improve communications, often with beneficial effects on compliance and recovery.

However the focus of the review has been on the narrow one of communications directed at individual patients, which is only one small, although important, part of a complex situation. Not only is the information flow in health care much wider than this (see Fletcher, 1973 for an excellent review), but the giving of information to patients is only one factor in the doctor-patient encounter.

Several other investigators are researching into different aspects of the situation. For example, doctors' perceptions of consultations are being investigated, e.g. Bennett *et al.* (1978), Pendleton and Jaspars (1979), and some attempts are being made to investigate the interaction between patient and physician. The research of Korsch *et al.* (1971) and Hulka (1979) provide good examples of this. To date most of these investigations have been correlational, and it is not yet clear whether the findings will be useful in improving clinical interaction. However, the field is attracting a great deal of research effort, and this should lead to better theoretical models and to improvements in practice.

References

Aitken-Swan, J. and Easson, E. C. (1959). 'Reactions of cancer patients on being told their diagnosis', *British Medical Journal,* **1,** 779–781.

Alfidi, R. J. (1971). 'Informed consent: a study of patient reaction', *Journal of the American Medical Association,* **216,** 1325–1329.

Allen, W. (1952). 'Readability of instruction film commentary', *Journal of Applied Psychology,* **36,** 164–168.

Anderson, J. L. (1979). 'Patients' recall of information and its relation to the nature of the consultation', in Oborne, D. J., Gruneberg, M. M., and Eiser, J. R. (eds), *Research in Psychology and Medicine,* vol. 2. Academic Press, London.

Azrin, N. H., and Powell, J. (1969). 'Behavioral engineering: the use of response priming to improve prescribed self-medication', *Journal of Applied Behavior Analysis,* **2,** 39–42.

Barofsky, I. (1980). *The Chronic Psychiatric Patient in the Community.* Plenum Press, New York.

Becker, M. H. (ed.) (1974). *The Health Belief Model and Personal Health Behavior.* Slack, New Jersey.

Bendick, M., and Cantu, M. C. (1978). 'The literacy of welfare clients', *Social Service Review*, March 1978, pp. 56–68.

Bennett, A., Knox, J. D. E., and Morrison, A. T. (1978). 'Difficulties in consultations reported by doctors in general practice. *Journal of the Royal College of General Practitioners*, **28**, 646–651.

Benson, H., Gordon, L., Mitchell, C., and Place, V. (1977). 'Patient education and intra-uterine contraception: a study of two package inserts', *American Journal of Public Health* **67**, 446–449.

Blackwell, B. (1979). 'The drug regimen and treatment compliance', in Haynes, R. B., Taylor, D. W., and Sackett, D. L. (eds), *Compliance in Health Care*. Johns Hopkins University Press, Baltimore.

Boyd, J. R., Covington, T. R., Stanaszek, W. F., and Coussons, R. T. (1974). 'Drug defaulting'. Part II: 'Analysis of non-compliance patterns', *American Journal of Hospital Pharmacy*, **31**, 485–491.

Boyle, C. M. (1970). 'Differences between patients' and doctors' interpretation of some common medical terms', *British Medical Journal*, **2**, 286–289.

Bradshaw, P. W., Ley, P., Kincey, J. A., and Bradshaw, J. (1975). 'Recall of medical advice: comprehensibility and specificity', *British Journal of Social and Clinical Psychology*, **14**, 55–62.

Brown, J. I. (1952). 'The Flesch Formula through the looking glass', *College English*, **13**, 393–394.

Butt, H. R. (1977). 'A method for better physician–patient communication', *Annals of Internal Medicine*, **86**, 478–480.

Campbell, R. K., and Grisafe, J. A. (1975). 'Compliance with the Washington State Patient Information Regulation', *Journal of the American Pharmaceutical Association*, **15**, 494–495.

Cappon, D. (1962). 'Attitudes of and towards the dying', *Canadian Medical Association Journal*, **87**, 693-700.

Carter, R. E. (1955). 'Cross-cultural application of four Flesch formulas', *Journalism Quarterly*, **32**, 487–489.

Cartwright, A. (1964). *Human Relations and Hospital Care.* Routledge & Kegan Paul, London.

Cartwright, A. (1967). *Patients and Their Doctors.* Routledge & Kegan Paul, London.

Cartwright, A., Hockey, L., and Anderson, J. L. (1973). *Life Before Death.* Routledge & Kegan Paul, London.

Dale, E., and Chall, J. S. (1948). 'A formula for predicting readability' *Educational Research Bulletin*, **27**, 37–54.

De Castro, F. J. (1972). 'Doctor–patient communication', *Clinical Pediatrics*, **11**, 86–87.

Dwyer, F. M. (1972). *A Guide for Improving Visualized Communication.* Learning Services, Pennsylvania.

Eklund, L. H., and Wessling, A. (1976). 'Evaluation of package enclosures for drug package, *Lakaridningen*, **73**, 2319–2310.

Ellis, D. A., Hopkin, J., Leitch, A. G., and Crofton, J. (1979). 'Doctors' orders: controlled trial of supplementary written information for patients', *British Medical Journal*, **1**, 456.

Fischbach, R. L., Bayog, A. S., Needle, A., and Delbanco, T. L. (1979). 'The co-authored medical record: a means to promote patient–practitioner communication and collaboration'. Mimeo: Beth Israel Hospital, Boston.

Fischbach, R. L., Bayog, A. S., Needle, A., and Delbanco, T. L. (1980). 'Having given the patient his medical record: a follow-up on a proposal to improve the system', *Patient Counseling and Health Education.*

Fisher, E. (1971). 'Patients' evaluation of out-patient medical care', *Journal of Medical Education,* **46,** 238–248.

Fitts, W. T., and Ravdin, I. S. (1953). 'What Philadelphia physicians tell their patients with cancer', *Journal of the American Medical Association,* **153,** 901–904.

Fleckenstein, L. (1977). 'Attitudes towards patient package inserts', *Drug Information Journal* **11,** 23–29.

Flesch, R. (1948). 'A new readability yardstick', *Journal of Applied Psychology,* **32,** 221–233.

Fletcher, C. M. (1973). *Communication in Medicine.* Nuffield Provincial Hospitals Trust, London.

Food and Drug Administration (1976). 'Oral contraceptives: patient labeling revision', *Federal Register,* **41,** 53630–53632.

Food and Drug Administration (1979). 'Prescription drug products: patient labeling requirements', *Federal Register,* **44,** 40016–40041.

French, C., Mellor, M., and Parry, L. (1978). 'Patients' views of the ophthalmic optician', *Ophthalmic Optician,* 28 October, pp. 784–786.

Friedman, H. S. (1970). 'Physician management of dying patients: an exploration', *Psychiatry in Medicine* **1,** 295–305.

Gerle, B., Lunden, G., and Sandblom, P. (1960). 'The patient with inoperable cancer from the psychiatric and social standpoints', *Cancer,* **13,** 1206–1211.

Gilbertsen, V. A., and Wangensteen, O. H. (1962). 'Should the doctor tell the patient that the disease is cancer?' *Ca: A Cancer Journal for Clinicians,* **12,** 82–86.

Gilinsky, A. S. (1948). 'How valid is the Flesch readability formula?' *American Psychologist,* **3,** 261–263.

Golodetz, A., Ruess, J., and Michaus, R. L. (1976). 'The right to know: giving the patient his medical record', *Archives of Physical Medicine and Rehabilitation,* **57,** 78–81.

Greenwood, R. D. (1973). 'Should the patient be informed of innocent murmurs?' *Clinical Pediatrics,* **12,** 468–477.

Grennan, D. M., Taylor, S., and Palmer, D. G. (1978). 'Doctor–patient communication in patients with arthritis', *New Zealand Medical Journal* **87,** 431–434.

Haynes, R. B. (1979). 'Strategies to improve compliance with referrals, appointments and prescribed medical regimens', in Haynes, R. B., Taylor, D. W., and Sackett, D. L. (eds), *Compliance in Health Care.* Johns Hopkins University Press, Baltimore.

Haynes, R. B., and Sackett, D. L. (1977). 'An annotated bibliography of compliance studies', in Sackett, D. L., and Haynes, R. B. (eds), *Compliance with Therapeutic Regimens.* Johns Hopkins University Press, Baltimore.

Hermann, F. (1973). 'The out-patient prescription label as a source of medication erors', *American Journal of Hospital Pharmacy,* **30,** 155–159.

Hermann, F., Herxheimer, A., and Lionel, N. D. W. (1978). 'Package inserts for prescribed medicines: what minimum information do patients need?' *British Medical Journal,* **2,** 1132–1135.

Hospital Affiliates Inc. (1978). *Hospital Care in America.* Hospital Affiliates Inc., Nashville, Tennessee.

Hulka, B. S. (1979). 'Patient–clinician interaction', in Haynes, R. B., Taylor, D. W., and Sackett, D. L. (eds), *Compliance in Health Care.* Johns Hopkins University Press, Baltimore.

Hulka, B. S., Kupper, L. L., Cassel, J. C., and Mayo, F. (1975a). 'Doctor–patient communication and outcomes among diabetic patients', *Journal of Community Health*, **1**, 15–27.

Hulka, B. S., Kupper, L. L., Cassel, J. C., and Babineau, R. A. (1975b). 'Practice characteristics and quality of primary medical care', *Medical Care*, **13**, 808–820.

Johnson, J. E. (1975). 'Stress reduction through sensation information', in Sarason, I. G., and Spielberger, C. D. (eds), *Stress and Anxiety*, vol. 2. John Wiley & Sons, New York.

Johnson, J. E., Morrissey, J. F., and Leventhal, H. (1973). 'Psychological preparation for an endoscopic examination', *Gastro-intestinal Endoscopy*, **19**, 180–182.

Johnson, J. E., Kirchhoff, K. T. and Endress, M. P. (1975). 'Altering children's distress behavior during orthopedic cast removal', *Nursing Research*, **24**, 404–410.

Johnson, J. E., Rice, V. H., Fuller, S. S., and Endress, M. P. (1977). 'Sensory information, behavioral instruction and recovery from surgery'. Paper presented to the American Psychological Association, San Francisco, California.

Jolly, C., Held, B., Caraway, A., and Prystowsky, H. (1971). 'Research in the delivery of female health care: recipients' reaction', *American Journal of Obstetrics and Gynecology*, **110**, 291–300.

Jonsen, A. R. (1979). 'Ethical issues in compliance', in Haynes, R. B., Taylor, D. W., and Sackett, D. L. (eds), *Compliance in Health Care*. Johns Hopkins University Press, Baltimore.

Joubert, P., and Lasagna, L. (1975). 'Patient package inserts. 1: Nature, notions, and needs', *Clinical Pharmacology and Therapeutics*, **18**, 507–513.

Joyce, C. R. B., Caple, G., Mason, M., Reynolds, E., and Mathews, J. A. (1969). 'Quantitative study of doctor–patient communication', *Quarterly Journal of Medicine*, **38**, 183–194.

Keeran, C. U., and Bell, G. R. (1968). 'Reading Ease as a factor in improved communication effectiveness', *Journal of Psychology*, **68**, 49–53.

Kelly, W. D., and Friesen, S. R. (1950). 'Do cancer patients want to be told?' *Surgery*, **27**, 822–826.

Kincey, J. A., Bradshaw, P. W., and Ley, P. (1975). 'Patients' satisfaction and reported acceptance of advice in general practice', *Journal of the Royal College of General Practitioners*, **25**, 558–566.

Kintsch, W. (1979). 'Comprehension and memory of text', in Estes, W. K. (ed.), *Handbook of Learning and Cognitive Processes*, vol. 6. Erlbaum, Hillsdale, NJ.

Kintsch, W., and Van Dijk, T. A. (1978). 'Toward a model of text comprehension and production', *Psychological Review*, **85**, 353–394.

Kintsch, W., and Vipond, D. (1979). 'Reading comprehension and readability in educational practice and psychological theory', in Nilsson, L. G., (ed.), *Perspectives on Memory Research*. Erlbaum, Hillsdale, NJ.

Klare, G. R. (1963). *The Measurement of Readability*. Iowa State University Press, Iowa.

Klare, G. R. (1974). 'Assessing readability', *Reading Research Quarterly*, **10**, 62–102.

Klare, G. R., Mabry, J. E., and Gustafson, L. M. (1955). 'The relationship of style difficulty to immediate retention and acceptability of technical material', *Journal of Educational Psychology*, **46**, 287–295.

Klare, G. R., Shuford, E. H., and Nichols, W. M. (1957). 'The relationship of style difficulty, practice, and ability to efficiency of reading and retention', *Journal of Applied Psychology*, **41**, 222–226.

Knapp, D.A., Wolf, H. H., Knapp, D. E., and Rudy, T. A. (1969). 'The pharmacist as a drug advisor', *Journal of the American Pharmaceutical Association*, **9**, 502–505.

Koenig, R. R. (1969). 'Anticipating death from cancer', *Michigan Medicine*, **68**, 899–905.

Korsch, B., Freemon, B., and Negrete, V. (1971). 'Practical implications of doctor–patient interactions: analysis for pediatric practice', *American Journal of Diseases of Children*, **121**, 110–114.

Kupst, M. J., Dresser, K., Schulman, J. L., and Paul, M. H. (1975). 'Evaluation of methods to improve communication in the physician–patient relationship', *American Journal of Orthopsychiatry*, **45**, 420–429.

Leventhal, H. (1979). 'A perceptual-motor processing model of emotion', in Pliner, P., Blankstein, K., and Spigel, I. M. (eds), *Advances in the Study of Communication and Affect*. Plenum Press, New York.

Leventhal, H., and Everhart, D. (1979). 'Emotion pain and physical illness', in Izard, C. E. (ed.), *Emotion and Psychopathology*. Plenum Press, New York.

Leventhal, H., Brown, D., Shacham, S., and Engquist, G. (1979). 'Effects of preparatory information about sensations, threat of pain and attention on cold pressor distress', *Journal of Personality and Social Psychology*, **37**, 688–714.

Levy, J. M., and McGee, R. K. (1975). 'Childbirth as crisis: a test of Janis's theory of communication and stress resolution', *Journal of Personality and Social Psychology*, **31**, 171–179.

Ley, P. (1972a). 'Complaints made by hospital staff and patients', *Bulletin of the British Psychological Society*, **25**, 115–120.

Ley, P. (1972b). 'Primacy, rated importance and the recall of medical information', *Journal of Health and Social Behavior*, **13**, 311–317.

Ley, P. (1972c). 'Comprehension, memory and the success of communications with the patient', *Journal of the Institute of Health Education*, **10**, 23–29.

Ley, P. (1973). 'The measurement of comprehensibility', *Journal of the Institute of Health Education*, **11**, 17–20.

Ley, P. (1974). 'Communication in the clinical setting', *British Journal of Orthodontics*, **1**, 173–177.

Ley, P. (1976). 'Towards better doctor–patient communication', in Bennett, A. E. (ed.), *Communications between Doctors and Patients*. Oxford University Press for the Nuffield Provincial Hospitals Trust, London.

Ley, P. (1977). 'Psychological studies of doctor–patient communication', in Rachman, S. (ed.), *Contributions to Medical Psychology*, vol. 1. Pergamon Press, Oxford.

Ley, P. (1978). 'Psychological and behavioural factors in weight loss', in Bray, G. A. (ed.), *Recent Advances in Obesity Research*, vol. 2. Newman Publishing, London.

Ley, P. (1979a). 'Improving clinicial communication: effects of altering doctor behaviour', in Oborne, D. J., Gruneberg, M. M., and Eiser, J. R. (eds), *Research in Psychology and Medicine*, vol. 2. Academic Press, London.

Ley, P. (1979b). 'Memory for medical information', *British Journal of Social and Clinical Psychology*, **18**, 245–256.

Ley, P. (1979c). 'The psychology of compliance', in Oborne, D. J., Gruneberg, M. M., and Eiser, J. R. (eds), *Research in Psychology and Medicine*, vol. 2. Academic Press, London.

Ley, P. (1980). 'The psychology of obesity', in Rachman, S. (ed.), *Contributions to Medical Psychology*, vol. 2. Pergamon Press, Oxford.

Ley, P. (1981). 'Professional non-compliance: a neglected topic', *British Journal of Clinical Psychology*, **20**, 133–136.

Ley, P., Bradshaw, P. W., Eaves, D., and Walker, C. M. (1973). 'A method for increasing patients' recall of information presented by doctors', *Psychological Medicine*, **3**, 217–220.

Ley, P., Bradshaw, P. W., Kincey, J. A., and Atherton, S. T. (1976a). 'Increasing patients' satisfaction with communications', *British Journal of Social and Clinical Psychology*, **15**, 403–413.

Ley, P., Goldman, M., Bradshaw, P. W., Kincey, J. A., and Walker, C. (1972). 'The comprehensibility of some X-ray leaflets', *Journal of the Institute of Health Education*, **10**, 47–53.

Ley, P., Jain, V. K., and Skilbeck, C. E. (1975). 'A method for decreasing medication errors', *Psychological Medicine*, **6**, 599–601.

Ley, P., Pike, L. A., Whitworth, M. A., and Woodward, R. (1979). 'Effects of source, context of communication, and difficulty level on the success of health educational communications concerning contraception, and the menopause', *Health Education Journal*, **38**, 47–52.

Ley, P., Skilbeck, C. E., and Tulips, J. G. (1975). 'Correlates of reported satisfaction and compliance in general practice'. Unpublished manuscript.

Ley, P., and Spelman, M. S. (1965). 'Communications in an out-paitent setting', *British Journal of Social and Clinical Psychology*, **4**, 114–116.

Ley, P., and Spelman, M. S. (1967). *Communicating with the Patient*. Staples Press, London.

Ley, P., Swinson, R., Bradshaw, P. W., and Kincey, J. A. (1974). 'Satisfaction with communication amongst surgical patients'. Unpublished manuscript.

Ley, P., Whitworth, M. A., Skilbeck, C. E., Woodward, R., Pinsent, R. J. F. H., Pike, L. A., Clarkson, M. E., and Clark, P. B. (1976b). 'Improving doctor–patient communications in general practice', *Journal of the Royal College of General Practitioners*, **26**, 720–724.

Liguori, S. (1978). 'A quantitative assessment of the readability of PPIs', *Drug Intelligence and Clinical Pharmacy*, **12**, 712–716.

Lockman, R. F. (1956). 'A note on measuring understandability', *Journal of Applied Psychology*, **40**, 195–196.

Lovius, J., Lovius, B. B. J., and Ley, P. 'Comprehensibility of the literature given to children at a dental hospital', *Journal of Public Health Dentistry*, **33**, 23–26.

Ludwig, M. C. (1949). 'Hard words and human interest: their effects on readership', *Journalism Quarterly*, **26**, 167–171.

McIntosh, J. (1974). 'Processes of communication, information-seeking and control associated with cancer', *Social Science and Medicine*, **8**, 167–187.

McIntosh, J. (1977). *Communication and Awareness in a Cancer Ward*. Croom Helm, London.

Maguire, G. P., and Rutter, D. R. (1976a). 'Training medical students to communicate', in Bennett, A. E. (ed.), *Communications between Doctors and Patients*. Oxford University Press for the Nuffield Provincial Hospitals Trust, London.

Maguire, G. P., and Rutter, D. R. (1976b). 'History taking for medical students: 1. Deficiencies in performance', *Lancet*, **2**, 556–558.

Maguire, G. P., Clarke, D., and Jolley, B. (1977). 'An experimental comparison of three courses in history taking skills for medical students', *Medical Education*, **11**, 175–182.

Marcel, T., and Barnard, P. (1979). 'Paragraphs of pictographs: the use of non-verbal instructions for equipment', in Kolers, P. A., Wrolstad, M. E., and Bouma, H. (eds), *Processing of Visible Language*, vol. 1. Plenum Press, New York.

Marshall, J. S. (1957). 'The relationship between readability and comprehension of high school physics text books', *Dissertation Abstracts*, **17**, 64.

Mayou, R., Williamson, B., and Foster, A. (1976). 'Attitudes and advice after myocardial infarction', *British Medical Journal*, **1**, 1577–1579.

Mazzullo, J. M., Cohn, K., Lasagna, L., and Griner, P. F. (1974). 'Variations in interpretation of prescription instructions', *Journal of the American Medical Association,* **227,** 929–931.

Midgley, J. M., and Macrae, A. W. (1971). 'Audio-visual media in general practice', *Journal of the Royal College of General Practitioners,* **21,** 346–351.

Miller, G. A. (1963). *Language and Communication.* McGraw Hill, New York.

Moll, J. M. H., and Wright, V. (1972). 'Evaluation of the Arthritis and Rheumatism Council Handbook on gout', *Annals of Rheumatic Diseases,* **31,** 405–411.

Moll, J. M. H., Wright, V., Jeffrey, M. R., Goode, J. D., and Humberstone, P. M. (1977). 'The cartoon in doctor–patient communication', *Annals of Rheumatic Diseases,* **36,** 225–231.

Morris, L. A., and Halperin, J. (1979). 'Effects of written drug information on patient knowledge and compliance: a literature review', *American Journal of Public Health,* **69,** 47–52.

Morris, L. A., Mazis, M., and Gordon, E. (1977). 'A survey of the effects of oral contraceptive patient information', *Journal of the American Medical Association,* **238,** 2504–2508.

Morris, L. A., Thilman, D. G., Myers, A., and Muniz, N. (1979). 'Consumer oriented drug information: reactions and readability', Paper read at *Second International Congress on Patient Counselling and Education.* The Hague.

Myers, E. D., and Calvert, E. J. (1973). 'Effects of forewarning on the occurrence of side-effects and discontinuance of medication in patients on amitriptyline', *British Journal of Psychiatry,* **122,** 461–464.

Myers, E. D., and Calvert, E. J. (1976). 'Effect of forewarning on the occurrence of side-effects and discontinuation of medication in patients on dothiepen', *Journal of International Medical Research,* **4,** 237–240.

Myers, E. D., and Calvert, E. J. (1978). 'Knowledge of side-effects and perseverance with medication', *British Journal of Psychiatry,* **132,** 526–527.

Newcomer, D. R., and Anderson, R. W. (1974). 'Effectiveness of a combined drug self-administration and patient teaching program', *Drug Intelligence and Clinical Pharmacy,* **8,** 374–381.

Novack, D. H., Plumer, R., Smith, R. L., Ochitil, H., Morrow, G. R., and Bennett, J. M. (1979). 'Changes in physicians' attitudes towards telling the cancer patient', *Journal of the American Medical Association,* **241,** 897–900.

Oken, D. (1961). 'What to tell cancer patients: a study of medical attitudes', *Journal of the American Medical Association,* **175,** 1120–1128.

Parkin, D. M. (1976). 'Survey of the success of communications between hospital staff and patients', *Public Health (London),* **90,** 203–209.

Parkin, D. M., Henney, C. R., Quirk, J., and Crooks, J. (1976). 'Deviation from prescribed drug treatment after discharge from hospital', *British Medical Journal,* **2,** 686–688.

Paulson, P. T., Bauch, R., Paulson, M. L., and Zilz, D. A. (1976). 'Medication data sheets—an aid to patient education', *Drug Intelligence and Clinical Pharmacy,* **10,** 448–453.

Pendleton, D. A., and Jaspars, J. M. F. (1979). 'Assessment and theory of communication difficulties in general practice'. Mimeo, Oxford: Department of Experimental Psychology.

Peterson, M. J. (1956). 'Comparison of Flesch readability scores with a test of reading comprehension', *Journal of Applied Psychology,* **40,** 35–36.

Powers, R. D., Sumner, W. A., and Kearl, B. E. (1958). 'A recalculation of four readability formulas', *Journalism Quarterly,* **25,** 339–343.

Pyrczak, R., and Roth, D. H. (1976). 'The readability of directions on non-prescription drugs. *Journal of the American Pharmaceutical Association,* **16,** 242–243 and 267.

Raphael, W., and Peers, V. (1972). *Psychiatric Patients View their Hospitals.* King Edwards Hospital Fund, London.

Reynolds, P. M., Sanson-Fisher, R. W., Harker, J., and Byrne, M. J., (1979). 'Towards improved doctor–patient communication: back to basics', Mimeo, Sir Charles Gairdner Hospital, Western Australia.

Riley, C. S. (1966). 'Patients' understanding of doctors' instructions', *Medical Care,* **4,** 34–37.

Roter, D. L. (1977). 'Patient participation in the patient–provider interaction: the effects of patient question-asking on the quality of interaction satisfaction and compliance', *Health Education Monographs,* **5,** 281–315.

Rowles, B., Keller, S. M., and Gavin, P. W. (1974). 'The pharmacist as compounder and consultant', *Drug Intelligence and Clinical Pharmacy,* **8,** 242–244.

Russell, D. H., and Fea, H. R. (1951). 'Validity of six readability formulas as measures of juvenile fiction', *Elementary Schools Journal,* **52,** 136–144.

Rutter, D. R., and Maguire, G. P. (1976). 'History taking for medical students: II. Evaluation of a training programme', *Lancet,* **2,** 558–60.

Sackett, D. L., Haynes, R. B., Gibson, E. S., Hackett, B. C., Taylor, D. W., Roberts, R. S., and Johnson, A. L. (1975). 'Randomized clinical trials of strategies for improving medication compliance in primacy hypertension', *Lancet,* **1,** 1205–1207.

Scoville, B. A. (1975). 'Review of amphetamine-like drugs by the Food and Drug Administration', in Bray, G. A. (ed.), *Obesity in Perspective.* Department of Health, Education and Welfare, Publication No. NIH 75–708, Washington, DC.

Shenkin, B. N., and Warner, D. C. (1973). 'Giving the patient his medical record: a proposal to improve the system', *New England Journal of Medicine,* **289,** 688–692.

Sime, A. M. (1976). 'Relationship of pre-operative fear, type of coping and information received about surgery to recovery from surgery', *Journal of Personality and Social Psychology,* **34,** 716–724.

Snowman, J., and Cunningham, D. J. (1975). 'A comparison of pictorial and written adjunct aids in learning from text', *Journal of Educational Psychology,* **67,** 307–311.

Stevens, D. P., Staff, R. N., and Mackay, I. R. (1977). 'What happens when hospitalized patients see their records', *Annals of Internal Medicine,* **86,** 474–477.

Suveges, L. (1977). 'The impact of counseling by the pharmacist on patient knowledge and compliance'. *Proceedings of the McMaster Symposium on Compliance with Therapeutic Regimens.* McMaster University, Hamilton, Ontario.

Svarstad, B. L. (1974). 'The Doctor–Patient Encounter'. PhD thesis, University of Wisconsin.

Swanson, C. E. (1948). 'Readability and readership: a controlled experiment', *Journalism Quarterly,* **25,** 339–343.

Tring, F. C., and Hayes-Allen, M. C. (1973). 'Understanding and misunderstanding of some medical terms', *British Journal of Medical Education,* **7,** 53–59.

Webb, B. (1976). 'The retail pharmacist and drug treatment', *Journal of the Royal College of General Practitioners,* **26,** Supplement 1, 81–88.

Weibert, R. T. (1977). 'Potential distribution problems', *Drug Information Journal,* **11,** Special Supplement, 45s–48s.

Willows, D. M. (1978). 'A picture is not always worth a thousand words: pictures as distractors in reading', *Journal of Educational Psychology,* **70,** 255–262.

Wilson, J. F. (1977). 'Coping styles influencing the effectiveness of preoperative intervention procedures'. Paper presented to the American Psychological Association, San Francisco, California.

Social Psychology and Behavioral Medicine
Edited by J. Richard Eiser
© 1982 John Wiley & Sons Ltd

Chapter 15

Behavioral psychotherapy for compulsions and addictions

RAY J. HODGSON

The aim of this chapter is to discuss recent behavioral approaches to compulsions and addictions and, at the same time, to consider the current status of behavioral psychotherapy. What is behavioral psychotherapy? Is it behavioristic? What was it, and what is it becoming?

At the turn of the century, psychology was defined as the 'science of mental life, both of its phenomena and of their conditions. . . . The phenomena are such things as we call feelings, desires, cognitions, reasonings, decisions and the like' (James, 1890). During the last 80 years the pendulum has been swinging, and we have witnessed a number of paradigm shifts, a dozen or more schools of psychology and various approaches to psychotherapy. Watson (1919) argued that, for the behaviorist, 'psychology is that division of natural science which takes human behavior—the doings and the sayings, both learned and unlearned—as its subject matter'. Today most psychologists do not accept the radical behaviorist position with its abhorrence of mediating variables and hypothetical constructs. Psychology is now most commonly defined as the scientific study of behavior *and* experience. 'Its subject matter includes behavioral processes that are observable, such as gestures, speech and physiological changes, and processes that can only be inferred such as thoughts and dreams' (Clark and Miller, 1970).

The pendulum has swung from the mental to the behavioral, but is now beginning to swing less violently between these two poles. I believe that exactly the same shifts have now occurred in psychological approaches to psychotherapy. The mentalistic and psychodynamic approaches gradually gave way to a behaviorist approach which focused as strictly as possible upon behavior and behavior change. Today there is a very strong movement towards the middle ground (Meichenbaum, 1977; Mahoney, 1974; Beck *et al.*, 1979). There is no doubt that the majority of behavior therapists are concerned with thoughts, beliefs, expectations, and the attitudes of their patients, so it would seem reasonable to ask to what extent is behavioral psychotherapy behavioristic.

Is Behavioral Psychotherapy Behavioristic?

Eysenck (1972) has distinguished three kinds of behaviorism, namely the metaphysical, analytical, and methodological which are defined as follows: METAPHYSICAL (or radical) BEHAVIORISM is the view that minds (or mental events or states) do not exist. ANALYTICAL (or logical) BEHAVIORISM is the view that all statements ostensibly about the mental can be translated into statements about behavior or behavioral dispositions. METHODOLOGICAL BEHAVIORISM is the view that psychologists should, for methodological reasons, abjure completely the use of mentalistic explanations. Some methodological behaviorists say that the mind, whether it exists or not, cannot be studied scientifically; others say merely that there are sound methodological reasons for not treating mental events as independent variables, although they may be studied as dependent variables. Mental events can be effects, but not causes.

Although one or more behaviorisms have been espoused by some behavior therapists, many others would reject these philosophical positions as being too restrictive and also at odds with the conceptual framework which guides their clinical practice. For example, behavior therapists involved in the treatment of obsessional–compulsive problems have always been interested in the bizarre beliefs and expectations that are characteristic of this particular disorder (Meyer, 1966; Beech, 1974; Beech and Vaughan, 1978; Rachman and Hodgson, 1980). It is of crucial importance that we know, for example, whether a hand-washing ritual is linked to a fear of contaminating oneself, or a fear of contaminating others, or is simply an attempt to keep distressing thoughts at bay (Rachman and Hodgson, 1980). Now an expectation is not a behavior and it is not a behavioral disposition, although of course it has behavioral correlates. On a particular occasion we cannot predict with absolute certainty a particular behavior from a particular set of expectations. An alcoholic's drinking behavior in a social situation cannot be predicted from the fact that he expects to feel anxious in that situation and that he expects alcohol to reduce his anxiety. Expectations are not reducible to statements about behavior; however, they are an important domain for most behavior therapists. There is no reason why a behavior therapist should voluntarily limit the range of explanatory concepts at his disposal through an allegiance to a highly disputable philosophical position.

So metaphysical and analytical behaviorism are not the philosophical cornerstones of behavioral psychotherapy. What about he methodological behaviorist position? The methodological behaviorist would argue that an expectation is not a cause, but is itself caused and is therefore simply a mediating link which can and should be ignored (Skinner, 1963). In practice, the expectation is often the only solid evidence available to the clinician. If an obsessional patient experiences a feeling of contamination on waking and expects all sorts of terrible consequences if he does not wash, then why should we deny that the feeling and the expectation are important elements in the causal chain and important data for the behavioral scientist? It could be argued that we should look for the observable events A, B, and C, which produce this feeling, but why stop there? What caused A, B, and C? This line of thinking would lead to an infinite regress and, in any case, the clear subjective report is probably more strongly predictive of future behavior than the putative publicly observable antecedents.

Erwin (1978) has very cogently argued against analytical and methodological behaviorism as the cornerstones of behavior therapy and concludes that:

> behaviourism persists within the behaviour therapy framework only as an unjustifiable, a priori restriction on what is to count as acceptable scientific research. It once served a useful purpose insofar as it encouraged experimental rigour and discouraged an unbridled mentalism, but it is no longer needed for that purpose. Behaviourism is false and, for that reason, should be rejected; it is time to get behaviourism out of behaviour therapy (p. 82).

Erwin goes on to suggest that we use the label 'pragmatic behaviorism' to refer to the one assumption, shared by most behavior therapists, which is one of the strengths of the behavioral approach. Most behavior therapists believe that it is useful to look for behavioral correlates of clinical concepts, such as depression, fear, paranoia, and schizophrenia. They believe that a strong emphasis on behavioral assessment and behavior change has very important consequences. Scientific rigor is increased and new approaches to treatment are suggested. There is no need to strip psychology and psychotherapy of mentalistic concepts. The behavioral psychotherapist emphasizes the importance of behavior in a full assessment; asks quesions about the relationship between the environment, cognitions, feelings, and behavior; but above all believes that psychotherapy can be an applied science based upon empirical testing of competing theories.

One important area of behavioral medicine is concerned with compulsive and addictive behaviors. Cigarette and alcohol dependence, over-eating, compulsive television watching, and obsessional–compulsive problems can all have deleterious effects on mental and physical health. Before considering the ways in which behavioral psychotherapists have approached these problems, I will briefly consider the concepts of compulsion and loss of control.

Compulsion and Loss of Control

'One drink–one drunk' is the catch-phrase which every member of Alcoholics Anonymous has on the tip of his tongue whenever he experiences the first signs of an urge to drink. This notion that one drink inevitably leads to *loss of control* is often considered to be the backbone of a disease model of alcoholism, and is the basis of the total abstinence pledge (Jellinek, 1960). Jellinek (1952) states that:

> loss of control means that any drinking of alcohol starts a chain reaction which is felt by the drinker as a physical demand for alcohol. This state, possibly a conversion phenomenon, may take hours or weeks for its full development; it lasts until the drinker is too intoxicated or too sick to ingest more alcohol (p. 679).

Actually, this simple, rather mechanical view turns out to be wide of the mark. An alcoholic given 1 oz. of vodka within a hospital environment does not typically take a second available drink (Engle and Williams, 1972), nor does he show increased consumption on a taste test (Marlatt *et al.*, 1973). It has been noted that alcoholics who are given moderate or large amounts of alcohol within a hospital environment do not tend to abscond in order to continue a drinking binge (Parades *et al.*, 1973), and that alcoholics taking part in experimental drinking programs often opt for abstinence in the final week or two (Gottheil *et al.*, 1972). Moreover, in the studies of prolonged drinking carried out by Mello and Mendelson (1971), the interesting discovery was made that alcoholic volunteers who are given the opportunity to work for alcohol frequently remain abstinent for the whole day in order to accumulate enough alcohol to sustain their next binge. On these abstinent days blood alcohol levels are minimal or zero, withdrawal symptoms are clearly observed, and yet the alcoholic does not drink, apparently preferring to spend a whole day working for a new stock of alcohol rather than mixing business with pleasure. It would appear that these planned days of abstinence are better described as periods of self-control rather than loss of control. Other studies have shown that within the hospital environment the alcoholic controls his drinking if loss of control is associated with the loss of privilege (Cohen *et al.*, 1971) and that even after discharge from hospital some alcoholics are able to drink in a controlled way (Davies, 1962; Sobell and Sobell, 1976; Orford *et al.*, 1976).

All of these studies indicate that loss of control is not the inevitable consequence of one drink or even a few drinks, but that the control of drinking, like any other behavior, is a function of cues and consequences, of set and setting, of psychological and social variables, in short, control, or the loss of it, is a function of the way in which the alcoholic construes his situation. If the concept of 'loss of control' is to be retained, then we must speak of a relative loss of control, an increased probability of consuming drink, or an increase in craving.

Although the *simple* loss of control notion has been discredited, it still makes sense to speak of an impairment of control, and a comprehensive theory of compulsion and addiction must be able to cope with this phenomenon.

One useful conceptualization is based upon the difference between *cue control* and *self-control*. We can be said to be in control of our behavior if it is not going against a master plan or a long-term goal. Very often the smoker, the heavy drinker, and the over-eater would prefer to resist their particular compulsion, but find themselves responding to stimuli or cues with behavior that conflicts with other goals to do with health, self-esteem, and interpersonal relationships.

The power of cues, whether they be mainly internally or externally generated, is clearly recognized by the excessive drinker, the smoker, and the over-eater. If we are to develop methods of desensitizing the broad range of cues which influence compulsive behavior, then it is essential to have some understanding of the way in which cues influence behavior.

Cue Control

A common misconception is that a cue mechanically switches behavior like a billiard cue striking a ball. For example, a traditional view, linked with the tension-reduction theory of alcohol consumption, maintains that a cue leads to an increase in anxiety which then triggers a desire for alcohol. Certainly alcohol can reduce anxiety (Hodgson, *et al.*, 1979) and anxiety can increase the probability of alcohol consumption in the heavy drinker (Marlatt, 1978), but cues are not necessarily anxiety-arousing. The heavy drinker may consume drink before a social occasion, while feeling quite relaxed in order to cope with the *future* anxiety that he expects. Alcohol is frequently consumed before going to bed, in order to avoid insomnia. The heavy drinker will feel like drinking in drinking situations because it has become a habit and he enjoys the feeling of bonhomie. A cue is not simply a mechanical prod. A cue has meaning. It serves as a signal which warns of future consequences, the consequences which follow from sobriety and from drinking. Each cue is associated with a whole set of response–consequence expectations which have to be modified if cue control is to be reduced. An assessment of these expectations is usually called 'a functional analysis' (Sobell and Sobell, 1978) or a payoff matrix (Orford, 1977) and it is this assessment of 'subjective expected probabilities' that gives meaning to a cue or a cue complex and furthers our understanding of a particular individual's drinking behavior. One person drinks mainly in social situations and another usually at home when alone. Some people drink heavily at night to unwind; others drink all day long. A proportion of severely dependent alcoholics always keep a bottle of spirits beside their bed in order to ward off withdrawal symptoms first thing in the morning, whereas others can wait for their local pub to open. This variability can best be understood by identifying important cues and the response–consequence expectations associated with each. If we try to translate the 'one drink–one drunk' notion into psychological terminology, it could be argued that the consumption of some drink produces cognitive and perhaps physiological cues which increase the disposition to drink. If this is correct, then we have two types of cues: those which can increase the desire for a drink after a period of abstinence (stage 1 cues) and those which result from the consumption of a drink (stage 2 cues). Nobody doubts that compulsive and addictive behavior can be influenced by stage 1 cues. For example, it is very clear that obsessional–compulsive rituals are often elicited by contamination, bumping into another person, hearing a suspicious bang when driving, the smell of gas or a speck of brown dirt (Rachman and Hodgson, 1980; Hodgson, 1981). Similarly, the cues which can influence appetite are multifarious, but include food cues and mood cues, as well as situations and occasions (Stuart and Davis, 1972).

More contentious is the notion that *stage 2 cues* can increase desire. The arguments relating to this hypothesis have been particularly lively in the literature on alcoholism (Keller, 1972; Marlatt, 1978). Can a few drinks prime a craving for more? We now know that the consumption of a few drinks does not lead inevitably to loss of control, but there is an increasing amount of evidence to support the view that a few drinks can have a priming effect at least in the severely dependent alcoholic (Ludwig *et al.*, 1974; Hodgson *et al.*, 1979).

Although the alcoholic is not literally one drink from the gutter, there is evidence that a few drinks can prime a desire for more. This is probably an example of a more general phenomenon. In one recent study (Hodgson and Greene, 1980) it was demonstrated that a small amount of chocolate would prime salivation, but only when subjects were ready to eat having gone without food for 4 hours. There is also evidence from animal research that behavior which is rewarded by electrical stimulation to the central nervous system can be primed by pretrial electrical stimulation (Gallistel, 1974).

The fact that priming effects probably do occur has many implications for models of addictions and compulsions and, therefore, for the field of behavioral medicine.

So one way of approaching 'loss of control' is to identify the antecedent cues which are associated with an increase in craving, desire, or compulsion. However, this can only be one component of a comprehensive model. The alcoholic often reports that he no longer tries to resist temptation. He has given up. The self-control strategies that people use when they are tempted are no longer used. But what are these self-control strategies? What does it mean to give up?

Self-control

'Tis one thing to be tempted, Escalus, another thing to fall.'
(*Measure for Measure*).

Although the last section has covered problem areas such as over-eating, problem drinking and obsessional–compulsive disorders, it would appear that the cues which lead us into temptation are at the very heart of the human condition. A major slice of our early childhood learning concerns self-control. We have to learn to do without sweets, to resist the urge to kick our brother, and to shout at the teacher. The moral development of young children can be seen from a self-control perspective (Bijou, 1974), although the specific actions that have to be controlled vary widely from culture to culture (Thoreson and Mahoney, 1974). John Dewey (1939) has suggested that the aim of education should be the development of the 'power of self-control', in other words, the ability to evaluate conflicting desires and goals in terms of their long-term and short-term consequences, to be able to decide what actions should be taken to achieve desired objectives, and to be able to cope with temptation (Thoresen and Coates, 1976).

The psychology of self-control is, therefore, an important area of enquiry with far-reaching implications for the helping professions, for teachers and for parents, as well as the man on the Clapham omnibus idly planning his day or his life. It is of crucial importance in the area of behavioral medicine, where people are asked to achieve self-control in the face of a wide array of powerful, potentially destructive temptations.

Walter Mischel (1979) has made a start in the investigation of self-control by studying the conditions which make it easy or difficult for children to delay gratification (e.g. Mischel, 1974; Mischel and Moore, 1973, 1980). It was initially suggested (Mischel, 1974) that attention to anticipated rewards should enable children to wait for them. Actually, this prediction turned out to be wrong, since it was shown that preschool children were able to wait ten times longer when the rewards were not available during the delay period (Mischel and Ebbesen, 1970); however, attention to *pictures* of the rewards made it easier to delay (Mischel and Moore, 1973). The ability to delay could also be increased by altering cognition. Thinking about a reward in consummatory (goal-directed) ways made delay more difficult, whereas 'cool' ideation focusing on the abstract features of the reward made it easier. Mischel and his colleagues have gone on to show that children have an increasing awareness of self-control procedures between the ages of 4 and 10. They learn to turn their attention away from rewards, prefer distraction when tempted, use self instructions and prefer cool ideation about the rewards.

These developmental shifts seem to reflect a growing recognition by the child of the principle that the more cognitively available and hot a temptation, the more one will want it and the more difficult it will be to resist. Armed with this basic insight into the nature of motivation, the child can generate a diverse array of strategies for effectively managing otherwise formidable tasks and for overcoming 'stimulus control' with 'self-control' (Mischel, 1979).

A number of questions are posed by this research. What are the basic principles of self-control? Is the adult aware of these principles, or can we assume that self-control is a cognitive competence that can be learned, a skill that some people lack and some have developed to a high degree? What strategies are used by those who are able to resist temptation, delay gratification, and fight compulsions? These are questions that cry out to be researched, and we don't have many hard facts on which to base our counselling procedures, although a number of psychologists have made some sensible proposals.

According to Bandura (1977), self-control operates principally through two cognitively based sources of motivation; proximal goal-setting and the representation of future consequences in thought. The first operates through planning or goal-setting and self-evaluating reactions to one's own performance. Now we must differentiate betweeen general intentions and explicitly defined goals. We must also distinguish between end-goals and sub-goals. It is argued that immediate goals rather than end-goals can strongly mobilize effort and direct our actions in the here and now. In order to test this hypothesis, Bandura and his colleagues studied the influence of proximal goals and distal goals on over-eating (Bandura and Simon, 1977). All subjects, except those in a control condition, were told that by recording and reducing the number of mouthfuls of food and beverage consumed, they would be able to regain control over their eating habits. Subjects used a wrist counter to keep a tally of the number of mouthfuls. Now one group of subjects were told to keep a cumulative record of mouthfuls per week and then aim for a weekly reduction of 10 percent over a 4-week period. Another group recorded intake during four periods each day and were then set the goal of reducing intake by 10 percent in each of these four periods. Actually, this is an experimental test of the Alcoholics Anonymous (AA) principle 'one day at a time', except that the day is further subdivided. It was found that those subjects who were focusing upon proximal goals were the only subjects to lose weight, and subjects focusing upon a change in their weekly intake did no better than a control group.

In the same paper Bandura and Simon also describe an individual case study in which an overweight woman successfully used 'proximal goal-getting' as a short-term coping strategy at various times during a period of 76 weeks, in order to reverse any weight increases.

Translating long-term goals into short-term sub-goals is a strategy that we all use on some occasions. It would seem that the AA advice to concentrate on one day at a time is a basic principle of self-control. Perhaps it is also appropriate in some situations (e.g. resisting a cream cake) to focus upon a few minutes at a time.

The second cognitively based source of motivation is the representation of future consequences in present thought. Whenever an alcoholic is tempted to drink there are many other options open to him, but often he will 'give in' to temptation, his drinking tends to be 'mindless' and he is not concerned about future long term consequences. A successful treatment must reverse this state of learned helplessness, and bring future consequences to bear upon present actions. One component of the Sobells' individualized behavior therapy treatment for problem drinkers (Sobell and Sobell, 1978) was designed to facilitate this kind of thoughtful, planning, problem-solving approach to craving. Alcoholics were encouraged to identify the thoughts, feelings, events, and situations which were associated with their heavy drinking and then to consider a number of alternative actions, along with the long-term and short-term consequences of each. This was intended to develop a self-control skill rather than a rigid set of rules. The Sobells' broad-spectrum treatment turned out to be significantly better than traditional treatment with clients who were considered to be suitable for a controlled drinking goal. Furthermore, the problem-solving component was given good ratings by the clients themselves. Unfortunately, however, the treatment package involved so many components that we cannot be certain that any one in particular helped at all.

With the rapid growth of cognitive–behavioral approaches to therapy (Beck *et al.*, 1979, Meichenbaum, 1977), we must hope that Bandura's ideas will soon be given the testing that they deserve. Can addicts be helped to focus upon the first step rather than the journey of 1000 leagues, and can they be helped to think about the long-term consequences of their actions? More importantly, do such strategies help people to change their behavior?

I have used self-control to mean those cognitive and behavioral coping strategies which are put into operation in the presence of temptation, craving, or compulsion. Another approach to compulsive and addictive problems involves gradual changes in lifestyle, in order to reduce the frequency of occurrence of cues and to reduce their influence when they do occur (Hunt and Azrin, 1973; Stuart, 1980).

Changing Lifestyles

Richard Stuart (1980) has argued against approaches which seek to control addictions and compulsions without changing the forces that maintain the urge. He suggests that we should use an indirect approach rather than a direct approach.

> The direct approach is much in keeping with the protestant Ethic which stresses the virtue of working now for reward later, and little in common with the

Buddhist belief that 'suffering ends when craving ceases' (Mikulas, 1978, p. 62). It implies that suffering may be a necessary dimension of all constructive change, but it essentially ignores much of our understanding of the hedonistic dimension of much human behavior. Rather than bucking the tide in our efforts to find constantly higher levels of satisfaction and lower levels of stress, behavior modifiers would do well to build this realisation into their models of intervention by adopting an indirect model of intervention, Simply stated:

> The principle of indirection requires two stages of therapeutic planning: (1) an effort should be made to modify the conditions that create and maintain the urge to behave in a problematic way; and (2) an effort should be made to promote alternative positive actions when the problem urge is under control (p. 156).

The lifestyle changes that need to be made will depend upon the cues which have the strongest influence on the problem behavior. For instance, there is good evidence that many heavy drinkers are particularly influenced by social cues (Marlatt, 1978) and it has been suggested that this is an area in which the significance of a cue can be altered through the development of social competence in a wide variety of situations (Chaney et al., 1978). Social skills training (Trower et al., 1978) or personal effectiveness training (Liberman et al., 1975) has been shown to be effective with some groups, although the supportive evidence has sometimes been overrated and the approach over-sold.

Typically, social skills training involves the identification of specific deficits followed by the repeated practice of graded tasks with the aim of gaining important skills. Sessions involve the role-playing of person-to-person situations, such as conversations, being firm with subordinates, job interviews, expressing affection to a loved one, and expressing annoyance without being insulting. Feedback (sometimes videotaped) is given after each interaction and the therapist makes suggestions about eye contact, the content of communications, etc., usually emphasizing positive feedback and encouraging every small improvement. Graded real-life assignments between treatment sessions are an essential component of these training methods.

The problem drinker often reports that not only does he lack a broad range of social skills, but that he does not have a ready answer when drink is offered in a number of situations. The finding that a large proportion of treated alcoholics give as their reason for relapse the social pressure exerted by others to get them to take a drink has stimulated a number of therapists to advocate that the problem drinker should be taught how to say 'no' effectively, Chaney et al., (1978) have shown that social skills training does help alcoholics cope more effectively with difficult psychosocial situations and increases the length of sobriety.

Since some people with drinking problems are unemployed and, furthermore, have a feeling of helplessness about their job-finding abilities, one indirect approach involves helping them to obtain a reasonably satisfying job. Azrin and his colleagues have achieved this by use of self-help job-finding clubs (Azrin *et al.*, 1975). Job-finding was viewed as an activity requiring a number of complex skills which could be developed in a structured learning situation. The program assisted the job-seeker in every area that was believed to be influential in obtaining a job, emphasis being placed upon mutual assistance among job-seekers, encouragement of family support, sharing job leads, and role-playing of interviews and telephone conversations. Within 2 months, 90 percent of the counselled job-seekers (not necessarily problem drinkers) had obtained employment, compared with 55 percent of a control group; furthermore, the average salary was one-third higher for the counselled group.

It has been argued that if the problem drinker is interacting well with his community, then sobriety will be reinforced and excessive drinking will be curtailed (Hunt and Azrin, 1973). Two trials have now been completed which suggest that increasing social and job-finding skills and improving marital relationships can have a strong beneficial effect on drinking (Hunt and Azrin, 1973; Azrin, 1976).

Cue Exposure

Now I would like to mention a recent advance in the treatment of compulsive behavior (Meyer, 1966; Rachman *et al.*, 1971; Rachman and Hodgson, 1980). The treatment, which goes under a number of labels such as flooding, exposure, participant modeling, and response prevention, is based upon the simple notion that a strong urge to carry out a compulsion will go away if the urge is resisted. This decay is clearly shown in Figure 15.1 (from Rachman, *et al.*, 1976). Eleven subjects were exposed to idiosyncratic cues (e.g. contamination) and then asked to perform their ritual. They were then re-exposed and asked to resist the urge to carry out a ritual for 3 hours. During this response-prevention period there was a clear reduction in the strength of the compulsive urge; in fact, for most subjects 3 hours resisting was as effective as a few minutes carrying out the ritual. So cue exposure treatment involves a functional analysis to identify the relevant cues and then exercises designed to produce exposure to these cues along with strong encouragement to resist the compulsion. A person experiencing a strong urge to wash after walking past a hospital will be repeatedly encouraged to visit hospitals and then resist his compulsion. A mother's obsessive compulsive urge to check her child's eyes after cutting her fingernails, because she feared that she might have harmed the child, is treated by the repeated use of scissors and needles in the presence of the child and then resisting the urge to check.

But why does repeated cue exposure result in the extinction of compulsive behavior? Obsessive–compulsive rituals are usually considered to be avoid-

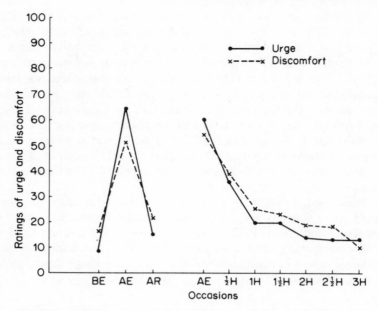

Figure 15.1 Mean ratings for urge and discomfort across occasions
($n = 11$). The measurement occasions plotted on the horizontal
axis are: BE, before exposure to provoking stimulus; AE after
exposure; AR after ritual; AE after second exposure; and half-
hourly intervals up intervals up to 3 hours. Reproduced with
permission from Rachman, De Silva, and Röper (1976)

ance responses and we know that active avoidance responses can be
extinguished by exposure to cues or discriminatory stimuli which elicit the
avoidance behavior. Also there are many similarities between phobic and
obsessive states and exposure treatment has been shown to be an effective
method of helping the phobic person. Recent theories of extinction have
emphasized 'reality testing' and changing expectations. According to these
theories the basis of human and animal operant learning involves the learning
of 'cue–response–consequence' chains. Whether these chains are altered or
strengthened after a particular repetition of the cue–response sequence will
be a function of the consequent feedback. Perceptual theorists have postulated the existence of a *perceptual analyzer* which is continually analyzing
afferent stimulation and coding it into known perceptual categories. Novel
stimuli immediately trigger the alerting response when the actual input does
not match the expected input. If recent theories of avoidance behavior are
correct, then it is necessary to postulate the existence of a feedback or
reinforcement analyzer. Every cue–response chain is associated with an

expected set of consequences (E) and the reinforcement analyzer compares the actual consequences (A) which are produced on a particular occasion with these expected consequences. If there is a difference between actual and expected consequences then E is updated. This is a cybernetic approach to the analysis of avoidance behavior, actual feedback is compared with a set standard based upon past experience and the standard is modified accordingly.

Whether this is a satisfactory model of obsessive–compulsive behavior remains to be seen. The fact is that for whatever reason cue exposure is an effective form of treatment for many obsessive–compulsive problems. Is it possible that such cue exposure practice along with coping skills training might also be the best way to extinguish an addiction once and for all? Models of compulsions and addictions overlap to such an extent that we must at least entertain the idea that a method which has revolutionized the treatment of obsessional–compulsive complaints might also be applicable to addictions and other types of compulsive behavior.

Applying this model to the problem of alcoholism the following program emerges. Firstly the therapist identifies those events that act as signals or cues for the alcoholic to drink. These could be internal feelings, such as anxiety or depression, or external stimuli such as particular pubs, or just the sight of a bottle of whiskey. The model then dictates the second part of the program, namely exposing the alcoholic to these cues and helping him to resist any subsequent urge to drink. Hodgson and Rankin (1976) report a case study in which a severe alcoholic received such treatment. A number of cues were related to his desire to drink but one of the most potent of these was the consumption of a moderate amount of alcohol (four vodkas). Once the patient had drunk four vodkas he experienced a very strong craving for more drink. He was therefore exposed to this situation by giving him four vodkas and then giving support as he resisted continuing drinking. Although craving was initially moderately high it diminished over time and lessened at an increasing rate across sessions so that at the end of the 12th session virtually no craving was present immediately after cue exposure. A second individual case study (Hodgson and Rachman, 1976) successfully applied the cue exposure approach to a case of compulsive masturbation. These case studies taken together strongly suggest that the approach is an appropriate form of treatment for compulsions other than the obsessive–compulsive and that, if not actually the treatment of choice, cue exposure could be an adjunct to other types of intervention.

Conclusion

Although self-control training, social skills training, and cue exposure may appear to be simple approaches, in practice they turn out to be rather complicated. The individual functional analysis requires a great deal of probing detective work and also a good knowledge of compulsions and addictive problems. Asking the right questions and building up a clear and accurate picture of one person's compulsions is a creative problem-solving exercise and not a mechanical assessment procedure.

Treatment must focus to some extent on the compulsion and related behavior, but the basic aim must be to alter the cognitive as well as the behavioral and physiological components. Recent cognitive approaches have not yet been systematically applied to compulsive and addictive problems, but there is now enough evidence to suggest that we should be busily testing their efficacy.

Behavioral psychotherapy is an applied science, and as such it will change with changes in psychological knowledge. The recent rapid developments in social and cognitive psychology must be integrated into psychotherapeutic practice. Behavioral psychotherapy is no longer behavioristic if behaviorism refers to metaphysical, analytical, or methodological behaviorism. It is behavioral in the sense that every clinical problem (even 'existential neurosis') is viewed as a system involving *behavior* as well as environmental and personal variables. By analysing behavior in great detail, its antecedents and consequences as well as attributions and expected consequences, there is a better chance that the clinical problem will be understood, there will be more objective ways of measuring change, and different treatment possibilities are generated.

References

Azrin, N. H. (1976). 'Improvements in the community reinforcement approach to alcoholism', *Behaviour Research and Therapy*, **14**, 339–348.

Azrin, N. H., Flores, T., and Kaplan, S. J. (1975). 'Job-finding club: a group assisted program for obtaining employment', *Behaviour Research and Therapy*, **13**, 17–27.

Bandura, A. (1977). *Social Learning Theory*. Prentice Hall, Englewood Cliffs, NJ.

Bandura, A., and Simon, K. M. (1977). 'The role of proximal intentions in self-regulation of refracting behaviour', *Cognitive Therapy and Research*, **1**, 177–193.

Beck, A. T., Rush, A. J., Shaw, B. F., and Emery, G. (1979). *Cognitive Therapy of Depression*. John Wiley & Sons, Chichester.

Beech, H. R. (1974). *Obsessional States*. Methuen, London.

Beech, H. R., and Vaughan, M. (1978). *Behavioural Treatment of Obsessional States*. John Wiley & Sons, Chichester.

Bijou, S. W. (1974). 'Moral development in the preschool years: a functional analysis'. Unpublished manuscript. University of Illinois at Champaign-Urbana.

Chaney, E. F., O' Leary, M. R., and Marlatt, G. A. (1978). 'Skill training with alcoholics', *Journal of Consulting and Clinical Psychology*, **46**, 1092–1104.

Clark, K. E., and Miller, G. A. (eds) (1970). *Psychology*. Prentice-Hall, Englewood Cliffs, NJ.

Cohen, M., Liebson, I. A., and Faillace, L. A. (1971). 'The modification of drinking in chronic alcoholics', in Mello, N. K., and Mendelson, J. H. (eds), *Recent Advances in Studies of Alcoholism*, pp. 745–766. US Government Printing Office, Washington, DC.

Davies, D. L. (1962). 'Normal drinking in recovered alcohol addicts', *Quarterly Journal of Studies on Alcohol*, **23**, 94–104.

Dewey, J. (1939). *Experience and Education*. Macmillan, New York.

Engle, K. B., and Williams, T. K. (1972). 'Effect of an ounce of vodka on alcoholics' desire for alcohol', *Quarterly Journal of Studies on Alcohol*, **33**, 1099–1105.

Erwin, E. (1978). *Behavior Therapy. Scientific, Philosophical and Moral Foundations*. Cambridge University Press, Cambridge.

Eysenck, H. J. (1972). 'Behavior therapy is behavioristic', *Behavior Therapy*, **3**, 609–613.

Gallistel, C. R. (1974). 'Motivation as central organising process: The psychophysical approach to its functional and neurophysiological analysis', *Nebraska Symposium on Motivation*, **22**, 183–250.

Gottheil, E., Murphy, B. F., Skoloda, T. E., and Corbett, L. O. (1972). 'Fixed interval drinking decisions', *Quarterly Journal of Studies on Alcohol*, **33**, 325–340.

Hodgson, R. J. (1981). 'A psychological theory of obsessional–compulsive behaviour', in Hand, I. (ed.), *Obsessions and Compulsions: Recent Advances in Behavioural Analysis and Therapy*. Springer, Berlin.

Hodgson, R. J., and Greene, J. B. (1980). 'The saliva priming effect, speed of eating and the measurement of hunger', *Behaviour Research and Therapy*, **18**, 243–247.

Hodgson, R. J., and Rachman, S. J. (1976). 'Modification of compulsive behaviour', in Eysenck, H. J. (ed.), *Case Studies in Behaviour Therapy*. Routledge & Kegan Paul, London.

Hodgson, R. J., and Rankin, H. J. (1976). 'Modification of excessive drinking by cue exposure', *Behaviour Research and Therapy*, **14**, 305–307.

Hodgson, R. J., Rankin, H., and Stockwell, T. R. (1979). 'Alcohol dependence and the priming effect', *Behaviour Research and Therapy*, **17**, 379–387.

Hodgson, R. J., Stockwell, T. R., and Rankin, H. J. (1979). 'Can alcohol reduce tension?' *Behaviour Reserach and Therapy*, **17**, 459–466.

Hunt, G. M., and Azrin, N. H. (1973). 'The community reinforcement approach to alcoholism', *Behaviour Research and Therapy*, **11**, 91–104.

James, W. (1980). *The Principles of Psychology*. Holt, New York.

Jellinek, E. M. (1952). 'Current notes—phases of alcohol addiction', *Quarterly Journal of Studies on Alcohol*, **13**, 673–684.

Jellinek, E. M. (1960). *The Disease Concept of Alcoholism*. Hillhouse Press, New Brunswick.

Keller, M. (1972). 'On the loss of control phenomenon in alcoholism' *British Journal of Addiction*, **67**, 153–166.

Liberman, R. P., King. L. W., De Risi, W. J., and McCann, M. (1975). *Personal Effectiveness*. Research Press, Champaign, Illinois.

Ludwig. A. M., Wikler, A., and Stark, L. H. (1974). 'The first drink', *Archives of General Psychiatry*, **30**, 539–547.

Mahoney, M. J. (1974). *Cognition and Behavior Modification*. Ballinger, Cambridge, Mass.

Marlatt, G. A. (1978). 'Craving for alcohol, loss of control, and relapse: a cognitive–behavioral analysis', in Nathan, P. E., Marlatt, G. A. and Loberg, T. (eds), *Alcoholism: New Directions in Behavioral Research and Treatment*. Plenum Press, New York.

Marlatt, G. A., Demming, B., and Reid, J. B. (1973). 'Loss of control drinking in alcoholics: an experimental analogue', *Journal of Abnormal Psychology*, **81**, 233–241.

Meichenbaum, D. (1977). *Cognitive–Behaviour Modification*. Plenum Press, New York.

Mello, N. K., and Mendelson, J. H. (1971). 'Drinking patterns during work contingent and non-contingent alcohol acquisition', in Mello, N. K., and Mendelson J. H. (eds), *Recent Advances in Studies of Alcoholism*. National Institute of Mental Health, Washington, DC.

Meyer, V. (1966). 'Modification of expectations in cases with obsessional rituals', *Behaviour Research and Therapy*, **4**, 273–280.

Mikulas, W. L. (1978).'Four noble truths of Buddhism related to behavior therapy', *The Psychological Record*, **28**, 59–67.

Mischel, W. (1974). 'Process in delay of gratification' in Berkowitz, L. *Advances in Experimental Social Psychology*, vol. 7. Academic Press, New York.

Mischel, W. (1979). 'On the interface of cognition and personality', *American Psychologist*, **34**, 740–754.

Mischel, W., and Ebbesen, E. (1970). 'Attention in delay of gratification', *Journal of Personality and Social Psychology*, **16**, 329–337.

Mischel, W., and Moore, B. (1973). 'Effects of attention to symbolically presented rewards upon self-control', *Journal of Personality and Social Psychology*, **28**, 172–179.

Mischel, W., and Moore, B. (1980). 'The role of ideation in voluntary delay for symbolically presented rewards', *Cognitive Therapy and Research*. (In press.)

Orford, J. (1977). 'Alcoholism: what psychology offers', in Edwards, G., and Grant, M. (eds), Alcoholism: *New Knowledge and New Responses*. Croom Helm, London.

Orford, J., Oppenheimer, E., and Edwards, G. (1976). 'Abstinence or control: the outcome for excessive drinkers two years after consultation', *Behaviour Research and Therapy*, **14**, 409–418.

Parades, A., Hood, W. R., Seymour, H., and Gollom, M. (1973). 'Loss of control in alcoholism: an investigation of the hypothesis with experimental findings', *Quarterly Journal of Studies on Alcohol*, **34**, 1146–1161.

Rachman, S., Hodgson, R. J., and Marks, I. M. (1971). 'Treatment of chronic obsessive–compulsive neuroses', *Behaviour Research and Therapy*, **9**, 237–247.

Rachman, S., De Silva, P., and Roper, G. (1976). 'The spontaneous decay of compulsive urges', *Behaviour Research and Therapy*, **12**, 311–318.

Rachman, S., and Hodgson, R. (1980). *Obsessions and Compulsions*. Prentice Hall, Englewood Cliffs. NJ.

Skinner, B. F. (1963). 'Behaviorism at fifty', *Science*, **140**, 951–958.

Sobell, M. B., and Sobell, L. C. (1976). 'Second-year treatment outcome of alcoholics treated by individualized behavior therapy: Results. *Behaviour Research and Therapy*, **14**, 195–215.

Sobell, M. B., and Sobell, L. C. (1978). *Behavioral Treatment of Alcohol Problems*. Plenum Press, New York.

Stuart, R. B. (1980). 'Weight loss and beyond: are they taking it off and keeping it off?', in Davidson, P. O., and Davidson, S. M., (eds) *Behavioral Medicine: Changing Health Life-styles*. Brunner Maze, New York.

Stuart, R. B., and Davis, B. (1972). *Slim Chance in a Fat World*. Research Press, Champaign, Illinois.

Thoresen, C. E., and Coates, T. J. (1976). 'Behavioral self-control: some clinical concerns', in Hersen, M., Eisler, R. M., and Miller, P. M. (eds), *Progress in Behavior Modification*, vol. 2. Academic Press, New York.

Thoresen, C. E., and Mahoney, M. J. (1974). *Behavioral Self-control*. Holt, New York.

Trower, P., Bryant, B., Argyle, M., and Marzillier, J. (1978). *Social Skills and Mental Health*. Methuen, London.

Watson, J. B. (1919). *Psychology from the Standpoint of a Behaviourist*. J. B. Lippincott, Philadelphia.

Social Psychology and Behavioral Medicine
Edited by J. Richard Eiser
© 1982 John Wiley & Sons Ltd

Chapter 16

Behavioral applications of the restricted environmental stimulation technique

PETER SUEDFELD

Historical Introduction

The first documented use of reduced sensory stimulation in psychotherapy occurred several thousand years ago. Both at Delphi and at Trophonius, the oracle was approached by entering a cave in which the supplicant was isolated and sensorially deprived. While the major purpose for consulting the oracle was to divine the future, there apparently were instances of psychological problems being treated (Kouretas, 1967; Papageorgiou, 1975). A number of non-Western cultures have also used stimulus reduction in connection with psychotherapy. Among such methods are the rituals of native healers in sub-Saharan Africa (Margetts, 1968) and the northwest coast of America (Jilek, 1974).

When 'sensory deprivation' became a popular research technique among Western psychologists in the early 1950s, among the earliest suggested applications was its use in a therapeutic context. A team of researchers at Allan Memorial Institute in Montreal found schizophrenic, depressive, and neurotic patients exhibiting improvement after several days of sensory deprivation (Azima and Cramer-Azima, 1956, 1957). One review (Suedfeld, 1980) cites reports of successful treatment using this technique in cases of schizophrenia, stuttering, snake phobia, childhood autism, and anorexia nervosa. Conditions closely related to stimulus restriction have been useful in the treatment of manic and depressed patients (Fitzgerald and Long, 1973), acting-out children (Pendergrass, 1971) and colicky infants (Wilcox, 1957). Various other investigators have found that sensory reduction, either by itself or in conjunction with appropriate messages, resulted in improved scores on measures of such characteristics as state anxiety (Antista and Jones, 1975) and ego strength (Gibby *et al.*, 1960; Kammerman, 1977). These and the

393

more recent applications of the technique are now usually categorized under the term Restricted Environmental Stimulation Therapy (REST).

Work using stimulus restriction in a clinical context can be divided into four major categories. The first is the use of input-restricting methods in what one may call quasi-therapeutic situations; that is, those involving spiritual experiences, promoting creativity, enhancing self-esteeem, and heightening awareness. The second is in the treatment of behavioral disturbances exhibited by children. The third is seclusion and stimulus reduction with hospitalized psychiatric patients. The last application, which is the most closely related both to social psychology and to behavioral medicine, is in the modification of health-dysfunctional habits and conditions such as smoking and obesity.

Until recently it was very difficult to find any single source that discussed all of the uses of environmental restriction in therapeutic and quasi-therapeutic contexts. Specific users or participants have written about their own experiences and findings, referring perhaps to some of the most obviously relevant literature but without integrating their approach into the larger pattern of research and application. We have not only had a diversity of uses, as mentioned in the previous paragraph, but there have also been many methodological variations. Some of the more frequently used techniques have included being left alone in one's room; sitting alone facing a blank wall; lying on a bed in a dark, quiet room; floating in a tank of water (sometimes mixed with chemicals to the consistency of a gel); being continously stimulated by diffuse light and white noise; and combinations and variants of all of these. Obviously, it is difficult to obtain highly replicable data with this kind of variability, particularly since on any measurable dimension that is conceptually relevant these techniques produce different results. There is some doubt as to whether the diffuse light–white noise procedure is at all compatible with the others. This procedure provides a constant and at least moderately high level of input even though that input is unpatterned; in contrast, most of the other techniques involve substantial reductions of the absolute level of stimulation. Similar inconsistencies are found when one looks at other procedural factors such as different types of briefing and debriefing, confinement duration, measures of the dependent variable, timing and type of follow-up, and so on. And, of course, this situation is further complicated by the fact that much of the literature is anecdotal, autobiographical, and in some cases purely historical.

One other, rather interesting, source of diversity is the theoretical or conceptual model upon which the use of stimulus restriction is based in a particular instance. What I find intriguing about this is that so many approaches have led to the same general prescription; the reduction of input. The rest of this chapter describes some of the major conceptual sources that have led to the application of REST to personal betterment. It also discusses the specific types of situations in which this kind of treatment has been considered appropriate by the proponents of the various models.

Conceptual Bases of the Use of REST

The application of REST in different situations has been based on various traditions and ideas. Among these have been the spiritual–religious model, which uses REST as a road to transcendental experiences and personal insights, and psychotherapeutic models deriving from learning theory and depth psychology. For this chapter, however, the most relevant sources are those rooted in cognitive and social psychology. One of these is the proposal that stimulus reduction serves as a 'reverse quarantine' situation, in which individuals are removed from excessive stimulation and information loads that are endemic in their normal environments. The theory is that this removal enables them to develop or learn more adaptive ways of behaving. The other is a persuasion model, which argues that the REST environment makes participants more open to new information and more capable of considering such information without becoming defensive. If the information provided advocates changes in habits and attitudes related to health, such changes may be more likely to occur as a result of this heightened persuasibilty and motivation to change.

The Spiritual–Religious Model

Perhaps the oldest root of the restricted environmental stimulation technique is the realization of the religious, spiritual, mystical qualities that experience can accrue under such conditions. As has already been mentioned, specifically therapeutic uses on a religious model were noted millennia ago, and were considered to be ancient even by the Romans (Garrison, 1921). It should be noted that the therapeutic aspect of stimulus reduction was a relatively minor one in this context; the more important events were those that led to contact with the deity.

Social isolation, usually in a monotonous and not highly stimulating environment, has been an established practice for those seeking transcendental experiences throughout many centuries and in many places. As one example, we may note the role that isolation in the wilderness has played in the development of the major contemporary religions. Moses first encountered God and was inspired to return to Egypt and free his people during a prolonged sojourn in the wilderness. During a similar period of wandering, Jesus rejected the temptations of Satan and returned to carry out his ministry.

Mohammed withdrew to a cave to find his vocation. The Buddha achieved the great insights that would form the basis of his teachings while contemplating, solitary, in the forest. Many other saints and prophets emerged from the deserts, mountain-tops, jungles, and prairies; and thousands of monks, hermits, mystics, and meditators sought out these environments as being the most conducive to their spiritual exercises and devotions (see, for example, Potter, 1958).

One interesting aspect of all of this is that the specific object of the quest, transcendental experience, apparently occurs with equal facility in deserts, forests, jungles, ice fields, and grassy plains. The crucial characteristics are the relative homogeneity and unchangingness of the environment. Similarly, what one finds appears to be extremely variable. It can be an encounter with a supernatural being (including a totemic animal, a spirit, or God), the learning—or making up, depending on how one looks at it—of a magic song or formula; the dreaming of a meaningful and magical dream; a peak experience of oneness with the universe; or enlightening discoveries within the inner self. This literature is closely related to the relatively recent but increasingly popular use of water-immersion tanks (Lilly, 1977) to facilitate fantasy, creativity, and self-exploration. This model—as well as 'reverse quarantine', which is discussed later in this chapter—also brings to mind the massive amount of autobiographical evidence that solitude, preferably in a relatively monotonous environment, is highly conducive to the incubation of creative ideas in science, philosophy, literature, and the arts.

To be sure, the spiritual–religious model has been adapted to psychotherapy in the narrower sense. Morita therapy (see Reynolds, 1976), developed in Japan, has its roots in Zen meditation techniques. However, whereas the meditator seeks solitude in order to reach enlightenment beyond that which rationality can bring, the patient in Morita therapy and other 'quiet' therapies uses the setting to obtain a better understanding of his own maladaptive reactions. It is for this reason that patients participating in such treatments spend up to a week alone in a mildly to moderately stimulus-impoverished environment. Very positive effects have been reported with various kinds of behavioral problems, although the transferability of these methods to Western cultures is questionable.

Therapeutic REST may also be seen as a rite of passage by clients in systematic projects, just as it is by adolescent tribesmen and religious seekers. Many participants in our own smoking-cessation and weight-reduction studies, described later in this chapter, have had this reaction. They repeatedly refer to their REST experience as a marker that delineated their earlier self from the new, healthier, self-efficacious individual who is successfully coping with problems that previously left him helpless. In this sense, some kind of rebirth can occur in REST, just as it can happen to people who undergo ritual stimulus-reduction in other cultures.

The Conditioning Model

This approach to the use of reduced stimulation, derived from simple learning theories, uses stimulus attenuation as an aversive or as a negative reinforcer. People who behave in ways that are inappropriate by some standard are 'punished' by being put into situations that are relatively low in general stimulation and usually completely lacking in social stimulation. Since this is presumed to be an unpleasant experience, the knowledge that misbehavior will lead to isolation is expected to reduce the probability of misbehavior occurring in the future. Solitary confinement in prisons, seclusion in psychiatric hospitals and educational institutions, 'time out from positive reinforcement' in the treatment of behaviorally disturbed children and mentally retarded adults, and being sent to one's room by parents are some common examples of this punitive approach.

In general, there seems to be no evidence that the likelihood of undesired behavior really is diminished by such treatment. Most segregation cells in prisons are populated by people who have been there before and recidivism is similarly high in the other instances. This is not surprising, given the generally unconvincing evidence about the long-term effectiveness of aversive reinforcement.

What is more interesting is the fact that, if one looks beneath the surface, the supposedly aversive condition frequently turns out to have been deliberately chosen. In a series of interviews with convicts who had had experience in isolation, we have found several who claimed that they had repeatedly violated institutional regulations precisely in order to be put into solitary confinement. They periodically felt that this environment was much more tolerable than the regimen of the general prison population (Suedfeld *et al.*, 1976). Similar experiences have been noted by administrators of such 'punishment' in other settings (see Suedfeld, 1980). In fact, one might argue that where seclusion and stimulus reduction do have the effect of restoring self-control, calmness, and appropriate behavior, they do so not necessarily because the individual is motivated to avoid the restricted environment in the future. No doubt there are some cases where this is true, since there are people for whom low stimulation levels are stressful; but it seems likely that the beneficial effects occur because negative features of the normal environment which had been the antecedent causal conditions for tension and misbehavior have now in fact been removed. This argument would imply that, from a conditioning viewpoint, restriction is actually a positive reinforcer, and therefore its use as punishment would increase the undesired behaviors. The conditions under which this may be true have not been explored; my guess is that they are quite specific and rare, and that a simplistic operant conditioning explanation of the effects of isolation and monotony is inadequate.

The Psychodynamic Model

Clinicians who proceed from a psychodynamic theoretical standpoint have described the REST situation as one in which childhood experiences are vividly relived. Among such theorists have been a team led by the late Hassan Azima (e.g. Azima *et al.*, 1961). These workers hypothesized that stimulus reduction could be used in what they called 'anaclitic therapy', a therapeutic procedure in which regression was fostered by returning the patient to a childlike condition. This consisted of the patient's dependence on the experimenter for food, approval, social contact, and stimulation, supposedly in the same way as very young children are dependent upon their parents for these things. Furthermore, the body schema hypothetically becomes disorganized and fluid in reduced stimulation just as it was in childhood. In using this technique with psychiatric patients, Azima's team did note evidence of regression (e.g. changes in figure drawings). Furthermore, they found better rapport with a therapist and improvement in symptomatology in a substantial proportion of these patients. On the other hand, the technique appeared to be counterproductive with obsessive–compulsive neurotics. A few such patients manifested psychotic symptoms during the session and were given electroconvulsive shock treatment to counteract the effect.

A somewhat different version of the theory has been used by Janov (1970), who recommends the use of a day or more of isolation and sensory restriction for patients beginning primal therapy. Coupled with sleeplessness, and sometimes with food-deprivation, this experience is supposedly so stressful as to facilitate the letting-down of cognitive controls and thus initiates the regression that is the hallmark of this school of therapy. 'Rebirthing', a new and not very well tested therapeutic procedure, accomplishes sensory restriction by the technique of water-immersion to regress the individual to the experience of birth. Unlike the original experience, this situation is carefully made low in stress, so that the after-effects of traumata that were induced during the actual birth of the individual are extinguished. Incidentally, the Leboyer (1976) method of obstetrics, if universally adopted, may spell the end of rebirthing since the use of greatly reduced stimulation in the delivery room would presumably just about eliminate the unpleasant experiences that rebirthing attempts to rectify.

In a derivation from ego psychology, Goldberger and Holt (e.g. 1961) argue that regression in the service of the ego, a shift in emphasis from secondary to primary process, is an adaptive response to stimulus-impoverished situations. Such a shift may encourage dreaming and fantasizing, which may be turned to therapeutic use. There has not been a good test of the therapeutic utility of this idea, but there has been considerable support for the prediction that individuals who can relax and enjoy primary process functioning, or can continue to control it even in REST, are those who tolerate the condition best and experience it as least aversive. There seems to be no doubt that daydreaming, fantasy, vivid dreams, and other forms of imagery are especially vivid and frequent under REST conditions, and that for some subjects they are a source of serious stress (Zuckerman, 1969). Given the recent interest in the use of imagery by therapists (e.g. Singer, 1974), it is high time that attempts be made to use the impact of REST on such phenomena in a clinically beneficial way.

The Cognitive–Social Models

The two major cognitive–social models that have been used to explain the beneficial effects of REST are discussed below. The reader will note that one is based on information-processing capacities and intrinsic motivation, while the other emphasizes the cognitive aspects of belief and opinion change. Thus, both of the theoretical positions are essentially cognitive, fitting handily into current trends within social psychological theory-building. In fact, they are not alternative but rather complementary positions. This approach is clearly the most closely related to the two themes of this book. It views REST as a form of applied social psychology, and the problems to which it has been applied are the most likely to be included under the rubric of behavioral medicine as opposed to the more traditional concerns of practitioners in psychiatry, clinical psychology, and the mental health field in general. Even so, the reader will note that large areas of behavioral medicine to which REST logically seems applicable have been untouched, so that there is great scope for innovative research and application in this area.

The Reverse Quarantine Model

By 'reverse quarantine' I mean the idea that stimulus reduction works through the removal of the individual from environmental conditions that trigger clinical symptoms or other adverse behavior, or that prevent better functioning by flooding the information-processing channels. A considerable body of literature has accumulated which either explicitly states or implicitly assumes that the stimulus levels commonly encountered in modern society are too much for some people to handle, that maladaptive reactions to the situation of overload will occur, and that these reactions can be avoided, reduced, or eliminated by taking the individual out of the environment and putting him into a less demanding one. This conceptual model is related to the one emphasizing persuasion (see next section), since the processing of information is a crucial part of both the information-overload problem and the destabilization of the attitude structure. However, there is one major theoretical and procedural difference. The persuasion model uses the effects of REST to increase the potency of other treatment techniques; in the reverse quarantine approach, REST in itself is considered to be sufficient to obtain the desirable results. One relevant theory is that certain types of psychopathology involve the malfunctioning of the information-processing system. More specifically, there is a breakdown in that part of the system which is responsible for selecting portions of the total environmental data array for further consideration. As a consequence, the cognitive mechanisms are flooded with an excess of stimulation and informational input, with which they are unable to cope adaptively. It has been proposed that schizophrenia and childhood autism, among other forms of disturbance, are based on this sequence. It is logical that a severe reduction in the amount of environmental stimulation should be beneficial in such cases, and REST has in fact been shown to be effective in the treatment of this kind of patient (see Suedfeld, 1980).

The use of REST as reverse quarantine has been successful in serious and difficult cases. 'Time-out', which is commonly defined by theorists as an essentially punitive technique, is viewed very differently by many patients and practitioners. In fact, it may serve as a welcome period of escape from overload, enabling the individual to calm down and restore self-control. REST has been used in this way for a long time (see e.g. Dercum, 1917; Suedfeld, 1980), and it continues to be used because it is an effective, economical, and safe procedure. In more ambitious studies with young patients, several projects have reported that the use of prolonged periods of stimulus reduction and partial social isolation has had good long-term effects in the treatment of autistic children (e.g. Schechter et al., 1969) as well as with some mentally retarded patients and with children suffering from learning and behavioral disturbances (e.g. Cohen, 1963; Glynn, 1957; Janz, 1978; Suedfeld, 1980).

It is this aspect of REST that probably makes it a useful treatment for people going through episodes of drug-induced psychosis. This effect has been most saliently noted in cases of PCP (phencyclidine) overdose for which darkness, silence, and social isolation constitute the treatment of choice (Luisada, 1978). LSD psychosis has been successfully treated in the same way (Adams, 1980).

Therapeutic success with adult psychiatric patients has been reported in several studies. Harris (1959) used very brief exposures to stimulus restriction on two successive days with schizophrenic in-patients, most of whom reacted positively to the situation and some of whom manifested reduced symptomatology. Similar findings were reported by Luby et al. (1962) and by Smith et al. (1961).

However, the most extensive series of studies with hospitalized patients was performed by a clinical research group in Virginia (summarized in Adams, 1980). Using individuals in a variety of diagnostic categories, these investigators reported that 6 hours of stimulus reduction (lying in a bed with eyes covered, ears plugged with cotton, and head wrapped in gauze) led to significantly more reductions than increases in symptomatology, with the beneficial changes persisting through the 1-week follow-up while the adverse ones disappeared. This result was interpreted as indicating that there were adaptive and durable mental reorganizations during the session while increased symptoms reflected temporary arousal of anxiety and emotional disturbance. In formal interviews before and after the session, the effects of REST were reported to include an increased desire for social contacts and therapeutic relationships, greater awareness of internal conflicts, and better insight about personal difficulties and the patient's own responsibility for his problems. Repressive and inhibitory defences were used less rigidly. In addition to these effects, testing showed increases in ego strength and in IQ score.

In a second study, using only 3 hours of stimulus reduction and adding a matched control goup, the researchers found more symptom-reduction in the REST group, which—unlike the controls—often showed better ego functioning, self-acceptance, and utilization of defence mechanisms. It was also reported that, as in the pilot study, those patients who had been the most severely disturbed prior to the session seemed to benefit the most from the treatment.

In the next step (Adams et al., 1966), the REST without message treatment was used as a control condition. Patients undergoing this treatment did show significant improvements on dominance, ego strength, depression, self-acceptance, and signs of increased personal adequacy. It should be noted here that the group that received messages while in REST also showed positive reactions, but their major areas of improvement were more concentrated on conscious insight and self-awareness. An attempt to use monotonous rather than reduced stimulation in the same way (Cleveland et al., 1963) found no positive results with a group of schizophrenics; neither did an experiment by Moran (1969), who added a social isolation condition as a comparison with monotonous stimulation.

Using a somewhat different design, Cooper et al. (1975) systematically manipulated interviewer behavior prior to a brief period of REST. They found that this treatment resulted in increased dominance and affiliation in the subject's interaction with the interviewer afterward. There were also long-term improvements on various behavioral rating scales and a significant reduction in hypochondriacal complaints.

In the context of habit-modification, this model served as the basis of one of the comparison conditions in two studies on smoking cessation (Suedfeld et al., 1972; Suedfeld and Ikard, 1974). In both of these studies the treatment of major interest combined REST and messages. Groups receiving REST without messages, messages without REST, and no treatment at all were included in the design. The authors were quite surprised to find that significant long-term reductions in cigarette smoking were reported by individuals who had spent 24 hours in the stimulus-reduction chamber without receiving any persuasive or informational inputs about smoking. In fact, in neither case was there a statistically significant difference between the REST–message and REST–no message groups. Both demonstrated significant decreases in smoking rate over as long as 2 years, in contrast to the non-confined groups who indicated little if any alteration in smoking.

Recent work in environmental psychology (Mehrabian and Russell, 1974; Russell and Pratt, 1980) has identified the qualities of arousal and pleasantness to be major polarities in environmental assessment. It appears quite likely that, in the absence of anxiety-arousing set, sensory reduction would be placed in the relaxed (low-arousal) and pleasant quadrant of such a two-dimensional space. In this, it has commonalities with the various kinds of relaxation and meditation training. There are similar parallels with the environmental circumstances that are considered to be conducive to the success of other treatment procedures. These factors are common to techniques of traditional psychotherapy, such as psychoanalysis; behavior-modification, as in systematic desensitization; and behavioral medicine, including biofeedback and relaxation training. To the extent that these conditions foster refocusing of attention, one would expect that individuals undergoing reduced stimulation would become more aware of, and perhaps more able to cope with, their behavioral problems.

In support of this hypothesis, several studies have shown that REST by itself, not combined with any other form of intervention, has had significant positive effects on self-concept. Antista and Jones (1975) found that university students undergoing as little as 45 minutes of stimulus reduction became less anxious and showed a significant reduction in the discrepancy between their perception of their actual and ideal selves. This demonstration of improvement in self-acceptance is supplemented by the findings of Kammerman (1977), whose water-immersion subjects manifested increased enthusiasm and optimism, greater feelings that they were able to cope with threatening and novel experiences, and a possible increase in ego strength, findings that are highly compatible with the positive self-reports of participants in both flotation and chamber confinement.

Some of the other applications of this model are closely related to the spiritual quests discussed elsewhere in this chapter. In fact, the model may serve as a scientifically more orthodox equivalent of the spiritual explanation of REST effects. If we reject the idea that the isolated monk or mystic opens himself to actual contact with an external supernatural force, we may hypothesize that he is becoming more aware of internal affects, motives, and intuitions. These are usually submerged because of the need to cope with the constant input of information from the normal environment. Another way of looking at it is that there is some optimal level of information and stimulation.

When the everyday world provides a very high level of these needs, internal sources are ignored, but when the individual leaves that situation for a more homogeneous and quiet one, internal sources will claim more attention and will be more likely to surpass some kind of attention threshold. For this reason, the relevant consequence of REST has also been identified as relaxation, refocusing of attention, and cognitive restructuring (Suedfeld, 1980).

The specific applications of this model in health psychology have included the use of flotation tanks. These have become very popular; tanks (or kits with which to build tanks) can be bought, and tank time rented, in many major cities throughout North America. The procedure usually consists of having the client floating in a shallow tank of water heavily loaded with Epsom salts to induce a feeling of weightlessness. The tank is completely enclosed, dark, and soundproof. Thus, a very low level of stimulation from the outside world is available. There has been relatively little systematic research done in this context, although many anecdotal reports have been published. Participants have described experiences of self actualization, increased creativity, improved self-esteem, deeper and better understanding of personal problems, and so on (e.g., Lilly, 1977). It appears probable that the commerical success of this approach, in the absence of major advertising campaigns or of an obvious vital need, must be based on the satisfaction and favorable recommendation of participants.

Early experiments using the immersion procedure reported it to be relatively stressful, and to be associated with disturbances of cognitive functioning, affect, and imagery. It can be supposed that, like the more standard chamber-confinement techniques, the immersion procedure was accompanied by experimental artifacts that induced anxiety and a negative set in the subjects (Suedfeld, 1980). The strangeness of the tank situation is quite likely to exacerbate these problems beyond the level that is usually found in REST chambers. On the other hand, appropriate expectations and instructions can apparently induce feelings of great relaxation and enjoyment, both in the chamber and in the immersion tank.

Introspective reports in these studies, as well as in the tank reports mentioned, support the view that a massive reduction in environmental stimulation leads to increased focusing on internal information-processing. Many participants in reduced-stimulation experiments have emphasized that they experienced an unusual ability to delve into their problems and concerns while in the chamber, an ability that went much further and deeper than that manifested in the normal environment (see for example, Suedfeld and Best, 1977). This, incidentally, may be one reason why monotonous stimulation is less effective as a therapeutic tool than reduced stimulation: it is quite possible that the relatively high levels of input, even if that input is meaningless, homogeneous, and unpatterned, provide enough of a load on the processing system to prevent any significant shifting of attentional focus toward internal productions. Although more data should be collected in which the refocusing and relaxation experiences are explicitly measured, there seems to be good reason even now to include REST as having much in common with relaxation and re-orienting techniques in psychotherapy and behavioral medicine (Suedfeld, 1980).

The Persuasion Model

The basic assumptions of this explanatory system lie in the various ways that REST can enhance the processing of information that is incompatible with the recipient's existing beliefs, opinions, and behavior patterns. Individuals normally ward off, dismiss, or rationalize away such information even against their own best interests.

The fact that stimulus restriction increases persuasibility was reported in the original set of experiments dealing with the experimental use of stimulus-poor environments with human subjects (Bexton, 1953). In succeeding years, when one after another of the more dramatic findings reported by early researchers was found to be non-replicable, contaminated with artifact, or greatly restricted in scope, this particular one continued to be consistently supported by the vast majority of relevant evidence. Experiments have shown increased suggestibility in the motor and perceptual realms, using such measures as body-sway, the autokinetic effect, and figure-copying. Much of the literature on visual 'hallucinations' appears also to have been reporting the after-effects of suggestion (Suedfeld, 1969).

There were early attempts to turn this phenomenon to practical use in clinical applications. Adams and his co-workers at the Richmond VA Hospital moved on from a model implicitly based on the reverse quarantine idea that underlay their earliest studies to a series of experiments (summarized in Adams, 1980) in which they presented messages to hospitalized psychiatric patients during a REST session lasting from 2 to 4 hours. This portion of the work of Adams *et al.* was based on an hypothesis that environmental reduction aroused a state of stimulus hunger (Lilly, 1956). Stimulus hunger would make the individual more open to information that would normally be avoided, a prediction that has been supported with great consistency in a number of studies (see Zubek, 1969). The relevant inference is that therapeutic messages, which may normally be warded off by some patients, would also become more acceptable and therefore presumably more potent.

The messages differed from study to study. In some cases a standard message was presented to all subjects; in others individual presentations were designed for each patient on the basis of his own symptoms and background. With standardized messages whose goal was to improve the patient's self-concept, the combined treatment was significantly more successful in obtaining change than was either REST without a message or the message presented in less restrictive conditions (Gibby and Adams, 1961). The effect was consistent across four separate sets of self-concept ratings. An experiment using a standardized message directed at improving the ability of patients to make decisions (Hogan, 1963) again showed significantly more positive change with the REST–message combination.

Adams *et al.* (1966) prepared individually designed messages, based on patients' patterns of responses to the MMPI and the Leary Interpersonal Check List. The messages described the patient's interpersonal behavior, his self-description, his covert attitudes, his concept of what the ideal person is like, and the meaning of discrepancies among these four factors. The messages also presented a preview of the therapeutic procedures that would be followed after the REST treatment. Messages took approximately 15 minutes. The individuals who heard the message during a 2-hour REST session showed improved realism of ideals, fewer symptoms, better internal controls, and less defensiveness and repression than the other groups. As mentioned in the previous section, a treatment group undergoing REST only, without the message, also demonstrated some improvements.

Another study with individualized messages (Robertson, 1964) used three brief REST sessions, with a different message heard during each. The usual message-only, REST-only, and no-treatment controls were included. In this study all three treated groups did better than the controls but there were no significant differences among treatment effects. A long time-interval between various measures of change may have been responsible for this failure to replicate earlier findings (Adams, 1980); but if this is in fact the correct explanation, one may wonder about the long-range therapeutic effectiveness of these procedures. No delayed follow-ups were performed by Adams or his co-workers. There seem to be good reasons to think that such effects may actually be obtained, although the short duration of REST in most of these studies (2–4 hours) should perhaps be extended for maximal impact. Incidentally, it should be noted that positive findings were again obtained only in studies using reduced stimulation (darkness and silence). Several attempts to obtain clinical improvement under monotonous-stimulation conditions (diffuse light, white noise) were unsuccessful.

One other series of studies designed to take advantage of stimulus hunger in a therapeutic way was effective in reducing fear of snakes. In this design, snake phobic subjects spent 5 hours in REST and then were permitted to press a button in order to view slides of snakes. The hypotheses were that stimulus hunger would induce the subjects to expose themselves to stimuli that would normally arouse fear; that because of stimulus hunger the stimuli would be less aversive after REST; and that this reduction in aversiveness would be further enhanced by the need to eliminate cognitive dissonance (the knowledge that they had chosen to view these slides would be dissonant with the knowledge that they were afraid of snakes, a situation that could be reduced by the changed cognition that they were not really afraid). The results showed a high degree of success, with significant changes in the direction of lowered fear both on self-report measures and on actual approach to a live 2-meter boa constrictor. Psychophysiological changes were significantly correlated with the other measures (e.g. Suedfeld and Hare, 1977).

Stimulus hunger is one component of Suedfeld's (1972) two-factor theory. This theory argues that while REST may indeed arouse a desire for stimulation and therefore a greater receptivity to messages designed to teach new ways of thinking, feeling, and acting, the impact of persuasive inputs is heightened primarily by a destabilization of belief systems which occurs under stimulus-reduction. This destabilization is the result of the impairment of complex cognitive functioning that has been found in REST (see Suedfeld, 1969). One cognitive theory of attitude change (Koslin *et al.*, 1971) proposes that change is a function of the extent to which a particular message (or any other factor) reduces the individual's ability to integrate new inputs into his existing belief system. To the extent that REST disrupts complex cognitive performance in general, it would also disorganize this process in particular.

In terms of Lewin's (1952) classic analysis of opinion change, the two-factor theory would argue that REST acts as an unfreezer of the existing attitude structure. Change is then brought about by the messages that are presented, as well as by the subject's own cognitions and motivation, by material that is remembered from previous exposures, and so on. Refreezing in the new pattern probably comes about after release from REST. In the behavioral medicine context, refreezing needs to be specifically fostered in order to avoid relapse, the fatal flaw of most clinical techniques in this area.

Unfreezing, the necessary first step, is a function of the amount of confusion and instability induced in the belief system. This variable can be measured by a scaling technique that indicates the degree to which respondents are clear about the implications of various attitude-related statements (Koslin *et al.*, 1971). The one experiment that has been performed so far specifically testing the role of REST as an unfreezer showed that it does indeed significantly increase the amount of measured belief instability, even when no persuasive message has been presented during the session (Tetlock and Suedfeld, 1976).

The persuasion hypothesis has been the basis of a number of habit-alteration projects. In three pilot studies:

(1) relaxation training followed by REST led to substantial drops in the blood pressure of three hypertensive patients (Suedfeld *et al.*, 1981);
(2) a derogatory message emphasizing the personal shortcomings of people who depend on alcohol was successful in reducing the alcohol intake of heavy social drinkers who heard the presentation during REST (Cooper *et al.*, 1977); and

(3) a very brief and mundane message presented toward the end of 24 hours of REST was associated with a 38 percent reduction in smoking rate on a 3-month follow-up.

In another, more elaborate, procedure, psychologically addicted smokers showed significant decreases in the use of cigarettes throughout a 2-year follow-up (Suedfeld et al., 1972; Suedfeld and Ikard, 1974). However, the theory was not differentially supported as compared to the reverse quarantine model, since REST-only treatment groups in both of these studies showed reductions in smoking rate essentially identical to those of the clients receiving REST plus messages. Non-confined subjects failed to show significant improvement in either study. Clearer support for the persuasion model specifically was obtained in a study by Borrie and Suedfeld (1980). In this experiment messages teaching relaxation and self-management techniques, and presented toward the beginning and near the end of a 24-hour REST situation, represented the only condition that led to significant and continued weight loss throughout a 6-month follow-up.

Although no specific test has been made, it is plausible to use unfreezing as a mediating construct in the ability of REST to increase the potency of other treatment techniques. Aside from the literature cited earlier, in which stimulus-reduction was combined with such standard procedures as psychoanalyis and behavior-modification, there have been two specific studies confirming this phenomenon. In one of these, grossly obese patients who received stimulus-reduction, appropriate messages, and prolonged individual follow-up therapy (primarily behavior-modification techniques promoting self-management) evidenced significant weight loss, with reductions of well over a pound a week for as long as 6 months (Borrie and Suedfeld, 1980; Suedfeld, 1980). In the other study (Best and Suedfeld, in preparation; Suedfeld, and Best, 1977), REST and messages were combined with satiation smoking and behavioral self-management instructions to constitute one of the most highly successful smoking cessation techniques ever reported. Six months after the treatment, 75 percent of the participants were completely abstinent from cigarettes. It seems logical to argue that the greater openness to information and instruction that results from REST can extend not only to the messages presented during the session but also to material that is presented as part of the same treatment package and is designed to help the client to reach his or her therapeutic goal.

To leave the discussion at this level is, I think, somewhat inadequate. The fact is that subjective reports of individuals emerging from the REST treatment indicate a much deeper impact than one would infer from paper-and-pencil measures of attitude or of belief instability. There appears to be a major change in motivation. Facts that were previously known but whose implications were never drawn in relation to the individual's own life become central in awareness, strong resolutions are made (and, as it turns out, maintained) concerning self-protective changes in habits and lifestyle, and clients come out expressing amazement at their previous lack of involvement with these obviously very important issues.

It should be recalled that normally anxiety-arousing stimuli apparently may become less so in REST. The impact of this phenomenon has been noted in this chapter as it related to visual stimuli in the case of snake phobia. However, it is also important for understanding the possible reasons that explain the increase both in persuasibility and in concentration on, and insight into, personal problems. As a general rule, messages arguing that one's important behavioral patterns are destructive (as in the case of anti-smoking campaigns for cigarette users, or exercise/dieting arguments in the case of the overweight) are anxiety-arousing. People therefore prefer to avoid thinking for any prolonged period of time or in any depth about their own self-damaging behaviors. For this reason most individuals who are confronted by such presentations tend to take advantage of the many distractions that are available in the normal environment and switch their attention from the unpleasant issue of health-dysfunctional habits. In REST, there are few, if any, good distractors, and none that is pressing enough to justify the ignoring of the central purpose for which the individual is undergoing the treatment.

These reports imply that the openness to new response patterns based on previously ignored information, and the willingness to restructure one's behavior in accordance with these patterns, may be based on a combination of unfreezing and the refocusing of attention. REST seems to promote a cognitive restructuring process which is more inner-directed, in which emotions are more appropriately attached to health-endangering habit patterns than is normally the case, and which enables the client to derive conclusions that lead to drastically modified behaviors. Obviously, the technique is not a panacea. It does not work for every problem, nor for every participant; but it does seem to provide one of the most powerful demonstrations of the importance of environmental and informational characteristics in the role that cognitive factors (including attitudes) can play when one is trying to solve problems in the area of behavioral medicine. Cognitive restructuring has been recognized from the beginning as a central part of the health psychology–behavioral medicine approach; REST may be a way to achieve such restructuring more efficiently and thoroughly than many of those currently in use.

Conclusion

A recent review of the literature on REST, with an emphasis on its clinical uses (Suedfeld, 1980), has shown that reduced stimulation is indeed a powerful and flexible therapeutic tool. Only a portion of these findings was reviewed here, but even these suffice to establish REST as a technique whose effectiveness has been at least as well documented as that of many more widely used treatments. In addition, it has been shown to have essentially no serious risks of major side- or after-effects, to be quite acceptable to the great majority of participants, and to be remarkably cost-effective in time and money. REST is also capable of increasing the power of other treatment procedures. The fact that it has not been more widely adopted is probably due to the unfamiliarity of most clinicians and researchers with its past successes and with the ease of application, and perhaps partly to an aura of strangeness and mystery that has clung to it. It is to be hoped that the myths with which the technique has been surrounded will not be permitted to keep behavioral medicine from using a valuable and readily available procedure.

The widely disparate theoretical and methodological backgrounds that have led to the use of this technique are impressive. However, this diversity of origins does point to one problem with adopting a theoretical approach to the literature. None of the theories has been stated in specific enough terms to permit the deduction of hypotheses that could be pitted against each other in a strong inference chain. Thus, the fact that REST leads to better rapport with the therapist can be equally well explained by the conditioning model, the psychoanalytic model, or the social-cognition model. There is probably not a single datum in the literature reviewed here that would have been predicted (or at least could be explained) by only one of the theories.

Although this chapter was organized to show the historical–conceptual roots that have converged in the adaptation of reduced-stimulation procedures to therapy, this is only one possible taxonomy. One could just as easily analyze the material in terms of the kinds of behavioral problems treated, including psychotic states, neuroses, mild difficulties of adaptation, habit control, and so on; on the basis of client type, by age, demographic characteristics, and personality traits; or by procedure, including confinement duration, specific type of stimulus alteration, and the use of other components such as messages or more orthodox psychotherapeutic techniques. The findings, obviously, would remain the same regardless of how one chose to categorize them. The clinical application of REST in psychotherapy and behavioral medicine tends to be largely pragmatic: the technique works, even if there are several widely different explanations of why that should be so. This may be adequate for the practitioner, but the development of more sophisticated theories and more definitive tests of theories is important not only for a better understanding of what is actually happening, but also for designing better applications.

References

Adams, H. B. (1980). 'Effects of reduced stimulation on institutionalized adult patients', in Suedfeld, P. (ed.), *Restricted Environmental Stimulation: Research and Clinical Applications*. Wiley, New York.

Adams, H. B., Robertson, M. H., and Cooper, G. D. (1966). 'Sensory deprivation and personality change', *Journal of Nervous and Mental Diseases*, **143**, 256–265.

Antista, B., and Jones, A. (1975). 'Some beneficial consequences of brief sensory deprivation'. Paper read at the meeting of the Western Psychological Association, Sacramento, California.

Azima, H., and Cramer-Azima, F. J. (1956). 'Effects of partial isolation in mentally disturbed individuals', *Diseases of the Nervous System*, **17**, 117–122.

Azima, H., and Cramer-Azima, F. (1957). 'Studies on perceptual isolation', *Diseases of the Nervous System*, **18**, 80–85.

Azima, H., Vispo, R. H., and Cramer-Azima, F. J. (1961). 'Observations on anaclitic therapy during sensory deprivation', in Solomon, P. *et al.* (eds), *Sensory Deprivation*. Harvard University Press, Cambridge.

Best, J. A., and Suedfeld, P. 'Treating smokers with a combination of self-management techniques and restricted environmental stimulation: additive effects', (In preparation.)

Bexton, W. H. (1953). 'Some effects of perceptual isolation in human subjects'. Ph.D. dissertation, McGill University.

Borrie, R. A., and Suedfeld, P. (1980). 'Restricted environmental stimulation therapy in a weight reduction program', *Journal of Behavioral Medicine*, **3**, 147–161.

Cleveland, S. E., Reitman, E. E., and Bentinck, C. (1963). 'Therapeutic effectiveness of sensory deprivation', *Archives of General Psychiatry*, **8**, 455–460

Cohen, R. L. (1963). 'Developments in the use of isolation therapy of behavior disorders of children', in Masserman, J. H. (ed.), *Current Psychiatric Therapies*, vol. 3. Grune & Stratton, New York.

Cooper, G. D., Adams, H. B., Dickinson, J. R., and York, M. W. (1973). 'Interviewer's role-playing and responses to sensory deprivation: a clinical demonstration', *Perceptual and Motor Skills*, **40**, 291–303.

Cooper, G. D., McGraw, J., Pasternak, R., Pasnak, R., and Adams, H. B. (1977). 'A new treatment for alcohol abuse: preliminary report'. Unpublished manuscript, George Mason University.

Dercum, F. X. (1917). *Rest, Suggestion and other Therapeutic Measures in Nervous and Mental Diseases*. P. Baliston's Son & Co., Philadelphia.

Fitzgerald, R. G., and Long, I. (1973). 'Seclusion in the treatment and management of severely disturbed manic and depressed patients', *Perspectives in Psychiatric Care*, **11**, 59–64.

Garrison, F. H. (1921). *An Introduction to the History of Medicine*, 3rd edn. Saunders, Philadelphia.

Gibby, R. G., and Adams, H. B. (1961). 'Receptiveness of psychiatric patients to verbal communication: an increase following partial sensory and social isolation', *Archives of General Psychiatry*, **5**, 366–370.

Gibby, R. G., Adams, H. B., and Carrera, R. N. (1960). 'Therapeutic changes in psychiatric patients following partial sensory deprivation', *Archives of General Psychiatry*, **3**, 33–42.

Glynn, E. (1957). 'The therapeutic use of seclusion in an adolescent pavilion', *Journal of the Hillside Hospital*, **6**, 156–159.

Goldberger, L., and Holt, R. R. (1961). 'Experimental interference with reality contact: individual differences', in Solomon, P. *et al.* (eds), *Sensory Deprivation*. Harvard University Press, Cambridge.

Harris, A. (1959). 'Sensory deprivation and schizophrenia', *Journal of Mental Science*, **105**, 235–237.

Hogan, T. P. (1963). 'The effects of brief partial sensory deprivation and verbal communication on decision-making ability'. Unpublished Ph.D. dissertation, Catholic University of America.

Janov, A. (1970). *The Primal Scream*. Dell, New York.

Janz, G. (1978). [Functional relaxation therapy applied to children suffering from disturbances of concentration.] *Praxis der Kinderpsychologie und Kinderpsychiatrie*, **27**, 201–205.

Jilek, W. G. (1974). *Salish Indian Mental Health and Culture Change: Psychohygienic and Therapeutic Aspects of the Guardian Spirit Ceremonial*. Holt, Rinehart & Winston, Toronto.

Kammerman, M. (1977). 'Personality changes resulting from water suspension sensory isolation', in Kammerman, M. (ed.), *Sensory Isolation and Personality Change*. Thomas, Springfield, Illinois.

Koslin, B. L., Pargament, R., and Suedfeld, P. (1971). 'An uncertainty model of opinion change', in Suedfeld, P. (ed.), *Attitude Change: The Competing Views*. Aldine-Atherton, Chicago.

Kouretas, D. (1967). 'The Oracle of Trophonius: a kind of shock treatment associated with sensory deprivation in ancient Greece', *British Journal of Psychiatry*, **113**, 1441–1446.

Leboyer, F. (1976). *Birth Without Violence*. Knopf, New York.

Lewin, K. (1952). 'Group decision and social change', in Swanson, G. E., Newcomb, T. M., and Hartley, E. L. (eds), *Readings in Social Psychology* (revised edn.). Holt, New York.

Lilly, J. C. (1956). 'Mental effects of reduction of ordinary levels of physical stimuli on intact, healthy persons', *Psychiatric Research Reports No. 5*. American Psychiatric Association, Washington, DC.

Lilly, J. C. (1977). *The Deep Self*. Simon & Schuster, New York.

Luby, E. D., Gottlieb, J. S., Cohen, B. C., Rosenbaum, G., and Domino, E. F. (1962). 'Model psychoses and schizophrenia', *American Journal of Psychiatry*, **119**, 61–67.

Luisada, P. V. (1978). 'The phencyclidine psychosis: phenomenology and treatment', in Petersen, R. C., and Stillman, R. C. (eds). *Phencyclidine (PCP) Abuse: An Appraisal*. US Government Printing Office, Washington. NIDA Research Monogrph 21.

Margetts, B. L. (1968). 'African ethnopsychiatry in the field', *Canadian Psychiatric Association Journal*, **13**, 521–538.

Mehrabian, A., and Russell, J. A. (1974). *An Approach to Environmental Psychology*. MIT press, Cambridge, Mass.

Moran, T. C. (1969). 'The effects of brief sensory deprivation on the learning efficiency of chronic schizophrenic patients'. Unpublished Ph.D. dissertation, St. John's University.

Papageorgiou, M. G. (1975). 'Incubation as a form of psychotherapy in the care of patients in ancient and modern Greece', *Psychotherapy and Psychosomatics*, **26**, 35–38.

Pendergrass, V. E. (1971). 'Timeout from positive reinforcement of persistent, high-rate behavior in retardates', *Journal of Applied Behavior Analysis*, **5**, 85–91.

Potter, C. F. (1958). *The Great Religious Leaders*. Simon & Schuster, New York.

Reynolds, D. K. (1976). *Morita Psychotherapy*. University of California Press, Berkeley.

Robertson, M. H. (1964). 'Facilitating therapeutic changes in psychiatric patients by sensory deprivation methods'. Final progress report to Research Foundation of the National Association for Mental Health.

Russell, J. A., and Pratt, G. (1980). A description of the effective quality attributed to environments. *Journal of Personality and Social Psychology*, **38**, 311–322.

Schechter, M. D., Shurley, J. T., Toussieng, P. W., and Maier, W. J. (1969). 'Sensory isolation therapy of autistic children: a preliminary report', *Journal of Paediatrics*, **74**, 564–569.

Singer, J. L. (1974). *Imagery and Daydream Methods in Psychotherapy and Behavior Modification*. Academic Press, New York.

Smith, S., Thakurdas, H., and Lawes, T. G. G. (1961). 'Perceptual isolation and schizophrenia', *Journal of Mental Science*, **107**, 839–844.

Suedfeld, P. (1969). 'Changes in intellectual performance and in susceptibility to influence', in Zubek, J. P. (ed.), *Sensory Deprivation: Fifteen Years of Research*. Appleton-Century-Crofts, New York.

Suedfeld, P. '(1972). 'Attitude manipulation in restricted environments: V. Theory and research', Paper read at the XXth International Congress of Psychology, Tokyo.

Suedfeld, P. (1980). *Restricted Environmental Stimulation: Research and Clinical Applications*. Wiley, New York.

Suedfeld, P., and Best, J. A. (1977). 'Satiation and sensory deprivation combined in smoking therapy: Some case studies and unexpected side-effects', *International Journal of the Addiction*, **12**, 337–359.

Suedfeld, P., and Hare, R. D. (1978). 'Sensory deprivation in the treatment of snake phobia: behavioral, self-report, and physiological effects', *Behavior Therapy*, **8**, 240–250.

Suedfeld, P., and Ikard, F. F. (1974). 'The use of sensory deprivation in facilitating the reduction of cigarette smoking', *Journal of Consulting and Clinical Psychology*, **42**, 888–895.

Suedfeld, P., Landon, P. B., Pargament, R., and Epstein, Y. M. (1972). 'An experimental attack on smoking: attitude manipulation in restricted environments, III'. *International Journal of the Addictions*, **7**, 721–733.

Suedfeld, P., Ramirez, C., Clyne, D., and Deaton, J. E. (1976). [The effects of involuntary social isolation on prisoners.] Paper read at the XVIth Interamerican Congress of Psychology, Miami Beach, Florida.

Suedfeld, P., Roy, C., and Landon, P. B. (1981). 'Reducing blood pressure of hypertensive patients by the use of restricted environmental stimulation therapy'. Unpublished paper. The University of British Columbia.

Tetlock, P. E., and Suedfeld, P. (1976). 'Inducing belief instability without a persuasive message: the roles of attitude centrality, individual cognitive differences, and sensory deprivation'. *Canadian Journal of Behavioral Science*, **8**, 324–333.

Wilcox, J. W. (1957). 'A practical approach to treatment of colic'. Paper read at the meeting of the Southwestern Paediatrics Society.

Zubek, J. P. (ed.) (1969). *Sensory deprivation: Fifteen years of research*. Appleton-Century-Crofts, New York.

Zuckerman, M. (1969). 'Hallucinations, reported sensations, and images', in J. P. Zubek (ed.), *Sensory deprivation: Fifteen years of research*. Appleton-Century-Crofts, New York.

Social Psychology and Behavioral Medicine
Edited by J. Richard Eiser
© 1982 John Wiley & Sons Ltd

Chapter 17

Social influence and compliance of hospital nurses with infection control policies

BERTRAM H. RAVEN and ROBERT W. HALEY

Introduction

Nosocomial Infections: Background of the Problem

A medical practitioner from the turn of the century would doubtless be dumbfounded by the developments in medical science and technology of the last 80 years: the elimination of the scourge of smallpox from the face of the earth; almost complete prevention of the debilitating effects of poliomyelitis; successful transplantation of human organs—corneas, kidneys, and even hearts; the amazing developments in X-rays and axial tomography scanning. Perhaps these very advances would leave him even more amazed at the fact that a partially preventable medical problem which was extant a century ago is still very much with us today—namely the problem of control of infections acquired in the hospital, or nosocomial infections. In the 1840s, Dr Ignaz Semmelweis in Vienna and, almost simultaneously, Dr Oliver Wendell Holmes in the United States discovered that maternal mortality in hospitals could be attributed to the spread of disease via the unwashed hands of physicians. How surprising that in the 1980s diseases are still spread in hospitals by the patient-care practices of hospital personnel.

Our nineteenth-century physician would, of course, also be amazed at the tremendous increase in hospital costs. Numerous articles have examined the factors which contribute to such increases: increased costs of malpractice insurance, increased costs of newly developed medical equipment, increased costs of physicians, wages of hospital staff members, utility bills. In recent years greater attention has been paid to the increased costs which result from hospital-acquired infections (Bennett *et al.*, 1971; Bennett, 1978; Sencer and Axnick, 1975; Polakavetz *et al.*, 1978).

Nosocomial infections (the word 'nosocomial' is derived from the Greek word for hospital) are defined as those infections that develop during (or sometimes following) hospitalization and are not present or incubating prior to the patient's admission. It is estimated that, of the 32 million patients admitted to hospitals in the United States each year, approximately 5 percent will acquire a nosocomial infection. The immediate costs of hospitalization alone would then add over a $1 billion to the nation's hospital bills. The costs of complications involving additional medical treatment would increase the costs considerably further. Of course, of even greater concern is the injury to the patients—15,000 US hospital patients per year will die from nosocomial infections, and even greater numbers will undergo needless suffering.

With the discovery of penicillin in the 1940s, medical experts believed that the problem of infections was finally under control. This optimism was heightened by the development of even more powerful antibiotics. However, this medical solution has not proved successful for several reasons. First, there is evidence that more powerful, resistant strains of bacteria have developed because of the over-use of antibiotics, often resulting in complicated 'suprainfections'. Further, the antibiotics, of course, are effective only on bacterial infections, which comprise 90 percent of nosocomial infections, leaving an additional 10 percent which are unaffected (Dixon, 1978).

An alternative approach to prevention of nosocomial infections focused on the inanimate environment, on the equipment, furnishings, walls, floors, air ducts, which may harbor nosocomial pathogens. Such an approach, popular in the 1960s, was characterized by a particular emphasis on environmental culturing—the routine sampling of the general environment for culture studies which might indicate the location of the infection-producing pathogens. This was accompanied by considerable efforts to develop and utilize antiseptic soaps and other means to sterilize the environment. There was, of course, some logic in trying to locate and destroy the pathogens in the environment before they could be transmitted to the patient. However, it is now generally conceded that the approach was of limited effectiveness for the effort and costs expended (Mallison, 1979).

Both the use of antibiotics and the monitoring and disinfection of the inanimate environment may ironically have contributed to present problems of nosocomial infections by giving a false sense of security to hospital personnel. For example, the over-use of antibiotics may encourage the emergence of pathogenic strains of bacteria that are highly resistant to the usual antibiotic regimens (Eickhoff, 1979). It has also been suggested that a heavy emphasis on environmental culturing may take the place of apparently more effective infection surveillance and control methods (American Hospital Association, 1974; Haley and Shachtman, 1980). In addition, simple measures, such as care in handwashing, wearing masks in isolation rooms, and disposing of hypodermic needles and soiled dressings, are not always being emphasized in educational programs nor followed with the necessary degree of care and precision (Hewitt and Sanford, 1974; Eickhoff, 1975). The problem then can be seen as falling within the realm of social psychology, and particularly social influence analysis. How can hospital personnel be influenced to engage in behaviors which tend to minimize the risks of nosocomial infections and to refrain from activities which tend to increase those risks. This problem is then analogous to accident prevention in industry—one can attempt to design the factory or shipyard or to develop equipment which is more likely to minimize the risk of industrial accidents; alternatively, or concurrently, one can attempt to encourage that behavior of workers which safeguards against industrial accidents (Misumi, 1974; Trist and Bamforth, 1951).

The Development of Infection Surveillance and Control Programs

The urgency of the problem of nosocomial infections became particularly salient following hospital epidemics of staphylococcal infections which spread through the United States in the 1950s (Communicable Disease Center, CDC, 1958). In the 1960s and 1970s many hospitals, guided and encouraged by the Center for Disease Control (CDC), the American Hospital Association (AHA), and other organizations, began extensive voluntary 'Infection Surveillance and Control Programs' (ISCPs). By 1976 the Joint Commission on Accreditation of Hospitals (JCAH, 1976), a private accrediting organization, issued a set of guidelines for the implementation of ISCPs for hospitals as a condition of accreditation. It was, of course, recognized that such programs themselves would involve considerable effort and expense. However, it was estimated that if they resulted in as little as a 6 percent reduction in the nosocomial infection rate, these programs would be justified financially, and even more importantly, in terms of the health and lives of hospital patients (Sencer and Axnick, 1975). Actually, though no-one is so optimistic as to expect that nosocomial infections could be completely eliminated, authorities have argued that is should be possible to reduce them by 50 percent (Sencer and Axnick, 1975; Bennett, 1978).

Past guidelines on infection control from CDC (CDC, 1968) and AHA (AHA, 1968) suggested that hospitals monitor the frequency, kinds, and locations of nosocomial infections in the hospital, develop policies and procedures for communicating information about infection control to the hospital staff, and employ effective means for implementing the recommended policies within the hospital. According to these guidelines, the ISP would include the following personnel:

(1) An *Infection Control Nurse* (ICN), usually a registered nurse with clinical experience and knowledge of epidemiology and infectious diseases. The ICN would be responsible for detecting and recording nosocomial

infections, analyzing the data, advising hospital personnel about correct policies and practices, and taking other necessary measures to reduce nosocomial infections.

(2) A *Hospital Epidemiologist* (HE), usually a physician with knowledge and interest in epidemiology, infectious diseases, and fundamental statistics. The HE would work closely with the ICN, giving direction, guidance, and support, and would also assist in the development of infection surveillance and control measures. The HE would preferably serve as chairperson of the Infection Control Committee.

(3) An *Infection Control Committee*, which would include, in addition to the HE and the ICN, representatives of the major clinical departments, the pathologist, the director of nursing, an administrative representative, and various other *ex officio* members (from Pharmacy, Housekeeping, Inhalation Therapy, Housestaff, etc.). The Infection Control Committee would meet regularly and would play a major role in determining hospital infection control policy. It would provide for meaningful implementation of policy, providing guidance and support for the HE and the ICN. It would also review surveillance data and other important findings and recommendations of the ICN and the HE.

The recommended guidelines were widely adopted by hospitals throughout the United States (Haley and Shachtman, 1980). As might be expected, the exact form in which the programs were implemented has varied with such factors as the size and activities of the hospital, the nature of the patient population, and various differences in the hospitals' administration, infection control personnel, and staff (Haley *et al.*, 1980; Emori *et al.*, 1980). Although it is widely speculated that their implementation has, in fact, contributed to some reduction in the nosocomial infection rate, there has not been any controlled evaluation of the ISCPs' effectiveness.

The Study on the Efficacy of Nosocomial Infection Control

Over the past 25 years, CDC has studied the problems of infection control in hospitals. It has been among the leading proponents of incorporating surveillance, or monitoring, of infections as an important and necessary adjunct to successful infection control and has provided consultation to hospitals in solving their infection control problems and in developing effective ISCPs. Thus, at the beginning of 1974, CDC initiated a major effort to evaluate the ISCPs, the Study on the Efficacy of Nosocomial Infection Control (SENIC Project). The specific objectives of the SENIC Project include enumerating the different approaches to infection control that have been practised in the United States over the past several years and determining their effectiveness by an in-depth study in a representative sample of US hospitals (Haley *et al.*, 1980).

The initial phase of the SENIC Project utilized a Preliminary Screening Questionnaire which was mailed to approximately 6500 general hospitals in the United States. A representative sample of 433 of these hospitals was later selected for the second phase of the study, the Hospital Interview Survey (HIS). It was in this phase that the Institute for Social Science Research of UCLA collaborated. A third phase of the study, the Medical Records Survey, which will not be a discussed here, was designed to determine the rates of infection in the sample of hospitals based on a review of approximately 1000 patients' records per hospital—500 from patients admitted around 1970 before the initiation of the ISCP, and a second 500 from those admitted approximately 6 years later. The purpose of the HIS has been to examine the characteristics of each hospital's ISCP and to determine which characteristics are related to successful programs. The data required for this undertaking were generated through interviews and questionnaires administered to occupants of twelve different positions in each hospital, including the Chairperson of the Infection Control Committee, the ICN, the hospital administrator, the director of nursing, plus a self-administered questionnaire given to a representative sample of staff nurses involved in direct patient care. Data reported here are based on the Hospital Interview Survey. Elsewhere we have discussed the ICN (Emori et al., 1980) and the Chairperson of the Infection Control Committee or the HE (usually physicians) (Haley et al., 1980; Raven et al., 1981). This paper will focus particularly on the interrelationship between the ICN and the staff nurses.

The SENIC Sample of ICNs

Of the 433 hospitals included in the SENIC sample, 347 had individuals who were assigned to the position of ICN, or an equivalent title. In the remaining 86 hospitals we interviewed the member of the nursing staff who was assigned to the infection control committee and who was most knowledgeable about infection control activities. In a few hospitals, two persons were assigned to the position of ICN, and in such cases we interviewed both, but in our present analysis we are considering only the one person per hospital who had principal responsibilities for that position. All but 4 percent of the ICNs were, in fact, trained as nurses, with the remainder having generally been trained as medical technologists, microbiologists, or sanitary engineers (Emori et al., 1980).

The interviews with the ICNs required an average of $3\frac{1}{2}$ hours and were divided into two sessions. Though they included a large number of questions about the history and current operations of the infection control program in the hospital, knowledge about infection control procedures, hospital regulations, etc., we will present here only those data relevant to the examination of social influence of staff nurses.

The SENIC Sample of Staff Nurses

Within each of the 433 SENIC hospitals, a random sample of staff nurses was selected to fill out HIS nurse questionnaires. Full- or part-time registered nurses (RNs), licensed practical nurses (LPNs), or licensed vocational nurses (LVNs) in staff-level positions involving direct patient care were eligible for participation. The pool of eligible nurses was stratified by service (medical/surgical) and shift (day/evening/night). For hospitals with 100 eligible nurses or less, every fourth nurse was sampled in each cell using a random starting point. For hospitals with more than 100 eligible nurses, the sampling fraction was adjusted to yield a sample of approximately 24 medical/surgical nurses. If the hospital had an intensive-care unit (ICU), one RN for each shift was sampled for each ICU. A single RN was selected from the operating room staff (day shift only). A total of 7188 staff-nurse questionnaires were collected. The number of nurses sampled per hospital ranged from 3 to 63 and averaged 17 (± 9 SD).

The sampled nurses were predominantly female (98 percent), Anglo-White (84 percent), and less than 30 years old (57 percent). The majority of them worked full time (87 percent) on a variety of different wards and services (61 percent), but 20 percent worked exclusively on medical services, and 17 percent exclusively on surgical services. Forty-eight percent of the nurses worked in hospitals that rotated shifts, but 52 percent generally worked on the day shift, 28 percent the evening shift, and 21 percent the night shift. Most of the sampled nurses had the RN license (68.8 percent); of these RNs, 24 percent had an associate degree (2-year program), 61 percent a diploma degree (3-year program), and 15 percent a baccalaureate degree (4-year program).

Results

In earlier reports (Haley *et al.*, 1980, Appendix A; Raven and Haley, 1980), we described the basic model which guided our analysis of data from the SENIC study. In those reports we also discussed the importance of the support of higher-level administrators for the ISCPs and the resulting authority of the ISCP staff to take appropriate action; in this chapter we will present a broader range of information about the social influence characteristics and practices of the ISCP staff and other groups of hospital personnel. In our discussion of the various analyses, all relationships reported are significant at the 0.001 level of confidence, unless otherwise indicated.

Availability and Visibility of the ICNs

Hospitals varied considerably in the extent to which their ICNs were visible to the staff nurses and the extent to which nurses recognized them or went to them for information on infection control. Staff nurses estimated that half of all staff nurses would recognize the ICN if they saw her*, and slightly less than half would know what her job is. On the average, they estimated that they saw her a bit more frequently than once a week and might talk to her on the average of several times a month.

The visibility of the ICN was measured indirectly in a series of the 16 questionnaire items in which staff nurses were asked to assess the characteristics of their ICN. For each item the nurse could abstain from answering by checking the alternative 'insufficient contact to answer'. The number of such responses was combined into an 'insufficient contact' score, which showed considerable variability among individual nurses and among hospitals. When asked whether they had ever sought information about infection control from the ICN, a majority (55 percent) reported that they had not or that they were unaware of such a position in the hospital. These relationships, of course, varied considerably with the other characteristics of the hospital. ICNs were apparently more likely to be visible in small hospitals, in those with larger numbers of staff per patient, and in those with medical school affiliations. Also, as might be expected, ICNs were more visible and available to nurses who worked on the day shifts than to those on night shifts. Analysis of all the responses of the staff nurses on this series of items resulted in the following four indices:

(1) Availability and example-setting qualities of the ICN (five items, such as 'Makes herself available for questions and discussions about infection control matters'; 'Is quiet and hardly noticeable when he/she makes the rounds on my ward' (scored negatively)).
(2) Active–didactic role (six items, such as 'Provides infection control information and explanations of policies which are clear and understandable'; 'Discusses infection control information in such a way that we are able to apply it to our patient care').
(3) Knowledgeability (two items: 'Does not seem to know what to do when outbreaks occur' (negative); 'Lacks information which would really be useful for infection control' (negative)).
(4) Personal abrasive qualities (two items: 'Is overbearing in discussions and questions when he /she comes on the ward', and 'Often puts people off with her/his discussion of the way they are observing infection control procedures').

The ICN's Perceptions of Herself and Infection Control

In the previous section we examined some measures of the manner in which the staff nurses see the ICN and their relationship to her. Our data also give

* Since only 6 percent of ICNs are men, we will refer to the holder of this position as 'her'.

measures of the ways in which the ICN perceives herself, the staff nurses, and the infection control problem.

It is well to keep in mind that 18 percent of the hospitals in the SENIC sample did not have a person formally assigned to the ICN position. In such cases the person, other than the HE, who was most knowledgeable and involved in that area was interviewed (Emori *et al.*, 1980). Of course, the 'most knowledgeable person' might not be expected to be as effective as someone formally appointed to the position of ICN, as our data bear out.

A series of items on our interview schedule asked how the ICN perceived and evaluated herself, her role, and her effectiveness in infection control. Considerable variation was found in the extent to which the ICN felt that she was doing a good job. A particularly sensitive measure was derived from a series of six items in which the ICN indicated the extent to which a replacement for her should have different characteristics (training, personal characteristics, personality), from herself. A score of six 'no's' would indicate that the ICN was very pleased with herself in her role. Other items asked how effective she felt she had been in implementing the program, how effective the program itself had been, and how effective she felt in influencing others.

A measure of internal/external control over infection control was developed from another four items, which essentially asked whether the ICN felt that infection control was largely a matter of chance or luck (external control), rather than a function of her own ability or contribution (internal control) (e.g. 'When infections are under control around here, I think it's due partly to a run of good luck.' 'Part of the time I feel that I have little influence over the kinds of problems which are brought to my attention.')

A number of the above items were related to one another, as one might expect. ICNs who felt that they were right for their job (that their replacement should have similar characteristics) were more likely to feel that they were aware of nosocomial infections when they occurred. Such ICNs were also rated as being visible and available by the nurses in their respective hospitals and as being helpful in dealing with hospital infection problems. ICNs who felt that they were personally effective were likely to see infection control as a matter of internal control, rather than a matter of whim or chance. Significantly related to a number of measures of perceived effectiveness was the ICN's belief that she could turn for support to the HE or the infection control chairperson assistance and counsel.

The Effects of Status on Compliance with Infection Control Policy

A question of particular interest is the extent to which hospital staff are, in fact, seen as complying with infection control policies, and, where there is non-compliance, which staff members are seen as violating policy. An overall measure of the extent to which nurses follow proper infection control policies was developed from a series of seven items which focused on isolation policy, proper method of care for patients with indewelling catheters, preparation of patients for abdominal or thoracic surgery, and proper use of intravenous catheters, A review of these items indicates that the perceived compliance with proper policy tends to be the rule rather than the exception.

Two items which measured the degree of compliance with isolation policy are presented in Table 17.1. We asked both staff nurses (and HEs or infection

Table 17.1 Mean reported adherence to isolation policy by various staff members

1. *As reported by staff nurses (n = 433)*

	Staff person				
Situation*	Attending physicians	Head nurses	Staff nurses	Laboratory technicians	Marginals
Skin infection	2.01	2.80	2.83	2.67	2.58
Tuberculosis	2.23	2.83	2.84	2.75	2.66
Marginals	2.12	2.82	2.84	2.71	2.62

2. *As reported by HEs (n = 406)*

	Staff person				
Situation*	Attending physicians	Head nurses	Staff nurses	Laboratory technicians	Marginals
Skin infection	2.04	2.84	2.82	2.73	2.61
Tuberculosis	2.30	2.89	2.88	2.84	2.73
Marginals	2.17	2.87	2.85	2.79	2.67

* The two situations were: (a) a patient with widespread skin infection with Group A streptococci, requiring that *all* who enter patient's room wear mask, gloves, and gown; (b) patient with tuberculosis, requiring that all entering wear masks. Responses ranged from 0 = 'definitely would not', to 3 = 'definitely would'.

Note: For both the nurses' responses and HEs' responses, all main effects and interaction effects were significant by repeated measures analysis of variance ($p < 0.001$).

control committee chairpersons) to rate the extent to which head nurses, staff nurses, attending physicians, and laboratory technicians adhered to policy in two hypothetical situations involving patients isolated with widespread skin infection and tuberculosis, respectively. As we can see, these staff members were rated as being almost certain to comply (2.6 on a scale from 0 to 3). However, there was some difference between compliance of attending physicians and others, with the attending physicians being rated as 'probably' rather than 'definitely' complying. Lest this be seen as a bias in the perception of nurse respondents, we note that the ratings by the HEs (physicians themselves) are very similar.

Readiness to Take Action with Violators of Infection Control Policy

Here we will focus particularly upon differential actions related to the status of the violators. To assess such tendencies, questions were included in the interview schedule for the ICNs and in the questionnaires for the staff nurses. The ICNs were asked, 'On your ward rounds you may have observed members of the staff not following good infection control practices. How often would you say something to the staff member about the following incidents?' Three incidents were included: 'Entering a strict isolation room without masking; discarding an unprotected hypodermic needle in a wastebasket; after handling a contaminated dressing or article, proceeding to a "clean" procedure without first washing your hands.' The hypothetical violators were either head nurses, staff nurses, attending physicians, or laboratory technicians. Responses could range from 0 = 'in few or no instances', to 3 = 'in every instance'. As we see in Table 17.2, the overall means indicate that ICNs report that, as a rule, they *would* speak up to the violator in nearly every instance (mean = 2.68), though there is some variation as a function of the type of violation and the status of the target.

Table 17.2 Readiness of ICN to speak up to violator as function of status and violation (means*; $n = 431$)

Violation	Target person				
	Attending physician	Head nurse	Staff nurse	Laboratory technician	Marginals
Enter a strict isolation room without masking	2.08	2.77	2.79	2.72	2.59
Discard an unprotected hypodermic needle in the wastebasket	2.47	2.84	2.85	2.82	2.74
After handling a contaminated dressing or article, proceed to a 'clean' procedure without first washing your hands	2.30	2.85	2.86	2.78	2.70

* Means are based on responses of the ICN to the question: 'On your ward rounds you may have observed members of the staff not following good infection control practices. How often would you say something to the staff member about the following incidents?' Scores ranged from 0 = 'in few or no instances', to 3 = 'in every instance'.

Note: Main effects for target person and violation variables and interaction effects were all significant ($p < 0.001$) by repeated measures analysis of variance (BMDP2V).

Again, we find that attending physicians are least likely to be spoken to. Head nurses, staff nurses, and laboratory technicians are more likely to be spoken to, and there is no substantial difference in tendency to take action with respect to any of these three target persons.

In a parallel question, ICNs and HEs were presented with hypothetical situations of nurses and physicians violating policy. In this question the respondents were asked, 'Would you request that other hospital staff do something about it, or deal directly with the (physician, nurse)?' In this case there were striking differences between the answers of the ICNs and those of the HEs. Eighty-six percent of the HEs said that they would deal directly with the physicians who violated policy, while only 40 percent said that they would deal directly with nurses. For the ICNs there was a greater tendency overall to deal directly with violators, but such direct action was less likely with physicians (65 percent) than with nurses (83 percent). Since the ICNs were generally nurses and the HEs physicians, the data suggest a greater tendency to deal directly with members of one's own profession. As we shall see, there are similar tendencies reported by staff nurses.

The effects of the status of violator on the actions of the observer are also evident in the reports of staff nurses. In this case the nurses were presented with three hypothetical situations in which they saw hospital personnel:

(1) disconnecting a urinary catheter in order to take a urine specimen (though not discouraged in all hospitals, this is clearly a violation of published guidelines, since opening the catheter usually allows the entrance of bacteria);
(2) performing various duties with a boil on their arms, a possible source of infection; and
(3) handling an infected wound or dressing and then proceeding to handle a patient without first washing their hands.

In some cases, the hypothetical violator was another staff nurse, in others an attending physician or some other hospital staff member (aide, housekeeper, or orderly). Would they speak up to the violator? As we can see in Table 17.3a, the mean overall responses indicate that the staff nurses believe that they were more likely to speak up than not speak up; although, again, it was far from certain that such action would be taken. Furthermore, when physicians were the violators, the mean responses fell on the 'probably would *not* say something' side of the scale. The effect of the status of the target on likelihood of saying something is highly statistically significant.

A second part of the question asked: 'If you decided *not* to speak directly to the person . . . would you report them to a staff supervisor or other hospital authority?' Comparing the means in Tables 17.3a and 17.3b, we note that staff nurses report different preferences for speaking directly versus reporting, as a function of the status of the violator. If the violator is a physician

Table 17.3 Mean* likelihood of staff nurses' speaking up to or reporting†
violators of differing status

(a) *Mean likelihood of speaking up to violators* (*n* = 7137)

Violation	Violators			
	Attending physician	Staff nurse	Other	Marginals
Disconnecting catheter	0.84	1.41	1.58	1.28
Performing patient care with boil on arm	0.78	1.56	1.41	1.25
Failing to wash hands between dealing with patients	1.20	1.83	1.93	1.65
Marginals	0.94	1.60	1.64	1.39

(b) *Mean likelihood of reporting violators* (*n* = 6903)

Violation	Violators			
	Attending physician	Staff nurse	Other	Marginals
Disconnecting catheter	1.02	1.06	1.36	1.15
Performing patient care with boil on arm	1.25	1.50	1.50	1.42
Failing to wash hands between dealing with patients	1.50	1.65	1.63	1.60
Marginals	1.26	1.40	1.50	1.39

* Based on nurses' responses to question regarding whether they would say
something to or report another nurse, a physician, or other hospital personnel
(aide, housekeeper, orderly): (a) improperly disconnecting a catheter to collect a
urine specimen; (b) performing duties with patients with a boil on their arm; (c)
handling a contaminated dressing or wound and then proceeding to care for
patients without washing hands. Responses ranged from 0 = 'Probably would not
say something to (or report) . . .', to 2 = 'Probably would say something to (or
report) . . .'.
   † Respondents in this question indicated 'if you decided·not to speak directly to
the person . . . would you report them to a staff supervisor or other hospital
authority'.

Note: All main effects and interaction effects significant by repeated measures
analysis of variance ($p < 0.001$).

they are more likely to report than to speak to directly; if the violator is a staff
nurse or other staff member the preference is to speak to the violator directly.
Nevertheless, the staff nurses would be less likely even to report the violator
if the violator is a physician rather than another staff member.

One might have expected that talking to the violator or reporting a violator would be alternative strategies—that a respondent who does not speak up to a violator would be more likely to report him instead. Thus, we would have expected a negative correlation between these two strategies. Instead, we find a positive correlation ($r = 0.55$; $p < 0.001$)—staff nurses who say they would speak up to a violator also say that they would report violators. For the three items in which the physician was seen violating policy, an average of 54.6 percent of the staff nurses reported that they would probably either say something to the physician or report the violation to a third party—thus, nearly half could not say with certainty that they would take any action.

A measure of assertiveness of nurses was constructed from the nine items which measured the readiness of staff nurses to speak up to violators of infection control policy. A factor analysis indicated that these nine items (three status levels by three violation situations) were sufficiently intercorrelated so that they could constitute one scale (Stevens *et al.*, 1979). A similar scale was constructed from the parallel series of items, indicating assertiveness in reporting a violator to other authorities. We will discuss these two assertiveness measures at later stages of this chapter, but we might note here that nurses are most likely to speak up to a violator of prescribed patient-care practice if the nurse reports that she herself practices the correct technique, and alternatively she is quite unlikely to speak up to the violator if she herself would violate the prescribed practice. The assertiveness of staff nurses was also significantly higher in hospitals in which the staff nurses reported that the ICN was visible and available, where the staff nurses were familiar with the ICN control nurse and her job, and where the ICN was someone whom they felt that they could turn to if théy had an infection control question or problem. Such assertiveness was also correlated with nurses seeing other nurses as complying with isolation policy in the hospital. A number of other relationships to these assertiveness measures have been presented elsewhere (Redfearn, 1980; Reeder and Stevens, 1980; Stevens *et al.*, 1979).

The Perceived Power of the ICN to Influence Others

A key factor in the effectiveness of the ICN would seem to be her belief in her ability to influence others to comply with infection control policy. We therefore included in our interview schedule several questions aimed at measuring this perception. In one series we asked ICNs: '. . . suppose that on the basis of strong recommendations of leading research organizations the following were adopted as policies in this hospital . . . how successful would you be in getting the hospital staff to comply with the policy?' There followed a series of six hypothetical policy changes affecting nurses, physicians, and other staff members, such as 'All nurses must wear a hairstyle that is neatly combed and "off the collar" while on duty; all X-ray tables must be disinfected after each patient; use of antibiotics by physicians must be

SOCIAL PSYCHOLOGY AND BEHAVIORAL MEDICINE

reviewed regularly by the chairperson of the infection control committee', with possible ratings of 'very successful' (2), 'somewhat successful' (1), or 'not at all successful' (0). An overall score for all six questions was developed to represent perceptions of ability to influence others. As with our earlier items there was an overall tendency for ICNs to believe that they would be somewhat successful in effecting compliance (mean = 1.07), the ICNs believing, however, that they would be significantly less successful in influencing physicians (mean = 0.80) than nurses (mean = 1.20). The status comparison, however, must be considered cautiously, since the types of hypothetical changes in behavior differed somewhat for the three target groups.

Our interview schedule also included two single items which measured the ICN's perceived success in influencing physicians and nurses. ICNs were asked to indicate the degree of agreement (from 'strongly disagree' (0) to 'strongly agree' (3)) with the statements:

(1) 'it is sometimes difficult to have much influence over an established physician's compliance with infection control procedures';
(2) 'success in obtaining a nurse's compliance with infection control procedures sometimes is more a matter of the nurse's mood and feelings at the time than the effectiveness of any actions on my part.'

Overall, the ICNs tended to agree with the first (mean = 2.1) and to disagree with the second (mean = 1.3). These two single items showed the expected negative correlations with the previous items on compliance. Though, in both sets of questions, the ICNs generally felt that it was more difficult to influence physicians than nurses, those ICNs who felt capable of influencing nurses also felt more capable of influencing physicians. The ICNs' confidence in their ability to influence specific staff persons is also reflected in their feelings of internal control over the infection control situation—internal control is positively correlated with being able to influence nurses and physicians, and is negatively correlated with finding such influence difficult.

The ICN's evaluation of her ability to influence nurses is also reflected in the staff nurses' perceptions of the ICN. When the ICN believes she can effectively influence staff nurses, the nurses tend to report that she is helpful in infection matters and fulfills an active–didactic role ($p = 0.03$).

Bases of Power Utilized by ICNs

In a series of preliminary informal interviews conducted during the development of the interview survey forms, we asked ICNs what methods they would use in influencing staff nurses and other hospital staff members to follow infection control policy. The anecdotal responses were sometimes brief and undeveloped ('I simply tell them and expect that they will follow through . . .'), but at other times they represented a carefully planned strategy with alternative methods depending on the degree of success in initial attempts. Some ICNs emphasized subtle diplomacy and indirect influence approaches; others suggested that if their first request was not successful they would refer the matter to higher authority for more drastic action. One ICN reported that she would always base her requests on 'hard data' and careful instruction, and would always back up her requests with facts. Others reported that they would like to have used 'tougher methods' if these were backed up by the hospital authorities. As later supported by our statistical data, there seemed a clear indication that ICNs felt that they would be less successful in influencing physicians than in influencing staff nurses. Sometimes the frustration in dealing with physicians was quite evident. Several ICNs reported that indirect approaches and diplomacy were particularly important in dealing with physicians. For example, one reported that rather than informing a physician that he should be wearing his gloves, she would instead quietly hand him his gloves, presumably suggesting that she was merely assisting him in his examination.

Unfortunately, it was not possible to tap the more elaborate influence strategies in the large field survey, nor could we include all of the variety of influence attempts in our fixed alternative questions. We, therefore, limited ourselves to six bases of power which have been presented in greater detail elsewhere (French and Raven, 1959; Raven, 1974; Raven and Rubin, 1976). As in French and Raven (1959), social power is defined in terms of social influence. *Social influence* is a change in the cognitions, attitudes, or behavior of a person (target) which is attributable to the actions of another person (influencing agent). The *social power* of the agent over the target is then simply defined as the *potential* ability to exert such influence. The six bases of power can be illustrated below by the alternatives which we presented to ICNs as possible means which we might use to change the behavior of a nurse who 'repeatedly breaks technique and exposes patients to a high risk of infection.'

(1) *Coercive power* is that which stems from the ability of the influencing agent to mediate punishment for the target: 'Warn the nurse of possible disciplinary action or possible dismissal.'

(2) *Reward power* stems from the ability to mediate rewards: 'Point out to the nurse that your evaluations carry some weight; that you might be able to help the nurse in the future.'

(3) *Legitimate power* grows out of the target's acceptance of a role relationship with the agent that obligates the target to comply with the request of the agent: 'Emphasize your position as ICN and the nurse's obligation to comply with your recommendation in this matter.'

(4) *Referent power* occurs when the target uses others as a 'frame of reference', as a standard for evaluating his/her behavior: 'Emphasize that other nurses in the hospital follow proper procedures.'

(5) *Expert power* stems from the target's attributing superior knowledge or ability to the agent—in other words, the agent knows best, knows what is correct. 'Emphasize your expertise regarding infection control procedures.'

(6) *Informational power* is a result of the persuasiveness of the information communicated by the agent to the target; 'Indicate the basis for techniques, citing available evidence, hospital data, or journal references, and so forth.'

The ICN was asked to rate each of these bases of power on a three-point scale of 'very likely' (2), 'somewhat likely' (1), and 'unlikely' (0) and then to select the basis of power which she was most likely to use. She was also asked to rate these bases on a three-point scale of 'very effective' (2), 'somewhat effective' (1), and 'ineffective' (0) and to select the most effective base. A parallel set of six social-power alternatives was then presented for dealing with a physician who, counter to established hospital policy, refuses (on grounds of psychological damage) to isolate a paitent with hepatitis. A third set of questions asked how the ICNs would deal with a head of the inhalation therapy department when evidence indicates that the department is lax in its cleaning of inhalation therapy equipment. The data for the inhalation therapy items parallel closely those for the physician and will not be discussed further in this chapter. For all three target persons we found high and significant correlations between the ratings of likelihood and ratings of effectiveness for each of the social influence strategies. Thus, we will limit our discussion here to the ratings of likelihood.

The likelihood of use of each of the six power bases for the nurse and physician violator are presented in Table 17.4. Overall, informational power is preferred, followed by expert and referent power. Reward power seems least preferred, and coercive power also is not seen as very likely. In comparing the use of power in influencing staff nurses as compared to physicians, we find highly significant interaction effects. Though informational power is seen as most likely in dealing with both targets, expert power is a second choice in influencing physicians, while referent and legitimate power come in second when dealing with nurses. That expert power is seen as so likely in dealing with physicians is somewhat surprising. It may be that the ICNs believe that they can best rely on their training in epidemiology and formal education in infection control to convince physicians that they know best when it comes to questions on infections; this base is further strengthened by the fact that hospital epidemiology has generally not been included in the curricula of medical schools or postgraduate medical training programs (Neu, 1978; Eickhoff, 1978). However, it may also be that their choice of expert power is due to their seeing other means of influence (especially coercion and reward) as being quite ineffective in dealing with physicians, so

Table 17.4 ICNs' reports of use of differing power bases in influencing nurses and physicians. Likelihood of use (means*; $n = 427$)

Power base	Target person		
	Physician	Nurse	Marginals
Coercive	0.17	0.71	0.44
Reward	0.06	0.57	0.32
Legitimate	0.65	0.86	0.76
Expert	1.54	0.70	1.12
Referent	0.88	0.86	0.87
Informational	1.79	1.88	1.84
Marginals	0.85	0.93	0.89

* Scores ranged from 0 = 'unlikely', to 2 = 'very likely'.
Note: Main effects and interaction effects significant by repeated measures analysis of variance ($p < 0.001$) (BMDP2V).

that expertise is one of their few remaining choices. When dealing with nurses it appears that the ICNs feel that they have access to a greater variety of influence strategies. While they do not see expertise as being influential in dealing with nurses (it is their fourth choice), they see legitimacy as more likely, and even coercive and reward power are in the realm of possibility when dealing with nurses.

After the ICNs rated each basis of power in terms of how likely they would be to use it and how effective they felt that basis of power would be they were then asked to pick the one basis which they would be most likely to use and the one which they would consider most effective. Given the focus of this chapter, we describe here only the data relative to a staff nurse target. As we see in Table 17.5, paralleling the ratings, informational power was ranked as most likely and most effective. There are again some discrepancies between these two choices—17.8 percent of the ICNs felt that coercive power was most effective, while only 5.6 percent rated it as most likely to be used. This discrepancy supports the findings of an earlier study (Rosenberg and Pearlin, 1962) on the choice of bases of power in a hospital setting; these investigators' subsequent interview indicated that the use of coercive power did not correspond to its rated effectiveness because it was seen as involving too much effort.

Even more striking is the discrepancy between reported usages of social power by ICNs and the effectiveness of such usage as reported by staff nurses (Table 17.5). Staff nurses were asked: 'Suppose the ICN . . . recommends that you change the procedures you are using for collecting specimens from indwelling urinary catheters. Which one of the following would be the *most*

Table 17.5 Percentage of ICNs who rate each power base as most likely and most effective in influencing staff nurses; percentage of staff nurses who rate each power base as most effective in influencing them

Power base	ICNs' ratings (%)		Staff nurses' ratings (%)
	Most likely ($n = 431$)	Most effective ($n = 432$)	Most effective ($n = 7069$)
Coercive	5.6	17.8	0.3
Reward	1.8	2.5	0.1
Legitimate	5.6	3.5	2.1
Expert	0.9	0.5	56.1
Referent	1.4	0.9	4.4
Informational	84.7	74.1	36.9

likely reason why you might go along with what the ICN recommended?' The social influence situation presented to the staff nurses, we should note, is somewhat more specific than that presented to ICNs (changing the behavior of a nurse who 'breaks technique'), and our comparison should be made with this in mind. However the differences are nonetheless striking: less than 1 percent of the ICNs say that they would be most likely to rely on their expert power to influence staff nurses or see it as the most effective. They would rely overwhelmingly on informational power. The majority (56.1 percent) of the staff nurses, by contrast, say that if they complied with the ICN's request it would be because of her expert power; a much smaller 36.9 percent say that the information imparted by the ICN would be most influential.

One would ordinarily expect that a person who selects a given power base in influencing the target does so because she/he feels that it would be the most effective and most economical method of bringing about change. There are, of course, other factors which enter into such a decision. As Rosenberg and Pearlin (1962) indicated, sometimes we will not use the basis of power which we consider most effective because we feel that it is too much trouble. There is also some indication that our own sense of insecurity or lack of confidence may effect our choice (Kipnis, 1976; Raven and Kruglanski, 1970; Raven and Rubin, 1976). A person who does not have self-confidence may feel that he/she will not be able effectively to present a persuasive case to a target. Or a more subtle factor may operate: a person with low self-confidence or self-esteem may increase feelings of power by using a stronger basis of influence. If we present information to a target and the target is thereby influenced, the locus of control still appears to come from the target—he/she listens to our information and then exercises a choice to change on the basis of the information. If we threaten the target, or if we appeal to our legitimate authority, and we observe the target complying, then we can assume that the locus of control is in ourselves—the target does not seem to have much choice in the matter (Litman-Adizes *et al.*, 1978). In our current study we did find some evidence in line with such an interpretation. ICNs who felt secure in their position (who felt that any replacement should have the same characteristics that they have) were significantly more likely to say that they would use informational power in influencing others; they would be less likely to say that they would use coercive power or legitimate power.

Staff Nurses' Compliance with Potentially Inappropriate Requests from Physicians

Our discussion thus far has focused upon the exercise and effectiveness of social influence which would tend to decrease infection risks. In our preliminary informal interview in the survey design phase, we heard of occasional instances in which physicians would request other staff members to engage in activities that were counter to the hospital's infection control policy and that would tend to *increase* risk of infection. On the basis of these early interviews, we included in our nurses' questionnaire three hypothetical situations in which physicians might make such requests:

(1) a doctor writes a transfer order to move a child out of isolation for psychological reasons even though the child still had a staphylococcal infection which was oozing pus;
(2) a doctor needs to send a patient's urine specimen to the laboratory immediately and instructs you to continue with a catheterization even though the doctor is aware that you have accidentally contaminated the catheter;
(3) a doctor asks you to allow a child to keep a pet turtle in his room as a morale booster despite a hospital policy which prohibits turtles because of the risk of salmonella.

We asked the respondents: '. . . how frequently do you feel doctors in fact ask nurses to carry out practices such as these which are against hospital policy?' In response to this item, 5 percent of the nurses responded that doctors do make such requests 'frequently', 33 percent responded 'sometimes', 62 percent 'rarely or almost never'. When asked how frequently they would comply with such requests which appeared to them to be against hospital policy, 11 percent replied 'almost always', 19 percent 'frequently', 44 percent 'sometimes', and 27 percent 'rarely or never'. Such a finding is consistent with an earlier field experiment by Hofling *et al.* (1966) in which it was found that, on a telephone order from a physician, 21 of 22 nurses were prepared to give a patient medication that was far beyond the maximum dosage clearly indicated on the medicine bottle. (The nurses were, of course, interrupted before they could actually administer the medication.)

The staff nurse respondents were also asked for each of the three

Table 17.6 Nurses' reports of compliance (%) with improper orders from physicians—individual situations

| | Situation | | |
Response category	Transfer patient out of isolation although still infectious	Continue with contaminated catheterization	Allow child to keep per turtle ' in room
Follow order	2.6	4.2	4.3
Follow order, express reservations	36.7	18.3	20.1
Refuse, state reasons	57.1	41.6	62.0
Just refuse	3.6	35.9	13.6
(n)	(7066)	(7131)	(7089)

hypothetical situations, what they personally would do when asked to perform these activities. The results are presented in Table 17.6. We note that the majority report that they personally would refuse in each case, some stating their reasons, the refusals ranging from 60.7 percent to 77.5 percent. However, the fact that an average 28.7 percent reported that they would comply with policies that would clearly seem to place patients at risk, gives grounds for concern. Of course the responsibility of the physician to determine in an individual case the course of action most conductive to patients' well-being must be considered: sometimes mitigating circumstances may require a physician to countermand hospital infection control policy because of a more immediate threat to life or health and in such cases the nurses should rightly comply.

This medical prerogative was indeed supported by our data. We specifically asked nurses why they would comply with inappropriate requests from physicians, again using the six bases of power. The results paralleled and were, indeed, significantly correlated with, the reasons given for complying with the ICN's appropriate request. The most frequently reported basis for compliance was the expert power of the physician (46.2 percent) followed by informational power (40.1 percent). A distant third was coercive power ('. . . if I didn't the doctor might make things difficult or unpleasant for me'), seen as the most likely reason by only 5.3 percent of the respondents. That such coercive power, though an uncommonly stated reason, is nonetheless a significant factor, is attested by several other significant correlations: reported degree of compliance with a physician's inappropriate request is positively correlated with the indication that coercive power is a significant factor. Attributed coercive power is also positively correlated with a six-item index which measures the extent to which nurses believe physicians will indicate displeasure if a nurse informs them of their errors, or otherwise shows assertiveness.

Elsewhere (Redfearn 1979a, 1979b, and 1980), data show that the degree of compliance with a physician's inappropriate request is negatively correlated with the extent to which the staff nurse is educated and knowledgeable about infection control policy. Of particular interest is the finding that it is not only the individual staff nurse's characteristics that are important but also the characteristics of other nurses who comprise the hospital staff. If the *other* nurses are knowledgeable and assertive and tend to resist the inappropriate requests of the physician, then the individual nurse will be similarly assertive and non-acquiescent (Redfearn 1980).

Effects on Practices which Minimize Infection Risk

The major concern of the SENIC study was to determine the extent to which various factors in the hospital affect behavior of staff members which, in turn, would tend to minimize the risk of infection. Ultimately, we plan to relate hospital policies and practices to actual infection rate data. For the present we have developed a 'Preventive Patient-Care Practices' (PPCP) index from responses in the staff nurses' questionnaire. This is composed of a series of seven items which deal with techniques for collecting urine specimens from catheterized patients, handling the catheters when the patient ambulates, routine irrigation of indwelling catheters, handwashing before urinary catheterization, frequency of replacing intravenous administration sets, and teaching preoperative patients proper breathing techniques to be used after surgery. The questions were constructed on the basis of information from CDC's infection control experts, which indicated that these are practices that nurses sometimes perform incorrectly. The CDC experts also provided the correct answers to these questions, so that we could score each nurse's response from zero to seven on the extent to which she engages in correct practices. As we examine this PPCP measure in relation to other data in our study, an interesting pattern develops.

First, it seems that when a staff nurse reports that she is aware of, and follows, proper infection control practices, she is also more likely to say that she would speak up to others who violate policy or to report them to hospital authorities. In addition, her relationship with the ICN is closer—there is a greater tendency to recognize the ICN when she sees her on the ward, she is more likely to be able to answer questions about her (a significantly negative correlation with the 'insufficient contact' measure), and she more likely knows what the ICN's job entails. The nurse also is more likely to see the ICN as available as a model ($p = 0.002$), sees her as playing an active–didactic role ($p = 0.008$), and feels that she can turn to her for information about infection control problems.

From the ICN's perspective, there are parallel findings in a significant correlation between the PPCP measure and the ICN's feeling that she has been personally effective in reducing infections ($p = 0.002$) and that she has the qualities which are necessary for her job ($p = 0.01$). The nurses' reports that they are following proper practices is also positively correlated with the ICN's feeling that she has the support of the HE and/or infection control committee chairperson ($p = 0.03$), and that she has the authority to take independent infection control action when a patient's physician is not present ($p = 0.005$). In terms of the bases of power that the ICN utilizes we find staff nurses reporting more correct patient-care practices when the ICN deals with them with informational power, giving them reasons for complying with proper policies ($p = 0.002$)—the PPCP measure is negatively correlated with the ICN's seeing legitimate and coercive power as effective means of implementing policy.

Summary and Discussion

Our discussion examines the social influence factors which might affect the extent to which patients in hospitals are exposed to the risk of nosocomical infection. In contrast to earlier approaches to preventing these infections, which emphasized medical remedies or changes in the physical environment, evidence indicates that in many instances it is more valuable to examine why some hospitals are more effective than others in influencing staff members to carry on their activities in line with policies that have been demonstrated to reduce infection risks. In this paper we focused upon the social influence variables which affect the behavior of staff nurses, particularly in their interaction with the ICN, a key member of the ISCP staff. Our data indicate that an important factor in this interaction is.the degree and form in which the ICN is available to the staff nurses. Hospitals which do not have a regularly designated ICN are, of course, handicapped in implementing an infection surveillance and control program. Not infrequently, however, an appointed ICN is not seen as playing an active role: she is not recognizable to the nurses; they are less likely to know what her job entails; they do not know her well enough to answer specific questions about her; and they do not see her as available for consultation or playing an active, didactic role. In such cases, it appears from our present analysis that staff nurses are less likely to comply with hospital policies.

The activities and effectiveness of the ICN are reflected in her view of herself, her role in infection control, and the infection control problem itself. If the ICN did not see herself as effective, felt that she had not been too successful in implementing an infection-control program, and felt that she did not have the characteristics which were best for her position, such a negative evaluation seemed related to the staff nurses' perception that she was not as readily available and effective on several of the measures which we had described. Related to these, in turn, was a tendency on the part of the ICN to rate infection control as externally caused—that is, to see infections as a matter of chance or luck or due to factors over which one has little control. Since we have presented a correlational analysis, we cannot be certain as to the relative importance of the multiple apparent influencing factors or the direction of causality: does the ICN's perception of her efficacy affect her interaction with nurses, which in turn leads them to feel that she is not available or effective, or is the reverse the case?

An important variable in determining compliance with hospital infection control policies is the status of the hospital staff member. Our data indicate that hospital physicians are seen as less likely to comply with the hospital's isolation policies than are other hospital staff members. Perhaps one might say that their higher levels of training would justify their using discretion in determining whether a particular hospital policy is indeed necessary in a given instance. However, our informal interviews suggested that such flexibility is a matter of some concern for hospital infection control officers. It is also of concern that both staff nurses and ICNs are less likely to speak up to a physician, as compared with other staff members who violate infection control policy, and indeed are more reluctant to report the physician violator to other authorities. Furthermore, when physicians requests that staff nurses carry out activities which are clearly counter to infection control policy and which would tend to increase infection risk, most staff nurses report that they would not comply, but a sizable minority (as many as 39 percent in some cases) report that they would follow orders, though usually expressing reservations while doing so. In explanation of their compliance, staff nurses most frequently report that this is due to the expertise which they attribute to the physician. In this regard, one might suggest that an approach to reducing the infection risk in hospitals would entail an educational program for physicians which would make them more aware of the necessity for infection control policies and a program for staff members encouraging them to question requests to engage in activities that tend to increase infection risk. However, one might also hope that the social power of the physician could be harnessed in the direction of fostering a greater overall compliance with infection control policy in the hospital.

In influencing violators of infection control policy, ICNs reported that they were most likely to use informational power—giving the target the reason for compliance; they were also most likely to consider informational power as most effective. The use of expert power was also rated quite highly, followed by referent power. The choice of power base differed, however, with differing targets. Expert power was a strong second choice in influencing physicians, but referent and legitimate power were rated second for dealing with nurses. Of particular note is the finding that while expert power is not rated very highly by ICNs in dealing with staff nurses, staff nurses are especially likely to attribute their compliance to the expertise of the ICN. It would seem appropriate to make ICNs aware of this discrepancy and suggest that a greater reliance on their status as experts in their dealing with staff nurses might be called for—or, perhaps, their use of informational power could be improved by making their persuasive communications more effective, e.g. systematic development and use of informational materials on a broad range of commonly encountered subjects. It is interesting theoretically to find that when coercive and legitimate power are selected by an ICN, such usage is correlated with a general feeling of insecurity and inefficiency, while use of informational power is correlated with a more positive self-evaluation. Such results are consistent with previous research by Kipnis (1976).

From these findings we would hope that we could gain greater theoretical understanding of the operations of social influence in hospital settings, and also begin to develop guidelines for the improved social influence processes in the implementation of hospital infection surveillance and control programs.

References

American Hospital Association (1968). *Infection Control in the Hospital*, 1st edn, AHA, Chicago, Ill.

American Hospital Association, Committee on Infections Within Hospitals (1974). 'Statement on microbiologic sampling in the hospital', *Hospitals, Journal of the American Hospital Association*, **48,** 125–126.

Bennett, J. V. (1978). 'Human infections: economic implications and prevention', *Annals of Internal Medicine* (Supplement), **89,** 761–763.

Bennett, J. V., Scheckler, W. E., Maki, D. G., and Brachman, P. S. (1971). 'Current national patterns, United States', in *Proceedings of the International Conference on Nosocomial Infections*, pp. 42–49. Center for Disease Control, Atlanta, GA.

Center for Disease Control (1968). 'Outline for Survillance and Control of Nosocomial Infections'. CDC, Atlanta, GA.

Communicable Disease Center (now Center for Disease Control) (1958). 'Hospital-Acquired Staphylococcal Disease', in *Proceedings of the National Conference on Nosocomial Infections*. Atlanta, GA.

Dixon, R. E. (1978). 'Effect of infections on hospital care', *Annals of Internal Medicine*, **89** (2), 749–753.

Eickhoff, T. C. (1975). 'Nosocomial infections', *American Journal of Epidemiology*, **101,** 93–97.

Eickhoff, T. C. (1978). 'Standards for Hospital Infection Control', *Annals of Internal Medicine* (Supplement), **89,** 829–831.

Eickhoff, T. C. (1979). 'Antibiotics and nosocomial infections', in Bennett, J. V., and Brachman, P. S. (eds), *Hospital Infections*, pp. 195–221. Little, Brown, Boston.

Emori, T. G., Haley, R. W., and Stanley, R. C. (1980). 'The infection control nurse in the U.S. hospitals, 1976–1977: characteristics of the position and its occupant', *American Journal of Epidemiology*, **111,** 592–607.

Haley, R. W., Quade, D., Freeman, H. E., Bennett, J. V., and the CDC SENIC Planning Committee (1980). 'The study of the efficacy of nosocomial infection control (SENIC Project): summary of study design', *American Journal of Epidemiology*, **111,** 472–485.

Haley, R. W., and Shachtman, R. H. (1980). 'The emergence of infection surveillance and control programs in U.S. hospitals: an assessment, 1976', *American Journal of Epidemiology*, **111**, 574–591.

Hewitt, W. L., and Sanford, J. P. (1974). 'National Institutes of Health workshop on hospital-associated infections', *Journal of Infectious Diseases*, **130**, 680–686.

Hofling, C. K., Brotzman, E., Dalrymple, S., Graves, N., and Pierce, C. M. (1966). 'An experimental study in nurse–physician relationship', *Journal of Nervous and Mental Diseases*, **143**, 171–180.

Joint Commission on the Accreditation of Hospitals (1976). 'Infection control', in *Accreditation Manual for Hospitals*, pp. 49–56.

Kipnis, D. (1976). *The Powerholders*. University of Illinois Press, Chicago, Ill.

Litman-Adizes, T., Fontaine, G., and Raven, B. H. (1978). 'Consequences of social power and causal attributions for compliance as seen by powerholder and target', *Personality and Social Psychology Bulletin*, **4** (2), 260–264.

Mallison, G. F. (1979). 'The inanimate environment', in Bennett, J. V., and Brachman, P. S. (eds), *Hospital Infections*, pp. 81–92. Little, Brown, Boston, Mass.

Misumi, J. (1974). 'Action research on the development of leadership, decision making processes and organizational performance in a Japanese shipyard'. Paper presented at the 19th International Congress of Applied Psychology, Munich, Federal Republic of Germany.

Neu, H. C. (1978). 'How is the medical student being trained in microbiology and infection?', *Annals of Internal Medicine* (Supplement), **89**, 818–820.

Polakavetz, S. H., Dunn, M. E., and Cook, J. S. (1978). 'Nosocomial infection: the hidden cost in health care', *Hospitals, Journal of American Hospital Association*, **52**, 101–106.

Raven, B. H. (1974). 'The comparative analysis of power and power preference', in Tedeschi, J. T. (ed.), *Perspectives on Social Power*. Aldine-Atherton, Chicago, Ill.

Raven, B. H., Freeman, H. E., and Haley, R. W. (1981). 'Social sciences perspectives in hospital infection control', in Johnson, A. W., Grusky, O., and Raven, B. H. (eds.), *Contemporary Health Services: a Social Science Perspective*. Auburn House, Boston, Mass.

Raven, B. H., and Haley, R. W. (1980). 'Social influence in a medical context: hospital-acquired infections as a problem in medical social psychology', in Bickman, L. (ed.), *Applied Social Psychology Annual*, vol. 1. Sage Publications Beverly Hills, California.

Raven, B. H., and Kruglanski, A. W. (1970). 'Conflict and power', in Swingle, P. G. (ed.), *The Structure of Conflict*, pp. 69–109. Academic Press, New York.

Raven, B. H., and Rubin, J. Z. (1976). *Social Psychology: People in Groups*. Wiley, New York.

Redfearn, D. J. (1979a). 'Individual-level and group-level determinants of nurses' compliance with physicians' inappropriate medical orders.' Paper presented at the Annual Convention of the American Psychological Association New York, 2 September.

Redfearn, D. J. (1979b). 'The application of hierarchical analysis techniques to hospital data'. Paper presented at the Annual Convention of the American Psychological Association, New York, 2 September.

Redfearn, D. J. (1980). 'Exploration in hierarchical analysis: Determining individual-level and group-level predictors of nurses' compliance with physicians' inappropriate orders.' Unpublished doctoral dissertation, University of California, Los Angeles.

Reeder, S. J., and Stevens, S. (1980). 'Assertive behavior in nurses and collegial staff relations: Implications for patient care practices.' Unpublished manuscript. UCLA Institute for Social Science Research, Los Angeles.

Rosenberg, M., and Pearlin, L. I. (1962). 'Power-orientations in the mental hospital', *Human Relations*, **15,** 335–349.

Sencer, D. J., and Axnick, N. W. (1976). 'Utilization of cost/benefit analysis in planning prevention programs', *Acta Medica Scandinavica*, **556,** (Supplement), 123–128.

Simmons, H. E. (1972). Testimony at hearings of the U.S. Senate Committee on Small Business. *Advertising of Proprietary Medicines. Part 3: Cough and Cold Remedies, Misuse of Antibiotics,* 5–8 and 13–14 December. 92nd Congress, pp. 1041–1042. Government Printing Office, Washington, DC.

Spengler, R. F., and Greenough, W. B. (1978). 'Hospital costs and mortality attributed to nosocomial bacteremia', *Journal of the American Medical Association*, **240** (22), 2455–2458.

Stevens, S., Reeder, S., Yokopenic, P., and Rakow, S. (1979). 'Nurse assertiveness and patient-care practices.' Paper presented at the Annual Meetings of the American Psychological Association, New York, 2 September.

Trist, E. L., and Bamforth, K. W. (1951). 'Social psychological consequences of the longwall method of goal-setting'. *Human Relations*, **4,** 3–38.

PART V

Reactions to Illness, Treatment, Aging, and Bereavement

Social Psychology and Behavioral Medicine
Edited by J. Richard Eiser
© 1982 John Wiley & Sons Ltd

Chapter 18

Placebo effects in medical research and practice

MICHAEL ROSS and JAMES M. OLSON

A placebo is a substance or procedure that is administered with suggestions that it will modify a symptom or sensation, but which, unknown to its recipient, has no specific pharmacological impact on the reaction in question. A placebo effect occurs when the administration of the placebo alters the recipient's condition in accordance with its presumed impact.

The medical profession has viewed standard placebo effects as a psychological phenomenon. Because such effects, by definition, are not caused by the pharmacological impact of the administered substance, explanations have involved psychological concepts such as expectancies, faith, and demands. Moreover, placebo effects are similar to phenomena that have been studied in the psychological literature, including self-fulfilling prophecies, expectancy effects, and demand characteristics.

In this chapter, we examine the nature of placebo effects and the psychological processes that underlie them. In so doing, we address the following issues:

(1) How pervasive are placebo effects?
(2) What accounts for the variation in the magnitude of placebo effects?
(3) By what mechanisms do placebos produce their effects?
(4) Finally, can (and should) placebo effects be utilized deliberately in medical practice?

Physicians have employed placebos for centuries to alleviate human suffering. Indeed, until the beginning of this century, most medicines had no specific pharmacological properties that would assist healing (Honigfeld, 1964a; Houston, 1938; Shapiro, 1971; Shapiro and Morris, 1978). The assortment of therapies employed by healers was astonishingly diverse, including such delicacies as 'lizard's blood, crocodile dung, the teeth of swine, the hoof of an ass, putrid meat, and fly specs' (Honigfeld, 1964a, p. 145).

As an example of the medical treatment lavished on our forefathers, consider the following attempts to cure George Washington of what was probably a throat infection compounded by pneumonia:

> Because he could afford the the best cure available, he was given a mixture of molasses, vinegar, and butter, and then made to vomit and have diarrhea. But he lapsed. In desperation, his physicians applied irritating poultices to blister his feet and his throat, while draining several pints of blood. Then he died (Lawrence Power, *San Francisco Chronicle,* 15 March 1978, p. 24).

Remedies of true value were introduced only rarely, such as when fresh fruits were used to cure scurvy.

Some astute observers questioned the efficacy of medical treatments; note, for example, the disdain with which the French playwright, Molière, treated physicians. Nevertheless, healers attained high standing in all cultures. How was this possible, if the medications were useless? The usual speculation is that the treatments were indeed effective, owing to placebo effects (e.g. Beck, 1977; Honigfeld, 1964a; Lowinger and Dobie, 1969; Shapiro and Morris, 1978; Wolf, 1959). It is also conceivable that the 'cures' often did more harm than good, but when (if) patients eventually recovered, their improvement was inappropriately attributed to the treatment—a salient and unambiguous agent—rather than to 'nature'.

Though modern medical practice rests on firmer scientific foundations, therapeutics of dubious pharmacological value are still employed. Studies suggest that up to one-third of the drugs prescribed by physicians in the United States may be placebos (Byerly, 1976). Further, folk medicines still abound in many countries. For example, in China there is a pill called Pien Tzu Pian, 'the pill for the manly man'. The pill consists of 200 grains of powdered penis from deer, donkeys, or dogs. It is sold as a 'nourishing tonic for men and is recommended for everything from a general weakness and sores in waists and backs to overwork, untimely senility, and pale faces (Johnson, 1980, p. 36).

Scientific investigation of placebos has occurred most extensively in pharmacological research. Placebo control conditions were first used in drug studies early in this century, but this practice did not gain wide acceptance until the 1950s (Haas *et al.,* 1963). Placebo conditions are now employed almost routinely as baselines against which to test the effects of drugs. Consequently, there has been considerable discussion of placebo effects in the medical literature (e.g. Beecher, 1955; Haas *et al.,* 1963; Honigfeld, 1964a,b; Wolf, 1959).

One inference that is typically drawn from this research is that placebo effects can be strong and enduring (e.g. Beck, 1977; Beecher, 1955; Haas *et al.,* 1963; Honigfeld, 1964a,b; Wolf, 1959). Placebos seem to have some value in the treatment of radiation sickness, dental pain, headaches, coughing, asthma, postoperative pain, multiple sclerosis, the common cold, diabetes, ulcers, arthritis, sea sickness, parkinsonism, and much more.

Nevertheless, medical researchers are typically interested in the effects of drugs or therapeutic procedures, not in the effects of placebos. Therefore, the studies rarely include baseline conditions (such as no-placebo conditions, in which improvement could only reflect spontaneous recovery) against which to evaluate the impact of the placebos that are presented as active drugs. Before–after assessments provide the usual measure of placebo effectiveness. As a result, placebos are given credit for effects that conceivably are due to the passage of time, spontaneous recovery, and the like. With this caveat in mind, we will now briefly review the relevant research (more extensive reviews can be found in Haas *et al.*, 1963; Honigfeld 1964a,b; Jospe, 1978; Shapiro and Morris, 1978).

Review of the Literature

Research has suggested that placebos are efficacious in the treatment of a wide variety of disorders. Thus Shapiro (1971) has observed that, comparing across experiments, 'uncontrolled studies [i.e. those lacking placebo conditions] of drug efficacy are reported effective four to five times more frequently than controlled studies' (p. 598). In other words, including a placebo baseline condition greatly reduces the probability that a drug will be declared effective; placebos often produce as much improvement as the drug being studied.

Some of the most dramatic illustrations of placebo effects come from reports of sham operations conducted in the United States during the 1950s. One example concerned patients with angina pectoris. During the twentieth century many panaceas for angina pectoris have been proposed, only to be abandoned eventually as ineffective (Benson and McCallie, 1979). In the mid- to late-1950s, ischemic heart disease was often treated in the United States by the ligation of the internal mammary artery. Two studies were conducted to assess the effectiveness of this surgery (Cobb *et al.*, 1959; Dimond *et al.*, 1960). Patients with angina pectoris were anesthetized and their internal mammary artery was exposed. They were then randomly assigned either to the operation group, in which case the artery was ligated, or a placebo control group, in which case the incision was closed without ligation. Following the operation, the patients were examined by cardiologists who were unaware of which procedure had been used. In the Dimond *et al.* study, the subjective sensation, angina, was considerably lessened in all of the patients immediately following the operation, and this improvement was maintained in 83 percent of the patients. Daily logs indicated a decreased need for nitroglycerin and an increased tolerance for exercise. (Interestingly, though, the amount of exercise required to produce an abnormal electro-cardiographic response was not affected by the surgery in either condition.)

There were no differences between subjects in the sham operation and mammary ligation groups on any of the measures.

Similarly, Cobb *et al.* found improvements in both the placebo and ligation groups in postoperative reports of anginal episodes and in the average number of nitroglycerin tablets used. Once again, the ligated group was not superior on any of the measures, and neither group showed an improvement in the amount of exercise required to produce electrocardiographic abnormalities.

Jerome Frank (1975, p. 129) has described the features of the hospital setting that might contribute to the placebo effects of surgery:

> inside he [i.e. the patient] would find a complex structure with certain areas open to the public, such as wards, others where members of the staff perform arcane healing rituals and to which they alone have access, such as laboratories, operating rooms, radio therapy rooms, and intensive care units. These rooms contain spectacular machines that beep and gurgle and flash lights, or emit immensely powerful but invisible rays, thereby impressively invoking the healing powers of science. The operating rooms are the Holy of Holies where the most dramatic and difficult healing rituals are conducted and which even the priests can enter only after donning special costumes and undergoing purification rites known as scrubbing. So jealously guarded are the mysteries of the operating rooms that patients are rendered unconscious before entering them

Wilmer (1962) has termed the tendency to invest the hospital with healing functions the 'edifice complex'.

It may be an oversimplification to attribute the effects of sham operations entirely to placebo effects, however. The impact of bed rest, sedation, anesthesia, changes in weight, and hospital habits must also be considered. Moreover, changes in the patients' daily activities and habits may persist after hospitalization. On the basis of current research, it is difficult to disentangle the consequences of these non-placebo-effect factors from placebo-effect factors.

As noted earlier, there are hundreds of studies that have used placebos. On reviewing this research it becomes apparent that, although placebo effects can be quite dramatic, the percentage of patients responding to placebos varies tremendously from study to study (see Haas *et al.*, 1963, and Jospe, 1978, for summaries of the relevant literature). For example, in one study on multiple sclerosis, 73 percent of the patients showed some improvement while being administered placebos (Blomburg, 1957); in a second experiment on multiple sclerosis, none of the patients responded to placebos (Nagler, 1957).

There are a number of factors that may contribute to this variability, including small sample sizes and differences in how the placebos are administered and how their impact is assessed. A closer examination of the research findings suggests, however, that the nature and strength of placebo effects are influenced in important ways by the type of drug to which the placebos are compared. Thus, the variability in placebo responsiveness reflects, in part, variability in the impact of the comparison drugs. This is exemplified by the following five patterns in the data.

First, the *direction* of the placebo effect seems to be related to the drug under study (Haas *et al.*, 1963). For example, Seligman *et al.* (1953) compared quinine with placebos and found that both decreased blood pressure; on the other hand, Goodman and Housel (1954) compared placebos with dexedrene and found that both increased blood pressure.

Second, the *strength* of the placebo effect is proportional to the strength of the drug effect (Evans, 1974; Lowinger and Dobie, 1969). Thus, a placebo compared with morphine would prove to be more effective in reducing postoperative pain than would a placebo compared with aspirin.

Third, the '*side-effects*' of placebos are often similar to the side-effects of the drugs to which they are being compared (Green, 1964; Pogge, 1963; Shapiro and Morris, 1978). Side-effects include objective manifestations such as sweating, vomiting, and rashes, as well as subjective reports.

Fourth, the short-term *time–effect curves* have been found to be similar in drug and placebo treatments. Lasagna *et al.* (1958) compared the impact of aspirin and placebos on postpartum pain. Patients were interviewed at differing time-intervals after medication. Parallel patterns of increases, followed by decreases, in reports of relief were obtained in the aspirin and placebo conditions.

Finally, drug and placebo treatments show similar *dose* effects. Drugs usually become more efficacious as the dosage level increases. This effect is generally considered to be a result of the increasing concentration of the drug in the body. However, Lasagna *et al.* (1958) found parallel build-up effects with placebos. Hospitalized turberculosis patients were told that the placebo pills would increase their appetite and improve their pep and energy. Subjects ingested the pills daily and reported a gradual improvement over days. Similarly, there is some evidence that the simultaneous administration of two placebo pills, rather than one, or of a large rather than a small placebo pill, is more effective (Gruber, 1956; Honigfeld, 1964a; Rickels *et al.*, 1970).

To this point, we have considered only the positive effects of placebos. Is there any evidence that placebos can have deleterious consequences? Some studies report that the health of a small proportion of placebo-treated patients worsened (cf. Shapiro and Morris, 1978; Wolf and Pinsky, 1954). Storms and Nisbett (1970) and other researchers (e.g. Snyder *et al.*, 1974) have cited work by Rickels and his colleagues (Rickels *et al.*, 1965; Rickels and Downing, 1967; Rickels *et al.*, 1966) in this regard. For example Storms and Nisbett note:

A study by Rickels *et al.* (1966) shows that both prolonged experience with the anxiety state and extensive experience with tranquilizing drugs increase the likelihood that treatment with placebos will produce a worsening of the anxiety state. Whereas 80% of such patients improved when treated with tranquilizers, fewer than 30% improved on placebos. Although it is not completely clear from the presentation of the data, it seems likely that the majority of the placebo treated subjects got worse. In contrast, over 70% of the acutely ill patients with no previous experience with tranquilizers actually improved on placebos. Other work, by Rickels and Downing (1967) and Rickels *et al.* (1965) indicates that the higher the anxiety level of the patient, the more likely it is that his condition will worsen when placed on placebos (p. 327).

The data from the Rickels *et al.* studies are not clear, however. First, the classification of subjects in the published articles does not distinguish subjects whose condition failed to improve from those whose condition deteroriated. Rickels (personal communication) has indicated that, of those placebo patients who complete a 4–8-week study, only a few actually get worse (i.e. most who do not improve exhibit a null effect for the placebo). Of course, it is possible that certain kinds of patients are less likely to complete the full study period, due to lack of improvement or actual worsening while on the placebo treatment. Nonetheless, the empirical evidence for worsening is minimal. Second, and more important, these studies lack an appropriate baseline (no-drug, no-placebo) control condition (as noted earlier, the same criticism can be applied to many studies showing positive placebo effects). Conceivably, the condition of particular subjects (e.g. those with high anxiety levels and previous drug experience) would have worsened even if placebos had not been administered. Without such controls, one cannot attribute any worsening or failure to improve to the placebo *per se*.

There is some evidence, as indicated above, that placebos can produce undesirable side-effects that are similar to the side-effects of the drugs to which the placebos are being compared. Green (1964) has observed, however, that symptoms that are labeled as side-effects of the placebo or drug are sometimes symptoms of the condition being treated. Thus, similar side-effects for placebos and active drugs might simply reflect that they are administered to the same population of patients.

In summary then, there is little indication in the pharmacological literature that placebos cause harmful effects. On the other hand, there is evidence that placebos can be effective in the treatment of a variety of illnesses. Further, the magnitude of the placebo effect is directly related to the strength of the drugs to which placebos are being compared.

Theoretical Explanations for Placebo Effects

If we can explain the link between placebo and drug effects, then we may be a step closer to understanding the mechanisms underlying placebo effects. Although this relation can be interpreted in various ways, subjects' expectancies seem likely to play an important role in each of the five trends identified above. For example, the physician generally knows the direction in which the active drug should act and the presumed potency of the drug. This knowledge is likely to be communicated to the patients and influence their responding.

Thus, the direction and strength findings may be attributable to the fact that placebos are described in a similar fashion to the active drug being studied; subjects' expectancies then produce effects (or perceptions of effects). The 'side-effects' findings are more complex. Sometimes, specific expectations concerning side-effects may be communicated to the patients. Alternatively, administration of the placebo may cause subjects to introspect and discover ailments that, otherwise, they would not have noticed (Shapiro and Morris, 1978). Finally, the 'side-effects' may simply be symptoms of the illness being treated. Turning to the effects of time and drug dosage, subjects' expectancies again seem relevant, but in this case the expectancies may not come from the physician. We all know that drugs take time to become effective, that their effects gradually wear off, and that larger doses are more potent than smaller ones. These implicit expectations could produce time and dosage effects for placebos that parallel those for active drugs.

It is one thing to identify placebo effects with expectancies; it is another to explain how expectancies produce these remarkable effects. Below, we summarize the major explanations that have been proposed.

One common speculation is that placebos alleviate patients' anxiety about their symptoms and thereby effect an improvement in their condition. This argument assumes that worrying about a problem only makes it worse; by reducing such anxiety, placebos can improve the condition. In support of this reasoning, there is evidence that anxiety increases the subjective experience of pain (Evans, 1974). In addition, Storms and McCaul (1976) obtained some evidence that worrying about stuttering exacerbated the problem.

A second and related possibility is that individuals accentuate the positive after receiving plecebos. They may observe small improvements in their condition that they would have failed to notice in the absence of the placebo, and they may downplay the significance of negative changes that would otherwise have caused them considerable concern (Lick and Bootzin, 1975). In addition, placebo recipients may label equivocal somatic sensations as positive changes. Along these lines, Dinnerstein and his colleagues have suggested that active drugs used in the treatment of pain or anxiety often produce ambiguous sensations that patients interpret in view of their expectancies (Dinnerstein and Halm, 1970; Dinnerstein et al., 1966).

A third explanation is that recipients of placebos do not truly perceive any changes in their condition, but simply comply with the 'demands' of the situation. Subjects in experiments, and patients being treated with placebos, know the effects that the placebos 'should' have. They may feel that it is important, either for the sake of science or for their own well-being, that the experimenter's or therapist's prognosis be affirmed. The demand interpretation implies that respondents are essentially 'faking' their improvement. There is considerable evidence against this proposition, however. Placebos can apparantly alter such 'objective' responses as blood pressure (Goodman and Housel, 1954), the contractile activity of the stomach (Wolf, 1950), and the galvanic skin response (Loftis and Ross, 1974a,b). In addition, placebo responses can be obtained in laboratory animals, as noted below.

A fourth speculation views placebo reactions as conditioned responses, dependent on previous experience with true medication. There is evidence from animal studies that placebo reactions can, indeed, be conditioned. Pavlov (1960, pp. 35–36) described research by Krylov, who demonstrated a conditioning effect upon injecting morphine in dogs. Hypodermic injection of morphine produces nausea, followed by vomiting, and then sleep. Krylov found that, after five or six daily injections, the dogs would react with all of these symptoms to such preliminaries of injection as opening the box containing the syringe and wiping the skin with alcohol.

> In the most striking cases, all the symptoms could be produced by the dogs simply seeing the experimenter. . . the greater the number of previous injections of morphine, the less preparation had to be performed in order to evoke a reaction simulating that produced by the drug (p. 36).

Similarly, Reiss (1958) induced insulin shock by injecting rats with large doses of insulin. When the insulin was subsequently replaced by a saline injection, all of the animals continued to show the body twitchings and state of collapse associated with an overdose of insulin. The saline injections were continued; by the sixth trial, no responses were elicited from any of the rats. Presumably, the conditioned response to the hypodermic needle and associated environmental stimuli had extinguished.

The above studies are vulnerable to methodological criticisms: the observers were not 'blind' to treatments (indeed, there was only one condition) and evaluations of the subjects' responses were relatively subjective. Better-controlled, though less dramatic, examples of conditioned placebo responses have been obtained by other investigators. For example, Hernstein (1962) showed that injections of scopalamine hydrobromide inhibit bar-pressing responses in rats. Injections of a saline solution did not affect responding prior to any administrations of scopolamine; alternate administrations of the two substances in a series of injections, however, also yielded an inhibition following the saline injections.

These data suggest that the pharmacological effects of a drug can be evoked by the stimuli associated with its administration, through a process of classical conditioning. It is likely that conditioning also plays a role in placebo responses in man. Wolf (1950) repeatedly provided his favorite experimental subject, Tom, with prostigmine, which induces abdominal cramps and diarrhea. (Tom, a New York janitor, had a gastric fistula that enabled direct observation of his stomach. He was apparently willing to suffer repeated unpleasant experimentation for the sake of science.) 'Each day, following the prostigmine, regardless of what substance was administered to Tom (e.g. tap water), he displayed gastric hyperfunction, abdominal cramps, and diarrhea'

(p. 108). Stanley and Schlosberg (1953) reported that tea influenced the reaction times of habitual tea-drinkers immediately after its ingestion— before the caffeine could have produced pharmacological effects. Hilgard and Hilgard (1975) suggested that a person who takes aspirin for a headache 'máy find the pain diminishing almost immediately, far too soon for the aspirin to be absorbed by the bloodstream' (p. 50).

It is unlikely that conditioning accounts for all instances of placebo effects, however. For example, placebo effects can occur in the absence of previous experience with a drug. Indeed, it has been suggested that the effectiveness of non-active drugs is *reduced* by prior experience with an active drug (e.g. Byerly, 1976; Frank, 1974; Hurst *et al.*, 1973; Knowles, 1963; Rickels *et al.*, 1966). The evidence typically adduced in support of this proposition is actually quite weak, sometimes based on trends in the data that were either non-significant or not subjected to statistical test (e.g., Lasagna *et al.*, 1954; Meath, *et al.*, 1956; Segal and Shapiro, 1959). Nevertheless, the occasional result does receive statistical confirmation (e.g. Rickels *et al.*, 1966; Zukin *et al.*, 1959). Thus, prior experience with a drug does not necessarily enhance the magnitude of placebo effects, as the conditioning hypothesis would suggest. Perhaps experience with an effective, active drug sometimes enables the recipient to distinguish an inert agent, which then seems unsatisfactory (Frank, 1974).

As noted above, placebos can sometimes induce actual somatic changes. Although these changes may be related to previous experience with drugs and conditioning, the mechanisms by which expectancies are translated into bodily changes are obscure. Recent research on pain, however, offers some intriguing speculations on a physiological mechanism that may mediate the relation between expectancies and pain perception. Briefly, there are morphine-like compounds in the brain and pituitary called endorphins, which may be related to pain perception (Goldstein, 1976; Hughes *et al.*, 1975; Levine *et al.*, 1978; Pasternak *et al.*, 1975). A number of researchers have suggested that painful stimuli activate the endorphin system thereby reducing the pain. In support of this hypothesis, dental postoperative pain has been reported to increase with the administration of naloxone, an opiate antagonist that blocks the release of endorphins (Levine *et al.*, 1978).

This leads to the exciting possibility that placebo expectancies might also activate the endorphin system and, hence, reduce the pain associated with noxious stimulation. If this were the case, then placebo effects should be attenuated by the administration of naloxone; and there is some evidence with dental postoperative pain that naloxone indeed counteracts placebo analgesia (Levine *et al.*, 1978). These data are consistent with the speculation that endorphin release mediates placebo analgesia.

The picture is not entirely clear, however. There have been a number of studies employing experimentally induced pain that have failed to find an effect of naloxone on pain perception in humans (Dostrovsky and Wall, 1976; Grevert and Goldstein, 1977). These findings suggest that the perception of experimentally induced pain may not be affected by endorphin release. In addition, there is some debate about the effect of naloxone on the central nervous system (Henry, 1979). Conceivably, naloxone influences pain perception independently of its effect on the release of endorphins.

In the next few years we shall probably learn a great deal more concerning the relation between pain perception and endorphins. At the present time we can only speculate about an intriguing relation between mind and body, between expectancies and endorphin release.

Finally, a great deal of conjecture has focused on personality factors that may predispose one to be a 'placebo reactor'. Yet attempts to relate standard placebo responses to differences in intelligence, suggestibility, and a host of personality variables, have generally proven unsuccessful (Evans, 1967, 1974; Haas et al., 1963; Honigfeld, 1964a,b; Jones, 1977; Shapiro, 1971; Shapiro and Morris, 1978). In addition, a number of studies have shown that individuals react differently across situations, at times showing placebo effects and at other times not (Fisher, 1967; Liberman, 1964; Wolf et al., 1957). The hunt continues (e.g., Moertel et al., 1976; Shapiro et al., 1973); at the present time, however, there is little evidence that individual differences variables are related strongly to placebo responding.

This analysis of the psychological processes that mediate placebo effects suggests the following characterization of such effects in humans. Placebo recipients anticipate specific somatic reactions because either (a) they believe that the placebo is identical to a previously administered drug, or (b) they are provided with implicit or explicit suggestions as to the impact of the placebo. The expectancies may then alleviate the recipients' anxiety about their condition and/or induce actual somatic changes, possibly involving the endorphin system and sometimes in the form of conditioned responses. Alternatively, individuals may interpret ambiguous or minor somatic sensations in light of their expectancies, and they may become more introspective and notice small changes in their condition that they would have failed to notice in the absence of the placebo.

Placebo Effects in Medical Practice

To this point, we have focused on placebo effects in the pharmacological literature and the unintentional use of placebos in medical practice. We will now examine placebo effects from the standpoint of medical practitioners. Can placebo effects be utilized to the advantage of patients? What are the ethical issues that arise?

To provide a perspective on how practitioners view the deliberate use of placebos, we have excerpted the following panel discussion, which was reported recently in *Patient Care*, 1978, vol. 12, no. 14, pp. 205–207.* The discussion concerns the utility of placebos in the treatment of chronic pain. The moderator is William Manahan, MD; the participants are Edgar Dawson, MD, Lawrence Halpern, PhD, John Loeser, MD, Terence Murphy, MD, Wilbert Fordyce, PhD, and J. Jerome Wildgen, MD.

MODERATOR: Many physicians feel that a placebo is worth a therapeutic trial. Some physicians even use placebo as a diagnostic tool '. . . to see if the pain is real or not'. What do you all think of using placebo medication for the patient with chronic pain?

DAWSON: Placebo may very well have some benefit, but it'll cause far more harm than any potential for good if the patient finds out. We've had some bad experiences. The patient makes good progress until he finds out he's on a placebo. This totally destroys his confidence in treatment. The problem is that it's just not that difficult for the patient to figure out what he's getting. We were getting great results with an antiarthritic medication until the pharmacy changed its policy and started putting the ingredient—aspirin—on the label.

HALPERN: Aspirin is not a placebo, but I do agree that you can get an additional placebo effect if the patient thinks his medication is more exotic. Familiarity has bred contempt.

LOESER: Put the patient on propoxyphene HCl [Darvon, Dolene, Progesic-65, etc.]. The patient will be on placebo but think it's a powerful drug.

MURPHY: Placebo is an effective analgesic.

MODERATOR: Isn't the use of a placebo basically dishonest?

MURPHY: Oh, no. With first administration, you can't tell the difference between a placebo and morphine in an acute pain situation. It's only down the track in acute pain management that morphine has a better record of response. As long as you're not financially exploiting the patient, there's nothing wrong with giving him a colored pill or colored water. It may do the job as well as pentazocine, for example.

LOESER: Well, pentazocine is another placebo when it's given by mouth. But the question actually begs the point. You can't determine why Mrs Jones feels better when you put her on any medication. Without a sophisticated study, how can you figure out how much of her response is placebo effect and how much is pharmacologic effect? If the patient is feeling better, why worry as long as you can be honest in your explanation to the patient?

FORDYCE: The important distinction is whether you use placebo for short-term diagnosis or for long-term management.

LOESER: That's a good point. There's nothing wrong with a placebo test to find out if the patient's pain is primarily environmental.

FORDYCE: But in the long haul, suggestibility is unlikely to have an enduring effect. Those colored pills may control pain for several days, but they probably won't hold the line for several weeks.

WILDGEN: What about intermittent flare-ups?

FORDYCE: Placebo is sometimes helpful for that type of chronic pain.

DAWSON: But most chronic pain patients have been on enough different medications to recognize the effects of a pharmacologically active agent. You can't fool these people when you give them aspirin or sugar.

FORDYCE: And you lose your credibility in a hurry.

DAWSON: Absolutely. When you lose that, you might as well send the patient somewhere else.

LOESER: I agree with that 100 percent. I wouldn't play games with the placebo. If you use a placebo, you should tell the patient.

WILDGEN: I often prescribe a brown-and-white capsule of APC instead of tetracycline for URI. I don't find anything wrong with that type of placebo to keep the patient off more harmful medications.

LOESER: Just as long as you're honest with the patient. People are critical of behavior modification because they see it as manipulative. The fact is, however, that behavior modification is right up front. Everyone—including the patient and the family—knows exactly what is going on and why. The same thing holds true for medication. If you taper a patient off a medication, let him know what to expect.

FORDYCE: Even if you wean a patient off medication entirely so he's taking nothing but cherry syrup, don't hesitate telling him. It's something of a myth that patients are all that vulnerable; they don't panic.

MODERATOR: What do you tell the patient?

FORDYCE: I might say: 'You've been off active drugs for pain for 24 hours now. Do you want to keep on taking the cherry syrup or would you like to stop?'

LOESER: And most answer—with full knowledge that it's nothing but cherry syrup: 'I need it?'

A number of points emerge from the above discussion. Three major ones are worthy of comment:

(1) Be honest with the patient if you use a placebo.

The ideal is laudatory, and the concern about losing credibility is valid. Presumably, many physicians view the deliberate prescription of placebo pills as unethical because it involves deception. Will a placebo work, however, if a patient believes it is pharmacologically useless? The answer would appear to be 'no'. All of the theoretical interpretations of placebo effects require that recipients have clear expectations that the placebo will have some impact. Of course, it may be impossible to persuade the patient that a drug is truly ineffective. Why would the physician suggest that he take such a thing? If this is the case, then the placebo may continue to work despite the physician's disclaimers concerning its effectiveness. The physician's ethical dilemma would remain, however.

A study that is often cited as relevant to the issue of whether pills labeled as placebos can be effective was conducted by Park and Covi (1965). These investigators provided neurotic patients with sugar pills that were explicitly labeled as such. Thirteen of fifteen patients showed improvement on a symptom checklist after taking the sugar pills, and, on the average, subjects reported that they felt 'quite a bit better'.

It is difficult to know what to conclude from this study, however. First, there is no control group and the improvements could reflect spontaneous recovery rather than genuine placebo effects. Second, although the sugar content of the pill was disclosed, it was nevertheless described as effective: 'Many people with your kind of condition have also been helped by what are sometimes called "sugar pills" and we feel that a so-called sugar pill may help you, too. Do you know what a sugar pill is? A sugar pill is a pill with no medicine in it at all. I think that this pill will help you as it has helped so many others. Are you willing to try this pill?' To the layman, the physician's assurances concerning the impact of the pill might be much more important than its content. Who cares what the pill contains as long as it works? Thus, the conditions are set for placebo effects.

To return to the initial question, can a physician deliberately evoke a placebo effect without being deceptive? Again, our answer would be 'no', if the idea is to describe the pill as inert. An alternative, though, is to present drugs that have proved effective with appropriate (and genuine) enthusiasm. The pharmacological impact of the drug can thus be supplemented by the placebo effect that results from the physician's obvious confidence in the therapy.

(2) Placebos are beneficial as a short-term diagnostic technique, but will not provide long-term relief.

Loeser suggests that there is nothing wrong 'with a placebo test to find out if the patient's pain is primarily environmental'. The implication in this statement and that of the moderator's is that one can use placebos to test if the pain is somehow 'real' (i.e. somatically based) or not. We question the utility of placebos in this regard. There is every reason to believe that placebo effects will occur with somatically based pain; that is, the pain is no less real if placebo effects do occur. This is particularly clear when one considers that placebo expectancies may induce actual somatic changes; for example, they conceivably may activate the endorphin system.

As to the issue of the long-term *versus* short-term value of placebos, we have been unable to find much evidence in this regard. On the the basis of our reading of the literature, we would say that the question is an open one and warrants examination in research.

(3) Most chronic pain patients have ingested sufficient medication to recognize a placebo when they receive one. Thus, these patients are unlikely to benefit from placebo effects.

The assumption that previous experience with active drugs will eliminate placebo effects runs directly counter to the conditioning account of such phenomena. Recall that this interpretation views placebo reactions as conditioned responses, dependent on previous experience with active medication. In discussing the conditioning hypothesis, we noted that the data are mixed. Nevertheless, there is some evidence in support of the panelists' contentions: prior experience with an active drug sometimes causes recipients to view placebos as ineffective.

It seems to us that there are two particular dangers inherent in prescribing ineffective medication (in this instance, placebos). First, it may destroy the patient's confidence in his treatment and in his physician. Second, and perhaps more important, the patient may attribute his failure to improve to the severity of his illness, rather than to the impotence of the drug. This misattribution could have important consequences for his mental and physical well-being.

Should placebos, then, be utilized deliberately in medical practice? It is impossible to answer this question unequivocally. Most of our knowledge of placebos comes from the pharmacological literature, where placebos are employed to assess the effectiveness of drugs. As a result, there is a dearth of directly relevant information. Certainly, physicians must be cautious about utilizing placebos deliberately in medical practice. Nevertheless, placebos seem to have value in the treatment of many disorders. What is particularly clear is that there is a need to take placebo research out of pharmacological settings, so that assessments of more utility to medical practitioners can be made. The placebo has long played an often unacknowledged role in medicine. It is time to acknowledge that role and scrutinize the value of placebos more thoroughly.

References

Beck, F. M. (1977). 'Placebos in dentistry: their profound potential effects', *Journal of the American Dental Association*, **95**, 1122–1126.

Beecher, H. K. (1955). 'The powerful placebo', *Journal of the American Medical Association*, **159**, 1602–1606.

Benson, H., and McCallie, D. P. (1979). 'Angina pectoris and the placebo effect', *The New England Journal of Medicine*, **300**, 1424–1429.

Blomburg, L. H. (1957). 'Treatment of disseminated sclerosis with active and inactive drugs', *The Lancet*, **1**, 431–437.

Buchsbaum, M. S., Davis, G. C., and Bunney, W. E., Jr. (1977). 'Naloxone alters pain perception and somatosensory evoked potentials in normal subjects', *Nature*, **270**, 620–622.

Byerly, H. (1976). 'Explaining and exploiting placebo effects', *Perspectives in Biology and Medicine*, **19**, 423–436.

Cobb, L. A., Thomas, G. I., Dillard, D. H., Merendino, K. A., and Bruce, E. A. (1959). 'An evaluation of internal-mammary-artery ligation by a double-blind technic', *The New England Journal of Medicine*, **260**, 1115–1118.

Dimond, E. G., Kittle, C. F., and Crockett, J. E. (1960). 'Comparison of internal mammary artery ligation and sham operation for angina pectoris', *American Journal of Cardiology*, **5**, 483–486.

Dinnerstein, A. J., and Halm, J. (1970).'Modification of placebo effects by means of drugs: effects of aspirin and placebos on self-rated moods', *Journal of Abnormal Psychology*, **75**, 308–314.

Dinnerstein, A. J., Lowenthal, M., and Blitz, B. (1966). 'The interaction of drugs and placebos in the control of pain and anxiety', *Perspectives in Biology and Medicine*, **10**, 103–117.

Dostrovsky, J. C., and Wall, P. D. (1976). 'Lack of an effect of naloxone on pain perception in humans', *Nature*, **263**, 783–784.

Evans, F. J. (1967). 'Suggestibility in the normal waking state', *Psychological Bulletin*, **67**, 114–129.

Evans, F. J. (1974). 'The placebo response in pain reduction', *Advances in Neurology*, **4**, 289–296.

Fisher, S. (1967). 'The placebo reactor: thesis, antithesis, synthesis, and hypothesis', *Diseases of the Nervous System*, **28**, 510–515.

Frank, J. D. (1975). 'The faith that heals', *Johns Hopkins Medical Journal*, **137**, 127–131.

Frank, J. D. (1974). *Persuasion and Healing: A Comparative Study of Psychotherapy* (revised edn.). Schocken Books, New York.

Goldstein, A. (1976). 'Opioid peptides (endorphins) in pituitary and brain', *Science*, **193**, 1081–1086.

Goodman, E. L., and Housel, E. L. (1954). 'The effect of D-amphetamine sulphate in the treatment of the obese hypertensive patient', *American Journal of Medical Science*, **227**, 250–254.

Green, D. M. (1964). 'Pre-existing conditions, placebo reactions, and "side-effects", *Annals of Internal Medicine*, **60**, 255–265.

Grevert, P., and Goldstein, A. (1977). 'Effects of naloxone on experimentally induced ischemic pain and on mood in human subjects', *Proceedings of the National Academy of Science*, USA, **74**, 1291–1294.

Gruber, C. M. (1956). 'Interpreting medical data', *Archives of Internal Medicine*, **98**, 767–773.

Haas, H., Fink, H., and Hartfelder, G. (1963). 'The placebo problem', *Psychopharmacology Service Center Bulletin*, **8**, 1–65.

Henry, J. L. (1979). 'Naloxone excites nociceptive units in the lumbar dorsal horn of the spinal cat', *Neuroscience*, **4**, 1485–1491.

Hernstein, R. J. (1962). 'Placebo effect in the rat', *Science*, **138**, 677–678.

Hilgard, E. R., and Hilgard, J. R. (1975). *Hypnosis in the Relief of Pain*. William Kaufman, Los Altos, Calif.

Honigfeld, G. (1964a). 'Non-specific factors in treatment. I. Review of Placebo reactions and placebo reactors', *Diseases of the Nervous System*, **25**, 145–156.

Honigfeld, G. (1964b). 'Non-specific factors in treatment. II. Review of social-psychological factors'. *Diseases of the Nervous System*, **25**, 225–239.

Houston, W. R. (1938). 'The doctor himself as a therapeutic agent', *Annals of Internal Medicine*, **11**, 1416–1425.

Hughes, J., Smith, T. W., Kosterlitz, H. W., Fothergill, L. A., Morgan, B. A., and Morris, H. R. (1975). 'Identification of two related pentapeptides from the brain with potent opiate agonist activity', *Nature*, **258**, 577–579.

Hurst, P. M., Weldner, M. F., Radlow, R., and Ross, S. (1973). 'Drugs and placebos: drug guessing by normal volunteers', *Psychological Reports*, **33**, 683–694.

Johnson, B. (1980). 'X-rated items abound in Chinese medicines', *The Globe and Mail*, 1 January.

Jones, R. (1977). *Self-fulfilling Prophesies: Social Psychological, and Physiological Effects of Expectancies*. Lawrence Erlbaum Associates, Hillsdale, NJ.

Jospe, M. (1978). *The Placebo Effect in Healing*. D. C. Heath and Co. Lexington, Mass.

Knowles, J. B. (1963). 'Conditioning and the placebo effect: the effects of decaffein-ated coffee on simple reaction time in habitual coffee drinkers', *Behavior Research Therapy*, **1**, 151–157.

Lasagna, L., Laties, V. G., and Dohan, J. L. (1958). 'Further studies on the "pharmacology" of placebo administration', *Journal of Clinical Investigation*, **37**, 533–537.

Lasagna, I., Mosteller, F., von Felsinger, J. M., and Beecher, H. K. (1954). 'A study of the placebo response', *American Journal of Medicine*, **16**, 770–779.

Levine, J. D., Gordon, N. C., and Fields, H. L. (1978). 'The mechanism of placebo analgesia', *The Lancet*, **2**, 654–657.

Liberman, R. (1964). 'An experimental study of the placebo response under three different situations of pain', *Journal of Psychiatric Research*, **2**, 233–246.

Lick, J., and Bootzin, R. (1975). 'Expectancy factors in the treatment of fear: methodological and theoretical issues', *Psychological Bulletin*, **82**, 917–931.

Loftis, J., and Ross, L. (1974a). 'Effects of misattribution of arousal upon the acquisition and extinction of a conditioned emotional response', *Journal of Personality and Social Psychology*, **30**, 673–682.

Loftis, J., and Ross, L. (1974b). 'Retrospective misattribution of a conditioned emotional response', *Journal of Personality and Social Psychology*, **30**, 683–687.

Lowinger, P., and Dobie, S. (1969). 'A study of placebo response rates', *Archives of General Psychiatry*, **20**, 84–88.

Meath, J. A., Feldbert, T. M., Rosenthal, D., and Frank, J. D. (1956). 'Comparison of reserpine and placebo in treatment of psychiatric outpatients', *American Medical Association Archives of Neurology and Psychiatry*, **76**, 207–214.

Moertel, C. G., Taylor, W. F., Roth, A., and Tyce, F. A. J. (1976). 'Who responds to sugar pills?', *Mayo Clinic Proceedings*, **51**, 96–100.

Nagler, B. (1957). 'Isoniazid in treatment of multiple sclerosis: report on Veterans Administration Cooperative Study', *Journal of the American Medical Association*, **163**, 168–172.

Park, L. C., and Covi, L. (1965). 'Nonblind placebo trial: an exploration of neurotic patients' responses to placebo when its inert content is disclosed', *Archives of General Psychiatry (Chicago)*, **12**, 336–345.

Pasternak, G. W., Goodman, R., and Snyder, S. H. (1975). 'An endogenous morphine-like factor in mammalian brain', *Life Science*, **16**, 1765–1769.

Pavlov, I. P. (1960). *Conditioned Reflexes*. Dover Press, New York.

Pogge, R. C. (1963). 'The toxic placebo', *Medical Times*, **91**, 773–781.

Reiss, W. J. (1958). 'Conditioning of a hyperinsulin type of behavior in the white rat', *Science*, **51**, 301–303.

Rickels, K., Baumm, C., Raab, E., Taylor, W., and Moore, E. (1965). 'A psychopharmacological evaluation of chlordiazepoxide, LA-1 and placebo, carried out with anxious, neurotic medical clinic patients', *Medical Times*, **93**, 238–242.

Rickels, K., and Downing, R. (1967). 'Drug- and placebo-treated neurotic outpatients', *Archives of General Psychiatry*, **16**, 369–372.

Rickels, K., Hesbacher, P. T., Weise, C. C., Gray, B., and Feldman, H. S. (1970). 'Pills and improvement: a study of placebo response in psychoneurotic outpatients', *Psychopharmacologia*, **16**, 318–328.

Rickels, K., Lipman, R., and Raab, E. (1966). 'Previous medication, duration of illness and placebo response', *Journal of Nervous and Mental Diseases*, **142**, 548–554.

Segal, M. M., and Shapiro, K. L. (1959). 'A clinical comparison study of the effects of reserpine and placebo on anxiety', *American Medical Association Archives of Neurology and Psychiatry*, **81**, 392–398.

Seligmann, A. W., Ferguson, F. C., Jr., Garb, S., Gluck, J. L., Halpern, S. L., and Goodgold, M. (1953). 'Evaluation of treatment in hypertension: effects of cinchona alkaloids'. *American Journal of Medical Science*, **226**, 636–644.

Shapiro, A. K. (1971). 'Placebo effects in medicine, psychotherapy, and psychoanalysis', in Bergin, A. E., and Garfield, S. L. (eds), *Handbook of Psychotherapy and Behavior Change: Empirical Analysis*. Wiley, New York.

Shapiro, A. K., Mike, V., Barton, H., and Shapiro, E. (1973). 'Study of the placebo effect with a self-administered test', *Comprehensive Psychiatry*, **14**, 535–548.

Shapiro, A. K., and Morris, L. A. (1978). 'The placebo effect in medical and psychological therapies', in Garfield, S. L., and Bergin, A. E. (eds), *Handbook of Psychotherapy and Behavior Change: An Empirical Analysis*, 2nd edn. Wiley, New York.

Snyder, M., Schultz, R., and Jones, E. E. (1974). 'Expectancy and apparent duration as determinants of fatigue', *Journal of Personality and Social Psychology*, **29**, 426–434.

Stanley, W. C., and Schlosberg, H. (1953). 'The psychophysical effects of tea', *Journal of Psychology*, **36**, 435–448.

Storms, M. D., and McCaul, K. D. (1976). 'Attribution processes and emotional exacerbation of dysfunctional behavior', in Harvey, J. H., Ickes, W. J., and Kidd, R. F. (eds), *New Directions in Attribution Research*, vol. 1. Lawrence Erlbaum Associates, Hillsdale, NJ.

Storms, M. D. and Nisbett, R. E. (1970). 'Insomnia and the attribution process', *Journal of Personality and Social Psychology*, **16**, 319–328.

Wilmer, H. (1962). 'Transference to a medical center', *California Medicine*, **96**, 173–180.

Wolf, S. (1950). 'Effects of suggestion and conditioning on the action of chemical agents in human subjects—the pharmacology of placebos', *Journal of Clinical Investigation*, **29**, 100–109.

Wolf, S. (1959). 'The pharmacology of placebos', *Pharmacology Review*, **11**, 689–704.

Wolf, S., Doering, C. R., Clark, M. L., and Hagans, J. A. (1957). 'Chance distribution and the placebo "reactor"', *Journal of Laboratory Clinical Medicine*, **49**, 837–841.

Wolf, S., and Pinsky, R. H. (1954). 'Effects of placebo administration and occurrence of toxic reactions', *Journal of the American Medical Association*, **155**, 339–341.

Zukin, P., Arnold, D. V. G., and Kessler, C. R. (1959). 'Comparative effects of phenaglycodol and meprobamate on anxiety reactions', *Journal of Nervous and Mental Diseases*, **129**, 193–195.

Social Psychology and Behavioral Medicine
Edited by J. Richard Eiser
© 1982 John Wiley & Sons Ltd

Chapter 19

The effects of chronic illness on children and their families

CHRISTINE EISER

A relatively new development in psychology has been the emergence of closer liaisons between pediatricians and psychologists involved in the care of chronically sick and dying children. The involvement is aimed at providing a more sensitive and complete treatment program, not only for the child, but also for his whole family. For many children in hospital or undergoing long-term treatment from home, such a goal is far from realized. In this chapter, I attempt to describe why such an involvement in professional staff is important and necessary, and to document particularly the contributions made by psychologists so far.

At the outset it is important to realize that the numbers of children suffering from long-term chronic illnesses are increasing, and likely to continue to do so. Improvements in medical care have led to the survival of children with gross and severe malformations, and the extension of life for children suffering from diseases that were previously fatal (e.g. leukemia or spina bifida).

Pless and Douglas (1971) have estimated that approximately 111 in 1000 children below the age of 15 years are undergoing treatment for a wide variety of diseases requiring long-term medical attention, and ranging in disability from the non-life-threatening to fatal, from the minimally handicapping to the seriously disabling. Clearly the problems faced by such children and their families are many, and it is therefore not surprising that several studies have reported that children with chronic illnesses are more likely to show a behavior problem or psychiatric disturbance than normal children. Three large-scale studies are of relevance here. In both the National Survey of Child Health and Development (Pless and Douglas, 1971) and the Rochester survey (Pless and Roghmann, 1971), a consistent although non-significant excess of difficulties in school among chronically sick compared with healthy children was reported. In the Isle of Wight survey (Rutter *et al.*, 1970) it was shown that chronically ill children had a higher rate of specific reading retardation, and a greater frequency of psychiatric disturbance compared with normal children. Further, both the Rochester and National surveys indicated that children with more permanent, and those with more severe, conditions had a higher incidence of maladjustment.

In terms both of reducing the incidence of maladjustment among sick children, and rehabilitating those already affected, it is not sufficient simply to document a relationship between chronic illness and mental handicap. Rather one must attempt to identify the mechanism whereby this relationship arises. In this respect, both developmental and social psychology has much to offer pediatrics. Understanding of the growth and development of the normal child is of central importance. At the same time it is essential to consider the role of alterations in family interactions and peer relationships as they affect sick children and consequently alter their expectations and adequacy of their developing self-concepts. Finally a knowledge of the differences between diseases and exactly how they limit the child's lifestyle can be derived from the field of pediatrics. In this chapter I hope first to examine in more detail the incidence and form that maladjustment can take among sick children; and second, to make some attempt to identify characteristics of the child or his disease which may predict the degree of severity of the maladjustment. Primarily, however, it is necessary to consider some of the theoretical approaches to understanding the development of the relationship between childhood chronic illness and maladjustment.

Theoretical Approaches

The Self-concept Model

Bodily physique and health status are seen by some workers (e.g. Barker *et al.*, 1953) as contributing to the formation of an individual's self-concept. A child with chronic illness is required to function in two worlds: that of the normal and healthy and that of the handicapped. The extent of his disability determines the world in which he functions; yet because of the partial nature of most illness, the child is required to function in both worlds. New situations pose a challenge both in terms of how the child sees himself able to handle them, and in the extent to which society is prepared to consider him 'normal'. Traditionally, three patterns of response are described: withdrawal, rejection, and adjustment.

A major determinant of how a child approaches a new situation relates to the extent that the child allows knowledge of his illness to interfere with his behavior in a new situation, even though his illness is irrelevant to it. According to Wright (1960) this 'spread' phenomenon ultimately leads to a devaluing of the child's self-concept. As the fact of his illness affects the child's behavior in situations where it is irrelevant, so it is also likely to affect the responses made to him by others. Green and Solnit (1964) have identified a 'vulnerable child syndrome', arguing that a comparable spread occurs in parents' restrictions of a child's activities following earlier illness. The self-concept approach therefore suggests that the child's behavior is affected by the formation of an inadequate self-concept, this occurring as the result of restrictions on his activity being imposed by himself and others, and affecting all aspects of his behavior, even those to which his illness should be irrelevant.

The Coping Model

An alternate approach is that an individual's adjustment to his illness develops as a function of processes which complement the type of coping behavior that follows stress of any kind. Lipowski (1970) argues that an individual's coping style (his disposition to deal with challenges of any kind) and his coping strategy (the techniques used to handle the illness specifically) can be affected by a number of factors. These include *intrapersonal* factors (his age, personality, and timing of the illness), *disease-related* factors (its rate of onset and prognosis) and *environmental* factors (family and peer attitudes). This model therefore attempts to describe how a variety of environmental events modify the nature of the child's fundamental personality. Unlike the self-concept model, the coping model does not imply that illness is inevitably associated with negative outcomes. Rather, a crisis such as chronic illness can provide an opportunity for the individual to develop coping mechanisms, in some cases mechanisms which are superior to those he might have achieved in more normal life circumstances. Life crises can provide opportunities for maturation if they are responded to appropriately (Kaplan, 1970). Indeed, it has been claimed that some individuals overcome disabilities and achieve goals they might never have done following severe handicapping illnesses (Pless and Satterwhite, 1975).

In both models emphasis is placed on how environmental influences, particularly social interactions, affect the individual's subsequent approach to new situations, either by devaluing his self-concept or by determining his coping strategies. Perhaps both models fail to bring out the essentially dynamic and continuing nature of the adjustment process. Before considering how some of the factors identified by Lipowski (1970) help determine coping, we should look in more detail at the nature of the maladjustment that has been identified in children with a range of physical illnesses.

The Incidence and Nature of Maladjustment among Children with Chronic Illness

It is worth noting at the outset that there appears to be little or no relationship between type of maladjustment shown by a child and specific illnesses

(Rutter, 1979). It would appear that it is the fact of being ill rather than having to take drugs, be on special diets, or have limitations placed on physical activity, that contributes primarily to a child's maladjustment. Nevertheless, the first problem is that of deciding how maladjustment is to be measured. Pless and Pinkerton (1975) have identified four areas which can be considered measures of adjustment. The first can be described as *scholastic*; the extent to which the child's achievements in school are compatible with those of his peers and comparable with estimates of his ability given his general intelligence level. One advantage of this indicator is that reliable and well-validated measures of academic achievement are available. On the other hand it must be remembered that sick children are likely to miss schooling because of the illness and perhaps be restricted in the lessons they can attend (e.g. Eiser, 1980). In addition, academic achievement is likely to be affected by drugs (Stores, 1978) or other aspects of the treatment, and some conditions are inevitably associated with central nervous system (CNS) complications. A second indicator of adjustment can be seen in the child's *social behavior*, his maturity or popularity with peers. Again, some well-established measures of social adjustment can be identified. Several measures of social behavior are available which can be completed by teachers (Stott, 1966; Rutter and Graham, 1970) or by parents (Rutter and Graham, 1970). Social maturity can be assessed by the Vineland Scale (Doll, 1956). Other scales to measure personality (Eysenck, 1965), anxiety (Castaneda *et al.*, 1956) and self-concept (Piers and Harris, 1964) can also be used. All these scales enable the clinician to obtain a general guide to the child's social functioning. Thirdly, we may consider the individual's *marital or sexual status* as an indicator of his adjustment, and finally his *vocational status*—the extent to which he obtains steady employment appropriate to his achievements or ability level.

Measures of Adjustment among Chronically Sick Children

Scholastic Attainments

A child with a chronic illness is at considerable disadvantage in school. He is likely to miss more schooling than others, either due to his increased susceptibility to minor illnesses or in order to attend hospital for medical check-ups. A child receiving long-term medication may constantly function under par, suffering from side-effects of sickness or drowsiness related to his drugs. Indirectly, parents and teachers may expect less of the child academically, and consequently the child too may come to accept lower standards of achievement than his healthy peers.

Given the range of disadvantages faced by the chronically sick child, it is hardly surprising that many studies report that these children have attainments considerably below their chronological age, despite normal levels of general intelligence. Where attempts have been made to assess the cause of such lowered attainments, changes in parental attitudes and expectations appear critical. Burton (1975), for example, reported that a group of children with cystic fibrosis had a normal mean IQ (104). Despite this, 55 percent of boys and 66 percent of girls were retarded by at least 12 months in two or more school subjects; 25 percent of parents interviewed stated that they expected less of the child than was expected from other children in the family. A direct relationship between physical appearance and others' expectations was reported for a group of short-stature children, including a number who suffered from growth hormone deficiency, by Dorner and Elton (1973). Among these children who look so much younger than their real age, nearly 50 percent were retarded in reading achievement by more than 20 months. Similar relations between low achievements and chronic illness have been reported among children with hemophilia (Olch, 1971a), and with physical disability (Allen, 1967), although in neither case did the authors attempt to explain the reasons for their findings. Gath et al. (1980) studied a group of 76 diabetic children and reported that 20 were at least 2 years behind in reading, and six were between 1 and 2 years behind.

In many cases the situation becomes more complex in that the disease requires treatment by drugs which are known to affect brain function, or in that the disease itself is associated with CNS dysfunction. There are several indications that children with epilepsy have attainments in the order of 2 years below their chronological age. Among children with uncomplicated epilepsy, 18 percent were found to have reading ages 2 years below their chronological age, compared with only 6.8 percent of children in a control group (Rutter et al., 1970). Green and Hartlage (1971, 1972) reported that children with epilepsy had academic achievements 1 or 2 years below the expected, with reading being the least affected (13 months below) and arithmetic the most affected (21 months below). Stores (1978) has argued that the type of epilepsy, drug treatment and sex are critical determinants of intellectual functioning. In particular, children with left temporal spike discharge had reading skills below those of normal controls, while children with right temporal spike discharge did not differ from normals (Stores, 1978). In the same report, Stores presented some evidence that children prescribed phenytoin for at least 2 years had lower reading skills than children prescribed barbiturates or other drugs over a similar period. Like children treated for epilepsy, those with leukemia undergo several years of drug treatment, and there is some evidence that both methotrexate (Meadows and Evans, 1976) and radiation therapy (Eiser, 1979) are associated with reduced intellectual functioning.

Among children with chronic illness there are some indications that those acquiring a disease at younger ages are more seriously affected than those acquiring the same disease later in childhood. This applies, for example, to children with epilepsy (Dikmen, *et al.*, 1975), leukemia (Eiser and Lansdown, 1977, Eiser, 1980) and diabetes (Ack *et al.*, 1961; Worden and Vignos, 1962). These findings may well indicate that metabolic or structural changes occur in the immature brain which pose real limits to subsequent intellectual growth, and which operate in addition to factors such as school absences and altered parental expectancies.

If under-achievement is accepted as a measure of poor adjustment in chronically sick children, the conclusions must be that many such children are not satisfactorily integrated into the normal school setting. While there is no doubt that many sick children function very adequately in school, several factors appear to increase the risk that the child will not succeed. Type of disease, age of onset, and some drug treatments appear particularly to increase the child's vulnerability to poor academic performance.

Social Behavior

The following section does not claim to be a comprehensive review of the literature concerned with social adjustment and behavior among children with chronic illness; rather it attempts to describe the range of procedures used to investigate the problem and the limitations that each alone entails. The most commonly used measures of adjustment include scales to measure anxiety and self-concept. In addition, there are several methods used to investigate general behavior, either in school (Rutter, 1967; Conners, 1970) or at home (Rutter *et al.*, 1970). Other workers who object to the development of scales such as these have attempted to use projective techniques (e.g. Goodenough and Harris, 1950; Rotter, 1950; Symonds, 1964), arguing that it is only by such indirect means that the child's real feelings can be explored.

Personality Measures

Although it might be argued that only deviant *behavior* is worthy of investigation, the assumption that underlying personality deficits are predictive of later behavior disorder has led to a continued attempt to assess various aspects of personality disorder among children with chronic illness. As it may affect the child's performance on other tests, one of the most widely used measures is that of *anxiety*. Both the children's Manifest Anxiety Scale (Castaneda *et al.*, 1956) and the Test Anxiety Scale for Children (Sarason *et al.*, 1958) have been used in the study of children with chronic illness. Waechter (1971), for example, compared four groups of 6–10-year-olds, and found that only children with a fatal illness scored higher on anxiety test scales. Despite the assumption that higher anxiety scores will interfere with the child's performance on other tasks, there has been little attempt to investigate this relationship among groups of chronically sick children.

Self-concept Scales

It has been suggested that chronic illness effects a child's body-image, and this in turn is detrimental to psychological growth. Both Lipsett (1958) and Piers and Harris (1964) have developed scales that have been used extensively to study self-concept among sick children. For example, Downing *et al.* (1961) used a modified semantic differential technique to investigate 41 children aged between 7 and 19 years and hospitalized during treatment for Legg-Perthes disease. Research on the sick child's self-concept has probably been studied most extensively in relation to children with heart disease. Green and Levitt (1962) compared 25 children aged between 8 and 16 years of age with 25 normal children. The test was simply to draw a picture of the self and one of a peer. By contrasting the height and area of the two drawings, Green and Levitt concluded that the self drawings of children with heart disease were significantly smaller than those of normal children. The implication is that smaller self-drawings mirror a constricted self-image on the part of the sick child, but while such inferences may be plausible, they clearly require additional confirmatory evidence.

Tavormina *et al.* (1976) used the Piers–Harris (1967) self-concept scale, to compare four groups of children. One group was being treated for asthma, one for cystic fibrosis, one for diabetes, and the fourth group was hard of hearing. Despite the fact that all children had mild forms of the illness, the score for the group as a whole was significantly higher than would be predicted from the published norms. Analyzing separately for each illness type, Tavormina *et al.* found that children with asthma, cystic fibrosis, and diabetes had significantly poorer self-concepts than the norm, but children who were hard of hearing did not differ from normal. Children were also divided into three age-groups; the 5–10- and 11–13-year age-groups had poorer self-concepts than would be expected, but the 14–19-year age group was comparable with normals. Tavormina *et al.* note that the children in their sample suffered from mild forms of their illnesses. Nevertheless, it is perhaps encouraging that the older group of children appeared not to deviate from the norm.

Behavior in School

Several scales have been devised which require teachers to check a number of statements of behavior as they apply to a given child. The Teacher's Behavior Questionnaire devised by Rutter (1967), for example, consists of 26 statements rated as 'certainly applies', 'applies somewhat', and 'doesn't apply' (scored 2, 1 and 0 respectively). Items such as 'fidgets, bites nails, truants, steals' are included. It has been used in studies of children with phenylketonuria (Stevenson *et al.*, 1979), asthma (Graham *et al.*, 1967), uncomplicated epilepsy (Rutter *et al.*, 1970) and brain lesions (Seidel *et al.*, 1975). Although the scale has been widely used in studying sick children, it was in fact only standardized for 9-year-olds. A further criticism is that the scale is exclusively concerned with items of behavioral deviance, and teachers often feel reluctant to describe a child in such a totally negative fashion.   ·

Similar scales have, however, been devised by Stott (1966), Cowen (1961), and Conners (1969). This last scale consists of 39 items rated by teachers on a four-point scale, and yields four factors: aggression, withdrawal, anxiety, and hyperkineticism, and has been most extensively used in studies of behavior changes in children treated by drugs (Conners, 1969).

Behavior at Home

Complementing those scales to describe behavior in school, several scales have been published for use with parents. Clearly, such scales represent the only means of identifying behavior problems for children below school-age. Richman and Graham (1971) have published a standardized questionnaire to be completed by parents of 3-year-olds, but to date the scale has not been used in studying sick children.

Rutter *et al.* (1970) devised a scale to be completed by parents to complement the scale already described for use with teachers. Despite a low concordance between the two scales, Rutter *et al.* used the scale to compare the frequency of behavior problems among children with chronic physical illness and normal controls. A parent scale has also been devised by Conners (1970), but failed to identify many qualitative differences between normal and psychiatrically ill children. The lack of relationship between parent and teacher scales suggests that each measures behavior in a very specific situation, rather than indicating underlying personality traits.

Projective Measures

Despite the many objections that have been made to the use of projective measures (e.g. Mischel, 1968), such methods have been used quite extensively in studying sick and dying children. One of the most widely used measures is the Draw-A-Person (Machover, 1951) where the assumption is that distortions in the drawing reflect abnormalities in the child's self-concept. This measure has been used in the study of children with renal disease (Khan *et al.*, 1971) and cerebral palsy (Abercrombie and Tyson, 1966). The Rotter Incomplete Sentences Blank (1950) test has been used in the study of children with various physical disorders (Cruikshank, 1952) and in the Rochester group of studies. The child's sentence completions can be scored according to the number of negative comments the child makes, and the number of references to sickness or disability.

Projective measures have most appeal in describing the inner feelings of the child with a terminal illness, although some workers (e.g. Vernick, 1973) claim that the use of such techniques is to save embarrassment for the researcher, rather than the child. Perhaps not surprisingly, reports of increased levels of anxiety and interpersonal isolation have been described among fatally ill children using projective measures (Spinetta et al., 1973, 1974).

Marital and Sexual Status

A third indicator of adjustment is the frequency of marriage and normality of sexual relationships among individuals who suffered a chronic illness during childhood. Although a lower incidence of marriage, or higher divorce rate than among normal individuals, might be taken to indicate a degree of maladjustment, there is probably no other area in which the prejudices of others play such a critical part. Much work supports the notion of prolonged batchelorhood among those with a chronic illness, although these findings remain somewhat difficult to interpret in the absence of satisfactory control groups.

Not surprisingly, lowest marriage rates occur among those with the more severe physical disabilities. Brieland (1967) found only 24 percent of 67 students with orthopedic handicaps to be married, while Lambert et al. (1969) reported a rate of 49 percent among a group of juvenile amputees. Among 1000 hemophiliacs, Katz (1963) reported that 46 percent had married, and only 2.2 percent were divorced or separated. Rainer et al. (1963) report a higher incidence of non-married people among the deaf, and further that deaf individuals tend to marry others with hearing problems. Lindsay et al. (1979) followed a group of children suffering from temporal lobe seizures. Female survivors, if not handicapped, were nearly all married, but males tended more often to remain single.

Recent reports concern marriage rates among individuals recovered from childhood cancers. Holmes and Holmes (1975) investigated 124 individuals who had survived at least 10 years following cancer. At the time of study, 60 had married, of whom 8 were divorced. Of 41 individuals who had never married, 36 stated that their reason for not marrying related to the illness or subsequent disability. Among those who had married 34 had children, and 6 were sterile. One patient stated he would not have children because he was unclear about the risk his own cancer conferred to his offspring. These studies are in some contrast to those in which adolescents with chronic illness are asked about their aspirations and expectations for the future. Children with diabetes, for example, appear to have a fairly optimistic outlook on life. Fallstrom (1974) reports that they develop occupational goals earlier than healthy peers. On the whole they hope to marry and have children (Davis et al., 1965; Khurana and White, 1970), and do not believe that their illness will affect their future plans (Gil *et al.*, 1977). That sick children may have seriously distorted ideas about how their illness will affect their future is emphasized in a paper by Dorner (1976) concerned with the psychosocial functioning of adolescents with spina bifida.

Despite the optimistic outlook on life described by these children, the evidence, such as it is, suggests that the scope of their social activities is likely to be curtailed compared with healthy individuals. The indications are that a chronic illness in childhood reduces the likelihood of an individual's marrying. At the same time, the data suggest that for those who do marry, there is considerably less risk of the marriage ending in divorce than among individuals with no history of illness.

Vocational Status

In general, individuals with chronic illness are less likely to be in permanent employment than the healthy, and also to hold more manual positions. These remarks appear to relate especially to those with the more severe handicaps, and to those of lower intelligence levels. For example, Vernon (1969) reports that 80 percent of the deaf are in some form of manual labour (a figure which he contrasts with 50 percent of the normal population). At the same time, only 17 percent of the deaf are in white-collar employment compared with 46 percent of the general population. Despite the relatively mild nature of the handicap with regard to employment, Katz (1963) reported that only 53 percent of 1000 hemophiliacs were employed; 20 percent were not, or had never been, in permanent employment. Further, among those employed, only 24 percent held white-collar positions.

Given the relatively poor rates of employment among those with mild disorders, it is not surprising that much higher rates of unemployment occur among the more severely disabled. Pollock and Stark (1969) investigated 75 individuals with cerebral palsy. Of 48 individuals over school-leaving age, only nine were in employment, one was at university and five were in sheltered employment. Similarly, Ingram *et al.* (1964) found that only 21 percent of 200 individuals with cerebral palsy were employed, and 44 percent unemployed. Laurence and Beresford (1976) reported that 36 of 51 individuals with spina bifida were employed or carrying out normal duties of a housewife or mother. All but two of these in employment were in light manual, clerical, or managerial positions. In a follow-up study of children treated for brain tumors, Eiser (1979) reported considerable variability in employment among 25 patients who had completed their education. Although one attended university, seven were unemployed and five worked in unskilled positions. The remainder were in clerical positions, with only two individuals following a profession. Klapper and Birch (1966) reported that only 15 of 80 patients over 18 years and suffering from cerebral palsy were in employment, and of these only three were financially independent.

As a measure of adjustment following chronic illness, employment rates are subject to the same criticism as marital rates; the incidence among the chronically ill may reflect society's attitudes and prejudices as much as the individual's abilities. Clearly, however, employment prospects are relatively poor following illness in childhood, and the individual's chance of achieving self-sufficiency may be limited in comparison with the normal.

Characteristics of the Child and his Illness that Determine the Degree of Maladjustment

Lipowski (1970) has argued that the degree to which the child accepts his illness is dependent on a number of factors, of which three main groups can be defined. These are *disease-related* factors: for example, its severity, degree of disablement, or restriction of activities; *intrapersonal* factors: the child's personality, intelligence, or social class; and *environmental* factors: the attitudes of parents and significant others to the illness. In examining the influence of each of these to the child's mental health, the dynamics of the interaction process between the variables cannot be over-emphasized. Most researchers have tended to examine one factor in isolation. It is noteworthy that where an attempt has been made to examine the relations between the different components of the coping process, workers have concluded that the child's attitudes very closely reflect those of his family (Tropauer *et al.*, 1970).

Disease-related Factors

Severity

For a number of diseases there appears to be a curvilinear relationship between severity of the handicap and the child's adjustment process. It appears that the more severely handicapped the child, the less he attempts to compete in the normal world and the more accepting he becomes of his position. The child with less disabling conditions attempts to operate in both the world of the normal child and that of the sick child, and this 'imagined status' leads to conflict and reduced effectiveness of functioning. The constant failure associated with the child's dealings in the normal world lead to a poorer self-image and less adequate adjustment. These findings have been reported for partially hearing compared with deaf children (Sussman, 1966; Rodda, 1970; Williams, 1970) and for partially sighted compared with blind children (Cowen *et al.*, 1961). It also applies to children with physical disabilities. Those most severely affected by juvenile arthritis (McAnarney *et al.*, 1974) or by thalidomide (McFie and Robertson, 1973) were reported to be better adjusted than those less disabled. Bruhn *et al.* (1970) has reported similar results for hemophiliacs.

Type of Disease

Although there have been no systematic reports of an association between type of disorder and type of maladjustment, the incidence of maladjustment appears to increase with certain disorders. Rutter *et al.* (1970) reported that among children with chronic diseases of various forms, there was a three-fold increase in disturbed ratings of behavior compared with healthy children, and a five-fold increase among children with neuroepileptic disorders.

One vexed question in pediatric research is whether the child's understanding of his illness can improve his adjustment and acceptance of its routine. Despite the heavy emphasis often placed by medical staff on the need to inform the child and his family about the nature of the illness, there have been few reports to confirm that increasing the child's understanding also improves his behavior. In fact, reports that have occurred suggest there is little or no relationship. Both Tietz and Vidmar (1972) and Koski (1969) failed to find a relationship between diabetic control and level of knowledge, for example. Such a lack of reported relationship does not necessarily imply that informing the child about his disease is of little value. Rather, care should be taken in deciding exactly what information is appropriate for children of different ages and ability levels; it is likely that if attempts were made to match the level of information given to the child's developmental state, more positive outcomes might result.

Demands of the Treatment Regime

Many children with chronic illness undergo intensive medical treatment for many years, and it is not surprising that resistance to the treatment regimes can frequently occur. Adolescents particularly identify adherence to treatment regimes as extending their dependence on adults, and may sabotage their medication as a result. Reports of such defiance are particularly likely to occur among diabetics (Mattson *et al.*, 1966, 1971) and cystics (Pinkerton, 1974; Tropauer *et al.*, 1970). Family life is much disturbed; Burton (1975) has described sympathetically the trials for a family of having a child with cystic fibrosis, and Korsch *et al.* (1973) have commented in the same vein with regard to the child undergoing renal dialysis.

Intrapersonal Factors

The child's age at disease onset, personality, and intelligence are thought to be predictive of adjustment, although with few exceptions it is difficult to investigate these variables systematically. It is rarely possible, for example, to have available measures of premorbid personality against which to assess the child's functioning.

Age at Onset of Disease

The long-standing implications of a chronic illness in childhood are thought to vary with the age at which the onset of the disease occurs, since it is at this time that the child is likely to be more ill than at any other time, as well as forced to undergo the most intensive forms of treatment. For many diseases, such as leukemia or other cancers, for example, the child is also likely to undergo hospitalization or surgery following diagnosis, while later treatment occurs almost exclusively on an out-patient basis. The degree of trauma associated with the illness is therefore greater on diagnosis than at any other time. Among young handicapped children, for example, there has been some concern about social development, given the deprivation that can occur during the child's early life. Battle (1974), argues that there may be critical periods for acquiring certain skills, and notes that the differences between handicapped and normal children increase with age. Williams (1970) reports that, the younger deaf children are when diagnosed, the less well adjusted they subsequently tend to be, and offers an explanation for this in terms of altered parental expectations for the younger handicapped child. Both Taylor and Falconer (1968) and Gudmundsson (1966) reported a higher rate of psychiatric disturbance in adults with temporal lobe epilepsy who had their first attack in childhood compared with adulthood, although this may clearly be the result of longer-standing social effects of the disease rather than genuinely due to earlier age of onset. Shaffer et al. (1975) failed to find an association between age at injury and psychiatric referral in a group of children who received head injuries between 6 months and 12 years of age.

Maddison and Raphael (1971) hypothesize that the onset of chronic illness at different ages in childhood is associated with specific adverse consequences in different area of functioning. Illness in the 1–3-year age-range may limit the child's opportunity for self-expression, increase maternal control, and thereby promote passive and helpless behavior. In the 4–6-year age-range the effect of chronic illness is to lead to the development of extreme guilt and inhibition of initiative. From 6 to 11 years the child is most likely to develop a sense of inadequacy and insecurity, and illness occurring during adolescence is most likely to interfere with the establishment of role and identity.

Although long-standing psychological effects of illness during childhood have been widely reported, there is little to support psychodynamic consequences of the type outlined above. Although age of onset is clearly a powerful determinant of the child's adjustment, subsequent environmental influences are likely to modify greatly the individual's coping behavior. It is also unlikely that age at diagnosis is an important variable in itself. Whether or not it contributes negatively to the child's social development will depend on the specifics of the disease in question.

Intelligence

There is some evidence to suggest that the more intelligent child is more adaptive in dealing with his illness (Vignos *et al.*, 1972). Hardy (1968), for example, found that among blind children, the higher the verbal IQ, the lower the child's score on a measure of anxiety. It need not necessarily be assumed that the more intelligent child will adjust better to his illness than the less intelligent. Increased intelligence may lead to enhanced understanding of the disease process and personal risk, exaggerating anxiety. Many parents and children express a wish to be told as little as possible about their disease, specifically to reduce anxiety. It may well be a situation in which a little knowledge is a desirable thing, and clinicians should not assume that factual information will in all circumstances lead to better acceptance of disease.

Social Class

Good adjustment among blind children was found to increase with social class (Cowen *et al.*, 1961). Presumably, factors such as improved parenting or higher income are more directly responsible for such improvement, rather than social class itself. Some work suggests that the more critical requirement is group support, i.e. working-class people who have a good network of friends and relations may be as well adjusted as middle-class people with comparable support systems.

Age at Assessment

Little attention has been given to the child's behavior on assessment and relation to chronological age. One exception is the study of hemophiliacs by Olch (1971b). She reported that 5–7-year-old showed a high degree of anxiety and social unease; 8–12-year-olds were passive and lacking in spontaneity, while young adolescents were resistant and independent, often displaying excessive risk-taking behavior. The extent to which these findings would apply to healthy children in these age-groups, or if they would be appropriate for children with other chronic illnesses, is not clear from Olch's report. However, such age-related differences in behavior need to be noted, particularly with regard to whether or not they also apply to the child's behavior in other situations.

Environmental Factors

While many workers acknowledge the influence of the child's family in molding his own attitudes to his illness, little research has been undertaken. Tropauer et al. (1970) showed that the behavior of very young children with cystic fibrosis was predictive from their parents' attitudes, as did McFie and Robertson (1973) working with thalidomides. The intimate nature of family coping mechanism was also documented by Orbach (1955) who showed that a father's adjustment to the illness of his child was related to his wife's well-being rather than the physical health of the child. This remains, however, an area open to much future research. It might be expected that those adolescents with diabetes or renal failure, for example, who rebel against their treatment regimes, may also be those whose families showed worst adjustment to their illness during the preceding years. Longitudinal studies concerned with such issues are needed.

The impact of chronic illness on the child's family is reported to vary from the very adverse, resulting in disturbed family relations and divorce, to the more positive, in which relationships may be warm and enhanced. The factors which lead a family to adopt either style have not been specified, nor is it altogether clear what proportion of families fit in to either category. Most researchers have tended to focus on the family during periods of crisis, particularly around the diagnosis (Burton, 1975); and during the terminal stage of the illness (e.g. Lewis, 1967).

There have been fewer attempts to describe the day-to-day life of families living with an extended illness of one of its members. There has been little attempt to describe psychological mood changes related to the child's health, or, with few exceptions, how restrictions such as special diets (Bentovim et al., 1970) or treatments (Burton, 1975) affect the family functioning and mood.

Changes in the quality of parent–child interaction, usuallly in the direction of over-protection (e.g. Fife, 1978) are well documented for children with chronic illness. However, two studies have emphasized the essentially normal approaches to child-rearing which can still occur despite childhood illness. Barsch (1968) interviewed the parents of 177 children who were blind or deaf, had cerebral palsy or were mongoloid or suffered some other central nervous system disorder. Hewett et al. (1970) interviewed the parents of 180 children with cerebral palsy. In both studies the authors emphasized that parents continued to rear their children according to their own beliefs, regardless of the handicap. In contrast, Shere (1957) studied interactions between mothers and twin children, where one twin suffered from cerebral palsy. Mothers were more directive to the twin with cerebral palsy and, in turn, the child was less involved in family decisions. It would clearly be useful to extend this type of study to include groups of children with other illnesses, and to investigate the relationship (if any) between the parents' reports of their behavior and their actual child-rearing practices. While the attitudes of the parents are clearly central in molding the child's beliefs and behavior, there has been a tendency to ignore the considerable influence that may also develop from grandparents, siblings, teachers, peers and medical personnel.

Conclusions

Chronic illness, having its onset during childhood, is clearly a traumatic event, very much influencing the child and his family in their adjustment to his adult life and independence. It would be a mistake, however, to assume that the effects of long-term illness are necessarily detrimental. A number of factors interact with the course of the illness to determine the psychological outcome in each individual case and, according to Rutter (1979), such adverse factors are multiplicative rather than additive. In discussing the repercussions of birth complications on the child's development, Pasamanick and Knobloch (1961) identify a 'continuum of reproductive casualty'. Extending this principle further, Sameroff and Chandler (1975) have stressed the plastic character of both the environment and organism in actively participating in mental growth. The child is in a constant state of active organization of the environment, and as such cannot be regarded as maintaining a disadvantage associated with disease or other trauma. This view implies that the child has a self-righting tendency, and will continue on a normal psychological growth path following a single trauma, provided a supportive environment is available. The child is unable to adopt such a self-righting policy where multiple traumas exist. Sameroff and Chandler (1975) note the contradiction between the wide range of influences on development and the small number of outcomes. The human organism appears able to develop within normal limits in all but the most severe conditions. Given such self-righting tendencies there are two mechanisms whereby deviations might occur. It is possible that the child's ability to organize and adapt to the environment may be damaged by physical means (e.g. severe anoxia following birth injury) or that, despite an intact nervous system environmental forces are so damaging that normal development is prevented. Given a single trauma, this view implies that normal adjustment and growth is possible in a highly supportive environment, but becomes less likely the poorer the quality of the child's environment. Although the theory itself may be criticized (St James Roberts, 1979) no-one can doubt the general tendency for children to recover in very adverse circumstances.

Such a view may therefore be consistent with the range of psychological outcomes following illness in childhood, but it leaves begging one of the most challenging of questions; notably, what constitutes the more supportive environment? Variables such as social class, intelligence, or personality may be associated with a supportive environment, but their relationship has not been established with clarity. Part of the problem lies in the lack of originality with which researchers have approached the problem. Reliance on established measures of personality, for example, may be acceptable from a research design point of view, but do not get at the less tangible issue of parent–child involvement and closeness factors that are more likely to be of critical value.

The relatively new alliance between pediatrics and psychology has already achieved considerable success. Already, the yardstick whereby cure is measured is not simply survival. More and more, the concern is with a child's total 'quality of life'. The goal is not just to prevent death, but to ensure that a child achieves a personal, social, and cognitive level of attainment that is indistinguishable from his believed potential. Objectives such as these require comprehensive and consistent medical care, social work support for the family, and psychological intervention to ensure the integration of the sick child into a normal school setting as far as possible, and to reduce the probability of behavior disturbance.

A second achievement is undoubtedly the realization that a child does not live in a vacuum, and that it is not possible to treat him in isolation from his family. The role of the parents in the medical care of their child is being encouraged (Rachman and Phillips, 1975). At the same time, the disruptive nature of most illness on family life is being recognized. For example, reports of the impact of cystic fibrosis (Burton, 1975), leukemia (McCarthey, 1975), and spina bifida (Tew et al., 1974) have been made. Although most researchers have so far been content to describe the adverse consequences of such diseases, practical recommendations are increasingly being made (e.g. Peck, 1979). The literature may have set out to document the hazards of a sick child as far as normal family life is concerned, yet its most notable achievement has been to document the positive aspects of human coping resources. Much remains to be done, however, before we will be able to predict which families are likely to cope most satisfactorily. This question is not simply a theoretical one. In the treatment of some illnesses, limited medical and technical resources make it essential that services are offered preferentially to some patients. The enormous cost and burden of renal dialysis, for example, means that not all children requiring such treatment are able to have a kidney machine in their own homes. In order to ensure that most use is made of the equipment that is available, physicians attempt subjective appraisals of a family's ability to cope. Any research findings which could indicate a more objective basis for making such decisions are clearly highly desirable.

Finally, psychologists have made real contributions to improvements in therapy. Lask and Weir (1979), for example, have shown that in a controlled trial of family therapy in childhood asthma a group treated by family therapy did significantly better than a control group, at a 1-year follow-up.

The range of problems to be tackled by pediatric psychologists is wide. It is perhaps unfortunate that advances in medicine are likely to increase even further the need for psychological involvement in the care of sick children and their families.

References

Abercrombie, M. L. J., and Tyson, M. C. (1966). 'Body image and a draw-a-man test in cerebral palsy', *Developmental Medicine and Child Neurology*, **8**, 9–15.

Ack, M., Miller, I., and Weil, W. B. Jr. (1961). 'Intelligence of children with diabetes mellitus', *Peadiatrics*, **28**, 764–770.

Allen, G. H. (1961). 'Aspirations and expectations of physically impaired high school seniors', *Personnel and Guidance Journal*, **47**, 59.

Barker, R. G., Wright, B. A., Myerson, L., and Gonick, M. R. (1953). 'Adjustment to Physical Handicap and Illness. A Survey of the Social Psychology of Physique and Disability', *Social Science Research Council (Revised)*, New York.

Barsch, R. H. (1968). *The Parent to the Handicapped Child*. Thomas, Springfield, Illinois.

Battle, C. U. (1974). 'Disruptions in the socialization of a young, severely handicapped child', *Rehabilitation Literature*, **35**, 130.

Bentovim, A., Clayton, B. E., Francis, D. E. M., Shepherd, J., and Wolff, O. H. (1970). 'Use of an amino acid mixture in treatment of phenylketonuria', *Archives of Disease in Childhood*, **45**, 640–650.

Brieland, D. (1967). 'A follow-up study of orthopedically handicapped high school graduates', *Exceptional Children*, **33**, 555.

Bruhn, J. G., Hampton, J. W., and Chandler, B. C. (1970). 'Clinical marginality and psychological adjustment in hemophilia', *Journal of Psychosomatic Research*, **15**, 207.

Burton, L. (1975). *The Family Life of Sick Children*. Routledge & Kegan Paul, London.

Castaneda, A., McCandress, B . R., and Palermo, D. S. (1956). 'The children's form of the manifest anxiety scale', *Child Development*, **27**, 317.

Conners, C. K. (1969). 'A teacher rating scale for use in drug studies with children', *American Journal of Child Psychiatry*, **126**, 884–888.

Conners, C. K. (1970). 'Symptom patterns in hyperkinetic, neurotic, and normal children', *Child Development*, **41**, 667–682.

Cowen, E. L., Underberg, R. P., Verrillo, R. T., and Benhan, F. G. (1961). *Adjustment to visual Disability in Adolescence*. American Foundation for the Blind, New York.

Cruikshank, W. M. (1952). 'A study of the relation of physical disability to social adjustment', *American Journal of Occupational Therapy*, **1**, 100.

Davies, F. (1963). *Passage Through Crisis. Polio Victims and Their Families*. Bobbs-Merrill, Indianapolis.

Davis, D. M., Shipp, J. C., and Pattishall, E. G. (1965). 'Attitudes of diabetic boys and girls toward diabetics', *Diabetes*, **14**, 106–109.

Dikmen, S., Mathews, C. G., and Harley, J. P. (1975). 'The effect of early vs. late onset of major motor epilepsy upon cognitive intellectual performances', *Epilepsia*, **16**, 73–81.

Doll, E. A. (1956). *Vineland Social Maturity Scale*. American Guidance Service, Inc., Circle Pines, Minnesota.

Dorner, S. (1976). 'Adolescents with spina bifida: how they see their situation', *Archives of Disease in Childhood*, **51**, 439–444.

Dorner, S., and Elton, A. (1973). 'Short, taught and vulnerable', *Special Education*, **62**, 12.

Downing, R. W., Moed, G., and Wright, B. W. (1961). 'Studies of disability: a technique for psychological measurement or effects', *Child Development*, **32**, 561.

Eiser, C. (1979). '*Irradiation and intellectual ability among children*', in Oborne, B. J., Gruneberg, M. M., and Eiser J. R. (eds), *Proceedings of the Conference on Psychology and Medicine*. Academic Press.

Eiser, C. (1980). 'The effects of chronic illness on intellectual development: a comparison of normal children with those treated for childhood leukaemia and solid tumours', *Archives of Disease in Childhood*, **55**, 766–770.

Eiser, C., and Lansdown, R. A. (1977). 'Retrospective study of intellectual development in children treated for acute lymphoblastic leukaemia', *Archives of Disease in Childhood*, **52**, 525–529.

Eysenck, S. B. G. (1965). 'A new scale for personality measurement in children', *British Journal of Educational Psychology*, xxxv, 362.

Fallstrom, K. (1974). 'On the personality structure in diabetic school children', *Acta Paediatrica Scandinavica*, Supplement 251, pp. 5–71.

Fife, B. L. (1978). 'Reducing parental overprotection of the leukaemic child', *Social Science and Medicine*, **12**, 117, 122.

Gath, A., Smith, M. A., and Baum, J. D. (1980). 'Emotional, behavioural, and educational disorders in diabetic children', *Archives of Disease in Childhood*, **55**, 371–375.

Gil, R., Frish, M., Amir, S., and Galatzer, A. (1977). 'Awareness of complications among juvenile diabetics and their parents', in Laron, Z. (ed.), *Psychological Aspects of Balance in Diabetics*.

Goodenough, F. L., and Harris, D. B. (1950). 'Studies in the psychology of children's drawings: II, 1928–1949', *Psychological Bulletin*, **47**, 369–433.

Graham, P., and Rutter, M. (1970). 'Psychiatric aspects of physical disorder', in Rutter, M., Tizard, J., and Whitmore, K. (eds), *Education, Health and Behavior*. Longman, London.

Graham, P., Rutter, M., Yule, W., and Pless, I. B. (1967). 'Childhood asthma a psychosomatic disorder? Some epidemiological considerations', *British Journal of Preventive and Social Medicine*, **21**, 78–85.

Green, J. B., and Hartlage, L. C. (1971). 'Comparative performance of epileptic and non-epileptic children and adolescents', *Disease of the Nervous System*, **32**, 418–421.

Green, J. B., and Hartlage, L. C. (1972). 'The relation of parental attitudes to academic and social achievement in epileptic children', *Epilepsia*, **13**, 21.

Green, M., and Levitt, E. E. (1962). 'Constriction of body image in children with congenital heart disease', *Pediatrics*, **29**, 438.

Green, M., and Solnit, A. S. (1964). 'Reactions to the threatened loss of a child. A vulnerable child syndrome', *Pediatrics*, **34**, 58.

Gudmondsson, G. (1966). 'Epilepsy in Iceland; a clinical and epidemiological investigation', *Acta Neurologica Scandinavica*, Supplement 25.

Hardy, R. E. (1968). 'A study of manifest anxiety among blind residential school students', *New Outlook for the Blind*, **48**, 173.

Hewett, S., Newson, J., and Newson E. (1970). *The Family and the Handicapped Child*. Aldine, Chicago.

Holmes, H. A., and Holmes, F. F. (1975). 'After ten years, what are the handicaps and life-style of children treated with cancer', *Clinical Paediatrics*, **14**, 819–823.

Ingram, T. T. S., Jameson, S., Errington, J., and Mitchell, R. G. (1964). *Living with Cerebral Palsy*. Heinemann, London.

Kaplan, H. B. (1970). 'Self-derogation and childhood family structure: family size, birth order and sex distribution', *Journal of Nervous and Mental Disease*, **151**, 13.

Katz, A. H. (1963). 'Social adaptation in chronic illness: a study of haemophilia', *American Journal of Public Health*, **53**, 166.

Khan, A. V., Herndon, C. H., and Ahmadian, S. Y. (1971). Social and emotional adaptations of children with transplanted kidneys and chronic hemodialysis. *American Journal of Psychiatry*, **127**, 114.

Khurana, R., and White, P. (1970). 'Attitudes of the diabetic child and his parents towards his illness', *Postgraduate Medicine*, **48**, 72–77.

Klapper, Z. S., and Birch, H. C. (1966). 'The relation of childhood characteristics to outcome in young adults with cerebral palsy', *Developmental Medicine and Child Neurology*, **8**, 645–656.

Korsch, B. M., Negrette, V. F., Gardner, J. F., Weinstock, C. L., Mercer, A. S., Grushkin, C. M., and Fine, R. N. (1973). 'Kidney transplantation in children: psychological follow-up study on child and family', *Journal of Pediatrics*, **83**, 399–408.

Koski, M. L. (1969). 'The coping processes in childhood diabetes', *Acta Paediatrica Scandinavica*, Supplement 198, 7–56.

Lambert, C. N., Hamilton, R. C., and Pillicare, R. J. (1969). 'The juvenile amputee program: its social economic value', *Journal of Bone and Joint Surgery*, **51A**, 1135.

Lask, B., and Weir, (1979). 'Childhood asthma: family therapy as an adjunct to routine management', *Journal of Family Therapy*, **1**, 33–50.

Laurence, K. M., and Beresford, A. (1976). 'Degree of physical handicap, education, and occupation of 51 adults with spina bifida', *British Journal of Preventive and Social Medicine*, **30**, 197–202.

Lewis, I. C. (1967). 'Leukaemia in childhood: its effects on the family', *Australian Paediatric Journal*, **3**, 244–247.

Lindsay, J., Ounsted, C., and Richards, P. (1979). 'Long-term outcome in children with temporal lobe seizures. 1: Social outcome and childhood factors', *Developmental Medicine and Child Neurology*, **21**, 285–298.

Lipowski, Z. J. (1970). 'Physical illness, the individual and the coping process', *Psychiatry in Medicine*, **1**, 91.

Lipsett, L. P. (1958). 'A self-concept scale for children and its relationship to the children's form of the Manifest Anxiety Scale', *Child Development*, **29**, 463.

McAnarney, E., Pless, I. B., Satterwhite, B., and Friedman, S. (1974). 'Psychological problems of children with chronic juvenile arthritis', *Paediatrics*, **53**, 523–528.

McCarthey, M. (1975). 'Social aspects of treatment in childhood leukaemia', *Social Science and Medicine*, **9**, 263–269.

McFie, J., and Robertson, J. (1973). 'Psychological test results of children with thalidomide disorders', *Development Medicine and Child Neurology*, **15**, 719–727.

Machover, K. (1951). 'Drawings of the human figure: a method of personality investigation, in Anderson, H. A., and Anderson, G. L. (eds), *An Introduction to Projective Techniques*. Prentice Hall, New York.

Maddison, D., and Raphael, B. (1971). 'Social and psychological consequences of chronic disease in childhood', *Medical Journal of Australia*, **2**, 1265.

Mattson, A., and Gross, S. (1966). 'Adaptational and defensive behaviour in young haemophiliacs and their parents', *American Journal of Psychiatry*, **122**, 1349.

Mattson, A., Gross, S., and Hall, T. W. (1971). 'Psychoendocrine study of adaptation in young haemophiliacs', *Psychosomatic Medicine*, xxxiii, 215.

Meadows, P. T., and Evans, A. E. (1976). 'Effects of chemotherapy on the central nervous system. A study of parenteral methotrexate in long-term survivors of leukaemia and lymphoma in childhood', *Cancer*, **1**, 1079–1085.

Mischel, W. (1968). *Personality and Assessment*. Wiley, New York.

Olch, D. (1971a). 'Effects of haemophilia upon intellectual growth and academic achievement', *Journal of Genetic Psychology*, **119**, 635.

Olch, D. (1971b). 'Personality characteristics of haemophiliacs', *Journal of Personality Assessment*, **13**, 635.

Orbach, C. E., Sutherland, A. M., and Bozemann, H. F. (1955). 'Psychological impact of cancer and its treatment', *Cancer*, **8**, 20–33.

Pasamanick, B., and Knobloch, H. (1961). Epidemiological studies on the complications of pregnancy and the birth process, in Caplan, G. (ed). *Prevention of Mental Disorders in Children*. Basic Books, New York.

Peck, B. (1979). 'Effects of childhood cancer on long-term survivors and their families', *British Medical Journal*, **1**, 1327–1329.

Piers, E. V., and Harris, D. B. (1964). 'Age and other correlates of self-concept in children', *Journal of Educational Psychology*, **55**, 91.

Pinkerton, P. (1969). 'Managing the psychological aspects of cystic fibrosis', *Arizona Medicine*, **26**, 348.

Pinkerton, P. (1974). 'Psychological problems of children with chronic illness', in *The Care of Children with Chronic Illness* (Proceedings of 67th Conference Paediatric Research). Ross Laboratories, Columbus, Ohio.

Pless, I. B., and Douglas, J. W. B. (1971). 'Chronic illness in childhood. 1 : Epidemiological and clinical characteristics', *Paediatrics*, **47**, 405.

Pless, I. B., and Pinkerton, P. (1975). *Chronic Childhood Disorder, Promoting Patterns of adjustment*. Henry Kimpton, London.

Pless, I. B., and Roghmann, K. J. (1971). 'Chronic illness and its consequences: observations based on three epidemiological surveys', *Journal of Paediatrics*, **79**, 351–359.

Pless, I. B., and Satterwhite, B. (1975). '*Chronic illness*', in Haggerty, R. J., Roghmann, K. J., and Pless, I. B. (eds), *Child Health and the Community*. Wiley, New York.

Pollock, G. A., and Stark, (1969). 'Long-term results in the management of 67 children with cerebral palsy', *Developmental Medicine and Child Neurology*, **11**, 17.

Rachman, S. J., and Phillips, C. (1975). *Psychology and Medicine*. Temple Smith, London.

Rainer, J. D., Altschuler, K. Z., and Kallman, F. J. (1963). *Family and Mental Health Problems on a Deaf Population*. Columbia University Press, New York.

Richman, N., and Graham, P. J. (1971). A behavioural screening questionnaire for use with three-year-old children. Preliminary findings. *Journal of Child Psychology and Psychiatry*, 1971, **12**, 5–33.

Rodda, M. (1970). *The Hearing Impaired School Leaver*. University of London Press, London.

Rotter, J.B. (1950). *Incomplete Sentence Blank*. Psychological Corp., New York.

Rutter, M. (1967). 'A children's behavior questionnaire for completion by teachers: preliminary findings', *Journal of Child Psychology and Psychiatry*, **8**, 1–12.

Rutter, M. (1979). 'Maternal deprivation, 1972–1978: new findings, new concepts, new approaches', *Child Development*, **50**, 283–305.

Rutter, M., and Graham, P. (1970). 'Psychiatric aspects of intellectual and educational retardation', in Rutter, M., Tizard, J., and Whitmore, I. C. (eds), *Education, Health and Behaviour*. Longman, London.

Rutter, M., Graham, P. J., and Yule, W. (1970). *A Neuropsychiatric Study in Childhood*. Spastics International Medical Publications, Heinemann Medical Books, London.

St James Roberts (1979). 'Neurological plasticity, recovery from brain insult and child development', in Reese, H. W., and Lipsitt, L. P. (eds), *Advances in Child Psychology*, vol. 14. Academic Press, New York.

Sameroff, A. J., and Chandler, M. J. (1973). 'Reproductive risk and the continuum of caretaking casualty', in Horowitz, F. D. (ed.), *Review of Child Development Research*. University of Chicago Press, Chicago.

Sarason, S. B., Davidson, K. S., Lighthall, F. F., and Waite, R. R. (1958). A test anxiety scale for children. *Child Development*, **29**, 105.

Seidel, U. P., Chadwick, O., and Rutter, M. (1975). Psychological disorders in crippled children: a comparative study of children with and without brain damage. *Developmental Medicine and Child Neurology*, **17**, 563–53.

Shaffer, D. (1977). 'Brain injury', in Rutter, M., and Hersov, L. (eds), *Child Psychiatry: Modern Approaches*. Blackwell, Oxford.

Shaffer, D., Chadwick, O., and Rutter, M. (1975). Psychiatric outcome of localised head injury in children. In Porter, R. and Fitz Simons, D. W. (eds). *Outcome of severe damage to the Central Nervous System*. CIBA Foundation Symposium No. 34. Amsterdam, Elsevier-Excerpta Medica-North-Holland.

Shere, M. O. (1957). 'The socio-emotional development of the twin who has cerebral palsy', *Cerebral Palsy Review*, **18**, 16–18.

Spinetta, J. J., Rigler, D., and Karon, M. (1973). 'Anxiety in the dying child', *Paediatrics*, **52**, 841–845.

Spinetta, J. J., Rigler, D., and Karon, M. (1974). 'Personal space as a measure of a dying child's sense of isolation', *Journal of Consulting and Clinical Psychology*, **42**, 751–757.

Stevenson, J. E., Hawcroft, J., Lobascher, M., Smith, I., Wolff, O. H., and Graham, P. J. (1979). 'Behavioral deviance in children with early treated PKU', *Archives of Disease in Childhood*, **54**, 14–18.

Stores, G. (1978). 'School children with epilepsy at risk for learning and behavior problems', *Developmental Medicine and Child Neurology*, **20**, 502–508.

Stott, A. (1966). *The Social Adjustment of Children*, 3rd edn. University of London Press, London.

Sussman, M. B. (1966). 'Sociological theory and deafness: problems and prospects', *ASHA: Journal of American Speech and Hearing Association*, **8**, 303.

Symonds, P. M. (1964). *Symonds Picture Study Test, 1964*. Teachers College, Columbia University, New York.

Tavormina, J. B., Kastner, L. S., Slater, P. M., and Watt, S. L. (1976). 'Chronically ill children: a psychologically and emotionally deviant population', *Journal of Abnormal Child Psychology*, **4**, 99–110.

Taylor, D. C., and Falconer, M. A. (1968). 'Clinical socio-economic and psychological change after temporal lobectomy for epilepsy', *British Journal of Psychiatry*, **114**, 1247–1261.

Tew, B., Laurence, K. M., and Samuel, P. (1974). 'Parental estimates of the intelligence of their physically handicapped child', *Developmental Medicine and Child Neurology*, **16**, 494–500.

Tietz, W., and Vidmar, J. T. (1972). 'The impact of coping styles on the control of juvenile diabetes', *Psychiatry in Medicine*, **3,** 67.

Tropauer, A., Franz, M. N., and Dilgard, V. W. (1970). 'Psychological aspects of the care of children with cystic fibrosis', *American Journal of Diseases of Children*, **119,** 424.

Vernick, J. (1973). 'Meaningful communication with the fatally ill child', in Anthony, J. E., and Koupernick, C. (eds), *The Child and His Family: The Impact of Disease and Death*, vol. 2. Wiley, New York.

Vernon, M. (1969). *Multiple Handicapped Deaf Children: Medical Education and Psychological Considerations*. Council for Exceptional Children, Research Monograph, Washington, DC.

Vignos, P. J. Jr., Thompson, H. M., Katz, W., Moskowitz, K. W., Fink, W., and Svec, K. H. (1972). 'Comprehensive care and psychological factors in rehabilitation in chronic rheumatoid arthritis: a controlled study', *Journal of Chronic Disease*, **25,** 457.

Waechter, E. H. (1971), Children's awareness of fatal illness. *American Journal of Nursing*, 1168–1172.

Worden, D. K., and Vignos, P. J. (1962). 'Intellectual function in childhood progressive muscular dystrophy', *Paediatrics*, 968–977.

Williams, C. (1968). 'Behaviour disorders in handicapped children', *Developmental Medicine and Child Neurology*, **10,** 736–740.

Williams, C. (1970). 'Some psychiatric observations on a group of maladjusted deaf children', *Journal of Child Psychology and Psychiatry*, **11,** 1.

Wright, B. (1960). *Physical Disability: A Psychological Approach*. Harper & Row, New York.

Wright, B. (1964). 'Spread in adjustment to disability', *Bulletin of the Menninger Clinics*, **28,** 198.

Social Psychology and Behavioral Medicine
Edited by J. Richard Eiser
© 1982 John Wiley & Sons Ltd

Chapter 20

The surgical patient: psychological stress and coping resources

COLETTE RAY

Fears and Concerns of the Surgical Patient

The early literature on psychological aspects of surgery reported the relatively frequent occurrence of psychiatric symptoms as a reaction to the experience (Lindemann, 1941; Stengel *et al.*, 1958). Titchener and Levine in 1956 claimed that 86 percent of their sample showed postoperative psychological disorder 'to the extent that a psychiatric illness could be diagnosed', and that one-third continued to show disturbance in the longer term. Current accounts present a more conservative impression of reactions to surgery; while it is recognized that many patients find the experience a distressing one, the distress is more likely to be described as a temporary elevation in anxiety than as a disturbance of psychiatric proportions. This discrepancy may be attributed to a number of factors. Firstly, there have been considerable changes in procedures over time, with improvements in hospital conditions and a reduction in the risks and discomforts associated with surgery. Attitudes within the general population have changed accordingly, and the expectation is now one of effective treatment and high standards of care rather than the reverse. Furthermore, 'the hospital' has provided a setting for many fictional dramatizations, and the popular presentation of themes relevant to hospitalization and surgery has probably done much to reduce the unfamiliarity, and hence the threat, of these. Finally, it may be that the orientation and expectations of researchers have shifted over time. Negative responses to illness and its treatment are generally reversible even without intervention, are at least as dependent upon the situation as upon the dispositional characteristics of the individual, and are the norm rather than the exception. The relevance of a clinical or psychiatric framework in this context is therefore questionable, and the descriptive terminology and theoretical concepts appropriate to this are less frequently employed now than they were in the past.

Surgery has been vividly described as a 'planned physical assault' upon the body (Gruendemann, 1965). The fact that the patient has generally consented to the assault does not substantially alter this, and there are few who do not view the prospect warily and with some trepidation. Early descriptions of the threats posed by surgery were primarily analytic in orientation. They emphasized the psychodynamic significance of the removal of specific organs and of the invasion of the body's boundaries, and pointed out that early childhood fears of loss, separation, and castration were likely to be reactivated at this time (Deutsch, 1942). There are, however, many aspects of the experience which are intrinsically threatening regardless of their possible symbolic relevance. Patients fear the administration of the general anaesthetic, worry that they might wake up or talk during the operation, and are concerned about postoperative vomiting, discomfort, and pain (Carnevali, 1966; Ramsay, 1972). Other common fears are that one might die while under the anaesthetic (Carnevali, 1966; Ramsay, 1972; Renshaw, 1974), or that the operation might unexpectedly reveal the presence of cancer (French, 1979; Ramsay, 1972). The relative importance of these different kinds of concern will depend in part upon the nature of the patient's illness and surgery. Certain operations entail problems which are different in both nature and degree from those more generally experienced. These will include procedures intended to treat or to confirm the existence of a malignant disease; procedures which in themselves carry a high risk to life; and procedures which result in mutilation or some impairment of function. They will not be dealt with in this review, but the psychological aspects of some of these have been discussed elsewhere (Doehrman, 1977; Ray, 1980; Sutherland, 1967).

Many of the stresses with which the surgical patient will be confronted are not specific to surgery and are shared by patients undergoing hospitalization for other reasons. These include separation from family and from work; dependency and loss of control; the symptoms of the illness for which hospitalization was required; enforced contact with the ill and the dying; and disturbed nights and disordered routines while in hospital. Stress may be particularly acute on admission when the patient is as yet unfamiliar with the staff, the facilities available, and with his or her own role within this framework (Franklin, 1974; Wilson-Barnett, 1978a), and may peak again on occasions such as ward rounds (Abrams, 1969; Cartwright, 1964). Volicer and Bohannon (1975) have developed a Hospital Stress Rating Scale for quantifying the psychosocial stress experienced as a result of hospitalization. The scale comprises 49 events, and patients are asked to check those which they have personally experienced while in hospital. Each event has a predetermined stress rating associated with it, and the total stress score for an individual patient is given by summing the ratings of those events checked. The items have been found to yield nine factors: unfamiliarity of surroundings; loss of independence; separation from spouse; financial problems; isolation from other people; lack of information; threat of severe illness; separation from family; and problems with medications.

Anxiety levels in surgical patients are generally higher before than after surgery (Auerbach, 1973; DeLong, 1970; Martinez-Urrutia, 1975; Spielberger *et al.*, 1973; Wolfer and Davis, 1970). Most of these studies have, however, included in the sample patients undergoing a variety of surgical procedures, so it is possible that there are exceptions which are masked within this trend. Different patterns might emerge if specific procedures were considered in isolation. For example, anxiety may in some circumstances be depressed pre-surgically by the presence of denial and other defenses, so that postsurgical assessments show an elevation before a decline. There is evidence of such a pattern among heart patients (Johnston, 1980), kidney donors and ortho-paedic patients (Chapman and Cox, 1977; Haselhorst, 1970). A related issue is that of the stress experienced by an individual before surgery *in relation to* postoperative adjustment. Two early and influential studies which were concerned with this are those of Titchener and Levine (1956) and Janis (1958). In the first of these, patients were interviewed preoperatively and then 3–6 months after their operation. Those who had been highly anxious prior to surgery were most likely to show an improved adjustment in later interviews; those who had experienced little preoperative anxiety tended to show signs of persisting maladjustment; while moderate anxiety at the first interview was associated with a subsequent deterioration in the patient's condition. Janis (1958) compared adjustment before surgery and in the immediate postoperative period, rather than several months later, and found that postoperative emotionality was *least* where preoperative levels had been moderate. High preoperative emotionality was associated with marked postoperative anxiety, while those who had been low in anxiety before surgery tended to be angry and resentful afterwards. It was suggested that the former reaction represents an oversensitization to the threatening aspects of the procedure, and that the latter reflects a lack of preparation and unrealistic expectations which, when not validated, give rise to hostility. It can be further argued that patients who show moderate concern, the optimal preoperative state, are vulnerable in neither of these ways: that they recognize the danger without being overwhelmed by it, and rehearse anxiety-producing images and coping strategies which protect them from future emotional disturbance.

This adaptive function of anxiety in preparing the individual for stress has been described as the 'work of worry'. The concept has proved an attractive one, but has not met with much empirical support in spite of many studies directed at the issue. Recent investigations which have compared relative anxiety levels before and after surgery have in fact found a simple linear relationship (Johnson *et al.*, 1971; Wolfer and Davis, 1970). Nor is there evidence of curvilinearity when physical rather than psychological indices of adjustment are employed. Several studies have failed to produce evidence of any relationship (Cohen and Lazarus, 1973; Johnson *et al.*, 1971; Wolfer and Davis, 1970), while in others recovery has been found to be a direct, linear function of preoperative anxiety (Chapman and Cox, 1977; Johnson *et al.*, 1978a; Sime, 1976).

One criticism that may be directed at this research is its exclusive focus on anxiety as an indication of preoperative status, while other factors relevant to the concept of 'work of worry' are ignored. One such factor is the individual's awareness of threat, which will be determined both by the information available to him and by his willingness to confront the possibility of danger. Janis suggested that low anxiety represents a blanket reassurance and avoidance, and will thus be associated with confusion and helplessness in the face of events that have not been anticipated. This assumption may not be generally valid. An absence of anxiety may be founded on a realistic assessment of the situation and of one's ability to cope with this, and here a favorable rather than an unfavorable postoperative adjustment would be predicted. Moreover, even ignorance or defensive denial may sometimes be adaptive, since anticipated dangers do not always materialize (Abrams, 1969; Cohen and Lazarus, 1973; Kennedy and Bakst, 1966) and with this outcome the work of worry would have been in vain. A second factor to be taken into account when considering the influence of the patient's preoperative status is the degree of anticipatory coping, reflected in a constructive preoccupation with the prospect of surgery and with the challenges which this will present. Extreme fear or anxiety may hinder the development of anticipatory coping, but low or moderate levels will not guarantee that it takes place. The two kinds of responses may indeed be broadly independent (Leventhal, 1970). In short, realistic expectations and anticipatory coping together represent the individual's cognitive preparation for surgery, and it is these which constitute the potentially adaptive aspects of worry. Preoperative emotionality will not in itself have a dynamic impact on adjustment. Although it may be empirically associated with the latter because of its relationship with denial and coping, the prediction of postoperative adjustment on the basis of preoperative anxiety alone is unlikely to be reliable in view of the complexity of this relationship.

Personality and Coping

Individuals do of course differ in their reactions to surgery. Deutsch (1942) referred not only to the importance of the presence or absence of neurosis, but also to that of the antecedent situation, and of the personal meaning of the operation within the framework of the individual's experience, lifestyle and value system. Most researchers who have concerned themselves with individual differences, while recognizing the role of such dynamic influences, have nevertheless focused their investigations exclusively on generalized personality constructs such as anxiety. Patients who show high levels of state anxiety are those who have high scores on trait measures of this construct (e.g. Johnson *et al.*, 1971; Wilson-Barnett and Carrigy, 1978), but the *elevation* in anxiety associated with surgery does not appear to differ between groups who are low and high in general trait anxiety (Auerbach, 1973; Martinez-Urrutia, 1975; Spielberger *et al.*, 1973). This negative finding accords with current conceptualizations of the latter as reflecting a vulnerability to ego threat but not to physical threat, and in one study a more specific trait measure designed to assess fear of surgery was found to be successful in predicting increases in anxiety preoperatively (Martinez-Urrutia, 1975). It is interesting to note that although general trait anxiety is not related to elevations in state anxiety, it is nevertheless related to postsurgical pain (Chapman and Cox, 1977; Martinez-Urrutia, 1975).

Two other personality traits investigated are more closely associated with coping than with vulnerability to stress. The first is perhaps better described as a cluster of related traits which have a common theme. It has been referred to alternatively as avoidance–coping (Goldstein, 1973), repression–sensitization (Byrne, 1964) and minimization–vigilant focusing (Lipowski, 1970). In each case the first pole refers to a tendency to avoid, ignore, deny, or otherwise blunt the significance of the threat, while the second refers to a tendency to approach, focus upon, or even exaggerate the threat. DeLong (1970) found that patterns of anxiety over time varied with this coping dimension. Avoiders when told of their operation were muted in their reaction, but stress then later increased. Copers showed an initial moderate increase in anxiety which was maintained throughout the period. Non-specific defenders, that is individuals who are not particularly predisposed to one coping style or another, responded with an initial surge in anxiety, followed by a decline. There were thus distinctly different gradients of stress in these three groups. Cohen and Lazarus (1973) looked at the relationship between coping style and postoperative physical recovery. They failed to find effects of either avoidance–coping or repression–sensitization as assessed by standard pencil-and-paper tests, but did find an effect of coping style when this was specifically defined in terms of the patient's apparent orientation to the surgical experience. The subjects were categorized as either vigilant or avoiding on the basis of their knowledge about the operation, their awareness of its threatening aspects, and their readiness to talk about these, and the vigilant group was found to have the most complicated postoperative course. It may be argued that these patients were over-sensitized to the possibility of danger, in view of the objective probability of its occurrence and the extent to which anticipatory coping was possible. The third dimension relevant to stress reactions and coping style is that of locus of control. This has been defined as the individual's tendency to attribute control over outcomes to either the self or to the outside world. The individual with an internal locus of control tends to seek information about situations and to manipulate these for desired ends, while an external locus of control implies a tendency to accept situations without exploration and to await outcomes passively (Phares, 1976). This dimension has been related to a number of preventive and sick role behaviors (see Wallston and Wallston, 1978). With regard to surgical patients, Johnson and colleagues (1971) found that internals received more drugs and had a longer hospital stay than an external group; this finding could be variously interpreted as reflecting either a more complicated postoperative course or a more active role in demanding and receiving care.

These trait studies have suggested some interesting hypotheses, but there is clearly scope for a more detailed and systematic consideration of individual differences in coping with the stress of surgery. From studies such as that of DeLong (1970) it is apparent that there are relatively subtle but distinct patterns of response over time, and the same may be true of the relationship between different kinds of response at any one moment in time. These distinctions will be lost in an aggregate analysis, yet will by their existence threaten the validity of conclusions derived from an averaging of the data. A trait approach is normally used to predict outcomes on isolated variables but might also be employed to direct the search for these more complex variations between subgroups within the sample. On the basis of evidence from both surgical and other contexts this strategy is most likely to be effective where the traits are conceived in terms directly relevant to the experience of surgery. This, however, raises an additional and much broader issue, and that is the utility of considering traits at all. As we become more specific in our conceptualization of the construct, so the distance between traits and actual behavior diminishes. If the aim is to be alert to, and to differentiate between, divergent responses and patterns of response, then it may be that this can be better accomplished by analyzing coping directly as it occurs *in* the situation than by making predictions about such differences on the basis of an assessment of the dispositions which the individual brings *to* the situation.

Coping is currently a subject of study and discussion in a variety of contexts, although research is still hampered by the breadth and complexity of the field and by the conceptual and methodological uncertainties to which this has given rise. Until recent years, concern has been disproportionately focused on the study of 'defence mechanisms', that is processes which are covert or intrapsychic, unconscious in their operation, and not accessible to introspection. Overt behaviors were correspondingly neglected as had those intrapsychic processes which are consciously directed. This emphasis has colored perceptions to the extent that an individual's claim to an absence of anxiety, in a situation which many would find stressful, is often quite readily interpreted as a defensive denial of threat or of its emotional implications. In fact an absence of anxiety may simply reflect a 'benign appraisal' (Lazarus, 1966) from the perspective of that individual's lifestyle and values or within the constraints of a limited experience and imagination. Not only has the significance of the role of psychological defence as a reaction to stress been exaggerated, but its adaptive function has, at the same time, been devalued. It has often been implied that defensive processes represent an absence rather than a form of coping, on the assumption that the latter is 'adaptive' while the former are 'maladaptive'. This will not always be the case. In the words of Haan (1977): 'coping does not insure success, nor [does] defending . . . entail failure, since outcomes depend on matches between situations and resources' (p. 79).

Several different approaches have been adopted in the assessment of coping. Pearlin and Schooler (1978), who were concerned with role strain and crisis in areas such as marriage and occupation, assessed responses to these problems by means of a questionnaire. Three basic coping functions were distinguished, comprising responses that control the situation, responses that modify the meaning of problems, and responses that are directed at the management of the stress itself. Weisman (1974) developed a scale which was used to assess coping in patients who were seriously ill or dying. The scale taps fourteen strategies which are regarded as being of 'intermediate generality', neither too broad nor too narrow, and covers a variety of forms of coping. Both of these approaches depend upon self-report. Others depend upon ratings made by an observer, where the observations are subjects' demeanor and expressed attitudes in interviews and the ratings are inferences about coping which are derived from these. Todd and Margarey, for example, interviewed women who had presented with breast symptoms that might or might not indicate cancer, and investigated their use of denial, suppression, rationalization, displacement, intellectualization–isolation, and reaction formation (1978). A more elaborate taxonomy of intrapsychic processes, both defensive and non-defensive, has been developed by Haan (1977). There are ten generic processes within this scheme, representing four kinds of function, and each of these may be reflected in three distinct modes of expression: coping, defence, or fragmentation. The coping mode is said to be characterized by purpose, choice, and flexibility and to have a basic correspondence with reality; the defensive mode implies compulsion, rigidity, and a distortion of reality; while fragmentation entails an automatic, ritualistic form of functioning which more blatantly violates inter-subjective reality.

None of the approaches mentioned is comprehensive in the range of responses with which it deals, while at the same time providing for a detailed analysis within this range. Both of these criteria are important in evaluating methods for analysing coping, if its complex nature is not to be denied. In any situation the options will be many and varied, as will be the resources and styles which individuals bring to the situation, and the resulting range and diversity of patterns of adjustment requires a system of classification which simplifies without impoverishing this complexity.

Once this fairly detailed description is obtained, it will be possible to look empirically for patterns which arise from the dynamic nature of coping. Firstly, we can anticipate functional relationships between specific responses; it may not be possible to determine the significance of any one of these in isolation but only in the context of those behaviors and processes with which it is associated. In other words, there may be *deeper structures* underlying surface coping, comprising response clusters which together have a meaning independent of their separate components. Secondly, coping will change over time; adjustment to the situation is not fixed in a single confrontation nor determined through a series of isolated transactions. It evolves in a continuous and presumably meaningful way, and there may be one or more *temporal themes* underlying surface changes. Thirdly, the individual will have a 'repertoire' of possible coping orientations, with the particular orientation adopted at any one time depending upon physiological, environmental, or social factors. For example, patients may behave differently, and express apparently inconsistent beliefs and attitudes, when with other patients on the ward, when talking with family and friends, when discussing his problem with nurses and doctors, and when being interviewed by a researcher. They may present a different image not only to others but even to themselves. Their perception of neither the situation nor of their own attitudes and capabilities will be stable. Both the substance and salience of particular beliefs will be influenced by the implicit demands and expectations associated with the setting and with the nature of the interaction in which they are involved. These potential orientations we can refer to as *coping roles*.

Table 20.1 represents a conceptual schema within which a wide range of quite narrowly defined behaviors are specified. The principal dimension for classification is the goal of the response. The three goals of coping distinguished are related to the three objects of change described by Pearlin and Schooler (1978), and comprise outcomes, meanings, and affect. The second dimension is that of the mode of expression, whether as a surface behavior which is observable or as an intrapsychic process which cannot be directly observed.

Controlling *outcomes* involves changing the objective impact of events Surface behaviors within this category may on the one hand be directed at factors in the situation, and take the form of challenge, escape, or, in a negative guise, a surrender to events. They may on the other hand be concerned with the development of coping resources. Seeking information and advice, social comparison, rehearsal of physical coping, and eliciting nurturance or support might all serve this end, while a passive variation on the theme would be represented by taking refuge in an unconditional dependency or withdrawal. Intrapsychic processes which change outcomes can have as their focus the refinement of expectations and of the ability to predict or, alternatively, the development of personal conttrol and coping

Table 20.1 Coping behaviors and processes: goals and modes of expression

	Surface behaviors	Intrapsychic processes
Control over outcomes	Search for information Search for advice Social comparison Rehearsal of physical coping Eliciting nurturance, support Passive dependency, withdrawal Challenge, protest Escape, withdrawal Giving up, surrender	Analysis of situation Rehearsal of stressor Tolerance of uncertainty Fatalism Analysis of coping options Internal rehearsal of coping Maintenance of morale Helplessness
Modification of meaning	Selective social comparison Search for supportive evidence Avoidance of threats Distraction	Optimism Attention deployment Denial of threat Denial of relevant needs, values Isolation Projection of threat Rationalization Suppression of awareness of threat
Regulation of affect	Social comparison Expression of affect Sharing concern Search for overt reassurance Search for advice Physical therapies Chemical therapies Avoidance of threats Distraction Social withdrawal Inhibition of affective expression Regressive dependency Physical pampering of self	Transformation of affect Denial of affect Suppression of affect Attention deployment Projection of affect Displacement Intellectualization Detachment Acceptance of affect Positive structuring of affect Martyr-like surrender to affect Psychological 'cosseting' of self

resources. The former would be reflected in attempts to analyze the situation, rehearsal of the stressor, and a measured tolerance of uncertainty, and the latter in an analysis of coping options, the internal rehearsal of coping, and maintenance of morale. Fatalism and helplessness respectively provide the passive alternatives to these positive orientations. The second principal goal of coping is to modify the *meaning* of the situation. This can be done intrapsychically by maintaining optimism and deploying attention from the situation's negative aspects; by denying threat or the needs and values which would be compromised; by isolating the former from the latter; and by processes such as the projection, rationalization, and suppression of threat. These meaning-oriented responses will often be supported by overt behaviors such as associating with others whose experiences or expectations are reassuring to one's own point of view; seeking confirmatory factual evidence; avoiding settings, persons, or sources of information which could present a challenge; and engaging in distracting activities which keep the realization of threat at bay. The third coping goal is the regulation of *affect*, that is of the stress associated with a given appraisal of the situation. A variety of surface behaviors and intrapsychic processes can serve to temper this emotional reaction, either by dampening the subjective experience of stress or by rendering the latter more tolerable. These range from the taking of medications to the employment of 'defence mechanisms' such as the projection of affect and displacement.

It is explicitly recognized within this framework that coping responses which are superficially similar may be directed at different ends. Social comparison, for example, encompasses a number of functions. One may observe others in a similar situation in order to gain information about anticipated stressors and to determine the coping behaviors appropriate to these; to validate one's interpretation of events; or to model one's emotional response upon that of others. Furthermore, responses that modify meanings and affects are given a weight equal to that of responses which control outcomes, and include behaviors and processes outside the range of defense mechanisms as traditionally conceived. They can be described as 'palliative' (Lazarus and Launier, 1978) in that their impact is primarily subjective or indirect, but they should not be regarded as a necessarily inferior form of adjustment. The adaptiveness of any response cannot be determined out of context, since it will depend upon the needs of the individual and the demands of the situation. In the case of the surgical patient, the responses which could bring about objective change are in fact likely to be limited in number.

There is a third dimension which does not appear in Table 20.1, and this is the awareness associated with coping. Surface behaviors and intrapsychic processes which reduce, or tend to reduce, stress can operate at varying levels of awareness. At one extreme, coping may reflect a deliberate and considered reaction to a recognition of threat, and an acknowledged intention of reducing stress. We can call this 'strategic' coping. At the other extreme, the response may have the consequence of controlling outcomes, modifying meaning, or regulating affect but without a corresponding intention on the part of the individual to achieve this end. Indeed, there may not even be an awareness of the factors on which the response is contingent. Coping in this case is 'reactive' rather than strategic in that, while it is elicited by the stressor and is a form of adjustment, it is not consciously directed to that purpose. Strategic and reactive coping may be regarded as two poles of a continuum, and responses which fall within the intermediate range may have both reactive and strategic components. The distinction bears some relation to that between conscious and unconscious processes, but the parallel is imperfect. The description 'unconscious' in the context of coping generally implies an underlying motivation which the individual chooses not to recognize, but the term 'reactive' does not have this implication. A lack of awareness of the significance of one's response as an adjustment to stress does not necessarily reflect a refusal or a reluctance to acknowledge this. It may merely indicate that the form and function of coping has in this instance not been articulated. It can be argued that further speculation about the nature of the motivation underlying responses to stress will not be profitable, in the absence of criteria for distinguishing operationally between motives which are unarticulated and those whose articulation is actively resisted.

This schema may be employed to generate items for self-rating, with the specific content of the items being determined by the context in which they are to be employed. It may also be used to guide observational analyses, determining the dimensions with regard to which subjects may be rated either in interview or in the situation itself. The outcomes of *both* self-report and observational approaches will be influenced by subjects' knowledge that they are being evaluated and by their probable desire to present an image of themselves as cooperative, mature, and socially acceptable. There is, however, an important difference in the nature of the data generated by these procedures (Cairns and Green, 1979). Observational methods produce data which, strictly speaking, have reference only to the setting or interaction in which the observations are made. They represent the subject's state on a given occasion and in a given context and unless a number of occasions and contexts are sampled they provide no indication of the consistency of this state. It is quite common for evasions or rationalizations observed in a single interview to be interpreted as evidence of a stable defensive style with regard to the topic under discussion, but such a generalization is unwarranted without further supporting evidence. It ignores the possibility that the subject may be displaying merely one of a number of coping roles at his or her command. Self-report techniques, in contrast, invite the subject to generalize over occasions and contexts, thus producing an account which refers directly to that individual's typical orientation with these other factors held constant. They cannot, however, yield much information about responses or intentions of which the subject personally is unaware; and are thus more appropriate to the assessment of strategic than reactive coping.

Social Support

A number of background factors will influence the particular coping responses that will be adopted by the individual and the effectiveness of these in enabling him or her to manage outcomes, meanings, and affects. One such factor will be personal resources and personality style. Characteristics such as flexibility, adaptiveness, and the ability to manipulate others and events, together with traits such as defensiveness, locus of control, anxiety, and aggressiveness, will influence both the form and product of coping. The physical environment will also have some effect on adaptation, discouraging the employment of some responses and hindering their operation, while facilitating others. A third factor is the social network of which the individual is a part, in particular the community of family and friends with whom he has a direct contact. Social relationships are widely recognized as a 'buffer' against the long-term effects of stress on mental and physical health (Cobb, 1976; Dean and Lin, 1977; Henderson, 1977) although the features mediating this protective influence have not been much discussed. Weiss (1974) has listed a number of functions by means of which relationships can contribute to psychological well-being. They comprise attachment, or a sense of security and belonging; social integration in the sense of shared information, activities, and services; the opportunity for nurturance, that is to take responsibility for others; reassurance of one's own worth; a sense of reliable alliance with the assurance of support when needed; and the ability to obtain guidance from others. A fully supportive network would be one in which the totality of relationships combined to furnish all of these provisions. Such support is important for adequate functioning in everyday situations, and will be particularly important in time of stress. Certain relational provisions will contribute dispositionally by fostering self-confidence and self-esteem, and reducing feelings of vulnerability. Others will be 'activated' in time of need and will thus more directly reduce the impact of stressful events by supplementing the individual's personal resources and enhancing the effectiveness of his coping.

Family and friends are not, however, the only source of social support for the individual under stress. There will normally be others available to whom he may turn for help, whether these are role figures who explicitly have this function, bystanders or fellow-'sufferers'. In the case of the surgical patient, for example, help might be sought from or offered by nurses, doctors, and other patients on the ward.

The primary responsibility of medical and nursing staff is the physical care of their charges, but the care of the 'whole patient' includes psychological as well as physical welfare (Skipper and Leonard, 1965). The physician's role is often regarded exclusively in terms of its instrumental aspects in effecting an appropriate diagnosis and treatment, although several writers have pointed to the importance of the surgeon–patient relationship in promoting compliance and psychological adjustment (Deutsch, 1942; Kraft, 1976), with the result that the patient's psychological needs are generally regarded as the particular concern of the nurse. These expressive aspects of the latter's role are often stressed alongside its instrumental function (Johnson and Martin, 1965) and both nurses and patients ascribe great importance to 'emotional' care (Anderson, 1973). There are several ways in which nurses may provide this emotional support: by imparting information and reducing uncertainty; by offering specific reassurances; by a general air of friendliness and acceptance; and by listening to the patient's worries and concerns. There is some evidence that nurses feel that the first of these is particularly valuable in reducing preoperative anxiety, but that patients themselves attach greater significance to those expressive activities which are even further removed from technical aspects of the nursing routine (Carnevali, 1966). The role of fellow-patients in alleviating stress has rarely been considered, in spite of much work on affiliation as a response to stress, following the research of Schachter (1959) who showed that subjects under threat of shock were more likely to prefer to wait with others than to wait alone. There are a number of possible motives for affiliation in such circumstances, including the reduction of uncertainty by seeking information about the nature of the anticipated experience, the evaluation of the appropriateness of one's own emotional response by comparing it with that of others, and a search for the reassurance that a sense of contact and company can afford. Not all stressful situations will increase affiliation. It seems that the effect is restricted to those which primarily involve physical threat, and does not occur for stressors which involve embarrassment, ridicule, or failure (Teichman, 1978). Surgery comprises many different kinds of threat and it is difficult to predict on an *a priori* basis whether the company of others would here be preferred or avoided. Rofé and colleagues, investigating a somewhat similar situation, found that the majority of mothers wanted to be alone during delivery, and that the greater the anxiety the more emphatic was this wish (1977). Childbirth involves an obvious physical threat; however, the mother-to-be may be experiencing emotional conflicts about the birth, and doubts about the adequacy with which she will perform her role, and these may be more salient than fears about her physical comfort and safety.

There has been a greater volume of research on affiliation as a response to stress than on the actual effect of affiliation on anxiety. Many subjects, when asked why they chose the company of others when under stress, give the reduction of anxiety as their reason, but does it in practice have this effect? The evidence suggests that it does in some, but not all, cases. The presence of another is more likely to reduce anxiety where he or she is in a similar situation to that of the subject (Amoroso and Walters, 1969; Glass *et al.*, 1970) and calm rather than displaying overt signs of distress (Buck and Parke, 1972; Kissel, 1965; Latané *et al.*, 1966). A friend may be of more help than a stranger (Kissel, 1965), but this effect will depend upon the kind of situation with which the stress is associated. If it involves embarrassment or ridicule then a friendly or supportive companion may be of less help, and their presence may even have an adverse influence (Buck and Parke, 1972; Glass *et al.*, 1970). On a cautionary note, these generalizations should be regarded as tentative only. There are few studies on this theme and there have seldom been attempts at replication; findings are not always consistent; and the setting has usually been limited to that of the laboratory.

In summary, research has demonstrated the potential contribution of both a supportive network of relationships and the physical presence of others in reducing vulnerability to stress, but the factors mediating either the long-term or immediate impact of this social context have not been clearly elaborated. A recent study attempted to deal with the second of these two issues within the context of surgery, focusing upon the different *types* of support provided by various role figures with whom the patient has contact while in hospital (Ray and Fitzgibbon, 1979). Several dimensions of support were distinguished, as suggested by the literature in this area: information, reassurance, guidance for coping, distraction, and ego-enhancement. The principal role figures investigated were nurse, fellow-patient, surgeon (or an equivalent figure with whom the patient had had contact), and spouse. Subjects were asked to rate, postoperatively, the extent to which each of these had contributed in terms of the dimensions listed; for every possible comparison between roles significant differences were obtained on at least two of the five dimensions. It appears from the ratings that the surgeon's primary role was seen as that of providing information, reassurance, and guidance for coping. Nurses and spouse also performed these functions. In addition, they catered for the patient's socially oriented needs, comprising distraction and ego-enhancement, and in this respect they differed from the surgeon but were similar to fellow-patients. The subjects were also asked to rate their anxiety in and after interaction with each of the role figures. These ratings were then correlated with perceptions of the support offered, with separate analyses being performed for each role and dimension of support. Information and reassurance were found to be negatively correlated with anxiety, but only where they were associated with the surgeon's role. Guidance for coping was negatively related to stress where this was offered by either the surgeon or a nurse. Distraction was associated with lower anxiety in interaction in the case of nurses and spouse, but it seemed that only nurses could reduce anxiety by means of ego-enhancement. The behavior of fellow-patients had no apparent effect on the anxiety experienced.

These rather complex findings suggest that not only do these figures differ in the nature of the support which they offer to the surgical patient, but that similar supportive behaviors will have different implications for stress depending upon their source or origin. The latter will probably determine the specific way in which any function is performed; for example, surgeons and nurses will both provide the patient with information, but there may be little overlap between them in terms of the topics to which this is related (Pender, 1974). Patients will, moreover, have prejudices regarding the appropriateness of behavior, depending upon the role of the figure concerned, and greater credibility may attach to some functions than to others according to these expectations.

Psychological Preparation for Surgery

Relatively little is known about the ways in which patients cope with the psychological challenges of surgery, or the kinds of support from which they might most benefit. It has, however, been commonly hypothesized that distress will be reduced and recovery facilitated by interventions which go beyond the care normally provided, and a great many studies can now claim to have demonstrated this empirically. Patients are typically exposed to the 'intervention' before they undergo the surgical, or some similar, procedure and its effectiveness is then subsequently determined by comparing their reactions with those of a control group. These investigations, apart from this common basic design, differ in terms of several important dimensions. The kinds of preparation attempted can take a variety of forms. These include general reassurance and emotional support; information about procedures; information about the nature of the sensations and experiences that will be associated with these; instructions for coping with physical discomfort and for speeding recovery; and advice on how to cope with psychological stress. Another major dimension in terms of which studies differ is the outcome measures they select. These have included ratings of emotions such as anxiety, hostility, and depression either by nurse, physician, interviewer, or by the patient himself; physiological indices of stress such as skin conductance, heart-rate, and urinary excretion of steroid hormones; and indices of physical recovery including pain, postoperative complications, requirements for medication, ambulation, and days to discharge.

The majority have in fact adopted a global approach to intervention, incorporating reassurance, information, and advice in their preparation. They may emphasize one rather than another component but do so without attempting to distinguish systematically between these. In Hayward's study (1975), for example, patients were given information about hospital routines and procedures, details of preoperative preparation, information about the degree of pain and discomfort that they might expect, and instructions on relaxation and exercises. These patients required fewer analgesics and were more quickly free of pain than a control group. Similarly, in Boore's study (1978) patients were informed about preoperative preparation, the induction of the anesthesia, and postoperative state, and they were also taught how to breathe and cough correctly and to perform leg exercises. Patients in the experimental group were significantly different from a control group in their pattern of steroid hormone excretion and in postoperative complications.

In another study the preparation took the form of 'crisis intervention therapy' undertaken by a pastoral counselor, and the effects of this were assessed in comparison with the effects of a non-therapeutic pastoral visit (Davis, 1973). Patients in the intervention condition had a shorter stay in hospital postsurgically and showed lower physiological reactions, although there were no differences between the groups in physician's ratings of stress or pain. Melamed and her colleagues have carried out a series of investigations with children, in which preparation for the surgical or other experience took the form of exposure to a fearful but coping model undergoing a similar experience on film (Melamed *et al.*, 1975; Melamed and Siegel, 1975). The children prepared in this way were less anxious and less disruptive in their behavior than a control group who had watched a film whose content was irrelevant to the experience at hand. One negative finding in the area is that of Field (1974). Here, orthopedic patients heard a tape which gave some information about the operation, but also made suggestions of relaxation, drowsiness, and comfort during the procedure and of a quick recovery afterwards. There were no significant differences between these patients and others who heard a recording which merely described the facilities available in the hospital.

In the above designs, the control group received the same attention as the experimental group; that is, they too were engaged in conversation, watched a film, or heard a tape-recording. Only the *content* of the communication was varied. There have been many other investigations, in the majority of which the intervention was associated with positive effects on at least some of the outcome measures employed, but where the control group received standard care. One of the best known is that of Egbert and colleagues (1964). Here patients who were given additional instructions and encouragement in preparation for the experience of pain required fewer narcotics postsurgically and were discharged earlier than patients who were treated normally. Other studies include those of Aiken and Henrichs (1971), Dumas and Leonard (1963), Gruen (1975), Leigh and colleagues (1977), Leonard and Elms (1965), Lindemann and Van Aernam (1971), Schmitt and Woolridge (1973), and Vernon and Bigelow (1974). With this research design the implications of a positive outcome cannot unfortunately be clearly determined. It can be attributed either to the specific content of the intervention or to contact alone regardless of its specific features, or it may be merely a placebo effect generated by an awareness that some kind of intervention was being attempted.

Where an adequate control group has been employed it is possible to claim that preparation had a positive effect over and above that of mere contact or of the placebo effect of the intervention. However, it is still often unclear which particular aspects of the preparation were instrumental in achieving this effect. Where the preparation comprises a 'package' it is not possible to disentangle the relative influence of the components which contribute to this, and relatively few studies have attempted to make a comparison between kinds of preparation. Exceptions are a number of studies by Johnson and her colleagues. One early investigation in this series focused upon preparation for the experimental induction of ischemic pain, comparing the effectiveness of information oriented toward procedures with that of information more directly relevant to the sensations that might be anticipated (Johnson, 1973), and it was found that subjects who received the sensation-oriented information were less distressed by the experience. This effect did not seem to be mediated by attention to sensations, by their perceived intensity, by the level of distress expected, nor by the degree of fear or helplessness. In another study either a description of sensations or behavioral instructions were presented, singly or in combination, to patients about to undergo a gastroendoscopic examination (Johnson and Leventhal, 1974). Sensory information reduced emotional reactions when presented either alone or in combination with behavioral instructions, but the latter were effective in facilitating the procedure only when paired with the sensory preparation. Subsequent research with surgical patients incorporated various combinations of sensory information, objective or procedural information, and instructions for physical coping (Johnson et al., 1978b). In this experiment mood states were influenced by all three interventions, but only sensory information was able to affect the rate of recovery. An extended replication not only supported these findings but showed that the effects of preparation were still apparent when patients were followed up after discharge (Johnson et al., 1978a). Fuller and colleagues (1978) presented either sensory information or instructions for relaxation, singly and in combination, to women having a gynecological examination. As in Johnson and Leventhal's study (1974), behavioral instructions did not reduce distress while the sensory preparation was successful in this respect. The findings of Langer and her colleagues are rather different in nature (Langer et al., 1975). Here information and reassurance had no significant effect, while coping instructions influenced not only nurses' ratings of the patients' anxiety but also the use of pain-relievers and sedatives. One explanation of the failure of the information condition to affect response may be the heterogeneous nature of the sample. This included patients admitted for minor and major surgery, and it is difficult to see how information appropriate for one group can have been similarly appropriate for the other. The relative effectiveness of the coping instructions in this particular study, while at first sight inconsistent with other findings, may be attributed to their psychological focus. They encouraged patients to develop coping devices such as cognitive reappraisal of anxiety-eliciting events, selective attention, and self-reassurance rather than providing advice on physical coping (relaxation, exercises etc.) as others have done.

There are some inconsistencies within this research, and it is difficult to draw general conclusions because of the variety of questions pursued. It does, however, seem that sensory information is more effective in reducing distress and promoting recovery than information about procedures; that behavioral instructions are most effective in combination with sensory information; and that advice on coping with stress can influence both distress and recovery. It may not, in fact, be appropriate to expect consistent findings concerning the relative efficacy of different types of preparation. Firstly, the outcome of any given intervention is likely to depend upon the context in which it is employed. Thus Lindemann and Stetzer (1973) found that patients who had undergone minor surgery responded less well to the preparation; Wilson-Barnett (1978b) obtained a positive effect where subjects were patients scheduled for a barium enema, but not for patients who were awaiting a less stressful barium meal; and it appears that results obtained with cholecystectomy patients cannot be generalized to those treated for hernia (Johnson et al., 1978a,b). Secondly, it will be difficult to standardize preparation materials between studies, and to equate these within studies, in terms of all dimensions other than that explicitly varied as part of the investigation. Finally, it may not in practice be possible to present different kinds of preparation independently, since sensory information must include some description of procedures, while behavioral instructions or advice on psychological coping will probably make reference to both.

One other theme to have been considered in relation to preparation is that of differences in response between individuals. The effect of anxiety has surprisingly not been widely investigated, but one study to have been concerned with this is that of Williams and colleagues (1975). Here the outcome of a detailed and supportive preoperative interview was compared with that of a briefer preparation, and it was found that, while both types of interview had a calming influence on patients who were already high in anxiety, the 'cursory' interview increased anxiety in patients who had initially been relatively calm. Several studies have found certain groups of patients who did not react favorably to the intervention employed. Andrew (1970) and DeLong (1970) both investigated the effect of patients' defensive style on their reaction to information, and found that those who tended generally to avoid threat showed, if anything, a negative reaction to the experimental manipulation. Similarly, dental patients with an external locus of control have been found to respond more positively to a general information tape than to one describing specific procedures, while the opposite was the case for those with an internal locus of control (Auerbach et al., 1976). A defensive orientation and an external locus of control can each be interpreted as a turning-away from an awareness of threat, and presenting information which forces confrontation with this may disrupt defenses adaptive for that individual. It will therefore be important to be alert to the possibility of such effects when planning an intervention, and to protect those patients whose reaction may be unfavorable.

Discussion

Psychological aspects of surgery have now been quite extensively investigated but research is, if anything, still gathering momentum. The setting provides a relatively rare opportunity for the systematic study of stress outside the laboratory, and lends itself to a variety of theoretical frameworks. Here coping can be explored in depth and over time, with the influence of factors such as role perspective, affiliation, and relational support being included within the analysis, whereas laboratory investigations can accommodate only short-term stressors and a restricted range of coping possibilities, and have little scope for incorporating complex and realistic social variables in their design. In addition to its potential contribution to theory, this research also offers the prospect of an immediate application to problems in the field. Findings should suggest effective means of alleviating patients' distress, speeding their postoperative recovery, and facilitating nursing care. Indeed, most studies have probably been undertaken with this as their primary goal.

There are some topics and issues within the area that have yet received scant attention. Few studies have been designed in a way that would adequately reflect variations in response, and in patterns of response, according to the individual patient or the type of surgical procedure. An undue concern with the general rather than the particular may compromise not only the validity of any theoretical account of the findings but also the value of the latter's practical application on the ward. Responses can vary with the time at which assessments are made, as well as with the patient and type of operation. Almost all studies have focused upon short-term postoperative reactions and have based conclusions about 'adjustment' upon assessments made at this time. However, some patients may experience a state of postoperative euphoria which is temporary and dissipates on being discharged, while others may be physically and psychologically weakened by the operation and the general anesthetic but quickly recover their morale. The relationship between immediate and longer-term reactions to surgery has yet to be established. Another possible source of distortion is that most research has focused upon anxiety and neglected other negative emotions commonly associated with stress. Anger and depression are alternative, and perhaps equally undesirable, states, but these are rarely assessed. Moreover, the blanket exclusion of positive and desirable responses from consideration, although more easily understood, may also be questioned. Many patients face the situation with equanimity and tackle it with confidence. These instances of successful coping are ignored, while attention is directed to negative reactions and coping failures.

There has been much research and discussion recently on the theme of doctor–patient and nurse–patient interactions, but the nature and effects of these have not often been investigated within the framework of stress. It seems that the capacity of doctors and nurses to reduce anxiety may be associated in a relatively complex way with aspects of both their role identity and the particular behavior carried out within that role (Ray and Fitzgibbon, 1979). If this effect were found to be general, then it would have important implications for the management of intervention procedures. In studies of psychological preparation for surgery, communications have been variously delivered by the anaesthetist, a nurse, a nursing researcher, or a psychologist, and sometimes by means of a booklet, tape-recording or film; little significance has been attached to the *source* of the communication as having a potential influence on its impact. It might, however, be the case that preparation in the form of information and specific reassurances will be effective in reducing anxiety only where delivered by the surgeon or an equivalent figure, and that the nurse's contribution in this respect derives more from giving advice for physical coping and providing general reassurance and comfort. It could also be hypothesized that preparation in booklet or taped form will have a high credibility, and an authority of its own regardless of who presents these materials. Interventions take place in a social setting to which complex meanings are attached, and their influence will depend upon the way they are appraised by patients within this context.

It may be assumed that, where instructions for physical or psychological coping are effective, they are likely to be so because of an influence on the development of the coping strategies which they explicitly encourage. The factors responsible for the effects of presenting information without such instructions are less clear. While the central role of ambiguity and its reduction in the instigation and resolution of stress is widely acknowledged (Shalit, 1977), the specific nature of its influence has not been clarified. A number of mediating factors could play a role in the context of surgery. Firstly, information may provide direct reassurance about the limits of threat, and correct distorted and over-vigilant expectations. Secondly, even in the absence of any prior distortions it may still reduce perceptions of vulnerability by establishing a confidence that one will not be 'taken by surprise', and by ensuring that demands which materialize have in fact been anticipated. It may indeed provide an 'illusion of control'. Constraints which are predicted and seen as legitimate may not be *experienced* as contraints; and external demands may be internalized, given an opportunity for their assimilation. Thirdly, information may change the set which the patient adopts toward his experience, so that the latter is encoded in terms of schemata appropriate to its objective rather than stressful aspects (Leventhal and Everhart, 1979). Finally, accurate expectations will provide a foundation for actual control, by making possible the planning and rehearsal of strategies for managing physical impairments and psychological stress. All of these influences could operate in combination, and it is possible that information simultaneously provides reassurance about the severity of threat, reduces feelings of vulnerability, encourages an objective approach to one's experience, and facilitates the development of coping.

References

Abrams, H. S. (1969). 'Psychological responses to illness and hospitalisation', *Psychosomatics*, **10**, 218–224.

Aiken, L. H., and Henrichs, T. F. (1971). 'Systematic relaxation as a nursing intervention technique with open heart surgery patients', *Nursing Research*, **20**, 212–217.

Amoroso, D. M., and Walters, R. H. (1969). 'Effects of anxiety and socially mediated anxiety reduction on paired-associate learning', *Journal of Personality and Social Psychology*, **11**, 388–396.

Anderson, E. (1973). *The Role of the Nurse*, Royal College of Nursing, London.

Andrew, J. M. (1970). 'Recovery from surgery, with and without preparatory *instruction for three coping styles*', *Journal of Personality and Social Psychology*, **15**, 223–226.

Auerbach, S. M. (1973). 'Trait–state anxiety and adjustment to surgery', *Journal of Consulting and Clinical Psychology*, **40**, 264–271.

Auerbach, S. M., Kendall, P. C., Cuttler, H. F., and Levitt, N. R. (1976). 'Anxiety, locus of control, type of preparatory information, and adjustment to dental surgery', *Journal of Consulting and Clinical Psychology*, **44**, 809–818.

Boore, J. R. P. (1978). *Prescription for Recovery*. Royal College of Nursing, London.

Brown, E. L. (1965). *Newer Dimensions of Patient Care*. Russell Sage Foundation, New York.

Buck, R. W., and Parke, R. D. (1972). 'Behavioural and physiological response to the presence of a friendly or neutral person in two types of stressful situations', *Journal of Personality and Social Psychology*, **24**, 143–153.

Byrne, D. (1964). 'Repression–sensitisation as a dimension of personality', in Maher, B. A. (ed.), *Progress in Experimental Personality Research*, vol. 1, pp. 169–220. Academic Press, New York.

Cairns, R. B., and Green, J. A. (1979). 'How to assess personality and social patterns: observations or ratings?', in Cairns, R. B. (ed.), *The Analysis of Social Interactions*, pp. 209–226. Lawrence Erlbaum, NJ.

Carnevali, D. L. (1966). 'Preoperative anxiety', *American Journal of Nursing*, **66**, 1536–1539.

Cartwright, A. (1964). *Human Relations and Hospital Care*. Routledge & Kegan Paul, London.

Chapman, C. R., and Cox, G. B. (1977). 'Anxiety, pain and depression surrounding elective surgery: a multivariate comparison of abdominal surgery patients with kidney donors and recipients', *Journal of Psychosomatic Research*, **21**, 7–15.

Cobb, S. C. (1976). 'Social support as a moderator of life stress', *Psychosomatic Medicine*, **38**, 300–314.

Cohen, F., and Lazarus, R. S. (1973). 'Active coping processes, coping dispositions, and recovery from surgery', *Psychosomatic Medicine*, **35**, 375–389.

Cottrell, N. B., and Epley, S. W. (1977). 'Affiliation, social comparison, and socially-mediated stress reduction', in Suls, J. M., and Miller, R. L. (eds), *Social Comparison Processes: Theoretical and Empirical Perspectives*, pp. 43–68. Halstead Press, New York.

Davis, H. S. (1973). 'The role of a crisis intervention treatment in the patient's recovery from elective surgery'. Doctoral Dissertation, Northwestern University.

Dean, A., and Lin, N. (1977). 'The stress-buffering role of social support', *Journal of Nervous and Mental Diseases*, **165**, 403–417.

DeLong, R. D. (1970). 'Individual differences in patterns of anxiety arousal, stress-relevant information and recovery from surgery.' Doctoral Dissertation, University of California, Los Angeles.

Deutsch, H. (1942). 'Some psychoanalytic observations in surgery', *Psychosomatic Medicine*, **4**, 105–115.

Doehrman, S. D. (1977) 'Psycho-social aspects of recovery from coronary heart disease: a review', *Social Science and Medicine*, **11**, 199–218.

Dumas, R. G., and Leonard, R. C. (1963). 'The effect of nursing on the incidence of postoperative vomiting', *Nursing Research*, **12**, 12–15.

Egbert, L. D., Battit, G. E., Welch, C. E., and Bartlett, M. K. (1964). 'Reduction of postoperative pain by encouragement and instruction of patients', *New England Journal of Medicine*, **270**, 825–827.

Field, P. B. (1974). 'Effects of tape-recorded hypnotic preparation for surgery', *International Journal of Clinical and Experimental Hypnosis*, **22**, 54–61.

Fisher, A. L. (1970). 'Psychiatric aspects of the pre- and post-surgical patient', *Psychosomatics*, **11**, 347–351.

Franklin, B. L. (1974). *Patient Anxiety on Admission to Hospital*. Royal College of Nursing, London.

French, K. (1979). 'Some anxieties of elective surgery patients and the desire for reassurance and information', in Oborne, D. J., Gruneberg, M. M., and Eiser, J. R. (eds), *Research in Psychology and Medicine*, vol. 2. Academic Press, London.

Fuller, S. S., Endress, M. P., and Johnson, J. E. (1978). 'The effects of cognitive and behavioral control on coping with an aversive health examination', *Journal of Human Stress*, 18–25.

Glass, D. C., Gordon, A., and Henchy, T. (1970). 'The effects of social stimuli on psychophysiological reactivity to a stressful film', *Psychonomic Science*, **20**, 255–256.

Goldstein, M. J. (1973). 'Individual differences in response to stress', *American Journal of Community Psychology*, **1**, 113–137.

Gruen, W. (1975). 'Effects of brief psychotherapy during the hospitalisation period on the recovery process in heart attacks', *Journal of Consulting and Clinical Psychology*, **43**, 223–232.

Gruendemann, B. J. (1965). 'The impact of surgery on body image', *Nursing Clinicians of North America*, **10**, 635–643.

Haan, N. (1969). 'A tripartite model of ego functioning values and clinical and research applications', *Journal of Nervous and Mental Diseases*, **148**, 14–30.

Haan, N. (1977). *Coping and Defending: Processes of Self-Environment Organisation*. Academic Press, New York.

Haselhorst, J. A. (1970). 'State-trait anxiety and the outcome of heart surgery.' Unpublished master's thesis, University of Illinois.

Hayward, J. C. (1975). *Information: a Prescription against Pain*. Royal College of Nursing, London.

Henderson, S. (1977). 'The social network, support and neurosis: the function of attachment in adult life', *British Journal of Psychiatry*, **131**, 185–191.

Hockey, L. (1976). *Women in Nursing: a Descriptive Study*. Hodder & Stoughton, Edinburgh.

Janis, I. L. (1958). *Psychological Stress: Psychoanalytic and Behavioural Studies of Surgical Patients*. Wiley, New York.

Janis, I. L., and Leventhal, H. (1965). 'Psychological aspects of physical illness and hospital care', in Wolman, B. B. (ed.), *Handbook of Clinical Psychology*, pp. 1360–1377. McGraw Hill, New York.

Johnson, J. E. (1973). 'Effects of accurate expectations about sensations on the sensory and distress components of pain', *Journal of Personality and Social Psychology*, **27**, 261–275.

Johnson, J. E., and Leventhal, H. (1974). 'Effects of accurate expectations and behavioral instructions on reactions during a noxious examination', *Journal of Personality and Social Psychology*, **29**, 710–718.

Johnson, J. E., Leventhal, H., and Dabbs, U. M. (1971). 'Contribution of emotional and instrumental processes in adaptation to surgery', *Journal of Personality and Social Psychology*, **20**, 55–64.

Johnson, J. E., Fuller, S. S., Endress, M. P., and Rice, V. H. (1978a). 'Altering patients' responses to surgery: an extension and replication', *Research on Nursing and Health*, **1**, 111–121.

Johnson, J. E., Rice, V. H., Fuller, S. S., and Endress, M. P. (1978b). 'Sensory information, instruction in a coping strategy, and recovery from surgery', *Research on Nursing and Health*, **1**, 4–17.

Johnson, J. E., and Rice, V. H. (1974). 'Sensory and distress components of pain', *Nursing Research*, **23**, 203–209.

Johnson, M. M., and Martin, H. W. (1965). 'A sociological analysis of the nurse role', in Skipper, J. K., and Leonard, R. C. (eds), *Social Interaction and Patient Care*, pp. 29–39. Lippincott, Philadelphia.

Johnston, M. (1980). 'Anxiety in surgical patients', *Psychological Medicine*, **10**, 145–152.

Kennedy, J. A., and Bakst, H. (1966). 'The influence of emotions on the outcome of cardiac surgery: a predictive study', *Bulletin of the New York Academy of Medicine*, **42**, 812–845.

Kissel, S. (1965). 'Stress-reducing properties of social stimuli', *Journal of Personality and Social Psychology*, **2**, 378–384.

Kraft, I. A. (1976). 'The surgeon's psychological management of his patient', in Howells, J. G. (ed.), *Modern Perspectives in the Psychiatric Aspects of Surgery*, pp. 637–658. Brunner Mazel, New York.

Langer, E. L., Janis, I. L., and Wolfer, J. A. (1975). 'Reduction of psychological stress in surgical patients', *Journal of Experimental Social Psychology*, **11**, 155–165.

Latané, B., Eckman, J., and Joy, V. (1966). 'Shared stress and interpersonal attraction', *Journal of Experimental Social Psychology*, Supplement 1, 80–94.

Lazarus, R. S. (1966). *Psychological Stress and the Coping Process*. McGraw Hill, New York.

Lazarus, R. S., and Launier, R. (1978). 'Stress-related transactions between person and environment', in Pervin, L. A., and Lewis, M. (eds), *Perspectives in Interactional Psychology*, pp. 287–327. Plenum Press, New York.

Leigh, J. M., Walker, J., and Janaganathan, P. (1977). 'Effect of preoperative anaesthetic visit on anxiety', *British Medical Journal*, 15 October, 987–989.

Leonard, R. C., and Elms. R. R. (1965). 'Nursing approaches to patients on admission to hospital', *Nursing Outlook*, **13**, 55.

Leventhal, H. (1970). 'Findings and theory in the study of fear communications', in Berkowitz, L. (ed.), *Advances in Experimental Social Psychology*, vol. 5, pp. 119–186. Academic Press, New York.

Leventhal, H., and Everhart, D. (1979). 'Emotions, pain and physical illness', in Izard, C. E. (ed.), *Emotions and Psychopathology*. Plenum Press, New York.

Lindeman, C. A., and Stetzer, S. L. (1973). 'Effect of preoperative visits by operating room nurses', *Nursing Research*, **22**, 4–16.

Lindeman, C. A., and Van Aernam, B. (1971). 'Nursing intervention with the presurgical patient—the effects of structured and unstructured preoperative teaching', *Nursing Research*, **20**, 319–332.

Lindemann, E. (1941). 'Observations on psychiatric sequelae to surgical operations in women', *American Journal of Psychiatry*, **98**, 132–139.

Lipowski, Z. J. (1970). 'Physical illness, the individual and the coping process', *Psychiatry in Medicine*, **1**, 91–102.

Martinez-Urrutia, A. (1975). 'Anxiety and pain in surgical patients', *Journal of Consulting and Clinical Psychology*, **43**, 437–442.

Melamed, B. G., Hawes, R. R., Heiby, E., and Glick, J. (1975). 'The use of filmed modelling to reduce uncooperative behaviour of children during dental treatment', *Journal of Dental Research*, **54**, 797–801.

Melamed, B. G., and Siegel, L. J. (1975). 'Reduction of anxiety in children facing surgery by modelling', *Journal of Consulting and Clinical Psychology*, **43**, 511–521.

Murphy, F., Bentley, S., Ellis, B. W., and Dudley, H. (1977). 'Sleep deprivation in patients undergoing operation: a factor in the stress of surgery', *British Medical Journal*, **2**, 1521–1522.

Pearlin, L. I., and Schooler, C. (1978). 'The structure of coping', *Journal of Health and Social Behaviour*, **19**, 2–21.

Pender, N. J. (1974). 'Patient identification of health information received during hospitalisation', *Nursing Research*, **23**, 262–267.

Phares, E. J. (1976). *Locus of Control in Personality*. General Learning Press, Morristown, NJ.

Pranulis, M. F., Dabbs, J. M., and Johnson, J. E. (1975). 'General anesthesia and the patients' attempts at control', *Social Behavior and Personality*, **3**, 49–54.

Ramsay, M. A. E. (1972). 'A survey of pre-operative fear', *Anesthesia*, **27**, 396–402.

Ray, C. (1980). 'Psychological aspects of early breast cancer and its treatment', in Rachman, S. J. (ed.), *Contributions to Medical Psychology*, vol. 2, Pergamon Press, Oxford.

Ray, C., and Fitzgibbon, G. (1979). 'The socially-mediated reduction of stress in surgical patients', in Oborne, D. J., Gruneberg, M. M., and Eiser, J. R. (eds), *Research in Psychology and Medicine*, vol. 2, Academic Press, London.

Renshaw, D. C. (1974). 'Postsurgical emotional reactions', *Journal of the American Osteopathic Association*, **73**, 843–848.

Rofé, Y., Lewin, I., and Padeh, B. (1977). 'Affiliation before and after child delivery as a function of repression-sensitisation', *British Journal of Social and Clinical Psychology*, **16**, 311–315.

Schachter, S. (1959). *The Psychology of Affiliation*. Stanford University Press, Stanford, California.

Schmitt, F. E., and Woolridge, P. J. (1973). 'Psychological preparation of surgical patients', *Nursing Research*, **22**, 108–116.

Shalit, B. (1977). 'Structural ambiguity and limits to coping', *Journal of Human Stress*, **3**, 32–45.

Shipley, R. H., Butt, J. H., Farbry, J. E. and Horowitz, B. (1977). 'Psychological preparation for endoscopy.' *Gastrointestinal Endoscopy*, **24**, 9–13.

Sime, A. M. (1976). 'Relationship of preoperative fear, type of coping, and information received about surgery to recovery from surgery', *Journal of Personality and Social Psychology*, **4**, 716–724.

Skipper, J. K., and Leonard, R. C. (eds) (1965). *Social Interaction and Patient Care*, Lippincott, Philadelphia.

Spielberger, C. D., Averbach, S. M., Wadsworth, A. P., Dunn, T. M., and Taulbee, E. S. (1973). 'Emotional reactions to surgery', *Journal of Consulting and Clinical Psychology*, **40**, 33–38.

Staub, E. and Kellett, D. S. (1972). 'Increasing pain tolerance by information about aversive stimuli', *Journal of Personality and Social Psychology*, **21**, 198–203.

Stengel, E., Zeitlyn, B. B., and Rayner, E. H. (1958). 'Postoperative psychoses', *Journal of Mental Science*, **104**, 389–402.

Sutherland, A. M. (1967). 'Psychological observations in cancer patients', *International Psychiatric Clinics*, **4**, 75–92.

Teichman, Y. (1978). 'Affiliative reaction in different kinds of threat situations', in Spielberger, C. D., and Sarason, I. G. (eds), *Stress and Anxiety*, vol. 5, pp. 131–144, Hemisphere, Washington.

Titchener, J. L., and Levine, M. (1956). *Surgery as a Human Experience: the Psychodynamics of Surgical Practice*. Oxford University Press, New York.

Todd, P. B., and Margarey, C. J. (1978). 'Ego defences and affects in women with breast symptoms: a preliminary measurement paradigm', *British Journal of Medical Psychology*, **51**, 177–189.

Vernon, D. T. A., and Bigelow, D. A. (1974). 'Effect of information about a potentially stressful situation on responses to stress impact', *Journal of Personality and Social Psychology*, **29**, 50–59.

Volicer, B. J., and Bohannon, M. W. (1965). 'A hospital stress rating scale', *Nursing Research*, **24**, (5), 352–359.

Wallston, B. S., and Wallston, K. A. (1978). 'Locus of control and health: a review of the literature', *Health Education Monographs*, **61**, 107–117.

Weisman, A. D. (1972). *On Dying and Denying*. Behavioral Publications, New York.

Weiss, R. S. (1974). 'The provisions of social relationships', in Rubin, Z. (ed.), *Doing unto Others*, pp. 17–26. Prentice Hall, NJ.

Williams, J. G. L., Jones, J. R., Workhoven, M. N., and Williams, B. (1975). 'The psychological control of preoperative anxiety', *Psychophysiology*, **12**, 50–54.

Wilson-Barnett, J. (1978a). 'In hospital: patients' feelings and opinions', *Nursing Times*, **74**, 29–32.

Wilson-Barnett, J. (1978b). 'Patients' emotional responses to barium X-rays', *Journal of Advanced Nursing*, **3**, 37–46.

Wilson-Barnett, J. and Carrigy, A. (1978). 'Factors influencing patients' emotional reactions to hospitalisation', *Journal of Advanced Nursing*, **3**, 221–229.

Wolfer, J. A., and Davis, C. E. (1970). 'Assessment of surgical patients' preoperative emotional condition and postoperative welfare', *Nursing Research*, **19**, 402–414.

Wolfer, J. A., and Visintainer, M. A. (1975). 'Pediatric surgical patients' and parents' stress responses and adjustment as a function of psychologic preparation and stress-point nursing care', *Nursing Research*, **24**, 244–255.

Social Psychology and Behavioral Medicine
Edited by J. Richard Eiser
© 1982 John Wiley & Sons Ltd

Chapter 21

Aging, health, and theoretical social gerontology: where are we and where should we go?

RICHARD SCHULZ

Good health is a valued commodity regardless of age, but it takes on a special significance for the aged; in part because for many persons the threat of losing it becomes imminent as one approaches the seventh, eighth and ninth decades of life. In the United States, for example, those aged 65 and over constitute one-tenth of the population, but account for one-fourth of the drug prescriptions, and over one-third of the nation's total health bill. The rate of chronic conditions is about three times higher for the aged than for younger groups (Brink, 1979).

The concern with health is reflected in the social and health services provided for the aged, as well as in the research priorities on aging. From Meals on Wheels to Medicare the emphasis is on promoting health in the aged, using both preventive and acute care strategies. In the research arena the emphasis is on chronic disease and on physical, social, and psychological determinants of well-being. Indeed, there are probably few groups receiving as much attention from so many different sectors as the aged are today.

Perhaps because of the variety and complexity of the problems associated with aging, the growth of gerontology has been characterized by multi-disciplinary approaches. This is particularly true in the area of health where one might expect a medical model to dominate. Instead, it has long been a tradition to study social and psychological, in addition to biological or physical, determinants of health status among the aged. The marriage between social psychology and health was an early one and has been fruitful for several decades.

The dominant research theme within social gerontology for the last three decades has been the identification of those factors which improve or aggravate the subjective and objective well-being of the aged. Research on stereotyping, morale, personal networks, disengagement, and so on, all fall within this category. Sociologists have been the major contributors of new knowledge, and as one would expect for a new and growing research domain, the early efforts are characterized by an Aristotelian approach to the problem: identification and classification of the relevant independent and dependent variables. The major assessment device has been the survey instrument. Occasionally, the descriptive and correlational approaches characteristic of these early efforts have been supplemented and guided by theories borrowed from other disciplines, particularly sociology. However, with the exception of the recent work on learned helplessness, few theories traditionally identified with experimental social psychology have been systematically applied to social gerontology.

It is the intent of this chapter to supplement and expand existing views on determinants of well-being among the aged with theoretical and methodological perspectives borrowed from experimental social psychology. This should not, however, be viewed as a unidirectional exchange. It is hoped that by applying existing social psychological theories, new light will be shed on aging and, reciprocally, existing knowledge about aging should point out strengths and weaknesses of social psychological theories.

Sociological Approaches

Disengagement and Activity Theories

Disengagement and activity theories have been the dominant theoretical influence in social gerontology for the last two decades, although their sovereignty has significantly waned in recent years.

Disengagement theory evolved in the late 1950s and was formally presented by Cumming and Henry in 1961. It posits a functional relationship between the aging individual and society, asserting that there is a process of mutual withdrawal or disengagement of the individual from society, and society from the individual. The individual withdraws because of his/her awareness of diminished capacities and the growing imminence of death. Society withdraws because it needs to fit younger persons into the slots once occupied by older individuals. These processes are said to be universal and inevitable and to promote system equilibrium. Operationally, the disengagement process is manifested by a decrease in the number and diversity of contacts between the older person and society. The fact that disengagement is thought to be a mutually satisfying process is in part reflected by data showing high morale among aged persons who withdraw from society both psychologically and behaviorally.

Almost from the moment it appeared, disengagement theory fired a controversy that persisted for over a decade. The major opposition came from proponents of activity theory who argued that social role participation or activity among the aged, while generally decreasing with age, correlated positively with life satisfaction (Lemon *et al.*, 1972). Thus, both theories assume that aging is characterized by a general decrease in social interaction, but they differ with respect to the predicted correlates of this process: disengagement theory predicts a positive relationship between life satisfaction and decreased social interaction; activity theory predicts the reverse (Dowd, 1975).

Choosing between these diametrically opposed theories would appear to be an easy task, but in fact it is not. Depending on which side of the fence one wants to be, a large literature can be found to support either perspective (cf. Gubrium, 1973). The fact that empirical support for either view is readily available or, even more problematic, that the same data can be interpreted as verifying either theory, suggests major shortcomings within these theories (Hochschild, 1976).

The fundamental problem with both theories is that they are not stated with enough specificity either in the original or revised versions to make them falsifiable (see Popper, 1968, for discussion of falsifiability criteria). Hochschild (1976) calls this the escape clause problem. For example, disengagement states that withdrawal is universal, inevitable, and intrinsic, but there will be variations in the 'form' and 'timing' of disengagement. Without specifying exactly the nature of the variation in form or timing, the door is left open for *post-hoc* reinterpretation of a myriad of disconfirming instances (see Hochschild, 1976, for examples).

Others (Lemon *et al.*, 1972) have justifiably criticized these theories as being based too much on linear models; they fail to capture the complex interplay between the individual and his/her social system. A related problem is that they are focused too much on the static relationship among elements rather than on the processes of adaptation to aging. Finally, there is the problem of meaning. Both disengagement and activity theories ascribe meaning to the behavior of aging individuals based on assumptions about the motives and desires of the individual and society. Yet neither theory really delves into the phenomenology of the actors involved, except when it is convenient to do so (e.g. *post-hoc* reinterpretation of disconfirming evidence). In sum, after more than two decades of existence, it seems appropriate to conclude that 'Neither the disengagement model [nor] the activity theory has so far proven to be as useful a predictive tool as social gerontologists are searching for' (Hendricks and Hendricks, 1977, p. 114).

Social Breakdown Model

In response to the need for a more dynamic model of normal aging, Kuypers and Bengtson (1973) proposed the social breakdown model. A systems approach with feedback loops and cyclical processes is emphasized in this model. The cycle is initiated when the aged individual becomes vulnerable to external evaluation and labeling, because of the loss of historically familiar sources of feedback such as roles, norms, and reference groups. The feedback or labels provided the aged individual are primarily negative since they are derived from socioeconomic utility models. The eventual consequence of the social labeling process is the acceptance of negative self-labels (e.g. incompetent) and the eventual atrophy of psychological and behavioral coping skills.

This model is replete with assumptions but relatively little data exist to support them. For example, the assumption that aging is associated with a loss of roles, norms, and reference groups is in part supported by Rosow (1967) but opposed, at least in principle, by advocates of age status (Cain, 1964) or age stratification (Riley, 1971) perspectives as well as by those who argue that the aged represent a unique subculture with its own group consciousness (Rose, 1964).

Even if we accept the assumption of normlessness, we must then show that the aged look to the values and attitudes of persons in their middle years and that these values are predominantly negative. The early stereotyping literature suggests that the latter may be true, although this too may be changing; but there is relatively little direct evidence showing that the aged view the middle-aged as their relevant reference group or that they accept the negative labels provided by this group. In fact, there is evidence suggesting the opposite: many older persons behave in ways to dissociate themselves from negatively valued stereotypic groups (e.g. Matthews, 1979). To this growing list of potential deficiencies one can add questions regarding the heuristic value of this theory: it is not clear how one would test it or how it could be falsified.

Finally, one must ask whether this is indeed a model of normal aging since the majority of aged persons do not perceive themselves as incompetent or as atrophied as this model would suggest.

Exchange Theory

Exchange theory (Dowd, 1975) is a more recent entry into the social gerontology theory pool. It attempts to explain the decreased social interaction of the aged in terms of economic exchanges à la Homans (1961), Blau (1964), and Emerson (1962, 1972). The basic assumption of all exchange theories is that interactions between individuals occur and are sustained because the rewards (e.g. money, esteem, compliance, novelty) are greater than the costs (e.g. time, boredom, anxiety). An interaction is imbalanced when one of the partners of a social exchange is unable to reciprocate the rewarding behavior of the other. According to Dowd, the aged become increasingly unable to enter into balanced exchange relationships with other groups because of the decline in power resources associated with age. The imbalanced exchange ratio ultimately forces the aged to exchange compliance—a costly generalized reinforcer—for their continued sustenance. Disengagement occurs when the costs of compliance and loss of self-respect reach a point 'beyond which additional costs become prohibitive' (Dowd, 1975, p. 591).

Dowd cautiously describes the aging exchange model as a 'preface' to theory. This seems wise since many questions are left unanswered. In addition to the problems of falsifiability raised with respect to disengagement, activity, and social breakdown theories, there are several specific problems intrinsic to this approach.

First, the heuristic value of the model is not clearly developed, although this may come with time. The process of retirement is used to illustrate components of the model but it is not clear what type of data one would collect in that context to test the model. The author does propose two specific hypotheses but these are relatively minor derivations from the model and do not represent critical tests. There are several hypotheses implicit in the theory but on face value they appear to have little credibility. For example, Dowd states that because of their limited power resources, the costs of remaining engaged for the aged (i.e. compliance and loss of self-respect) steadily increase. This suggests that the engaged aged individual should have lower self-esteem and a more inferior self-concept than the non-engaged older person. There is little support for this notion in the existing gerontological literature.

Second, there are conceptual problems inherent in the exchange approach in general and in this version of exchange theory in particular. One problem concerns the calculation of costs and benefits associated with social interaction. This may not be as straightforward as proposed by Dowd and others. For example, dissonance and self-attribution theory (Festinger, 1957; Worchel and Cooper, 1976; Bem, 1972) suggest that we value voluntary experiences *more* to the extent that the costs for engaging in them are high. The younger individual who perceives no clear extrinsic rewards for interacting with older persons may justify his/her behavior by generating *post-hoc* intrinsic reasons (e.g. genuine interest in older persons). Alternatively, one can argue that virtue has its own reward: interacting with the aged in a positive manner can be viewed as a credit to the younger person, especially if extrinsic rewards are absent. The point of all this is that the calculus for adding up costs and benefits is considerably more complex than the formulae suggested by Dowd.

Another conceptual problem concerns the absence of expectancies in the exchange model proposed by Dowd. How satisfied we are with social interactions is not so much a function of the absolute rewards and costs associated with that interaction, but rather the level of rewards and costs relative to the individual's expectation. If middle-aged persons have a negative stereotype of the aged, it follows that their expectations for rewards from interactions with the aged should be relatively low. This reasoning predicts reduced initiation of contact with the aged on the part of younger persons but, more importantly, it predicts high satisfaction for interactions that do occur. Viewed from this perspective, interaction between young and old would rarely be imbalanced, not because the young expect and receive large quantities of compliance but rather because the expectations for, and occurrence of, any kind of reward is low.

Other Principal Theories in Social Gerontology

The list of major theories within social gerontology would be incomplete without the inclusion of Rose's (1965) perspective of the aged as a subculture, the related views of Cain (1964) and Riley (1971) on age stratification and age status, and the notions of Neugarten et al. (1968) that individual adaptation to aging is best understood from a typology-of-personalities perspective. When compared to the previously described theories, these models are more descriptive than predictive. Thus, they may help us understand the process of aging but they may not necessarily improve our predictive ability with respect to individuals or groups—just as understanding what causes volcanoes does not necessarily allow us to predict when they will occur (Goodson and Morgan, 1976).

Rose (1965) proposes that a variety of demographic and social trends combined with biological changes contribute to the formation of a distinct aged subculture. Retirement policies, for example, make it difficult for older persons to remain integrated with the larger society and thereby promote greater identification with an aged peer group (Hendricks and Hendricks, 1977). According to Rose, if we are to understand adjustment to aging from this perspective, we must look to the values and attitudes of the aged subculture to define adjustment. As Hendricks and Hendricks (1977, p. 113) noted: 'From the standpoint of activity theory, the occasional person who expresses high morale but low activity levels is a deviant, while from a subcultural perspective he or she may simply be listening to an older drummer.'

The basic assumption of age status and age stratification approaches to the study of adjustment to late life is consistent with the aging subculture views, although much broader in perspective. The fundamental premise is that 'societies typically arrange themselves into a hierarchy of age strata complete with obligations and prerogatives assigned to members as they move from one stratum to the next' (Hendricks and Hendricks, 1977, p. 119). Each age stratum develops its own characteristic subculture as it moves through time, and these powerfully influence the behavior and attitudes of its members. This perspective immediately leads to questions concerning the nature of relationships within and between strata, movement from one stratum to another, and the impact on society as a whole of differences and conflicts between strata (Riley, 1971). While age stratification is certainly a valuable descriptive instrument and can within some cultural contexts serve as a valuable predictive tool, its explanatory power appears limited. Few social scientists would deny the validity of an age strata perspective but many would view it as something that *needs* rather than *does* a great deal of explaining.

Another approach to understanding adaptation to late life emphasizes individual differences and the stability of interaction and coping systems developed earlier in life. This is the personality or trait approach. According to this view, individuals develop over time characteristic styles for dealing with problems and adapting to new situations, and these persist into later years (Neugarten *et al.*, 1968). Several typologies of personality have been developed (e.g. see Reicherd *et al.*, 1962; Neugarten *et al.*, 1964, 1968; Neugarten, 1972) based on data collected from several aged populations. However, to date there are no prospective studies which document the predictive validity of these typologies. In addition, a trait approach alone would find it difficult to explain the discontinuities in activity levels between the middle-aged and the elderly.

We have omitted from this discussion several perspectives on adult development and aging that traditionally appear under the rubric of theoretical social gerontology. This would include theories of adult development such as those of Erikson (1950) and Bühler (1935) as well as a variety of specific theories dealing with person–environment fit (e.g. Lawton, 1975; Kahana, 1975). The developmental theories have generated little empirical interest beyond occasional anecdotal reports, probably because of a lack of specificity. Person–environment fit theories have thus far had only limited application to primarily institutional settings. At this point the value of this approach remains to be demonstrated.

Psychological Approaches

Learned Helplessness and Aging

Seligman (1975) first proposed learned helplessness theory as a model to explain depression in humans. According to this theory (Seligman, 1975; Abramson *et al.*, 1978), when individuals are exposed to uncontrollable outcomes they develop expectations that future outcomes will also be uncontrollable. This in turn leads to the motivational, cognitive, and emotional deficits associated with helplessness and depression.

The degree of helplessness will vary as a function of the type of attribution the individual makes about the cause of the non-contingency. Attributions about the cause can be classified along three orthogonal dimensions:

(1) internal/external—internal causes stem from the individual and external causes from the environment;
(2) stable/unstable—stable factors are long-lived and recurrent, whereas unstable factors are short-lived and intermittent;
(3) global/specific—global factors occur across situations, whereas specific factors are unique to a particular context.

Each type of attribution has specific consequences for the individual: attributions to internal/external factors should affect self-esteem; attributions to stable/unstable factors should determine the long-term consequences of a particular experience; and attributions to global/specific factors should determine the extent to which individuals will generalize a particular experience to other situations. In general, the most damaging effects are expected when an individual makes internal, stable, and global attributions concerning the cause of a non-contingent event. As an example, consider a man who loses his spouse, blames himself, and believes that the death was largely due to his uncaring and negligent nature (internal, global, stable attribution). Compared to another person who is convinced that he lost his wife because of a rare, incurable disease (external, unstable, specific attribution), the former should suffer greater self-esteem deficits, the experience should generalize to a larger variety of events and situations, and the negative impact of the loss should be longer-lasting.

Although this model has not been rigorously tested with an aged population, it has stimulated considerable research on aging in general and on the impact on aged individuals of institutionalization in particular. Several researchers (e.g., Schulz, 1976, 1978; Schulz and Brenner, 1977; Schulz and Hanusa, 1978, 1979; Langer and Rodin, 1976; Rodin and Langer, 1977) have suggested that aging is a process characterized by large decreases in the individual's ability to control important outcomes due to shrinking financial resources, decreased physical ability, loss of work role, etc. According to this view of aging, then, the withdrawal and high rates of depression observed among the aged are attributable to the shrinking sphere of environmental control. Several studies have been carried out, experimentally testing derivations from this model. In particular, data are now available demonstrating the positive impact of control-enhancing interventions on the institutionalized aged (Schulz, 1976; Rodin and Langer, 1976), the long-term effects of these interventions (Schulz and Hanusa, 1978; Langer and Rodin, 1976), the relationship between these interventions and individual differences (Schulz and Hanusa, 1980), and the relationship between competence and control in promoting health-related outcomes among the institutionalized aged (Schulz and Hanusa, 1979).

Like Dowd's exchange theory, the central idea of learned helplessness theory concerns the issue of power. In both theories the declining power resources of the aged are identified as the precipitating causes of withdrawal among the aged. Beyond this initial similarity, however, the theories are vastly different. Learned helplessness, because of its emphasis on attribution, delves deeply into the phenomenology of the individual. Exchange theory does not. Indeed this difference, more than any other, distinguishes psychological from sociological approaches to theoretical social gerontology. Psychological theories like learned helplessness focus on the person as the unit of analysis and ask the question: what goes on inside the head that would explain individual behavior? The unit of analysis for sociologists is often the group, and the major questions asked concern the phenomenology of collectives rather than individuals.

One purpose of this chapter is to show that both theories and their domain of application benefit when they are brought together. The case of learned helplessness illustrates this point well. The declines associated with aging are, from an attributional perspective, chronic (they are not reversible) and global (they affect many areas of a persons's life). However, whether or not the declines are attributed to internal or external (e.g. personal or universal) causes is an empirical question and represents an important area for future research. According to learned helplessness theory, the answer to this question depends on the ability of *relevant others* to control similar outcomes. The aged person who believes that relevant others can control outcomes which he or she cannot should make internal or personal attributions. External attributions should result if the aged individual believes that he or she and relevant others are in the same boat; that is, none of them can control important outcomes. Judging from the examples provided by Abramson *et al.*, defining relevant others appears to be a straightforward task. Thus, for example, graduate students in psychology compare their performances in school with other psychology graduate students. Applied to the aged, however, identifying relevant others is more problematic. Do middle-aged persons serve as the relevant reference group? Or is it other older persons? Or does it vary with the specific outcome or attribute being evaluated? These are important questions because the type of attribution generated ultimately determines the individual's level of self-esteem. At present there is no answer to this question. However, we will return to this issue when we examine social comparison processes.

Lest we present too one-sided a picture of learned helplessness theory, it should be noted that it, too, is beset with numerous problems. The theory is intended to explain depression in humans but falls short on several counts (cf. Wortman and Dintzer, 1978). Perhaps the most significant shortcoming is that if fails to account for the large variety of depression observed in clinical populations. Questions have also been raised concerning whether people actually make attributions, whether the attributional dimensions proposed

are adequate, what role expectations play, and so on. One of the strengths of
the theory is that it is stated with enough specificity to allow for critical tests;
however, many attempts to verify the theory have yielded contradictory
results (cf. Wortman and Dintzer, 1978). The theory has generated a
tremendous amount of research but much of it has undermined rather than
strengthened our faith in it. In sum, the picture of learned helplessness theory
isn't all that rosy either.

Social Comparison Theory

Over two decades ago Festinger (1954) proposed his theory of social
comparison processes. The underlying assumption of the theory is that there
exists in humans a basic drive to evaluate their opinions and abilities. In the
absence of objective evidence (e.g. physical reality) persons will compare
themselves with others to assess the validity of their views. In Festinger's
words: 'An opinion, belief, and attitude is "correct", "valid", and "proper"
to the extent that it is anchored in a group of people with similar beliefs,
opinions, and attitudes' (Festinger, 1950, p. 272). Sociological counterparts to
social comparison theory can be found in the work of Mead (1934) and
Cooley (1956).

The relevance of social comparison processes to an understanding of
adjustment to late life is evident once we recognize that there is no physical
reality that readily provides an answer to questions such as: How should I feel
about my life? How happy am I? With the possible exception of extreme
cases, how we respond to or feel about a wide array of circumstances and
outcomes depends on the opinion and beliefs of relevant others. Who are the
relevant others for the aged? This is a recurrent and pivotal question for
several of the theories (e.g. learned helplessness, discussed above). Social
comparison theory, along with a recent derivation, temporal comparison
theory (Albert, 1977), suggest two possible answers to this question. One
option is to identify similar others in the environment and use them as
reference persons. This is reflected in corollary III (A) of social comparison
theory which states that, given a range of possible persons for comparisons,
someone close to one's own ability or opinion will be chosen for comparison
(Festinger, 1954).

A second option is to make historical or temporal comparisons. This is an
intraindividual comparison in which present circumstances, outcome, abilities, etc. are compared with past circumstances, outcomes, abilities, and so
forth (Schulz, in press).

To the extent that any comparison yields negative discrepancies, the
individuals are likely to feel badly about themselves or their situation. Thus,
for example, the old person who perceives relevant others to be considerably
better off than him/herself or who finds his/her past to be better than the

present may experience negative affect. Positive affect should result when comparisons yield positive discrepancies.

Which of the two processes dominate should have important consequences for adjustment to late life. Given the many real declines associated with reaching old age (e.g. physical and cognitive ability, economic resources, etc.), comparisons based on the past are likely to yield negative discrepancies and hence negative affective states. Alternatively, the aged individual who uses his/her contemporaries as comparison—others should be less likely to experience negative discrepancies.

As an example, consider an institutionalized older person and the types of events he/she is likely to encounter. Clearly, if such an individual compares past housing conditions leisure activities, physical mobility and daily events in general with present condition, he/she is likely to experience negative affect. However, if the same individual uses as a basis for comparison the circumstances and outcomes of similar individuals in the immediate environment (other institutionalized older persons), there is less likelihood of experiencing negative discrepancies and hence negative affect.

The type of comparison processes older persons engage in can be inferred from some recent data reported by Zemore and Eames (1979). In their study, residents of old-age homes reported no more symptoms of depression than either a group of waiting-list controls or a non-institutionalized young group. This would be expected *if* individuals engage in contemporary rather than temporal comparison processes. A similar inference can be derived from the large number of studies on morale and well-being in the aged (for a review of this literature see Larson, 1978). Despite large differences in objective conditions of young, middle-aged and aged individuals, few studies report any age-related differences in self-report of well-being and morale. Apparently, individuals in different age groups adjust their expectancies in line with the prevailing conditions for that group. Such strategies are adaptive in that they minimize disappointment, but also tend to promote the *status quo*.

The social comparison approach to adjustment to late life illustrates again a fundamental difference between sociological and psychological approaches to social gerontology. Sociologists have for a long time asked questions concerning subjective well-being and its correlates. The social comparison approach asks the more rudimentary question: How does an individual figure out how he/she feels? At this point in time we know a great deal about the correlates of well-being among the aged but little about the process used by individuals to arrive at judgements of well-being.

Other Psychological Theories

Learned helplessness, attribution, and social comparison theories are only a few of the available psychological models for understanding adaptation to late life. To this list we can add a variety of other theories, including Self-perception (Bem, 1972), Just World (Lerner *et al.*, 1976; Walster, 1966), and Defensive Attribution (Shaver, 1970, 1975). These theories are particularly useful in understanding more circumscribed issues related to well-being in late life.

Lerner's Just World theory, for example, provides some fresh insight into the voluminous and largely atheoretical literature on attitudes toward the aged. In essence, Just World theory states that observers are motivated to blame victims for their misfortunes, in order to preserve for themselves the illusion that the world is a predictable, 'safe' place. Walster similarly suggests that persons may derogate victims in order to avoid the realization that they too are vulnerable to similar outcomes.

This theory was intended to explain negative attitudes toward rape and accident victims, but may also be relevant to aging if we make the assumption that the aged fall into a general category of victimized or stigmatized persons. This assumption is supported by researchers such as Ward (1977, p. 231) who concludes that 'Old age may be viewed as a stigmatized attribute—one to which negative meanings may be attached by people in general and by specific persons who "enter" the status.' The advantage of the Just World approach to studying attitudes toward the aged is that it provides both a specific experimental paradigm and a new set of mediating variables (e.g. similarity of target individual) to guide future research. Furthermore, the exchange between theory and application is a two-way street. The application of Just World theory to aging makes salient an important distinction and points to possible limitations of the theory. The aged may well be a stigmatized group, but of a particular type. As Schulz and Scheier (1978, p. 16) point out, 'membership in most stereotypic groups is either prescribed at birth or determined by a unique series of events which affect a relatively small proportion of the population. In contrast, becoming old is the normal culmination of the developmental process'. This raises the question, therefore, to what extent will young persons derogate someone whom they may become?

This serves as a good example of how both the domain of application—aging—and the theory are enriched by integrating social psychology with social gerontology. The same point can be made with respect to other theories such as social comparison theory. On the one hand, the theory leads to novel approaches to studying well-being in late life. On the other hand, the field of aging leads to new questions about social comparison theory. Older persons have available by definition a longer past for comparison purposes. One might ask, therefore, as we have done, does this fundamentally change the types of comparisons made?

The psychological theories described above are only a small sample of the possibilities available to social gerontologists. We could add to this list self-esteem theories (e.g. Epstein, 1973), illusory correlation (Hamilton and Gifford, 1976), the social contact hypothesis (Rokeach, 1968), mere exposure (Zajonc, 1968), theories of emotionality (Schulz, in press), and more. Given the present moribund status of theoretical social gerontology, recourse to these theories should bring new life to both gerontology and social psychology.

Discussion and Future Directions

We have examined a broad spectrum of theories aimed at enhancing our understanding of human adaptation to late life. Both the traditional sociological and the more recent psychological approaches to social gerontology were presented, with an eye toward identifying important problems characteristic of each. While it is admittedly easier to identify than to solve problems, theoretical social gerontology seems to be at a developmental stage where a clear assessment of where we stand is an essential prerequisite for further development. The remainder of this chapter is devoted to a general set of prescriptions designed to facilitate future theory development.

Breadth *vs.* Depth

The intent of many of the theories discussed above, particularly the sociological theories, is to explain and describe adaptation to late life, viewed either in terms of activity, self-concept, and/or a mixed assortment of specific indicators of subjective and objective well-being. Clearly, generating a theory that adequately accounts for human adaptation to late life is not an easy task. Indeed, it may be impossible given the large variability across both persons and contexts. One problem, then, is that existing theories are too broadly focused. What appears to be needed are theories that are more minutely focused and are specified in far greater detail than existing theories.

Contexts, Problems, or Processes

Social gerontology has been and continues to be a problem-oriented enterprise. Theories are developed in response to problems identified by researchers and practitioners. A second and slightly less frequent determinant of theory development has been specific contexts characteristic of the aged. Thus, for example, the fact that the aged are frequently institutionalized has spawned theories about the effects of institutionalization. A third and most underrepresented contributor to theory development is a concern for underlying processes. Theories based on problems and contexts frequently yield excellent descriptions and are necessary first steps toward the development of causal models. Theoretical social gerontology is now ripe for the next step, the development of causal explanation. This is best achieved by emphasizing processes rather than contexts or problems. The emphasis on processes is one of the strengths of experimental social psychological theories. Their application to aging should be particularly useful for facilitating a shift toward process models.

Increased Specificity

The need for greater specificity in stating theoretical ideas has been a recurrent theme throughout this chapter. Specificity has its own rewards. Theories that are not stated with sufficient precision to allow for empirical tests are unlikely to receive much attention. Basic ingredients for good social science theory, such as the specification of the unit of analysis (e.g. Is it the individual or the group?) are often glossed over by current theories. In fact, it might be a good idea to have theoreticians evaluate (and defend) their theories using a standard checklist of criteria. Such a system might eliminate a great deal of confusion and a number of bad theories as well.

Original Theories vs. Applications of Existing Theories

Will social gerontology ever have its own theories or is it destined to remain a domain to which theories from other disciplines can be applied? Throughout this chapter we have avoided referring to social gerontology as a discipline. Although the disciplinary status of gerontology is still a hotly debated topic, we feel that if fails to qualify as a discipline on two counts. It has neither an independent nor unique set of theories or methods. Gerontology is the multidisciplinarian's dream, bringing together the methods and theories of at least half a dozen disciplines all focused on a particular population roughly defined by age.

To answer the question posed above, social gerontology appears destined to remain an area of application rather than a fountainhead of original theory. However, gerontology raises important questions frequently overlooked by traditional disciplines. An implicit assumption inherent in sociological and psychological theories aimed at explaining behavior of the human adult is that there is little difference between the 20 and the 60-year-old. While this may be true in many cases, it should not always be assumed. In particular, persons applying social psychological theory about adult behavior to the aged must ask the following questions:

(1) Are there characteristic biological changes associated with age that are relevant to constructs or processes specified by the theory?
(2) Are there social–contextual changes typically associated with age that are related to specified components of the theory?

(3) Do biological and social–contextual factors interact with each other and/or with elements of the theory in such a way as to significantly alter the theory when applied to the aged?

Theory *vs.* Data

A final suggestion concerns the need for a balance between abstraction and empirics. Most of this chapter consists of 'abstractions about theory . . . [rather than] substantive principles or propositions about the nature of the relevant universe' (Sears, 1980, p. 304). Theory development and application ultimately depend on the collection of relevant data. If we are to facilitate a science of human development we must heed the logic of science but also put to work the elegant theories we develop.

References

Abramson, L. Y., Seligman, E. P., and Teasdale, J. D. (1978). 'Learned helplessness in humans: critique and reformulation', *Journal of Abnormal Psychology*, **87**, 49–74.

Albert S. (1977). 'Temporal comparison theory', *Psychological Review*, **84**, 485–503.

Bem, D. (1972). 'Self-perception theory', in Berkowitz, L. (ed.), *Advances in Experimental Social Psychchology*, vol. VI. Academic Press, New York.

Blau, P. M. (1964). *Exchange and power in social life*. John Wiley & Sons, New York.

Brink, T. L. (1979). *Geriatric Psychotherapy*. Human Sciences Press, New York.

Bühler, C. (1935). 'The curve of life as studied in biographies', *Journal of Applied Psychology*, **19**, 405–409.

Cain, L. E., Jr. (1964). 'Life course and social structure', in Faris, R. E. L. (ed.), *Handbook of Modern Sociology*. Rand McNally, Chicago.

Cooley, C. H. (1956). *Human Nature and the Social Order*. Free Press, Glencoe, Ill. (Originally published 1902.)

Cumming, E., and Henry, W. E. (1961). *Growing Old*. Basic Books, New York.

Dowd, J. (1975). 'Aging as exchange: a preface to theory'. *Journal of Gerontology*, **30**, 584–594.

Emerson, R. M. (1962). 'Power–dependence relations', *American Sociological Review*, **27**, 31–41.

Emerson, R. M. (1972). 'Exchange theory', Parts 1 and 2, in Berger, J., Zelditch, M., and Anderson, B. (eds), *Sociological Theories in Progress*, vol, II. Houghton-Mifflin, Boston.

Epstein, S. (1973). 'The self-concept revisited', *American Psychologist*, **27**, 404–416.

Erikson, E. H. (1950). *Childhood and Society*. Norton, New York.

Festinger, L. (1950). 'Informal social communication', *Psychological Review*, **57**, 271–282.

Festinger, L. (1954). 'A theory of social comparison processes', *Human Relations*, **7**, 117–140.

Festinger, L. (1957). *A Theory of Cognitive Dissonance*. Stanford University Press, Stanford, Calif.

Goodson, F. E., and Morgan, G. A. (1976). 'Evaluation of theory', in Marx, M. H. (ed.), *Theories in Contemporary Psychology*. Macmillan, New York.

Gubrium, J. F. (1973). *The Myth of the Golden Years*. Charles C. Thomas, Springfield, Ill.

Hamilton, D. L., and Gifford, R. K. (1976). 'Illusory correlation in interpersonal perception: a cognitive basis of stereotypic judgments', *Journal of Experimental Social Psychology*, **12**, 393–407.

Hendricks, J., and Hendricks, C. D. (1977). *Aging in Mass Society, Myths and Realities*. Winthrop, Cambridge, Mass.

Hochschild, A. R. (1976). 'Disengagement theory: a logical, empirical and phenomenological critique', in Gubrium, J. F. (ed.), *Time, Roles and Self in Old Age*. Human Sciences Press, New York.

Homans, G. C. (1961). *Social Behavior: Its Elementary Forms*. Harcourt, Brace & World, New York.

Kahana, E. (1975). 'A congruence model of person–environment interaction', in Windley, P. G., Byerts, T. O., and Ernst, F. G. (eds), *Theory Development in Environment and Aging*. American Gerontological Society, Manhattan; Kansas.

Kuypers, J. A., and Bengtson, V. L. (1973). 'Social breakdown and competence: a model of normal aging', *Human Development*, **16**, 181–201.

Langer, E., and Rodin, J. (1976). 'The effects of choice and enhanced personal responsibility for the aged: a field experiment in an institutional setting', *Journal of Personality and Social Psychology*, **34**, 191–198.

Larson, R. (1978) 'Thirty years of research on the subjective well-being of older Americans', *Journal of Gerontology*, **33**, 109–125.

Lawton, M. P. (1973). 'Competence, environmental press and the adaptation of older people', in Windley, P. G., Byerts, T. O., and Ernst, F. G. (eds), *Theory Development in Environment and Aging*. American Gerontological Society, Manhattan, Kansas.

Lemon, B. W., Bengtson, V. L., and Peterson, J. A. (1972). 'An exploration of the activity theory of aging: activity and life satisfaction among inmovers to a retirement community', *Journal of Gerontology*, **27**, 511–523.

Lerner, M. J., Miller, D. T., and Holmes, J. (1976). 'Deserving and the emergence of forms of justice', in Berkowitz, L. (ed.), *Advances in Experimental Social Psychology*, vol. X. Academic Press, New York.

Matthews, S. H. (1979). *The Social World of Old Women: Management of Self-identity*, (Sage Library of Social Research, vol. 78.), Sage, Beverly Hills, Calif.

Mead, G. H. (1934). *Mind, Self and Society*. University of Chicago Press, Chicago.

Neugarten, B. L. (1972). 'Personality and the aging process', *Gerontologist*, **12**, 9–15.

Neugarten, B. L., Crotty, W. J., and Tobin, S. S. (1964). 'Personality types in an aged population', in Neugarten, B. L., and Berkowitz, H. (eds), *Personality in Middle and Late Life*. Atherton, New York.

Neugarten, B. L., Havighurst, R. J., and Tobin, S. S. (1968). 'Personality patterns and aging', in Neugarten, B. L. (ed.), *Middle Age and Aging*. University of Chicago Press, Chicago.

Popper, K. R. (1968). *The Logic of Scientific Discovery* (rev. English edn.). Hutchinson, London.

Reicherd, S., Livson, F., and Peterson, P. G. (1962). *Aging and personality: A study of 87 older men*. Wiley, New York.

Riley, M. W. (1971). 'Social gerontology and the age stratification of society', *Gerontologist*, **12**, 79–87.

Rodin, J., and Langer, E. J. (1977). 'Long-term effects of a control-relevant intervention with the institutionalized aged', *Journal of Personality and Social Psychology*, **35**, 897–902.

Rokeach, M. (1968). *Beliefs, Attitudes and Values*. Jossey-Bass, San Francisco.

Rose, A. M. (1964). 'A current theoretical issue in social gerontology', *Gerontologist*, **4**, 25–29.

Rose, A. M. (1963). 'The subculture of the aging: a framework in social gerontology', in Rose, A. M., and Peterson, W. A. (eds), *Older People and their Social World*. F. A. Davis Co., Philadelphia.

Rosow, I. (1967). *Social Integration of the Aged*. Free Press, New York.

Schulz, R. (1976). 'The effects of control and predictability on the psychological and physical well-being of the institutionalized aged', *Journal of Personality and Social Psychology*, **33**, 563–573.

Schulz, R. (1978). *The Psychology of Death, Dying and Bereavement*. Addison Wesley, Reading, Mass.

Schulz, R. (in press). 'Emotionality and aging', in Blankenstein, K., and Polivy, J. (eds), *Communication and Affect*, vol. IX. Plenum Press, New York.

Schulz, R., and Brenner, G. (1977). 'Relocation of the aged: a review and theoretical analysis', *Journal of Gerontology*, **32**, 323–333.

Schulz, R., and Hanusa, B. H. (1978). 'Long-term effects of predictability and control enhancing interventions: findings and ethical issues', *Journal of Personality and Social Psychology*, **36**, 1194–1201.

Schulz, R., and Hanusa, B. H. (1979). 'Environmental influences on the effectiveness of control and competence enhancing interventions', in Perlmutter, L. C., and Monty, R. A. (eds), *Choice and Perceived Control*. Lawrence Erlbaum Associates, New York.

Schulz, R., and Hanusa, B. H. (1980). 'Experimental social gerontology: a social psychological perspective', *Journal of Social Issues*, **36**, 30–47.

Schulz, R. and Scheier, M. F. (1978). *Aging as stigma*. Unpublished manuscript.

Sears, R. R. (1980). 'A new school of life span?', *Contemporary Psychology*, **25**, 303–304.

Seligman, M. E. P. (1975) *Helplessness: On Depression, Development and Death*. W. H. Freeman, San Francisco.

Shaver, K. G. (1970). 'Defensive attribution: effects of severity and relevance on the responsibility assigned for an accident', *Journal of Personality and Social Psychology*, **14**, 101–113.

Shaver, K. G. (1975). *An Introduction to Attribution Processes*. Winthrop Publishers, Cambridge.

Walster, E. (1966). 'Assignment of responsibility for an accident', *Journal of Personality and Social Psychology*, **3**, 73–79.

Ward, R. A. (1977). 'The impact of subjective age and stigma on older persons', *Journal of Gerontology*, **32**, 227–232.

Worchel, S., and Cooper, J. (1976). *Understanding Social Psychology*. Dorsey Press, Homewood, Ill.

Wortman, C. B., and Dintzer, L. (1978). 'Is an attributional analysis of learned helplessness phenomenon viable? A critique of the Abramson, Seligman and Teasdale reformulation', *Journal of Abnormal Psychology*, **87**, 75–90.

Zajonc, R. B. (1968). 'Attitudinal effects of mere exposure', *Journal of Personality and Social Psychology*, **9**, 1–27. (Monograph supplement.)

Zemore, R., and Eames, N. (1979). 'Psychic and somatic symptoms of depression among young adults, institutionalized aged and noninstitutionalized aged.' *Journal of Gerontology*, **34**, 716–722.

Social Psychology and Behavioral Medicine
Edited by J. Richard Eiser
© 1982 John Wiley & Sons Ltd

Chapter 22

The effects of bereavement on mortality: a social psychological analysis*

WOLFGANG STROEBE, MARGARET S. STROEBE,
KENNETH J. GERGEN, and MARY GERGEN

Introduction

All married persons face the possibility of their mate's death. For half the married population widowhood will become a reality. Bereavement in most cultures can be a period of intense grief, uncertainty, stress, doubt, and self-criticism. Within recent years investigators have also begun to ask whether bereavement may not have more severe effects. Specifically, can loss of a mate affect the longevity of the survivor? If so, what is the magnitude and generality of such a *'loss effect'*? Who is at greatest risk of mortality following the death of the spouse? What factors differentiate those for whom loss has a major impact from those who remain more resilient? From what physical causes are the bereaved most likely to die? What is the duration of the risk period following bereavement? Can we identify physiological and/or psychological mechanisms to account for these potentially fatal effects of partner loss? In the present chapter, we shall first examine evidence relevant to various aspects of the loss effect, its magnitude, generality, and specific forms. We shall then discuss the cognitive and social psychological processes which are likely to contribute to the loss effect.

The Loss of a Spouse and Mortality

Cross-sectional Studies

In everyday life, intimations of the higher risks of the widowed are pervasive. The 'broken heart' notion is a recurrent theme and inexhaustible source of inspiration in literature and the arts. It would appear that there is very good

---

* Parts of this chapter are an extension of ideas formulated by the authors in a German publication (Stroebe *et al.*, 1980).

empirical support for these popular beliefs. Analysis of national mortality statistics, giving death rates by marital status, reveals a consistent relationship between bereavement and death. A simple analysis of census information published by the Office of Population Censuses and Surveys for England and Wales (OPCS) for the year 1974 illustrates this relationship. Included in Table 22.1 are the ratios of the death rates of the widowed to those of the married. These ratios indicate the magnitude of the excesses in widowed mortality over the married. The table shows that widowed mortality is excessive for every age-group, and for both sexes. The excesses for widowers compared with married men are consistently larger than the excesses for widows compared with married women. For example, widowed males in the 20–24 age category are 17 times more likely to die than their married counterparts, while widowed females in this same age category are 10 times more likely to die than married females. This high rate slowly declines until the later years when the ratio becomes less than 2 to 1.

Table 22.1 Mortality in England and Wales, all causes: ratios produced by dividing the mortality rate of the unmarried by the mortality rate of the married, 1974*†

Unmarried category (ratio)	Age-group											
	20–24	25–29	30–34	35–39	40–44	45–49	50–54	55–59	60–64	65–69	70–74	75+
Single												
Male	1.92	2.44	2.64	2.39	2.11	1.80	1.67	1.54	1.34	1.22	1.13	1.13
Female	1.63	2.74	2.78	2.13	1.92	1.29	1.44	1.32	1.27	1.15	1.12	1.46
Widowed												
Male	17.25	6.27	3.66	2.86	2.22	2.12	1.66	1.57	1.53	1.44	1.34	1.50
Female	10.01	4.25	4.20	1.24	1.94	1.47	1.44	1.30	1.29	1.19	1.18	1.59
Divorced												
Male	2.94	2.10	2.45	2.25	1.87	1.81	1.84	1.57	1.61	1.38	1.36	1.40
Female	3.59	1.60	1.67	1.77	1.61	1.43	1.43	1.30	1.28	1.15	1.06	1.53

* Population and mortality figures are taken from publications from the Office of Population Censuses and Surveys, DH1 No. 1, FM2 No. 2 (1977a,b).

† Ratios are dereived from the crude age- and sex-specific death rates (using total deaths registered in England and Wales, and total mid-year population estimates) for various marital status groups. These ratios are calculated by dividing the mortality rate of the unmarried status (for the specific age and sex group) by the comparable death rate for the married. Thus, a coefficient of 2.00 means that the mortality rate of the widowed is twice as high as that for the married.

However, it is also important to note that not only the widowed but also other single statuses—the never married and the divorced—have excessive rates compared with the married. The ratios also show similar patterns for these other unmarried statuses: more excessive rates are found for the younger, and for males, although these differences are generally not as marked as for the widowed. It seems, then, that the high risk of mortality is not unique to those who have lost their spouses to death. Other unmarried groups are similarly susceptible. Clearly, more extensive data are necessary to determine the existence of a loss effect.

What is the generality of these findings? Support for the basic pattern of excess mortality derives from a variety of sources. Over a century ago Farr (1859) noted the low mortality of the married compared to the widowed as evidenced in French national statistics. More recently, Kraus and Lilienfeld's (1959) epidemiological analysis of US death rates for 1949–51 indicated a pronounced tendency for the widowed to die prematurely, as compared to the married. There are many other studies of a cross-sectional nature generally confirming the loss effect, and the subsidiary findings that, compared with married counterparts, widowers have relatively more excessive rates than widows, and that younger widowed have more excessive rates than do older (for a review, see Stroebe *et al.*, 1981).

Although cross-sectional analyses are an asset because they give a general indication of the magnitude and range of potential loss effect, tracing of cause and effect sequences in such epidemiological or demographic surveys is not typically permissible. Further, if we do regard these cross-sectional results as indicative of a bereavement–mortality relationship, we are faced with a number of issues which are difficult to clarify. For instance, why should widowers be at higher risk than widows? One might easily generate the opposite hypothesis, that widows are faced with more overwhelming problems on the death of their husbands than vice-versa. And why should the young be more prone to a deleterious loss effect than the old? The old are more likely to be in poor health before bereavement than the young, so that this additional stressful event would be expected to have more extreme consequences. Let us then consider results from longitudinal research.

Longitudinal Investigations

One of the major advantages of longitudinal investigations is that, in contrast to cross-sectional studies, they provide information on the length of time that the widowed survive their spouses. If we postulate a loss effect, we would predict a *rise* in death rates in the period closely following the death of the spouse, when grief is most acute. In longitudinal studies one can compare the mortality experience of the recently bereaved with those of longer duration. Theoretically, there is also the possibility of more closely examining age and sex differences and causes of death in widowed mortality by relating these variables to duration of bereavement.

Unfortunately, longitudinal studies of the loss effect are rare, and those that exist are often marred by methodological problems. Such problems are due in large measure to the complexities of conducting such research. Sample size is, for example, a critical problem in tracing the loss effect on a longitudinal basis. To illustrate, the rate of mortality (per 100,000) for widowers age 70–74 shown in the 1974 census of England and Wales (OPCS, 1977a,b) is 8180.73. That is, 8 of these widowers per 100 would be expected to die in any given year. Among comparable married men, the mortality rate is 6114.32. That is, 6 per 100 would be expected to die in a similar period. Additionally, while the mortality ratios of the recently widowed to married would be expected to show a greater difference, the differences in actual numbers per 100 cases would still be unlikely to be large enough to be statistically reliable in a small sample. It is evident from these figures that longitudinal studies would need large samples for any statistically reliable difference to be observed.

Several longitudinal studies that have tried to assess the effects of widowhood on death rates do prove useful. Taking data from death certificates, Young *et al.* (1963) investigated the 'duration effect', that is, the time lapse between the deaths of a couple, among 4486 widowers whose wives had died in 1957. Unfortunately, widows could not be included in this study as death certificates of men do not identify their spouses in a way that enables them to be followed up, whereas widowers do feature on the death certificates of their wives. Mortality rates for the widowers for the first 6 months and for each year following bereavement for a period of 5 years were compared with those for married men. Young *et al.* reported that the only ratios which were consistently greater than unity (i.e. demonstrated a loss effect) were for those dying within 6 months of becoming widowed. After this period the rates fell back rapidly to the level for married men. The increment in the first 6 months was approximately 40 percent (i.e. a widowed to married ratio of 1.4).

A follow-up of this investigation was conducted by Parkes *et al.* (1969), who examined mortality rates of this sample for 4 additional years. They found that from the fifth year onwards the mortality rates of the widowers were slightly below those for the married men. Thus, the increase in mortality risk among older widowers does appear to be confined to the first 6 months of bereavement.

Additional support for these findings comes from a Swedish study (Ekblom, 1963) that included both widowers ($n = 351$) and widows ($n = 283$). All were aged 75 at the time of partner loss. Ekblom compared the frequency of mortality among this group with age- and sex-specific mortality rates for the married, as obtained from official Swedish statistics. In the first 6 months 26 of the widowed (14 males and 12 females) died, compared with an expected figure of 19 (a widowed to married ratio of 1.36). This increase thus supports the Young *et al.* (1963) finding that the loss effect for widowers occurs in the 6 months immediately following the death of a spouse. As in the Young *et al.* study, a decline in excess risk was noted during the following $1\frac{1}{2}$ years (the expected number of deaths in fact exceeded the actual for this period). However, in contrast to Young *et al.*, Ekblom found that in the third year of bereavement there was again an excess for the widowed. It is interesting to note that this was due entirely to death of widows and not widowers. Unfortunately, as the Young *et al.* study was confined to widowers, we cannot compare the Swedish and British studies for a sex difference in the duration of risk period. The basic patterns of results does seem very similar to the results of the British studies reported above, but it should be noted that the differences observed in the Swedish study were only tendencies, as Ekblom could not obtain large enough samples to furnish statistically significant results.

A further British study by Cox and Ford (1964) fulfils the requirement regarding sample size. The mortality among 60,000 widows under 70 years of age was examined for a period of 5 years following the deaths of their husbands. These investigators reported a rise in mortality over expected rates (derived by calculating the mortality rates for the entire period) in the second but not the first year of bereavement. After this peak in the second year the rates became comparable to the expected rates. As the study was based on widows who had applied for widows' pensions, it could have excluded those from the sample who died in the first year and thus had no time to apply for a pension. This might account for the similarity between observed and expected rates for the first year. It is also difficult to compare the Cox and Ford (1964) results with other studies, due to procedural differences and the time period under investigation (i.e. 1927).

However, McNeill (1973) designed a longitudinal study that promised to provide much needed information on sex and age differences in the loss effect. The investigation was planned on a large scale and included mortality data on 9247 widowed (6310 widows and 2937 widowers) in Connecticut, USA. This widowed mortality rate was compared with expected rates. In this investigation the latter were not the married rates but those of the general population of the state. The cohort was followed for $3\frac{1}{2}$ years, with the aim of determining for which of the sexes, at what age, and at what time interval after bereavement the risk of death was most excessive for the survivor.

The bereaved included in the study ranged in age from 20 to 74. Those over 44 were stratified into quinary age-groups; those under 45 were combined into one group so that it would be comparable in size to the older age categories. McNeill reported that the risk of death for the widowed compared with expected rates *declined* with age. Only under 60 years of age were observed deaths significantly excessive compared to expected rates. This decline is in line with the pattern found in cross-sectional surveys (cf. Table 22.1), and also the longitudinal study by Young *et al.* (1963), although these latter sources show *some* excess over expected rates even among the elderly. A sex difference in time-period of highest risk was also found by McNeill: for widowers under 60 years the peak in deaths was during the first 6 months, whereas for widows the greatest risk was during the second year of bereavement. As in other studies, observed rates after the first 2 years returned to a level that was generally comparable with expected rates.

In view of its scope (large sample, analyses by age, sex, and cause of death), the McNeill study promised more enlightenment on the bereavement–mortality relationship than any other longitudinal investigation. Interpretation of the above results is, however, severely hampered by the fact that the expected rates very often exceeded the observed (widowed) rates. In fact, taking the entire $3\frac{1}{2}$-year period, the overall excess of the expected to the observed rates for widowers was significant at the 1 percent level. Thus, one can hardly interpret this study as generally supportive of the bereavement–mortality relationship.

In a longitudinal study by Rees and Lutkins (1967), a significant loss effect has been found in a comparatively small sample. This ingenious study, conducted in a small town in South Wales, differed in several respects from the other longitudinal studies. First, it was carried out prospectively, for a period of 6 years, from 1960 onwards. Furthermore, Rees and Lutkins isolated 370 cases in which a death had occurred and extended the investigation of the impact of bereavement on mortality to include its effect on parents, siblings, and children. The total number of relatives included in this survey group was 903. The control group ($n = 878$) was composed of the relatives of a further group of 371 local residents ('hypothetical death group'), the latter being matched for age, sex, and marital status with the deceased individuals. This study found highly significant differences in mortality between the relatives in the bereaved and the relatives in the control group. During the first year, 43 (4.76 percent) of the bereaved group and 6 (0.68 percent) of the control group died, a difference that was highly significant. During the second year the excess was no longer significant, and in subsequent years it declined further, to the level of the control group.

Rees and Lutkins analyzed the mortality for the various relatives separately. For the widowed (51 widowers, 105 widows) the mortality rate was higher in the first year: 12.2 percent died compared with 1.2 percent of the controls. The mortality rate for widowers was reported to be significantly higher than for widows. In the first year 19.6 percent of the widowers and 8.5 percent of the widows died; but as males have a higher mortality rate than females, the sex difference may be more clearly expressed in terms of excesses over controls. If we do this, we find that widows to female controls have a higher excess (no control females died in the first year of 'bereavement') than widowers to male controls. This result is contrary to all our other findings. However, the Rees and Lutkins results confirmed the finding of Young *et al.* (1963) that the highest risk period for widowers was the first 6 months after the spouse's death.

Among the other close relatives, the risk of mortality was excessive during the first year, and this reached significance when the other relatives were combined, and for the children and siblings. The loss effect seems not to be confined to marital partners, though detailed stratification of the relative susceptibility of other close relatives is difficult to make from this study, as the sample sizes are not large enough, and as information on age distribution of the relatives was not given. Nor do we have details of causes of death for either spouse. It would be useful to replicate and to extend this study, particularly in view of a criticism by Parkes *et al.* (1969) that the differences in mortality rates between widowed and controls may be due in part to the surprisingly low rate of mortality for the controls—the latter is much lower than the mean for married persons of the same age from national statistics.

A few studies have reported no increase in death risk for the recently bereaved; but on close examination none of these investigations convincingly discredits the loss effect. In some (e.g. Clayton, 1974; Shepherd and Barraclough, 1974) small sample sizes and other methodological shortcomings are probably responsible for the discrepancy. In others (e.g. Ward, 1976) the loss effect may be reduced because bereavement followed an extended illness, and death of the spouse was expected. Such expected deaths typically lead to better bereavement outcomes than is the case for unexpected deaths (see, e.g., Parkes, 1972).

Conclusions

Most longitudinal studies do seem to point to a period of heightened risk in the first 6 months of bereavement. This relationship seems to be more pronounced for the widowers than for widows. Some studies have concluded that widows are most susceptible after a longer time-lapse. However, this conclusion must await more detailed study. Further investigations are also needed to compare the mortality risk according to duration of bereavement in widowed of different ages.

Causes of Death in the Widowed

Further support for the loss effect would be provided if the excess mortality rates of the widowed could be attributed to physical causes for which there is a strong psychological underpinning. Unfortunately, only limited information is available on the causes of death among the widows and widowers, and across age-groups. Governmental statisticians no longer list 'Griefe' as a cause of death, as was done, for example, in the mortality tables of the City of London in 1657 (McNeill, 1973). These deaths among the widowed were 'characterized by rupture of auricles and ventricles', and were attributed to a 'broken heart'. Limitations in possible inferences from present-day diagnoses still persist, in part because people seemingly die from only one disease, namely, the one considered by the attendant physician to be the most important in bringing about the demise of the patient. That such diagnoses are problematic is indicated in studies comparing cause of death as given on death certificates with postmortem examination. Parkes *et al.* (1969) reported a lack of concurrence to the extent of 28 percent from a national survey. One must hope, then, that the inaccuracies are spread evenly across the marital status groups. One further limitation in available data is that causes of death in marital partners are rarely listed together; therefore it is difficult to assess the contribution to the mortality rates of a number of alternatives to the loss effect (which we discuss in the next section) such as mutual infection, joint accident, or shared unfavorable environments.

One of the most detailed accounts of causes of death across marital status groups was published by the National Center for Health Statistics (NCHS) in 1970. Data for the total United States population for the 1959/61 period were included in this analysis. The report gives information not only on the leading causes of death among the widowed, but also specifies those causes for which risk of death shows an increase in comparison with the still-married. The discussion here will be confined to the data for white citizens, as mortality patterns for black citizens are remarkably different, and consideration of them is beyond our scope.

Interestingly, calculations made from the data show that the three *leading* causes of death for all widowed (white citizens) are identical to those for all married: arteriosclerotic heart and coronary disease is the major killer, followed by strokes, and then cancer of the digestive organs and peritoneum. However, those causes of death that show *excesses* for the widowed with the corresponding married rates are of interest. Table 22.2, compiled from the NCHS (1970) publication, shows widowed to married mortality ratios for specific causes of death, ranked according to magnitude of excess for the widowed. One characteristic of these results is that the two leading causes of death (arteriosclerotic heart disease, including coronary heart disease, and vascular lesions of the central nervous system) do *not* have the largest excesses. In fact, for widows they rank 3rd and 4th in excess over married women's rates, while for widowers, these rank only 7th and 8th in excess. However, the ratios do indicate that in equal-sized groups, for every two married people who die from heart attacks and strokes, three widowed people die. The most dramatic increases in risk come from suicide, accidents, liver cirrhosis, and tuberculosis. While the risk of dying of a 'broken heart' is high among the widowed, the risk of an unsavory death rises even more.

Carter and Glick (1976) presented comparable information for 15–64-year-olds. Low excesses (compared to the married) were found for coronary and other myocardial disease, but also notably for many of the cancers. Excesses among widowers ranging from four to seven times as high as married men's were found for accidental fire and explosion, suicide, and tuberculosis. For

Table 22.2 Mortality ratios of widowed to married. Standardized marital status–mortality ratios for white persons for selected causes of death:* in order of relative excess ratios of widowed to married, US, 1959–61†

Widowers		Widows	
1. Homicide	2.69	1. Accidents (other than motor vehicle	1.84
2. Liver cirrhosis	2.42		
3. Suicide	2.39	2. Suicide	1.66
4. Accidents (other than motor vehicle	2.27	3. Arteriosclerotic heart, including coronary, disease	1.48
5. Tuberculosis	2.17	4. Lesions of CNS	1.47
6. Motor accidents	1.99	5. Tuberculosis	1.43
7. Vascular lesions of central nervous system (CNS)	1.50	6. Liver cirrhosis	1.31
		7. Homicide	1.28
8. Arteriosclerotic heart, including coronary, disease	1.46	8. Cancer of digestive organs and peritoneum	1.23
9. Diabetes	1.41	9. Cancer of cervix	1.18
10. Cancer of digestive organs and peritoneum	1.26	10. Cancer of respiratory system	1.18
11. Cancer of respiratory system	1.26		

* The 'selected causes' are composed, for the most part, of categories which contribute to the four leading causes of death (ICD Nos. 400–402, 410–443, 140–205, 330–334, E800–E962). Also included are liver cirrhosis, diabetes, suicide, homicide and tuberculosis. For further details see NCHS (1970), p. 2.

† Source: NCHS, 1970 (Series 20, No. 8A, compiled from Tables 2, 10, 37, and 47).

widows the most extreme excesses were for motor vehicle accidents, homicide, and accidental fire and explosion. Overall, the widowed do seem to die from those causes in which psychological factors can be presumed to play a crucial role. This argument has been elaborated by Gove (1973). He concluded that the evidence on specific types of mortality suggests that the excesses among the unmarried:

can be largely attributed to characteristics associated with one's psychological state (p. 61).

More precisely, he argued that:

the variations in the mortality rates are particularly large where one's psychological state (1) appears to play a direct role in death, as with suicide, homicide, and accidents, (2) is directly related to acts such as alcoholism that frequently lead to death, and (3) would appear to affect one's willingness and ability to undergo the drawn-out and careful treatment required for diseases such as tuberculosis. In contrast, there is little difference between the marital status in the mortality rates for diseases such as leukemia and aleukemia, where one's psychological state has little or no effect on either the etiology of the disease or treatment (p. 61).

Gove's comments did not elaborate on the meaning of 'psychological state', and even more critically, omitted any reference to, or analysis of, the major causes of death: heart disease and strokes. Yet arteriosclerotic heart disease and vascular lesions of the central nervous system together account for approximately 50 percent of the total deaths in each group (i.e. for all marital statuses, males and females, white citizens over 15 years, 1959–61). The excess rate among the widowed (3 to 2) is sizeable, and may reflect the added psychological stress of bereavement on the widowed. While not as dramatic in excess as the relatively rare instances of homicide and suicide, the excess rate is quite substantial, particularly if one takes into account the vast numbers of people affected by these ailments, and the statistical problem of showing great excesses for such overwhelming causes of death.

Just as longitudinal investigations supplement the cross-sectional with regard to the incidence and the prevalence of mortality among the bereaved, so are they also desirable for obtaining information on causes of death in the recently bereaved. Comprehensive as the above cross-sectional data on causes of death are, it is important to remember that the 'widowed' in these statistics exclude all those who have remarried, and remarriage rates, particularly for males, are high. Carter and Glick (1976) provided some indication of the general magnitude of this 'reselection factor':

> Of the 15.3 million persons . . . whose first or last marriage had ended in widowhood, 11.7 million, or three-fourths, were still widowed at the time of the census (p. 438).

According to this information, then, we have to expect that a quarter of the widowed are no longer categorized in this marital status group, and that data concerning these individuals are not available for inclusion in the widowed sample.

Evidently, information is needed on causes of death in the recently bereaved (among whom remarriage is rare), but very little research is available that goes into sufficient detail for our purposes. Suicides and accidents appear to be very excessive among recently bereaved males (McNeill, 1973; MacMahon and Pugh, 1965). In contrast with the comparatively low *excesses* from diseases of the heart found in cross-sectional studies, death from these causes also accounts for a high proportion of the excess rates among recently bereaved widowers (McNeill, 1973; Parkes *et al.*, 1969). McNeill (1973) further reported that cancer accounted for a significant proportion of the excess mortality among widows in the second half-year of bereavement and that, similar to the cross-sectional data, there were significant excesses in death rates from liver cirrhosis and alcoholism for both males and females in the second and third years of bereavement.

Conclusions

Perhaps of particular significance is the finding that the widowed in general (that is, disregarding the duration of bereavement) have fairly low excess levels for deaths from heart diseases compared with the married, whereas among the recently bereaved, heart diseases feature not only as the main cause of death, but also as the disease which accounts for most of the excess in death rates. This seems highly consistent with research which has linked diseases of the heart with stress (e.g. Glass, 1977), for loss of a partner places great stress on the remaining spouse, especially in the first few months (of Lynch, 1977). Furthermore, in numerous studies of the recently widowed (e.g. Maddison and Walker, 1967; Maddison and Viola, 1968; Parkes and Brown, 1972) signs of depression and general emotional disturbances (restlessness, sleeplessness, inability to make decisions, etc.) and increased presence of physical disability have been demonstrated. The widowed are also found to drink more alcohol, smoke more, and generally to neglect their health more than the non-bereaved. And as we have seen, the widowed (as far as the evidence goes) frequently die from causes that are related to these symptoms.

Despite the lack of reliable or detailed research on causes of death among the widowed, taken together the analyses reported above seem to point towards an interpretation of the bereavement–mortality relationship which emphasizes the role of psychological factors. The widowed in general, but particularly the recently widowed, appear to be vulnerable to those specific types of mortality which are affected by psychological variables. Support comes not only from the pattern of highly excessive death rates from heart diseases in the recently bereaved, but also from such diseases as liver cirrhosis, cancer, and from suicide, in which (either directly or indirectly) psychological factors can affect the etiology to a far greater extent than is possible, for example, in the case of leukemia and aleukemia (cf. Gove, 1973). Precisely how psychological variables operate to affect the bereaved's life chances is our concern in the remainder of this chapter, after alternative explanations for the observed relationship between widowhood and mortality have been discussed.

Alternative Explanations to the Loss Effect

When viewed concomitantly, evidence from both the cross-sectional and longitudinal studies to date appears to furnish strong support for a loss effect. Yet, this conclusion must still be regarded with caution. For example, not least among the problems in measuring rates across marital statuses is the possibility of statistical artifact. Of special importance is the fact that the widowed may be as much as 1 year older than the married comparison group in surveys that divide the marital status groups into 10-year age-spans (Kraus and Lilienfeld, 1959; Registrar General's Review, 1967). In view of the close relationship between age and mortality, the fact that the widowed are older than the comparison group may be critical. In addition, cross-sectional surveys can exaggerate the mortality rates of the widowed: they are typically underrepresented at census and overrepresented at death counts (Registrar General's Review, 1967). It is easier to control for these methodological or statistical artifacts in longitudinal studies, particularly as comparison groups can be selected and matched for age, sex, and other demographic variables. But even here, caution is needed in interpreting differences (see Kastenbaum and Costa, 1977).

Apart from these statistical artifacts, the following factors have been discussed (e.g. Kraus and Lilienfeld, 1959; Parkes *et al.*, 1969) as potential alternative explanations to the loss effect (i.e. as explanations which deny a causal link between bereavement and mortality).

Selection for Remarriage

As we pointed out earlier, the validity of cross-sectional studies can be threatened by the possibility that a certain proportion of the widowed population remarry in a relatively brief period. In particular, the widowed mortality rates may be inflated because the fittest remarry, leaving in the widowed population mainly those who are in poor health, emotionally unstable, physically handicapped, or chronically ill. This possibility seems particularly salient inasmuch as the younger widowed partners and the males have the highest remarriage rates, and it is precisely these groups that have the highest mortality rates among the widowed. Must we look no further than this selection explanation to account for the high mortality rates among the young widowers?

To estimate the probable effect of remarriage, Kraus and Lilienfeld (1959) carried out a subsidiary analysis in which they first assumed that none of the widowed who had remarried had died and, for further safety, systematically overestimated the numbers of remarried widowed. This maximum estimate was then added to the widowed population (they used data for the young widowed male group, for whom remarriage is particularly high) and computed the mortality rate of this total group, whether remarried or not. In other words, instead of calculating the widowed mortality rate by dividing the total number of deaths in the specific widowed group by the total widowed population given at the census, they calculated an adjusted rate by dividing the same total of widowed deaths by the total widowed population *plus* the estimate of those who had remarried (and who had therefore been reclassified in the census as married). Kraus and Lilienfeld concluded that:

> the estimated maximum effect of the selectivity is slight, relative to the observed tenfold excess risk among those who had remained widowed, compared to the married (p. 213).

In longitudinal research, selection in remarriage is not so problematic as (a) the remarriage rates immediately after loss of a spouse are low, and (b) it is easier to trace or to estimate the numbers of remarriages and, therefore, to exclude this as a possible explanation of excess mortality risk. Thus, Ekblom (1963) reported a total of only three men and no women who remarried during the 3-year period following decease of the partner. McNeill (1973) used insurance company data on remarriage rates in the widowed by age and sex to control the influence of this factor on the mortality rates. Young *et al.* (1963) calculated how much the widower–married men differentials could be a result of selective remarriage of the fittest men by adding the remarried group to the total widower population. As Kraus and Lilienfeld (1959) indicated, the effect relative to the total excess proved slight, even for the younger widowed. It seems that we are justified in concluding that the excesses found in the longitudinal studies are not due to selective remarriage, as remarriage is either negligible or, when controlled for, alters the excess risk only minimally.

Homogamy

If we consider bad health a handicap, we are faced with the possibility that healthy individuals prefer to marry other healthy ones, and the unhealthy are left to marry each other. The proximity of the times or ages of death in the spouses would then be due to homogamy; that is, marrying a similar other. It is impossible from the available cross-sectional or longitudinal data to assess accurately the contribution of this factor to mortality rates as we have no information on the medical histories of the spouses. A 'tendency' found by Parkes *et al.* (1969) for spouses to die from similar causes of death might possibly be regarded as support for this explanation, but as the greatest concordance was not found for those diagnostic groups which accounted for the highest excesses, this seems unlikely to explain more than a small portion of the excess. Nevertheless, the contribution of homogamy to the mortality rates of the widowed cannot be disregarded.

Shared Unfavorable Environments

Living conditions may be so harmful as to endanger the lives of a couple and, again, if such pathogenic environmental conditions are responsible for death, one would expect the partners to die in close proximity to one another, and from the same or similar causes. While this is unlikely to be the main explanation for joint mortality effects, the possibility cannot be ruled out completely.

Joint Accidents

Also contributing to the excess rates of the widowed are accidents in which both partners were involved (e.g. motor-vehicle accidents). If one member of a couple outlived the other, however short the time-lag between the deaths, he or she is classified as widowed. Particularly among the younger adult age-groups, where accidents account for higher proportions of the mortality rates, joint accidents could be an important reason for the excessive rates. In Britain, accidents claim the lives of over 60 percent of all deceased male and female widowed between 25 and 34, and approximately 25 percent of those widowed between 35 and 44 (see Registrar General's Review, 1967). This rate is double that of their married counterparts. Again, we lack information on what proportion of these accidental deaths occurred jointly. However, accidental death may be responsible for the outstandingly excessive mortality rates among the young widowed.

Infectious Diseases

Marital partners are naturally at high risk of catching any infectious disease that one of them has, which may then ultimately cause the deaths of both. In fact, an early study by Ciocco (1940) found a tendency for partners to die from the same causes in the case of pneumonia, influenza, and tuberculosis. They are likely to account for a smaller portion of the variance today, however, as fatality rates and frequency of such diseases have decreased.

Conclusions

Although there seem to be grounds for the view that none of the above alternatives can fully explain the excesses in widowed mortality, the extent to which all of these alternatives in combination may account for the increases is very hard to assess. Our view is that the excess mortality is importantly related to psychological processes and is not predominantly a result of the combined effect of the above alternatives. After all, the relationship between bereavement and mortality has been found quite consistently, regardless of method of data-collection, for both sexes, across age-groups, for different generations and also in a variety of countries all over the world (see Stroebe *et al.*, 1981). Thus, while a definitive investigation has yet to be done, our conclusions appear, in the light of present knowledge, to be well supported.

Nevertheless, the high excess widowed mortality rates for the young and for males remain puzzling: are they reflective of a more acute loss effect for this group? As we noted, the evidence indicates that these excesses are not due to a remarriage artifact. Yet it is difficult to reconcile the finding that young widowers apparently suffer most extremely from loss of a partner (i.e.

have the highest mortality ratios compared with married men of the same age) with the fact that it is precisely among this group that the highest remarriage rates are found. It is also difficult to imagine that most deaths will occur among a young adult group in which the incidence of prior illness and disease is very low compared with a more elderly group. So how can these high excesses be explained? As deaths for younger adults are predominantly, and to a far greater extent than is the case for the older, due to accidents, it seems plausible that part of the excess is attributable to joint accidents, the survivor being classified at census as widowed, before dying as a result of injuries sustained at the accident from which the spouse previously died. Also, one caution is required in interpreting excesses for the young adults: death of a partner for the young adult age-groups is a comparatively rare event, and numbers are so small that statistics are likely to be unreliable (Registrar General's Review, 1967).

Perhaps, combined with a slight remarriage selection bias, these considerations explain the unusually excessive death ratios for the young, and particularly for the young widowers. Until further data are available which assess the contribution of the various factors more precisely, we cannot conclude that the high ratios for young widowers indicate greater vulnerability to the loss effect.

Tracing the Psychological Antecedents of the Loss Effect

Psychological Factors in Longevity: Hope and Hopelessness

One typically assumes that a medical explanation for mortality is the most appropriate one; death is, after all, a termination of one's biological functioning. Yet, in the present case, there is ample reason to take a psychological perspective. The death of one's spouse does not operate in the same manner on one's bodily system as the entry of some alien bacterium or lethal instrument. Merely being present at the death of another person does not itself produce biological deterioration. Rather, it would appear, the death of another person must be interpreted psychologically by the individual in order for it to have effects. One's definition of the other's death, one's view of its repercussions for oneself, one's interpretation of the meaning of the death in one's own life, and for one's self-definition must all be considered, for it is variations on this psychological level that determine what biological response will be made to the death of the spouse.

The importance of psychological factors in determining longevity has been underscored in research on the relationship between personal anticipation and mortality. For example, Phillips (1972) reported that before each presidential election in the United States since 1904 the mortality rate sank considerably; it appeared that people wished to know the result of the election before their death. A similar fall in mortality rate was found for Jewish citizens of New York and Budapest before Yom Kippur, the major Jewish holiday. Similarly, birthdays seem to have an impact on the length of life. In an analysis of the birth and death dates of 1251 famous Americans, Phillips (1972) found a notable dip in mortality in the month before the birthday, and a rise in the month following. Comparable results were reported by Labovitz (1974) for a sample of famous and non-famous Canadians (though without the dip before the birthday in the case of the famous citizens), and using a variety of sources by Kunz and Summers (1980).

Perhaps the most important of these results for our purposes were obtained from an analysis of British mortality statistics (Alderson, 1975). For married, widowed, and single men and women over the age of 74 (but not under this age), there was a distinct fall before, and a rise after, the birthday. Figures 22.1 and 22.2 are particularly instructive. As they show, within the male

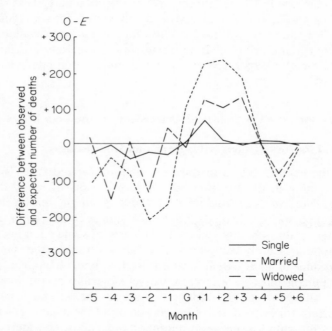

Figure 22.1 Differences between observed and expected deaths for *males* over 74 years of age, in relation to the month of birth (G) and marital status, England and Wales, 1972 (after Alderson, 1975)

sample the dip in mortality prior to one's birthday and the rise afterwards are most pronounced among the married and less so among the widowed and single. The pattern for the female sample is similar but less regular.

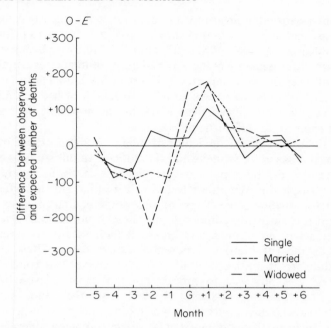

Figure 22.2 Differences between observed and expected deaths for *females* over 74 years of age, in relation to the month of birth (G) and marital status, England and Wales, 1972 (after Alderson, 1975)

Unfortunately, Alderson does not report whether these differences between marital statuses are statistically reliable. From the pattern of these data it would appear that at least for males (but to a lesser degree for females), the personal significance of adding another year to one's life may be vitally influenced by the social context. Specifically, when one resides in a social context where the event might be invested with significance, such as within the marital unit, the birthday becomes an important predictor of longevity. In effect, psychological factors seem to loom especially important within these results.

Unfortunately, a recent review and methodological critique of this literature (Schulz and Bazerman, 1980) has raised doubt as to the validity of these conclusions. However, there are further results in a somewhat different domain, which appear to be quite consistent with the notion that the will to live affects longevity. There is evidence which seems to indicate that lack of a will to live, a sense of hopelessness, negatively affects survival in crisis situations.

For example, Paloucek and Graham, 1965 (described in Schulz, 1978) attributed the unexpectedly poor response to treatment of cancer patients whom they studied to the patients' bleak, negative views on life. They divided patients into two treatment groups (comparable with regard to the state of their disease) according to whether they judged their future as positive, or as hopeless and unacceptable. Whereas patients in the first group responded well to treatment, the identical therapy had only minimal effects in the second group. Similar results were reported by Verwoerdt and Elmore (1967), who found a relationship between will to live and length of life among terminal patients. Patients who viewed their condition as hopeless, died months in advance of their more optimistic fellow-sufferers.

Perhaps the most convincing demonstration of the importance of hope for survival was published by Schmale and Iker (1966). In this study, psychiatrists used criteria of hope and hopelessness to diagnose cancer in patients who, on the basis of suspicious symptoms found in a routine smear test, had been transferred for further tests. Thus, at this point in time, cancer was only suspect, and this suspicion could still prove to be unfounded. Patients who viewed themselves as failures, and regarded their future as hopeless, were diagnosed by the psychiatrist as potential cancer cases. These predictions proved to be correct in 31 out of 40 cases. Of course, it is conceivable that hopelessness does not lead to cancer, but that cancer, even before it is diagnosed, leads to hopelessness. However, Schmale and Iker's (1966) interpretation receives support from the finding that the widowed die more frequently of cancer than the married or single of comparable ages (Carter and Glick, 1976; Dorn, 1943; Peller, 1952).

The Causes of Hopelessness: A Cognitive Approach

There seems to be a great deal of agreement in recent analyses (e.g. Mandler, 1975; Melges and Bowlby, 1969; Schulz, 1976; Seligman, 1975) that the feeling of having lost control over one's environment is one of the major causes of hopelessness. There is less agreement, however, regarding the assumptions about the processes that lead to a perception of loss of control. While Mandler (1975; Mandler and Watson, 1966) sees the interruption of integrated response sequences as a major cause, Seligman (1975) assumes that the experience of situations in which outcomes are independent of one's behavior may lead to a feeling of helplessness. In the following sections both these theories will be discussed.

The Interruption of Response Sequences

According to Mandler (1975; Mandler and Watson, 1966) the interruption of an integrated response sequence (behavioral or cognitive) produces a state of arousal that in the absence of certain alternative responses (completion or substitution) then develops into an emotional expression. Following Schachter (1964) Mandler understands emotion as a joint product of an unspecific arousal and environmental cues. While arousal is a consequence of the interruption, the *specific* emotional experience will depend on factors *other than the interruption itself*. Mandler admits that the conditions under which interruption may lead to pleasant emotions are somewhat unclear. He is quite specific, however, about the preconditions of anxiety. Whenever an individual feels unable to complete an interrupted sequence and has no alternative completion sequences available, interruption causes distress and anxiety. Interruption does not lead to anxiety if the individual expects to complete the sequence or has alternative response sequences available which he can substitute for the initially intended response.

The lack of adequate sequences and the absence of what, in another language, might be called purposeful behavior define the disorganized organism. Helplessness and disorganization *are* anxiety (Mandler and Watson, 1966, p. 266).

In Mandler's (1975) theory helplessness is perceived as an immediate response to a situation. The individual feels helpless if he does not know what to do in a particular instance. However, if this builds up over a number of situations to a generalized feeling of not knowing what to do in any situation, it leads to *hopelessness*. Hopelessness may also result from repeated failures (non-completion) of a single plan, if that plan is very important and ego-involving for the individual. Intense feelings of hopelessness, Mandler believes, are the basis of many depressive syndromes.

The relevance of response-disruption theory for the loss effect should be obvious. The loss of a partner and the ensuing disruption of interpersonal bonds must certainly be a unique source of anxiety and distress. A person who has just lost his or her partner will find over and over again that response sequences cannot be completed because completion would require some action or reaction from the lost partner. Such disruption should be particularly severe if the death of a partner was sudden and unexpected, so that the individual had little time to adjust to the loss and to search for acceptable alternate sequences. This is quite consistent with conclusions reported by Parkes (1975) that the unexpected loss of a partner leads to greater strain and distress than loss due to an extended illness. On the other hand the disruption may, to a greater or lesser extent, be alleviated if alternative persons are available to provide actions and reactions necessary for the completion of a response sequence, which had previously been carried out by the spouse. As the development of such projects as 'Preventive Intervention for the Newly Bereaved' and 'Widow to Widow' programs indicates, it has become well-recognized by theoreticians and clinicians alike that one of the major determinants of a good outcome following bereavement is the presence and support of family members or friends (see e.g. Lopata, 1973, 1978; Marris, 1958; Walker *et al.* 1977).

We have argued, earlier, that the higher widowed to married mortality ratio of the younger widowed (compared to the older age-groups) could be accounted for by the greater number of joint accidents in these age-groups. It should be pointed out, however, that response-disruption theory offers an alternative interpretation of this pattern. Since accidents are a more frequent cause of death in the younger age-groups, and furthermore, since death is anyway an unusual occurrence among young adults, it follows that sudden and unexpected loss experiences are also more prevalent and that response disruption should thus be more frequent and severe. This could partly account for the high mortality rate among the younger widowed.

Response-disruption theory could also be used to interpret the puzzling finding that divorce, though less noxious than widowhood, nevertheless tends to decrease life chances relative to a married status. Although divorce does not typically come unexpectedly, the break-up of a close interpersonal relationship should lead to a great deal of response disruption and thus be the cause of stress and anxiety. The consequences of divorce could therefore, at least for the partner who does not initiate the divorce and who is unlikely to move into an alternative relationship immediately, be quite similar to those of the loss through death of a partner after an extended illness.

Response-disruption theory has finally some interesting implications with regard to mourning and funeral rites. According to this theory, interruption of a planned response sequence should only cause distress and anxiety in the absence of alternative behavior sequences. It could be argued that with mourning and funeral rites, culture provides the individual with pre-planned response sequences which may serve as substitutes for the disrupted responses and should thus reduce the anxiety and distress resulting from the loss of a loved one. Unfortunately, as Mandler (1964) could demonstrate in animal experiments, the therapeutic effect of alternative behavior is transistory, and most of the rites are anyway completed within the first few months of bereavement.

The Perceived Non-contingency of Actions and Outcomes

While Mandler (1975) attributes the feeling of hopelessness to repeated experiences of response disruption and the unavailability of acceptable alternate response sequences, Seligman (1975) perceives the frequent experience of a non-contingency between one's actions and one's outcomes as a major cause of hopelessness. Seligman (1975) proposes that learning that outcomes are uncontrollable is a major precursor of deleterious emotional and physical effects, both in animal and human populations. As he argued, the belief that one's outcomes are independent of one's actions generates a state of *learned helplessness*. This state of learned helplessness is accompanied by a loss of motivation to act, a blockage of learning ability and a depressed emotional condition. Studies supporting this line of argument have been conducted with dogs (e.g. Seligman and Maier, 1967), cats (e.g. Masserman, 1971; Thomas and Dewald, 1977), rats (e.g. Maier et al., 1973; Maier and Testa, 1975), and adults (Glass and Singer, 1972; Hiroto, 1974; Klein et al., 1976; Krants et al., 1974; Rodin, 1976). In an attempt to cement the link between learned helplessness and depression, experiments have also compared depressed with normal subjects placed in a condition of helplessness. Such studies indicate that the two groups perform similarly on subsequent problem-solving tasks. In each case they are inferior to control subjects (Miller and Seligman, 1973, 1975; Klein et al., 1976).

The implications of this line of work for present concerns should be clear. When an individual loses a spouse, particularly through death, a decreased sense of outcome control may be generated, which in turn will be accompanied by depression and cognitive disorganization. Support for this position can be found in work with the elderly by Ferrari (1962), who reports on 55 females admitted to an old-age home in the midwest. Of the 17 who said they had no choice in this placement, 8 were dead after 4 weeks; 16 had died after 10 weeks. Of the 38 who said they had other alternatives, only 1 died in the 10-week period. Finally, Schulz and Aderman (1973) studied terminal cancer patients who had been transferred to a ward for the dying from other hospitals or from their homes. The investigators reasoned that those patients who had lived at home were most accustomed to controlling their environments—and would consequently be most deprived upon arrival at the ward. This loss of control would, in turn, lead to learned helplessness and a higher mortality rate. This reasoning was supported by the results of the study.

Yet, although perceived loss of outcome control may be generated by the loss of a close relation, it need not be. As Seligman and his colleagues make clear (Abramson et al., 1978), the state of learned helplessness depends importantly on the manner in which one interprets the impending situation. For example, as Klein et al. (1976) suggest, learned helplessness is affected by the degree to which one attributes his or her outcomes to internal or external sources. If external events produce undesirable outcomes, and no personal failure is implied, learned helplessness may be reduced; or when loss is perceived by an individual to be the result of unstable forces as opposed to a predictable and coherent plan of nature, or when one does not believe himself or herself to be uniquely helpless, feelings of depression and cognitive disorganization may be lessened. In effect, this line of argument suggests that there may be considerable variation in the degree to which one responds to loss with feelings of helplessness and resulting depression, inactivity, and physical vulnerability. Depending on whether one views the death as the result of controllable circumstances, or is able to locate other successful avenues of attribution, interpersonal loss may not propel one into a state of perceived helplessness. We may summarize this section with the working hypothesis that, as the death of a close relation increases the perception of personal helplessness, physical impairment and mortality rate will increase. To the extent that alternative interpretations of the loss may be located, and perceptions of helplessness avoided, physical well-being and longevity may be unaffected.

Conclusions

Both models presented above offer quite convincing interpretations of the processes linking partner loss to depression and hopelessness. The loss of a loved person, ending a close interpersonal relationship, is likely to lead to a great deal of disruption of well-learned response sequences and may thus foster a sense of helplessness and hopelessness. Similarly, the death of a loved person, especially if it comes suddenly and unexpectedly, could be experienced as a traumatic example of universal helplessness. Furthermore, the loss is likely to deprive one of a great many valued outcomes. But what kind of response sequences are disrupted and what are the outcomes lost through the death of a partner? Are there differences between losing a loved person and losing some loved object? If there are, what are they, and what are the consequences for response disruption and learned helplessness? The cognitive approaches discussed above can offer little guidance with regard to these questions. To answer them a social psychological analysis of the marriage relationship is needed. Such an analysis has recently been attempted by Stroebe *et al.* (1980) and some of their conclusions will be reported in the following sections.

The Causes of Hopelessness: A Social Psychological Approach

A marital couple can be considered a small social group in which members, as in any social group, fulfil certain functions for each other and in which each has certain tasks to perform. The loss of a partner should lead to deficits in a number of areas which can broadly be characterized as *social validation, social support, task performance,* and *social protection.* The surviving partner should experience problems in socially validating a wide range of his or her judgments, he or she should suffer a marked deficit in social and emotional support and, furthermore, will have to take over those parts of the group task which had formerly been performed by the partner. Finally, he or she may find deprivation of the social protection of the marital group anxiety-arousing.

Loss of Social Validation of Personal Judgements

Effective behavior, and the accompanying feeling of having control over one's own outcomes, requires an assessment of reality that may take place under highly ambiguous circumstances. So, too, one's assessment of self-worth is not always an easy one to accomplish with confidence. Such decisions may thus be maximally dependent on social comparison processes (Festinger, 1954). Loss of a partner, that is, of someone who fulfilled a central role in comparison processes, may lead to drastic instability of such judgments. In order to evaluate whether one has sufficient ability to solve a specific problem, one needs to have not only a realistic and stable assessment of one's own competence, but also an accurate judgment of the complexity of the task in question. According to Kelley (1967), consensus information (that is, information regarding others' reactions) is as important for the correct attribution of stable characteristics to the environment as it is for characteristics of the person himself. Due to the closeness of the relationship between marital partners, one's spouse is likely to be one of the main sources of consensus information. With the death of the partner, this important source of information is lost, and consequently, confident assessment of one's achievements and capabilities are far more difficult.

Social comparison processes may also play an important part in judging the appropriateness of one's own emotional responses (Schachter, 1959). When a spouse is lost, one may face a myriad of questions about what one should be feeling emotionally, what plans are appropriate, how one is to live a life alone, what level of spending is appropriate for a person of single status, and so on. Not the least of such questions may concern one's own sanity. As Glick *et al.* (1974) have shown, almost 40 percent of those bereaved are fearful at one time or another that they may be 'going crazy'. Matters of sanity are typically very ambiguous, and without a close relation to assure one that his or her actions, emotions, or thoughts are 'merely the result of temporary stress', as opposed, let us say, to 'deep emotional trauma', the fear that one is a borderline psychotic may continue unabated. In sum, to the extent that the survivor is unable to locate sources enabling a successful definition of reality, the negative effects on health and death rate may be increased.

Loss of Social and Emotional Support

Broad agreement exists within the helping professions concerning the central, if not critical, role played by self-esteem in the emotional well-being of the individual. The neo-Freudian analysts furnished perhaps the initial insights into the significance of self-regarding attitudes in the life of the individual. Horney's method of treatment was chiefly centered around the problem of reducing the patient's feelings of 'basic inferiority', which feelings were believed to be at the root of various neurotic patterns. Adler's concept of the 'inferiority complex' and Erikson's (1963) elaboration of the crisis between competence *versus* inferiority, underscores many of the same concerns. More recently, Carl Rogers (1959, 1968) has constructed a theory of therapy and personal growth based on the assumption that the major problems motivating the individual to seek therapeutic consultation most frequently stem from depleted feelings of self-regard. Much of the data generated by Rogers and his colleagues lends support to this assumption. Additional support emerges from other realms of the socio-behavioral sciences where theorists consistently point to the fulfilment of esteem-needs necessary to optimal human functioning (cf. Becker, 1967; Maslow, 1962; Adler, 1930; Horney, 1950). In general, then, it would appear that people are frequently concerned with their worth or value, and that feelings of personal worth are furnished primarily through social sources. Expression of regard or love, indications of trust, communications of praise, and even the other's provision of material resources may all serve to bolster one's feelings of self-worth or esteem.

This line of argument enhances our understanding of the loss effect. With the death of a close relation one often loses a major source of personal esteem. With their love and unconditional positive regard, partners in a happy marriage can repair many of the damages that the other's self-esteem may have suffered in the course of a day. Thus, with the loss of his or her partner, the individual may face a significant lowering of self-regard. This decrement may be accompanied by a lowered motivation to engage in health-sustaining activities, and an increased reliance on drugs (including alcohol and tobacco) for reducing suffering and furnishing a transient sense of security. All such outcomes should lend themselves to a decline in health. In effect, to the extent that the loss of a close relation is accompanied by a decrease in expressions of positive regard for the survivor, the survivor may experience a loss of self-worth and a decrement in personal health and increased vulnerability to death.

Loss of Material and Task Supports

Although little discussed in the traditional literature on bereavement, there is good reason to believe that a surviving spouse frequently confronts a substantial loss of material and task supports. Primary among the former, of course, may be the loss of a reliable income. However, additional material losses may frequently include one's living quarters, health insurance, the caretaking of one's home, and the provision of meals. In the traditional family, where role differentiation occurs, a spouse also has a number of tasks to fulfil, such as bringing up children, preparing food, cleaning the house, clearing snow, etc. The higher the specialization of these roles in a marriage, the more drastic are the effects of loss of one of the partners. For example, if a husband has never been concerned with running the household, the death of his wife may present a number of difficult problems. If a wife has never carried out heavy manual work or been responsible for financial accounting, she may also come under great strain. Although these difficulties may be minimized with the help of an extensive 'social support network' (Kobrin and Hendershot, 1977; Lopata, 1973; Walker *et al.*, 1977), such tasks may be highly stressful and thus lead to an increase in physical vulnerability.

Loss of Social Protection

In a scholarly analysis of functions of grief, Averill (1968, 1979) argued that

it is the biological function of grief to ensure group cohesiveness in species where a social form of existence is necessary for survival (p. 347).

This suggestion rests on the assumption that since such animals have a greater chance of survival in the group, where they are better protected against predators, there is evolutionary pressure to establish instinctual mechanisms which would make leaving the group painful for the individual animal. A similar suggestion has been made by Bowlby (1969) who postulated that children are born with an innate propensity to be near an attachment figure, a role usually taken over by their mothers. Separation anxiety, or—in the case of permanent loss—severe grief reactions, are thus assumed to have a biological function, ensuring cohesiveness, even if they lead to distress or physical detriment for the bereaved. This view, which is also shared by Parkes (1972), is in clear opposition to Freud's (1917) claim, that it is the function of grief to foster the detachment of the bereaved from the lost love object.

If it were the biological function of attachment to keep the individual protected against dangers, the question should be raised whether at a psychological level (a) there is an increase in need for affiliation in situations of threat, and (b) whether the presence of others actually reduces stress and anxiety.

With regard to the first point, research by Schachter (1959) clearly demonstrated that fear elicits affiliation. Subjects who expected to receive severe electric shocks showed a greater preference to wait with others than subjects who anticipated only mild shock treatment. While there is also evidence for the anxiety-reducing property of the presence of others in fear-arousing situations, the mechanisms which mediated fear-reduction have not yet been clearly identified (Cottrell and Epley, 1977; Epley, 1974). Nevertheless, the fact that the presence of a companion has been demonstrated to lessen the emotional reaction to fear-arousing situations suggests that the loss of a loved companion should make life more stressful for the surviving partner. Since, in this case, the noxious effects are not due to the loss experience itself, but to the absence of a partner, lack of socially mediated stress-reduction might be one of the factors contributing to the greater mortality of the never-married and divorced as compared with married persons.

A second process which may be important in this context is that of 'diffusion of responsibility'. Sharing decisions lessens the load of responsibility for the decision-makers. Although the evidence is less than clearcut (Lamm and Myers, 1978), the fact that under certain conditions groups make more extreme decisions than individuals may be partly attributed to a diffusion of responsibility among group members. Applied to a marital couple, this would mean that decision-making is likely to be experienced as more stressful if one of the partners should suddenly be faced with the necessity of arriving at decisions (or facing responsibilities) without being able to consult the other. In this way, the loss of a partner would add considerable strain to the life of the other.

The implications of this research for differential prediction of the loss effect are somewhat complex. With regard to the anxiety-reducing property of the presence of others, predictions would depend of the precise mechanisms mediating this effect. If the *mere* presence of others lessons anxiety, then partner loss should always have a deleterious effect. If, on the other hand, the anxiety-reducing effect is achieved by the other person serving as a calm model, consequences of partner loss are difficult to predict. With regard to decision-making, predictions can be arrived at more easily. Loss of a partner should be the more stressful, the more the couple has been used to arriving at decisions only after joint deliberation.

Conclusions

According to the analysis presented above the consequences of losing a marital partner should be the more severe, the closer the relationship between the partners, the greater the role differentiation within the marital group, and the fewer alternative persons are available who could serve part of the functions formerly fulfilled by the partner. While the absence of strong positive affective bonds between the partners may imply that they will no longer serve each other as sources of social and emotional support, it should leave their willlingness and ability to fulfil social-validational, task-related and social protection functions for each other unimpaired. Even if the marriage is no longer completely harmonious, the partners might still value the other's judgments and they will certainly still have to depend on each other for performing the tasks necessary to keep the family going.

Thus, it would follow from a social psychological model that the loss of a partner should lead to some of the same problems whether caused by death or divorce. This prediction is consistent with findings by Weiss (1976) that partners who had voluntarily separated reported frequent experiences of separation anxiety, uncertainty, disorientation and other reactions which are quite familiar from psychiatric studies of the widowed (Parkes, 1972). It also is consistent with the higher mortality rates of the divorced compared with the married.

The Relationship between Psychological and Physical Consequences of Partner Loss

Thus far we have considered a variety of psychological reactions to the loss of a partner which may contribute to the increase in widowed mortality. In this section an attempt will be made to analyze some of the mechanisms by which psychological reactions such as helplessness and hopelessness may cause a deterioration in the physical health of the surviving spouse.

In many cases it appears that the psychological state might lead to *behavioral changes* which are life-threatening. Because of the psychological state, the individual may increase drug intake (e.g. alcohol, tobacco, and tranquilizers), forego sleep, attend less to a proper diet, and in general take less care of his or her health. This type of apparently 'irrational' behavior becomes quite understandable if analyzed in terms of the changes in costs and rewards of health care eventuated by the loss of the partner. As the economist Gary Becker (1976) formulated succinctly:

> Good health and a long life are important aims of most persons, but surely no more than a moment's reflection is necessary to convince anyone that they are not the only aims: somewhat better health or a longer life may be sacrificed because they conflict with other aims. The economic approach implies that there is an 'optimal' expected length of life, where the value in utility of an additional year is less than the utility foregone by using time and other resources to obtain that year. Therefore, a person may be a heavy smoker or so committed to work as to omit all exercise, not necessarily because he is ignorant of the consequences . . ., but because the lifespan forfeited is not worth the cost to him of quitting smoking or working less intensively. . . . According to the economic approach, therefore, *most* (if not all!) deaths are to some extent 'suicides' in the sense that they could have been postponed if more resources had been invested in prolonging life (pp. 9–10).

It would follow from this type of analysis that less effort would be invested in health care, if the utility of an additional year of life has decreased and/or if the utility of actions which are deleterious to one's health has increased. From what we know, the loss of a partner has both these consequences. Not only does life seem less worthwhile to the surviving spouse, but the intense stress situation is also likely to increase his or her dependence on cigarettes, alcohol, and sleeping pills and decrease the satisfaction which might normally be derived from consumption of food. Thus, in terms of such an analysis, the behavioral changes observed in the widowed appear to reflect changes in their evaluation of life and health care caused by the loss of their partner. Consistent with this analysis is the finding that widowed persons have higher suicide rates than the married and that this difference is particularly marked during the first year after the death of the partner (MacMahon and Pugh, 1965).

In contrast to these forms of self-inflicted deterioration, however, are cases in which one's psychological condition is paralleled by certain physiological states, which themselves may hasten mortality. Although little is yet known about such processes of *physically-correlated deterioration* in the bereaved, some inroads have been made. At the most general level, many believe (cf. Engel, 1978; Fredrick, 1976) that the harmful effects of bereavement are not due to newly developing illnesses or diseases, but to an accelerated deterioration of already malfunctioning or defective systems. As Fredrick (1976) explains:

> The biochemical and physiologic concomitants of sustained or intense grief may directly or indirectly put under strain an already defective system (such as the effect on a damaged heart) or accelerate, precipitate, enhance or uncover pre-existing, sometimes latent, pathological process at a biochemical organ or system level (such as infection or neoplasia) (p. 298).

On the basis of animal studies, and a physiological investigation of parents whose children had died of leukemia (Hofer *et al.*, 1972a,b), Fredrick (1976) concludes that the stress of bereavement stimulates an increase in the production of adrenocorticotropic hormone from the pituitary gland. This hormone controls the release of corticosteroids which, among other effects, causes a suppression of the immune protective processes. This would explain the excessive susceptibility of the widowed to infectious and also malignant diseases.

In an attempt to explain the excess mortality rates from heart attacks in the widowed, Engel (1978) suggests that hopelessness, as a reaction to negative emotional situations, simultaneously activates two contradictory biological reactions to emergencies, namely the 'flight–fight' and the 'conservation–withdrawal' systems. The 'flight–fight' system mobilizes all resources for massive motor activity, in order to cope with threat. Activation of the 'conservation–withdrawal' system, on the other hand, leads to inactivity, to internal withdrawal from the situation, in order to save energy, to reduce the interaction with a threatening world. Normally, the two systems inhibit each other. Engel (1978) proposes, on the basis of animal experiments in 'learned helplessness' situations, that stress and hopelessness can lead to simultaneous activation for the two systems. In the case of healthy individuals, the result may be vasodepressor syncope, benign arrhythmias, or both. But for people who already suffer from heart trouble, this additional strain may lead to death.

Conclusions

Interest in the psychology of death and bereavement has grown at a rapid rate over the past decade. Both the *Annual Review of Psychology* and the

Psychological Bulletin published reviews in these domains in 1977 (Kastenbaum and Costa, 1977; Rowland, 1977). Two additional volumes (Kastenbaum and Aisenberg, 1972; Schulz, 1978) have summarized and integrated the psychological literature in the field, and an international journal for the study of 'dying, death, bereavement, suicide, and other lethal behaviors', namely, *Omega—The Journal of Death and Dying*, has been established. Yet, to our knowledge, there has been no systematic psychological investigation of the factors underlying the apparent risk of death among the widowed. As we have seen, many investigations have attempted to document the loss effect, but the reasons for its existence remained obscure. Since Freud's pioneering work, psychological research has primarily concentrated on problems of adjustment to death by the terminally ill, and on general attitudes towards death. Psychological investigations on loss and grief following the death of a loved one (e.g. see Lindemann, 1944; Schoenberg *et al.*, 1975) have been chiefly concerned with the dynamics and sequential character of the grieving process. The most detailed description and theoretical analysis of responses to loss through death—that by Bowlby (see 1969, 1973, 1980)—has focused on children (particularly on their responses to the loss of a parent). Adult responses to loss of a spouse were discussed mainly for the purposes of comparison with childhood grief and mourning. It was our aim, therefore, at this juncture to raise the question more specifically as to the underlying mechanisms of the loss effect among spouses, for only following an analysis of these cognitive and social psychological factors can effective ameliorative programs be planned and implemented.

We have seen that the mortality rates of the widowed are excessive compared with married controls of comparable age and sex; but it is most important for the planning of intervention measures among the bereaved to remember that only a small proportion of the bereaved population actually suffers psychological and physical reactions which eventuate in early death. The majority of the widowed recover from the grief process and return to normal life. Thus, there are clearly individual differences in reactions to bereavement, and, in our opinion, psychological investigations of these differences are now necessary in order to identify this high-risk group. In addition to the identification of the risk group, prevention requires the opportunity to administer therapy. Such a therapy program must, however, be constructed on the basis of a theoretical and empirical account of the processes responsible for the potentially fatal effects of widowhood.

Each of the factors discussed above probably contributes a small part to the development of pathological reactions in bereavement. Although epidemiological studies provide a preliminary foundation for development and examination of the effects of bereavement, such a theory will ultimately have to be buttressed by more thorough psychological investigation.

References

Abramson, L. Y., Seligman, M. E. P., and Teasdale, J. D. (1978). 'Learned helplessness in humans: critique and reformulation', *Journal of Abnormal Psychology*, **87**, 49–74.

Adler, A. (1930). 'Individual psychology', in Murchison, C. (ed.), *Psychologies of 1930*. Clark University Press, Worcester, MA.

Alderson, M. (1975). 'Relationship between month of birth and month of death in the elderly', *British Journal of Preventive and Social Medicine*, **29**, 151–156.

Averill, J. (1968). 'Grief: its nature and significance', *Psychological Bulletin*, **70**, 721–728.

Averill, J. R. (1979). 'The functions of grief', in Izard, C. E. (ed.), *Emotions in Personality and Psychopathology*. Plenum, New York.

Becker, G. S. (1976). *The Economic Approach to Human Behavior*. University of Chicago Press, Chicago.

Becker, H. S. (1967). 'History, culture and subjective experience: an exploration of the social bases of drug-induced experiences', *Journal of Health and Social Behavior*, **8**, 163–176.

Bowlby, J. (1969). *Attachment and Loss,* vol. 1: *Attachment*. Hogarth Press, London.

Bowlby, J. (1973). *Attachment and Loss*, vol. 2: *Separation: Anxiety and Anger*. Hogarth Press, London.

Bowlby, J. (1980). *Attachment and Loss,* vol. 3: *Loss: Sadness and Depression*. Hogarth Press, London.

Carter, H., and Glick, P. C. (1976). *Marriage and Divorce: a Social and Economic Study* (rev. edn.). Harvard University Press, Cambridge, MA.

Ciocco, A. (1940). 'On mortality in husbands and wives', *Human Biology*, **12**, 508–531.

Clayton, P. J. (1974). 'Mortality and morbidity in the first year of bereavement', *Archives of General Psychiatry*, **30**, 747–750.

Cottrell, N. B., and Epley, S. W. (1977). 'Affiliation, social comparison and socially mediated stress reduction', in Suls, J. M., and Miller, R. L. (eds), *Social Comparison Processes: Theoretical and Empirical Perspectives*. Wiley, Halstead Press, New York.

Cox, P. R., and Ford, J. R. (1964). 'The mortality of widows shortly after widowhood', *Lancet*, **1**, 163–164.

Dorn, H. F. (1943). 'Cancer and the marital status', *Human Biology*, **15**, 73.

Ekblom, B. (1963). 'Significance of psychological factors with regard to risk of death among elderly persons', *Acta Psychiatrica Scandinavica*, **39**, 627–633.

Engel, G. L. (1978). 'Psychologic stress, vasodepressor (vasovagal) syncope, and sudden death', *Annals of Internal Medicine*, **89**, 403–412.

Epley, S. W. (1974). 'Reduction of the behavioral effects of aversive stimulation by the presence of companions', *Psychological Bulletin*, **81**, 271–283.

Erikson, E. H. (1963). *Childhood and Society*. Norton, New York.

Farr, W. (1859). *Influence of Marriage on the Mortality of the French People*. Savill & Edwards, London.

Ferrari, N. A. (1962). 'Institutionalization and attitude change in an aged population: a field study and dissidence theory'. Unpublished doctoral dissertation, Western Reserve University.

Festinger, L. (1954). 'A theory of social comparison processes', *Human Relations*, **7**, 117–140.

Fredrick, J. F. (1976). 'Grief as a disease process', *Omega,* **7**, 297–305.

Freud, S. (1917). 'Mourning and melancholia', in *Collected Papers*. Basic Books, New York (1959), vol. 4, pp. 152–170.

Glass, D. C. (1977). *Behavior Patterns, Stress and Coronary Disease*. Lawrence Erlbaum, Hillsdale, NJ.

Glass, D. C., and Singer, J. E. (1972). *Urban Stress: Experiments on Noise and Social Stressors*. Academic Press, New York.

Glick, I., Weiss, R. S., and Parkes, C. M. (1974). *The First Year of Bereavement*. Wiley Interscience, New York.

Gove, W. R. (1973). 'Sex, marital status and mortality', *American Journal of Sociology*, **79**, 45–67.

Hiroto, D. S. (1974). 'Locus of control and learned helplessness', *Journal of Experimental Psychology*, **102**, 187–193.

Hofer, M. A., Wolff, S. B., Friedman, S. B., and Mason, J. W. (1972a,b). 'A psychoendocrine study of bereavement', *Psychosomatic Medicine*, **34**, 481–491 and 492–504.

Horney, K. (1950). *Neurosis and Human Growth: The Struggle Toward Self-realization*. Norton, New York.

Kastenbaum, R., and Aisenberg, R. (1972). *The Psychology of Death*. Springer Publications, New York.

Kastenbaum, R., and Costa, P. T. (1977). 'Psychological perspectives on death', *Annual Review of Psychology*, **28**, 225–249.

Kelley, H. (1967). 'Attribution theory in social psychology', in Levine, D. (ed.), *Nebraska Symposium on Motivation*. University of Nebraska Press, Lincoln, Nebraska.

Klein, D. C., Fencil-Morse, E., and Seligman, M. E. P. (1976). 'Learned helplessness, depression, and the attribution of failure', *Journal of Personality and Social Psychology*, **33**, 508–516.

Kobrin, F. E., and Hendershot, G. E. (1977). 'Do family ties reduce mortality? Evidence from the United States 1966–68', *Journal of Marriage and the Family*, **39**, 737–745.

Krantz, D. S., Glass, D. C., and Snyder, M. L. (1974). 'Helplessness, stress level and the coronary-prone behavior pattern', *Journal of Experimental Social Psychology*, **10**, 284–300.

Kraus, A. S., and Lilienfeld, A. M. (1959). 'Some epidemiological aspects of the high mortality rate in the young widowed group', *Journal of Chronic Diseases*, **10**, 207–217.

Kunz, P. R., and Summers, J. (1980). 'A time to die: a study of the relationship of birthdays and time of death', *Omega*, **10**, 281–289.

Labovitz, S. (1974). 'Control over death: the Canadian case', *Omega*, **5**, 217–221.

Lamm, H., and Myers, D. G. (1978). 'Group-induced polarization of attitudes and behavior', in Berkowitz, L. (ed.), *Advances in Experimental Social Psychology*, vol. 11. Academic Press, New York.

Lindemann, E. (1944). 'Symptomatology and management of acute grief', *American Journal of Psychiatry*, **101**, 141–148.

Lopata, H. Z. (1973). *Widowhood in an American City*. General Learning Corp., Morristown, NJ.

Lopata, H. Z. (1978). 'Contributions of extended families to the support systems of metropolitan area widows: limitations of the modified kin network', *Journal of Marriage and the Family*, **40**, 355–364.

Lynch J. J. (1977). *The Broken Heart: the Medical Consequences of Loneliness*. Basic Books, New York.

MacMahon, B., and Pugh, T. F. (1965). 'Suicide in the widowed', *American Journal of Epidemiology*, **81**, 23–31.

Maddison, D. C., and Viola, A. (1968). 'The health of widows in the year following bereavement', *Journal of Psychosomatic Research*, **12**, 297–306.

Maddison, D. C., and Walker, W. L. (1967). 'Factors affecting the outcome of conjugal bereavement', *British Journal of Psychiatry*, **113**, 1057–1067.

Maier, S. F., Albin, R. W., and Testa, T. J. (1973). 'Failure to learn to escape in rats previously exposed to inescapable shock depends on nature of escape response', *Journal of Comparative and Physiological Psychology*, **85**, 581–592.

Maier, S. F., and Testa, T. J. (1975). 'Failure to learn to escape by rats previously exposed to inescapable shock is partly produced by associative interference', *Journal of Comparative and Physiological Psychology*, **88**, 554–564.

Mandler, G. (1964). 'The interruption of behavior', in Levine, D. (ed.), *Nebraska Symposium on Motivation*. University of Nebraska Press, Lincoln, Nebraska.

Mandler, G. (1975). *Mind and Emotion*. Wiley, New York.

Mandler, G., and Watson, D. L. (1966). 'Anxiety and the disruption of behavior', in Spielberger, C. D. (ed.), *Anxiety and Behavior*. Academic Press, New York.

Marris, P. (1958). *Widows and their Families*. Routledge & Kegan Paul, London.

Maslow, A. (1962). *Toward a Psychology of Being*. Van Nostrand, New York.

McNeill, D. N. (1973). *Mortality among the Widowed in Connecticut*. Yale University, New Haven (MPH essay).

Masserman, J. H. (1971). 'The principle of uncertainty in neurotigenesis', in Kimmel, H. D. (ed.), *Experimental Psychopathology*. Academic Press, New York.

Melges, F. T., and Bowlby, J. (1969). 'Types of hopelessness in psychopathological process', *Archives of General Psychiatry*, **20**, 690–699.

Miller, W. R., and Seligman, M. E. P. (1973). 'Depression and the perception of reinforcement', *Journal of Abnormal Psychology*, **82**, 62–73.

Miller, W. R., and Seligman, M. E. P. (1975). 'Depression and learned helplessness in man', *Journal of Abnormal Psychology*, **84**, 228–238.

National Center for Health Statistics (1970). Series 20, No. 8. *Mortality from Selected Causes by Marital Status*. Government Printing Office, Washington DC.

Office of Population Censuses and Surveys (1977a). Series FM 2, No. 1. *Marriage and Divorce Statistics, 1974*. HMSO, London.

Office of Population Censuses and Surveys (1977b). Series DH 1, No. 1. *Mortality Statistics, 1974*. HMSO, London.

Paloucek, F. P., and Graham, J. B. (1965). 'The influence of psychosocial factors in the prognosis of cancer of the cervix', *Annals of the New York Academy of Science*, **125**, 814–819.

Parkes, C. M. (1972). *Bereavement: Studies of Grief in Adult Life*. Tavistock Publications, London.

Parkes, C. M. (1975). 'Unexpected and untimely bereavement: a statistical study of young Boston widows and widowers', in Schoenberg, B., Gerber, I., Wiener, A. et al. (eds), *Bereavement: its Psycho-social Aspects*. Columbia University Press, New York.

Parkes, C. M., Benjamin, B., and Fitzgerald, R. G. (1969). 'Broken heart: a statistical study of increased mortality among widowers', *British Medical Journal*, **1**, 740–743.

Parkes, C. M., and Brown, R. (1972). 'Health after bereavement: a controlled study of young Boston widows and widowers', *Psychosomatic Medicine*, **34**, 449–461.

Peller, S. (1952). *Cancer in Man*. International Universities Press, New York.

Phillips, D. (1972). 'Deathday and birthday: an unexpected connection', in Tanur,

J. M. (ed.), *Statistics: a Guide to the Unknown*. Holden-Doug, San Francisco.

Rees, W., and Lutkins, S. (1967). 'Mortality of bereavement', *British Medical Journal*, **4**, 13–16.

Registrar General's Statistical Review of England and Wales (1967). Part III. Office of Population Censuses and Surveys, London.

Rodin, J. (1976). 'Density, perceived choice and response to controllable and uncontrollable outcomes', *Journal of Experimental Social Psychology*, **12**, 565–578.

Rogers, C. (1959). 'A theory of therapy, personal and interpersonal relations, as developed in the client-centered framework', in Koch, S. (ed.), *Psychology: A Study of a Science*. McGraw-Hill, New York.

Rogers, C. (1968). 'The significance of the self-regarding attitudes and perceptions', in Gordon, C., and Gergen, K. (eds), *The Self in Social Interaction*. Wiley, New York.

Rowland, K. F. (1977). 'Environmental events predicting death for the elderly', *Psychological Bulletin*, **84**, 349–372.

Schachter, S. (1959). *The Psychology of Affiliation*. Stanford University Press, California.

Schachter, S. (1964). 'The interaction of cognitive and physiological determinants of emotional state', in Berkowitz, L. (ed.), *Advances in Experimental Social Psychology*, vol. 1. Academic Press, New York.

Schmale, A. H., and Iker, H. P. (1966). 'The affect of hopelessness and the development of cancer', *Psychosomatic Medicine*, **28**, 714–721.

Schoenberg, B., Gerber, I., Wiener, A., Kutscher, A. H., Peretz, D., and Carr, A. C. (eds) (1975). *Bereavement: its Psychosocial Aspects*. Columbia University Press, New York.

Schulz, R. (1976). 'Some life and death consequences of perceived control', in Carrol, J. S., and Payne, J. W. (eds), *Cognition and Social Behavior*. Erlbaum, Hillsdale, NJ.

Schulz, R. (1978). *The Psychology of death and dying*. Addison-Wesley, MA.

Schulz, R., and Aderman, D. (1973). 'Effects of residential change on the temporal distance of terminal cancer patients', *Omega*, **4**, 157–162.

Schulz, R., and Bazerman, M. (1980). 'Ceremonial occasions and mortality: a second look', *American Psychologist*, **35**, 253–261.

Seligman, M. E. P. (1975). *Helplessness: on Depression, Development and Death*. Freeman, San Francisco.

Seligman, M. E. P., and Maier, S. F. (1967). 'Failure to escape traumatic shock', *Journal of Experimental Psychology*, **74**, 1–9.

Shepherd, D., and Barraclough, B. M. (1974). 'The aftermath of suicide', *British Medical Journal*, **2**, 600–603.

Stroebe, M. S., Stroebe, W., Gergen, K. J., and Gergen, M. (1981). 'The broken heart: reality or myth?' *Omega*, **12**, 87–106.

Stroebe, W., Stroebe, M. S., Gergen, K. J., and Gergen, M. (1980). 'Der Kummer Effekt: psychologische Aspekte der Sterblichkeit von Verwitweten', *Psychologische Beiträge*, **22**, 1–26.

Thomas, E., and Dewald, L. (1977). 'Experimental neurosis: neuropsychological analysis', in Maser, J. D., and Seligman, M. E. P. (eds), Psychopathology: Experimental Models. Freeman, San Francisco.

Verwoerdt, A., and Elmore, J. (1967). 'Psychological reactions in fatal illness. I: The prospect of impending death', *Journal of the American Geriatrics Society*, **15**, 9–19.

Walker, K. N., MacBride, A., and Vachon, M. L. S. (1977). 'Social support
    networks and the crisis of bereavement', *Social Science and Medicine*, **11**, 35–41.
Ward, A. W. (1976). 'Mortality of bereavement', *British Medical Journal*, **1**, 700–702.
Weiss, R. S. (1976). 'The emotional impact of marital separation', *Journal of Social
    Issues*, **32**, 135–145.
Young, M., Benjamin, B., and Wallis, C. (1963). 'Mortality of widowers', *Lancet*, **2**,
    454–456.

Author Index

561

Subject Index